PHR®, PHRi® and SPHR®, SPHRi®

Human Resources Certification Complete

Study Guide

Sixth Edition

AF751726

PHR®, PHRi® and SPHR®, SPHRi®

Human Resources Certification Complete Study Guide

2024 Exams

Sixth Edition

Sandra M. Reed, SPHR, SHRM SCP

SYBEX
A Wiley Brand

Copyright © 2025 by John Wiley & Sons, Inc. All rights, including for text and data mining, AI training, and similar technologies, are reserved.

Published by John Wiley & Sons, Inc., Hoboken, New Jersey.
Published simultaneously in Canada and the United Kingdom.

ISBNs: 9781394276493 (paperback), 9781394276516 (ePDF), 9781394276509 (ePub)

No part of this publication may be reproduced, stored in a retrieval system, or transmitted in any form or by any means, electronic, mechanical, photocopying, recording, scanning, or otherwise, except as permitted under Section 107 or 108 of the 1976 United States Copyright Act, without either the prior written permission of the Publisher, or authorization through payment of the appropriate per-copy fee to the Copyright Clearance Center, Inc., 222 Rosewood Drive, Danvers, MA 01923, (978) 750-8400, fax (978) 750-4470, or on the web at www.copyright.com. Requests to the Publisher for permission should be addressed to the Permissions Department, John Wiley & Sons, Inc., 111 River Street, Hoboken, NJ 07030, (201) 748-6011, fax (201) 748-6008, or online at www.wiley.com/go/permission.

Trademarks: WILEY, the Wiley logo, and the Sybex logo are trademarks or registered trademarks of John Wiley & Sons, Inc. and/or its affiliates, in the United States and other countries, and may not be used without written permission. PHR, PHRi, SPHR, and SPHRi are trademarks or registered trademarks of the Human Resource Certification Institute, Inc. All other trademarks are the property of their respective owners. John Wiley & Sons, Inc. is not associated with any product or vendor mentioned in this book.

Limit of Liability/Disclaimer of Warranty: While the publisher and author have used their best efforts in preparing this book, they make no representations or warranties with respect to the accuracy or completeness of the contents of this book and specifically disclaim any implied warranties of merchantability or fitness for a particular purpose. No warranty may be created or extended by sales representatives or written sales materials. The advice and strategies contained herein may not be suitable for your situation. You should consult with a professional where appropriate. Further, readers should be aware that websites listed in this work may have changed or disappeared between when this work was written and when it is read. Neither the publisher nor author shall be liable for any loss of profit or any other commercial damages, including but not limited to special, incidental, consequential, or other damages.

For general information on our other products and services, please contact our Customer Care Department within the United States at (800) 762-2974, outside the United States at (317) 572-3993. For product technical support, you can find answers to frequently asked questions or reach us via live chat at https://sybexsupport.wiley.com.

Wiley also publishes its books in a variety of electronic formats. Some content that appears in print may not be available in electronic formats. For more information about Wiley products, visit our web site at www.wiley.com.

Library of Congress Control Number: 2024936007

Cover image: © Jeremy Woodhouse/Getty Images
Cover design: Wiley

SKY10147377_022026

To my husband Chris, whose three little words never fail to inspire me: "Go for it." To my children, Calvin and Clara, because the best part of me will eternally be each of you. I am filled with love and gratitude for having the three of you in my life.

Acknowledgments

I know I have said this before in other acknowledgments, but there really is no other way to put this: Writing a book is a group project, regardless of whose name is on the cover! The value of being able to call on thought leaders, scrub the Internet for perspective and fact checks, and leaning on my clients and online network for field research cannot be understated. I am truly indebted to my professional network for their insights and encouragement.

Thank you to my editors for helping to channel the chaos of my mind. I am especially grateful to Kenyon Brown for his availability and guidance, and to Brad Jones for his excellent project management skills and assistance in juggling multiple projects and timelines. I cannot thank them enough! A special thanks goes to James Galluzzo, my partner in crime, for his technical editing. Knowing that James would catch anything I missed gave me great comfort, allowing me to relax long enough to actually submit each chapter for review.

A book like this requires a great deal of time and diversity of thought, and the contributions from experts Dr. Erin Richard, Reut Schwartz-Hebron, Hector Alvarez, and Joanne Walters added different voices and critical perspectives to the exam content. I am in awe of and grateful for their contribution.

Finally, to the students, a brief mention of my own testing experience: I remember sitting in my hotel room the night before my SPHR exam, trying to cram in a few more details, desperate to figure out what I didn't already know. It was around Christmas time, and my youngest child was just two years old. Feeling guilty for being away from my family and with my confidence at an all-time low, I wondered if I was really up for the challenge. Then, surrounded by my books and flashcards, I suddenly "got" it. The pieces started fitting together, the processes had rationale, and the big picture came into clear focus. The next morning, I took a four-hour exam in just two hours and passed it on the first go-around. My excitement about being a part of this project is a reflection of that one "a-ha" moment, representing for me when HR crosses over from just being a job to an intelligent, strategic career choice. My hope is that with each pass through this material, you will get closer to your own enlightened moment when you suddenly just get it. Many thanks, and good luck in your career—this absolutely can happen for you!

Acknowledgments

About the Author

Sandra M. Reed, SPHR, **SHRM SCP** has more than 25 years of experience in human resources, the last 20 of which have been spent in training and instruction. She holds her undergraduate degree in industrial-organizational psychology and her graduate degree in Organizational Leadership. Fun fact: It took her 30 years to complete her college degrees! She was certified before her first degree, and it is this that fuels her passion to help others achieve HR certification, regardless of their educational level achieved. Sandra is a master practitioner of the MBTI, Working Genius, and the Profiles XT personality assessments. She is the author of *A Guide to the Human Resource Body of Knowledge (HRBoK™)*, *The Big Book of HR Exam Questions*, and other certification study guides, all available through John Wiley & Sons. Sandra is the owner and founder of sandrareed.co, a consulting firm that specializes in executive coaching and the unique needs of small to mid-sized organizations. Find her on the web at `https://sandrareed.co`.

You can also find the officially licensed companion app for this material at `https://learnzapp.com/apps/hr/index.html`. Use code **sandyHR** for 10 percent off any purchase.

About the Technical Editor

James J. Galluzzo, III, SPHR, PMP is a human resources strategic professional with nearly 30 years of experience. During his service in the U.S. Army, he found his professional calling in the HR branch, the Adjutant General's Corps, and retired as Chief of Leadership Development for the 40,000 Army HR professionals around the world. He has served as a director of human resources in government and private sector organizations and is a human resources subject matter and program manager helping to transform the Army's human resources training and development as it fielded the most comprehensive human resources information system (HRIS) in its history. Additionally, James has been an adjunct instructor, author, and content creator for training HR professionals.

Contents at a Glance

Contents

Introduction

Congratulations on taking the first step toward achieving your Professional in Human Resources (PHR), Professional in Human Resources International (PHRi), or Senior Professional in Human Resources (SPHR) or Senior Professional in Human Resources International (SPHRi) certification! The process you're embarking on is rewarding and challenging, and as more than 500,000 of your fellow human resource colleagues in more than 100 countries have already discovered, it's an excellent opportunity to explore areas of HR management with which you may not work every day. In the next few pages, you'll find some general information about HR certification, some suggestions for using this book, information about what to expect in the following chapters, and a discussion of the organizations involved in certification.

Before we begin, a word about what you should already know. This study guide was designed to serve as a refresher for experienced professionals who have practiced for several years or who have been educated in human resources. We assume that those who are pursuing certification have the basic HR knowledge that comes not only from education in human resources but also, more importantly, from professional-level experience. If your daily work is truly generalist in nature, you likely have touched on many of the topics I cover, but you may not have in-depth knowledge in all of them. Conversely, if you specialize in one or two areas of HR, you probably have extensive experience in those areas but may need to refresh your knowledge in other areas.

NOTE

In 2024, the Human Resource Certification Institute combined the exam content outlines for the PHR and PHR, international exams, and the SPHR, SPHR international exams. This book references them as follows:

- PHR and PHRi: PHR/i
- SPHR and SPHRi: SPHR/i

Any differences between the U.S. and international exams are called out in each chapter.

Additionally, for SPHR and SPHRi candidates, there is an assumption that you have the benchmark knowledge that PHR and PHRi candidates are learning. This means that there is likely opportunity within the PHR/i chapters for SPHR/i candidates to refresh their knowledge.

The goal of this study guide is to provide enough information about each of the functional areas of HR management to enable candidates in either situation to find what they need to prepare themselves for successfully completing the exam. More than 50,000 books related to human resources are listed on Amazon.com alone, and there is obviously no way we can cover all the aspects of HR in a single book. So, we've organized the information around the exam content outline (ECO) established by the Human Resource

Certification Institute (HRCI®), the certifying body for our profession. We'll talk more about the content outline in Chapter 1, "Certifying Human Resource Professionals," but for now, suffice it to say that the key to success on the exam is a thorough understanding of and ability to apply the test specs when answering questions on the exams.

About Human Resource Certification

What exactly *is* human resource certification? Briefly, certification is a way of acknowledging individuals who have met the standard of competency established by HR practitioners as that which is necessary to be considered a fully competent HR professional. To understand whether this book is for you, you'll want to know why you should become certified and how the certification process works.

Who Certifies HR Professionals?

Two organizations are involved in the certification of HR professionals: the Human Resource Certification Institute (HRCI) and Pearson VUE.

The Human Resource Certification Institute

HRCI is the certifying body for the HR profession. It was formed by the American Society for Personnel Administration (ASPA) in 1972, when it was known as the ASPA Accreditation Institute (AAI). In its early stages, HRCI was financially dependent on the Society for Human Resource Management (SHRM), but it's now financially independent. Both HRCI and SHRM have individual boards of directors that govern their operations. Although HRCI and SHRM have a long history of affiliation and mutual support, the certification process is a separate and distinct function of HRCI.

NOTE You can find HRCI's organizational mission statement at `www-dev.hrci.org/about-hrci/who-we-are`.

Pearson VUE

Pearson VUE is a computer-based testing administrator headquartered in the United States with locations in 180 countries, including the United Kingdom, Japan, Australia, India, Dubai, and China. More than 400 credential owners use their services to administer exams, including HRCI. `https://home.pearsonvue.com` is where certification seekers will register for their exam date and location.

We'll refer to these organizations frequently in Chapter 1 as we discuss the body of knowledge and the certification process.

Why Become Certified?

Over time, the certification offered by HRCI has become the industry standard for determining competence in the field of human resources. There are many reasons that individuals may decide to seek professional certification. Let's talk about just a few of them.

First, certification is an acknowledgment that you have met the standards of excellence determined by other HR professionals to be those that are necessary to be fully competent in the field. Because the standards are developed by working professionals, not just by those who teach and consult in the field, this credential demonstrates that you're a fully competent HR practitioner based on a standard set by your peers.

Second, certification is a way to increase your marketability. In difficult economic times, when there is tough competition for jobs, certification provides an edge that can be advantageous in your job search. With an abundance of job seekers for a limited number of jobs, whatever you can do to set yourself apart from the crowd can give you the edge when potential employers are making the final hiring decision. Additionally, a 2018 Payscale survey found that certified HR professionals rank the HRCI exams as #1 of all professional exams and that they are the most valuable. The survey also noted that "We found that for the most part, having an HR certification is beneficial from a pay perspective and a career advancement perspective." See the full survey results at `www.payscale.com/data/hr-certifications-pay`.

Third, those who spend the time to advance their own knowledge and achieve certification have demonstrated their ability to continue learning and growing as times and business needs change. A person who is willing and able to set a significant goal and do what is necessary to achieve it demonstrates characteristics that are in great demand in business today: results orientation, technical competence, commitment, and excellence.

Finally, certification enhances your credibility with coworkers and customers by demonstrating to the people you encounter during your workday that you have proven competence in the field.

Whether your reason for seeking certification falls into one of these categories or you're motivated to do so for some other reason, it can be a great opportunity to validate how much you already know about the practice of human resources as a profession.

How to Become Certified

To become a certified HR professional, you must pass either the PHR/i or the SPHR/i exam, both of which have been developed by HRCI in a comprehensive process described in Chapter 1.

Each exam has a different number of scored exam items and passing thresholds. You can find a detailed discussion of how the questions are developed and scored in the *HR Certification Institute's Certification Policies and Procedures Handbook*, which can be viewed and/or downloaded at the HRCI website (`www.hrci.org`). The handbook is an essential guide to all aspects of the exams and includes test dates, application deadlines, fee information, and answers to frequently asked questions about the certification process, as well as the full list of test specifications.

Chapter 1 explains in greater detail how much and what kinds of experience are required for each exam level and how the questions differ on each level.

How This Book Is Organized

We've talked a little about Chapter 1, which provides information about requirements for certification and the testing process. Chapter 1 also provides some suggestions on the best ways to study for the exam.

There are also several areas of foundational knowledge that HR professionals should understand at any stage of their career. These topics are covered in Chapter 2, "Shared Competencies." This chapter is a must-read, regardless of which exam you choose to sit for.

Chapters 3 through 9 get down to the specifics of each functional area of the PHR/i exams. Chapters 10 through 14 dive into SPHR/i exam content. Each of these chapters consists of a list of responsibilities (exam objectives) for each functional area. We have also provided appendices to facilitate your study.

Appendix A, "Answers to Review Questions," provides all of the answers to the questions at the end of every chapter.

Appendix B, "PHR | PHRi and SPHR | SPHRi Case Studies," gives you an opportunity to pull information from multiple functional areas to understand and solve typical HR challenges.

Appendix C, "Federal Employment Legislation and Case Law," is a listing of the federal legislation as well as significant court decisions with implications for human resources.

Appendix D, "Resources," is just that: a list of additional sources of information about each of the functional areas of human resources.

Appendix E, "Summarizing the Summaries: What Meta-Analyses Tell Us About Work Engagement," and Appendix F, "Neuroscience Principles and Applications for HR Leaders," provide further insights from leading experts in the field.

Finally, we've provided additional study tools, including sample tests, electronic flashcards, and a glossary of terms (an alphabetical listing of key HR terms with their corresponding definitions).

The Elements of a Study Guide

You'll see many recurring elements as you read this study guide. Here's a description of some of those elements:

Assessment Tests At the end of this introduction is an two assessment tests (PHR/i Assessment Test and SPHR/i Assessment Test) that you can use to check your readiness for the exam. Take this test before you start reading the book; it will help you determine the areas on which you may need to brush up. The answers to the assessment tests questions appear separately after the last question of the test. Each answer includes an explanation and a note telling you the chapter in which the material appears.

Summary The summary is a brief review of the chapter to sum up what was covered.

Exam Essentials The "Exam Essentials" section at the end of each chapter highlights topics that could appear on one or both of the exams in some form. Although we obviously don't know exactly what will be included in a particular exam, these sections reinforce significant concepts that are key to understanding the functional area and the test specs HRCI has developed.

Review Questions Each chapter includes 20 practice questions designed to measure your knowledge of key ideas discussed in the chapter. After you finish each chapter, answer the questions; if some of your answers are incorrect, it's an indication that you need to spend more time studying that topic. The answers to the practice questions can be found in Appendix A. The chapter review questions are designed to help you measure how much information you retained from your reading and are different from the kinds of questions you'll see on the exam.

Interactive Online Learning Environment and Test Bank

The interactive online learning environment that accompanies *PHR®, PHRi® and SPHR®, SPHRi® Human Resources Certification Complete Study Guide: 2024 Exams* provides a test bank with study tools to help you prepare for the certification exam—and increase your chances of passing it the first time! The test bank includes the following:

Sample Tests All the questions in this book are provided, including the chapter tests that include the review questions at the end of each chapter. In addition, there are two practice exams (one each for the PHR and SPHR) that have a variety of question formats that match the newly structured exams as of fall 2024. Use these questions to test your knowledge of the review guide material. The online test bank runs on multiple devices.

Flashcards Two sets of questions are provided in digital flashcard format (a question followed by a single correct answer); one set is for the PHR/i and the other set is for the SPHR/i. You can use the flashcards to reinforce your learning and provide last-minute test prep before the exam.

Officially Licensed Companion App John Wiley and Sons has partnered with LearnZapp to provide you with an on-the-go mobile resource to enhance your studying. The app is regularly updated, and it includes realistic test questions with explanations, flashcards, and a custom test builder to target specific content. Download the app at `https://learnzapp.com/apps/hr` and use promo code **SANDYHR** for 10% off any purchase.

Other Study Tools A glossary of key terms from this book and their definitions is available as a fully searchable PDF.

NOTE Like all exams, the Human Resources Certification from PHR, PHRi and SPHR, SPHRi is updated periodically and may eventually be retired or replaced. At some point after PHR, PHRi and SPHR, SPHRi is no longer offering this exam, the old editions of our books and online tools will be retired. If you have purchased this book after the exam was retired, or are attempting to register in the Sybex online learning environment after the exam was retired, please know that we make no guarantees that this exam's online Sybex tools will be available once the exam is no longer available.

NOTE Go to `www.wiley.com/go/sybextestprep` to register and gain access to this interactive online learning environment and test bank with study tools.

How to Use This Book and the Additional Study Tools

This book has a number of features designed to guide your study efforts for either the PHR/i or the SPHR/i certification exams. All of these features are intended to assist you in doing the most important thing you can do to pass the exam: understand and apply the test specs in answering questions. This book helps you do that by listing the current responsibilities and knowledge requirements at the beginning of each chapter and by ensuring that each of them is fully discussed in the chapter.

The practice questions at the end of each chapter and the practice exams (which can be found in the online test bank at `www.wiley.com/go/sybextestprep`) are designed to assist you in testing your retention of the material you've read to make you aware of areas on which you should spend additional study time. We've provided web links and other resources to assist you in mastering areas where you may require additional study materials. Here are some suggestions for using this book and study tools:

- Take the PHR/i or the SPHR/i assessment test before you start reading the material. These questions are designed to measure your knowledge and will look different from the questions you'll see on the exam. They will give you an idea of the areas on which you need to spend additional study time, as well as those areas for which you may just need a brief refresher.
- Review the exam content outline at the beginning of each chapter before you start reading. Make sure you read the associated knowledge requirements in the *HR Certification Institute's Certification Policies and Procedures Handbook* because they may help you in your study process. After you've read the chapter, review the requirements again to be sure you understand and are able to apply them.

- Answer the review questions after you've read each chapter. If you miss any of them, go back over the chapter and review the topic, or use one of the additional resources if you need more information. If in true learning mode, answer the questions open-book first.
- Download the flashcards and review them when you have a few minutes during the day.
- Take every opportunity to test yourself. In addition to the assessment test(s) and review questions, there are bonus practice exams. Take these exams without referring to the chapters and see how well you've done. Go back and review any topics you've missed until you fully understand and can apply the concepts.

Finally, find a study partner if possible. Studying for, and taking, the exam with someone else will make the process more enjoyable, and you'll have someone to help you understand topics that are difficult for you. You'll also be able to reinforce your own knowledge by helping your study partner in areas where they are weak.

How to Contact the Publisher

If you believe you have found a mistake in this book, please bring it to our attention. At John Wiley & Sons, we understand how important it is to provide our customers with accurate content, but even with our best efforts an error may occur.

In order to submit your possible errata, please email it to our Customer Service Team at `wileysupport@wiley.com` with the subject line "Possible Book Errata Submission."

PHR/i Assessment Test

1. According to the WARN Act, an employer with 200 employees is required to provide a 60-day notice of a mass layoff when which of the following is true?
   - **A.** The employer is seeking additional funding and will lay off 70 employees if the funding falls through.
   - **B.** A major client unexpectedly selects a new vendor for the company's products, and the company lays off 75 employees.
   - **C.** The employer lays off 5 employees a week for 3 months.
   - **D.** A flood requires that one of the plants be shut down for repairs, and 55 employees are laid off.

2. An employee has come forward with an allegation of quid pro quo harassment by her supervisor. As the HR manager, you are responsible for investigating the complaint. The supervisor in question is someone with whom you have become quite friendly. In this case, who is the best person to conduct the investigation?
   - **A.** You
   - **B.** The corporate attorney
   - **C.** The direct manager of the accused supervisor
   - **D.** A third-party investigator

3. As of 2024, the federal minimum wage is set at which of the following?
   - **A.** $5.15 per hour
   - **B.** $7.25 per hour
   - **C.** $10.50 per hour
   - **D.** $15.00 per hour

4. During the union-organizing process, how is the bargaining unit determined?
   - **A.** By the union organizers
   - **B.** Jointly, by the union and the employer
   - **C.** By the National Labor Relations Board
   - **D.** By the employees during the election

5. The motivation theory that suggests people are motivated by the reward they will receive when they succeed and that they weigh the value of the anticipated reward against the effort required to achieve it is known as what?
   - **A.** Vroom's expectancy theory
   - **B.** Adams' equity theory
   - **C.** McClelland's acquired needs theory
   - **D.** McGregor's Theory X and Theory Y

6. What is the most effective method of performance evaluation?
   A. A field-review process
   B. A continuous-feedback process
   C. A forced-ranking process
   D. A behaviorally anchored rating-scale process

7. Which of the following is an example of a nonqualified deferred-compensation plan?
   A. An excess-deferral plan
   B. A target-benefit plan
   C. A money-purchase plan
   D. A cash-balance plan

8. Which of the following is an example of a passive training method?
   A. Vestibule training
   B. Demonstration
   C. Distance learning
   D. Self-study

9. What is the purpose of the OSHA consulting service?
   A. Helps employers identify the OSHA standards that apply to their workplace
   B. Fines employers for violating OSHA safety standards
   C. Does not require compliance with OSHA standards
   D. Acts as a one-time service

10. Measuring staffing needs against sales volume could be done most effectively by using which of the following techniques?
    A. A multiple linear regression
    B. A ratio
    C. A simulation model
    D. A simple linear regression

11. What is an employer's responsibility when workplace conditions pose a threat to an unborn child?
    A. Do nothing. It is up to employees to protect their unborn children.
    B. Move the employee into a different job that does not pose a threat to the unborn child.
    C. Advise the employee of the potential threat and allow the employee to make the decision.
    D. Allow only sterile employees to work in jobs that pose a threat to unborn children.

12. What does the Health Insurance Portability and Accountability Act do?
   - A. Prevents HR from investigating claims issues
   - B. Requires continuation of health benefits
   - C. Establishes EPO networks
   - D. Limits preexisting condition restrictions

13. The concept that recognizes that businesses are social organizations as well as economic systems and that productivity is related to employee job satisfaction is known as what?
   - A. Human resource management
   - B. Strategic management
   - C. Human relations
   - D. Human resource development

14. Total quality management focuses all employees on producing activities that are of value to the organization. This is achieved by doing what?
   - A. Eliminating processes that waste time and materials
   - B. Developing a high level of expertise in all employees
   - C. Sharing information with all levels in the organization
   - D. Balancing the needs of all stakeholders in the organization

15. The correlation coefficient is a statistical measurement that is useful for which of the following?
   - A. Determining whether one variable affects another
   - B. Compensating for data that may be out-of-date
   - C. Determining which variables are outside acceptable ranges
   - D. Describing standards of quality

16. The process of identifying risks and taking steps to minimize them is referred to as what?
   - A. Liability management
   - B. Risk management
   - C. Qualitative analysis
   - D. Risk assessment

17. What is the most effective method to use when an employer wants to obtain insight into employee goals and job satisfaction and provide career counseling to those in the workgroup?
   - A. An employee survey
   - B. A skip-level interview
   - C. An employee focus group
   - D. A brown-bag lunch

18. Which of the following is an example of workplace ethics issues? (Choose all that apply.)
    A. Workplace privacy
    B. Conflicts of interest
    C. Whistleblowing
    D. Confidentiality

19. Which of the following statements about substance abuse policies is *not* true?
    A. Substance abuse policies identify who will be tested.
    B. Federal law requires all employers to implement substance abuse policies.
    C. An effective policy describes when tests will occur and what drugs will be tested.
    D. An effective policy describes what happens to employees who test positive.

20. Which one of the following statements is true of a hostile work environment?
    A. When a single incident of unwanted touching occurs, a hostile work environment has been created.
    B. A hostile work environment may be created when an individual witnesses the ongoing harassment of a coworker.
    C. Only a supervisor can create a hostile work environment.
    D. A grievance procedure/policy against discrimination protects employers from hostile work environment claims.

21. An HR audit is designed to help management do what? (Choose all that apply.)
    A. Improve employee morale.
    B. Analyze HR policies, programs, and procedures against applicable legal requirements.
    C. Improve HR effectiveness.
    D. Regulate employee behaviors.

22. A high-involvement organization is an example of what type of OD intervention?
    A. Human process
    B. Human resource management
    C. Techno-structural
    D. Strategic

23. Claims of disparate treatment for employees caring for elders, children, or disabled family members increased 450 percent between 1990 and 2005. Which of the following provides one of the bases for filing these claims?
    A. Sarbanes–Oxley
    B. Davis–Bacon Act
    C. Family Medical Leave Act
    D. Lily Ledbetter Act

24. Which of the following would be considered an extrinsic reward?
   A. Challenging work on a new project
   B. A 10 percent salary increase
   C. A feeling of accomplishment after completing a tough assignment
   D. Recognition by the CEO at a company meeting

25. According to the Copyright Act of 1976, which of the following is most likely to be considered a fair use of copyrighted material?
   A. Distributing 30 copies of a chapter in a book to a study group
   B. Copying a book for 10 staff members of a nonprofit organization
   C. Distributing 30 copies of a paragraph in a book to a study group
   D. Using 2.5 minutes of a popular song as part of a training video

26. Studies are showing that employers with written ethics policies are most likely to have employees ____________________.
   A. Report unethical behavior
   B. Require whistleblower protection
   C. Grow within the company
   D. Develop trusting relationships with coworkers

27. In the context of employee engagement, age, gender, and ethnicity are best represented by which description?
   A. Unlawful treatment
   B. Discriminatory criteria
   C. Surface-level diversity
   D. Deep-level diversity

28. Once a union begins an organizing campaign, managers may do all of the following *except*?
   A. A statement of the company's desire to remain union-free
   B. Factual statements about the disadvantages of unions in the labor/management relationship
   C. A description of what a union cannot do for the employees
   D. A promise of extended benefits if the company remains union-free

29. Which of the following is a form of bias that relates to the unintentional application of stereotypes to coworkers or customers?
   A. Face time bias
   B. Unconscious bias
   C. The halo effect
   D. The horn effect

30. OSHA requires which of the following plans to be provided in written form? (Choose all that apply.)

    A. Hazard communication

    B. Emergency response

    C. Fire prevention

    D. SDS

31. Which of the following tools would be the *best* first line of defense against employee embezzlement?

    A. A written policy

    B. Segregated job duties

    C. Accounting audits

    D. Computerized financial data

32. Which theory of motivation is built on the premise that the quality of motivation is just as important as the act of being motivated itself?

    A. Self-determination

    B. Hierarchy of needs

    C. Theory X and Y

    D. Acquired needs

33. Which of the following is an example of return-on-investment for a company training program?

    A. Improved customer experience

    B. Profit that is the result of training outcomes

    C. Reduced employee turnover

    D. Positive employee reactions

34. HR is being asked to consider a program that will track employees engaged in computer-based training. One feature is that HR will know precisely which quiz questions employees are missing. This is an example of which of the following? (Choose all that apply.)

    A. Workforce analytics

    B. Deep learning

    C. Program evaluation

    D. Training needs assessment

35. The need for adult learners to first unlearn old behaviors before they may replace them with new behaviors is the premise of which of the following sciences?

    A. Clinical psychology

    B. Applied psychology

    C. Neuroscience

    D. Biology

36. Why has trust emerged as a significant theme for leaders desiring to increase creativity in the workplace?

    A. Without trust, employees will be afraid for their ideas to fail.

    B. Without trust, employees fear they will not be rewarded for their innovation.

    C. Without trust, employees fear they will be ridiculed for ideas that are unconventional.

    D. Without trust, employees will not care enough to contribute to creative outcomes.

37. What is the purpose of identifying the percentage of internal candidates that fill leadership positions prior to implementing a leadership development program?

    A. Doing so allows for effectiveness to be measured.

    B. Doing so will determine whether the program is necessary.

    C. Doing so allows for a baseline comparison after an initiative has been implemented.

    D. Doing so will increase participation.

38. A sales employee is having a hard time understanding why he is required to "get off the phones" to attend classroom-based training on company culture. What is most likely missing in getting him motivated?

    A. Whole context

    B. A positive attitude

    C. Financial incentives

    D. Proper scheduling

39. Identifying the value that training created for an employer is the main purpose of which of the following business impact measures?

    A. Break-even analysis

    B. Return-on-investment

    C. Tactical accountability

    D. Learning evaluation

40. Andragogy refers to which of the following?

    A. How children learn

    B. How adults learn

    C. Cognitive functioning

    D. Behavioral sciences

41. Participants in a training program are asked to log into a website at their convenience, watch a video lecture, and take a quiz. This is an example of which of the following types of training?

    A. Vestibule

    B. Mobile learning

    C. Asynchronous

    D. The Delphi technique

42. How can chatbots influence employee learning and development? (Choose all that apply.)
    A. Chatbots provide instant access to learning resources and information, facilitating continuous learning and development on-demand.
    B. Chatbots offer personalized learning experiences by providing tailored recommendations, quizzes, and feedback based on individual learning preferences and performance.
    C. Chatbots can replace human trainers and instructors, delivering all learning content autonomously.
    D. Chatbots can only support very limited interactive experiences that do not require significant nuance.
43. Melissa recently facilitated companywide diversity training through a series of webinars. Prior to designing the training, she surveyed a sampling of employees to identify their experiences in the organization related to harassment, promotion opportunities, and equitable treatment. This is an example of which of the following?
    A. Summative evaluation
    B. Knowledge banking
    C. Attitude assessment
    D. Formative evaluation
44. One of your senior leaders has come to you with a career development plan for her employees. She would like your feedback to ensure that she has covered the future needs for the employee's development. The senior leader is displaying high degrees of what?
    A. Dependence
    B. Extroversion
    C. Autonomy
    D. Self-determination
45. Innovation by building one idea on top of another is the premise of which of the following?
    A. Creativity
    B. The Delphi technique
    C. Idea fluency
    D. The nominal technique

Answers to PHR/i Assessment Test

1. C. The WARN Act requires employers to provide a 60- day notice when 500 employees or 50 employees making up 33 percent of the workforce are laid off, and it requires the number to be counted over a period of 90 days. Five employees a week for 3 months is a total of 65 employees (5 employees times 13 weeks), which is 33 percent of the workforce. The three exceptions are the "faltering company exception" (option A) when knowledge of a layoff will negatively impact the company's ability to obtain additional funding, the "unforeseeable business circumstance" (option B) when unexpected circumstances occur, and the "natural disaster" (option D) exception. To learn more, see Appendix C.

2. D. In this case, the organization will be best served by a third-party investigator. The most important consideration in an investigation of sexual harassment is that the investigator is seen as credible and impartial. Because you have become friendly with the accused, it will be difficult to maintain impartiality during an investigation. While the corporate attorney (option B) may be selected to conduct investigations, this solution can lead to conflict-of-interest issues. The direct manager of the accused supervisor (option C) may not be viewed as impartial by the accuser or by regulatory agencies. To learn more, see Chapter 2.

3. B. As of 2024, the federal minimum wage is still $7.25 per hour. The minimum wage in some states and other localities may be different. To learn more, see Appendix C.

4. C. The National Labor Relations Board (NLRB) determines which jobs will be included in the bargaining unit based on the "community of interest" shared by the requirements of the jobs. To learn more, see Chapter 8.

5. A. Vroom explains his theory with three terms: expectancy (the individual's assessment of their ability to achieve the goal), instrumentality (whether the individual believes they are capable of achieving the goal), and valence (whether the anticipated goal is worth the effort required to achieve it). Adams's equity theory (option B) states that people are constantly comparing what they put into work to what they get from it. McClelland's acquired needs theory (option C) states that people are motivated by one of three factors: achievement, affiliation, or power. McGregor's Theory X and Theory Y (option D) explain how managers relate to employees. Theory X managers are autocratic, believing that employees do not want to take responsibility. Theory Y managers encourage employees to participate in the decision-making process, believing that they respond to challenges. To learn more, see Chapter 2.

6. B. A continuous-feedback review process is most effective because it provides immediate feedback to employees, enabling them to correct performance issues before they become major problems. In a field review (A), reviews are conducted by someone other than the direct supervisor. Forced ranking (C) is an evaluation method in which all employees are listed in order of their value to the work group. The BARS process (D) identifies the most important job requirements and creates statements that describe varying levels of performance. To learn more, see Chapter 2.

7. A. An excess-deferral plan makes up the difference between what an executive could have contributed to a qualified plan if there had not been a limit on contributions and how much

was actually contributed because of the discrimination test required by ERISA. These plans are nonqualified because they are not protected by ERISA; they are limited to a small group of executives or highly compensated employees. A target-benefit plan (option B) is a hybrid with elements of defined-benefit and money-purchase plans. A money-purchase plan (option C) defers a fixed percentage of employee earnings. A cash-balance plan (option D) combines elements of defined-benefit and defined-contribution plans. To learn more, see Chapter 2.

8. C. Distance learning is a form of lecture style presentation that does not necessarily require active participation. Vestibule training (option A) is a form of simulation training. Demonstration (option B) is an experiential training method. Self-study (option D) is an active training method. To learn more, see Chapter 5.

9. A. OSHA consultants provide free services to assist employers in identifying workplace hazards and the standards that apply in their workplaces. The consulting service requires employers to abate any hazards that are identified during the consultation but does not fine them for violations. To receive a free consultation, employers must agree to advise OSHA of changes in operating processes that may require additional consultations. To learn more, see Chapter 8.

10. D. A simple linear regression measures one variable against another, so it would be effective for measuring staffing needs against sales volume. Multiple linear regression (option A) measures more than one variable against others, which would not work in this case as there are not multiple variables. A ratio (option B) compares one number to another and is too simplified to provide more value than the correct answer. A simulation model uses a computer program (option C) to predict the possible outcomes of different business scenarios, which is not necessary in this scenario. To learn more, see Chapter 2.

11. C. The Supreme Court determined in *Automobile Workers v. Johnson Controls, Inc.* that it is the responsibility of prospective parents to protect their unborn children. Although employers must provide information about potential hazards, the employer may not decide for the employee whether they can work in a job that poses a risk to an unborn child, as this would be considered discriminatory. To learn more, see Chapter 2.

12. D. HIPAA prohibits health insurance providers from discriminating on the basis of health status and limits restrictions for preexisting conditions. HIPAA does not prevent HR from investigating claims issues (option A) as long as the employee provides written permission. COBRA requires continuation of health benefits (option B). EPO networks (option C) are established by physicians connected to a hospital. To learn more, see Appendix C.

13. C. The concept of human relations was first introduced in the 1920s and challenged previous assumptions that people work only for economic reasons and could be motivated to increase productivity simply by increasing monetary incentives. Human resource management (option A) is the business function responsible for activities related to attracting and retaining employees, including workforce planning, training and development, compensation, employee and labor relations, and safety and security. Strategic management (option B) is the process by which organizations look for competitive advantages, create value for customers, and execute plans to achieve goals. Human resource development (option D) is the functional area of human resources focused on upgrading and maintaining employee skills and developing employees for additional responsibilities. To learn more, see Chapter 7.

14. A. The TQM concept reviews processes to eliminate waste, relies on teamwork, and involves all members of the organization in meeting customer needs. Personal mastery, a high level of employee expertise (option B), is one of the five disciplines of a learning organization. Information sharing is one characteristic of a high-involvement organization (option C). The ability to balance stakeholder needs is a requirement of a change agent (option D). To learn more, see Chapter 2.

15. A. The correlation coefficient is useful in determining whether two factors are connected. For example, the correlation coefficient will tell you whether an increase in resignations is related to a change in location of the worksite and, if so, whether the change had a strong impact on resignations. To learn more, see Chapter 2.

16. B. Risk management is the process of controlling legal exposure for the organization and reduces those risks with preventive actions. Liability management (option A) occurs after a liability is incurred, while risk management seeks to prevent liability. Qualitative analysis (option C) covers several subjective tools for analysis. A risk assessment (option D) is used to determine how likely it is that an identified risk will actually occur. To learn more, see Chapter 2.

17. B. A skip-level interview provides an opportunity for a manager's manager to obtain insight into the goals and satisfaction of employees in the work group. An employee survey (option A) is best used to gather information about various issues that can be collated and summarized. A focus group (option C) can be used to involve employees in the decision-making process. A brown-bag lunch (option D) is an effective way for senior managers to meet with small groups of employees to answer questions about the company goals and mission and to obtain feedback about operations. To learn more, see Chapter 7.

18. A, B, D. Workplace privacy, conflicts of interest, and confidentiality are all examples of workplace ethics issues. Ethics are considered a standard of conduct and moral judgment defined by the processes that occur and the consequences of these processes. Whistleblowing occurs when an employee reports employer wrong doing, and is separate and distinct from ethical issues. To learn more, see Chapter 2.

19. B. The Drug-Free Workplace Act of 1988 requires only federal contractors and subcontractors to establish substance abuse policies. A fair and effective policy will describe which employees will be tested (option A) and whether it is all or specific job groups. The policy should describe (option C) when tests will be done (preemployment, randomly, on reasonable suspicion, or according to a predetermined schedule), what drugs are included in the process, and the consequences for employees who test positive (option D). To learn more, see Chapter 8.

20. B. A coworker who witnesses the ongoing harassment of another individual may have an actionable claim of a hostile work environment. A single incident of unwanted touching (option A), unless it is particularly offensive or intimidating, will not reach the threshold of a hostile work environment established by the courts. A hostile work environment may be created by any individual in the workplace, including customers, vendors, or visitors, in addition to supervisors or coworkers (option C). In the case of *Meritor Savings Bank v. Vinson*, the Supreme Court held that the mere existence of a grievance procedure and antiharassment policy (option D) does not necessarily protect an employer from hostile work environment claims. To learn more, see Chapter 2.

21. A, B, C. An HR audit is an organized process designed to identify key aspects of HR in the organization such as employee morale, HR policies, programs and procedures, and HR effectiveness. It is not designed to regulate employee behavior (option D). To learn more, see Chapter 2.

22. C. Techno-structural interventions address issues of how work gets done in an organization. A high-involvement organization is one in which employees at all levels are involved in making decisions about how work is accomplished. Human-process interventions (option A) are designed to build competencies at the individual level of the organization. HRM interventions (option B) focus on HR processes and programs such as selection procedures or performance management that address individual employee needs. Strategic interventions (option D) are used to execute changes to an organization's vision, mission, or values. To learn more, see Chapter 2.

23. C. According to guidance published by the EEOC, caregivers are not a protected class, but there are circumstances in which disparate treatment becomes unlawful based on violations of FMLA caregiving requirements. This can also be true of stereotyping prohibited by Title VII and association with disabled individuals prohibited by the ADA. Sarbanes–Oxley deals with financial reporting (option A), and the Davis–Bacon Act established minimum wages (option B). The Lily Ledbetter Act reset the amount of time a wage claim can be filed (option D). To learn more, see Appendix C.

24. D. Extrinsic rewards are non-monetary rewards where self-esteem comes from others, such as formal recognition for a job well done. Challenging work on a new project (option A) is an intrinsic reward. Salary increases (option B) are monetary rewards. A feeling of accomplishment after completing a tough assignment (option C) is another type of intrinsic reward. To learn more, see Chapter 6.

25. C. Four factors are considered in determining whether the use of published material is a fair use: the purpose of the use, the nature of the work being copied, how much of the work is copied, and what economic effect copying the material will have on the market value of the work. Using full chapters or an entire book, or a clip from a song would be violations of the Copy Right Act. To learn more, see Appendix C.

26. A. Employees that witness unethical behavior by others are the first line of risk management. Written ethics policies that both encourage reporting and prohibit retaliation have been shown to increase internal reporting, allowing employers to quickly respond and resolve issues before they get out of hand. To learn more, see Chapter 2.

27. C. Of the two types of diversity, surface-level refers to the observable traits of a specific demographic such as age, gender, or ethnicity. The other answers are not correct. To learn more, see Chapter 7.

28. D. Employers may be accused of an unfair labor practice (ULP) if they threaten, interrogate, promise, or spy on employees (TIPS). To learn more, see Chapter 8.

29. B. Unconscious bias occurs when people act on stereotypes that they are unaware that they have. Training employees to be aware that this bias is unconscious can help reduce and eliminate behavior that is built from this bias. To learn more, see Chapter 8.

30. A, B, C. There are several written plans that are required of employers in order to be compliant with the Occupational Safety and Health Act's standards. These written plans include hazard communication, emergency response, and fire prevention. Safety data sheets (SDSs) are a form of hazard communication, not a plan, and can be stored electronically. To learn more, see Chapter 2.

31. B. While written policies, audits, and the computerization of financial data for tracking purposes may all help reduce employee embezzlement, eliminating the opportunity by segregating job duties is the most effective as a first line of defense. For example, a single employee should not have the ability to receive, post, and physically deposit customer payments. Being able to do so would make it easier for an employee to alter the books to hide any deceit. To learn more, see Chapter 2.

32. A. The self-determination theory of motivation is built on the idea that the quality, depth, and origin of motivation matters just as much as how much motivation an employee has. Intrinsic motivators tend to have a stronger force than external motivators. To learn more, see Chapter 2.

33. D. Return on investment (ROI) may be measured using both tangible and intangible criteria. Examples may include hard costs, reduced turnover, improved employee retention, higher customer satisfaction, and improved employee reaction to training. To learn more, see Chapter 5.

34. A, B, C There are several advantages to using technology to evaluate training program outcomes. This example refers to the deep-learning techniques that allow for macro and micro data collection. This is a form of workforce analytics that is used to evaluate program design effectiveness. A training needs assessment is done prior to the design and development of a training program and its content to understand the learning objectives of training. To learn more, see Chapter 4.

35. C. The impact of neuroscience research on organizational and individual employee behavior is just beginning to scratch the surface of workplace breakthroughs. Neuroscience is making significant contributions toward the behavioral sciences in change management, decision making, and leadership development, just to name a few. To learn more, see Chapter 5.

36. A. The creative process requires a period of trial and error. Some ideas will simply not work. If a leader or a culture does not inspire trust from employees, employees will fear that these failures will result in a negative professional outcome and so are reluctant to speak up. To learn more, see Chapter 7.

37. C. Part of measuring the effectiveness of any L&D intervention activity is knowing what the "before" conditions are prior to implementation. This allows for periodic checks to ensure that the program is doing what it was intended to do. To learn more, see Chapter 4.

38. A. Some adults require a deeper level understanding of a training session's context and purpose—in short, the "why" behind a training initiative. By providing the sales employee with this information—such as how selling techniques are a reflection of what the company values—the company is more likely to gain his buy-in. To learn more, see Chapter 2.

39. B. With the cost of having employees ever on the rise, the value of any type of investment—training or otherwise—should be effectively measured and clearly communicated. Regularly calculating return-on-investment (ROI) allows for real-time adjustments, increasing the odds that the program will achieve the desired results. To learn more, see Chapter 2.

40. B. Malcolm Knowles introduced the concept that adults and children learn new things very differently. The term andragogy refers to the process by which adults learn. To learn more, see Chapter 5.

41. C. Asynchronous training is self-paced training that typically occurs using computer-based tools. Although timelines for completion may be preestablished (such as specifying that all assignments must be submitted no later than 11:59 p.m. Sunday evening), participants typically are able to set their own schedule for when they engage in learning the material. Vestibule training is a form of OJT (option A), mobile learning (option B) is a type of e-learning that occurs typically through mobile devices, and the Delphi technique (option D) is a decision-making or forecasting activity that relies on a group of experts to reach a consensus. To learn more, see Chapter 5.

42. A, B. Chatbots can influence employee learning and development by providing instant access to learning resources and information. They serve as virtual assistants that employees can interact with to quickly retrieve relevant learning materials, such as training modules, manuals, videos, or articles. By analyzing user interactions and preferences, chatbots can deliver tailored recommendations, quizzes, and feedback to individual learners. This personalization enhances engagement and effectiveness by providing content and activities that align with each learner's interests, goals, and skill levels, fostering a more impactful learning experience. Option C is incorrect because chatbots are not intended to replace human trainers and instructors entirely; human interaction remains valuable for addressing complex learning needs, providing mentorship, and facilitating interactive discussions and collaborative learning experiences. Option D is incorrect because modern chatbots are capable of supporting a wide range of learning needs and interactive learning experiences beyond basic information retrieval. To learn more, see Chapter 5.

43. D. Formative evaluation is a technique used prior to the commencement and during the design phase of training. It is used to gather data that will be used in training to ensure that the objectives are met and that the training meets the needs of the workgroup. This is different from summative evaluation (option A), which occurs after the training has taken place. Knowledge banking (option B) and an attitude assessment (option C) are not used in the evaluation of training. To learn more, see Chapter 5.

44. D. Self-determination is one of many theories of motivation. Research (and anecdotal evidence) has found that leaders who are self-determined rarely wait for others to drive their best behaviors. As a general rule, they strive to be proactive. To learn more, see Chapter 2.

45. C. Being fluid in the generation of ideas is the premise behind idea fluency. Similar to language fluency, ideas build on each other until a coherent concept emerges, rather like words build a sentence. To learn more, see Chapter 7.

SPHR/i Assessment Test

1. Which of the following negative outcomes best reflects the failure to align the human resource strategic plan with the organization's strategic plan?
   - A. Lack of plan management
   - B. Misdirection of the organization's human talent
   - C. Failure to respond to external market conditions
   - D. Out-of-compliance HR policies, procedures, and rules
2. Before selecting an HRIS system, which of the following questions should be answered? (Choose all that apply.)
   - A. What information will be converted to the HRIS?
   - B. Who will have access to the information stored in the HRIS?
   - C. Are there customer testimonials we can review?
   - D. How will the HRIS be accessed, i.e., remotely or through other platforms?
3. Which of the following is not a breach of a human resource professional's fiduciary responsibility?
   - A. Profiting from the HR role
   - B. Paying someone less based solely on their race
   - C. Conflicting duties
   - D. Acting in their own self-interest
4. Which of the following is not a component of a SWOT analysis?
   - A. Strengths
   - B. Weaknesses
   - C. Outsourcing
   - D. Threats
5. Adverse impact determines whether there is statistical evidence of unlawful discrimination by calculating selection ratios for a protected class group by using what percentage?
   - A. 10%.
   - B. 50%.
   - C. 80%.
   - D. It varies by group.
6. Succession planning is best described by which of the following?
   - A. A systematic approach to identify, assess, and develop talent for leadership roles in an organization
   - B. Predetermining employees within the company to fill management roles
   - C. Planning the career path of entry level employees to fill different roles in the company
   - D. A developmental program that offers promotion opportunity for internal candidates.

7. Which of the following describes deep-level diversity?
   - **A.** Biological variables that may or may not correlate to job attitudes or overall performance
   - **B.** Various people working together, often with differences in culture, race, generation, gender or religion
   - **C.** Individual differences in values or beliefs
   - **D.** A program for training employees in diversity awareness

8. Which of the following describes the difference between a STEP analysis and a PEST analysis?
   - **A.** A STEP analysis identifies opportunities, whereas a PEST analysis identifies threats.
   - **B.** A STEP analysis is part of a SWOT analysis, whereas a PEST analysis is independent.
   - **C.** There is no such thing as a PEST analysis.
   - **D.** There is no difference. They are the same thing.

9. A critical aspect of retaining quality employees in an organization is __________.
   - **A.** Rigid management that is focused on achieving business results
   - **B.** Limiting training to increase productivity of the workforce
   - **C.** A strong socialization and onboarding of new employees
   - **D.** Providing higher compensation or a raise in salary

10. Measuring how much a job is worth is known as __________.
    - **A.** Job analysis
    - **B.** Job evaluation
    - **C.** Job grading
    - **D.** Job ranking

11. Which of the following is not one of the four key questions of a strategic HR plan?
    - **A.** Where have we been?
    - **B.** Where are we now?
    - **C.** Where do we want to be?
    - **D.** How will we know when we arrive?

12. Which of the following collective-bargaining positions is a type of principled bargaining?
    - **A.** Positional bargaining
    - **B.** Interest-based bargaining
    - **C.** Concession bargaining
    - **D.** Distributed bargaining

13. A recent round of turnover has your executive team questioning the existing salary structure. What should be your first strategic approach?
    A. Recommend pay increases for critical staff positions.
    B. Implement exit interviews to find out if inadequate pay is the reason for leaving.
    C. Conduct a wage survey to compare your pay rates to those of similar employers in the area.
    D. Meet with employees to determine if they are satisfied with their pay.

14. The executive committee has asked HR to provide them with copies of all employee personnel files, EEO reports, collective-bargaining agreements, and the employee handbook. They are most likely engaged in the practice of executing which activity?
    A. Exercising due diligence
    B. Responding to a labor dispute
    C. Union busting
    D. A wage review

15. Strategic organizational design interventions would include making changes to which of the following business practices?
    A. Mission, vision, and values
    B. Tactical measures
    C. Organizational policies, procedures, and rules
    D. Management development

16. A strategic workforce plan allows an employer to accomplish which of the following?
    A. Determine what skill sets are needed to meet future training or staffing needs.
    B. Comply with affirmative action requirements.
    C. Identify recruitment sources based on skill sets required.
    D. Provide a framework to ensure that the right people are doing the right jobs when the employer needs them.

17. Which of the following provides the framework for collecting information to be used in strategic planning?
    A. Environmental scan
    B. SWOT audit
    C. Statistical model
    D. Force analysis

18. When privately held companies provide the benefits of employee ownership without actually granting stock, it is known as which of the following?
    A. Restricted stock
    B. Phantom stock
    C. Incentive stock options
    D. Nonqualified stock options

19. Computing the cost per hire is a way to determine which of the following?
    - **A.** HR's internal budget
    - **B.** The time needed to onboard a new employee
    - **C.** Staffing effectiveness
    - **D.** Budget shortfalls

20. Which of the following is the main type of strategic analysis? (Choose all that apply.)
    - **A.** Gap analysis
    - **B.** Supply analysis
    - **C.** Demand analysis
    - **D.** Workforce planning

21. Many companies have fiscal years that begin on July 1 and end on June 30 of the following calendar year. This function is guided by what?
    - **A.** SMART
    - **B.** LMS
    - **C.** ZBB
    - **D.** GAAP

22. A company located in Seattle, Washington, as part of the post-employment activities for a new employee residing in Boston, Massachusetts, may engage in which of the following?
    - **A.** Contact references to verify employment history.
    - **B.** Assist the employee with relocation.
    - **C.** Use online teleconferencing technology to facilitate the interviews.
    - **D.** Offer a signing bonus.

23. A statement of cash flows is a financial report that tells you which of the following?
    - **A.** The financial condition of the business at a specific point in time
    - **B.** Where the money used to operate the business came from
    - **C.** The financial results of operations over a period of time
    - **D.** How much money is owed to the company by its customers

24. One purpose of a diversity initiative is to do what?
    - **A.** Increase workplace creativity.
    - **B.** Increase the effectiveness of the workforce.
    - **C.** Increase the organization's ability to attract customers.
    - **D.** Increase surface-level diversity.

25. Billingswotth Entertainment recently joined forces with its largest competitor, WWE, combining assets into one functioning entity. This is an example of which of the following?

    A. Hostile takeover

    B. Corporate restructuring

    C. Merger

    D. Workforce expansion

26. Which of the following is the best example of a cross-functional stakeholder?

    A. Marketing specialist

    B. Sales representative

    C. Finance analyst

    D. Product manager

27. In what ways does an organizational chart support effective decision making? (Choose all that apply.)

    A. Clarifies reporting relationships

    B. Identifies gaps in the organization

    C. Facilitates communication channels

    D. Encourages siloed thinking

28. What is the key strategic difference between replacement plans and succession plans in organizational management?

    A. Replacement plans focus on long-term leadership development, whereas succession plans focus on immediate staffing needs.

    B. Replacement plans identify specific individuals to fill critical roles temporarily, whereas succession plans develop talent for long-term leadership roles.

    C. Replacement plans focus on training current employees, whereas succession plans focus on recruiting external candidates.

    D. Replacement plans are used only in emergencies, whereas succession plans are a regular part of strategic planning.

29. "Our company focuses on attracting and retaining top talent by offering competitive pay, benefits and opportunities for growth." This is the best example of which of the following?

    A. The employer brand

    B. An equity statement

    C. A compensation philosophy

    D. The company values

30. Which of the following statements best describes the primary role of a human resource leader in the collective bargaining process?

    A. Ensuring that all union demands are considered in a fair and impartial manner

    B. Representing the interests of the employer, negotiating employment terms, and ensuring compliance with labor laws

C. Acting as a neutral mediator between the union and the employer to resolve disputes

D. Organizing union meetings and advocating for the employees' concerns

31. Which of the following is *not* a key component of data security policies in the workplace? (Choose all that apply.)

A. Prohibiting employees from using their personal devices for work

B. Implementing strong password policies and requiring regular password changes

C. Limiting access to social media for all workers

D. Conducting regular security awareness training for all employees

32. What are the primary functions that employers should use employee self-service systems for? (Choose all that apply.)

A. To complete routine tax forms

B. To update personal information

C. To update progress on performance goals

D. To acknowledge harassment prevention and other compliance training

33. The manufacturing company you work for is redesigning the production line to be more efficient. This includes automating routine tasks, investing in robotics, and using AI systems for troubleshooting. Based on this, place the following digitization initiates in the order of importance:

1. Implementing an AI-powered talent management system

2. Developing an automated learning and development platform

3. Launching a digital employee self-service portal

A. 1, 2, 3

B. 2, 1, 3

C. 3, 2, 1

D. 1, 3, 2

34. An employee receives an email with an attachment that appears to be an invoice from a trusted vendor. After downloading and opening the attachment, the employee's computer becomes slow and unresponsive, and files start getting corrupted. The IT department discovers that malicious software has been installed, which is now spreading across the network. What type of attack does this scenario describe?

A. Phishing

B. Hacking

C. Malware

D. Ransom

35. Which of the following benefits strategies is most effective for a small startup company with under 100 employees?
    A. Offering flexible work arrangements and a comprehensive health benefits package
    B. Providing retirement plans and concierge wellness programs
    C. Implementing a structured, pension plan with generous employer contributions
    D. Offering a wide range of stock options and deferred compensation plans

36. In which situation would a service recognition reward be most effective?
    A. Celebrating an employee's five-year anniversary with the company to acknowledge their loyalty and contributions
    B. Recognizing an employee's completion of a short-term project ahead of schedule
    C. Rewarding an employee for attending a mandatory training session
    D. Incentivizing employees to participate in a new volunteer program

37. Which of the following best describes the job evaluation process?
    A. The method used to systematically study and document the duties, responsibilities, and requirements of a specific job
    B. The systematic process of determining the relative worth of jobs within an organization to establish fair compensation
    C. The annual review process where employees' performance is assessed and rated
    D. The method used to analyze the skills and qualifications required for a job

38. What should be the first step a senior HR leader should take when tasked with creating an annual human resource budget?
    A. Allocate funds for new employee benefits and compensation packages.
    B. Determine the expected costs of recruiting and hiring new employees.
    C. Review the previous year's budget and identify areas of overspending.
    D. Assess the company's strategic goals and align the HR budget with those objectives.

39. What communication strategy would be the most effective when addressing the remaining employees after a mass layoff?
    A. Announcing the layoffs in a brief email without providing further details
    B. Holding a companywide meeting to openly discuss the reasons for the layoffs, address concerns, and outline the future direction of the company
    C. Avoiding any formal communication
    D. Sending a memo to managers only, instructing them not to discuss the layoffs with their teams

40. Which factor of cultural integration will address employees after a merger when the employees are having interpersonal conflicts?
    A. Establishing new organizational policies and procedures
    B. Focusing on aligning business processes and systems

C. Promoting open communication and team-building activities to foster understanding and collaboration

D. Implementing a unified branding strategy for the new organization

41. Which of the following types of organizations is most likely to use sabbaticals as a form of employee development?

A. Academia

B. Healthcare

C. Manufacturing

D. Finance

42. Which of the following best illustrates how senior HR leaders can use Hofstede's dimensions of culture to form HR strategies?

A. Customizing employee recognition programs to reflect the levels of comfort with uncertainty prevalent in each culture

B. Emphasizing individual performance metrics in countries with high collectivism scores

C. Adjusting leadership development programs to align with the power distance levels of each country

D. Ignoring cultural dimensions and focusing solely on financial performance

43. Which of the following statements is *true* about an employee who scores high uncertainty avoidance?

A. The employee is an introvert.

B. The employee may be uncomfortable with change.

C. The employee is probably not creative.

D. The employee has low levels of stress.

44. Which of the following best describes a strategy to ensure HR policies are aligned with labor laws?

A. Establishing a flexible set of guidelines that can be adjusted based on geographic locations and norms

B. Conducting regular training sessions for HR staff on current labor laws and legal compliance requirements

C. Allowing each department to create its own HR policies independently

D. Prioritizing compliance with nondiscriminatory practices

45. Which of the following is a diversity strategy that is most likely to support inclusive hiring practices?

A. Implementing a strict seniority-based promotion system

B. Limiting job postings to internal candidates only

C. Using blind recruitment processes to remove bias from the hiring process

D. Requiring all applicants to have degrees from specific prestigious universities

Answers to SPHR/i Assessment Test

1. B. The human resources strategy should support the overall strategic direction of the organization by ensuring that the right people are in the right roles, and that they are motivated and capable of achieving the organization's objectives. Lack of plan management (option A) refers to the inability to effectively manage and execute a plan. While this can be a problem in any strategic initiative, it indicates a broader issue of poor management practices rather than the specific consequences of misalignment. Failure to respond to external market conditions (option C) is a broader organizational issue that can result from various factors, such as poor strategic planning, lack of market research, or inflexible business practices; it is not directly tied to the alignment of the HR strategic plan with the organization's strategic plan. Out-of-compliance HR policies, procedures, and rules (option D) refer to the HR department not adhering to legal and regulatory requirements. While this is a serious issue, it is not a direct consequence of the misalignment between the HR strategic plan and the organization's strategic plan. To learn more, see Chapter 10.

2. A, B, D. A needs analysis will provide answers to questions related to properly selecting an HRIS, as well as whether the HRIS will be integrated with payroll or other systems and what kinds of reports will be produced. To learn more, see Chapter 14.

3. B. The three breaches of a human resource professional's fiduciary responsibility include acting in their own self-interest, having conflicting duties, and profiting from their role. Paying someone less based solely on their race is not specifically a breach of the human resource professional's fiduciary responsibilities, although it is unethical and illegal. To learn more, see Appendix C.

4. C. The four components of a SWOT analysis include strengths, weaknesses, opportunities, and threats. To learn more, see Chapter 10.

5. C. Adverse impact is also known as the 4/5ths rule, which is also 80%. It is used to calculate the selection ratio for all protected class groups. To learn more, see Chapter 2.

6. A. Succession planning is a process to identify talent in the organization, assess their potential, and develop them over time. It does not preselect people for positions but ideally creates a pool that can be drawn from to fill roles that are vacated by senior employees who transition or separate from the company. To learn more, see Chapter 2.

7. C. Deep-level diversity refers to individual differences in values or beliefs. It is valuable in employee relations and behavior management because when employee values and attitudes are aligned with organizational culture and outcomes, job performance is enhanced. By contrast, more general diversity is a combination of various people working together, often with differences in culture, race, generation, gender or religion (option B), which is a form of surface-level diversity, the biological variables that may or may not correlate to job attitudes or overall performance (option A). To learn more, see Chapter 2.

8. D. A STEP analysis (also known as a PEST analysis) scans the external environment to identify opportunities and threats as part of the SWOT analysis. PEST/STEP is an acronym for social, technological, economic, and political factors. To learn more, see Chapter 10.

9. C. Companies that socialize and successfully onboard new employees integrate them into the culture of the organization. This builds brand loyalty and a shared sense of belonging and purpose, which strengthens an employee's commitment to the company based on values. These employees are more likely to be retained by a company in the future. To learn more, see Chapter 11.

10. B. Measuring how much a job is worth is known as job evaluation. Job analysis is a study of the major tasks and responsibilities of jobs to determine their importance and relation to other jobs in a company (option A). Job grading is a means of determining different job levels and pay scales based on the required knowledge, skills, and abilities (option C). Job ranking compares jobs to each other based on their importance to the organization (option D). To learn more, see Chapter 13.

11. A. The four key questions of a strategic HR plan are "Where are we now?," "Where do we want to be?," "How do we get there?," and "How will we know when we arrive?" These follow a natural order and are answered in the strategic-planning process. To learn more, see Chapter 10.

12. B. Interest-based bargaining (IBB) is when both sides in the negotiation have harmonious interests, which is a form of principled bargaining where both parties are more concerned with solving a problem than winning a position. Concession bargaining (option C) is when a union gives something up in return for job security. Positional bargaining (option A) and distributive bargaining (option D) are synonymous and refer to when each side's primary concern is winning their own position. To learn more, see Chapter 12.

13. C. Conducting equity surveys both internally and externally is necessary to determine if your pay structure is positively or negatively influencing turnover. Exit interviews are important, but they usually come too late to have an immediate effect on retention. To learn more, see Chapter 13.

14. A. Due diligence is described by HRCI as "the gathering and analysis of important information related to a business acquisition or merger, such as assets and liabilities, contracts, and benefit plans." Due diligence is a type of investigation that will take place as part of a merger or an acquisition. To learn more, see Chapter 11.

15. A. Mission, vision, and values statements are at the heart of strategic HRM. Implementing changes to these areas will result in the tactical and operational changes required to achieve the desired results. To learn more, see Chapter 2.

16. D. A strategic workforce plan will ensure that qualified employees are available when the organization needs them by forecasting business needs, assessing employee skill, bridging gaps between them, and embedding ways to engage to retain employees. To learn more, see Chapter 2.

17. A. An environmental scan includes activities related to both internal and external data collection. This data is used to determine the course of action for businesses once the goals and objectives have been developed. To learn more, see Chapter 10.

18. B. Phantom stock is used in privately held companies to provide the benefits of employee ownership without actually granting stock. Restricted stock is common stock offered to employees, typically executives or employees who demonstrate outstanding performance (option A). Nonqualified stock options can be used for consultants and external members of the board of directors (BOD) as well as for employees (option D). Incentive stock options are stock options that can be offered only to employees (option C). To learn more, see Chapter 13.

19. C. Staffing effectiveness can be measured in a variety of ways to ensure that the cost of human capital is not excessive for what duties and tasks are to be performed. Turnover ratios, cost per hire, and number of applicants to number of qualified applicants are metrics that can be used. To learn more, see Chapter 13.

20. A, B, C. Together, supply analysis, demand analysis, and gap analysis make up the three main types of strategic analysis. Workforce planning is a process that identifies current and future staffing needs. To learn more, see Chapter 10.

21. D. Generally Accepted Accounting Principles (GAAP) guide the use of a fiscal year that begins on July 1 and ends on June 30 of the following calendar year. SMART (specific, measurable, action-oriented, realistic, time-based) is a system used in establishing effective corporate goals (option A). A learning management system (LMS) streamlines the administration of employee training programs (option B). Zero-based budgeting (ZBB) is an approach to creating budgets (option C). To learn more, see Appendix C.

22. B. Among the myriad of tasks that HR might perform with new employees is to provide information on relocation or coordinate relocation services. This is done in the post-employment phase after an offer of employment has been made and accepted by the employee. To learn more, see Chapter 11.

23. B. A statement of cash flows provides information about the money that flowed through the business. It identifies whether the cash was received from customers, loans, or other sources; how much cash was spent to operate the business; and how much was reinvested in the business. A balance sheet describes the financial condition of the business at a specific point in time (option A). The income statement, or profit and loss statement, tells you the financial results of operations over a period of time (option C). An accounts-receivable ledger describes how much money is owed to the company by each customer (option D). To learn more, see Chapter 10.

24. B. The purpose of a diversity initiative is to increase the effectiveness of an already diverse workforce by educating the employee population about the benefits of a diverse workforce, which include increased creativity (option A) and an enhanced ability to attract customers (option C). Surface-level diversity (option D) refers to observable individual characteristics and is not a goal of diversity initiatives. To learn more, see Chapter 2.

25. C. A merger is similar to an acquisition as both result in a new, single business entity. A merger, however, is usually a mutual effort to leverage assets, whereas an acquisition is often

completed by the strategic purchase of the target's stock, allowing the purchaser to assume (or take over) control. To learn more, see Chapter 11.

26. D. A cross-functional stakeholder is an individual who collaborates with multiple departments or functions within an organization to achieve a common goal. A product manager is responsible for overseeing the development and lifecycle of a product. They interact with various departments, including marketing, sales, engineering, and finance, to ensure the product meets market demands and business goals. This role requires collaboration across multiple functions, making the product manager a cross-functional stakeholder. Options A, B, and C are incorrect as their roles are specific to a single function within the organization. To learn more, see Chapter 10.

27. A, B, C. An organizational chart is a visual representation of a company's structure, showing the relationships and relative ranks of its positions and departments. It helps to (A) define who reports to whom, helping to establish clear lines of authority and responsibility. By visualizing the structure, it becomes easier to spot missing roles or overburdened departments. An organizational chart shows formal communication pathways, aiding in efficient information flow across the organization. Option D is incorrect because although organizational charts can inadvertently contribute to siloed thinking, they are not designed to encourage it. To learn more, see Chapter 10.

28. B. Replacement plans are designed to provide immediate coverage for key positions in case of sudden vacancies, ensuring business continuity by having a ready list of candidates. In contrast, succession plans are focused on the long-term development of employees to prepare them for future leadership roles, aligning with the organization's strategic goals. Option A is incorrect as replacement plans are typically short-term solutions for immediate needs, whereas succession plans are long-term strategies for developing future leaders. Option C is incorrect because both replacement and succession plans generally involve internal talent. Option D is partially true but misleading. While replacement plans are often used in emergency situations, they can also be part of regular planning. To learn more, see Chapter 12.

29. C. A compensation philosophy describes the principles and strategies that guide how a company compensates its employees, aligning with the organization's overall goals and values. Option A is incorrect as the employer brand relates to how a company is perceived as a place to work, and it encompasses more than just compensation. Option B is incorrect because an equity statement typically addresses a company's commitment to fairness, diversity, and inclusion. Option D is incorrect because while the statement could reflect aspects of a company's values, such as valuing talent and growth, it is specifically focused on how the company compensates its employees, making it more accurately a compensation philosophy. To learn more, see Chapter 13.

30. B. The primary role of a human resource leader in the collective bargaining process is to represent the employer's interests during negotiations with the union. They work to reach an agreement that balances the needs of the employees with the company's operational and financial goals. The HR leader also ensures that the negotiation process complies with labor laws and company policies. To learn more, see Chapter 12.

31. A, C. Prohibiting employees entirely from bringing their own devices to work is impractical and difficult to enforce. Instead, HR leaders should write bring your own device policies to ensure employees are aware of data security best practices. Limiting access to social media will restrict marketing and other teams from using this resource to promote product and employer awareness. Options B and D are both critical steps to maintain data security in the workplace. To learn more, see Chapter 14.

32. A, B, D. Employee self-service (ESS) systems are typically used for administrative and informational functions that employees can manage independently. This includes completing routine tax forms, updating personal information and acknowledging compliance training like harassment prevention. Option C, updating progress on performance goals, is usually part of performance management systems rather than ESS systems, which focus more on administrative tasks. To learn more, see Chapter 14.

33. A. Given the company's investment in robotics and AI, the first priority should be an AI-powered talent management system (1). This system can help identify skills gaps, recommend training programs, and match employees to roles that align with the new technology. As the company moves toward more automated and technologically advanced production processes, an automated learning and development platform (2) can provide on-demand training modules, track progress, and offer certifications for various technical skills, ensuring that the workforce is capable of handling the new technology. A digital self-service portal (3) will streamline HR processes, allowing employees to manage their personal information, access pay stubs, request leave, and complete necessary paperwork. While important, this initiative ranks third because it focuses more on administrative efficiency rather than directly supporting the company's technological transition. To learn more, see Chapter 14.

34. C. The scenario describes a malware attack, where malicious software was unknowingly installed onto the employee's computer after opening a seemingly legitimate attachment. This software can cause various issues, such as slowing down systems, corrupting files, and spreading to other devices on the network. Option A, phishing, is a type of cyberattack where attackers send fraudulent emails or messages that appear to come from a legitimate source. Option B, hacking, refers to unauthorized access to computer systems or networks. Hackers exploit vulnerabilities to steal information, disrupt operations, or gain control of systems. While hacking can involve a variety of techniques, including using malware, option C is the more specific answer. Option D, ransomware attacks, is where malicious software encrypts the victim's data and demands payment in exchange for the decryption key. To learn more, see Chapter 14.

35. A. For a small startup company with limited resources, offering flexible work arrangements and a comprehensive health benefits package is an effective strategy. This approach balances cost management with providing valuable benefits that can attract and retain talent. The other options (B, C, and D) involve higher costs and commitments, which may not be sustainable for a startup with fewer resources and a smaller workforce. To learn more, see Chapter 13.

36. A. Service recognition rewards are most effective when celebrating significant milestones, such as anniversaries, as they acknowledge an employee's long-term commitment and contributions to the company. The other options (B, C, and D) might be more suited for different

types of recognition, such as performance bonuses, attendance awards, or participation incentives, respectively. To learn more, see Chapter 13.

37. B. The job evaluation process involves assessing various job positions within an organization to determine their relative value and establish a fair and equitable compensation structure. This process helps ensure that employees are paid appropriately based on the responsibilities and requirements of their roles. Option A describes job analysis, which focuses on identifying the specific duties and qualifications of a job. The other options refer to different HR processes, such as performance evaluation (option C) and skills analysis (option D). To learn more, see Chapter 2.

38. D. The first step in creating an annual HR budget is to assess the company's strategic goals and ensure the budget aligns with these objectives. This ensures that the HR initiatives and spending support the broader goals of the organization. While the other steps, such as reviewing previous budgets, determining recruitment costs, and allocating funds for benefits, are important, they should be informed by the company's overall strategy and priorities. To learn more, see Chapter 10.

39. B. After a mass layoff, it's important to address the remaining employees openly and transparently. Holding a companywide meeting allows leadership to explain the reasons behind the layoffs, address any concerns, and share the company's future direction. This approach helps rebuild trust, reduces uncertainty, and provides a sense of stability. The other options are less effective as they fail to provide necessary information, encourage misinformation, or prevent open communication. To learn more, see Chapter 11.

40. C. After a merger, promoting open communication and team-building activities is crucial for addressing interpersonal conflicts among employees. These initiatives help employees from different backgrounds understand each other, build trust, and work together more effectively. This approach can ease tensions and create a more cohesive and integrated work environment. The other options, while important, are less directly focused on resolving interpersonal conflicts. To learn more, see Chapter 11.

41. A. Sabbaticals are commonly offered in academic institutions to allow faculty members to take extended time off from their regular duties to focus on research, writing, and other forms of professional development. This practice helps educators stay current in their fields, contribute to academic knowledge, and bring new insights and innovations back to their institutions. Healthcare institutions (option B) typically rely on other methods, such as continuing education courses, conferences, and specialized training programs, to keep their staff updated on the latest medical practices and technologies. The focus in the manufacturing sector (option C) is often on technical training, skills development, and efficiency improvements through on-the-job training, workshops, and certifications. In the finance sector (option D), professional development is usually achieved through certifications, training programs, and continuous learning opportunities. To learn more, see Chapter 12.

42. C. Hofstede's power distance dimension measures how much less powerful members of a society accept and expect that power is distributed unequally. By aligning leadership development programs with the power distance levels, HR leaders can ensure their strategies are culturally appropriate and effective. Customizing employee recognition programs based on uncertainty (option A) is incorrect as employee recognition programs are more directly influenced by the individualism versus collectivism dimension. In cultures with high collectivism (option B), teamwork and group achievements are valued more than individual performance, so this strategy would not align well with the cultural values. Ignoring cultural dimensions and focusing solely on financial performance (option D) overlooks the importance of cultural factors in shaping effective HR strategies and can lead to policies that are culturally insensitive and less effective. To learn more, see Chapter 2.

43. B. Individuals (and cultures) that score high on Geert Hofstede's "uncertainty avoidance" dimension of culture are less likely to embrace change for the sake of innovation. These employees may require higher degrees of support as a company takes on creative or innovative endeavors. To learn more, see Chapter 2.

44. B. Regular training sessions is a proactive approach that helps to maintain compliance and reduces the risk of legal issues. By staying informed, HR staff can create and implement policies that align with labor laws, ensuring that the organization operates within legal boundaries. Establishing a flexible set of guidelines (option A) might lead to inconsistencies and potential noncompliance with labor laws. Labor laws are often specific and must be strictly followed, and too much flexibility can result in misinterpretation and unintentional violations. Allowing each department to create its own HR policies (option C) can lead to a lack of uniformity and increased risk of noncompliance with labor laws. While compliance with nondiscriminatory practices is legally required (option D), labor laws cover a wide range of issues beyond nondiscrimination, such as wage and hour laws, health and safety regulations, and employee rights. A comprehensive strategy is needed to ensure all aspects of labor law are addressed in HR policies. To learn more, see Chapter 10.

45. C. This strategy supports inclusive hiring practices by anonymizing candidate information that could lead to unconscious bias, such as names, genders, and ages, thus focusing on skills and qualifications. Implementing a strict seniority-based promotion system (option A) focuses on internal promotions based on seniority, which does not necessarily support inclusive hiring practices as it may overlook diverse external candidates. Restricting job postings to internal candidates (option B) reduces the opportunity for a diverse pool of applicants and therefore does not support inclusive hiring practices. Requiring all applicants to have degrees (option D) can limit diversity by excluding capable candidates from a variety of educational backgrounds and does not support inclusive hiring practices. To learn more, see Chapter 2.

Chapter 1

Certifying Human Resource Professionals

Human resources. Ask 10 different people what human resources (HR) is or does, and you'll get many different answers. Business partner, engagement officer, change agents, minister of culture, management adviser, recruiter, talent manager, employee advocate, event planner, union negotiator, counselor, policy police, coach, mediator, administrative expert, corporate conscience, and even "chief happiness officers"—these are just a few of the roles that we play, or that others within and outside of the organization think we should play. Some of these descriptions are based on misperceptions from nonpractitioners, others describe the roles we aspire to attain within our organizations, and some describe what we actually do each day. The HR Certification Institute (HRCI) provides the *HRBoK™ (A Guide to the Human Resource Body of Knowledge)*, which is the means by which we define ourselves to the larger business community and that communicates to them what roles are appropriate for the human resource function in an organization. The *HRBoK™* reflects the most current competencies of an HR professional.

HRCI, the agency responsible for the PHR/PHRi, SPHR/SPHRi, and many other human resource certifications, and the Society for Human Resource Management (SHRM) had a very large, and very public, split back in 2014. The stated reason for the separation was the need for a more competency-based exam. While HRCI was adamant that their exam suite was sufficiently competency based, the split represented a major shift in how HR is perceived in the field. It is under no dispute that HR professionals need a wide variety of knowledge, skills, abilities, and practical competencies in order to drive organizational performance. As David Ulrich, author of *Victory Through Organization* (McGraw-Hill Education), put it, "HR is not about HR. HR begins and ends with the business" (Ulrich, 2017, p. 3). In order to be credible business partners and an official management practice, we have to have a way to measure said competencies.

The benefits of professional human resource certification are many. The Academy to Innovate HR (AIHR) found that HR certifications improve lifetime earnings potential by as much as 44 percent,[1] and cite other studies showing that successful certification holders are more likely to get promoted. These promotions perpetuate the learning opportunities provided by on-the-job experience, creating even more opportunities for those without a formal college degree to compete.

HRCI certification holders report better employment prospects, higher annual salaries, faster income growth, and higher levels of career satisfaction. Additionally, businesses benefit from hiring certification holders, a point made clear by the fact that over 95 percent of Fortune 500 companies have HRCI-certified professionals among their leadership ranks.[2]

---

[1]www.aihr.com/blog/best-hr-certifications.

[2]www.hrci.org/amy-dufrane#:~:text=Over%2095%20percent%20of%20Fortune,professionals%20among%20their%20leadership%20ranks.

This chapter provides you with an overview of HR certification: the growth of human resources as a profession, a little history about the certification process, and a discussion of the types of professional HR certification. (There are eight—PHR, SPHR, GPHR, PHRca, PHRi, SPHRi, aPHR, and the aPHRi.) This chapter will also review the required eligibility standards for the PHR/i and SPHR/i, updated in March 2024 for the first time since 2018. Additionally, you'll learn about the HR body of knowledge and get a few tips to assist you in preparing for the PHR/i and SPHR/i exams.

The Human Resource Profession

By the end of the 19th century, the Industrial Revolution had changed the nature of work—businesses were no longer small organizations that could be managed by a single owner with a few trusted supervisors. As a result, many support functions were delegated to individuals who began to specialize in certain areas. One of these functions became known as *industrial relations* or *personnel* and evolved into what we know today as *human resources*.

As businesses continued to become even larger entities, standards began to develop as practitioners met and shared information about the ways they performed their jobs. The need for more formal training standards in various aspects of this new function became apparent, and colleges began to develop courses of study in the field. By the middle of the 20th century, the personnel function was part of almost every business, and numerous individuals worked in the field. A small group of these individuals got together in 1948 and determined that the personnel function was developing into a profession and was in need of a national organization to define it, represent practitioners, and promote its interests in the larger business community. Thus, the American Society for Personnel Administration (ASPA) was born.

For the first 16 years of its existence, ASPA was strictly a volunteer organization. By 1964, membership had grown from the small group of charter members in 1948 to more than 3,100—enough to support a small staff to serve the members. With membership growing, the discussion quite naturally turned to the topic of defining the practice of personnel as a profession. Although established professions have similar characteristics, such as a code of ethics, a specific and unique body of knowledge, and an education specific to the profession, there are aspects of most professions that set them apart from one another—and personnel was no different. To solicit the contribution of practitioners in this process, ASPA cosponsored a conference with Cornell University's School of Industrial Relations to determine how best to define the characteristics that made personnel a profession. This conference spawned a year of consideration and debate among ASPA members.

The culmination of this process was an agreement on five characteristics that would set personnel/HR apart as a profession:

- HR would need to require full-time practice.
- The HR profession must be defined by a common body of knowledge that defines a course of study at educational institutions.
- There must be a national professional association that represents the views of practitioners in the larger business community and in the legislative process.

- There must be a certification program for HR professionals.
- There must be a code of ethics for the HR profession.

Once ASPA had a clear definition of what was required for the practice of personnel to be considered a profession, the members knew what needed to be done to make this a reality: Develop a body of knowledge and a certification program to evaluate the competence of practitioners.

Development of the Human Resource Body of Knowledge

With its goal clearly set, ASPA went about the process of developing a body of knowledge for the profession. ASPA created a task force to study and report on the issues involved and recommend a course of action. The ASPA Accreditation Institute (AAI) was formed in 1975 with a mandate to define a national body of knowledge for the profession and develop a program to measure the knowledge of its practitioners.

Over time, as personnel evolved into human resources, ASPA changed its name to the Society for Human Resource Management (SHRM) to reflect changes in the profession. At that point, AAI became the HR Certification Institute (HRCI) for the same reason. These associations exist today to represent and certify the profession.

As with all previous exam content outline updates, HRCI began the 2024 review with the question, "What should a human resource practitioner know and be able to apply to be considered a competent HR generalist?" To answer this, every 5 or so years HRCI conducts a *practice analysis study* to obtain information from a variety of sources, including subject matter experts, journal articles, meta-analysis of job descriptions, one-on-one interviews with practitioners, and eventually, an in-depth focus group to identify field content. The culmination of this data collection is a comprehensive look at how HR is being practiced in the field and a relevant picture of what the business climate needs from its HR representatives. From this, exam content is developed.

Clearly, the nomenclature has changed over the past 30 years, yet the basic functional areas of HR have remained fairly stable. Significant changes have occurred to ensure the relevance of human resource practice to the changing needs of business in the 21st century.

In early 2024, HRCI announced a revision to the PHR, PHR International (PHRi) SPHR and SPHR International (SPHRi) Exam Content Outlines based on the results of the regularly scheduled practice-analysis study. The major change was the combination of the international exams with the generalist exam content. The PHR and PHRi (PHR/i) exams now share near identical content with the exception of the knowledge of U.S. labor laws. The SPHR and SPHRi (SPHR/i) exams also now share exam content, with minor differences in U.S. labor laws as well. Other highlights include:

- Elimination of the "Core Knowledge" requirements from the exam content outlines.
- Two new domains were added to the PHR/i, HR Information Management and Employee Engagement.

- Two new domains were added to the SPHR/i exams, HR Information Management, Safety and Security and Total Rewards.
- HRCI updated the exam content weights to be more reflective of a current HR practitioner.

Figure 1.1 presents a complete look at the 2024 changes.

FIGURE 1.1 The 2024 changes

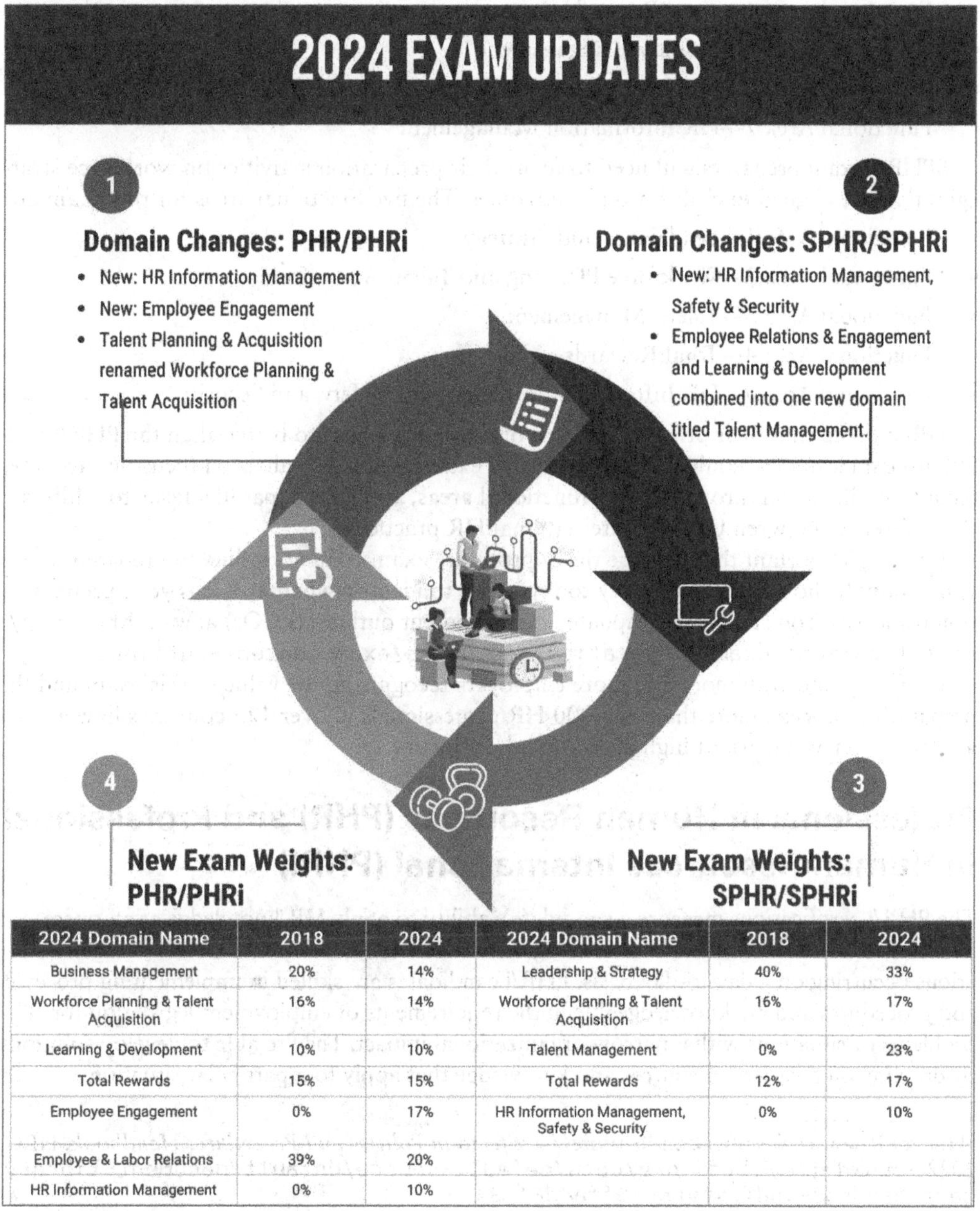

2024 Domain Name	2018	2024	2024 Domain Name	2018	2024
Business Management	20%	14%	Leadership & Strategy	40%	33%
Workforce Planning & Talent Acquisition	16%	14%	Workforce Planning & Talent Acquisition	16%	17%
Learning & Development	10%	10%	Talent Management	0%	23%
Total Rewards	15%	15%	Total Rewards	12%	17%
Employee Engagement	0%	17%	HR Information Management, Safety & Security	0%	10%
Employee & Labor Relations	39%	20%			
HR Information Management	0%	10%			

What hasn't changed is the expectation that PHR/i candidates should continue to understand the operational nature of human resources. This is reflected in the addition of two new domains, bringing the total from five to seven on the PHR/i exam:

- Functional Area 1—Business Management
- Functional Area 2—Workforce Planning and Talent Acquisition
- Functional Area 3—Learning and Development
- Functional Area 4—Total Rewards
- Functional Area 5—Employee Engagement
- Functional Area 6—Employee and Labor Relations
- Functional Area 7—HR Information Management

SPHR/i exam preparers will need to focus their preparation activities on workforce strategies that are aligned to clear business outcomes. The five functional areas for this exam are:

- Functional Area 1—Leadership and Strategy
- Functional Area 2—Workforce Planning and Talent Acquisition
- Functional Area 3—Talent Management
- Functional Area 4—Total Rewards
- Functional Area 5—HR Information Management, Safety, and Security

HRCI noted that their primary purpose of the changes was to better align the PHR/i and SPHR/i exams and streamline terminology. All exams will have enhanced focus on diversity, equity, and inclusion throughout the functional areas, and paired, parallel tasks to address the differences between U.S. and international HR practices.

It is very important that you use the appropriate exam content outline to prepare for your exam. It should be the primary tool you use to identify where to focus your preparation resources. You can find the updated exam content outlines (ECOs) at `www.hrci.org/certifications/exam-preparation-resources/exam-content-outlines`.

Currently, and with more and more employers recognizing the value of this exam and the preparation process, more than 500,000 HR professionals in over 125 countries have earned a certification as a mark of high professional distinction.[3]

Professional in Human Resources (PHR) and Professional in Human Resources International (PHRi)

The PHR/i certifications measure a candidate's ability to apply HR knowledge at an operational or technical level. These exams test a candidate's ability to apply HR knowledge to situations occurring on a day-to-day basis. PHR/i candidates are skilled in implementing processes and procedures and are knowledgeable in the requirements of employment legislation for problems or situations with a narrow organizational impact. They're able to develop solutions by drawing on a variety of sources and knowledge that apply to a particular situation.

---

[3] Human Resource Certification Institute. *Certification Policies and Procedures Handbook*. HRCI, 2022, sourced at `www.hrci.org/docs/default-source/default-document-library/cert-handbook.pdf?sfvrsn=5ffa4d61_34`.

The functional areas in the PHR/i exams are weighted to reflect the emphasis on the operational, administrative, and tactical application of the elements of the body of knowledge. Table 1.1 shows the functional area weightings for the PHR/i exams. Here is a brief overview of the seven functional areas of the PHR/i:

TABLE 1.1 PHR/i functional area weighting

Functional area	Exam weight
Business Management	14%
Workforce Planning and Talent Acquisition	14%
Learning and Development	10%
Total Rewards	15%
Employee Engagement	17%
Employee and Labor Relations	20%
HR Information Management	10%

Business Management—14% of Exam Content This content area asks candidates to apply their knowledge and skill to help reinforce employee expectations; make quality, data-driven decisions; and help avoid or manage organizational risk. It is here you will find content related to a company's mission, vision, and values; ideas about corporate governance and ethical behaviors; and how HR strategy cascades down from business strategy.

Workforce Planning and Talent Acquisition—14% of Exam Content Formerly known as Talent Planning and Acquisition, this functional area of the PHR/i exams focuses on the recruiting and selection stage of the employee lifecycle. Prepare for content related to all types of workforce plans; the availability, recruitment, and selection of qualified talent; and assessing/managing the talent once onboard.

Learning and Development—10% of Exam Content Learning and Development focuses on employee professional growth. Prepare to apply your skills toward questions related to learning and development theories, organizational development concepts and practices, coaching and mentoring techniques, and the need to upskill and reskill team members in response to changing organizational needs.

Total Rewards—15% of Exam Content Total Rewards continues to combine compensation and employee benefits as one functional area. New to the 2024 exams is content related to the impact of hybrid work schedules and how to use Total Rewards systems to enhance the employee experience. This means that you can expect to find questions related to compensation and benefits, labor laws, employee payroll processing, job analysis, and the application of non-monetary rewards.

Employee Engagement—17% of Exam Content Added as its own functional area in the 2024 update, PHR/i candidates can expect to see questions about designing HR programs that support the employee experience throughout the lifecycle. These systems include measuring engagement at all phases and stages of the employee experience, from communicating the employer brand to navigating separations.

Employee and Labor Relations—20% of Exam Content This functional area continues to hold the greatest amount of exam content for PHR/i candidates. You'll want to prepare accordingly on topics such as union organization and management, administration of collective bargaining agreements, employee health and safety, discipline, and the development of tools such as the employee handbook and standard operating procedures (SOPs) to ensure compliance with performance expectations.

HR Information Management—10% of Exam Content New for the 2024 exams, this content is all about data management and its use to support organizational results. This includes the use of human resource information systems (HRISs) as well as data collection on a macro scale to be used in evidenced-based decision making. Issues such as confidentiality, privacy, and cybersecurity are also covered in this section of the exams.

Senior Professional in Human Resources (SPHR) and Senior Professional in Human Resources International (SPHRi)

The SPHR and SPHRi certifications measure a candidate's strategic perspective and ability to pull information from a variety of sources to address issues with organizationwide impact. These exams measure the candidate's ability to apply HR knowledge and experience in developing policies that will meet the organization's long-term strategic objectives and impact the entire organization.

The senior-level exams measure a candidate's strategic ability to integrate HR processes into the big picture of an organization's needs and to develop policies to support the achievement of business goals. Table 1.2 demonstrates how the weightings for the functional areas reflect this. Here is a brief overview of the 2024 updates to the five functional areas of the SPHR/i exam:

TABLE 1.2 SPHR/i functional area weighting

Functional area	Exam weight
Leadership and Strategy	33%
Workforce Planning and Talent Acquisition	17%
Talent Management	23%
Total Rewards	17%
HR Information Management, Safety, and Security	10%

Leadership and Strategy—33% of Exam Content For SPHR/i candidates, this should be the primary focus for exam preparation as it makes up the most exam content. Questions will include heavy emphasis on strategy, such as strategic planning, risk management strategies, change management strategies, and efficacy measurements. This area also includes knowledge of management functions, corporate governance procedures, project management, and aligning HR strategy with business strategy to ultimately drive results.

Workforce Planning and Talent Acquisition—17% of Exam Content This functional area has a bit more content weight than the PHR/i exam, but with a slightly different focus. Workforce planning strategies, including forecasting to address talent shortages and surpluses, will most likely be found in this area, as will content related to sourcing, onboarding, and managing cultural integrations, the design of separation practices that address downsizing, mergers and acquisitions, divestitures, and global expansion.

Talent Management—23% of Exam Content Talent Management is a new functional area of the SPHR/i exam, and it combines the previously titled domains of Employee Relations and Engagement and Learning and Development. In 2012 the title of this domain was Human Resource Development and in 2018 it was Learning and Development; the title changes suggest practical shifts in this function over time. Expect to find questions about designing and supporting organizational learning and HR systems that engage employees to maximize individual, team, and organizational performance. This includes diversity, equity, and inclusion (DEI) initiatives and other strategic interventions around business strategy.

Total Rewards—17% of Exam Content SPHR/i candidates must be able to analyze and evaluate strategies related to compensation and benefits programs—a total rewards system. In the context of study plans, it may be helpful to use the term "analyze" to address activities such as identifying the company compensation philosophy and conducting job evaluation to properly price jobs. The term "evaluate" in the exam objectives relates to identifying how well a company's total rewards program is attracting, rewarding, and retaining talent. Both compensation and benefits strategies at the SPHR/i level will involve making decisions and managing risks associated with this practice.

HR Information Management, Safety and Security—10% of Exam Content Another new functional category, HR Information Management, Safety, and Security is interesting. For the PHR/i exams, this domain was also added in 2024 and titled HR Information Management, without the added *Safety and Security* as it's titled here. From this we can surmise that in addition to the fundamental aspects of HR information management, senior leaders are responsible for data protection strategies that address cybersecurity, social engineering, and the ethical use of data within the workplace.

NOTE HRCI's *Certification Policies and Procedures Handbook (aPHR, aPHRi, PHR, PHRca, SPHR, GPHR, PHRi, and SPHRi)* contains the most current listing of the HRCI exam requirements. Because the exams are built around these policies and procedures, we strongly urge you to review the handbook and familiarize yourself with the test specs for each functional area before reading the related chapter. The HRCI website (`www.hrci.org`) provides information on downloading or ordering this free publication.

Eligibility Requirements

As we've mentioned, complete information on eligibility requirements for the exams is available in the *Certification Policies and Procedures Handbook (aPHR, aPHRi, PHR, PHRca, SPHR, GPHR, PHRi, and SPHRi),* and HRCI, of course, makes the final decision as to whether or not a candidate meets them. In this section, we'll provide a broad overview of the requirements, along with some suggestions based on the experience of successful candidates.

The current eligibility requirements reflect a candidate's education and experience. According to HRCI, "professional-level experience" means that candidates have the following:

- The ability to use independent judgment and discretion in performing work duties
- Some authority for decision making
- In-depth work requirements, such as data gathering, analysis, and interpretation
- Interaction with people at multiple levels, including decision makers
- Individual accountability for results

It's important to note that almost all supervisors and managers perform some HR functions as part of their daily requirements, but because these activities aren't usually the major function of the position and constitute less than 51 percent of their time at work, this experience most likely would not meet the requirements established by HRCI. See Table 1.3 for the exam eligibility requirements.

TABLE 1.3 PHR/i and SPHR/i eligibility

	Professional-level experience	Education
PHR/i	1 year	Master's degree or global equivalent
	2 years	Bachelor's degree or global equivalent
	4 years	None
SPHR/i	4 years	Master's degree or global equivalent
	5 years	Bachelor's degree or global equivalent
	7 years	None

The minimum requirements are pretty simple, but let's be realistic for a moment. The PHR/i and SPHR/i exams don't measure just book knowledge. They measure your ability to apply that knowledge in work situations. The more experience you have in applying knowledge at work, the greater your chances of passing the test.

Professional Level Experience vs. Exempt Level Experience

"Professional-level experience" no longer means work that is exempt from overtime and other wage and hour requirements, although that is a common misperception. It is, however, a safe bet that if the work performed falls within at least one of the functional areas *and* is exempt level, it will likely meet the "professional" requirement.

Recommendations for PHR/i Candidates

To summarize the ideal PHR/i profile, HRCI suggests that candidates have 2–4 years of professional-level, generalist HR experience before they sit for the exam. These candidates generally report to a more senior HR professional within the organization and during the course of their daily work focus on implementation of programs and processes that have already been developed. PHR/i experience focuses on providing direct services to HR customers within the organization.

Recommendations for SPHR/i Candidates

The ideal SPHR/i candidate has 6–8 years of increasingly responsible HR experience. An SPHR/i needs to be able to see the big picture for the entire organization, not just what works best for the human resource department. This requires the ability to anticipate the impact of policies and decisions on the achievement of organizational goals. SPHR/i candidates are business-focused and understand that HR policies and processes must integrate with and serve the needs of the larger organization. Whereas a PHR's decisions and activities have a more limited effect within the operations of the organization, decisions made by SPHR/i candidates will have organizationwide impact.

Recommendations for New HR Professionals and Students

For new HR professionals such as recent graduates or individuals transitioning into human resources, HRCI offers the aPHR and aPHRi exams. These are strictly knowledge-based credentials and thus no previous HR experience is required. Candidates with a high school diploma or global equivalent are eligible to sit for the aPHR/i.

SPHRi Candidates Only

When applying for the SPHRi exam, you will have an additional question related to your knowledge of local employment laws. The criteria may be met by holding another HR certification (such as the PHR or the GPHR), holding a bachelor's degree or global equivalent in an HR field, or having successfully completed a course in employment law. Refer to the *Certification Handbook* for a complete list of how you can confirm this step in your knowledge.

Recertification

Until 1996, HRCI awarded lifetime certification to individuals who successfully recertified twice. At that time, the policy was changed to reflect the need for professionals to remain current with developments in the field. As a result, the lifetime certification program ended, and with the exception of those who were awarded lifetime certification prior to 1996, all PHRs and SPHRs are now required to recertify every 3 years by:

- Earning 45 hours of HR-related professional activities for the aPHR/i.
- Earning 60 hours of HR-related professional development activities for all other exams, including the PHR/i and SPHR/i. SPHR/i candidates must fulfill their 60 credit hours with at least 15 specified credits in business. From the *Recertification Handbook*, this can be done by the pursuit of results-focused experiences that enhance business strategy and HR expertise. This can also be achieved by logging activities with measurable business outcomes (such as driving revenue) or by engagement in experiential learning activities such as coaching or building strategy.

There are a number of ways to be recertified; they fall into two basic categories:

Recertification by Exam HR professionals may retake either exam to maintain certification at that level. Information on recertifying by exam is available in the *Certification Policies and Procedures Handbook,* but the process is similar to registering for the exam the first time—apply, pay the fees, schedule and sit for the test. Most individuals don't wish to sit for the exam again, and so they opt to recertify by completing professional development activities.

Professional Development To recertify on this basis, PHRs and SPHRs must complete 60 credit hours of professional development during the 3-year period. These 60 hours may be accomplished in a variety of ways. One of the most common is by attending continuing education courses, including workshops and seminars related to HR functions. These courses are often preapproved for credit, although you can submit a non-preapproved course for credit with proper documentation if requested. In 2021, HRCI required that all recertification applicants fulfill at least one credit in ethics.

Be sure to take a look at HRCI's *Recertification Policies and Procedures Handbook* for the most up-to-date recertification information. It can be found at `www.hrci.org/docs/default-source/document-control-2023/2023-hrci-recertificatin-handbook.pdf?sfvrsn=991c3f11_3`.

Another way to earn recertification credit is by developing and/or presenting HR-related courses, seminars, or workshops, or creating educational videos or writing blogs. Recertification credit for teaching a specific course is awarded only for the first time it's taught.

On-the-job experience can also be the basis for recertification credit: The first time you perform a new task or project that adds to your mastery of the *HRBoK™*, you may earn credits for the work if it meets the criteria established by HRCI.

Professionals who take on leadership roles in HR organizations or on government boards or commissions may earn certification for those activities if they meet the criteria established by HRCI. Certified professionals may also earn credits by volunteering in an HR-related group.

Finally, certified professionals may also choose to recertify their credentials by being a member of a professional association and reading HR or business-related books. Recommended books and associations that can fulfill the recertify requirements are found in Appendix D, "Resources."

The Test

Now, a little information about the test.

One question frequently asked by candidates preparing for the exam is, "What are the questions like?" The HRCI website provides a detailed explanation of testing theory and question development. In this section, we've summarized what we think is the most practical information for those preparing to take the exams. If you're interested in the details, you'll find more than you ever wanted to know about it on the HRCI website.

The questions in these tests are designed to measure whether candidates meet the objectives established by HRCI as the standard required for a minimally qualified human resource professional to achieve certification. The exam questions are designed to assess the depth and breadth of candidates' knowledge and their ability to apply it in practice. Questions at the basic level examine a candidate's ability to not only recall information but comprehend it as well. Questions designed to measure knowledge and comprehension (such as recalling facts) constitute the smallest percentage of questions on both the exams, but there are slightly more of them on the PHR/i exam. Questions at the next level, application and problem-solving, are more complex and require candidates to apply their knowledge in practical situations that require the ability to differentiate which information is most relevant to real-life situations. Questions of this type are prevalent on all the exams. Questions at the highest level of complexity, synthesis, and evaluation require candidates to use their knowledge in multifaceted situations by drawing on information from different areas of the body of knowledge to create the best possible result. They require the ability to review actions taken in a variety of situations and use critical thinking skills to solve a complex problem. This type of question appears on all exams but is more prevalent on the SPHR/i.

The exam questions, which HRCI refers to as *items*, are developed by subject matter experts (SMEs), all of whom are SPHR-certified professionals trained to write test items for the exams. These SME panels meet to review items that each member has written between meetings. Each volunteer generates about 50 questions annually, which are then reviewed by the entire panel. Questions that make it through the item-writing panel process move to an item-review panel for additional consideration. As a question travels through the panels, one of three things can happen to it:

- The item can be rejected as not meeting the criteria for the exam.
- The item can be returned to the writer for additional work.
- The item can be forwarded to the next step in the process.

When an item is accepted by the review panel, it moves on to the pretest process for inclusion as an unscored pretest question.

Each item consists of the *stem*, or premise, and four possible answers: One of these is the correct or best possible answer, and three others are known as *distractors*. There may be two answers that could be technically correct, but one of them is the best possible answer. As part of the item-development process, HRCI requires that the correct answers are documented and takes great care to ensure that the best possible answer is one that is legally defensible.

The PHR/i have 90 questions each, along with 25 pretest questions that are not included in your scaled score. You will have 2 hours to complete the PHR exam, and 2 hours, 15 minutes to complete the PHRi exam. The SPHR/i exams have 115 scored questions, and 25 pretest questions. You will have 2 hours and 30 minutes to complete the SPHR exams, and 2 hours and 45 minutes to complete the SPHRi exam. All exams also include 30 minutes for administrative tasks to get set up. This means you'll have just about one to two minutes to answer each question. You'll be surprised how much time this gives you to consider your answers if you're well prepared by your experience and have taken sufficient time to study the test specifications. As you answer practice questions in preparation for the exam, be sure to time yourself so you can get a feel for how much time it takes you to answer each question.

Test candidates often ask why the pretest questions are included on the exam, and the answer is simple: These items are included to validate them prior to inclusion on future exams as scored questions. Although the 25 pretest items aren't scored, you won't know which questions are the pretest questions while taking the exam, so it's important to treat every question as though it will be scored.

The more you know about how the questions are designed, the better able you will be to focus your study—which leads us to the next section: some tips on preparing for the exam and what to expect on test day.

NOTE If you're anything like the tens of thousands of HR professionals who have taken the certification exam since 1976, you're probably a little nervous about how you will do and the best way to prepare. In this section, we'll provide you with some hints and tips gathered from our experiences as well as from others who have generously shared their experiences in taking these exams.

It's Experiential and Federal

The most important thing to keep in mind—and this can't be stressed enough—is that these exams are *experiential*. That means they test your ability to *apply* knowledge, not just that you *have* knowledge. For this reason, memorizing facts isn't all that helpful. With a few exceptions, it's far more important to understand the *concepts* behind laws and practices and how they're best applied in real-life situations.

Another crucial factor to keep in mind is that these exams test your ability to apply knowledge of *federal* requirements, so you should be aware of legislation and significant case law that has developed since the 1960s. As experienced professionals are aware, federal law is very often different from the requirements of a particular state. This brings us to our first bit of advice from previous test candidates:

> Do not rely on your past experiences too heavily. Just because you have done it that way at one company doesn't mean it is the right (or legal!) way.
>
> —*Becky Rasmussen, PHR*

> Don't necessarily think of how you would do it at work. It is possible the way your company is doing it is wrong, so you will answer the question wrong. Look for the most correct answer, and take plenty of practice tests. The more you take, the more familiar you will become with test taking.
>
> —*Susan K. Craft, MS, PHR*

These tips apply to several situations: Your state requirements may be different from the federal requirements that are the subject of the test; your company practice may not be up-to-date with current requirements; and in some cases, you may be operating on the basis of a common myth about legal requirements or HR practices that is not, in fact, accurate. One way that HRCI tests candidates' depth of knowledge is to provide one of those commonly held myths as a distractor for a question. It's not really a trick question, but a candidate with minimal experience may not know the difference. As you study, think about why you do things in a particular way, how you got that information, and how sure you are that it's the most current and up-to-date approach. If it is current, great! You're a step ahead of the study game. If you aren't sure it's the most current, do a little research to find out whether it will apply on the exam, whether it's a state requirement, or whether it's possibly misinformation you picked up somewhere along the way.

What the Questions Look Like

As mentioned earlier, the HRCI website goes into a fair amount of detail about the technical aspects of test development. Much of that technical information won't help you in developing a study plan. However, you may find it useful to know the types of questions that the item-writing panels are trained to develop.

In the previous section, we discussed the different parts that make up a test item. Each item begins with a stem, which presents a statement or a question requiring a response. The stems will either ask a question or present an unfinished statement to be completed. Within that context, the stem can be categorized in one of the following ways:

Additionally, the item (question) structure has been updated to include all of the following:

- **Traditional Multiple Choice:** These items contain a stem (or premise) and four answer choices, including only one correct answer.
- **Multiple Choice, Multiple Response:** These are like multiple-choice items except there are two or more correct answers. The item will tell you how many correct options there are.
- **Fill in the Blank:** You will be asked to provide a numeral, word, or phrase to complete the sentence.
- **Drag and Drop:** You will be asked to click on certain pieces of information and drag them with your cursor to place them in the correct position.
- **Scenarios:** Scenario questions present typical HR situations, followed by a series of exam items based on the scenario. These scenarios require you to integrate facts from different subject areas.

> My experience was that the actual test differed from any of the prep materials or sample tests that I had seen. The exam questions were differentiated by nuance rather than clear distinctions. Studying from multiple sources helped me be better prepared for this unexpected approach.
>
> *—Lyman Black, SPHR*

Preparing for the Exam

A number of options are available to assist candidates in preparing for the exams. One option is a self-study program that you put together for yourself based on the test specifications. Another option, depending on your location, is to attend a formal preparation course. In the past few years, informal online study groups have become popular and effective ways to prepare for the exam. Regardless of the option you choose, the most important step is to know what you already know. Then figure out what you need to learn, and develop a study plan to help you learn it.

Study Options

Several study options are available for exam candidates. Here are the most common:

Study Partners No matter which study option works best for you, many have found that partnering with someone else is a critical part of the process. Find one or two others who are studying, develop a group study plan, and meet each week to review the material for that week. Working with a reliable study partner makes the process more enjoyable and helps you stay focused. The ideal study partner is one whose areas of strength coincide with your areas of weakness, and vice versa. One effective technique is to prepare the material and "teach" it to your study partner. Teaching your partner one of your weaker areas results in a deeper understanding than just reading or listening to someone else talk about it.

Online Study Groups If there is no one local for you to partner with, try an online study group. Join groups dedicated to the PHR/i SPHR/i exams such as those found on `LinkedIn.com` or `GoConqr.com`, and see if there are offerings for online study groups to help keep your efforts on track.

> I'd advise anyone to form a study group and meet on a regular basis to read, compare notes, quiz each other, and lend moral support! Not only did I learn a lot from my study partners, I gained some wonderful professional friendships—and we all passed!
>
> *—Julie O'Brien, PHR*

> Present the material yourself! Don't just listen—participate. If you teach it, you think of it much differently than if you are sitting passively and listening.
>
> *—Alicia Chatman, SPHR*

> I set up a very small study group: three people. We met once a week until a month before the test, when we met twice a week. It was good to have someone say, "Listen to the question." This made me slow down and review the phrasing and some key words like most, not, least, etc.
>
> *—Patricia Kelleher, SPHR*

Preparation Materials Several publications are designed to prepare candidates for the exams. This book (of course!) is an intense, focused overview of material you may find on the exam.

In preparing for these exams, a best practice is to take advantage of multiple preparation resources to ensure you get a full view of the exam content. `HRCI.org` dedicates a special section of their website to a list of preparation resources and offers bundled packages that include prep materials and exam fees.

In Appendix D of this book, "Resources," you'll find a list of additional materials that focus on specific functional areas, as well as many other excellent sources.

> If I felt it was beneficial I would look at it, listen to it, or read it. Anything from LinkedIn, to YouTube, to podcasts. I was determined that I was going to pass. I really got serious about studying when HRCI sent an email with a coupon code for FREE Second Chance Insurance . . . . So, I jumped on the train and rode it all the way to success.
>
> *Demetrius Q. Russell, PHR, SHRM CP*

Self-Study Self-study provides you with the greatest flexibility in deciding what areas to focus on. If you go this route, developing a study plan is crucial in keeping you focused. Equally important for this method is finding a study partner to share questions and ideas. There are lots of self-study online options as well, including companion courses to this book at the author's website, `https://catalog.mindedge.com/sandrareed`.

> Studying for the PHR is exactly like taking a final exam, you really need to read, apply and practice the material. Once you do this and pass the exam it is thrilling to be certified and solidify your knowledge of HR.
>
> *—Marcie Carleton, aPHR, PHR*

Formal Preparation Courses A number of organizations sponsor formal preparation courses designed specifically for the exam. These are offered by colleges and universities, local network affiliations, and independent exam preparers.

Developing a Study Plan

Although you may be tempted to jump in and immediately start reading books or taking classes, the best thing you can do for yourself at the outset is to identify where you are right now and what study methods have worked for you in the past, and then develop a study plan for yourself:

> The study technique that worked best for me was simply making preparation for the test a priority! I outlined a realistic study schedule for

myself and stuck to it as much as possible. Plus, I studied away from my everyday environment in order to avoid distractions. For me this was a local bookstore cafe, a table covered with notes, a latte in one hand, and a pack of flashcards in the other. . .and it worked!

—Julie O'Brien, PHR

Don't be discouraged if your first few practice test results are poor. A low practice score is SUCCESS—it means you've discovered gaps in your knowledge, and now you can fill them ahead of the real test!

—Ben Opp, SPHR

Where are you right now? The best way to answer this question is to take the self-assessment test immediately following the Introduction to this book. This will help you to see where your strengths and weaknesses lie. Based on the assessment test and on your work experience, make a list of areas you will need to spend the bulk of your time studying (your weaknesses) and the areas in which you simply need a refresher review (your strengths).

I'm glad I took the PHR exam first because it helped to divide my studying plan into the disciplines of HR and commit the tactical pieces to memory. It's important to have a recollection of those facts as you move on to the strategic questions that are a heavy portion of the SPHR and SHRM exams.

Hannah Vest, PHR, SHRM CP

What study methods have worked for you in the past? This may be easy or hard to determine, depending on how long it has been since you took a class. List study methods you have used successfully in the past.

Develop a study plan. Using your list of strengths and weaknesses and the study methods that work for you, create a study plan:

Develop a timeline. Decide how much time you need to spend on each functional area of the body of knowledge.

Working back from the test date, schedule your study time according to your strengths and weaknesses. You may want to leave time close to the test date for an overall review—be reasonable with yourself! Be sure to factor in work commitments, family events, vacations, and holidays so you don't set yourself up for failure.

Get organized! Set up folders or a binder with dividers to collect information for each functional area so that you know where to find it when you're reviewing the material.

Plan the work, and then work the plan. Make sure you keep up with the plan you have set for yourself.

Keep up with the reading; do it every week, faithfully. Take notes on what you don't understand, then ask someone about them.

—Becky Rasmussen, PHR

> Make sure you don't cram; at least a week before the test, take some days off or make extra time available to study so that you're not cramming the night before.
>
> —*Rose Chang, PHR*

When creating your study plan, did you do the following?

- Assess your strengths and weaknesses by taking the assessment test at the beginning of this book?
- Review the HRCI test specifications?
- Identify study methods that will work for you, such as self-study, working with a study partner, using a virtual (online) study group, or taking a formal preparation class?
- Identify useful study materials such as this study guide and website content, online HR bulletin boards, and current HR books and magazines?
- Develop a study timeline?
- Plan to start studying 12–16 weeks before the test?
- Allow more time to study weaker areas?
- Allow refresher time for stronger areas?
- Schedule weekly meetings with a study partner?
- Set up a digital file or a binder with space for each functional area to store all your study materials, questions, and practice tests?
- Allow two to three weeks before the test for a final review of everything you've studied?
- Simulate the test experience by finding a place to study that is free from distractions?
- Challenge yourself further by setting a timer to see how well you do?

Preparation Techniques

To begin with, the best preparation for the exam is solid knowledge of human resource practices and federal employment law combined with broad generalist experience. Because it's experiential in nature, your ability to use HR knowledge in practical situations is the key to success. This isn't a test you can cram for, regardless of the materials you use.

> Rewrite the book in your words! Use your experiences to explain the lesson. It will help you remember the lesson.
>
> —*Alicia Chatman, SPHR*

Preparation materials can help provide an organized way of approaching the material. In many cases, you already have the information; you just need a refresher of where it came from and the reason it's appropriate for a particular situation.

> A friend of mine used the practice tests to give me oral exams on the material. This was very helpful because I was not reading the questions,

> just listening to them and answering them, marking, of course, the ones that I answered wrong to emphasize my study on that specific topic.
>
> —*Marcela Echeverria*

> I found an "SQ3R" technique (Survey, Question, Read, Recite, Review) effective in studying the materials.
>
> —*Lyman Black, SPHR*

Possibly the best advice to give you is this: Don't rely on a single source of information in your preparation. If you have a limited budget, check out books about the various functional areas from your public library. If you're financially able and so inclined, take the opportunity to build your personal HR library (and don't forget to read the books while you're at it!). Take a preparation course. Form a study group. Ask questions of your peers at work. Find a mentor willing to answer your questions. Make use of online HR bulletin boards to ask questions and to observe what others ask and the responses they receive.

None of the people who create the preparation materials for the exams have special access to the test. The best any preparation materials can do is to provide you with a review of HRCI's test specifications. It's to your advantage to utilize as many sources of information as you can to obtain the broadest possible review of the HR body of knowledge.

Answer as many practice questions as possible! Whether or not they're the same format as the questions on the exam, they will assist you in recalling information, and that will benefit you during the exam. Aside from the practice questions provided with this book, a great source of questions is HRCI's online assessment exams. Because the questions used are retired from actual exams, HR professionals have the opportunity to prepare for the style and types of questions they're likely to encounter when taking the actual exam. Additionally, the assessment content is weighted in accordance with the exam requirements, allowing you the opportunity to identify strengths and weaknesses by functional area, resulting in a more meaningful study plan. Purchase the two-exam package and take one at the beginning of the study period and one before the exam itself for maximum value.

> I have worked in startup environments predominantly through my career, so it was nice to be able to hone in on the more tactical parts of HR that are less sought after in a startup environment to sharpen my skills. So many of us HR folks are self-taught!
>
> —*Kaylei Harkness, PHR*

Taking the Exam

One of the comments heard most often by candidates as they leave the test site is that the information in their preparation materials did not bear any resemblance to what was on the test. None of the questions in this book or in any other preparation materials will be exactly like the questions on the exam. The broader your preparation and experience, the greater will be your ability to successfully answer the exam questions.

Knowing the kinds of questions that may be asked, as described earlier in this chapter, can help you focus your study and be as prepared as possible.

One of the best pieces of advice we've heard about getting ready for test day is to stop studying two or three days before the test. By then, if you've been diligent about your study plan, you will be well prepared. The night before, get a good night's sleep. Allow yourself plenty of time to get to the test site.

> Go to bed early the night before and have a light breakfast the morning before the test, so you are alert . . . unlike me who kept falling asleep during the test!
>
> —*Rose Chang, PHR*

On Test Day

The PHR/i and SPHR/i exams are administered as a computer-based test (CBT) by Pearson VUE. This approach provides candidates with greater flexibility in scheduling the test and has other benefits as well.

Here are some time-tested hints and tips for exam day gathered from many who have gone before you and who were willing to share some of what they learned in the process. For the day of the exam, do the following:

- Get a good night's sleep the night before the test.
- Plan to arrive at least 30 minutes before your scheduled test time. This is part of the 30 minutes of admin time that is in addition to your test time.
- Bring your ID (your driver's license, your passport, or any other unexpired government-issued photo ID with a signature) and the test admission letter, along with any other required documents. Your ID must *exactly* match the exam application.
- Bring only items you must have with you. You won't be able to take anything into the testing area except your ID.
- Minor comfort aids such as tissues, cough drops, or eyeglasses are generally allowed, provided they are inspected by the greeter before you enter the exam room. Other accommodations must be approved in advance, usually when the application to test is submitted.
- Don't overeat in the morning or drink a lot of caffeine before the exam.

In certain geographic locations, a live-proctored, virtual, online exam administration is also available, where you can schedule your test 24 hours a day, 7 days a week and 365 days a year.

While taking the exam, do the following:

- Read the entire question carefully; don't skim it. Taking the time to do this can make the difference between a correct and an incorrect answer.

> I am a speed-reader, and missing one little word could change the entire question. Slow down and read every word.
>
> —*Marie Atchley, SPHR*

- Read all of the answer choices carefully; don't skim them or select an answer before you've read them all.
- If you're unsure of the answer, eliminate as many wrong answers as you can to narrow down your choices. Remember: One of them is correct!
- Very often, your gut instinct about the correct answer is right, so go with it.

- Don't overanalyze the questions and answers.
- Don't look for patterns in the answers. A myth has been circulating for a number of years that the longest answer is the correct one—it's just not true.
- If you don't know the answer to a question, *guess*. If you don't answer, the question will be counted as incorrect, so you have nothing to lose, and you might get it right.

> I was not surprised by the test at all. Everyone said it was hard; it was! Everyone said that it was subjective; it was! Everyone said that you will feel like you flunked; I did! (But I actually passed.)
>
> —*Patricia Kelleher, SPHR*

The Aftermath

The best thing about CBTs is that you will have a preliminary test result before you leave the test site. If testing at a physical exam center, you will receive the results right then and there, with official online results available in a few business days. If testing through an online proctor, you will not have the benefit of immediate notification, but rather will receive an email within 24–48 hours with your results. A little trick here is that you usually can log into your HRCI account (the one you used to register for the exam) and see your results within an hour after testing. See Figure 1.2 for the most recent exam pass rates available from HRCI.

FIGURE 1.2 Exam pass rates

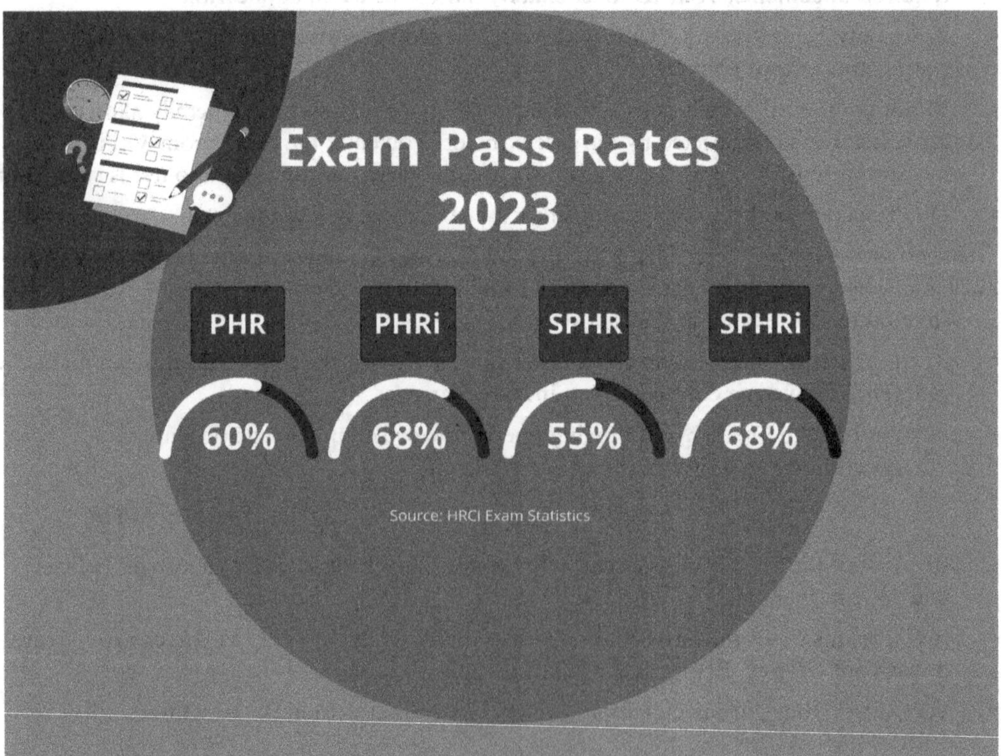

A Passing Score

Congratulations, you've passed! For many that sense of elation is accompanied by a strong sense of relief that the nerves and sleepless nights are finally over! Now for the fun part! Communicate your success by claiming a digital badge that confirms your new certification. This badge can be used to display the credential on your social media sites and other places with digital signatures. HRCI will send successful candidates an email with how to claim the badge. You can also order a paper copy of the certificate from HRCI's online store.

Be proud of this success! The time you spent studying, not to mention the years of your practical experience, have culminated in this career milestone.

Visualizing Success

Eighty-two-time PGA winner Tiger Woods described a visualization technique he used when he was nervous in a match. He would take a mental picture of the ball—its position from above and around—and then visualize himself putting it into the cup. Later, when under pressure, he would remind himself to just "putt to the picture." This is an example of visualizing success before a major performance to help stay focused on game day.

If you're reading this book right now, chances are you have not yet sat for the exam. This is the perfect time to engage in your own visualization technique that sets you up for success as you begin the next 10–12 weeks of studying. Do this now and as a regular part of your study efforts so that the imagery is embedded in your mind before the big day.

Take a moment to close your eyes, breathing deeply in and out. Feel your heartbeat slow, your shoulders drop, and your mind quiet. Visualize the following:

It's the early morning of test day and you are entering the exam room, focused amidst other candidates. You are calm, determined, and prepared. With each breath, you gather confidence. As the exam unfolds, questions emerge like puzzles waiting to be solved. You navigate each challenge with clarity and precision, drawing upon your diligent study. With every correct answer, a sense of accomplishment fills you, reaffirming your readiness. For those questions that you're unsure of, you mark for review and calmly focus on the next question, smiling to yourself knowing that the answer is in there, waiting to be recalled. After submitting your final answer, you feel satisfied knowing you've given your best effort. Stepping out, you feel successful, a result of your hard work and dedication. You carry yourself proudly, recognizing your achievements and the path you've paved for others.

A Non-passing Score

A scaled score of 500 is necessary to pass these exams. If you don't pass the test, you will receive a report that shows the areas where you underperformed so that you can use this as a guide for future study. I encourage you to retake the exam as soon as possible after the 90-day cooling-off period has passed. This is because it is best to test again while the information and the experience is fresh. I especially recommend this if your scaled score was close to 500—get back in there and try again; it absolutely can and will happen for you!

If you don't pass the test, knowing immediately probably won't make you feel any better about it, but there are a couple of consolations:

- The time and work you put into studying has already benefited you by increasing your knowledge about your chosen profession—congratulate yourself for investing in your career.
- Although the test is important to you, put it in its proper perspective—it's only a snapshot of your capabilities in the context of the 90–115 questions you happened to receive—it is not a measure of your performance or dedication to our industry. People take tests every day, and not all of them pass on the first attempt.

If you plan to take the test again, review HRCI's advice on retaking the exam at www.hrci.org. Browse the entire HRCI website—you'll find a lot of information about how the test is constructed and scored that may help you refine your study plan for better success.

NOTE

If you are really anxious about your ability to pass this exam on the first try, purchase the second-chance insurance offered by HRCI. This insurance allows candidates to prepurchase the ability to retake an exam if they are unsuccessful the first time. The insurance must be purchased when you first apply to take the exam, and it is nonrefundable.

Summary

Certification for HR professionals is a process that has been evolving for more than 50 years. The *HRBoK*™ was first developed in 1975 to define the profession and provide the basis for certification. Over the years, HRCI has updated the *BOK* to reflect current business needs and trends to ensure its viability in business. The PHR/i and SPHR/i exams are based on federal legislation and case law and are experiential, meaning that in order to pass them, candidates need to have exempt-level experience in the field.

Questions on the exams are developed by certified HR professionals who volunteer their time with oversight from test professionals. The questions go through levels of review prior to inclusion as unscored pretest questions on an exam. A question that is validated in this process goes into the pool of questions available for testing purposes. Questions that don't pass this rigorous process are either discarded or returned to the writer for additional work.

A number of methods can be used to prepare for the exam. The most important preparation methods are to use as many sources of information as possible and to study with a partner or group.

PHR | PHRi and SPHR | SPHRi Exams: Shared Competencies

The Professional in Human Resources (PHR), Professional in Human Resources International (PHRi) and the Senior Professional in Human Resources and Senior Professional in Human Resources International (SPHRi) exams, administered by the Human Resource Certification Institute (HRCI), assess a range of competencies and knowledge areas essential for HR professionals. While the PHR/i focuses on operational and technical aspects, the SPHR/i emphasizes strategic and policymaking considerations. What does this exactly mean? *Human resource operations* focuses on the day-to-day functions of the HR department. *Human resource strategy* seeks to align the management of an organization's workforce with its overall business goals and objectives.

While operations and strategy are the key distinctions between the exams, there are foundational knowledge components that must be understood and applied when answering questions for all exams.

Prior to the 2024 updates, the exam content outline included knowledge components at the end of each functional area. In 2024, these components were removed. Although the reasoning for this removal is not clear, understanding the foundational knowledge from which HR is practiced is key to understanding *context*, the situation or background information that helps explain or understand something. This chapter is different from the other chapters in the book in that it is not mapped to specific exam objectives. Rather, it is centered around the foundational knowledge necessary to understand context for successful exam performance and on the job. Regardless of which exam you have selected, you should rigorously study this content.

Business Management and Leadership and Strategy

In business management, leadership and strategy, staffing plans, recruiting strategies, legal compliance, risk management, total quality management (TQM), change management, and workforce planning all intersect operationally and strategically by ensuring smooth daily operations, minimizing risks, and driving continuous improvement. Competencies in strategic thinking, process optimization, legal knowledge, and adaptability are critical for HR professionals at all stages of their career. These competencies help to manage current business needs and align with long-term growth and transformation objectives.

Business management and strategy involve the planning, organizing, and directing of resources and operations to achieve the company's long-term goals and competitive advantage in the market.

Henri Fayol was a pioneering French mining engineer and management theorist. In his seminal work, *General and Industrial Management* (Martino Fine Books, 2013), Fayol identified five primary functions of management that provided a comprehensive framework for managing organizations effectively:

- **Planning:** Setting goals and determining the best course of action to achieve them
- **Organizing:** Arranging resources and tasks to implement the plans effectively.
- **Commanding (Directing):** Leading and motivating employees to execute the plans
- **Coordinating:** Ensuring all parts of the organization work together harmoniously toward common objectives
- **Controlling:** Monitoring progress and making necessary adjustments to stay on track with the goals

These five functions shape and help to execute organizational strategy while aligning with the company's mission, vision, and values.

Mission, Vision, Values

SPHR/i and PHR/i practitioners must serve as the company's role model of many different behaviors. This is especially true when it comes to communicating and reinforcing guidelines for behavior. For many companies, these standards are developed as mission, vision, and values (MVV) statements.

Mission Statement Effective mission statements describe the company, what it does, where it's going, and how it's different from other organizations. The message of the mission statement is generally directed at employees in the organization, and it should tell them where the company is headed in the mid to long term.

Vision Statement A vision statement should inspire the organization and inform customers and shareholders, describing what will carry the organization into the future and what it will accomplish. In a very concise way, the vision statement should communicate what the company does, for whom it does it, and what long-range success will look like.

Corporate Values Statement A statement of corporate values is a way for leaders to communicate their standards for how the organization will conduct business. The values chosen for this purpose should be those that will be true regardless of changes in product lines or business processes. A question to ask in selecting an organization's values is whether the value would hold true if the organization changed its focus entirely and began doing business in a completely different way. Values such as integrity, excellence, teamwork, customer service, and mutual respect are some of those that remain constant regardless of changes in business operations.

In addition to the MVV statements defined here, organizations often identify their *core competencies*: the parts of their operations that they do best and that set them apart from the competition. Many organizations believe that focusing on these core competencies makes it possible to expand their revenue streams. Competencies can be related to the technology used in operations, customer relationship management, product characteristics, manufacturing processes, knowledge management, organization culture, or combinations of these or other organizational aspects that work together synergistically and are difficult for others to replicate. When core competencies are identified, organizations can focus their strategy on ways to build related products or services instead of moving into unrelated areas. In many companies, HR becomes a core competency when it is embedded in operations rather than a segregated business unit. This involves HR leading change, fostering teamwork, developing staff, and contributing to organizational decision making and strategic planning.

Once the vision and mission statements have defined why the organization exists, corporate goals are needed to describe how the organization will get there in the mid to long term. Effective corporate goals follow the SMART model:

- **Specific:** The goal should be descriptive enough to guide business-unit managers in developing action plans that will accomplish the goal.
- **Measurable:** The goal must include a method for determining when it has been met.
- **Action-Oriented:** Goals must describe the actions that will be taken.
- **Realistic:** The goal must be high enough to challenge the organization or individual but not so high that it's not achievable.
- **Time-Based:** Goals must include a time frame for completion.

Once identified, these elements are combined into one strategic document, often called a *business plan*. The contents of a business plan may vary, but ultimately, it must match the purpose identified through the strategic planning process.

Organizations

Since ancient times, people have formed groups to achieve goals that they were unable to achieve on their own. Whether it was for protection, shelter, food, or profit, organizing gave people the means to achieve more than they could by acting alone. The modern organization evolved to coordinate the many different activities that are needed to produce the goods or services necessary to achieve its goals.

> 100% of customers are people. 100% of employees are people. If you don't understand people, you don't understand business.
>
> *Simon Sinek*

Because organizations consist of people, the HR function is impacted by everything that affects an organization, whether it's an external development (such as a competitor's technological development) or an internal change in a business process (such as a product design change). Whatever the impact, HR professionals are called on to implement the resulting changes.

External Business Environment

Many organizational changes occur as the result of forces outside an organization's control, and HR professionals must understand how these forces impact existing organizational strategies. These external forces affect the competition as well, and how different organizations respond to these forces plays a role in determining whether they succeed in the new environment.

Technological Developments Historically, developments in technology have driven the growth and decline of organizations. For example, family farms have largely been replaced by corporate farms as a result of improved techniques and equipment , and leveraging scale to control costs. Typewriters and mimeograph machines have been replaced by computers and plain-paper copy machines. Organizations that make a point of keeping abreast of these types of developments thrive, whereas others deteriorate when they ignore or dismiss the changes as insignificant.

Industry Changes Technological developments often lead to industry changes. For example, the methods used to distribute goods have evolved over the past 100 years or so from animal power (horse-and-wagon) to railcars, trucks, and airplanes. Very few companies that began distributing goods using horse-drawn wagons were able to adapt to these changes. One company that did, the West Motor Freight Company, successfully transitioned from horse-and-wagon deliveries that began in 1907 to a regional delivery service, celebrating more than 100 years of continuous operation because it has been able to embrace industry changes.

Economic Environment The economic environment impacts all organizations and individuals. When the economy is growing, there is a greater demand for business goods and services, and many companies are able to thrive and grow. When the economy is shrinking, companies survive, or may even prosper, when they're able to keep expenses in line with declining income. In this environment, tightly run companies (those able to eliminate redundancy and waste) are more likely to succeed.

Many factors impact economic conditions. Higher taxes mean customers have less cash to spend on goods and services and are more selective about their purchases. Stricter government regulations mean organizations must spend more of their money on mandated expenses, such as reducing the pollution created by manufacturing processes.

Labor Pool A significant aspect of the general business environment that affects organizations is the availability of skilled labor. A *labor pool* is a group of available workers in the general population with the skills and qualifications needed by employers for various job roles. The labor pool directly affects unemployment rates by determining the number of individuals available and actively seeking work. A larger labor pool with insufficient job opportunities leads to higher unemployment rates, while a smaller labor pool or a high demand for workers can result in lower unemployment rates, reflecting the balance between job availability and the number of job seekers.

Legal and Regulatory Activity The external business environment is affected by activities of federal, state, and local governments. In addition to basic protections for worker safety, minimum wage and the right to organize, American labor laws have evolved to address emerging workplace issues such as discrimination and family leave. This evolution is generally in response to changing societal values and economic conditions. HR professionals are responsible for ensuring compliance with these laws by staying informed about legal updates, implementing relevant policies, and advocating for a fair and safe workplace environment.

Internal Business Operations

As important as the general business environment is to the health of an organization, it's equally affected by internal business operations.

Every organization is unique in how it organizes itself, but some basic functions and structures are common to all of them. Many organizations have independent *departments*, specialized divisions responsible for a specific set of functions or activities. These include core competencies such as the production of goods or delivery of services, and also the back office functions such as human resources, accounting, sales, marketing and research and development, to name a few.

Organizational Design and Development

Organizational design and development involve the process of aligning an organization's structure, roles, and processes with its strategy and goals to enhance efficiency, effectiveness, and adaptability. This is accomplished through a series of planned interventions focused on desired results. These results often include addressing structural, team or individuals' needs to help the organization remain competitive. *Organizational design* refers to the creation and optimization of an organization's structure to ensure it can achieve its objectives effectively. Key elements include:

- **Structure:** Determining the most effective way to arrange departments, teams, and roles
- **Processes:** Establishing efficient workflows and communication channels
- **Roles and Responsibilities:** Clarifying job roles and expectations to ensure everyone knows their duties
- **Hierarchy:** Defining the levels of authority and decision-making processes

Organizational development (*OD*) is a field of research and practice focused on improving an organization's capacity to handle its internal and external functioning and relationships. This involves planned, systematic change in the values, attitudes, and beliefs of employees through various programs and initiatives to improve organizational effectiveness. Key elements include:

- **Change Management:** Implementing strategies to help employees adapt to organizational changes
- **Employee Development:** Providing training and development programs to enhance skills and competencies
- **Culture Change:** Initiating programs to evolve the organizational culture to support strategic objectives
- **Performance Improvement:** Using interventions to improve individual and group performance

Both organizational design and development aim to enhance the overall effectiveness and efficiency of an organization. They focus on aligning the structure and culture with strategic goals, improving communication, supporting innovation, and ensuring that employees are prepared to meet the demands of their roles.

Organization Values and Ethics

Business organizations have a responsibility, and sometimes a legal requirement, to interact with employees, shareholders, and the community at large in a trustworthy and ethical manner. These responsibilities range from making appropriate decisions about pollutants that are released into the environment; to treating employees, customers, and other stakeholders honestly and fairly; to working with and training disadvantaged individuals to become productive members of society. This section describes ways to approach some of the issues in these areas.

The Enron scandal, which unfolded in the early 2000s, involved the energy company Enron Corporation's fraudulent accounting practices that led to its collapse. The scandal exposed significant corporate corruption and accounting fraud, resulting in the bankruptcy of Enron and the dissolution of its auditing firm, Arthur Andersen. Since then, the issue of business ethics has come to the forefront of discussions about the behavior of corporate executives, auditors, attorneys, and board members. Subsequent revelations about possible accounting irregularities at other multinational corporations such as AOL, WorldCom, and Global Crossing made it clear that this was not simply a case of one company that ran amok, but a pervasive problem at the top levels of major corporations. The Sarbanes–Oxley Act (SOX) made many of the practices that occurred in these companies illegal and provided penalties for violations. Ultimately, SOX created regulations about ethical business practices to create safeguards for all stakeholders, including shareholders and employees.

Companies that are committed to ethical practices often create behavior codes as guidelines for employees to follow. In practice, the terms code of ethics and code of conduct are interchangeable, but each has a different purpose. A *code of ethics* is a statement of ideal standards that the organization is committed to uphold in its business practices. A *code of conduct* is a statement of behaviors that the organization expects from employees; inherent in the conduct is the idea that disciplinary action would be the result of violating the behavioral standard.

A code of conduct or ethics is a useful tool that can inform people in the organization about what behavior is expected and what is unacceptable. Some topics to consider when creating these statements are as follows:

Honesty The code of ethics should set an expectation of honesty in the workplace. As with all other aspects of an ethics code, the executive team must model honesty in the representations they make to employees, customers, suppliers, and all other stakeholders in order for the message to be taken seriously within the company.

Integrity *Integrity* is defined as a firm's adherence to a code of moral values. Integrity is demonstrated when an individual does the right thing, even when that "thing" is unpopular.

Confidentiality In most companies, confidential information can be found in every department: Marketing plans, new product development, financial statements, personal employee information, and email accounts can all contain highly confidential information. In HR, professionals work every day with confidential employee information and are sometimes pressured to share this information for one reason or another. However, information collected during the employment process, such as an employee's age, religion, medical condition, or credit history, may not be used to make employment decisions such as promotions, transfers, discipline, or selection for training. HR professionals and other employees with access to confidential information have a duty to maintain its confidentiality.

Conflicts of Interest As mentioned at the beginning of this section, employees must put the interests of the organization before their own. Any time an employee stands to gain personally from an action taken by the employer, there is a conflict of interest (except, of course, for payment of the employee's salary). At a minimum, these situations must be disclosed to the employer, or employees should remove themselves from the situation. The ethics statement should make it clear that even the appearance or perception of a conflict of interest is damaging to the company and should be avoided.

Insider Information Although insider information is most commonly associated with trading securities on the stock exchange, it can also apply to other areas. Insider information is any information that an employee has access to or comes into contact with that isn't available to the general public. Using this information in stock exchanges is illegal and can result in criminal prosecution and civil penalties.

The prohibitions against using insider information with regard to stock transactions apply to an employee who overhears the information as much as they apply to decision makers in the organization. Federal law requires that those with access to insider information may not act on it until the information is made public.

Gifts An ethics policy should address the issue of gift exchanges with customers, vendors, and employees. It should describe under what circumstances gifts are acceptable and define limitations on the amounts if they're to be allowed. When the receipt of a gift unfairly influences a business decision, the gift becomes unethical and should be refused.

For companies operating outside the United States, receipt of gifts can be a difficult issue because in some cultures exchanging business gifts is a standard and expected practice, and the failure to do so can be seen as an insult. The Foreign Corrupt Practices Act of 1977 was enacted by Congress in response to revelations by multinational corporations of the bribes that were paid to obtain business in some foreign countries. The act prohibits the payment of bribes and requires accounting practices that preclude the use of covert bank accounts that could be used to make these payments.

Personal Use of Company Assets A code of ethics should clearly state what the employer considers to be an appropriate and acceptable use of company assets. In some organizations, the receipt of any personal telephone calls or emails is considered inappropriate, whereas in other companies a limited number is acceptable. Copying and distributing copyright material from print or digital media and other company assets may also violate patents or copyrights, and employees should be made aware of the consequences if they use any of these assets inappropriately.

Fairness Actions taken by employers have the ability to significantly impact the lives of their employees. Whether decisions are being made about hiring or layoffs, or accusations of malfeasance or inappropriate behavior are being made, employers have an obligation to treat employees fairly in all their actions. Employees who have the power to make decisions, such as selecting suppliers or evaluating employee performance, have an equal responsibility to handle these decisions fairly.

A real test of an organization's fairness occurs when an employee makes a complaint to a federal agency, claiming that illegal activity has occurred. A person who does this is known as a *whistleblower*. Some federal statutes, such as the Occupational Safety and Health Act, Railroad Safety Act, Safe Drinking Water Act, and Toxic Substances Control Act provide protection for employees who "blow the whistle" on their employers. Even so, it's a true ethical test to see how the whistleblower who continues to work for the company is treated in the workplace once the complaint has been made.

As important as a code of ethics is, it's equally important to be aware of situations where conflicting needs and desires make doing the right thing less clear-cut. As those responsible for maintaining the confidentiality of personal employee information, HR professionals make ethical decisions on a regular basis and are in a position to model ethical behavior in the way they respond to inappropriate requests for information.

Businesses serious about establishing meaningful ethics programs have appointed ethics officers or facilitators charged with the responsibility to ensure that the organization adheres to the ethical standards set by the executive team. Ethics officers advise employees at all levels in an organization on ethical issues and manage programs designed to allow confidential reporting of ethical concerns by employees, customers, shareholders, or others, and they also investigate allegations of wrongdoing. Ethics officers provide periodic reports for the executive team to keep them apprised of ethical issues in the organization.

Total Quality Management

Total quality management (TQM) is a long-term intervention strategy requiring employees at all levels in an organization to focus on providing products that meet customer needs. This is done by continually improving an organization's practices, structures, and systems. A successful TQM implementation requires the commitment of top management to lead the process. Processes are reviewed to eliminate wasted time as well as materials that either don't contribute to or are obstacles to producing the end product. The most popular TQM tools to be familiar with include the following:

Check Sheet *Check sheets* are the simplest analysis tools, requiring only a list of items that might be expected to occur. In an HR setting, a check sheet might be used to keep track of the reasons people resign from their positions. Figure 2.1 is an example of a check sheet used for that purpose. When an item occurs, a check or tick mark is placed next to it on the list. The data collected with a check sheet may be graphically represented in a histogram to facilitate analysis.

FIGURE 2.1 Sample check sheet

Reason	Number of Occurrences	Total
Lack of advancement	𝍸	5
Lack of recognition	𝍸 𝍸 ||||	14
Long commute	\	1
Low pay	\\	2
Poor supervision	𝍸 𝍸 𝍸 \	16
		38

Histogram *Histograms* provide a way of looking at random occurrences to find out whether there is a pattern. Using the data from the check sheet provided in Figure 2.1, a histogram provides a visual image of the reasons for resignations, as illustrated by Figure 2.2.

FIGURE 2.2 Histogram

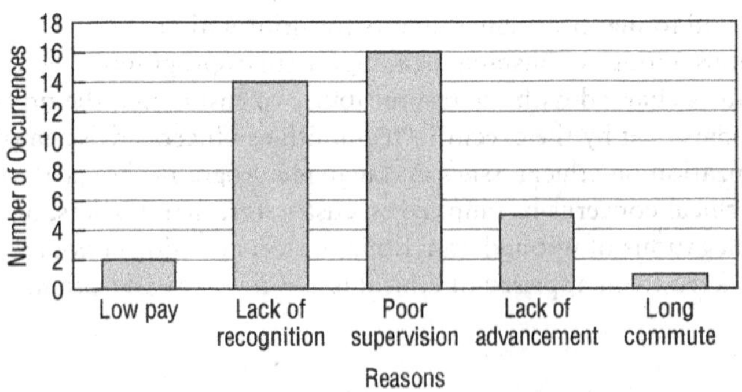

Pareto Chart The *Pareto chart* provides a graphical representation of the 80/20 rule: 80 percent of the problems are caused by 20 percent of the causes, a principle established by an Italian economist named Vilfredo Pareto. The Pareto chart points out which areas of concern will provide the greatest return when corrected. The difference between a Pareto chart and a histogram is that the Pareto chart arranges the data in descending order and includes a cumulative percentage on the right side of the chart. Figure 2.3 uses the Pareto chart to identify the most significant causes of resignations. In this case, poor supervision and a lack of recognition cause 80 percent of the resignations.

FIGURE 2.3 Pareto chart

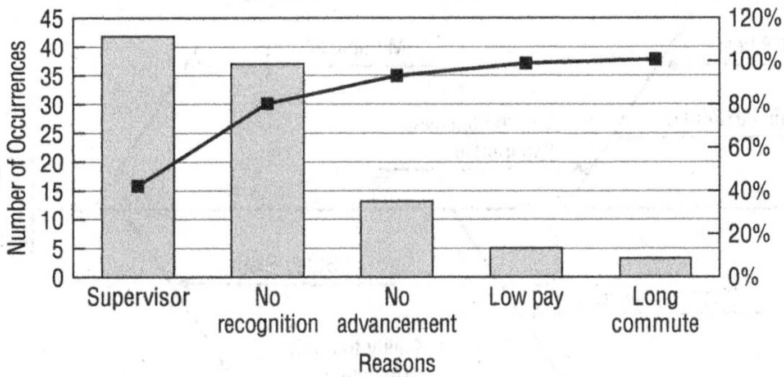

Cause-and-Effect Diagram A *cause-and-effect diagram* aids in organizing information during brainstorming sessions. This quality-analysis tool is also known as the *Ishikawa diagram* or *fishbone diagram*. Figure 2.4 analyzes what PHR candidates can do to maximize their chances for success on the exam.

Stratification To stratify something means to sort large amounts of data into smaller groups. *Stratification charts* show the individual components of a problem in addition to the total or summary. This aids in identifying possible strategies for correcting problems. Figure 2.5 is an example of a stratification chart. In the resignation example, the shorter bars represent components of each category, and the taller bar is the total amount. For example, the poor-supervision reasons could be broken down into categories for poor management skills and the inability to delegate. This kind of chart aids in the development of appropriate programs to solve the individual problems that make up a whole.

Process-Control Chart *Process-control charts* provide a graphical representation of elements that are out of the acceptable range by setting parameters above and below the range. This tool is most effective for determining variances in production processes over time. Although this tool is generally used in a production context, to help you understand how it works, let's look at how it could be applied in an HR context. Let's say your department has established that open positions will be filled within 30 days from the date of notification to the HR department, with a 5-day grace period. The sample process-control chart in Figure 2.6 shows you that two positions were out of the normal range: One took less than 25 days, and the other took more than 35 days. Both of these are considered to be "out of control" and warrant investigation to determine what caused the variance.

FIGURE 2.4 Cause-and-effect diagram

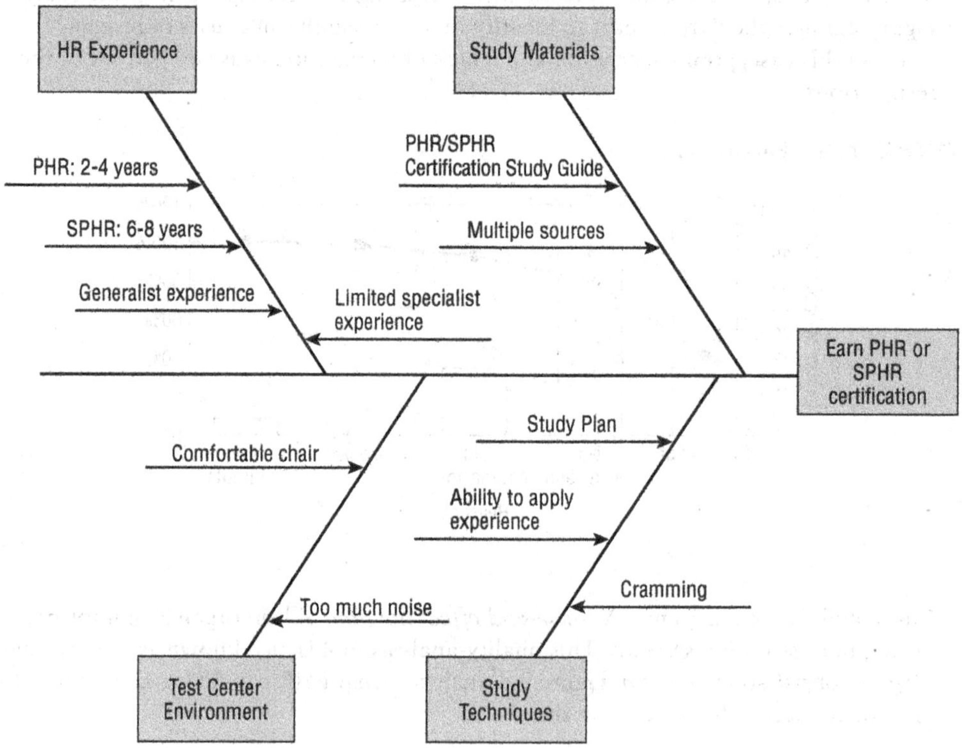

FIGURE 2.5 Stratification chart

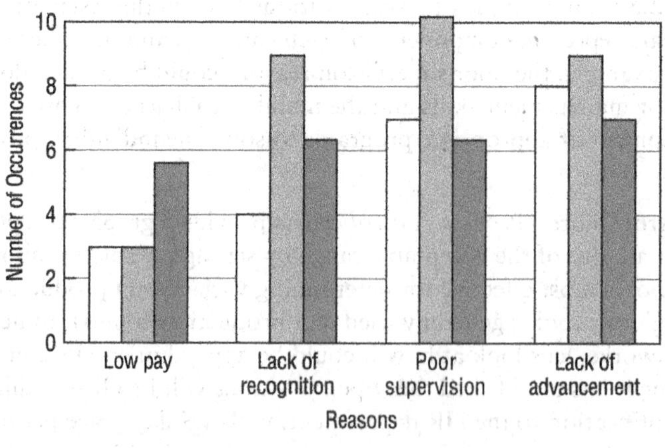

FIGURE 2.6 Process control chart

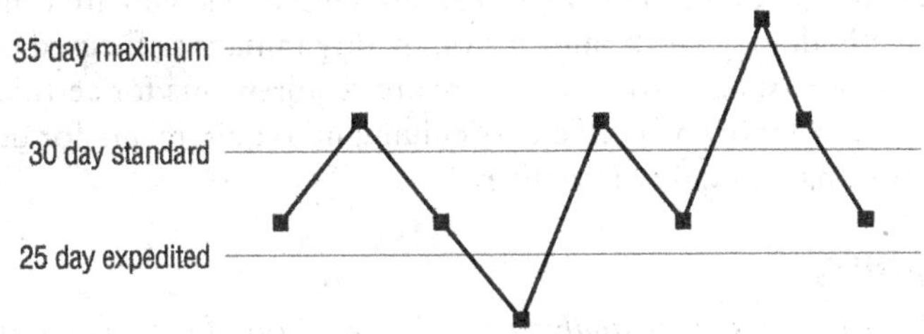

Philip B. Crosby

Philip B. Crosby's approach to quality, unlike that of Deming and Juran, focused on management as the key factor. His approach was based on strategic planning as the means to accomplish a high level of quality. Crosby advanced four absolutes of quality:

- **Conformance to Requirements:** Crosby believed that once management clearly described what was required, quality could be determined by whether the product met the standard.
- **Prevention:** "Do it right the first time" is a phrase Crosby associated with this absolute.
- **Performance Standards:** Zero defects is another term Crosby came up with to describe the quality standard that should be met.
- **Measurement:** In Crosby's view, quality should be measured by the additional cost of not producing zero-defect products the first time.

Although TQM originated in manufacturing environments, its concepts translate easily to service and other industries. For example, a public accounting firm can establish standards and then develop checklists and templates for accountants to follow when providing client services.

Six Sigma

Six Sigma is a quality philosophy developed by engineers at Motorola during the 1980s, when they were looking for a more precise way to measure process defects. The Six Sigma quality standard is measured on a "defects per million" basis, unlike previous standards that were measured on a "defects per thousand" basis. The Six Sigma methodology is referred to as DMAIC: Define, Measure, Analyze, Improve, and Control:

- **Define:** The first step is to define the customer and issues of importance to them, along with the process and project parameters.
- **Measure:** Once the process is defined, data about defects and other measures is collected and then compared to the original parameters to identify underperformance.
- **Analyze:** An analysis of the data is made to identify gaps between the goal and actual performance, explain why the gaps occurred, and rank possible improvements.
- **Improve:** Based on the analysis, solutions are created and implemented.
- **Control:** During the control phase, systems are revised to incorporate the improvements, and employees are trained in the new processes. The goal of this phase is to prevent backsliding into the previous process by ongoing monitoring.

A significant component of Six Sigma is the quality team structure used to develop, implement, and manage initiatives. In these organizations, employees who are trained and certified in the Six Sigma methodology work full-time on quality initiatives focused on continuously reviewing and revising business processes. There are requirements for certification at each level in the structure, including a specific curriculum and requirements for demonstrating effectiveness by working on quality initiatives.

Process Mapping

Defined by HRCI as a *process flow analysis*, this is a method of assessing critical business functions. A process map is a tool that visually represents workflow. It is useful to show the end result of a process, and all the steps and people involved in getting there. Visually relaying this information can be used to improve efficiencies and make decisions about resources. Additionally, a process flow map can be used as a training tool to show others how the work gets done, provide process documentation, and improve task consistency. It is also helpful in diagnosing bottlenecks, especially for more complex processes that require many steps.

Important to the workflow mapping are standard symbols to communicate steps in a workflow or process. Figure 2.7 shows a sample of flowchart symbols and what they represent on a process map.

FIGURE 2.7 Meaning of process flow symbols

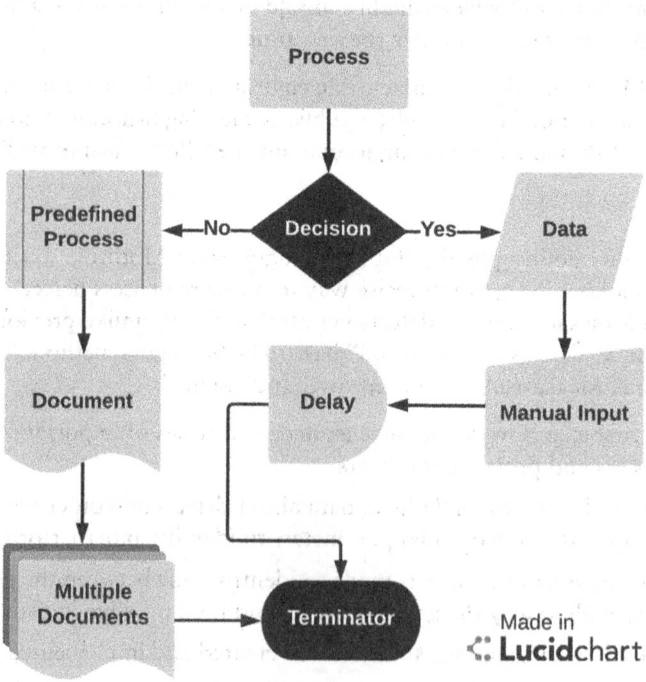

Job Design

Job design or redesign in the context of structural interventions involves structuring and organizing tasks, responsibilities, and relationships within a job to optimize efficiency, employee satisfaction, and organizational effectiveness. For example, organizations that seek to promote from within are often faced with a difficult dilemma—there aren't higher level jobs available for everyone. One solution is to employ a promote-from-within strategy that develops employees within the context of their current role. Job design can be accomplished in several ways:

Job Enrichment When an employee shows potential and is interested in growth opportunities, employers use *job enrichment* to assign new responsibilities or tasks that challenge the employee to use existing skills and abilities in new ways or to develop new ones as they tackle new assignments. Beginning with Frederick Herzberg, many social scientists have built behavior models that help incorporate job enrichment activities into job design. This strategy is based on the theory that when certain job factors are present, positive outcomes such as improved attendance, increased productivity, and greater levels of job satisfaction are the result. J. Richard Hackman and Greg Oldham's *Job Characteristics model* identified five job design factors that can improve four critical psychological states, including meaningfulness of work, responsibility for outcomes, knowledge of actual results, and employee growth needs. Here are the five job design factors used to achieve these positive states:

- **Skill Variety:** The ability of the employee to use multiple skill sets to complete a task
- **Task Identity:** The concept that the effort applied by the worker produces a whole identifiable unit or outcome, as opposed to a single part
- **Task Significance:** The inherent or perceived value of a job either internally to coworkers or externally to society
- **Autonomy:** The degree of independence or discretion allowed on the job
- **Feedback:** Communication to the employee by management related to how well the employee performs their duties

Job Enlargement *Job enlargement* is when additional tasks are added to the job without increasing the level of responsibility or skill. Job enlargement may be viewed positively by employees when it reduces job boredom by increasing the variety of tasks assigned. In other cases, employees may view this job design negatively if they perceive they're doing more work without a corresponding increase in pay.

Job Rotation Focused on giving employees a sense of the "bigger picture," *job rotation* allows employees to cross-train for jobs within other areas of the company. This strategy allows for skill variety while increasing the task identity, and potentially, the significance of their work as a whole.

Job Crafting In many cases, the design (or redesign) of jobs can be taken on by the employees themselves. *Job crafting* is a term that is used to describe the efforts employees take to (1) change the work itself, such as scope of job tasks, and (2) change the amount or quality of interaction with others, including coworkers and customers. Job crafting is a form of employee ownership achieved through autonomy and trust that can improve the meaning of jobs. Cautious employers may want to take a blended approach to job design and redesign, ensuring that employees have a voice while still controlling for productive outcomes.

Job Loading Built from Hackman and Oldham's job model, *job loading* seeks to redesign work in order to better serve employee psychological needs for understanding and meaning, thus increasing ownership of work outcomes. *Horizontal loading* involves adding different tasks to a job that are equal to other tasks, whereas *vertical loading* adds decision-making responsibility to a position. For example, a nursing job can be vertically loaded by giving employees a shared governance role over scheduling.

Corporate Social Responsibility

Corporate social responsibility (CSR) is a business behavior that is focused on building external strategic relationships. Identifying the CSR goals and resulting behaviors used for future decision making is an element of the strategic planning process.

CSR activities are interdependent on multiple department responsibilities that serve to link the external environment to the internal environment. Achieving the CSR objectives often requires the active participation and commitment of the entire organization.

The emerging stakeholders with an investment in the outcomes of CSR activities are often identified as those with a need for deeper participation and activity on the part of their business leaders (employees and the community), social initiatives, and the global landscape. These stakeholders typically are represented at a local, national, or global level.

Sustainability is defined by HRCI as "the capacity to endure over time." In other words, it speaks to company behavior that doesn't deplete the resources used to achieve an outcome. These resources include time, labor, and finances, all three of which have a significant impact on the long-term health of a corporation. Sustainability first became a widely recognized principle as the result of "green" initiatives, and companies now understand that the financial benefit of sustainable business practices is a long-term strategic solution that influences factors far beyond their environmental footprint.

Sustainability issues for many companies are often functionally still only a matter of complying with regulations, but true sustainability initiatives are undertaken regardless of the political climate. Companies that care about their environmental and social impact have taken steps to embed sustainability into their corporate behavior and brand. This means that regardless of changing regulations from the Environmental Protection Agency (EPA) or the Federal Communications Commission (FCC), sustainability efforts remain firmly rooted as a function of business strategy.

The use of the Internet in business continues to provide multiple opportunities for HR professionals to emerge as business leaders. HR practitioners must be able to establish relationships with individuals both inside and outside the organization to assist in the achievement of corporate responsibility initiatives.

One issue in which a partnership would be relevant is the "digital divide." This is characterized both economically and geographically: Roughly one-third of U.S. households with an annual income of under $30,000 do not have access to high-speed Internet, and in some cases, have no access to Internet at all. This "homework gap" highlights the ongoing digital divide that disproportionately affects lower-income, Black, and Hispanic households, leading to significant challenges in accessing educational resources and completing schoolwork. These issues must matter strategically to the businesses HR serves for many reasons:

Limited Internet access affects where companies may operate. A lack of digital infrastructure will keep companies from expanding where there is available talent and less expensive real estate. This affects the cost of goods and services, thus undermining profitability.

Access to the Internet is how many students are educated. A lack of access results in a less educated and qualified workforce to serve future staffing needs. This also means that the competition for talent will remain fierce in some industries, such as nursing and technology.

Professional growth is limited. The Internet provides many free and low-cost resources for individuals to develop professionally. This includes fundamentals such as reading skills, interviewing tips, and even language courses.

The Internet is a revenue stream. With the dominance of online shopping, the Internet is a source of revenue to which people must have access in order to make purchases. It behooves companies that sell or market anything online to partner with groups to aid in getting and keeping consumers connected.

HR can lead the efforts to partner with governments, nongovernmental organizations, and local community groups to bring infrastructure to underserved areas. HR may also get involved in lobbying efforts to help maintain a free Internet, allowing for innovation and fair competition.

Real World Scenario

Affordable Access Initiatives

Microsoft's Affordable Access Initiatives aim to bridge the digital divide by providing grants and resources to innovative businesses working on solutions for affordable Internet access. These initiatives focus on last-mile technologies, such as TV white spaces (unused television broadcast frequencies to provide internet access), and cloud-based services to reduce the cost of Internet connectivity, especially in underserved communities globally. Recipients receive seed funding, mentorship, and access to Microsoft's BizSpark tools, which include software, training, and technical support. This program not only supports connectivity but also fosters economic and educational opportunities by enabling Internet and energy access in remote areas.

For example, by extending fiber-optic connectivity from schools to homes in rural Virginia, Microsoft helped thousands of students gain Internet access at home, reducing the "homework gap" and providing equal educational opportunities (see `https://blogs.microsoft.com/blog/2015/12/17/microsofts-affordable-access-initiatives-partnering-for-impact`). In turn, this creates a future labor market of qualified potential employees with computer and Internet skills.

By addressing both the technological and socioeconomic barriers to Internet access, Microsoft's Affordable Access Initiatives help create more equitable opportunities for education, business, and personal development across the globe.

Diversity, Equity, and Inclusion

Diversity, equity, and inclusion (DEI) are interconnected concepts that collectively contribute to creating a more equitable and respectful environment within organizations. *Diversity* refers to the presence of a variety of identities and perspectives, encompassing factors such as race, ethnicity, gender, sexual orientation, age, ability, and socioeconomic background. *Equity* focuses on ensuring fairness and justice by addressing systemic barriers and providing resources and opportunities to level the playing field for all individuals, regardless of their background or identity. *Inclusion* emphasizes fostering a sense of belonging and acceptance, where all individuals are valued, respected, and empowered to contribute their unique perspectives and talents. While diversity recognizes differences, equity aims to rectify disparities, and inclusion promotes a sense of belonging, all three are essential components of creating a truly equitable and inclusive workplace culture.

DEI initiatives are not just ethical issues, but also strategic imperatives tightly linked to organizational success and results. A diverse workforce brings together individuals with varied perspectives, experiences, and skills, fostering innovation and creativity. By valuing equity, organizations ensure that all employees have equal access to opportunities for growth and advancement, which can enhance employee engagement, retention, and productivity. Fostering an inclusive workplace culture where every individual feels valued and respected can improve employee morale, collaboration, and teamwork, leading to better decision making and problem solving. Concepts you should be familiar with for the exams include:

- ***Employee Resource Groups (ERGs)***: An employee resource group (ERG) is a voluntary, employee-led organization within a company that provides support, networking, and advocacy for specific communities or affinity groups, such as women, LGBTQ+ individuals, or people of color.
- ***Unconscious Bias***: Implicit attitudes or stereotypes that influence our understanding, actions, and decisions in an unconscious manner, often leading to unintentional discrimination.
- ***Microaggressions***: Subtle, often unintentional, discriminatory remarks or actions directed toward marginalized groups, which can undermine their sense of belonging and well-being.

- ***Affirmative Action***: Policies and practices designed to address historical discrimination by promoting the hiring, promotion, and advancement of individuals from underrepresented groups.
- ***Cultural Competence***: The ability to effectively interact and communicate with people from different cultural backgrounds, understanding and respecting their perspectives and values.
- ***Allyship***: The practice of individuals from privileged or majority groups actively supporting and advocating for marginalized or underrepresented groups, often through education, advocacy, and amplification of voices.
- ***Intersectionality***: The interconnected nature of social categorizations such as race, gender, sexuality, and socioeconomic status, which can create overlapping systems of discrimination and disadvantage.
- ***Tokenism***: The practice of including a small number of individuals from underrepresented groups to give the appearance of diversity without addressing systemic inequalities or providing meaningful opportunities for advancement.
- ***Pipeline Problem***: The misconception that a lack of diversity within an organization is due to a shortage of qualified candidates from underrepresented groups, rather than systemic barriers or biases within the recruitment and hiring process.
- ***Inclusive Leadership***: Leadership styles and behaviors that prioritize diversity, equity, and inclusion, fostering an environment where all employees feel valued, respected, and empowered to contribute their unique perspectives and talents.
- ***Equity Audit***: A systematic review of organizational policies, practices, and procedures to identify areas where inequities may exist and develop strategies to address them, ensuring fairness and justice for all employees.
- ***Diversity Tax***: The additional burden or costs that individuals from underrepresented groups may face due to biases or systemic barriers in the workplace. It can manifest in various ways, such as women and minorities being disproportionately tasked with diversity-related responsibilities, experiencing microaggressions, or facing limitations in career advancement opportunities despite their qualifications.

For purposes of exam content, HRCI defines diversity as "a combination of various people working together, often with differences in culture, race, generation, gender, or religion." This definition aligns precisely with the I/O psychology term of *surface-level diversity*, which is thought of as the biological variables that may or may not correlate to job attitudes or overall performance.

The following sections will explore some key areas of diversity such as representation of women in leadership, LGBTQ rights, and cultural competence in the workplace.

Women in Leadership

According to the Center for Creative Leadership (CCL), factors such as gender bias, discriminatory practices, and inflexible organizational cultures all have resulted in a very low representation of women in executive leadership roles. Additionally, women themselves fail to believe in their own leadership abilities, often thinking that they must have the proven experience to lead, whereas men may be hired based solely on potential.[1] This lack of diversity has a negative impact on business decision making, creativity, innovation, and the diverse representation of nearly half of the workforce. HR must take the lead in identifying existing bias or practices that do not recognize the value of women at all levels of leadership. This may take on the form of several HR interventions, including an audit of hiring practices, demographics at all levels, or coaching and mentoring to develop future female leaders.

Sexual Orientation and Gender Expression/Identity

Statistically, the Lesbian, Gay, Bisexual, Transgender, and Queer (LGBTQ) community is one of the largest populations that experience discrimination in the workplace. Addressing issues that are specific to this community should be an important objective for senior-level HR leaders.

While Title VII of the Civil Rights Act of 1964 originally protected an employee's gender at birth, there has been some progress toward including LGBTQ employees for protection under antidiscrimination laws. Regardless, it is still an emerging issue, and guidance for employers is somewhat unclear. LGBTQ+ rights under Title VII and other federal antidiscrimination laws have seen significant developments in recent years, particularly with the landmark U.S. Supreme Court decision in *Bostock v. Clayton County* on June 15, 2020. In this decision, the Supreme Court ruled that Title VII also extends protections to LGBTQ+ employees. Specifically, it was determined that discrimination based on sexual orientation or gender identity is inherently a form of sex discrimination.

Justice Gorsuch, writing for the majority, clarified that an employer who fires an individual merely for being gay or transgender violates Title VII. The Court reasoned that because these forms of discrimination are intrinsically linked to the employee's sex, they fall within the prohibition of sex-based discrimination under Title VII. This decision harmonized previous conflicting lower court rulings and expanded federal employment protections nationwide.

HR must also be aware of the beliefs of employees who have religious opposition to this protection, being careful to not allow hostile, abusive, or discriminatory behaviors based on any characteristics that are not job-related.

Cultural Competence

HR professionals should also be familiar with cultural competence: the ability of a diverse group of people to achieve organizational aims, and a measure of a company's ability to work with individuals from multiple walks of life. Cultural competence is a necessary component of a corporate diversity management program and should focus not only on the operational needs of the workgroup but also on the more subjective realities of cross-cultural needs. HR has a broad influence in developing and assessing an organization's cultural competencies. Examples of this influence include addressing

---

[1] Ryan, J. [March, 2018] "Here's How to Propel More Women into the C-Suite," Center for Creative Leadership, `https://www.ccl.org/articles/leading-effectively-articles/heres-how-propel-women-in-c-suite`.

cross-cultural conflict, assessing the hiring patterns of managers, sensitivity training efforts, recruitment practices, leave policies, healthcare benefits design, and antiharassment policy development.

Difficulties also arise for employees whose backgrounds are dissimilar to the group. They may feel uncomfortable in situations requiring them to make major adjustments in order to be accepted by a group whose culture or demographic is different from their own, such as when managing a multigenerational workforce, for example. The workforce of today spans more generations than at any other time in history, with an average age-span difference ranging between 20 and 30+ years and many older workers unable or unwilling to retire. Although this is a boon in terms of talent availability based on work and life experiences, the result is a generational division that plays out in the hallways of the corporate landscape. Differing values, expectations, and cultural identities are the hallmarks of the type of factors influencing a company's ability to manage a multigenerational workforce. Examples of the HR factors that must be considered include training design, benefits utilization, and diversity management programs.

Diversity training seeks to educate all groups about the cultures, needs, and attitudes of other groups in the workforce to ensure the inclusion of all groups in workplace activities. One example many may remember is the 2018 training by Starbucks in which they closed all of their stores for four hours to address unconscious bias. Unconscious bias is a form of stereotyping that is so deeply embedded in a person's psyche that they are unaware of it, even as it influences behaviors. While humans are often unable to recognize bias in their own actions, they seem capable of recognizing it in others. For this reason, companies may wish to train institutionalized practices that encourage employees to "check" behaviors with a co-worker or supervisor before acting. For example, Starbuck's training was prompted by a racial profiling incident where an employee called 911 to report two African-American customers who were then falsely arrested. Had this employee understood the nature of unconscious bias and then, based on company practice, checked her desire to call 911, the profiling may not have occurred.

A *diversity initiative* seeks to increase the diversity of the workforce or to increase the effectiveness of an already diverse workforce. As with any companywide objective, top management support is essential for the success of the initiative, as is a clear picture of the challenges the initiative will address. Communicating the purpose of the initiative and providing feedback mechanisms for employees to ask questions will help ease any fears about the changes taking place in the organization. The initiative may begin with training designed to educate employees about the need for and benefits of diversity for the organization and to explain the benefits of diversity to them as individuals. As with any HR program, an evaluation of its effectiveness should be conducted at an appropriate time.

On the exams, DEI has a significant place throughout many of the functional areas. The following is a summary of each:

Business Management In business management, DEI focuses on integrating diverse perspectives and equitable practices into strategic planning and decision-making processes. This ensures that all employees, regardless of their background, have equal opportunities to contribute to and benefit from the company's success. It involves creating policies and practices that promote an inclusive workplace culture where diversity is valued and leveraged for organizational growth.

Talent Planning and Management DEI in talent planning and management involves implementing strategies to attract, recruit, retain, and develop a diverse workforce. This includes creating equitable hiring practices, reducing bias in recruitment, and ensuring diverse representation at all levels of the organization. It also encompasses succession planning and leadership development programs that provide equal opportunity for advancement to all employees.

Learning and Development Within learning and development, DEI ensures that training programs are inclusive and address the needs of a diverse workforce. This includes providing DEI training to raise awareness and foster a culture of inclusion, as well as developing training materials and opportunities that are accessible and relevant to employees from different backgrounds.

Total Rewards DEI in Total Rewards involves creating compensation and benefits programs that are fair and equitable for all employees. This includes ensuring pay equity across different demographic groups, offering benefits that cater to diverse needs, and recognizing and rewarding employees in ways that are inclusive and nondiscriminatory.

Employee Engagement In employee engagement, DEI focuses on creating an inclusive workplace culture where all employees feel valued, respected, and connected to the organization. This includes implementing initiatives that promote belonging, such as employee resource groups, mentorship programs, and inclusive communication practices. It also involves regularly measuring and addressing employee engagement across diverse groups to ensure that all voices are heard and considered.

Legal and Regulatory Requirements DEI in legal and regulatory requirements involves ensuring compliance with laws and regulations related to diversity, equity, and inclusion. This includes adhering to antidiscrimination laws, equal employment opportunity regulations, and other legal mandates that protect the rights of employees. It also involves staying informed about changes in legislation and implementing required policies and practices.

Company Culture

Company culture refers to the shared values, beliefs, attitudes, and behaviors that characterize an organization and guide its practices. It includes the work environment, company mission, leadership style, ethics, expectations, and goals, shaping how employees interact with one another and stakeholders. A strong company culture aligns with the company's objectives and drives employee engagement and overall business success. Culture is often reflected in the company's policies, communication styles, and daily operations, creating a sense of identity and belonging among employees.

Company culture is often impacted by industry. For example, in healthcare, company culture emphasizes teamwork, empathy, and patient care. In academia, it focuses on intellectual curiosity, research, and collaboration. Manufacturing environments prioritize efficiency, safety, and continuous improvement. Retail cultures often stress customer service, sales goals, and employee adaptability. Many HR policies are crafted around company culture, often incorporating the company's mission, vision, values.

Geert Hofstede's dimensions of culture provide a framework for understanding cultural differences across countries and within organizations. These dimensions help explain how values in the workplace are influenced by culture. The six dimensions are:

- ***Power Distance Index (PDI)***: This dimension measures the extent to which less powerful employees in an organization accept and expect that power is distributed unequally. High-PDI workplaces have a hierarchical order with significant gaps between authority and subordinates, whereas low-PDI workplaces strive for equality and participative decision making.
- ***Individualism* vs. *Collectivism***: Individualism in a workplace refers to environments where employees are expected to take care of themselves and their immediate tasks. In contrast, collectivism pertains to workplaces where employees are integrated into strong, cohesive teams that support each other. High-IDV workplaces value personal achievement and individual rights, whereas low-IDV workplaces emphasize group harmony and collective well-being.
- ***Masculinity*** vs. ***Femininity***: This dimension examines the distribution of roles and values in a workplace. Masculine workplace cultures value competitiveness, assertiveness, and material success, whereas feminine workplace cultures place more importance on relationships, quality of life, and caring for others. High-MAS workplaces prioritize ambition and performance, whereas low-MAS workplaces value cooperation and modesty.
- ***Uncertainty Avoidance (UAI)***: This dimension measures an organization's tolerance for uncertainty and ambiguity. High-UAI workplaces have strict rules and regulations to minimize uncertainty, showing a low tolerance for unconventional behaviors. Low-UAI workplaces are more relaxed and open to change and innovation.
- ***Long-Term Orientation*** vs. ***Short-Term Orientation***: Long term–oriented workplaces focus on future rewards, valuing perseverance and thrift. In contrast, short term–oriented workplaces are more concerned with maintaining traditions and achieving quick results.
- ***Indulgence*** vs. ***Restraint***: Indulgence in a workplace stands for an environment that allows relatively free gratification of employees' desires related to enjoying life and having fun. Restraint, on the other hand, reflects a workplace culture that suppresses gratification of needs and regulates behavior through strict social norms.

These dimensions help businesses and organizations develop culturally appropriate strategies. Discover more at `https://geerthofstede.com`.

Change Management

The result of almost everything covered in the previous sections—developing a company's mission, vision and values statements, establishing ethical guidelines, total quality management, and DEI—is *change*. Although, intellectually, many people understand the need for such changes, how they're personally affected has a direct impact on employee morale and productivity. The following are some of the structural changes that can significantly affect workforce populations today:

Reengineering Reengineering involves looking at the entire organization to simplify or eliminate unnecessary processes with the goal of increasing customer satisfaction through improvements in efficiency.

Corporate Restructuring Corporate restructuring looks at individual units in the organization to reduce or eliminate redundancy or bureaucratic processes in order to reduce costs and increase production.

Workforce Expansion Workforce expansions create their own type of stress in an organization. When a large number of employees enter an organization within a short period of time, it can be difficult for them to assimilate into the existing culture and climate. The resulting clashes of operating styles (face-to-face versus email communication, team orientation versus individual contributors, or authoritarian versus laissez-faire management style, for example) can create mistrust and reduce productivity.

Workforce Reduction Workforce reductions, also known as *reductions in force (RIFs)*, *downsizing*, or *rightsizing*, are used to decrease expenses by reducing the size of the workforce. One way RIFs are used is to lower expenses for short-term improvements in net profits in order to meet previously stated earnings targets for stock-market analysts.

Change Theories

Several theories of change are commonly used to guide organizational and social change initiatives. Here are the most prominent ones:

Kurt Lewin's Change Process Theory An early model of *change process theory*, developed by a social psychologist named Kurt Lewin, described three stages for change:

- **Unfreezing:** This stage creates the motivation for change by identifying and communicating the need for the change. In this stage, it's important to create a vision for the outcome of the change and a sense of urgency for getting to the new outcome.
- **Moving (Change):** During this stage, resistance is examined and managed, and the organization is aligned with the change. Communication remains an integral part of the process.
- **Refreezing:** In the final stage of the theory, the change becomes the new norm for the organization, the outcome is evaluated, and additional changes occur to adjust the actual outcomes to those that are desired.

Kotter's 8-Step Change Model John Kotter's model provides a more detailed approach with eight steps:

1. Create a sense of urgency.
2. Form a powerful coalition.
3. Create a vision for change.
4. Communicate the vision.
5. Remove obstacles.
6. Create short-term wins.
7. Build on the change.
8. Anchor the changes in corporate culture.

ADKAR Model The ADKAR Model, developed by Prosci, focuses on five key building blocks for successful change:

1. Awareness of the need for change
2. Desire to participate in and support the change
3. Knowledge on how to change
4. Ability to implement the required skills and behaviors
5. Reinforcement to sustain the change

The Change Curve Based on Elisabeth Kübler-Ross's Grief Cycle, the Change Curve model is widely used to understand the stages of personal transition in response to significant change:

- **Shock and Denial:** An initial reaction to a significant change or loss, characterized by disbelief and avoidance as a defense mechanism
- **Anger:** A stage where individuals express frustration and resentment about the change or loss, often questioning its fairness
- **Bargaining:** A phase where individuals attempt to negotiate or make deals to avoid the change or mitigate its effects
- **Depression:** A period of deep sadness and despair as the reality of the situation sets in, leading to a withdrawal from activities and people
- **Acceptance:** The stage where individuals come to terms with the change or loss, acknowledging its reality and starting to adjust
- **Integration:** The final phase where individuals incorporate the change into their lives, finding ways to move forward and grow from the experience

Elements for Successful Change

People dislike change for a variety of reasons: Change moves them out of the comfort zone to which they have become accustomed, and they may be fearful of the unknown.

The politics of the organization may make change undesirable in one group or another, and employees may perceive that they will lose status or control. Changes fail most often because the people who are expected to implement them aren't prepared to do so. Organizations can take steps to ensure the success of change initiatives, including the following:

Prepare for Change The only constant in the current business environment is change. Organizations must be aware of situations developing in the industry or geographic areas in which they operate so they can be ahead of the curve in developing strategies that will effectively handle changes in the environment.

Communicate To enhance the likelihood of a successful implementation, leaders must communicate effectively and repeatedly with employees well in advance of any planned implementation. Soliciting ideas from those who are closest to operations may provide insight into better solutions and increase buy-in when it's time to implement the change. Communication at every stage of the process will enable employees to get used to the idea of the change gradually, increase the level of acceptance, and build commitment for the process.

Develop a Plan A comprehensive plan that clearly defines the goals of the change, addresses all of its implications, and includes tools for evaluating its success is essential. Scheduling training for employees who may need to upgrade skills, integrating processes from different areas of the organization, upgrading equipment, and developing a plan to address resistance to the change and reduce stress will increase the chances for successful implementation.

Have an Executive Sponsor The CEO or another senior executive who is committed to and enthusiastic about the change must be able to inspire employees to commit to the implementation.

Motivate Direct Supervisors Employees want to know how their supervisors feel about changes and will be influenced by what the supervisors say about the change. When direct supervisors and managers are motivated to implement a change, employees will be more likely to accept it.

Recruit Unofficial Leaders Every organization has unofficial leaders who are able to influence co-workers; obtaining their commitment to the change will influence others. HRCI defines a *change agent* as a person or department that deliberately causes change within an organization. In OD interventions, this is at the direction of strategy.

Implement Put the change into action. Ensure that employees have the tools needed to successfully implement the change, whether that is new equipment, facilities, training, or support.

Evaluate Compare results to the evaluation criteria developed during the planning stage to determine whether the change was successfully implemented.

HR professionals are in a unique position to act as change agents during this process. A *change agent* must be able to balance the needs of various stakeholders in the process, listen to their concerns, and move them toward acceptance of and commitment to the change.

Business Metrics

All strategies must be periodically measured to assess progress, success or failure. The HRCI exams focus primarily on human resource metrics, although there are a few non-HR metrics that HR teams should understand. These include the following:

- **Revenue:** The total amount of money generated by the company from its business activities.
- **Profit Margin:** The percentage of revenue that remains as profit after all expenses are deducted.
- **Customer Satisfaction:** A measure of how happy customers are with the company's products or services, often gathered through surveys.
- **Market Share:** The percentage of an industry's sales that a particular company controls.
- **Cash Flow:** The amount of cash coming in and going out of the business, indicating the company's financial health.
- **Return on Investment (ROI):** This measures the financial return on investments made by the company, such as training programs or new technology.
- **Key Performance Indicators (KPIs):** Key performance indicators (KPIs) are measurable values that demonstrate how effectively an organization is achieving its key business objectives.

General HR department metrics that all practitioners should have a grasp of include:

- **Employee Turnover Rate:** Measures how many employees leave the company over a certain period
- **Employee Engagement:** Measures how motivated and satisfied employees are with their work and the company
- **Time to Hire:** Measures how long it takes to fill an open position from the time the job is posted
- **Employee Productivity:** Measures how much work employees accomplish in a certain amount of time
- **Full-Time Employee Ratio (FTE):** A measure that calculates the proportion of full-time employees relative to the total workforce, often used to assess staffing levels and resource allocation
- **Absenteeism Rate:** The percentage of workdays missed due to employee absence
- **Training and Development:** The average number of training hours per employee and the effectiveness of training programs
- **Diversity and Inclusion:** Measures related to the diversity of the workforce and the inclusiveness of the workplace
- **Benefits Participation Rate:** The percentage of eligible employees who are enrolled in various benefit programs offered by the organization

Risk Management

The inclusion of risk management as an exam topic has fluctuated in representation over the years. Originally highlighted as "Health, Safety and Security," it morphed into its current title of Risk Management in the 2012 updates. In 2018, it lost its status as its own functional area and was absorbed into the topics of Business Management and Employee and Labor Relations. In 2024, it is accounted for in the functions of Business Management/Leadership and Strategy, Employee and Labor Relations, and HR Information Management. What this suggests is that there are many areas of risk that an HR practitioner should be aware of and be prepared to manage. While topic-specific risk management practices are covered in their relevant chapters ahead, the basics are covered here.

Risk Identification

An argument could be made, and often is, that risk is inherent in any activity. The magnitude of the risk often determines whether an activity is pursued, and this of course is true for human resource activities. HR risks can be classified into one of the following five areas:

Legal Compliance Employers are at risk for potential lawsuits arising from employment practices that are out of compliance with laws and regulations designed to protect employees from unlawful activities such as discrimination, wrongful termination, and sexual harassment. Failure to comply with legal requirements has the potential to cost employers millions of dollars in legal expenses, judgments, penalties, and fines.

Safety and Health Risks for illness and injury exist in virtually every workplace, not just those involving the operation of heavy equipment or dangerous situations such as those faced by first responders. Employees who work in pleasant, climate-controlled environments face the possibility of repetitive stress injuries (RSIs), emotional and physical stress, and ergonomic strains.

Security Security risks can affect financial operations and practices, physical assets such as buildings and equipment, information assets such as documentation and data storage, and the people who work in organizations. At times, people may be the source of risk, as in the case of a hacker or an embezzler; at other times, they may need to be protected from a risk, such as a fire or natural disaster.

Business Continuity The ability to continue operating a business can be adversely affected by environmental disasters, organized or deliberate disruptions, loss of utilities and public services, equipment or system failures, serious information security incidents, or other emergencies. The HR responsibility for mitigating risks in this area is to develop programs that protect human assets.

Workplace Privacy In most organizations, HR is responsible for maintaining the privacy of highly confidential employee information. Risks to this information range from identity theft to the release of private health information and improper workplace-monitoring procedures.

Safety and Health Risks

Any discussion of managing safety and health risks must begin with the Occupational Safety and Health Administration (OSHA), because it sets standards that exert overwhelming influence on those issues in the workplace.

The Bureau of Labor Statistics (`http://.bls.gov`) reported that there were more than 1.8 million nonfatal workplace injuries and illnesses reported by private employers in 2022, a significant decrease from 30 years ago, when this number was 3.0 million. The purpose of assessing risk for environmental health and safety issues is to prevent those illnesses and injuries from occurring in the first place, to protect workers, and in the long run, to reduce the costs of turnover and workers' compensation, as well as to increase productivity and eliminate OSHA fines and penalties.

Environmental Health Hazards

Environmental health hazards in the modern workplace come in many forms, from physical hazards such as noise and extreme temperatures to chemicals used for everything from making copies to manufacturing products to biological hazards from viruses and bacteria. The effects of these various hazards differ between individual employees—some are more affected than others—so employers must take steps to prevent serious health consequences in the workplace. Table 2.1 lists some of the more common environmental health hazards.

TABLE 2.1 Examples of environmental health hazards

Chemical	Physical	Biological
Asbestos	Ergonomic design	Bacteria
Battery acid	Stress	Contaminated water
Corrosives	Extreme temperatures	Dusts
Gas fumes	Light, noise	Fungi
Pesticides	Electrical currents	Molds
Polyurethane foam	Radiation	Plants
Solvents	Vibrations	Viruses

Chemical Health Hazards

Many of the OSHA standards deal with specific chemical health hazards in the workplace. Every chemical present in the workplace should have a *safety data sheet (SDS)* from the chemical manufacturer to provide information on how to both prevent and treat an injury.

The SDS identifies the ingredients in the substance, how the substance reacts to changes in the atmosphere (such as at what temperature it will boil or become a vapor), and information about its explosive and flammable qualities. The SDS tells employees whether the substance is stable or unstable, what materials it must not be in contact with, and what additional hazards are present when it decomposes or degrades.

Most importantly for safety programs, the SDS provides information about how the chemical may be absorbed by the body; whether it can be inhaled, can be ingested, or can enter through the skin; whether it's carcinogenic; and what protective equipment is required to prevent illness when handling the substance.

Some chemicals, known as teratogens, have no effect on a pregnant woman but do affect an unborn child. Some employers, concerned about the health of the employee and her child as well as about potential liability, have developed policies to protect the fetus. These policies, although well intentioned, violate the Pregnancy Discrimination Act (PDA), which prohibits sex-specific fetal protection policies.

Physical Health Hazards

Many physical health hazards are easy to identify and remedy. One such hazard would be an open hole without any warning signs or barriers to prevent someone from accidentally falling. Another would be an electrical or telephone cord that isn't covered or secured to prevent someone from tripping. Another physical hazard would be a walk-in freezer storage unit that couldn't be opened from inside the unit. Many physical health hazards are addressed by the Occupational Safety and Health Act, covered in detail in Appendix C, "Federal Employment Legislation and Case Law." Mitigation techniques include eliminating the hazard, or reducing the likelihood of injury through controls such as machine guards or personal protective equipment.

Job-Related Stress

In 1999, the National Institute for Occupational Safety and Health (NIOSH) published the results of a study titled *Stress at Work*, which defined job *stress* as "harmful physical and emotional responses that occur when the requirements of the job do not match the capabilities, resources, or needs of the worker." When job stress is added to personal factors in an employee's life, such as a sick child or financial concerns, the effect on job performance can be magnified. Dr. Hans Selye, an endocrinologist, is generally credited with identifying stress as an influencer of health and well-being. He identified three stages of stress: arousal, resistance, and exhaustion.

In 2019, the World Health Organization identified stress (specifically, burnout) as an "occupational phenomenon," characterized by three dimensions:

- **Feelings of Energy Depletion or Exhaustion:** This dimension reflects the chronic fatigue and lack of energy resulting from prolonged stress at work.
- **Increased Mental Distance from One's Job, or Feelings of Negativism or Cynicism Related to One's Job:** This dimension involves developing a negative or detached attitude toward one's job and colleagues.
- **Reduced Professional Efficacy:** This dimension includes a decline in feelings of competence and successful achievement in one's work.

High levels of job stress can result in increased turnover, low morale, increased tardiness and absenteeism, reduced productivity, poor product quality, and increased accidents on the job. All of these negatively affect the bottom line.

The NIOSH study recommends a two-pronged approach to reducing job stress: organizational change and stress management. Organizational changes can take the form of employee-recognition programs, career development, a culture that values individual employees, and employer actions consistent with the organization's stated values. Stress management programs are, to a certain extent, dependent on the needs of individual employees, because people react differently to job stressors. These programs include training for employees about the sources of stress and how it affects health and teaching stress reduction skills. Managers can encourage employees to reduce the effects of stress by balancing their work with private activities, maintaining an exercise program, and building a support network at work and at home.

The full NIOSH study is available free of charge at `https://www.cdc.gov/niosh/stress/about/?CDC_AAref_Val=https://www.cdc.gov/niosh/topics/stress`.

Biological Health Hazards

Biological health hazards come in many forms, from unsanitary conditions in a food-preparation area to serious diseases contracted through needlestick injuries. Infectious diseases are spread by different means to employees, but the resulting impact on the health of the workforce or the community can be substantial. Although the healthcare and food-preparation industries are at greater risk than other industries, the entire world learned that in global pandemics, no industry is exempt from the need for preparedness and rapid response plans. HR professionals should understand the implications of infectious disease whether bloodborne pathogens, zoological, and plant-based hazards in all workplaces, and have established protocols for prevention and response. These include personal protective equipment, realistic sick time policies, handwashing, and other sanitation practices.

HR professionals can play a role in preparing their organizations to cope with a pandemic by establishing plans to maintain essential functions if a large number of employees are absent from work. The CDC encourages employers to prepare guidelines for minimizing face-to-face contact; secure vaccines for employees to prevent outbreaks; modify sick-leave policies to allow ill employees time to recover so they don't spread the disease; use telecommuting, flexible work hours, and work shifts to minimize contact; and establish knowledge-management programs to ensure business continuity during a health crisis. Additional information on preparing for a pandemic is available at `www.pandemicflu.gov`. For COVID-19 specific support, go to `www.cdc.gov/covid/index.html`.

Employees with infectious diseases who don't pose a threat to coworker health and safety are protected by the Americans with Disabilities Act (ADA) requirements for reasonable accommodation and may not be subjected to adverse employment actions because of their disease.

Business Continuity Risks

Ensuring an organization's ability to continue despite a disruption is one of the many challenges facing business leaders today. Whether the threat to operations is natural or human-made, accidental or intentional, the goal of business continuity planning is to protect the organization from unforeseen emergencies and other circumstances. Risks to business continuity can generally be classified as natural, human-made, or biological. In some cases, disasters such as fires or floods can be either natural or human-made, but response is similar in either situation. Examples of conditions that may trigger business continuity plans are covered next.

Environmental Disasters Environmental disasters come in many forms, from extreme weather conditions such as hurricanes, tornadoes, or blizzards, or from other causes such as floods, earthquakes, fires, volcanic eruptions, toxic gas releases, and chemical spills. For some environmental disasters, such as volcanic eruptions and floods, there is usually some advance warning, such as rising water levels in a river or gradually increasing volcanic activity. In these cases, businesses are able to take precautionary steps to secure people, data, and physical assets. At other times, natural disasters are unexpected, such as a major earthquake or toxic gas release. At those times, people must react instantly to save lives and business assets; the best way to do this is with a preestablished plan for people to follow so they don't have to make decisions under stressful conditions.

Organized or Deliberate Disruptions Organized and/or deliberate disruptions can be the result of acts of terrorism, major thefts, sabotage, or labor disputes. Major thefts and acts of sabotage come with little or no warning and can disrupt operations and, in the case of sabotage, potentially injure people. Terrorism also comes with little or no warning. In addition to the devastation to people and infrastructure, this disruption has the additional element of creating fear in people who may not have even been on the same continent where the attack occurred. In addition to the loss of life and infrastructure, management must be able to calm employee fears to continue operating the business.

On the other hand, labor disputes generally occur after a period of notice by a union and provide an opportunity to plan for continued operations. Even so, the disruption is costly and can be dangerous for employees who cross picket lines.

Loss of Utilities and Public Services The loss of utilities can occur as the result of a demand for electricity that exceeds the capacity of the power grid as the result of an oil shortage or as the result of a failure of the communication system, any of which can be caused by an environmental disaster or an organized disruption. In some cases, such as excessive demand on the power grid, the utility company may have a system in place to notify business owners of a potential loss of power prior to the loss. At other times—as the result of a terrorist act, for example—the disruption could be immediate and unexpected.

Equipment or System Failures Equipment breakdowns, such as a failure of production equipment or water pipes bursting and causing a flood, can halt production and disrupt operations unexpectedly. Other internal systems, such as the company's Internet service, communication system, or building power, can fail as well, disrupting operations.

Serious Information Security Incidents Cyberattacks by hackers, or the unleashing of a major email virus, can compromise sensitive and confidential information, shut down the customer-ordering website, or cause the IT system to fail. In 2024, a massive update to Windows programs caused major disruptions to many employers and airlines.

Other Emergencies Other emergencies vary widely in the amount of disruption caused to business operations. At one extreme, a biological disaster such as a serious epidemic could affect much of the workforce, reducing the ability of the company to function. Biological disasters can be either natural, such as the swine flu outbreak in 2010, or human-made, as the result of a bioterror attack. These types of disasters pose different challenges than some others because they affect the people who would otherwise be available to reduce the impact of the emergency. The unexpected loss of a key employee might not have an immediate impact but could cripple an organization's forward movement, regardless of the cause. In some cases, such as a resignation, there is some opportunity for transitioning to a replacement, including the transfer of essential knowledge. At other times, because of an accident, terrorist attack, or other type of disaster, the circumstances would rule out any time for transition, and remaining employees would need to reconstruct critical information in order to move forward. A public transportation strike or gas shortage is another situation that could either prevent employees from getting to work at all or significantly increase commute times.

Planning for these eventualities is a process known as a *business continuity plan (BCP)*, which results in a written document used to describe possible disruptions to operations and actions to be taken to minimize those disruptions and assign responsibility for executing the plan to specific individuals.

A BCP is often an umbrella term that includes other emergency plans, such as the emergency response plan and disaster recovery plan. In some organizations, these terms are interchangeable, whereas in others each describes a specific process. For the purposes of this discussion, the BCP is treated as an umbrella term covering different aspects of the business continuity process.

A successful BCP begins with a commitment from the CEO so that sufficient resources are provided for the process. When the CEO is committed to the process, a planning committee that includes representatives from each business function is appointed and defines the scope of the plan. There are several activities that occur as part of the BCP process. These are covered next.

Risk Assessment By their very nature, emergencies occur with little or no warning and can devastate individuals, single organizations, or whole communities. The BCP planning process identifies those risks most likely to occur based on the organization's location, industry, and other considerations. The risks are then assessed for the level of disruption each would cause and the impact on different business functions, as well as an estimate of the cost to reestablish or maintain them in the event of each risk.

Identify vital processes and key employees. Another element of the BCP is a review of each functional business area. This review identifies vital business processes, key employees necessary to maintain operations in each critical area, and records essential for the continuation of the business. If emergency plans currently exist, the planning team will review them at this time and determine what revisions are needed for different risks. At this stage, the BCP team will identify critical vendors and suppliers and how to move forward if one or more of them are incapacitated. Alternative locations and equipment resources for use in the event that the building is destroyed are also identified.

Develop a disaster recovery plan. A disaster recovery plan (DRP) describes activities that take place once the initial response to the emergency is over. Planning for this phase develops alternatives for reestablishing operations when property, processes, information systems, and people have been disrupted. If the building is unusable, what are the arrangements for temporary facilities? If the computer systems are inoperable, how and where will the off-site backups be reinstalled to continue operations? If transportation systems and roadways are damaged, how will employees get to work?

One important factor to consider in the DRP is a list of alternative vendors, suppliers, and service providers that can provide materials or support when normal sources are affected by emergencies and unable, either temporarily or permanently, to continue in the aftermath. This may make the difference in an organization's ability to continue servicing customers after an emergency.

Prepare a continuity of operations plan. The continuity of operations plan (COOP) generally refers to plans created to move from the disaster recovery phase, during which critical business functions are maintained but normal operations may not be taking place, back to pre-emergency service operating levels.

Maintain business continuity plans. Too often, organizations go through the process of creating plans and, once they're completed, never look at them again, assuming that the plans will work when needed. A critical component of a BCP is the need to test the plan, train employees to use the plan, and revisit it annually to keep the information current. An evaluation of the test results provides information about any necessary changes so that the plan can be refined.

Once the risks have been identified and plans have been developed, it's imperative that the affected employees have a clear understanding of the plan components through communication and training. Effective and frequent communication of the BCP allows the employees to respond to emergency situations properly, mitigate the risks associated with the crisis, and handle emergency situations when the owner/manager isn't present. Methods include classroom training of the procedures, hands-on training such as drills, and simulation of disasters such as data breaches and loss of power.

Addressing Risks

Members of the management team look to the HR function for guidance in complying with employment laws and regulations. HR also takes the lead in establishing compliant policies and procedures and is responsible for ensuring that members of the management team are aware of laws and regulations governing employment practices and the potential costs to the organization for failing to comply. In general, risks can be managed in one of the following ways:

- **Mitigation:** The company minimizes the risk.
- **Acceptance:** The company manages the risk if it occurs.
- **Avoidance:** The company eliminates the risk.
- **Transfer:** The company uses insurance to cover the risk.

Baseline for all risk management efforts is the requirement for different types of emergency response plans; these are covered next.

Emergency Action Plans

The OSHA emergency action plan standard requires, at a minimum, that the employer define the preferred method for reporting fires and other emergencies, an evacuation policy and procedure, and floor plans or maps that define escape procedures and assign evacuation routes. The plan must have contact information for individuals who can provide additional information during an emergency and provide procedures for employees who will remain behind to perform essential services during the emergency. Employees who will perform rescue and medical duties are to be included in the plan as well. The plan requires alarm systems to notify all employees, including those who are disabled, of the need to evacuate.

Real World Scenario

Sample Emergency Action Plan

Section 1: Responsibilities

In this section is a description of everyone who has a role to play during an emergency. Who will make the decision to evacuate the building? If critical machinery must be shut down, who will do that? Who is responsible to "take roll" and ensure that all employees have been safely evacuated from the building? Which employees are certified to perform first aid until medical personnel arrive on the scene? How will the emergency be reported to authorities, and who is responsible for doing that? Finally, this section should include the names of those who have been designated to answer questions and explain duties required by the plan.

Section 2: Emergency Escape Procedures

This section of the plan identifies the emergency escape procedures that employees are to follow and provides a diagram of the building showing escape routes from each floor and each area. In this section, special procedures for evacuating persons with disabilities, visitors to the building, and others with special needs should be spelled out. A safe meeting area should be designated so that all employees know where they should go in the event of an evacuation.

Section 3: Critical Plant Operations

Particularly in manufacturing operations, there are processes that must be shut down according to specific protocols. This section should identify these processes, along with instructions for employees on recognizing when they must evacuate themselves, even if the operation is not yet complete.

Section 4: Accounting for Employees

In the event of an evacuation, it's critical that rescue personnel know whether people are trapped in the building. Equally important is that rescue personnel not endanger themselves if everyone has been successfully evacuated. This section of the plan should describe the procedures to be followed, including where employees will meet and who will account for employees and visitors to the area.

Section 5: Reporting Emergencies

This section describes how emergencies are to be reported to the appropriate authorities.

Section 6: Identifying Emergency Contacts

In this section, the plan should identify who should be contacted for specific information. This may be a single person, or it may be several individuals who are responsible for different sections of the plan.

Section 7: Alarm System

This section of the plan should describe how employees will be notified of an emergency, where alarms are located, if there are different alarms for different emergencies, what they sound like, and whether the alarm system automatically notifies emergency personnel.

Section 8: Types of Evacuations

If the building is located in an area in which the potential for different types of emergencies exists, such as fires, tornadoes, and floods, this section of the plan describes the evacuation plan for each type of emergency.

Section 9: Training Requirements

In this section, the plan should describe how employees will be trained in emergency procedures and how often. The person responsible for training employees should be identified, along with a schedule for emergency drills.

Section 10: Recordkeeping

In this section, the plan should include documents that might be required in an emergency. This could include information on SDSs for chemicals in the worksite, maintenance records for safety equipment, equipment inspection records, building plans, and OSHA forms.

The emergency action plan begins with the common elements described previously and adds the following:

- Emergency escape procedures, including a floor plan or diagram for employees to follow
- Procedures for shutting down critical plant operations
- A process to account for employees after an evacuation
- A description of the alarm system that will notify employees of an emergency, including how persons with disabilities, visitors, and temporary employees will be notified
- Procedures to follow for different types of emergencies, such as fires, tornadoes, earthquakes, and terrorist attacks

Fire-Prevention Plan

The fire-prevention plan may be included as part of the emergency action plan. Whether the plan is included with it or separate, it must provide information about the following:

- All major fire hazards, how they should be handled and stored, a description of possible causes of igniting them and how to prevent that from happening, and a description of the appropriate equipment to suppress each hazard
- The location of fire-extinguishing systems or portable fire extinguishers
- The procedure describing how waste materials that are flammable or combustible will be stored before disposal

Injury and Illness Prevention Programs

Injury and illness prevention plans (IIPPs) (also called safety health management plans) are required by OSHA and designed to protect employees from preventable workplace injuries and illnesses. OSHA describes several plans with different purposes.

The IIPP includes several core elements essential for workplace safety. These elements are:

- **Management Commitment and Employee Involvement:** Establishing a safety culture supported by management and actively involving employees
- **Hazard Identification and Assessment:** Regularly inspecting the workplace to identify and assess potential hazards
- **Hazard Prevention and Control:** Implementing measures to prevent and control identified hazards
- **Safety Training and Education:** Providing ongoing training to employees on safety practices and procedures
- **Program Evaluation and Improvement:** Continuously evaluating the effectiveness of the IIPP and making necessary improvements

Generally, employers with 10 or fewer employees aren't required to provide written plans unless they have been notified by OSHA to do so.

To ensure the safety of employees and business assets, an emergency action plan, combined with ongoing employee training, is essential. By developing a plan and having regular drills to reinforce the steps to be taken, employers can improve the chances that all employees will be safe in an emergency.

Safety Training Programs

OSHA has developed guidelines to assist employers in developing effective training programs that reduce work-related injury and illness. The following guidelines can be modified to fit the specific industry and worksite requirements for individual businesses:

1. Determine whether training is needed. In other words, is the safety problem something that can be corrected with training or is another correction necessary?
2. Identify the training needs. What should employees be doing that they aren't doing? The program should inform them of appropriate methods for doing the job.
3. As with any other training program, develop objectives for the training.
4. When the learning needs and objectives have been identified, methods for delivering the training can be developed. Will classroom training be best? One-on-one training with an experienced employee? Demonstration and practice? This will depend on the specific training needs for the organization.
5. Conduct the training.
6. Evaluate how well the training worked, using training evaluation methods discussed in Chapter 4, "PHR | PHRi Exam: Workforce Planning and Talent Acquisition."
7. Based on the evaluation, adjust the training to improve its effectiveness.

NOTE

OSHA has various training programs unique to specific industries, such as general industry, construction, maritime and healthcare. You can find out more about these certification programs by going to `www.osha.gov/training/outreach`.

Elements Common to All Plans

Some elements are important enough for inclusion in each of the plans:

- A clear statement of the company policy regarding the program
- The commitment and full support of senior management
- A process for including employees in the process, whether through the establishment of a safety committee or some other means
- Identification of those with responsibilities under the plan, including employees, vendors, and public health and safety officials, and contact information for those individuals

- A clear, unambiguous process for reporting hazards or concerns to the responsible parties
- A description of the process to be used in training employees
- Procedures for maintaining records required by OSHA

Sexual Harassment

Recent events have shown a spotlight on industry and workplace incidents of egregious acts of sexual harassment. In particular, they have highlighted how confidentiality agreements can suppress the natural reporting mechanism of claims, creating systemic issues that are far deeper than single employer incidents.

And yet, this type of behavior has been prohibited since 1964 by Title VII of the Civil Rights Act subsequent amendments. Issues such as same-sex harassment, the implied obligation of supervisor-employee propositions, and whistleblower protections will continue to be important HR practices to be managed. The heart of the law remains, however, in which employers have an obligation to prevent two forms of sexual harassment: quid pro quo and hostile work environment.

Quid pro quo is a legal term that means, in Latin, "this for that." Quid pro quo harassment, therefore, occurs when a supervisor or manager asks for sexual favors in return for some type of favorable employment action. *Sexual favors* is a broad term that covers actions ranging from unwanted touching to more explicit requests.

A *hostile work environment* has been defined by the EEOC as one in which an individual or individuals are subjected to unwelcome verbal or physical conduct "when submission to or rejection of this conduct explicitly or implicitly affects an individual's employment, unreasonably interfere with an individual's work performance, or creates an intimidating, hostile, or offensive work environment." When investigating these charges, the EEOC looks at many factors. In most cases, a single incidence of inappropriate and unwelcome behavior doesn't rise to the level of a hostile work environment, but in some cases when the actions or behavior are particularly offensive or intimidating, the EEOC may find that harassment has occurred. A hostile work environment can also be found to exist for victims who have been affected by unwelcome offensive conduct toward someone other than themselves.

NOTE Unlike the quid pro quo form of harassment, a hostile work environment can be created by coworkers, suppliers, customers, or other visitors to the workplace.

Courts have held employers responsible for the harassing actions of their employees, whether or not the employer was aware of the harassment. Beginning in 1986, the Supreme Court issued a number of rulings to clarify employer responsibilities in the prevention of sexual harassment. The most commonly cited of these for HR purposes are *Meritor Savings Bank v. Vinson* (1986), *Harris v. Forklift Systems* (1993), and two cases decided at the same time in 1998, *Burlington Industries v. Ellerth* and *Faragher v. City of Boca Raton*; these are covered next.

Meritor Savings Bank v. Vinson (1986)

Mechelle Vinson applied for a job at a branch of Meritor Savings Bank in 1974 when Sidney Taylor was a vice president and manager of the branch. Taylor hired Vinson, who worked at the branch for four years, starting as a teller trainee and working her way up to assistant branch manager, based on her performance in the jobs she held. Once she passed her probationary period as a trainee, Vinson claims that Taylor began to harass her, requesting that they go to a motel to have sexual relations. Although Vinson refused Taylor's advances initially, she gave in eventually because she believed she would lose her job if she didn't. Vinson claims that Taylor's harassment escalated to the point that she was fondled in front of other employees and expected to engage in sexual relations at the branch both during and after work. In September 1978, Vinson took an indefinite medical leave, and the bank terminated her in November 1978.

The Supreme Court issued its opinion in June 1986, finding that a claim of "hostile environment" sex discrimination is actionable under Title VII. The Court rejected the idea that the "mere existence of a grievance procedure and a policy against discrimination" is enough to protect an employer from the acts of its supervisors. The opinion indicated that a policy designed to encourage victims of harassment to come forward would provide greater protection.

Harris v. Forklift Systems (1993)

In April 1985, Teresa Harris was employed by Forklift Systems, Inc. as a manager, reporting to the company president, Charles Hardy. Hardy insulted Harris frequently in front of customers and other employees and made sexually suggestive remarks. When Harris complained in August 1987, Hardy apologized and said he would stop the conduct. But in September of that year, Hardy once again began the verbal harassment, and Harris quit on October 1.

Harris then filed a lawsuit against Forklift, claiming that Hardy had created a hostile work environment on the basis of her gender. The district court found that although Hardy's conduct was offensive, it didn't meet the required standard of severity to seriously affect her psychological well-being.

The Supreme Court agreed to hear the case in order to resolve conflicts in the lower courts on what conduct was actionable for a hostile work environment. The Court found that the appropriate standard is one that falls between that which is merely offensive and that which results in tangible psychological injury. Although this isn't a precise guideline, it does allow courts to take into consideration a number of factors about the work environment, the frequency and severity of the conduct, the level of threat or humiliation to which the victim is subjected, and whether the conduct interferes unreasonably with performance of the employee's job.

Faragher v. City of Boca Raton (1998)

Beth Ann Faragher and Nancy Ewanchew were two of six females out of more than 40 lifeguards for the city of Boca Raton in Florida from 1985 to 1990. During their tenure, they were verbally and physically harassed by two supervisors, Bill Terry and David Silverman. They both complained to a third supervisor, Robert Gordon, about the harassment but didn't file a formal complaint, and no corrective action was taken. Ewanchew resigned in 1989 and wrote to the city manager in 1990 to complain about the harassment. The city investigated, and when it found that both Terry and Silverman had acted inappropriately, reprimanded and disciplined both supervisors.

The Supreme Court found that employers are responsible for actions of those they employ and have a responsibility to control them. Going further, the Court determined that a supervisor need not make an explicit threat of an adverse *tangible employment action* (TEA), which the Court defined as "a significant change in employment status, such as hiring, firing, failing to promote, reassignment with significantly different responsibilities, or a decision causing a significant change in benefits" in order for harassment to be actionable. The Court determined that subordinates know that the possibility of adverse supervisory actions exists whenever requests are made, even if the adverse actions aren't stated.

Burlington Industries v. Ellerth (1998)

Kimberly Ellerth worked for Burlington Industries in Chicago as a salesperson from March 1993 to May 1994. During that time, Ellerth claims that she was subjected to ongoing sexual harassment by Ted Slowick, who wasn't her direct supervisor but did have the power to approve or deny a TEA with regard to her employment. Although Ellerth was aware of Burlington's policy prohibiting sexual harassment during her employment, she didn't complain about the harassment until after she resigned. After resigning, she filed a complaint with the EEOC and, when she received a right-to-sue letter in October 1994, filed suit against Burlington.

A key issue in this case was that of *vicarious liability* (an element of the legal concept of *respondeat superior*), which, in this context, means an employer may be held accountable for the harmful actions of its employees, whether or not the employer is aware of those actions. The Supreme Court decided in part that "An employer is subject to vicarious liability to a victimized employee for an actionable hostile environment created by a supervisor with immediate (or successively higher) authority over the employee."

Bostock v. Clayton County (2020)

Bostock v. Clayton County is a landmark Supreme Court case decided on June 15, 2020. The case consolidated three separate cases involving employees who were dismissed from their jobs for being gay or transgender. The Supreme Court ruled in a 6-3 decision that Title VII of the Civil Rights Act of 1964, which prohibits employment discrimination "because of sex," extends to discrimination based on sexual orientation and gender identity. This decision significantly expanded the protections under Title VII, affirming that employers cannot legally terminate or discriminate against employees for being gay or transgender, thus ensuring broader workplace equality and civil rights.

EEOC Guidelines for the Prevention of Sexual Harassment

The EEOC has developed detailed guidelines titled "Enforcement Guidance: Vicarious Employer Liability for Unlawful Harassment by Supervisors" to assist employers in developing policies that clearly express the employer's prohibition against harassment and conducting investigations that meet EEOC standards.

To summarize the guidelines, employers are encouraged to develop antiharassment policies, along with complaint procedures for those who believe they have been harassed. The policy should clearly explain unacceptable conduct and reassure employees who complain that they will be protected against retaliation. The complaint process should describe multiple avenues for reporting harassment and provide assurances of confidentiality to the extent it's possible. Investigations of allegations should be prompt and impartial, and if the investigation finds that harassment did indeed occur, the policy should provide for immediate corrective action.

These guidelines are fully described at `www.eeoc.gov/policy/docs/harassment.html`.

Workplace Investigations

Workplace investigations are necessary under various conditions, including allegations of harassment, discrimination, misconduct, violations of company policies or laws, conflicts between employees, grievances, and complaints regarding workplace safety or ethical concerns. Investigations may be initiated in response to reports of theft, fraud, or other illegal activities that impact the organization's integrity and operations.

HR professionals handling workplace investigations must possess strong communication, problem-solving, and conflict resolution skills. They need knowledge of ethics, laws, and attention to detail to conduct thorough and compliant investigations. Emotional intelligence is also important for maintaining neutrality and managing confidentiality. Effective time management and continuous learning are essential for staying updated and adaptable in this dynamic field. These competencies are engaged throughout the workplace investigation process:

- **Promptness and Confidentiality:** Investigations should be initiated promptly upon receiving a complaint or noticing potential misconduct. HR should ensure confidentiality throughout the process to protect the privacy of all parties involved and prevent retaliation.
- **Impartiality and Objectivity:** HR professionals must approach investigations with neutrality, setting aside personal biases and preconceptions. They should focus solely on gathering facts and evidence to make fair and unbiased determinations.
- **Clear Policies and Procedures:** Clear guidelines and procedures for conducting investigations should be established and communicated to all employees. This ensures consistency and transparency in handling complaints and allegations.
- **Thorough Documentation:** HR should meticulously document all stages of the investigation, including interviews, evidence collection, and findings. Detailed records serve as a safeguard against legal challenges and provide a clear trail of actions taken.
- **Interviewing Techniques:** When interviewing parties involved in the investigation, HR professionals should use open-ended questions to elicit detailed responses and avoid leading or suggestive questioning that could compromise the integrity of the process.

- **Evidence Gathering:** HR should gather and analyze all available evidence, including documents, emails, witness statements, and electronic communications. It's crucial to assess the credibility and relevance of each piece of evidence to reach a well-informed conclusion.
- **Maintaining Confidentiality and Privacy:** HR must respect the privacy of all individuals involved and refrain from disclosing sensitive information to unauthorized parties. Information should only be shared on a need-to-know basis to preserve confidentiality.
- **Fair and Timely Resolution:** Once the investigation is complete, HR should make a timely decision based on the findings and take appropriate action, which may include disciplinary measures or remedial actions to prevent future incidents.
- **Prevention:** After the investigation, HR should conduct a thorough review of the process to identify any areas for improvement. Feedback from stakeholders should be solicited to enhance future investigations and prevent similar issues from arising.

NOTE: An after action review (AAR) is a structured process used to evaluate the outcomes of a project, event, or activity after it has been completed. It involves gathering relevant stakeholders to reflect on what went well, what didn't, and what lessons can be learned for future improvement. The goal of an AAR is to identify successes and areas for improvement, capture insights and best practices, and make recommendations for enhancing performance in similar situations in the future.

Workforce Planning and Talent Acquisition

Workforce planning and talent acquisition involves strategically forecasting an organization's future staffing needs and implementing processes to attract, recruit, and retain the best talent to meet those needs. Operationally, this involves analyzing current workforce capabilities, identifying gaps, and managing recruitment processes to fill immediate vacancies. Strategically, this involves long-term planning to align workforce capabilities with future organizational goals, anticipating changes in market conditions, and developing talent pipelines to ensure sustained organizational growth and competitiveness.

Forecasting talent involves predicting future talent needs based on organizational goals and market trends. This process includes analyzing current workforce data, identifying potential skill gaps, and developing strategies to recruit and retain talent effectively to align with anticipated business demands.

Workforce Analysis

Workforce analysis involves evaluating the current workforce's composition, skills, and capabilities to understand how well they align with the organization's needs. This process includes examining the following:

- **Employee Demographics:** Statistical data of the workforce, including age, gender, ethnicity, education level, and other relevant characteristics that help understand the diversity and composition of the organization's employees
- **Skills Inventories:** Comprehensive lists or databases of the skills, qualifications, and competencies possessed by employees within an organization, used to identify existing capabilities and plan for future training and development needs
- **Turnover Rates:** The rate at which employees leave an organization and are replaced by new hires over a specific period, indicating the stability and retention effectiveness of the workforce
- **Productivity Metrics:** Quantitative measures used to assess the efficiency and performance of employees, helping to identify areas where the workforce excels and areas that require improvement
- **Gap Analysis:** The process of comparing the current state of the workforce's skills and capabilities with the desired future state, identifying discrepancies and formulating strategies to bridge these gaps

In addition, employers collect data for many other functions of HR. *Quantitative analysis* involves the use of numerical data and statistical methods to identify patterns, relationships, and trends. It is objective and often employs tools like surveys, experiments, and computational models. For example, analyzing employee turnover rates using statistical software to determine the average tenure of employees is a quantitative approach.

In contrast, *qualitative analysis* focuses on understanding the meaning and characteristics of human behavior and experiences. It is subjective and often uses methods like interviews, focus groups, and content analysis. For instance, conducting in-depth interviews with employees to understand their job satisfaction and reasons for leaving provides qualitative insights. Here are other examples:

- **Quantitative:** Using a survey to collect data on employee satisfaction levels and analyzing the results using statistical techniques to identify correlations between satisfaction and productivity
- **Qualitative:** Conducting focus groups to explore employee perceptions of company culture and analyzing the discussion to identify common themes and sentiments

HR teams use quantitative analysis for workforce metrics, turnover rates, and compensation benchmarking, whereas qualitative analysis is used for employee feedback, conflict resolution, and understanding change resistance. Both methods help in operational efficiency and strategic planning.

Translating Organization Goals into Staffing Plans

Translating strategic workforce goals and objectives into a tactical action plan is accomplished with the use of a *staffing needs analysis*. This tool is used to determine the numbers and types of jobs forecasted in the organization's strategic plan.

The strategic plan identifies two key pieces of information for HR: the work that needs to be done and how many people are needed to do it. From here, the process of creating the plan can begin:

1. **Collect Data:** HR collects information about current employees who may be ready to assume new tasks and responsibilities and any training needed to prepare them for new roles.
2. **Identify Gaps:** Building on the data collected from individual business-unit managers, HR develops a comprehensive list of the knowledge, skills, abilities and other (KSAO) competencies required to meet future needs for the organization. Factored into this list should be contingencies for retirements or unexpected resignations of current employees based on prior history of turnover, transfers, and promotions.
3. **Analyze Options:** Once the list of numbers, types, and timing of future openings is available, HR identifies options for filling the positions, whether from internal transfers or promotions, external hires, or the use of alternative staffing methods.
4. **Select/Implement Solutions:** Conducting a cost-benefit analysis of the options identified in the previous step provides a means for comparison between the available options.
5. **Evaluate Results:** After the solution has been implemented, an evaluation of its success is conducted to ensure that it meets the needs of the organization.

Recruitment and Staffing Strategies

Recruitment strategies refer to the methods and approaches used to attract and hire qualified candidates to fill organizational roles. These strategies include defining job requirements, sourcing candidates, leveraging employer branding, using various recruitment channels, and implementing selection processes that ensure the best talent is recruited efficiently and effectively.

Offshoring is the process of moving production or service processes to other countries to realize cost savings. For example, India has become a popular offshore site for U.S. service processes, such as customer support call centers.

Outsourcing contracts internal business services to outside organizations that specialize in the specific process, such as payroll processing, IT, or janitorial services.

Either decision generally results in a reduction in staff for employees who previously did the work that will now be done externally. In some cases, an outsource firm may hire those employees, who will continue to do the same work as members of the new organization.

Other Legal and Regulatory Issues

In addition to the federal labor laws covered in Appendix C, it is important for PHR and SPHR candidates to understand a few other concepts related to the legal and regulatory environment.

For example, *nepotism* is the practice of favoring relatives or friends, especially by giving them jobs, promotions, or other advantages within an organization, regardless of their qualifications or merit. Nepotism itself is not inherently illegal in most jurisdictions. However, in the United States, certain federal, state, and local governments have laws or policies prohibiting nepotism, particularly to avoid conflicts of interest and ensure fairness in public service. Private companies may also have their own policies against nepotism to maintain a fair and merit-based work environment. If an employer chooses to hire relatives, it is a best practice to ensure that they do not have direct reporting lines to each other.

Moonlighting occurs when an employee holds a secondary job outside of their primary employment. In some cases, this may present a conflict of interest, particularly if the second job is with a competitor. *Noncompete clauses* are agreements in which the employee agrees not to enter into competition with the employer during or after employment, restricting them from working with competitors or starting a similar business within a specified period and geographic area after leaving the company. The enforceability of these agreements has come under recent scrutiny, with general agreement that no entity has the right to prohibit an individual from making a living. In the European Union and Canada, noncompete agreements can be enforceable if they are reasonable and protect legitimate business interests. They often require compensation for the restricted period and must comply with local labor laws. HR teams should develop clear policies on their position on moonlighting, including requiring disclosure and addressing any compliance issues if they arise.

Finally, romantic or close personal relationships between coworkers or between supervisors and subordinates can lead to conflicts of interest, perceived favoritism, and potential legal issues if the relationship ends poorly. HR should have clear policies in place regarding workplace relationships and require disclosure of such relationships to manage potential conflicts.

The Uniform Guidelines on Employee Selection Procedures (UGESPs)

The UGESPs state that any selection tool must be both job-related and a valid predictor of success in the position. Records are to be kept by sex, race, and ethnic group, using categories consistent with the EEO-1 report (Hispanic, White, Black or African-American, native Hawaiian or other Pacific Islander, Asian, American Indian or Alaska native, and two or more races) and EEO reporting purposes.

One report required by the UGESPs is a determination of whether selection procedures have an adverse impact on one or more protected groups. An *adverse impact* occurs when the selection rate for a protected class is less than four-fifths, or 80 percent, of the selection rate for the group with the highest selection rate. This is often referred to as the 4/5ths rule or the 80 percent rule. Table 2.2 illustrates an adverse-impact calculation.

TABLE 2.2 Calculating adverse impact

Group	Applicants	Hired	Selection rate	4/5 of highest rate
Males	255	48	19%	15%
Females	395	52	13%	
Total	650	100		

The UGESPs direct that if employers have access to more than one selection tool, the tool that has the least adverse impact is the one to be used.

In this example, the company advertised 100 openings. Applications were received from 255 males and 395 females for the position. Adverse impact is calculated as follows:

1. For each group, divide the number of applicants hired by the total number of applicants:

   Males: 48 ÷ 255 = 19%

   Females: 52 ÷ 395 = 13%

2. Multiply the highest selection rate by 80%:

   Males: 19% × 80% = 15%

3. Compare the selection for the other group(s) to determine whether adverse impact has occurred:

   Females: 13%

   Males: 15%

In this example, female applicants were adversely impacted by the selection process because 13% is lower than the resulting 15%.

Applicant Tracking

The UGESPs require employers to keep records of individuals who apply for open positions based on their sex and race/ethnicity as previously described for the EEO-1 report. In 1974, the UGESPs defined an applicant as "a person who has indicated an interest in being considered for hiring, promotion, or other employment opportunities. This interest might be expressed by completing an application form or might be expressed orally, depending on the employer's practice."

Reliability and Validity

The UGESPs require that selection tests be reliable and valid predictors of success on the job:

Reliability *Reliability* measures whether a test or other measurement produces consistent results so that, over time, the scores won't vary greatly. Test reliability is enhanced by several factors, including wording instructions and test questions clearly. Providing optimal conditions for administering the test contributes to its reliability, as does making sure it's long enough to accurately test the candidate's knowledge.

In essence, measuring reliability can be done by administering the same test to the same respondents after a set amount of time has passed, and seeing if there is a correlation between the test questions and predicted behaviors. This is called "test-retest" reliability.

Another method, called the "internal consistency" method, is used when questions from the same content domain are constructed in different ways, and the items are evaluated for respondent consistency.

Finally, a third way to measure test reliability is the "parallel forms" method, used when two tests from the same content domain are constructed and results are compared for consistency.

Validity *Validity* considers the characteristics being measured by a test and whether the test is measuring the characteristics accurately. There are several different measurements of validity, including the following:

- ***Content Validity*:** This is the simplest of the three validation measures. Job analysis is a key element of the content-validity process, which confirms that a selection procedure samples significant parts of the job being tested. For example, a driving test given to a delivery person who would drive a truck 80 percent of the time if hired for the job is a test with content validity.
- ***Construct Validity*:** This determines whether a test measures the connection between candidate characteristics and successful performance on the job. According to the DOL, construct validity is a method of testing that measures an applicant's abstract future behaviors. In order for a test to be legally defensible, it must show that it measured the proper characteristic and that it accurately predicted future success on the job.
- ***Criterion Validity*:** A criterion is a trait or work behavior that is predicted by a test. Criterion validity is established when the test or measure either predicts or correlates the behavior:
- ***Predictive Validity*:** This compares the test scores of a test given at the beginning of a job before new employees have experience to the same criterion collected at some future time. When the employees have had some experience (e.g., 6 months or 1 year) with the job, the manager evaluates their performance. The original test scores are then measured against the criterion (the evaluation ratings), and the test is validated if they're similar.
- ***Concurrent Validity*:** The process for determining concurrent validity is similar to that of determining predictive validity. The difference is that the criterion measurement occurs at the same time the test is given and not at a later time.

Learning and Development and Talent Management

Effective talent management in HR involves both operational and strategic considerations, particularly in areas like succession planning, performance management, and leadership development. These processes ensure day-to-day continuity and optimal employee performance while also strategically cultivating future leaders and aligning talent development with long-term organizational goals.

Learning and development (L&D) and talent management both focus on enhancing employees' skills and competencies to drive organizational success and support career growth. For HR professionals at all stages of their career, an important contribution is made by helping employees manage their career. This includes understanding the fundamentals of career management and managing employee performance.

Career Management

Career management is a term used by HRCI to describe the preparation, implementation, and monitoring of the professional development of employees while still focusing on the goals and needs of an organization. Career management is generally achieved by engaging in career planning and development.

Career planning is a process that helps employees take steps to improve professional skills and create new opportunities. It begins by identifying gaps between where an employee is currently in their career and where they wish to be. A plan, often called a path, can then be developed to help employees move forward toward their career goals.

The career planning process uses an assessment of individual strengths and weaknesses, both in their current role and in the context of a future role. From this data, individual intervention strategies, including training, coaching, and mentoring, can then be put into motion.

Instructional Design

Instructional design is the systematic process of creating educational experiences and materials that facilitate learning and improve performance. It is often used in *skills training*, which provides employees with specific information that is needed to do their jobs. In some cases, skills training is job-specific; for example, to teach accounting staff how to use new accounting software, or to provide a software engineer with training in a new language that will be needed to develop a product. Training in soft skills is often used to assist employees; for example, training on meeting management might be provided to reduce the amount of time spent in meetings and make them more productive.

In the context of instructional design, ADDIE, SAM, Agile, and Bloom's Taxonomy are frameworks used to guide the design, development, and implementation of training and educational programs.

ADDIE (Analyze, Design, Develop, Implement, Evaluate) The ADDIE model progresses through five stages used to create training programs. These five stages are:

1. **Analyze:** Identify the learning needs, objectives, and audience characteristics.
2. **Design:** Plan the learning experiences, content structure, and assessment methods.
3. **Develop:** Create the instructional materials and activities.
4. **Implement:** Deliver the training to the target audience.
5. **Evaluate:** Assess the effectiveness of the training and make necessary revisions.

SAM (Successive Approximation Model) The SAM model is used for instructional design to create effective training programs through iterative development. It emphasizes rapid prototyping, continuous feedback, and multiple iterations to refine and improve instructional materials and learning experiences efficiently. There are generally three phases to SAM:

1. **Preparation Phase:** Gather information, define goals, and develop initial project plans.
2. **Iterative Design Phase:** Create prototypes, review, and refine them through multiple iterations based on feedback.
3. **Iterative Development Phase:** Develop the final product in stages, continually testing and refining it until it meets the desired standards.

Agile Agile in instructional design borrows principles from Agile software development, focusing on flexibility, collaboration, and iterative development. Key features include:

- **Iterative Development:** Create learning solutions in small, incremental cycles or sprints.
- **Collaborative Approach:** Involve stakeholders and learners in the design and development process.
- **Rapid Prototyping:** Develop quick prototypes for immediate feedback and continuous improvement.
- **Adaptive Planning:** Adjust plans based on ongoing feedback and changing requirements.

Bloom's Taxonomy Bloom's Taxonomy is a classification system for categorizing educational goals, objectives, and skills into levels of complexity and specificity. It helps trainers design curriculum and instructional activities that promote higher-order thinking skills. The taxonomy is divided into six hierarchical levels:

1. **Remember:** Recall facts and basic concepts (e.g., define, list, memorize).
2. **Understand:** Explain ideas or concepts (e.g., describe, explain, summarize).
3. **Apply:** Use information in new situations (e.g., demonstrate, solve, use).
4. **Analyze:** Draw connections among ideas (e.g., compare, contrast, examine).

5. **Evaluate:** Justify a decision or course of action (e.g., argue, defend, judge).
6. **Create:** Produce new or original work (e.g., design, construct, formulate).

Each model has its strengths and is chosen based on the specific needs, timelines, and constraints of the instructional design project:

ADDIE: A linear and systematic approach, suitable for projects with clear, well-defined goals and requirements. It provides a comprehensive framework but can be time-consuming and less flexible.

SAM: Focuses on rapid prototyping and iterative design, allowing for more flexibility and quicker adjustments. It is effective for projects needing frequent feedback and revisions.

Agile: Emphasizes adaptability and collaboration, making it ideal for dynamic environments where requirements may evolve. It supports continuous improvement and responsiveness to stakeholder needs.

Bloom's Taxonomy: Bloom's Taxonomy is most effective when the focus is on designing curriculum and assessments that promote higher-order thinking and comprehensive learning outcomes. ADDIE, SAM, and Agile are more focused on the overall process of instructional design, development, and implementation, rather than specifically on categorizing and promoting different levels of cognitive skills.

In addition to these frameworks, *content chunking* is an instructional design technique that breaks down information into smaller, manageable units, or "chunks," to enhance comprehension, retention, and recall for learners.

Coaching Programs

Although formal training can be useful in providing information for managers, one of the best ways to develop them is by assigning a mentor or coach. A coach is typically a specialist who becomes involved, often at the organization's expense, in developing an employee in a particular area: for example, to hone leadership skills or to improve communication skills. Some coaches can offer guidance in many areas.

Too often, employees with strong operational skills but very little leadership skill are promoted into management. Yet with the changing workforce and increased demands on employees, the ability to influence others is rapidly becoming a benchmark of effective management techniques. Identifying strengths and weaknesses, discovering latent talent or aptitudes, personal development, and recognizing elements of the job that are most enjoyable to the individual are outcomes from successful coaching methods. Other more technical outcomes of these programs include the analysis of orientation toward learning, emotional intelligence scores, cognitive processing skills, and measuring levels of motivation.

Non-skill or work-related deficiencies that are unrelated to an employee's skill set can also be addressed through the coaching process. These include issues such as work burnout, career plateaus, lack of personal accountability, and struggles with work/family balance.

As with all training design, a needs assessment should first be conducted to evaluate the specific deficiencies to be addressed. Depending on the need, various approaches to coaching can then be applied in an effort to modify and strengthen a leader's ability. The decision of how to deliver the coaching process—internally, externally, or virtually—must then be made.

Internal Sources Internal sources for coaching can be effective for several reasons. Peer-to-peer coaching is useful when the values or behaviors desired are shared within a workgroup or management tier. For example, some organizations create training initiatives that focus on the achievement of strategic aims such as increasing retention or forecasting growth. Having an internal peer network that can identify with the unique company culture is helpful for managers who are having difficulty achieving specific organizational objectives.

External Sources External coaching sources are appropriate when the need is for a one-on-one experience or the focus of the coaching is highly technical/psychological in nature. The individual seeking the executive coaching may have a need to hone one or two specific skill sets, and the organizational hierarchy doesn't have an internal source or tools to provide meaningful, real-time feedback and analysis.

Virtual Coaching Virtual coaching techniques combine the concepts of self-paced learning with typical coaching outcomes. The mode of delivery varies and can include a combination of email relationships, telephone consulting, videoconferencing, webinars, tests that simulate workplace experiences and measure reactions, discussion boards, and industry-specific forums.

Mentoring Programs

In a business context, a *mentor* is generally an experienced individual who acts as a teacher, guide, counselor, or facilitator and provides personalized feedback and guidance to a more junior colleague. In many cases, a mentor is someone who takes an interest in an employee's career and acts as a sponsor for them, providing a sounding board for issues and decisions. Traditionally, the mentor relationship is based more on an informal personal interest than on a formal program. *Mentoring programs* formalize this concept and ensure that the benefits of mentoring are available to a diverse group of employees who demonstrate leadership potential.

Formal mentors are those approved by an organization to take on protégés after being screened to ensure that only those who are best suited for mentor relationships enter the program. Mentors in formal programs receive training to develop skills in mentoring, and both mentors and mentees receive training to ensure that everyone understands what to expect from the relationship.

A relatively new feature of mentoring is the *reverse mentor*. These are young individuals who help older coworkers understand technology and the culture of the younger generation.

Coaching vs. Mentoring

There are several definitions of coaching and mentoring in the business lexicon. For purposes of the exams, focus on HRCI's definitions as follows:

> **Coaching:** A method of developing specific skills in which a coach gives information and objective feedback to a person or group (guiding, giving information or training)
>
> **Mentoring:** When an experienced person shares knowledge with someone who has less experience (helping a person learn)

Learning Development Plans

A *learning development plan* is a structured framework designed to support employees in their professional growth and skill enhancement. It outlines an individual's learning objectives, identifies relevant training and development opportunities, and establishes a timeline for achieving goals. The plan may include a variety of learning activities such as workshops, seminars, online courses, on-the-job training, and mentorship programs tailored to the employee's career aspirations and organizational needs. By investing in employees' continuous learning and development, organizations can enhance employee engagement, job satisfaction, and overall performance while ensuring they remain competitive and adaptable in a rapidly changing business environment.

A common challenge for human resource teams is the need to engage young professionals just starting out in their careers. With cost of living out of reach for many, and student loan debt at a historic high, early career employees often prioritize career growth and development as key factors in their job satisfaction and engagement. They value opportunities for learning, advancement, and skill acquisition, seeking roles that offer clear pathways for professional growth and advancement.

Career Pathing

A career path is important for every employee, not just those who are high potential or seeking a management role. Helping employees develop their personal and professional skills will lead to better business outcomes, from loyalty (retention), customer satisfaction, and productivity. There is not necessarily only one way to design a career path program for your employer, but all systems should share an outcome that gives employees skills that will transfer on the job—current or future.

High-Potential Employees

Some of the individuals identified as future organization leaders in this process are known as high-potential employees (HiPos) and are provided with extensive training opportunities to prepare them for future roles. Identifying HiPos can be difficult, because future performance can't always be predicted from current performance (as described in *The Peter Principle*, by Dr. Laurence Peter [1968, Harper Business] that explains how organizations tend to promote people until they rise to their level of incompetence and leave them in that position). Many selection procedures can be used to screen candidates for the HiPo track, including assessment centers, behavioral interviews, and observation. See the Holland's RIASEC Model to learn about how career inventories such as the RIASEC (Holland Codes, or the Holland Occupational Themes) can be useful in evaluating individuals for a HiPo development program. Note that early identification can create a disadvantage when diverse factors and assessment tools are not considered and implemented.

Dual-Career Ladders

For some employees, the idea of moving into a supervisory role is not palatable. While loyal and talented, they may prefer to take on new responsibilities that allow them to build or use different skills. For these employees, dual-career ladders are an effective tool. Characterized by advanced training, certification, or licensing, these employees progress in their current role by becoming subject matter experts (SMEs) rather than managers.

Holland's RIASEC Model

The RIASEC inventory developed by John Holland helps individuals identify what types of careers they may prefer based on certain characteristics. The inventory sorts individuals according to their three most preferred "types," and the combination/order of the letters may help to predict satisfaction in certain careers. The groupings are:

Realistic: Also known as "the doers," these individuals prefer jobs that require the use of concrete (versus abstract) skills. They may include careers in the culinary arts or outdoor education.

Investigative: These folks prefer to use their thinking skills at work, gravitating toward jobs where they can work with data or models. These individuals are suited for work such as counseling or engineering.

Artistic: Also known as creators, people who prefer to use their artistic skills are drawn toward industries such as graphic design or teaching.

Social: Not surprisingly, those with a dominant social preference are usually found in careers where they may use their people skills to help others. Careers such as nursing or clergy may be well suited for these individuals.

Enterprising: Enterprising individuals are most noted for both their people skills and power of persuasion. They are often working in fields such as customer service or human resources.

Conventional: Those known for their preference for data and rules are most likely exercising their conventional preferences for career choice. You will find many conventional personalities in jobs such as business training and web developing.

For a look at how the RIASEC Model is used in career development, check out the Department of Labor's job database. Search `http://onetonline.org` for their career codes, and you can see how they apply to specific jobs. Click Advanced Search, and then browse by Interests for a more robust review of the RIASEC Model in action.

Succession Planning Through Leadership Development

The Center for Creative Leadership (CCL) describes the goal of succession planning as having the talent necessary to meet future goals and challenges. Organizations of today have had to respond to pressures from mergers and acquisitions, downsizing, layoffs, corporate restructuring, government mandates, political shifts, corrupt business practices, demographic migrations, an opioid crisis, and medical marijuana—the list seems nearly endless. Though it's impossible to predict the nature of future challenges, HR practitioners know that they will need a pipeline of future leaders to call on when the time comes. This section briefly reviews a few of the more popular and emerging strategies for building a leadership pipeline.

Developmental Multisource Feedback Similar to building a developmental network, HR can help leaders identify areas for development by seeking feedback from multiple sources. Tools such as the 360-degree feedback assessment provide feedback to managers about specific skills or behaviors from subordinates, peers, managers, and even outside sources such as customers or vendors. HR helps leaders navigate the process and provide the feedback necessary to then develop plans for growth.

Developmental Assignments Many developmental assignments can be taken on simultaneously with existing job responsibilities. Asking future leaders to take on a new assignment or project, lead a team, or become a subject matter expert are all ways employees can develop skills for their next role. Job rotation may also work well here, particularly for future leadership teams that are focused on operational learning.

Personal Growth So much of the research in leadership development directly relates to the human condition. Research has consistently shown that the impact a program has on people is directly linked to the quality of the emotional experience—the effect of a leadership experience is stronger when it is bound with an emotion. Some examples include Tony Robbins events, leadership workshops using Patrick Lencioni's work on vulnerability-based trust in teams, and Dale Carnegie's leadership breakthrough plans. Personal growth programs designed to increase self-awareness have many advantages, not the least of which includes emotional intelligence, personality factors, and emotional labor.

Management by Objectives A management by objectives (MBO) intervention aligns individuals with organization goals and measures the successful attainment of objectives as well as the quality and/or quantity of performance. Because it's an effective way of tying results to goals, MBO is often used as a performance appraisal tool. Its application and acceptance results, at least in part, from its philosophy that rewarding people for what they accomplish is important.

The MBO process is built on the concepts of mutual involvement in setting performance goals, ongoing communication during the performance period (usually one year), measurement, and reward for accomplishments at the end of the period. The process identifies and clarifies expectations and provides for a broad assessment of individual performance.

The use of an MBO process to tie individual goals to corporate goals and objectives has value but must take into account the rapid pace of change in the current business environment and use goals that are broad enough to be meaningful for the entire review period or that allow for revision as business objectives change.

Supervisory Training When the organization is successful in advancing employees, very often they end up in positions with supervisory responsibility. Some organizations make the mistake of assuming that a person who excels in a technical area will automatically be able to supervise employees in that area, but that is rarely the case. Providing training for new supervisors gives them the tools they need to succeed at their new responsibilities.

Supervisory training usually involves topics related to interactions with employees, such as performance management, progressive discipline, performance appraisals, workplace safety, interviewing, and training. New supervisors also benefit from training on topics such as legal requirements for employers (such as exemption status, leave policies, equal employment opportunity [EEO], the Americans with Disabilities Act [ADA], the Family and Medical Leave Act [FMLA], and so on) and policies and procedures specific to the organization. Other topics that help supervisors accomplish more and improve effectiveness include the following:

- Effective management skills
- Financial analysis
- Business basics
- Technology management
- Decision-making skills
- Conflict management
- Team building
- Influence and negotiation skills
- Communication skills
- Time management
- Interview skills
- Delegation

- Planning
- Motivation skill

Job Movement Within the Organization

Job movement within an organization can support an employee's career path in various ways. Promotion offers upward advancement, providing opportunities for increased responsibility and recognition. Lateral moves allow employees to gain diverse skills and experiences without vertical progression. Expatriate assignments offer international exposure and cultural immersion, enhancing global competency. Other forms of job movement, such as cross-functional projects or temporary assignments, broaden expertise and networks, contributing to overall career development and adaptability.

Too often, employees moving positions throughout the organization are left unsupported. It is important to remember that a current employee in a new position should be addressed similarly to a new hire, with the orientation and onboarding process. The orientation and onboarding process should provide clear guidance on the expectations, resources, and support systems available to employees during transitions, whether they are experiencing promotions, lateral moves, expatriate assignments, or other career shifts. Orientation sessions can offer insights into the company's culture, values, and career development pathways, ensuring that employees understand how their new roles fit into the broader organizational context. Onboarding programs should facilitate seamless integration into new teams or departments, fostering connections with colleagues and mentors who can provide guidance and support throughout the adjustment period. This may include a 30/60/90 day feedback, and clarity on whether the employee will have the option to move back into their former position should the new role not be a good fit.

Performance Management

Performance management is an ongoing process of providing feedback for employees about their performance to develop them into increasingly productive contributors to the organization, and to align them with the company's mission, vision, values and culture. Although only one element of a robust talent management program, *performance management programs* begin by defining employee jobs and end when an employee leaves the organization. The performance management process provides for an employee's professional development in the context of organizational needs.

Effective performance management must be based on an agreement between the manager or supervisor and the employee about what the job requires. This information comes from the organization's strategic plan, the manager's goals and objectives, and the employee's essential job functions as contained in an accurate job description. With these elements, the parties can develop individual goals and objectives and agree on the standards of performance to be used in measuring results.

Meaningful feedback that can be used to improve performance is specific, describing the behavior so the employee is clear about what is being done correctly or incorrectly. For example, instead of saying "Good job," you can tell an employee, "The way you handled

Bob Kent's complaint yesterday was professional and effective. I was impressed with how quickly you were able to calm him down by remaining calm yourself and solving his problem." Feedback should also focus on behaviors, not personal attributes.

Corrective feedback should be given privately to avoid embarrassing the employee—the point of feedback is to improve behavior, not to alienate the employee. The employee should also be able to respond, explain, or ask for clarification.

On the other hand, positive feedback given more publicly can motivate the recipient and observers to repeat the positive behavior and receive additional recognition.

Performance management isn't a once-a-year proposition. For maximum effectiveness, it must be an ongoing process that enables a manager to intervene in the early stages if an employee is getting off track.

The following sections will take a closer look at the elements, timing, and methods of conducting performance appraisals, training performance evaluators, and how to improve performance and deal with workplace behavior issues.

Performance Appraisal

One important aspect of performance management is the *performance appraisal*, *performance evaluation*, or *performance review* process. These three terms are used interchangeably to describe the process of reviewing how well employees perform their duties during a specified period of time. The appraisal process has the potential to be a powerful tool for building the important relationship between supervisors and their direct reports.

When used well, appraisals provide a structured means for communication, helping to build working relationships. This structure provides for positive performance feedback, recognition of accomplishments during the review period, honest discussion of areas for improvement, and development opportunities for the future.

Another important function of the performance appraisal process is the documentation it provides for employment decisions—positive or negative. For example, appraisals that document a history of achievement and positive contribution provide the basis for promotion decisions or inclusion in a high-potential employee (HiPo) development program. Conversely, appraisals that document a history of mediocre or below-average performance are crucial when making adverse employment decisions.

Three factors in the appraisal process are important to understand. These are the elements included in an appraisal process, the timing of review cycles, and the methods used.

Elements of a Performance Appraisal

Several elements should be included as part of an effective annual review. These include:

Supervisor Assessment The supervisor's assessment begins with a review of the goals and objectives set at the beginning of the review cycle and whether the anticipated results were achieved. The supervisor must then evaluate whether any deficiencies occurred because of inadequate performance by the employee or whether they were the result of circumstances outside the employee's control, such as a change in the organization's direction. The supervisor must then develop a plan to address the discrepancies.

Employee Self-Assessment Because this process is meant to be a two-way conversation, employees should be asked to assess their own performance as part of the appraisal. Giving employees advance notice of the scheduled review meeting allows time for reflection about their past performance as well as goals they may have for the future and areas of professional development that are of interest to them.

Assessment from Others It's important for supervisors to obtain feedback from those with whom the employee has contact each day to find out whether there are areas of concern or outstanding performance about which the supervisor may not be aware. This includes *360-degree feedback*, which HRCI defines as "employee appraisal data gathered from internal and external sources (such as peers, subordinates, supervisors, customers and suppliers); also known as *multi-rater* feedback."

Goal Setting A key component of the review is planning for the future using changes to the strategic plan and the supervisor's goals and objectives to help plan the employee's goals. It's important for employees to participate in the setting of their own goals to facilitate their commitment to achieving them.

Development Goals As part of the review, supervisors can provide development opportunities for employees to address any areas of deficiency or to prepare them for the next level.

Timing Performance Appraisals

Performance appraisals can be conducted either on employee anniversary dates or during an organizationwide focal review period. In organizations that time reviews to coincide with employee anniversary dates, managers conduct individual reviews throughout the year. The advantage of this process is that there are fewer reviews to conduct at one time; disadvantages occur when awarding salary increases and when using comparative appraisal methods. Managers who don't plan adequately for salary increases or other compensation awards may find that rewards for high performers don't exceed—or, worse, are lower than—what average performers received earlier in the year. It's also difficult to use comparative appraisal methods when appraisals occur on individual employee anniversary dates because the manager will need to consider the performance of employees not up for review at the same time.

During a *focal review period*, all employees in the organization are reviewed at the same time. This is more difficult for managers, as well as for HR, because of the sheer volume of reviews that must be completed. On the other hand, the focal process provides managers with an opportunity to allocate salary increases, equity grants, bonuses, and other rewards in a way that appropriately reflects individual performance levels. Comparative appraisal methods are more easily conducted during a focal review as well.

Performance Appraisal Methods

Employee performance appraisal may be based on quantitative data, such as whether specific goals were accomplished, or on more qualitative factors. There is currently much discussion in the HR field about the effectiveness of traditional performance appraisal processes. Some HR texts suggest that appraisal systems be abolished and replaced with more effective methods of providing feedback and developing employees.

A number of methods have been developed for use in evaluating employee performance. All of them can be placed in one of these four basic categories:

Comparison Methods Comparison appraisal methods compare the performance of individuals or employees to one another. The most common methods of comparison are ranking, paired comparison, and forced ranking:

- ***Ranking*:** Employees are listed in order from the highest to the lowest performer. This method works well for small groups of employees but becomes increasingly difficult as the size of the group increases.
- ***Paired Comparison*:** All employees in the group are compared to one employee at a time. For example, if there are three employees in the workgroup—Susan, Jack, and Rachel—then Susan's performance is compared to Jack's and Rachel's, Jack's performance is compared to Susan's and Rachel's, and finally, Rachel's performance is compared to Susan's and Jack's.
- ***Forced Ranking*:** Also known as *forced distribution* or *forced choice*, forced ranking requires managers to rank employees according to the bell curve, rating a small group of employees at the high end, a small group at the low end, and the bulk of the employees in the average range. This appraisal tool can be used as part of any of the appraisal methods to reduce the effects of the leniency or harshness biases.

Rating Methods Common rating methods for performance appraisal include the use of rating scales and checklists:

- ***Rating Scales*:** Rating scales may be numeric, with scales ranging from 3 to 10 ratings to differentiate levels of performance, or may use phrases such as "exceeds expectations," "meets expectations," or "does not meet expectations." Rating scales attempt to quantify what is a very subjective process, but because of the different ways in which the descriptors are interpreted by raters, these scales aren't as objective as they may appear at first glance.
- ***Checklists*:** A performance checklist is a list of statements, phrases, or words that describe levels of performance, such as "always finishes work on time." The reviewer checks off those that best describe the employee. The various descriptions may be weighted and used to calculate a rating score.

Narrative Methods Narrative methods of appraisal require managers to describe the employee's performance. These include critical incident, essay, and field reviews:

- ***Critical Incident*:** The *critical incident review* process requires that during the review period supervisors make notes of successful and unsuccessful performance issues for each employee. At the time of the review, the supervisor is able to review these critical incidents and present them to employees in a written narrative.
- ***Essay*:** An *essay review* requires the reviewer to write a short description of each employee's performance during the year. This format provides maximum flexibility for managers to cover areas they see as most important to improving employee performance.
- ***Field Review*:** A *field review appraisal* may be conducted by someone other than the supervisor. This can be an HR practitioner or someone from outside the organization.

Behavioral Methods The best-known behavioral review method is the *behaviorally anchored rating scale (BARS)*. This is defined by HRCI as "a type of performance rating scale designed to combine both qualitative and quantitative data to the employee appraisal process. The BARS compares an individual's performance against specific examples of behavior that are attached to numerical ratings." The BARS method uses the job description to create dimensions that represent the most important requirements of the job. For each dimension, anchor statements are created to represent varying levels of performance behaviors that describe rating numbers on a scale. For example, a job dimension for a receptionist might be greeting customers. Table 2.3 shows the anchors that could be used to measure the behaviors associated with this job dimension.

TABLE 2.3 Sample BARS anchor statements

Rating	Anchor statement
5	Greets customers warmly and makes them feel welcome
4	Pleasant to customers and answers their questions
3	Courteous to customers
2	Finishes other work before greeting customers
1	Rude to customers when they approach the desk

Regardless of the review method used in an organization, raters should be aware of the various biases that can impact the fairness of a review. When bias is a concern, organizations can use a process known as inter-rater reliability, which uses multiple raters to reduce the possibility of rating errors due to bias. The scores of all raters are averaged, with the goal of providing a review that is as free from bias as possible.

Training Performance Evaluators

It's unfortunate that the performance appraisal process is disliked by so many supervisors and employees, because when well used it provides a structure for building positive, productive working relationships. One of the concerns many employees have about the appraisal process is their perception of its fairness, or lack of fairness. Some employees may think their boss is much tougher than other managers, and some managers have developed reputations for being "easy graders." Those perceptions may never go away entirely, but providing training for those who conduct appraisals will at least ensure that everyone is beginning from the same place. Evaluators should be made aware of the purpose of performance evaluations (it's not just for wage increases), the methods of providing feedback (formal and informal), the behaviors being rated (and how to tell the difference between employees), and the common rater errors such as leniency and bias that can affect the appraisal.

The training should provide information for activities before, during, and after the actual appraisal meeting.

Before the Meeting

Preparation prior to meeting with employees helps alleviate some of the stress and discomfort that many evaluators feel, particularly when they're new to providing feedback. The goal of the process is to make sure employees know they're valued team members and to motivate them to continue positive performance and improve any areas in which they may be deficient.

Schedule the meeting for a mutually convenient time and allow sufficient time for an open conversation. Give the employee advance notice, which is ideally one week minimum. Don't schedule the meeting for a time when other pressures, such as deadlines or other commitments, will be a distraction.

Provide the employee with a self-appraisal form or questionnaire to complete prior to finalizing the evaluation to ensure that the employee's input is considered; at least one day before the meeting, provide the employee with a copy of the completed appraisal. If reviewing multiple employees in the same job category, use the same appraisal criteria for all of them.

Prepare for the meeting by reviewing the job description, performance standards, goals set during previous appraisals, and the critical-incident log or other notes about specific performance issues (positive and negative) that occurred during the review period.

Complete the review form using specific, job-related comments to describe positive and negative performance issues. This helps the employee see what to continue doing that is successful and how to improve other areas as needed.

Make sure the appraisal is balanced. Keep in mind that few employees are all good or all bad; in most cases, even those with serious performance deficiencies are usually doing some things right, and outstanding performers can improve in some area.

Whenever possible, use quantitative measurements, such as on-time project completions, missed deadlines, production data, and so on. Describe how the behaviors impacted the organization.

If improvements are needed in some areas, provide specific information on what is expected from the employee and how feedback will be given. Don't sugarcoat problems—appraisals that neglect to document performance problems make future adverse employment actions difficult and expose the organization to litigation.

Arrange a private area to conduct the meeting; even if the evaluator has an office, the use of a conference room may be advisable to eliminate interruptions and create a neutral atmosphere conducive to open dialogue.

During the Meeting

Adequate preparation is essential and demonstrates that the supervisor values the employee. It's equally important for evaluators to make full use of that preparation during the meeting. This is an opportunity to communicate about issues that are important to both participants such as feedback, expectations, goals, and, in some cases, rewards.

Most employees enter an appraisal meeting wanting to know how they're doing, what the supervisor expects from them, and what their reward for previous performance will be. Some will approach the meeting as though it were a guillotine, whereas others see it as an opportunity to learn the positive and negative information provided to continue developing their careers.

The evaluator's goal during the meeting is to acknowledge the employee's value to the organization and provide them with constructive feedback to enhance their productivity. Training for evaluators should include the following information:

Set a tone of mutual respect. It's up to evaluators to ease anxiety by creating an open atmosphere and giving employees their full attention.

Discuss the appraisal forms that were exchanged prior to the meeting. If there are areas of disagreement, seek to understand the employee's perspective; be willing to revise the appraisal if warranted due to any oversights or misunderstanding of the facts. Don't, however, change an appraisal to avoid confrontation about accurate facts.

Discuss training options and development needs. Find out what career direction the employee wants to take and provide realistic guidance about how that may be achieved.

Set goals for the next review period. Be sure to include the employee in developing the goals instead of merely assigning them. Keep in mind that the goal of the appraisal is to enhance performance; giving employees a voice in setting their goals helps them to feel invested in the outcome.

Communicate expectations clearly. If attendance or tardiness is an issue, say so flat out; don't leave anything to interpretation.

Give the employee an opportunity to ask questions about the appraisal, expectations, or goals. When they leave the meeting, they should be clear about any next steps.

Once the appraisal part of the meeting is completed, in many organizations the discussion turns to rewards, whether that is a salary increase, a bonus, a promotion, or another reward.

Have the employee sign any necessary paperwork required for the appraisal or reward.

After the Meeting

Provide information to supervisors about how to complete the appraisal process. In most cases, this will include submitting paperwork to HR for retention and processing salary changes. In addition, encourage supervisors to make continuous feedback part of their daily interaction with employees. This reduces the level of stress involved in annual appraisals because the feedback becomes a regular part of the daily routine instead of an annual review of what should have been done differently during the year. An appraisal with no surprises is easier on supervisors and their employees.

Nonsupervisory Evaluators

Evaluators are generally supervisors or managers, but in the case of 360-degree appraisal systems, coworkers may be asked to provide feedback as well. These evaluators should receive training on the organization's appraisal process and the importance of keeping the feedback related to job activities. They should also be made aware of the biases that can affect the appraisal process.

Total Rewards

Compensation practices in HR require a careful balance between operational efficiency and strategic alignment, which is evident in the interconnected processes of salary surveys, benchmarking, job evaluation, and job pricing.

Compensation strategies are approaches and policies implemented by organizations to determine and manage employee compensation, which includes wages, salaries, bonuses, benefits, and other financial and nonfinancial rewards. These strategies aim to attract, motivate, and retain employees while aligning compensation with organizational goals, budget, and market standards. Key components of compensation strategies include:

- **Pay for Performance:** Linking compensation to individual, team, or company performance to encourage productivity and achievement of goals
- **Competency-Based Pay:** Rewarding employees based on their skills, knowledge, and competencies rather than their job title or tenure
- **Market-Based Pay:** Setting compensation levels based on market surveys and benchmarking against similar positions in other organizations
- **Internal Equity:** Ensuring fair and consistent compensation within the organization, taking into account job responsibilities, experience, and performance

Pay History Bans

Several states, including Alabama, Georgia, Massachusetts, California, Colorado, Illinois, Maine, and Oregon (22 states total as of 2024), have addressed pay inequity by passing laws banning employers from asking applicants about their salary history. This means that HR will need to base compensation offers on the value of the jobs in the marketplace, not on what an applicant was making at their previous job. This makes an even stronger case for a systematic approach to creating wage bands using market data and the need for HR practitioners to understand the unique laws of the states in which they pay employees.

Operationally, employee wages and benefits make up a large portion of an employer's cost of doing business. For this reason, HR professionals must work closely with line managers and finance professionals to build the total rewards budget for the organization. Compensation and benefit budgets are projected during the annual budget process and must consider increases to base salaries as well as adjustments to the salary structure to keep salary ranges competitive with current labor market trends. Budgets are also projected for incentive pay programs and planned promotions.

Job Evaluation

Job evaluation is the process used traditionally to determine the value of jobs relative to each other in the organization. It's an inexact science that attempts to remove subjectivity from the process as much as possible by replacing opinions and preconceived ideas with more objective criteria. Job evaluations are normally conducted when a job is developed, when the job duties change, or as part of a routine job-evaluation process. HR professionals partner with line management when conducting job evaluations; defined job-evaluation methods allow for a repeatable process for this key component of the compensation system.

Job-evaluation methods identify and define the compensable factors of each job that are most relevant for the organization. *Compensable factors* are characteristics that define and distinguish jobs from one another. For instance, a junior-level engineer's compensable factors might include the following:

- Bachelor's degree in electrical engineering
- Two years of industry-related experience
- Two years of experience testing products for quality and reliability

The two methods discussed in this chapter for job evaluation include the ranking method and the classification method. Let's examine each of these in greater detail.

Ranking Method

The *ranking method* requires evaluators to compare the value of jobs to one another. Because this is a subjective method for evaluating jobs, evaluators can be influenced by any preconceptions they may have about different positions or job duties, and this impacts the way in which jobs are ranked. Although ranking is a simple and cost-effective method for use in small organizations, it can become a very complicated process in a complex organization with many positions to evaluate. In this method, it's also difficult to compare unrelated jobs.

Classification Method

The *classification method* involves identifying key *benchmark positions*. Benchmark positions are jobs common to organizations regardless of size or industry, such as accountants or administrative assistants. Once a job is matched to a benchmark position, it may be classified according to value on a vertical scale. Benchmark positions are then associated with a grade on a hierarchical salary structure. Positions with similar characteristics are slotted into the same grade or level, which are identified by a similar level of knowledge, skills, and abilities.

To use the classification method, companies must determine *internal equity*, or the value of jobs to each other relative to their value to the organization.

Job Pricing

Job pricing occurs when a new job is created or an existing job has undergone changes and is a common practice when administering compensation. Many organizations, especially those going through high-growth periods, use job pricing to ensure pay is competitive. A four-step process is used to determine the appropriate pay level for a position:

1. Review the job description, and understand the level and scope of the job and its required responsibilities and skills.
2. Select a salary survey. When selecting a salary survey, it's important to consider the type and number of survey participants. For example, if you're pricing a job in Austin, Texas, it may not be appropriate to use data from a salary survey if most of the participants are located in Silicon Valley. Most compensation managers like to see several competitors or other premier employers as part of the survey so that the data is perceived as valid.
3. Review compensation components, such as base pay, variable pay, equity pay, and so on. At this time it's also important to review a number of matches for a certain position. The more matches, the better, because the data will be more reliable and less likely to be skewed by outliers (jobs that are paid significantly above or below the average).
4. Recommend a salary range. The recommendation should be in alignment with your organization's compensation philosophy of leading, matching, or lagging the market. In addition to a salary range, it may be appropriate to recommend incentive pay or special pay programs.

It's important for HR professionals to review job-pricing results with management to validate that the survey positions and data match the job. Once a job is priced, it's appropriate to slot the job into the appropriate pay range and grade.

Terms to be Familiar With

Job benchmarking is the process of comparing internal jobs with similar jobs in the relevant labor market. This creates an anchor point from which to determine whether to lead, lag, or match the market in pay rates.

Job ranking compares jobs to each other based on their importance to the organization.

Job classification is an arrangement of different types of employment or grades within an organization according to skills, experience, or training.

Job-content-based job evaluation is a method used to estimate how much a person should be paid based on what they do.

Additionally, pricing jobs based on survey data requires that the source of the data is highly credible. HR should be sure to consider how the survey administrators match the jobs that will be used for comparisons. For example:

- Is it only by job titles, or is a more robust method used to ensure an accurate comparison of job responsibilities and tasks?
- Do the survey administrators offer descriptions of each job used in the comparisons?
- Are HR professionals the ones validating job descriptions, or are line managers involved as well?
- Does the survey administrator publish the names of the employers who participate in the survey?

These important considerations will help HR draw in the relevant data to craft pay structures that result in competitive job pricing. This in turn will improve hiring and retention.

There are some legal concerns in sharing compensation information. *Wage setting* or *price fixing* is a violation of antitrust laws that can get employers into trouble. For example, in 2017, Animation workers reached a $100 million settlement with Disney and affiliates for wage setting (*Nitsch v. DreamWorks Animation SKG Inc.*, 14-cv-04062). The charges addressed competitors in the industry agreeing to not poach each other's talent by cold calling or counter-offering higher wages if an employee gave notice. In a similar case dealing with high-tech employers in the Silicon Valley, the complaint noted that these types of agreements "interfered with the proper functioning of the price-setting mechanism that otherwise would have prevailed in competition for employees" (The United States Department of Justice, 2010 `https://casetext.com/case/nitsch-v-dreamworks-animation-skg-inc-11`). This is another reason to participate in formal surveys as opposed to attempting to gather the data through more informal (and less expensive) methods.

Benchmarking

Before embarking on the salary survey journey, HR must have a thorough understanding of the tasks, duties, and responsibilities of each job being priced. Compensation *benchmarking* is the process of validating existing job descriptions in order to identify the external market rate for each position. It is not enough to search based on job titles; benchmarking requires the data obtained through the job analysis process defined in Chapter 4, "PHR/PHRi Exam: Workforce Planning and Talent Acquisition."

It is considered a best practice to use three-to-five sources to ensure you have accurate descriptions from which to conduct market research. Reliable sources for job and salary data includes O*NET OnLine, the job database maintained by the DOL. The job descriptions on O*NET are linked to Career One Stop, which will sort salary data by state. This and other local and regional resources are also valid sources to access pay trends by geographic location.

Salary Surveys

Salary surveys allow organizations to gather compensation and benefits data that reflects current trends in the labor market. Surveys are often provided by professional services' vendors or compensation consulting firms. The vendor provides a confidential data-collection process by administering the survey and compiling data into a usable, aggregated format. Salary surveys identify trends in labor costs and are integral in ensuring that compensation and benefits programs continue to attract, retain, and motivate employees. Here are different types of salary surveys for an organization to consider:

Employee Surveys Polling the internal workforce is one method companies can use to gauge employee satisfaction with their pay structures, measure perceptions of pay equity, and identify the needs of the current workforce as it relates to compensation and benefit offerings.

Government Surveys A great source for compensation data is the Bureau of Labor Statistics (BLS), an independent national statistical agency whose mission is to collect, analyze, and distribute statistical data. The BLS is a statistical resource to the Department of Labor (DOL) as well as a source for salary survey data.

Industry Surveys For certain jobs, it may be important to consider industry-specific salary surveys for greater validity. For example, the high-tech and hospitality industries are two that provide specific surveys for companies in their sectors.

Commissioned Surveys Many organizations operate in industries with very specific skill requirements that may be difficult to match in readily available surveys, or they may want to find out how their compensation practices stack up against several specific competitors. This information can sometimes be collected by commissioning a third party to conduct a survey, aggregate the data, and supply the results to the participating organizations. Commissioning a survey can be very costly and time-consuming but may provide the best data for building a competitive salary structure.

An alternative way to collect some of this data is to use an informal process where HR professionals exchange information on pay practices with their counterparts in other organizations. Another informal option is to work with a local/regional HR or compensation association and have the group facilitate the collection of pay practice data from participating members.

When conducting or participating in a salary survey, one of the first decisions to be made is which jobs will be priced in the survey. The most accurate data would be obtained by including all the organization's jobs, but this may not be practical. Generally, including 65–70 percent of organization jobs in a survey provides a solid base for use in creating a salary structure.

It's important for HR professionals and employees to keep salary survey data confidential in order to comply with legislative mandates. Over the years, there have been a number of lawsuits against organizations and individuals who are not properly managing their pay scales.

Overtime Compensation Rules

The Biden-Harris administration finalized a rule that increases the salary thresholds for overtime eligibility:

- Effective July 1, 2024, the salary threshold will rise to $43,888 per year, up from $35,568.
- On January 1, 2025, the threshold will further increase to $58,656 per year.
- The highly compensated employee (HCE) threshold will also rise to $151,164 by January 1, 2025.

The rule will update these thresholds every three years to keep up with changes in earnings data.

Employee Engagement

Employee engagement is another exam content area that was updated in 2024. Interestingly, it went from an SPHR content area (Employee Relations and Engagement in 2018) to a stand-alone functional area for the PHR/i in 2024. This suggests that employee engagement is not just a corporate strategy, but rather measurable tactical activities that have a significant impact on organizational health.

Human relations refer to the way people interact with each other in a workplace, focusing on building positive relationships between employees and management. Good human relations can boost employee engagement, making workers feel more valued and motivated to do their best. There are several areas of knowledge overlap in the area of human relations and employee engagement between generalist and senior HR roles. These are covered next.

Theories of Motivation

Engaged employees are motivated workers. These individuals show up with enthusiasm, take initiative, and contribute positively to the workplace. There are two functional types of motivation:

Intrinsic motivation is driven by internal rewards, where individuals engage in activities for their inherent satisfaction, enjoyment, or personal fulfillment. Examples include taking on a challenging project for the satisfaction of mastering new skills or contributing to a team effort because of the enjoyment of collaboration.

Extrinsic motivation is driven by external rewards or pressures, where individuals perform tasks to earn rewards or avoid negative consequences. Examples include working for a paycheck, receiving bonuses, or avoiding disciplinary action.

Several main theories of motivation in the workplace have been developed to understand what drives employees to perform and stay engaged. These theories are:

Maslow's Hierarchy of Needs This theory proposes that individuals are motivated by a hierarchy of needs starting from basic physiological needs, progressing through safety, social belonging, esteem, and culminating in self-actualization. In the workplace, this means employees need to have their basic needs met before they can be motivated by higher-level needs like recognition and personal growth.

Herzberg's Two-Factor Theory Also known as the Motivation-Hygiene Theory, it suggests that job satisfaction and dissatisfaction are influenced by two independent sets of factors. Hygiene factors (such as salary, company policies, and working conditions) can prevent dissatisfaction but do not motivate, whereas motivators (such as achievement, recognition, and responsibility) drive job satisfaction and performance.

Vroom's Expectancy Theory This theory states that an individual's motivation is based on the expected outcome of their actions. It suggests that employees are motivated when they believe their effort will lead to effective performance and, subsequently, to desirable rewards. It emphasizes the importance of clear goals, attainable performance standards, and meaningful rewards.

McClelland's Theory of Needs This theory focuses on three specific needs that drive motivation: the need for achievement, the need for affiliation, and the need for power. Employees are motivated by the need that is most important to them. For example, those with a high need for achievement seek challenging tasks, whereas those with a high need for affiliation seek cooperative and supportive work environments.

Self-Determination Theory (SDT) SDT posits that people are motivated by intrinsic factors when their basic psychological needs for autonomy, competence, and relatedness are met. In the workplace, this theory suggests that providing employees with a sense of choice, opportunities to develop their skills, and a sense of belonging can drive higher motivation and engagement.

Equity Theory This theory argues that employees are motivated by fairness and will compare their inputs and outcomes with those of others. If they perceive an imbalance, they may be motivated to adjust their efforts or seek changes to restore equity. Fair treatment and transparent communication are crucial for maintaining motivation under this theory.

Human relations theories, such as those proposed by Maslow, Herzberg and others, emphasize the importance of social interactions and employee needs in the workplace. These theories suggest that when employers focus on building strong, supportive relationships and addressing employees' basic and psychological needs, workers are more likely to feel engaged and committed to their jobs. This positive environment fosters better communication, teamwork, and a sense of belonging, all of which contribute to higher levels of employee engagement and overall job satisfaction.

High-Involvement Organizations

In *high-involvement organizations (HIOs)*, employees are involved in designing their own work processes, are empowered to take the actions necessary to complete their work, and are accountable for the results. HIOs are characterized by broadly defined jobs in flat hierarchies in which continuous feedback is provided and information flows between and among self-directed work teams.

Edward E. Lawler, III, founder of the Center for Organizational Effectiveness at the University of Southern California and author of numerous books on organizational effectiveness, identified four elements needed to create an HIO:

Power Traditional organization structures are built on a "command and control" model in which decisions are made at the top with little or no input from lower levels in the hierarchy. HIOs grant decision-making power down to the employees assigned to carry out the decision and hold them accountable for the results.

Information "Information is power," and in traditional organizations that often means individuals hold on to information that could be used to improve results instead of sharing it with the individuals who could use it to make improvements. In an HIO, a variety of information (production statistics, sales, expenses, profits, customer feedback, and so on) is disseminated so that everyone can use it to direct their efforts toward improving results.

Knowledge Increasing the knowledge, skills, and abilities (KSAs) available in the organization enhances the ability of all employees to contribute to bottom-line success. Providing training and development opportunities increases the organization's capability for making decisions and taking actions that improve operating effectiveness.

Rewards Tying pay to performance compensates employees according to the level of effort they expend to accomplish their goals and objectives and contribute to organizational success. When employees know that their contributions will be recognized, they're encouraged to go "above and beyond" normal job requirements. These rewards can be based on individual or team contributions.

The return on the investment for HIOs is significant. They include higher levels of reported customer satisfaction, reduced turnover, and reduced employee complaints.

Communication Skills and Strategies

Communication skills are critical for HR professionals, from specialists to generalists, individual contributors and leaders alike. Effective communication skills enable HR professionals to clearly convey policies, mediate conflicts, provide constructive feedback, and build strong relationships within the organization. Strategies such as active listening, empathetic engagement, and clear, concise messaging are essential.

An HR professional needs to balance clarity with empathy, assertiveness with approachability, and consistency with flexibility. Clarity ensures messages are understood, while empathy fosters trust and understanding. Assertiveness helps in addressing issues effectively, whereas approachability encourages open communication. Consistency maintains fairness, and flexibility allows adaptation to individual situations and needs. Balancing these elements is crucial for effective and compassionate HR communication. There are several strategies to build effective communication skills:

- **Active Listening:** Practice active listening to fully understand and respond to employees' needs and concerns, showing empathy and respect.
- **Regular Training:** Provide ongoing communication skills training for HR staff and employees, covering topics such as conflict resolution, feedback techniques, and effective presentation skills.
- **Clear Messaging:** Develop and use clear, concise messaging in all communications to avoid misunderstandings and ensure important information is conveyed effectively.
- **Feedback Culture:** Encourage a culture of regular, constructive feedback to help team members improve their communication skills and address any issues promptly.
- **Open Door Policy:** Implement an open-door policy to foster open, transparent communication, making employees feel comfortable sharing their thoughts and concerns.
- **Technology Utilization:** Leverage communication tools and platforms to streamline information sharing and collaboration within the team and organization.
- **Empathy and Emotional Intelligence:** Cultivate empathy and emotional intelligence to better understand and connect with employees, improving interpersonal communication and relationships.

Summary

Foundational knowledge of the HR topics covered in this chapter is important not only for exam day, but for excelling in the day-to-day running of an HR department. For HR exams, understanding these topics provides a comprehensive framework to answer questions accurately and demonstrate a holistic grasp of HR functions.

Consider Bloom's Taxonomy as a lens through which to understand the importance of this content. Understanding these core concepts allows you to progress through its levels—from basic knowledge and comprehension to more advanced application, analysis, synthesis, and evaluation. Initially, you can recall and explain the fundamental principles of business management, risk management, workforce planning, learning and development, Total Rewards, and employee engagement. As you advance, you can apply this knowledge to real-world HR scenarios, analyze complex situations to identify patterns and underlying issues, and synthesize information to develop innovative HR strategies. Ultimately, you can evaluate the effectiveness of these strategies, make data-driven decisions, and provide expert recommendations to improve organizational performance.

Business management, risk management, workforce planning and talent acquisition, learning and development, Total Rewards, and employee engagement are interconnected areas that drive the work of human resource teams. Business management provides strategic direction and oversight, seeking to align HR activities with business goals. Risk management identifies and mitigates potential threats, safeguarding organizational stability. Workforce planning and talent acquisition focus on identifying and attracting the right talent to meet current and future needs. Learning and development ensure employees have the skills needed for their roles, current and future. Total Rewards and employee engagement strategies aim to motivate and retain employees through compensation, benefits, and a positive work environment. HR teams must possess skills in strategic planning, analytical thinking, communication, and empathy to effectively integrate these areas.

Exam Essentials

Master key concepts in business management, leadership, and strategy. HR teams seek to align strategy with operations to achieve business results. This includes designing programs that support the company mission, vision, and values. They are responsible for evaluating and applying these principles to enhance organizational effectiveness and ethical decision making.

Assess and effectively manage risk. Effective risk management involves identifying potential risks, assessing their impact, and implementing strategies to mitigate them. This process requires continuous monitoring and updating to address new and evolving threats. A proactive approach protects human, physical, and financial assets.

Comply with laws and best practices to manage sexual harassment and conduct workplace investigations. Understanding and adhering to legal requirements and best practices for managing sexual harassment is an important element of human resource management. Conducting thorough and impartial workplace investigations ensures that issues are addressed fairly and promptly. This helps in upholding organizational integrity and reducing liability risks.

Understand business metrics and interpret workforce analysis data. Proficiency in business metrics and workforce analysis involves understanding key performance indicators (KPIs) and data analytics. This skill helps in making informed decisions regarding workforce planning, productivity, and overall business performance. Interpreting this data accurately can lead to improved organizational strategies and outcomes.

Support employee performance through learning and development initiatives. Learning and development initiatives are essential for enhancing employee skills and performance. Effective support includes identifying training needs, providing relevant resources, and evaluating the impact of development efforts.

Understand how to properly evaluate and price jobs. Proper job evaluation and pricing involve assessing the relative value of positions within an organization and determining fair compensation. This process ensures internal equity and market competitiveness. Accurate job evaluation helps in attracting and retaining talent while maintaining budgetary control.

Advise employers on how to apply motivation and human relations theories to engage workers. Advising on motivation and human relations theories involves using psychological principles to enhance employee engagement and satisfaction. Understanding theories such as Maslow's hierarchy of needs or Herzberg's two-factor theory can help in creating a motivating work environment.

Review Questions

You can find the answers in Appendix A.

1. Which of the following best describes the main differences between a company's mission, vision, and values?
   - A. The mission defines long-term goals, the vision outlines daily operations, and values describe the company's products.
   - B. The mission describes what the company does today, the vision outlines what it aims to achieve in the future, and values represent the principles guiding its actions.
   - C. The mission explains financial strategies, the vision details market expansion, and values focus on employee benefits.
   - D. The mission outlines marketing strategies, the vision defines competition, and values address customer satisfaction.
2. Which of the following best describes what a 13% unemployment rate in the United States means?
   - A. 13% of the total population is not working.
   - B. 13% of the labor force is actively seeking employment but unable to find work.
   - C. 13% of the employed population is working part-time jobs.
   - D. 13% of companies are experiencing labor shortages.
3. Which of the following are example of quantitative analysis? (Choose all that apply.)
   - A. Focus group
   - B. Surveys
   - C. Interviews
   - D. Statistical review
4. The company you work for is using a new sales aptitude test to predict current sales performance, validated by correlating it with existing performance metrics. This is the best example of which of the following types of validity?
   - A. Criterion
   - B. Construct
   - C. Predictive
   - D. Concurrent
5. Which of the following best illustrates an example of workplace reengineering?
   - A. Implementing a new employee recognition program to boost morale
   - B. Restructuring a company's workflow by eliminating unnecessary steps and automating repetitive tasks to improve efficiency
   - C. Organizing team-building activities to enhance collaboration among employees
   - D. Offering flexible work hours to improve work-life balance for employees

6. Which of the following statements are true regarding organizational design and development? (Choose all that apply.)
   - **A.** Organizational design focuses on aligning the structure of an organization with its business strategy.
   - **B.** Development of an organization primarily involves short-term planning and immediate problem solving.
   - **C.** Effective organizational development can lead to improved employee engagement and overall performance.
   - **D.** Organizational development is concerned with creating hierarchies and reporting structures.
7. Which theory of motivation suggests that employees are motivated when they believe their effort will lead to effective performance and subsequently to desirable rewards?
   - **A.** Maslow's hierarchy of needs
   - **B.** Herzberg's two-factor theory
   - **C.** Vroom's expectancy theory
   - **D.** Equity theory
8. According to Herzberg's two-factor theory, which of the following is considered a motivator rather than a hygiene factor?
   - **A.** Salary
   - **B.** Company policies
   - **C.** Working conditions
   - **D.** Recognition
9. Which of the following instructional design models emphasizes iterative development? (Choose all that apply.)
   - **A.** ADDIE
   - **B.** SAM
   - **C.** Agile
   - **D.** Bloom's Taxonomy
10. The olive oil producer that you work for has 43 warehouse positions to fill for the harvesting season. Out of the 105 applications received, 45 were women and 60 were men. After the selection process was completed, offers were made to 16 women and 27 men. Using the 4/5ths rule, what is the selection ratio for the female candidates, and did adverse impact occur?
    - **A.** 30 percent, yes
    - **B.** 30 percent, no
    - **C.** 35 percent, yes
    - **D.** 35 percent, no

11. Calculate the training cost per employee using the following data: $2,000 for the training design and facilitator; $2,500 for the facility; 20 full-time employees (40 hours per week) and 10 part-time employees (20 hours per week).
    - **A.** $150
    - **B.** $180
    - **C.** $200
    - **D.** $300

12. What is the primary purpose of the job evaluation process?
    - **A.** To create job descriptions
    - **B.** To identify the physical and mental health requirements
    - **C.** To accurately place jobs in a pay band
    - **D.** To compare jobs to external market conditions

13. Which of the following organizational scientists was responsible for the fishbone, also called cause-and-effect, diagram?
    - **A.** Juran
    - **B.** Ishikawa
    - **C.** Deming
    - **D.** Taylor

14. Which of the following total quality management tools would be best suited to complete production time studies?
    - **A.** Check sheet
    - **B.** Cause-and-effect diagram
    - **C.** Stratification chart
    - **D.** Process-control chart

15. What is the primary distinction between job enrichment and job enlargement?
    - **A.** Job enrichment involves adding more tasks of a similar nature, whereas job enlargement includes increasing the complexity of tasks.
    - **B.** Job enrichment focuses on increasing the depth of a job by adding more responsibilities and opportunities for growth, whereas job enlargement focuses on increasing the breadth of a job by adding more tasks at the same level.
    - **C.** Job enrichment is about offering higher pay for additional responsibilities, whereas job enlargement is about providing more training for existing tasks.
    - **D.** Job enrichment aims to improve job satisfaction through job rotation, whereas job enlargement aims to increase productivity through job sharing.

16. In your role as the HR manager, you can make decisions independent of the executive team in order to maintain the integrity of the position. This is the best example of which feature of the job characteristics model?

A. Feedback

B. Autonomy

C. Task significance

D. Ethics

17. Which of the following is the best definition of corporate social responsibility?

A. The practice of maximizing profits for shareholders through ethical business practices

B. The obligation of a corporation to prioritize the interests of its employees above all other stakeholders

C. The responsibility of a corporation to operate in a manner that benefits society and the environment, while balancing the interests of various stakeholders

D. The requirement for corporations to adhere strictly to legal regulations and industry standards

18. What is the key distinction between quid pro quo harassment and hostile workplace harassment?

A. Quid pro quo harassment involves threats, whereas hostile workplace harassment involves physical violence.

B. Quid pro quo harassment is based on a power differential, whereas hostile workplace harassment involves creating an intimidating or offensive environment.

C. Quid pro quo harassment is always pèrpetrated by a coworker, whereas hostile workplace harassment is always perpetrated by a supervisor.

D. Quid pro quo harassment is defensible in certain circumstances, whereas hostile workplace harassment is always illegal.

19. The company you work for has recently installed machine guards to a piece of equipment on the production line. This is the best example of which of the following risk management techniques?

A. Avoid

B. Mitigate

C. Transfer

D. Accept

20. Who should be consulted to build a workplace business continuity plan? (Choose all that apply.)

A. The CEO

B. The IT department

C. Employees

D. Local first responders

Chapter 3

PHR | PHRi Exam: Business Management

PHR AND PHRi RESPONSIBILITIES:

USING INFORMATION ABOUT THE ORGANIZATION AND BUSINESS ENVIRONMENT TO REINFORCE EXPECTATIONS, INFLUENCE DECISION MAKING, AND AVOID RISK.

- ✓ **1.1 Interpret and apply information related to general business environment and industry best practices**
- ✓ **1.2 Understand the role of cross-functional stakeholders in the organization and establish relationships for effective decision making (for example: org charts, span of control, shared services, centers of excellence)**
- ✓ **1.3 Identify risks and recommend best practices (for example: compliance audit, mitigation, internal/external threats, safety, conflict of interest, employee relations, change management [automation, digitalization, gap analysis])**
- ✓ **1.4 Understand metrics and interpret data to support business initiatives and recommend strategies (for example: attrition rates, diversity in hiring, time-to-hire, time-to-fill, ROI, success of training, promote continuous improvement using data)**
- ✓ **1.5 Understand and reinforce organizational culture, core values, and ethical and behavioral expectations (for example: identify opportunities and make recommendations, contribute to diversity, equity, and inclusion [DEI], employer branding)**

The current business environment, with its emphasis on the ability to compete in multiple markets and respond to rapidly changing conditions, requires more effort from its leaders and managers than ever before. They must seek and develop a competitive advantage in their marketplaces and continuously create new processes, products, and services to meet the ongoing challenges presented by several key forces, including economic changes, modes of service delivery, customer expectations, and the rapid changes to technology. As each challenge is met, successful managers are already forecasting the next challenge on the horizon, looking for an advantageous market position. This ongoing process of innovation, advantage, value creation, and reassessment is known as *strategic management*. PHR and PHRi (PHR/i)-level candidates must be able to use information about the business environment to influence decision making, create and reinforce expectations, and manage risks associated with all business functions.

The General Business Environment

Business is essentially the engine that drives economies—it's about creating value, whether through selling products, providing services, or developing innovative solutions to meet people's needs. Business is the process of making decisions, taking risks, and managing resources to generate profit and sustain growth. From small local enterprises to multinational corporations, businesses play a vital role in shaping our society, driving progress, and fostering economic development.

Businesses often involve goods or services. *Goods* refer to tangible, physical products that are produced, distributed, and exchanged in the market, such as clothing, electronics, or vehicles, characterized by their material form and ability to be inventoried. *Services* are intangible offerings that involve providing labor, expertise, or experiences to meet specific needs, such as consulting, healthcare, or transportation services, often consumed at the point of delivery. While goods are standardized and can be mass-produced, services are often customized to meet individual preferences and require direct interaction between service providers and consumers, leading to differences in production, distribution, and marketing strategies between the two.

The Commercial Landscape

The environment in which business gets done is often referred to as the *commercial landscape*. The general business environment encompasses the conditions and factors that influence businesses' operations and performance. These factors include:

- **Economic Indicators:** Statistical data used to gauge the performance and health of an economy, such as unemployment rates or gross domestic product (GDP); for instance, a human resources department might monitor unemployment rates to anticipate changes in labor market conditions and adjust recruitment strategies accordingly.
- **Regulations:** Rules and guidelines set by state, federal, and local governments to govern behavior and ensure compliance, such as labor laws or industry-specific regulations; in a business context, for example, companies must adhere to environmental and privacy regulations.
- **Technology and Analytics:** Tools, systems, and innovations used to improve efficiency and effectiveness in business operations, such as human resource information systems (HRISs) or artificial intelligence (AI) recruitment software; HR departments may utilize technology to streamline administrative tasks, enhance employee engagement, and optimize talent management processes.
- **Sociopolitical Factors:** Pertaining to the combination of social and political factors influencing society, such as demographic shifts or government policies; for example, HR professionals might analyze sociopolitical trends such as the migration of employees outside of certain states to anticipate changes in workforce demographics.
- **Market Trends:** Patterns and movements in consumer preferences, industry dynamics, or economic conditions that impact businesses' performance and strategies, such as shifts toward remote work or increasing demand for sustainable products; in HR, monitoring market trends helps organizations adapt their talent acquisition, retention, and development strategies to remain competitive.

Within the commercial landscape, HR professionals play an important role. With the ongoing challenges presented by global uncertainties and technological advancements, HR professionals are tasked with ensuring that businesses have the right talent, skills, and organizational culture to thrive. They are instrumental in devising strategies for recruitment, training, and retention, adapting to the evolving needs of the workforce and the demands of the market. HR professionals are increasingly focused on fostering diversity, equity, and inclusion within organizations, recognizing the importance of creating inclusive workplaces for both employee well-being and business success. In addition to the traditional functions of human resource management, HR teams today are at the forefront of addressing emerging issues such as remote work arrangements, mental health support, and adapting HR policies to accommodate changing regulations and the social forces shaping the workplace. These actions by HR have a direct effect on the organization's stakeholders.

Cross-Functional Stakeholders

A *stakeholder* is any individual or group with a vested interest or concern in the activities, decisions, or outcomes of an organization. In the context of HR, stakeholders include employees, managers, executives, shareholders, regulatory bodies, labor unions, customers, and the broader community. Employees are key stakeholders as HR functions directly impact their employment experience, development, and well-being. Managers and executives rely on HR for strategic workforce planning and talent management. Shareholders (stock owners) have an interest in HR's role in maximizing organizational performance and profitability. Regulatory bodies set standards and guidelines that HR must adhere to in areas such as employment law and workplace safety. Labor unions represent employee interests and negotiate collective bargaining agreements with HR. Customers indirectly benefit from HR practices that ensure quality products and services. The broader community may be impacted by HR's efforts in corporate social responsibility and community engagement. Each stakeholder group influences and is influenced by HR decisions, highlighting the importance of stakeholder management in HR strategy and operations.

Tools that help to establish relationships and aid in decision making are directly related to the roles and responsibilities of cross-functional stakeholders. For example, an organizational (org) chart is a visual representation of the relationships within an organization, illustrating authority, reporting lines, roles, and responsibilities. It identifies the *span of control,* which is the number of subordinates or employees that a manager or supervisor directly oversees and is responsible for managing within an organization. The org chart helps stakeholders understand the hierarchy, communication channels, and decision-making processes, which in turn facilitates clarity, transparency, and collaboration across the organization.

Company culture is an internal component that affects company stakeholders. For example, a company's values and ethics directly impact business results by influencing customer loyalty, employee morale, and investor confidence, ultimately shaping the organization's reputation and long-term success. Company culture shapes the employee experience, impacting factors such as job satisfaction, engagement, and retention by fostering a sense of belonging, purpose, and alignment with organizational values and goals. A PHR/i candidate should be able to understand and reinforce the company culture. Chapter 2 "Shared Competencies" covers this concept in more detail.

The role of human resource professionals and its impact on business results and stakeholders is greatly influenced by how HR departments are structured.

Human Resources' Role in Organizations

The concept of VUCA describes the environment in which HR must be able to perform: volatile, uncertain, complex, and ambiguous. This demands sharp business focus with aligned HR initiatives that are at once stable and fluid—stable in that they always serve business strategy and fluid in that they may be adapted as needs dictate. Successful VUCA managers are characterized by an ability to align structures, processes, culture, and people with organizational objectives while responding to the external realities of the competitive landscape.

Competent HR professionals will be able to synthesize their knowledge of labor laws, the company culture, and the business needs to formulate a rapid response to the—quite often, unpredictable—nature of their day-to-day activities.

Today, although the roles are ever-changing, the role of HR exists as strategic, administrative, and operational.

Strategically, HR professionals contribute to decisions that build on employee strengths to meet corporate goals. Establishing recruiting and retention plans to attract the best-qualified employees and keep them in the organization is a key contribution that HR is uniquely qualified to make. Developing performance-management systems to motivate employees and providing continuous development opportunities are other areas that provide strategic advantages to organizations. Managing change and leading or participating in reengineering or restructuring programs to ensure the retention of key employees furthers the organization's ability to meet its goals.

Administratively, HR manages compliance issues related to government regulations, maintains employee and benefit records, and ensures the confidentiality of employee information.

Operationally, HR professionals manage the entire lifecycle of the employee, from recruiting to separation.

Additionally PHR/i candidates should understand the impact of metrics on organizational and HR department level decision making. For example, the results of an employee engagement survey should drive recommendations for new HR services. In a tight labor market, understanding the time-to-hire metric directly influences decisions about budgets and recruiting sources. Understanding operational business metrics helps organizations track performance, identify areas for improvement, and make informed decisions by providing valuable insights into the day-to-day operations and effectiveness of their processes.

Managing the strategic, administrative and operational elements of the employee lifecycle requires that an HR department is properly set up for maximum efficiencies and service excellence.

Operational Structure of Human Resource Departments

The lifecycle of an employee spans from recruitment and onboarding to voluntary and involuntary separations. At each stage, HR teams are responsible to curate a positive, personalized employee experience aligned with organizational effectiveness.

HR professionals are responsible for attracting top talent through strategic recruitment and sourcing and structured onboarding processes that integrate new hires into the company culture. Throughout the employee's tenure, HR oversees performance management, career development, and training initiatives to nurture talent and drive engagement. HR addresses employee concerns, provides support for work-life balance, and fosters a culture of inclusion and diversity. As employees progress in their careers, HR guides succession planning and talent management strategies to ensure continuity and succession within the organization. During transitions or separations, HR manages offboarding procedures in a professional manner, preserving relationships and knowledge transfer.

A well-structured HR department must be organized to address each stage of the employee lifecycle effectively, with functional systems (talent and technical) focusing on recruitment, employee development, employee relations, and strategic planning. The PHR and PHRi (PHR/i) functional area 01 "Business Management" is about organizing the delivery of these HR services within the framework of the business landscape.

HR Service Delivery

HR departments need to be structured in a way that aligns with business strategy and also in a way that optimizes service delivery. Variables to how to deliver HR programs include the number of employees, the specific industry, and where the organization itself is within the business lifecycle of infancy, growth, maturity and decline. Three common structural approaches for an HR department are as follows:

- **Functional Structure:** In this arrangement, HR functions are grouped based on specialized areas such as recruitment, compensation and benefits, employee relations, training and development, and so on. Each function is headed by a manager or director who oversees the respective area. This structure allows for deep expertise and efficiency within each function.
- **Matrix Structure:** A matrix structure combines functional and project-based reporting lines. HR professionals may be organized by function (e.g., recruitment, training) while also working on cross-functional teams or projects (e.g., diversity initiatives, organizational development). This structure facilitates collaboration, flexibility, and the ability to address complex, multidisciplinary challenges.
- **Shared Services Model and Centers of Excellence (COEs):** The main difference between a shared service model and a COE lies in their focus and function within the organization. A shared service model involves consolidating administrative functions such as payroll, benefits administration, and HR inquiries into a centralized service center to streamline processes and improve efficiency. A *center of excellence (COE)* is a specialized team within the HR department focused on developing and implementing best practices, policies, and strategies in specific areas such as recruitment, talent development, or employee relations, aiming to centralize expertise, drive consistency, and enhance HR effectiveness. While both models aim to optimize HR operations, shared service models focus on centralizing transactional activities, whereas COEs focus on centralizing expertise and driving excellence in specific HR functions.

In some cases, it may be strategically advantageous for an organization to outsource individual HR systems, such as payroll and benefits administration; to shift the entire function to an HR *business process outsource* (BPO) provider; or to lease employees through a *professional employer organization* (PEO). When this is the case, selecting the appropriate vendor for an organization is crucial. As with any other strategic decision, the first step is to clearly define the services required of the provider as well as the organization's service expectations to ensure that business needs are met. It's also important to identify the responsibilities of both parties so that there is a framework for addressing situations that aren't specifically covered in the agreement.

HR Roles and Responsibilities

How an HR department is structured impacts the roles and responsibilities of each HR team member. A traditional department may include some combination of the following HR roles:

Director of HR Responsible for overseeing the overall strategic direction and operations of the HR department, aligning human resources initiatives with organizational goals and ensuring compliance with relevant laws and regulations.

HR Manager Responsible for supervising and coordinating the daily activities of the HR team, including recruitment, employee relations, performance management, and policy implementation, while also serving as a strategic partner to senior management.

HR Generalist Responsible for handling a variety of HR tasks across multiple functional areas, including recruitment, onboarding, benefits administration, employee relations, and compliance, providing comprehensive support to both employees and management.

HR Specialist Responsible for focusing on a specific area within HR, such as compensation and benefits, training and development, recruitment, or employee relations, bringing in-depth expertise and specialized knowledge to address complex issues and implement best practices.

HR Department of One An HR department of one refers to a scenario where a single individual manages all aspects of human resources within an organization, encompassing tasks such as recruitment, employee relations, benefits administration, training, and compliance, often requiring multitasking and resourcefulness to meet the needs of the organization effectively. An HR to full-time employee ratio (HR:FTE) is about 1:80, although this number can vary significantly based on many factors.

Human Resource Budgets

An operational HR budget is a comprehensive financial plan that outlines the expenses associated with managing the workforce and supporting HR functions within an organization. Such a budget includes various components to ensure effective management of *human capital*, the collective value of employee skills and knowledge. A review of the key elements of an HR budget that PHR/i candidates should understand follows.

Labor Costs This encompasses salaries, wages, bonuses, and benefits for HR staff, including compensation for HR managers, recruiters, trainers, and administrative personnel.

Recruitment and Hiring Expenses This includes costs associated with sourcing, advertising, screening, interviewing, and selecting candidates for job openings. It may also cover expenses related to background checks, drug testing, and pre-employment assessments.

Training and Development Budget allocation for employee training programs, workshops, seminars, and professional development initiatives aimed at enhancing skills, knowledge, and performance. This may also include expenses for external training providers or online learning platforms.

Employee Benefits Funds allocated for employee benefits such as health insurance, retirement plans, paid time off, sick leave, and other perks. This also includes employer contributions to insurance premiums and retirement accounts. Employers must offer workers compensation insurance, and account for unemployment and disability insurance costs in compliance with various state laws.

Compliance and Legal Costs Budget provisions for ensuring compliance with labor laws, regulations, and industry standards. This may involve expenses related to legal consultations, audits, workplace safety programs, and compliance training.

HR Technology and Systems Budget allocation for HR software, platforms, and systems used for recruiting, onboarding, performance management, payroll processing, and data analytics. This may include subscription fees, licensing costs, implementation expenses, and IT support.

Employee Relations Funds set aside for managing employee relations, including expenses for employee engagement initiatives, recognition programs, conflict resolution, and employee assistance programs.

Contingency and Miscellaneous Expenses Reserve funds for unforeseen HR-related expenses, emergencies, or special projects that may arise during the budget period. This may also include miscellaneous expenses such as office supplies, travel costs, and communication expenses related to HR operations.

In managing an HR budget, both HR generalists and operational HR teams play active roles. They monitor expenses to ensure they stay within budget limits. This involves implementing cost-saving strategies, negotiating vendor contracts, and refining processes while maintaining quality and compliance standards. HR specialists handle vendor relationships, ensuring services are delivered effectively within budgetary constraints. They also allocate funds for employee training initiatives, aligning investments with organizational goals. HR generalists assist in coordinating training logistics and tracking attendance, ensuring resources are utilized efficiently.

Real World Scenario

Whistle-Blowing in the Wake of the Enron Scandal

In the wake of the Enron scandal, and particularly during the month when congressional hearings into the bankrupt corporation's activities were televised each day, the SEC saw a marked increase in complaints. This trend has continued over the last decade. For example, in fiscal year 2023, the SEC received more than 18,000 complaints, an increase of more than 50 percent from the prior record-breaking year (`https://www.sec.gov/files/fy23-annual-report.pdf`).

Sherron Watkins, who is credited with blowing the whistle on the Enron accounting practices that eventually led to its bankruptcy in December 2001, may have inspired the increased reports. Ms. Watkins followed a path typical of whistleblowers by meeting with Enron CEO Kenneth Lay long before she went to regulators. Her desire was to advise him of the wrongdoing so he could put an end to it. That unfortunately did not happen, and the company filed for bankruptcy a few months after their meeting.

Although some whistleblowers have statutory protection from retaliation, courts are divided on just what whistleblowing activity is protected; those who go to regulators are often unable to work in their chosen profession after taking the action.

One whistleblower who paid the price for his actions is Dr. Jeffrey Wigand, a former tobacco executive who was fired by Brown & Williamson Tobacco Corporation in 1993 after the company refused to remove a known carcinogen from its cigarette products. After his termination, Dr. Wigand testified against tobacco companies in civil lawsuits and appeared in an interview on the television show *60 Minutes*; his former employers launched a campaign to discredit him. Dr. Wigand was a key witness in the lawsuit brought by 46 states against tobacco companies that was settled when they agreed to pay $206 billion to reimburse the states for medical expenses related to smoking.

The good news is that regardless of the evolution of regulations, whistleblower protection since the Enron and Brown & Williamson examples continues to gain traction, largely due to the impact of media. Consider the 2018 whistleblower report to the *Wall Street Journal* by Theranos employee Tyler Shultz of the company's potential manipulation of data. The result was, by several accounts, the beginning of the end for Theranos and company founder Elizabeth Holmes. In today's world, whistleblowing to the media has significant impact (often more so than to state or federal regulators) because of the viral nature of news delivered and then shared online.

Enterprise Risk Management

All businesses have operational and strategic risks that need to be accounted for, although the degree of and impact on organizational results varies based on company size, industry and type of operation. For some businesses, safety and security are separate business functions; for others, it is part of an HR Generalist or Specialist role. Regardless of where the task-level responsibilities lie, HR makes important contributions. *Enterprise risk management (ERM)* is a practice of forecasting possible risks to the organization and taking steps to mitigate their impact on operations. In exam content terms, objective 1.3 relates to

HR recommending and implementing best practices to reduce risk in the workplace. The first step in accomplishing this is to identify the risks; for HR, that means conducting an audit of HR practices to identify areas of potential loss.

HR Audits

An *HR audit* identifies areas that may be out of compliance with legal requirements or that are in need of updating because of strategic changes within the organization, and it defines elements that are working well. First identifying the exposure factors and then developing an audit system to measure the current levels based on behaviors and outcomes (not the intent) are important contributions of HR within the scope of ERM. Examples of the types of audits conducted include the following:

Compliance Audits These audits assess whether the organization is compliant with relevant employment laws and regulations at the federal, state, and local levels. Areas of focus may include wage and hour compliance, discrimination and harassment policies, employee classification (exempt vs. nonexempt), and recordkeeping practices.

Workers Compensation Class Audit These audits evaluate the classification of employees to ensure that they are correctly categorized based on the type of work they perform, which directly impacts the calculation of workers' compensation premiums. The audit verifies that employees are appropriately classified into categories such as administrative roles, which typically carry lower risk and thus lower premiums, versus high-risk roles like those involving heavy machinery, which incur higher premiums due to the increased likelihood of injury. Misclassification can lead to financial penalties and under- or overpayment of premiums.

Cybersecurity Audits A risk audit focused on information technology (IT) or cybersecurity would assess the organization's digital infrastructure, systems, and protocols to identify vulnerabilities, compliance gaps, and potential threats related to HR data and operations in digital environments. An HR-specific risk audit may also include a review of HR processes and systems, such as digital HRISs (human resources information systems), to identify any specific risks or weaknesses in handling employee data digitally.

Policy and Procedure Audits Reviewing HR policies and procedures ensures they are up-to-date, comprehensive, and legally sound. This includes policies related to equal employment opportunity, antidiscrimination, harassment prevention, disciplinary actions, termination procedures, and employee handbook policies.

Documentation Audits Assessing the accuracy and completeness of employee documentation is crucial in predicting potential lawsuits. This includes personnel files, performance evaluations, disciplinary records, and documentation related to employee grievances or complaints.

Training Audits Evaluating the effectiveness and consistency of employee training programs, particularly on topics such as harassment prevention, diversity and inclusion, and workplace safety, can help identify areas where additional training or reinforcement may be needed to mitigate legal risks.

Leave and Accommodation Audits Ensuring compliance with laws related to employee leave (such as the Family Medical Leave Act) and reasonable accommodations for disabilities is essential. Audits in this area can help identify any gaps or inconsistencies in leave administration and accommodation processes that could lead to legal challenges.

Personnel File Audits Personnel file audits involve a comprehensive review of employee records to ensure accuracy, completeness, and compliance with legal requirements. This includes verifying that all required documents are present in each employee's file, such as job applications, résumés, offer letters, performance evaluations, disciplinary records, and signed acknowledgment forms for company policies. Additionally, personnel file audits may assess whether sensitive information is appropriately safeguarded and whether access to employee records is restricted to authorized personnel only.

Many organizations grapple with the question of who is responsible for conducting the audits. Using internal HR resources for audits offers familiarity with organizational culture and cost-effectiveness, but may lack objectivity and expertise, and face resource constraints. External auditors provide objectivity, specialized expertise, and confidentiality, but at a higher cost and with potential limitations in understanding organizational dynamics. Internal audits foster continuous improvement but risk bias, whereas external audits ensure impartiality but may lack organizational insight. Combining internal and external resources can optimize audit effectiveness, balancing cost and objectivity to mitigate HR risks comprehensively.

By conducting these types of HR audits regularly and proactively addressing any areas of concern or noncompliance, organizations can reduce the likelihood of employee lawsuits and mitigate potential legal risks.

Risk Management Techniques

Once possible risks are identified and analyzed, options to mitigate the risks are reviewed, and recommendations for handling the risk are made. Depending on the level of risk and its possible impact on operations, decisions can be made about how to handle each risk. There are four primary ways to address risks:

- **Mitigate:** This technique involves taking actions to reduce the impact or likelihood of identified risks.
- **Transfer:** Risk transfer entails shifting the burden of potential losses to another party, such as through insurance or contracts.
- **Avoid:** The strategy of avoidance involves circumventing risks entirely by refraining from engaging in activities that pose potential harm or negative outcomes.
- **Accept:** Acceptance involves acknowledging the existence of risks and their potential consequences without taking active measures to mitigate, transfer, or avoid them.

HR professionals play a role in each of the above risk management techniques. In mitigating risks, HR professionals develop and implement policies and procedures aimed at reducing the likelihood of potential hazards in the workplace, such as safety protocols and training programs. They also facilitate risk transfer by negotiating and managing insurance policies and contracts, ensuring that the organization is adequately protected against financial and legal liabilities. HR professionals contribute to risk avoidance by advising on regulatory compliance and ethical standards, guiding decision-making processes that steer clear of activities with high-risk implications. In risk acceptance, HR professionals assess and communicate potential risks to relevant stakeholders, ensuring that leadership is informed and prepared to make informed decisions about accepting certain risks as part of the organization's strategic objectives.

When a risk has been identified and contained, HR is then tasked with taking steps to prevent the issue from occurring again. The following are examples of audits HR can use to minimize exposure and to demonstrate a good-faith effort toward compliance:

Hiring and Diversity Statistics at All Levels of Employees Check what percentage of your management team includes protected-class individuals. This measures diversity and inclusion in leadership roles. By tracking and improving these statistics, HR can minimize the risk of discrimination claims and demonstrate a commitment to equal opportunity.

Recruiting Sources Identify which recruiting sources offer the most diverse pool of qualified applicants. This ensures a wider range of candidates for open positions. Utilizing diverse recruiting sources can reduce the risk of biased hiring practices and show a proactive approach to building a diverse workforce.

Data Security Review the security of confidential information, check for breaches, and verify the effectiveness of control measures. This protects sensitive employee data from being compromised. Data security measures minimize the risk of data breaches and demonstrate a strong (and compliant) commitment to protecting employee privacy.

Form I-9 Audits Verify procedures and review forms to reduce penalties from improperly completed documents. This ensures compliance with employment eligibility verification laws. Conducting regular Form I-9 audits helps avoid legal penalties and shows good faith in adhering to immigration and employment laws.

Harassment Claim Management Review training records, conduct employee surveys to ensure claims are taken seriously, and check policies for compliance with state and federal laws. This ensures a safe and respectful workplace. Effective harassment claim management minimizes the risk of legal action and demonstrates the company's commitment to maintaining a respectful and compliant work environment.

For some risks, the purchase of an insurance policy will adequately protect the organization. *Employment practices liability insurance (EPLI)* provides protection for employers to help them reduce the potential loss associated with various employment-related claims. Sexual harassment, discrimination, and wrongful discipline are some examples of the types of protection EPLI offers. In cases where the risk is low, a plan for self-insuring—that is, to pay out-of-pocket should the risk occur—may make sense. It may be possible to reduce the level of risk for some practices, such as unsigned I-9 forms, by implementing checklists or reviewing procedures. The potential exposure from other risks may be so high that eliminating the practice would provide the best protection for the organization.

Summary

The role of HR in the 21st century is changing into one that is more strategic and involved with planning the future direction of the organization and driving the achievement of business results. As a result, it's crucial for HR professionals to have a working knowledge of the general business environment in order to provide the operational and administrative support necessary to attract and retain qualified employees in each area.

Operations are just as important as business strategy because they translate strategic goals into tangible actions, ensuring efficient resource allocation, effective processes, and timely execution, ultimately determining the organization's ability to deliver value to customers and achieve its strategic objectives.

PHR/i candidates use their knowledge to reinforce organizational values and ethics and support HR service delivery. HR oversees various functions such as recruitment, talent development, performance management, compensation and benefits, employee relations, and compliance with employment laws and regulations. These functions make up the framework for the domain of human resources and the HR exams.

By attracting, retaining, and developing top talent, HR contributes to organizational success and competitiveness. HR fosters a positive work environment, promotes diversity and inclusion, and ensures fair and equitable treatment of employees.

Human resources' risk management efforts focus on identifying, assessing, and mitigating risks associated with the workforce to ensure organizational resilience and compliance. HR professionals proactively analyze potential risks such as legal liabilities, employee relations issues, workplace safety concerns, and talent shortages. They develop and implement policies, procedures, and training programs to mitigate these risks, promoting a safe, fair, and productive work environment. HR conducts regular audits and assessments to identify areas of vulnerability and compliance gaps, taking corrective actions as necessary and steps necessary to prevent future exposure.

This chapter is best summed up by HRCI's definition of the Business Management function of the exam: "Using information about the organization and business environment to reinforce expectations, influence decision making, and avoid risk."

Exam Essentials

Understand the general business environment. HR professionals must understand the general business environment and the forces that shape how goods are manufactured or services are offered, and how they interact with each other and with HR.

Understand HR's role in the organization. The role of HR is evolving into one that provides strategic, administrative, and operational services for the organization. HR must understand the role of cross-functional stakeholders and establish relationships to influence organizational decision making.

Be able to identify risks and recommend best practices. HR audits are effective tools used to identify risks and make decisions on how to address those risks. Protecting the company's physical digital and human assets are a high priority for all businesses, regardless of size or industry.

Review Questions

You can find the answers in Appendix A.

1. Which of the following factors is *not* considered part of the general business environment?
   A. Economic conditions
   B. Social trends
   C. Organizational culture
   D. Technological advancements
2. Which of the following best illustrates the impact of sociopolitical forces on human resources in a multinational enterprise (MNE)?
   A. Implementing a new HRIS software to streamline employee data management across global offices
   B. Adapting recruitment strategies to comply with local regulations on diversity and inclusion
   C. Promoting a companywide initiative to foster a more collaborative and inclusive work culture
   D. Monitoring fluctuations in the unemployment rate to anticipate changes in labor market conditions
3. Which of the following best defines a stakeholder?
   A. An individual or group that invests money into a company
   B. A person who works for the company in a managerial role
   C. An individual or group with an interest or concern in the success or performance of an organization
   D. A person responsible for making all the decisions in an organization
4. Which of the following best describes a human resources center of excellence (COE)?
   A. A centralized HR department responsible for managing day-to-day administrative tasks such as payroll and benefits administration
   B. A specialized team within the HR department focused on developing and implementing best practices and strategies in specific areas such as recruitment, talent development, or employee relations
   C. An external consulting firm hired by organizations to provide HR services on a project basis
   D. A cross-functional team consisting of employees from various departments tasked with improving organizational effectiveness and efficiency

5. What is the primary distinction between the strategic and operational roles of human resources?
   A. The strategic role focuses on day-to-day tasks and transactional activities, whereas the operational role involves long-term planning and alignment with organizational goals.
   B. The strategic role involves setting organizational objectives and developing HR initiatives to support business strategies, whereas the operational role involves implementing HR policies and procedures to meet immediate needs.
   C. The strategic role primarily deals with compliance and legal matters, whereas the operational role focuses on talent acquisition and employee development.
   D. The strategic role emphasizes employee relations and engagement, whereas the operational role centers on budgeting and resource management.
6. Which of the following is a practical benefit for measuring diversity in hiring practices?
   A. The findings may allow HR to correct an issue before it is litigated.
   B. The findings may allow HR to save money on attorney fees.
   C. The findings will make HR practitioners better business partners.
   D. The findings will allow HR to comply with affirmative action laws.
7. Which of the following is an appropriate use for an HR audit?
   A. To determine which employees no longer have the skills needed by the organization
   B. To determine the employee productivity and turnover rates
   C. To determine whether the employee handbook is in compliance with current government regulations
   D. To ensure that employees are properly classified under workers' compensation codes
8. Which of the following best describes a matrix structure within an HR department?
   A. A structure where HR functions are divided based on job roles
   B. An organizational structure where HR professionals report directly to the CEO
   C. A cross-functional approach where HR staff report to both functional managers and project managers
   D. A structure where HR functions are outsourced to external agencies
9. The company you work for has asked you to get requests for proposals on employment practices liability insurance. This is an example of which of the following risk management techniques?
   A. Avoidance
   B. Acceptance
   C. Mitigation
   D. Transfer

10. Which of the following factors are shaped by an HR service culture?
    A. Employee engagement
    B. Productivity
    C. Quality
    D. Legal compliance

11. Which of the following is *not* a method used by organizations to communicate the expected standards of behavior to employees?
    A. Written policies
    B. HR behavior modeling
    C. Mentor programs
    D. Employee handbook

12. You are an HR Generalist in a growing technology company, responsible for managing vendor contracts and ensuring that services are delivered according to the agreed-upon terms. The staffing agency you work with has consistently failed to meet the expectations outlined in the HR budget. Despite their promises of providing high-quality candidates within specified timelines, they have been delivering subpar candidates, often missing deadlines, and causing delays in the hiring process. How should you handle this situation?
    A. Continue working with the vendor, hoping they will improve their performance over time.
    B. Confront the vendor directly, providing specific examples of their shortcomings and demanding immediate improvements.
    C. Seek alternative vendors without informing the management, to avoid unnecessary scrutiny of the HR budget.
    D. Document the vendor's failures and gather evidence to present a comprehensive report to senior management.

13. An HR audit enables an employer to do which of the following? (Choose all that apply.)
    A. Evaluate the effectiveness of current HR practices in alignment with strategic goals.
    B. Identify exposure factors and the employer's potential risk due to compliance failures.
    C. Conduct a knowledge assessment of the current workforce.
    D. Measure levels of employee engagement.

14. Which of the following types of audits is most likely to identify exposure to confidentiality breaches in the workplace?
    A. Behavioral training audit
    B. Phishing vulnerability audit
    C. Compliance audit
    D. Cybersecurity audit

15. What is the purpose of an HR budget?
    A. To determine how much cash is required to achieve a goal
    B. To hold departments accountable for outcomes
    C. To ensure that the outcomes match the strategic plan
    D. To evaluate the effectiveness of HR strategy

16. What is the primary difference between a stakeholder and a shareholder?
    A. Shareholders own a stake in the company through stock ownership, whereas stakeholders are individuals or entities affected by the company's actions and decisions but may not necessarily own shares.
    B. Stakeholders primarily focus on financial returns and profitability, whereas shareholders have a broader range of interests, including social, environmental, and ethical considerations.
    C. Stakeholders have legal rights as owners, such as voting in meetings and receiving dividends, whereas shareholders have no legal rights within the company.
    D. Shareholders are directly involved in the ownership and financial success of the company, whereas stakeholders are only interested in the company's performance for external reasons.

17. Fill in the blanks: __________ are customized support activities designed to improve business or customer outcomes whereas __________ are consumable products.
    A. Goods; deliverables
    B. Solutions; products
    C. Products; services
    D. Services, goods

18. Which of the following best describes the purpose of funds allocated for employee relations within a company's budget?
    A. Funds allocated as part of a collective bargaining agreement
    B. Funds set aside for expenses related to recognition programs, conflict resolution, and employee assistance programs
    C. Funds specifically reserved for mitigating employment practice liability risks
    D. Funds allocated for employee training and development programs

19. Implementing regular safety inspections and providing comprehensive training on hazard identification and emergency procedures to reduce workplace accidents is the best example of which of the following risk management techniques?
    A. Avoid
    B. Mitigate
    C. Transfer
    D. Accept

20. Salaries, payroll taxes, and benefits are all examples of which of the following HR activities?

    A. Conducting a business impact measure

    B. Creating an HR budget

    C. Creating a compensation strategy

    D. Analyzing the cost of recruiting

Chapter 4

PHR | PHRi Exam: Workforce Planning and Talent Acquisition

PHR RESPONSIBILITIES:

IDENTIFYING, ATTRACTING, AND EMPLOYING TALENT WHILE FOLLOWING ALL FEDERAL LAWS RELATED TO THE HIRING PROCESS.

- ✓ **2.1 Apply US federal laws and organizational policies to adhere to legal and ethical requirements in hiring (for example: Title VII, nepotism, disparate impact, FLSA, independent contractors)**
- ✓ **2.2 Identify and implement sourcing methods and techniques to attract talent (for example: employee referrals, social media, diversity, equity, and inclusion [DEI] metrics, agencies, job boards, internal postings, job fairs, college recruitment, remote/hybrid work solutions)**
- ✓ **2.3 Manage the talent acquisition lifecycle (for example: interviews, job offers, background checks, job descriptions, onboarding, orientation, assessment/skills exercises, employee integration)**

PHRi RESPONSIBILITIES:

THE PHRi RESPONSIBILITIES ARE THE SAME AS THOSE FOR THE PHR, EXCEPT FOR 2.1.

- ✓ **2.1 Apply relevant labor laws and understand their impact to organizational hiring policies to adhere to legal and ethical requirements**

In today's fast-paced business environment, HR professionals must be able to "turn on a dime," adjusting workforce plans and lifecycle employment activities to meet the changing needs of their organizations. Workforce Planning and Talent Acquisition is the functional area of the *human resource body of knowledge* (*HRBoK*™) that tests your knowledge of workforce planning and the associated employment activities.

Workforce planning involves strategically analyzing and forecasting an organization's future staffing needs to ensure it has the right talent in place. *Talent acquisition* focuses on the strategic process of identifying, attracting, and hiring top-quality candidates to fulfill those workforce needs.

This chapter reviews the responsibility and knowledge requirements for PHR and PHRi (PHR/i)-level candidates. Note that many of the functions of this area, such as Title VII and the Fair Labor Standards Act (FLSA), require practical knowledge of labor laws; you will find this information in Appendix C, "Federal Employment Legislation and Case Law." Also note that the PHRi responsibility 2.1 differs from the PHR in the scope of labor law. PHRi candidates will need to be familiar with general concepts and "relevant" regulations as opposed to being able to cite U.S. federal laws.

Workforce Planning

The goal of workforce planning is to ensure that qualified employees are available when the organization needs them. An effective workforce planning process is based on the following:

- Workforce goals and objectives that forecast the organization's future workforce needs
- Job analysis and description that identifies the knowledge, skills, and abilities needed to meet future needs
- Identification of qualified employees beginning with the organization's current workforce demographics
- Translating the goals and objectives into tactical staffing plans to build the future workforce

The workforce plan resulting from this process provides the framework for targeting and prioritizing future staffing requirements, remaining flexible enough to allow HR to respond rapidly to changing business needs.

The Talent Acquisition Lifecycle

Once there is an understanding and action plan around current and future staffing needs, the talent acquisition process is engaged. This process is positioned as a lifecycle, illustrating the series of stages an HR professional must manage when hiring talent. It begins with identifying the skills necessary to achieve organizational goals by conducting job analysis and writing job descriptions. This is followed by *recruiting*, which is the process of identifying and attracting suitable candidates for job vacancies within an organization. *Selection* refers to the process of interviewing, assessing, and hiring individuals to fill positions within an organization, ensuring that the right people are in the right roles to meet business objectives. The talent planning and acquisition cycle is completed once an employee has been successfully onboarded. *Onboarding* is the structured process of integrating and orienting new employees into an organization, facilitating their transition into their roles and ensuring they understand the company culture, policies, and procedures.

Throughout the talent acquisition lifecycle, clear communication and effective coordination among recruiters, managers, and new hires helps to create a positive and supportive introduction to the company and defined expectations of their new role.

Predicting Fit

An important function of the talent acquisition process is predicting "fit"—the compatibility of a person to job and person to organization. Fit is determined using many data inputs, including the following:

- The organizational culture and norms (the work environment)
- The tasks, duties, and responsibilities of the job identified through job analysis (the job)
- The characteristics of people identified in the selection process through preemployment testing (the individual)
- Compliant practices with relevant labor laws

Person-to-Organization Fit

Predicting person-to-organization fit includes the identification and communication of the cultural norms and social mores of a company and its climate. In some cases, it is about the specific product or services offered. Many individuals, for example, would prefer not to work for vice businesses such as alcohol or tobacco, whereas others are not bothered by it. In other examples, the norm of 80+ hour workweeks may be prohibitive to individuals seeking work-life balance, whereas some would find the workload stimulating.

Person-to-Job Fit

Once the tasks, duties, and responsibilities (TDRs) of the job and the *knowledge, skills, abilities, and other (KSAOs)* characteristics necessary for successful performance have been established, it becomes necessary to find nondiscriminatory methods to predict an applicant's ability to perform. One way this is done is through the use of preemployment tests. Note that equal employment opportunity (EEO) laws define any preemployment requirement as a test that must be job-related and nondiscriminatory in both intent and effect. This includes employment applications, interview questions, psychological tests, in-box tests, and any other requirement of the selection process.

Offering a *realistic job preview (RJP)*, defined by Human Resource Certification Institute (HRCI) as "a strategy for introducing job candidates to the realities of the position, both good and bad, prior to making a hiring decision," may help improve person-to-job fit. Job previews must be realistic in that they clearly and honestly portray the organizational culture and expectations. This will aid in that critical retention period of the first 30–90 days. Predicting fit during the recruitment process is dependent on the identification of the characteristics of people (discovered during the recruiting and selection process) and the characteristics of jobs (identified through job analysis).

Predictive analytics is another method employers are increasingly leveraging to improve their quality of hires. Built from models using specific hiring criteria, these types of analytics can help larger employers sift through the thousands of résumés received each year, targeting the selection process to maximum effect. Smaller employers may also benefit from streamlining the hiring process using technology.

The continued rise in the use of the Internet and social media to recruit talent is an indication that online recruiting has replaced the more traditional sources for candidates. However, the efficiency of technology has in many cases compromised the candidate experience. Many job applicants report frustration at applying for jobs online and then never hearing back. Progressive companies recruiting in a tight labor market know that improving the applicant experience sends a message about how the company values its employees—even before they are hired.

NOTE

The role of technology—a broad concept in the scope of all that HR has responsibility for at the best of times—has a particular application for the talent acquisition process. Many companies are using chatbots, for example, to allow candidates to have a conversation with a computer without even realizing it. Other companies are leveraging technology by building databases that allow applicants to complete preassessments that do not require face-to-face interaction. While many companies use technology to enhance the customer experience, so also must HR use technology to enhance (not erode) the applicant experience.

The Employer Brand

The *employer brand* refers to the reputation and image an organization projects as an employer. It includes the company's values, behaviors and culture, and is used to enhance the employee experience and to attract and retain talent.

The employer's brand identity sets the stage for many aspects of the recruiting process. Each organization has a brand identity in the marketplace, whether or not it has been consciously developed. The reputation established with employees, current and former, along with the way the organization presents itself in the general marketplace, contribute to the brand.

Simply developing a catchy PR campaign isn't enough to make an effective employer brand. For a brand to be useful in attracting high-quality employees to the organization, it must first match the reality of working in the organization and describe what is unique about it. When that happens, every employee becomes an ambassador, creating interest among friends, neighbors, former colleagues, or others in working for the organization.

Building an employer brand begins with identifying unique elements of the organization culture. This may include answering the following questions:

- What values are important to the company?
- How are employees treated?
- Is the company on the leading edge in its industry?
- Is risk-taking encouraged or frowned upon?
- Are employees involved in the decision-making process?
- Is the performance-management process perceived to be fair? Do employees receive regular feedback?
- How does the company respond to economic downturns?

An accurate brand message gives candidates an idea of what it would be like to work in the organization and positively influences retention. If the employer has differentiated its organization as an employer of choice with a clearly defined message about the benefits of working there, then attracting the quality of candidates desired by the organization becomes less difficult. It's critical, however, that the "official" brand message is an accurate reflection of the organization. To ensure that this is the case, an employee survey can be conducted to find out whether current employees perceive the organization the way the brand portrays it. If there is a discrepancy, the organization can choose whether to adjust the brand message or make operational changes that address the differences between employee perceptions and the branding message.

In a tight labor market, many employers are using their brand to drive HR practices. Salesforce, for example, is known for their innovation and customer service. They have applied these characteristics to their staffing programs by treating the recruiting process as a customer service function. Résumés are submitted online, with a real-time, near-immediate response of "yes, we will proceed" or "no, not qualified." Other companies are similarly looking to embed their brand where it matters, actively seeking out employee ratings and reviews on Internet job boards.

An effective employer brand that accurately portrays the organization's culture benefits the organization in any economic climate. During times of economic growth when high-quality employees are in great demand, the brand both attracts and retains them. In an economic downturn, the brand becomes a vehicle for fostering communication and improving morale. For example, the unemployment offices in California were under great strain in March 2020 due to the high volume of claims related to COVID-19 shutdowns. One manufacturing company in central California chose to continue paying their employees their full salaries during the shutdown, demonstrating their commitment to taking care of their teams. This kept morale high and ensured a full return to work when the employees were needed.

Job Analysis and Descriptions

Job analysis systematically identifies and documents the duties, responsibilities, and required qualifications for a job position. This foundational step in the talent acquisition lifecycle ensures a clear understanding of the role and guides the subsequent processes of attracting, assessing, and selecting the right candidates. There are three primary methods used to conduct job analysis:

- **Observation:** This method involves directly watching employees perform their job duties to understand the tasks, skills, and requirements involved. It is particularly useful for jobs that involve manual or observable activities.
- **Interviews:** This method entails conducting structured or unstructured conversations with employees, supervisors, and other stakeholders to gather detailed information about the job. Interviews provide insights into the nuances of job tasks, responsibilities, and necessary qualifications.
- **Questionnaires:** This method uses standardized forms filled out by employees and supervisors to collect data on job duties, responsibilities, and required skills. Questionnaires can cover a wide range of job elements and are efficient for gathering information from a large number of respondents.

There are several challenges in the job analysis process to be aware of. One issue is the potential for bias and inaccuracy in the data collected. Employees and supervisors might provide subjective or incomplete information, leading to a distorted understanding of the job. The process itself can be time-consuming and resource-intensive, and require substantial effort to observe, interview, and compile information from various sources.

Another challenge is the dynamic nature of job roles, particularly in rapidly changing industries. Job descriptions can quickly become outdated, failing to accurately reflect current requirements and responsibilities.

Job inflation is another challenge, where roles are described in exaggerated terms to attract higher salaries or more prestigious titles, resulting in unrealistic or misleading job descriptions. In some cases, a manager may arbitrarily change a job title of an employee, resulting in lack of alignment with benchmarked job data such as that found in the U.S. Department of Labor's (DOL's) job database, O*NET OnLine (`www.onetonline.org`).

The output from job analysis is typically a formal, written *job description*. The job description outlines the essential responsibilities of a job, including the tasks and duties, along with the KSAOs necessary to perform. Job analysis and the resulting descriptions serve as the foundation for most HR activities, including recruiting, selection, establishing pay rates, and identifying training and development. In short, the process identifies the performance criteria for success.

Recruiting

Recruiting is the process of identifying and attracting qualified candidates for job positions within an organization. It is similar to the function of marketing in that it involves promoting the organization's brand and opportunities to appeal to potential candidates, much like how marketing aims to attract customers. An effective recruiting strategy is ongoing. Even during times when few positions are open, continuing to communicate with potential candidates, educational institutions, search firms, and other sources can help shorten the time needed to fill positions when they do occur and result in better service to internal customers.

From a strategic perspective, HR leaders are responsible for the overall *sourcing* (defined by HRCI as "identifying candidates who are qualified to do a job by using pro-active recruiting techniques") strategy. This is different from the operational efforts of recruiting and selection activities. HR leaders are called upon to help organizations clearly define both the need for the job and the qualifications necessary to successfully perform it. In some cases, HR will advise managers on the need to build the talent; in others, it may be best to externally recruit.

HR may also advocate for job restructuring. Redesigning jobs is an effective way to capitalize on existing skill sets while potentially making a job simpler. This, in theory, should increase the talent pool and make the recruit quicker and more effective. This approach will not work where there is a shortage of entry-level workers or where entry-level pay rates are cost-prohibitive.

Organizations have three options for locating the talent they need to achieve business goals: internal transfers or promotions, external hires, and alternative staffing methods. HR professionals evaluate the options by deciding which option is best in a given situation. Are there sufficient skills within the organization that can be redirected to the new requirements through transfers or promotions? Is it best to bring in full-time employees? Will some other staffing alternative provide the best solution? Let's take a brief look at these alternatives and discuss the strategic implications of each source.

Internal Hiring

There are a number of advantages to filling jobs internally, or "promoting from within." Management has an opportunity to evaluate candidates and determine their suitability for advancement over an extended period of time as they perform current duties, and the possibility of future promotion can encourage employees to maintain a high level of performance. Investing in employees through learning and development and then providing advancement opportunities for them communicates to employees that the organization values and rewards their contributions.

When promotion from within is an organizational practice, many external hiring becomes entry level. These hires tend to be easier to find, and the process allows new employees to become acclimated to the organization's culture and operating procedures early in their careers, leading to greater success when they move into positions with greater responsibility.

Of course, some disadvantages are associated with relying solely on promotion from within to fill positions of increasing responsibility:

- There is the danger that employees with little experience outside the organization will have a myopic view of the industry.
- Although the morale of those promoted will be high, employees who have been passed over or lost out on promotions may have lower morale and be less motivated in performing their jobs.
- When several people are being groomed for promotion, the competition can lead to a breakdown in teamwork and jockeying for political position.
- If the organization lacks diversity in its workforce, overreliance on promoting from within can perpetuate the imbalance.
- Reduced recruiting costs will be offset by an increase in training costs to prepare employees for positions with increased technical responsibilities or for supervisory or management positions.

In some cases, supervisors are unwilling to promote a high performer because the job the promoted employee leaves behind may not be done as well by a new employee. This is not a best practice because high performers may leave the organization altogether if their talents, skills, and career goals are not supported.

Skills Inventories

A *skills inventory* is an HR management tool used to collect and store information that would otherwise be obtained only after many hours of research by HR staff. An effective skills inventory collects information on special skills or knowledge, performance appraisals, fluency in foreign languages, educational qualifications, previous experience in or outside of the company, credentials or licenses that may be required, and any continuing education employees have obtained through training classes, seminars, or educational institutions. When collecting this information is one of the functions of an automated Human Resource Information Systems (HRIS), obtaining a report with detailed information about the internal talent pool can be accomplished in minutes.

Once possible internal candidates for openings are identified using the skills inventory, replacement chart, or succession plan , two methods are used to publicize current openings throughout an organization:

Job Posting A *job posting* is an internal job announcement that provides basic information about the opening, including the title; a brief description of the competencies, duties, responsibilities, and specifications; the salary range; and the application procedure.

Job Bidding *Job bidding* provides a means by which interested employees express interest in a position before it's available. This gives the supervisor and HR department an opportunity to review the job qualifications with the employee, provide training opportunities, let the employee gain additional experience if needed to meet the position requirements, and add the employee's name to the replacement or succession plan as appropriate.

Succession Planning

A well-thought-out *succession plan* identifies individuals in the organization who have the talent and ability to move into management and executive positions in one to five years. Once these individuals are identified, development plans are created to ensure that they're mentored and have opportunities to obtain education, training, and experience in areas that will enhance their ability to move into senior positions when the organization needs them.

Organizations might also choose to develop, implement, and use a *replacement chart*. This tool is useful at all organization levels and helps HR and line managers identify staffing needs by categorizing current employees in one of four categories:

Ready for Promotion Employees in this category demonstrate the KSAOs to assume additional responsibilities and are ready to move forward in the organization.

Develop for Future Promotion This group includes employees who are proficient in their current positions and, with additional training opportunities and experience, will be ready to move forward in the organization.

Satisfactory in Current Position These employees are proficient in their current positions but don't demonstrate the KSAOs or interest to assume greater responsibility in the organization.

Replace Employees are placed in this category for a variety of reasons, such as transfer or promotion, impending retirement, short-term disability, or unsatisfactory performance.

Talent pools continue to emerge as a strategic source for leadership roles. Some define talent pools as a 21st century alternative to the traditional succession plan. This is because most organizations across the globe can no longer offer a "career for life" track for any worker, and many workers no longer value that as a retention factor. A talent pool instead tracks the availability of people from diverse sources that may be used to backfill multiple roles as opposed to a linear option. In a pool approach, instead of a single successor for a single role, three or more potential candidates are identified, all with various levels of readiness for promotion. Often, criteria-based organizations with proper tracking mechanisms may also recruit externally for the talent pool should the size, skill set, or availability of internal candidates shrink. HRCI has a bit more specific definition of a talent pool that reads as "a group of available skilled workers, or database of resumes, that a company can use to recruit in a particular location." This suggests that talent pools can refer to talent available not only internally, but externally as well.

External Talent

At some point, organizations need to look outside for new employees. Even if the organization has a policy or practice of promotion from within, entry-level positions must be filled as employees are promoted or transferred. There are, of course, advantages to bringing new people into the organization:

- Experienced professionals bring new ideas with them and can revitalize operations.
- It's usually easier and more cost-effective to hire individuals with highly specialized skills than it is to develop them within the organization.
- If there is an urgent need for someone with particular skills, it's usually faster to hire those skills than to provide on-the-job training.
- Looking outside the organization to fill positions provides opportunities to increase the diversity of the workforce.

Looking outside the organization also has several disadvantages:

- Current employees who have been passed over for promotion will very likely have lower morale.
- It's always difficult to know how someone from outside the organization will fit into an existing team.
- The new hire is an unknown. Until the person begins doing the job, it's very difficult to know what their performance level will be.

Recruiting Methods

A variety of recruiting methods can be considered for finding new employees. The appropriate method depends on the type of employee needed by the organization in a particular situation. This means that a number of methods may be used in a single organization at any given time:

Media Sources Until the advent of Internet job boards, the most prevalent means for recruiting was newspaper advertising; for some jobs it's still the preferred method. Advertising jobs on the radio is used much less often than newspaper ads, but it can be effective if a company is trying to fill a large number of positions in a short period of time or for a targeted audience such as individuals with bilingual skills. Television advertising is rarely used to advertise individual positions; when used, it's most often by agencies that accomplish a dual purpose with the ads—attracting candidates and soliciting clients.

Internet Job Boards and Community Sites Advertising open positions on Internet job boards such as `https://indeed.com`, `https://ziprecruiter.com`, and `https://dice.com` has become prevalent in recent years. Its popularity as a recruiting source is growing because it's often more cost-effective than traditional media advertising. A downside for employers using this method is that some job seekers are indiscriminate when responding to posted jobs, which results in a large number of résumés from unqualified applicants that must be sorted through to find appropriate candidates.

Mobile Devices The popular Internet job board CareerBuilder found that more than 70 percent of candidate traffic and job applications come from mobile devices. Yet many employers still do not have their career pages mobilized. These numbers highlight the need for HR to take the lead in ensuring that applicants can find open jobs and easily apply online. To view additional insights related to the candidate experience, visit `https://resources.careerbuilder.com/employer-blog`.

Social Media Recruitment Social media is quickly becoming a cost-effective way to recruit for many staff positions. Using social media to recruit involves leveraging platforms like LinkedIn, Facebook, and X (formerly known as Twitter) to attract and engage potential candidates. A Society for Human Resource Management (SHRM) research spotlight reported that more than 80 percent of the companies polled were using social media sites to recruit. An advantage of using social media to recruit is its vast reach, enabling access to a diverse pool of candidates worldwide. However, a disadvantage is the potential for information overload and difficulty in filtering relevant candidates, not to mention having access to information that should not be used to make hiring decisions. For example, scanning a potential candidate's social media accounts can reveal protected-class characteristics such as race, age, status as a parent or sexual orientation, none of which should be used to make a hiring decision.

Other studies have reported that organizations that posted a short video with the job information had a 34 percent higher application rate than those who posted jobs without video. These behaviors indicate that the current and future workforce continues to be online and mobile, marking a need for HR to respond. One example of a type of corporate response is the use of an external applicant-tracking system. This outsourced activity involves hiring a social media recruiting service that tracks how many times an employee refers a job through their personal network. The originating employee and the final referring "friend" both share a referral bonus.

Other examples of social media recruiting and selection activity include the use of the following:

- School alumni sites
- Personal networks used to mine passive and active job seekers, such as LinkedIn, Facebook, X, TikTok, and Instagram
- Corporate social-media campaigns
- Search engine optimization (SEO) ranking, brand management, and career sections on web pages
- Mobile technology
- Job alerts and mobile-friendly web pages
- Videos

- Job postings with video
- Virtual interviewing
- Skype and GoToMeeting

Company Websites Most companies with a web presence have a "career" or "opportunities" page on their websites where they post current openings. When combined with recruiting software that requires applicants to enter their own information into the recruiting database, this recruiting method can greatly reduce the time spent wading through résumés from applicants who don't qualify for positions.

Colleges and Universities Colleges and universities are a good source for entry-level hires in areas such as accounting, engineering, and human resources. An effective college recruiting program capitalizes on school ties by sending alumni to the campus as recruiters. Recruiters are carefully chosen for their enthusiasm about the students as well as for the company. Key factors for recruiting success are delivering informative presentations about the organization and being honest about the job opportunities currently available in the organization. College recruiting has become a reliable source for locating minority applicants in recent years.

Job Fairs Job fairs are events designed to bring employers and job seekers together in a single location. This format gives employers a chance to meet many potential job applicants in a short period of time. Including line managers and other employees with HR reps in the booth gives job seekers an opportunity to talk directly to hiring managers and find out about the organization without going through a formal interview process.

Alumni Employees Building and maintaining professional relationships with former employees who left in good standing and on good terms can be a cost-effective, worthwhile source for re-recruiting. Particularly if they enjoyed their experience in the organization, they may be enticed to return if an appropriate opportunity presents itself, and they can be good sources for referrals.

Previous Applicants Often during the recruiting process, a recruiter may remember a candidate who wasn't the best fit for one position but left an impression as someone who would be good elsewhere in the organization. Maintaining professional contact with such individuals can pay off when an appropriate position becomes available.

Employee Referrals Current employees are a great resource for potential candidates. Recommendations from this source can result in long-term hires, because employees will remain longer with a company where they have established a social network. Moreover, a referral program that provides nominal cash awards after the new hire has remained with the company for a specific period of time (normally 90 to 180 days) encourages such referrals and keeps cost per hire under control.

Vendors and Suppliers Individuals who provide goods or services to the company are often aware of potential candidates for openings. Particularly when there has been a long-term relationship, the vendor is aware of the organization's culture and needs and may prove to be a good source for applicants.

Labor Unions In union environments, the union hiring hall can be a good source for qualified employees.

Professional Associations Relationships developed in connection with attendance at professional association functions or conferences often provide leads for qualified applicants. In addition, many associations provide job-posting opportunities on websites or sell job advertisements in their publications.

Employment Agencies Each state has an agency dedicated to providing services to job seekers, including job counseling and training opportunities. There is no charge for employers to list job openings with the agency, which then screens, tests, and refers appropriate candidates. Contingent employment agencies generally focus on jobs in a specific profession or job category, such as accounting professionals or administrative employees. Fees, paid by the employer only when a candidate is hired, are usually based on a percentage of the first year's salary and vary widely with different agencies. The fee is often negotiable. Retained employment agencies are often referred to as *headhunting firms* or *executive search firms*. When these agencies are engaged by an organization, a fee for recruiting services is paid whether or not any of the candidates are hired. A *retained search firm* is generally used for executive-level positions; these firms specialize in sourcing candidates from the passive labor market.

Walk-in Candidates Candidates may come into the business in person to fill out applications and apply for jobs.

During the process of creating job competencies, descriptions, and specifications, HR works with line managers to ensure that the job requirements are accurately presented. In the recruiting process, HR works with line managers to create a candidate profile so that applicants who go through the selection process fit the requirements of the position. In developing this profile, line managers often want to describe an "ideal candidate" who possibly even exceeds the requirements of the position. It's up to HR to work with line managers in developing candidate profiles that are realistic, given the working conditions and salary range offered for the position. At the same time, it's also effective to work with line managers to develop alternatives to the candidate profile, possibly substituting years of experience for education requirements or lowering experience requirements if the experience is in the same industry. This expands the pool of available candidates and increases the chances of success in the recruiting process.

Continuous Recruitment

Continuous recruitment is an ongoing process of proactively sourcing, engaging, and nurturing potential candidates to fill positions as they arise, rather than waiting for specific job openings to occur. This approach is often used by organizations that operate in highly competitive markets or industries with high turnover rates, where the demand for skilled talent is constant. Continuous recruitment helps maintain a pipeline of qualified candidates, reducing time-to-hire and ensures that the organization is as prepared as can be to fill vacancies quickly.

To implement continuous recruitment, companies should focus on building a strong employer brand, and leverage various channels such as social media, job boards, and professional networks to reach potential candidates. It is also useful to maintain a database of prospective candidates and regularly communicate with them through newsletters and events. Personalized outreach can keep them engaged and interested in future opportunities.

Alternative Staffing Methods

To expand the pool of available candidates with the desired skills, consider alternative staffing methods. A wide range of alternatives provides varying levels of flexibility to the organization. Particularly when staffing needs require specialized skills or when the labor market is tight, these methods can provide access to highly qualified candidates who might otherwise be unavailable to the organization:

Telecommuting Due to advances in technology, *telecommuting*, which allows employees to work at home and connect to the office electronically, has become a viable solution for individuals who don't want to commute or who have other reasons to work at home. This option continues to grow in popularity as the United States reduces unemployment rates and the competition for talent heats up. A 2024 Gallup trend report noted that hybrid work has become the norm for *remote-capable jobs*, which are roles within an organization that can be performed effectively from a location outside of the traditional office setting, facilitated by the use of technology and communication tools.

Remote-Hybrid Remote-hybrid work, often referred to as a flexible work arrangement, combines elements of remote work and in-office presence. Employees have the flexibility to work from home or another location outside the traditional office setting for part of the week, while also having scheduled times to work on-site. This model offers increased autonomy and work-life balance, while still allowing for face-to-face collaboration and interaction when necessary.

Job Sharing *Job sharing* is an alternative that allows two people with complementary skills to share the duties and responsibilities of a full-time position.

Part-Time Employees *Part-time employees* are those who work less than a regular workweek. This staffing strategy can be a cost-effective solution for organizations needing particular skills on an ongoing but not full-time basis.

Internships *Internship programs* are usually designed to give students opportunities to gain experience in their chosen fields prior to graduation. Successful programs provide meaningful work and learning experiences for the students, including opportunities to meet with senior executives. The student gains a valuable learning experience, and the organization benefits by developing low-cost access to employees and the chance to observe the intern's performance prior to making an offer for full-time employment. In 2018 the DOL made changes to the Fair Labor Standards Act internship program requirements. All seven factors in the test of whether an employee is an intern or student are built on the premise that the "primary beneficiary" is the intern—not the employer.

Temporary Workers The temporary worker category covers a wide range of flexible staffing options:

> **Traditional** In a traditional arrangement, an individual is employed by an agency that screens and tests candidates prior to sending them to a work site for variable periods of time, from short, one-day assignments to assignments lasting for long periods of time. Under certain circumstances, these assignments can be converted to a regular, open position. These arrangements allow organizations to observe and evaluate a worker's performance prior to making an offer of full-time employment.
>
> **On-Call Workers** *On-call workers* are employed by the organization, available on short notice, and called to work only when they're needed.
>
> **Payrolling** *Payrolling* allows the organization to refer to an agency those individuals they want to hire. The agency hires the individuals to work for the organization and provides payroll and tax services for either a fixed fee or a percentage of the salary, which is generally less than a traditional temp agency fee.
>
> **Seasonal Workers** *Seasonal workers* are hired only at times of the year when the workload increases, such as the holiday shopping season or when it's time to harvest agricultural products.
>
> **Contract Workers** *Contract workers* provide another solution for acquiring talent. There are two types of contract workers:
>
> > **Independent Contractors:** *Independent contractors* are self-employed individuals who work on a project or fee basis with multiple customers or clients. Both federal and state governments have guidelines to determine the difference between an independent contractor and an employee. Misclassifying an employee as an independent contractor can result in substantial penalties to the employer, so it's important to ensure that the guidelines are followed.
> >
> > **Contingent Workforce:** A *contingent workforce* is made up of nontraditional workers, including part-time and seasonal as well as temporary or leased employees. Employment agencies or brokers will typically act as the employer of record on behalf of many contract workers, providing payroll, mandated benefits, and other services to this classification of workers.

Professional Employer Organization

A *professional employer organization* (PEO) operates as the organization's HR department. The PEO becomes the employer of record and then leases the employees back to the organization. PEOs provide full-service HR, payroll, and benefit services and can provide a cost-effective solution that enables smaller companies to offer benefits comparable to those offered by much larger organizations.

Outsourcing

Outsourcing moves an entire function out of the organization to be handled by a company specializing in the function. For example, *human resource outsourcers (HROs)* may be used for one or more HR functions, such as benefits administration or recruiting. On a larger scale, NASA announced that Space X—an Elon Musk company that was the first privately held entity to launch an unmanned spacecraft—was awarded the contract to build a rocket ship to fly astronauts to and from the space station. This solution can be beneficial by allowing the organization to focus on its basic business operations and potentially reduce costs.

Real World Scenario

Employee or Independent Contractor?

The Internal Revenue Service (IRS) has established guidelines for determining whether an individual can be considered an independent contractor or an employee. Recently, the IRS clarified the factors it uses to determine the appropriate status for an individual. These standards fall into three categories:

- *Behavioral controls* establish whether the organization has the right to direct and control tasks completed by the worker and how the work is evaluated. This includes the following:
  - When and where to do the work
  - What tools or equipment to use
  - What workers to hire or to assist with the work
  - Where to purchase supplies and services
  - What work must be performed by a specified individual
  - What order or sequence to follow when performing the work
  - Whether training is provided

- *Financial controls* establish whether the organization controls the business aspects of the individual, including the following:
  - The extent to which business expenses are not reimbursed
  - The extent of investment made by the worker in the business
  - The extent to which the worker makes services available to the relevant market versus a single business
  - How the worker is paid
  - The extent to which the worker can realize a profit or loss
- The type of relationship that exists between the parties is demonstrated by the following:
  - The existence of a written contract
  - The existence of benefits such as insurance, a pension, and vacation and sick pay
  - The permanency of the relationship—that is, an indefinite period of time (employee) or a specific project or period of time (contractor)
  - The extent to which the services performed are a key aspect of the regular business of the organization

Additional information about the IRS guidelines is available at `https://www.irs.gov/businesses/small-businesses-self-employed/independent-contractor-self-employed-or-employee`.

Many states have established their own rules for determining the appropriate status for workers. As with all employment laws and regulations, the highest standard is the one with which employers must comply, so be sure to familiarize yourself with the standards for the state(s) in which you practice.

Selection

The result of the recruiting phase of the employment process should be résumés and application forms from job seekers hoping to be selected for the position. Screening these candidates to find those who best meet the qualifications of the position begins with establishing procedures that ensure equal employment opportunities.

Screening Tools

The goal of the assessment process is to narrow the candidate pool into a manageable group including those candidates most qualified for a position. A variety of tools are used to assess candidate qualifications:

Résumés Many organizations rely on candidate résumés as a first step in the assessment process. Although they generally contain relevant information, it can be difficult to compare qualifications of different candidates because of the lack of uniformity of style and content. Résumés generally present information about the applicant in the most favorable light and don't always contain all the information necessary to determine whether the applicant is qualified for the position. For those reasons, having all applicants complete an employment application is a good practice.

NOTE

Is the résumé outdated? Many companies are looking beyond written work history in applications for jobs. These companies are replacing the traditional résumé with game-playing scenarios scientifically designed to measure candidates' abilities in communication, creativity, problem-solving, multitasking, conscientiousness, and altruism—all factors of success in many roles. Other companies accept social media profiles such as LinkedIn or short videos as applications for open positions.

Employment Applications Because application forms are considered employment tests by the Equal Employment Opportunity Commission (EEOC), employers must be certain that the information requested on them is both job-related and a valid predictor of success in the position. A key benefit to using a standard application form is the inclusion of a statement signed by the applicant stating that the information contained in the document is true and complete. This statement can be useful in the event that an employer becomes aware of misstatements or discrepancies subsequent to hiring a candidate.

There are four basic types of application forms to consider using; one will suit the needs of the specific position or organization:

Short-Form Employment Application As its name implies, the short-form application is less extensive than other application forms. The term *short* is relative—it describes application forms that range from one to five pages. Short-form applications are often used by employees who are applying for transfers or promotions and are useful for prescreening candidates or for positions with minimal skill requirements.

Long-Form Employment Application The long-form application provides space for additional information related to the job requirements, such as advanced degrees and longer employment histories.

Job-Specific Employment Application If the organization hires a substantial number of employees for positions with similar requirements, the application form can be designed to gather specific information related to the position or profession. This type of form would be appropriate for teaching, scientific careers, or volume hiring in similar professions.

Weighted Employment Application The weighted application form was developed to assist recruiters in evaluating candidate qualifications. The form is developed using the job description; aspects of the job that are more important for success are given higher weights than other, less critical requirements. Weighted applications tend to reduce bias in the screening process, but they're expensive to maintain because they must be redesigned whenever job requirements change.

Screening Interviews

After reviewing the application forms and choosing those applicants who meet the job specifications and candidate profile, the recruiter conducts screening interviews to decide which candidates will be forwarded to the hiring manager. The purpose of these interviews is to both discover facts about the candidate and provide information about the position. The recruiter can assess the candidate's interest in the position and begin the process of determining which candidates are the best fit for the requirements. Screening interviews may be conducted by telephone or in person, and are relatively short, lasting from 15 to 30 minutes.

Once HR has screened the applicants for a position and narrowed the candidate pool to those who meet job requirements and fit the candidate profile, the next step in the process of selecting the best candidate for the position begins. This may include several elements, such as an in-person interview, a realistic job preview, an in-box test, or participation in an assessment-center process. By far the most common selection tool is an in-depth interview conducted by hiring managers and others who know what the successful candidate will need to do in the position. The best interview process begins with an interview strategy.

The purpose of an interview strategy is twofold. First, it ensures that everyone on the interview team knows the candidate profile as well as what requirements the hiring manager has for the job. Second, when several interviewers will be interviewing candidates for a position, it ensures that everyone is using the same criteria to evaluate candidates. During the strategy-development phase, HR professionals work with hiring managers to decide the appropriate type of interview for the position.

Conducting Effective Interviews

Job interviews are stressful situations for interviewers and candidates alike. The interviewer has a very short period of time to determine whether the candidate is the best choice for the position, and the candidate wants to make a good impression with the ultimate goal of obtaining a job offer. To reduce the stress and improve the chances of obtaining the information needed to make the best hiring decision, preparing for the interview is essential. HR can assist interviewers in this process by providing advice on structuring an effective interview and developing an interview strategy:

Select the interview team. HR's role in selecting the interview team is to work with the line manager to ensure that everyone who needs to be involved in the interview process is involved. In a team environment, it may be appropriate for all members of the team to participate; in other situations, employees from other business units who have frequent contact with the person in the position may be invited to participate in the process, along with employees who are knowledgeable about the work to be done.

Hold a pre-interview strategy meeting. Conducting a pre-interview strategy meeting with the interview team provides an opportunity for the hiring manager to share what will be required of the successful candidate and to ensure that all interviewers are on the same page for the interviews. Topics for discussion can include the job description, specifications, and competencies. At this time, a discussion of the type of interview to be conducted and of common interview biases is also appropriate. This is a good opportunity for HR to share best interview practices with interviewers, such as not making notes on the application form or résumé, and to review appropriate interview questions.

Complete candidate evaluation forms. During the pre-interview strategy discussion, HR can review the candidate evaluation form with the interview team. This form provides consistency in the interview process by providing interviewers with a list of topics to cover during the interview. The form is useful in rating candidates on job requirements and acts as a reminder of what to discuss during the candidate-evaluation phase of the selection process.

Conduct interviews. Interviewers should prepare to meet the candidates by reading the application forms or résumés and making notes of any items that need explanation. During the interview, the candidate should be treated with dignity and respect, beginning with starting the interview on time and giving full attention to the candidate during the course of the interview. This includes screeners putting away their phones and focusing exclusively on the candidate. Setting the candidate at ease in the first few minutes will set the stage for a productive and informative interview. Providing a clear explanation of the organization's mission, values, and culture; details concerning the position; and what will be expected of the successful candidate early in the interview gives prospective employees a context in which to answer questions. Listening carefully to the candidate's answers, taking notes as appropriate, and following up on points that need clarification indicate a genuine interest in what is being said and encourage an open and honest exchange. Be honest with candidates about the workplace environment and give them time to ask their own questions. End the interview with an explanation of the next steps in the process.

Evaluate candidates. When everyone on the interview team has met with all the candidates, a final meeting takes place. During this meeting, the interviewers review the candidate-evaluation forms and share their thoughts on each candidate.

Types of Interviews

Several types of interviews are available for selecting candidates. Not all of them are appropriate for every situation, and it's up to HR to counsel the hiring manager on what will work best in each situation:

Behavioral Interviews These interviews are based on the premise that past behavior is the best predictor of future behavior. This interview type asks candidates to describe how they have handled specific situations in previous jobs or life experiences. Candidates are expected to be able to describe a situation or problem, the actions they took to resolve it, and what outcome resulted. Interviewers skilled in this type of questioning are able to drill down into the answers to determine the candidate's depth of experience.

Situational Interviews It is helpful to note that the key distinction between behavioral and situational interviews is the past and the future. Situational interviews are future-focused, often beginning with a variation of the question "How would you address . . . " followed by a realistic example of a likely work encounter. For example, a candidate for a customer service position may be asked "How would you handle an angry customer who called in to complain about our product?" These types of questions are appropriate for jobs in which there are consistent situations that applicants will be required to manage in their new role. Employers are trying to predict the candidate's decision-making style, critical thinking skills, ability to probe for more information, and ultimately, how the candidate would take action.

Structured/Directive Interviews As the name implies, a structured or directive interview is very much controlled and guided by the interviewer, with a predetermined set of questions asked of all candidates. This style allows for consistent questioning, thus reducing the potential for bias or discrimination.

Nondirective Interviews In this interview style, the interviewer asks broad questions and allows the candidate to guide the conversation. This style may produce a great deal of information relating to the candidate's qualifications, and that can become a problem during the candidate-evaluation phase, as well as in substantiating or defending the final hiring decision.

Patterned Interviews A patterned interview is structured to cover specific areas related to the job requirements. The interviewer covers each area with all candidates but may ask different questions of them.

Panel Interviews In a panel interview, several interviewers interview the candidate at the same time.

Stress Interviews In some positions, such as airline pilots, law enforcement officers, and astronauts, employees encounter highly stressful situations on a regular basis. A stress interview subjects candidates to an intimidating situation to determine how they will handle stress in the position.

Equal opportunity legislation and regulations require that questions asked of candidates during the selection process be constructed to obtain only job-related information. Some topics, such as race, may never be a consideration in a selection decision. Others, such as age, are *bona fide occupational qualifications (BFOQs)* that may be asked in a nondiscriminatory manner (for example, state laws may require that a bartender be at least 21 to serve alcoholic beverages). Table 4.1 illustrates appropriate and inappropriate ways to obtain job-related information in an interview.

TABLE 4.1 Appropriate and inappropriate job-related questions

Inappropriate interview questions	Appropriate interview questions
Affiliations	
What clubs or social organizations do you belong to? Do you go to church?	Do you belong to any professional or trade associations or other organizations that you think are relevant to this job?
Age	
How old are you? When did you graduate from high school?	Are you 18 or older? Can you, after employment, provide proof of age?
Arrest Record	
Have you ever been arrested?	Have you ever been convicted of ___________? (Name a crime that is plausibly related to the job in question.)
Disabilities	
Do you have any disabilities? Have you had any recent or past illnesses or operations? If yes, list them and give dates when these occurred. How's your family's health? When did you lose your vision/arm/hearing? How did it happen?	After reviewing the job description, are you able to perform all the essential functions of the job, with or without accommodation? Any job offer will be made contingent on a medical exam. Are you willing to undergo one if we offer you a job?
Marital/Family Status	
What is your marital status? With whom do you live? What was your maiden name? Do you plan to have a family? When? How many children will you have? What are your child-care arrangements?	Are you willing to relocate?* This job requires frequent travel. Are you willing and able to travel when needed?* Is there anything that will prevent you from meeting work schedules?*

Inappropriate interview questions	Appropriate interview questions
Military Service	
Were you honorably discharged? What type of discharge did you receive?	In what branch of the armed services did you serve? What type of training or education did you receive in the military?
National Origin/Citizenship	
Are you a U.S. citizen? Where were you/your parents born? What is your race? What language did you speak in your home when you were growing up?	Are you authorized to work in the United States? What language(s) do you read/speak/write fluently? (Acceptable if related to essential functions.)
Personal	
How tall are you? How much do you weigh? Would working on weekends conflict with your religious beliefs?	This job requires the ability to lift a 50-pound weight and carry it 100 yards. Are you able to do that? This job will require work on the weekends. Are you able to do so?

* Acceptable if asked of every candidate

Interviewer Bias

Any interviewer may bring preconceived ideas or biases into an interview situation; these can have an unintended impact on the hiring decision. The following list includes some of the types of interview bias that can occur. Once interviewers are aware of these, it's possible to reduce their impact on the selection process:

Average/Central Tendency The *average bias* becomes apparent when the interviewer has difficulty deciding which candidate is best and rates them all about the same.

Contrast The *contrast bias* occurs when an interviewer compares candidates to each other or compares all candidates to a single candidate. For example, if one candidate is particularly weak, others may appear to be more qualified than they really are.

Cultural Noise *Cultural noise bias* occurs when candidates answer questions based on information they think will get them the job—what they think the interviewer wants to hear. For example, a candidate who has been an individual contributor may tell an interviewer that they prefer working as part of a team if the interviewer stresses teamwork as a key job requirement.

First Impression This bias can work either for or against a candidate, depending on the interviewer's *first impression*. A candidate who is very nervous and stutters during the first few minutes of the interview may be viewed as less qualified even if during the remainder of the interview they are poised and well spoken.

Gut Feeling The *gut feeling bias* occurs when the interviewer relies on an intuitive feeling that the candidate is a good (or bad) fit for the position without looking at whether the individual's qualifications meet the criteria established by the job specifications and candidate profile.

Halo Effect The *halo effect bias* occurs when the interviewer evaluates a candidate positively based on a single characteristic. For example, a candidate's self-confident attitude may overshadow a lack of experience in a particular requirement.

Harshness/Horn Effect *Harshness bias*, or the *horn effect*, occurs when the interviewer evaluates a candidate negatively based on a single characteristic.

Knowledge-of-Predictor *Knowledge-of-predictor bias* occurs when the interviewer is aware that a candidate scored particularly high (or low) on an assessment test that has been shown to be a valid predictor of performance.

Leniency *Leniency bias* occurs when an interviewer tends to go easy on a candidate and give a higher rating than is warranted, justifying it with a rationalization.

Negative Emphasis The *negative emphasis bias* occurs when the interviewer allows a small amount of negative information to outweigh positive information.

Nonverbal Bias *Nonverbal bias* occurs when an interviewer is influenced by body language. For example, a candidate who frowns when answering questions could be rated negatively even though the answers were correct.

Question Inconsistency *Question inconsistency bias* occurs when an interviewer asks different questions of each candidate. Although this is acceptable to a certain extent in order to delve more deeply into each candidate's qualifications, there is no baseline for comparison if there are no questions that were asked of all candidates.

Recency The *recency bias* occurs when the interviewer recalls the most recently interviewed candidate more clearly than earlier candidates.

Similar-to-Me The *similar-to-me bias* occurs when the candidate has interests or other characteristics that are the same as those of the interviewer and cause the interviewer to overlook negative aspects about the candidate. For example, an interviewer who played college football may select a candidate who did so even though the candidate's qualifications aren't the best for the position.

Stereotyping The *stereotyping bias* occurs when the interviewer assumes candidates have specific traits because they are a member of a group. For example, an interviewer may assume that a woman would not be able to successfully perform in a job that requires frequent lifting of packages weighing 50 pounds.

In-depth interviews are the cornerstone of the selection process, used in virtually all hiring decisions. However, interviews aren't the only tool available for candidate selection. Equally important information that adds different perspectives to candidates can be obtained by using in-box tests and assessment centers.

In-Box Test

An in-box test provides candidates with a number of documents describing problems that would typically be handled by an employee in the position, with instructions to prioritize the problems and/or decide how the problems should be handled. Candidates are evaluated on the appropriateness of their decisions as well as on the length of time it takes for them to complete the test.

Assessment Centers

Assessment centers are characterized by multiple tests designed to measure different aspects of the job. Generally used to assess candidates for management potential and decision-making skills, they have been demonstrated to be valid predictors of success on the job. Used extensively by state and local governments and large organizations for assessing internal candidates for promotion, their use is limited due to the high cost of conducting them. Typical assessments include interviews, testing and problem-solving skills, in-basket tests, leaderless group discussions, and role-playing exercises.

Candidate Testing Programs

The use of preemployment tests has become more prevalent in recent years. These tests take many forms and have a variety of purposes. Physical tests and drug screens are used by employers to manage risk, and yet, improper use of these tests can actually increase an employer's risk for discriminatory practices. HR professionals must lead the effort to ensure that what is being measured in these tests is correlated with future success on the job. HR must also keep up with emerging law in this area, such as legalized marijuana on a state-by-state level.

The key issue to keep in mind with regard to preemployment tests is the requirement that they must be job-related and, should they be challenged by an EEOC complaint, defensible as valid predictors of success in the position. Candidates for PHR/i certification should be aware of the following types of selection tests:

Aptitude Tests These tests are designed to measure an individual's knowledge and ability to apply skills in various areas, such as mathematics, typing, language, and reasoning. Properly constructed aptitude tests have been shown to be valid predictors of job success.

Cognitive Ability Test (CAT) CATs measure an individual's ability to analyze and solve problems and draw conclusions from a set of facts. They also measure an individual's potential for learning, thinking, and remembering.

Personality Test Personality tests assess how a candidate will "fit" into a specific job. If, for example, an employer uses a personality test that has shown particular characteristics to be valid predictors of success—such as extroversion or conscientiousness—in sales positions, and an applicant doesn't reflect those characteristics when tested, the test would indicate an area to be explored with the candidate prior to making the hiring decision.

Integrity Tests Also known as *honesty tests*, integrity tests assess a candidate's work ethic, attitudes toward theft and drug and alcohol use, and similar traits. According to the EEOC, professionally developed integrity tests don't create an adverse impact for protected classes as long as the tests are administered equally to all candidates.

Psychomotor Assessment Tests A psychomotor assessment tests an individual's coordination and manual dexterity.

Physical Assessment Tests Physical assessment tests are used to determine whether candidates are physically capable of performing specific job duties. The tests generally require that tasks be completed within a predetermined period of time and most often simulate activities that regularly occur on the job. A common physical assessment test is one that is given to potential firefighters to ensure that they're capable of lifting and carrying heavy weights for predetermined periods of time in a variety of circumstances.

As previously discussed, a key requirement for selection tools is that they be both related to specific job requirements and valid predictors of successful job performance. To determine whether an employment test meets those criteria, employers must ensure that tests are both reliable and valid.

In preemployment testing, *reliability* means that the test gives consistent results every time it is used. For example, if someone takes the same test on different days and gets similar scores each time, the test is reliable. *Validity* means that the test actually measures what it is supposed to measure. For example, if a test is designed to assess math skills, it should accurately show how good a person is at math. Both reliability and validity are important to ensure that preemployment tests are nondiscriminatory and job-related.

Real World Scenario

The Courts Address Employment Tests

Once Title VII of the Civil Rights Act of 1964 was enacted, employees who thought they had been subjected to unlawful employment discrimination were able to initiate lawsuits to resolve their grievances. Preemployment testing practices were the subject of a number of cases, the most prominent of which are described here.

1971: *Griggs v. Duke Power Co.* Duke Power Company, located in North Carolina, employed 95 workers in its Dan River Steam Station in 1964. There were five departments at the plant: Labor, Coal Handling, Operations, Maintenance, and Laboratory and Test. The Labor Department was the lowest-paid department in the company; in fact, the highest-paying job in the department paid less than the lowest-paying job in the other four. In 1955, the company began to require that employees in all departments except Labor have a high school diploma, but prior to that time employees could be hired into any of the departments without one. On July 2, 1965, the effective date of Title VII, Duke added a requirement that all new employees must pass two aptitude tests and that an employee wanting to transfer from Labor to another department needed a high school diploma.

Willie Griggs was one of 14 black employees working in the Labor Department at the plant. There were no black employees in any of the other departments. Mr. Griggs filed a class-action lawsuit on behalf of himself and 12 of the black employees, alleging that the requirement for a high school diploma and satisfactory scores on the aptitude tests discriminated against them. The district court that first heard the case dismissed it. The court of appeals found that Griggs had not shown that there was a discriminatory purpose to the requirements and that a discriminatory purpose was required to show discrimination. The Supreme Court granted *certiorari* (agreed to review the case) and heard oral arguments in December 1970.

Because a number of the white employees who didn't have high school diplomas had been hired prior to the requirements for the diploma or the aptitude tests, and those employees performed well on the job, it was clear that the requirements didn't predict job performance, and Duke Power didn't dispute this fact. The Supreme Court found that "good intent or absence of discriminatory intent" in the face of a job requirement that adversely impacts a protected class isn't a sufficient defense against discrimination. The job requirement must be shown to be job-related in order to be lawful, and it's up to the employer to prove this.

The HR significance of *Griggs v. Duke Power Co.* is that discrimination doesn't need to be intentional to exist. It's up to employers to prove that job requirements are related to the job.

1975: *Albemarle Paper v. Moody* In 1966, a group of current and former black employees at Albemarle Paper's mill in Roanoke Rapids, North Carolina, filed a lawsuit against both their employer, Albemarle Paper, and the union representing them with the company. The group asked the court for an injunction against "any policy, practice, custom, or usage" at the mill that was in violation of Title VII. When the case dragged on for several years, a demand for back pay was added to the injunction request in 1970. One of the policies in question was the employment testing practice used by Albemarle Paper. The district court denied the claim for back pay and refused to consider the testing procedure, saying that the tests had been validated.

The court of appeals reversed the ruling, finding that the absence of bad faith wasn't sufficient grounds to deny back pay and that the validation process had four serious flaws:

- It had not been used consistently.
- It had compared test scores to the subjective rankings of supervisors, which couldn't be tied to job-related performance criteria.
- The tests were validated against the most senior jobs and not entry-level positions.
- The validation study used only experienced white employees, not the new job applicants, who were mostly nonwhite.

The HR significance of *Albemarle Paper vs. Moody* is that test validation must be in accordance with the Uniform Guidelines on Employee Selection Procedures. Subjective supervisor rankings aren't sufficient for criterion validation; the criteria must be able to be tied to the job requirements.

1975: *Washington v. Davis* In 1970, two applicants for the police department in Washington, D.C., filed suit against the city, claiming that the written personnel test given to applicants had an adverse impact on black applicants. The Supreme Court upheld the district court's finding that the test was a valid predictor of successful performance in the police-training program.

The HR significance of *Washington v. Davis* is that tests that have an adverse impact on a protected class are lawful if they are valid predictors of success on the job.

Preemployment Inquiries

Preemployment inquiries or background checks cover a range of activities designed to ensure that candidates who receive employment offers are who they represent themselves to be during the selection process. Information collected during these processes should be protected from inappropriate dissemination and, at the appropriate time, disposed of in a way that ensures its security. Preemployment inquiries verify information collected from candidate résumés and/or interviews during the selection process. Some of the information is relatively easy to verify, such as educational degrees and previous employment, and provides insight into earlier educational and employment experiences.

Preemployment inquiries may also include a check of the candidate's financial records, driving record, and any previous criminal behavior, depending on the type of job. Any background or reference check conducted by a third party is considered to be a consumer report and is therefore subject to requirements of the Fair Credit Reporting Act (FCRA). When employers conduct their own reference checks, those requirements don't apply.

Reference Checks

An organization may ask for several types of references from potential employees. Types of references may include the following:

Employment References To make an informed decision about a potential employee, employers should obtain all the information they can from previous employers. Information collected during the reference-checking process includes previous employment history, dates, job titles, and type of work performed. Many employers are reluctant to provide more information than this for privacy reasons, but as long as the information is factual and given in good faith, most states consider it "qualifiedly privileged," which protects the employer from legal action. It's desirable to obtain additional information about the employee's work habits and interpersonal skills and find out if the employee is eligible for rehire.

Educational References Depending on the position applied for and the length of time since graduation, some employers request high school, college, and postgraduate transcripts to verify the accuracy of information presented during the selection process.

Financial References Financial references are generally used only when candidates will be handling large sums of cash. As with all other selection tools, a financial reference must be shown to be job-related *and* a valid predictor of success in the position. When required, financial references, generally provided by credit-reporting agencies, are subject to requirements of the federal FCRA.

Criminal Record Checks

Criminal record checks can uncover information about substance abuse, violent behavior, and property crimes such as theft and embezzlement. Because private employers don't have access to a central database that collects information from every level of government (federal, state, county, and local), it can be difficult to do a comprehensive check. When applicants have lived or worked in several states, counties, or municipalities, records in each jurisdiction must be checked to ensure completeness.

Negative information obtained through criminal record checks should be carefully reviewed on a case-by-case basis, considering all of the relevant information:

- How does the type of crime relate to the position applied for?
- How recent was the conviction?
- How old was the applicant when the conviction occurred?
- What is the level of risk to customers, coworkers, and others in the workplace if the applicant is hired?

Criminal record checks are considered consumer investigations and must comply with related FCRA requirements. Additionally, "ban the box" laws prohibit employers from asking about a candidate's criminal history on initial job applications, allowing applicants to be evaluated based on their qualifications first. These laws aim to reduce discrimination against individuals with criminal records and provide them with a fairer chance at securing employment. States such as California, New York, and New Jersey have enacted these laws for most employers. U.S. federal agencies and contractors are subject to similar regulations under the Fair Chance Act of 2019.

When an employer considers making an adverse hiring decision based on negative information received in an investigative consumer report, the applicant must be notified in writing and given a chance to respond. Should the negative information be the result of a mistake, the applicant can provide information to clear the record. If the employer decides to proceed with the adverse action, the applicant must receive a second written notice stating that the adverse action has been taken.

Medical Examinations

As with all other assessment tools, medical examinations are allowable after extending a job offer or conditional job offer if their purpose is job-related and they're required of all candidates. These exams are used to ensure that the employee will be fully capable of performing the requirements of the job and, in some cases, may be part of an employer's health and safety program. Under the ADA, employers may make a job offer conditional on a medical examination before the candidate begins working as long as all applicants for positions in the same job category must undergo the exam. If the offer is rescinded as a result of the medical exam, the employer must be able to demonstrate that the job requirement eliminating the candidate from consideration is related to a business necessity.

Drug-Screening Tests

Drug screens in preemployment testing are used to ensure that prospective employees do not use illegal substances. Studies conducted by the Occupational Safety and Health Administration (OSHA) indicate that drug-screening programs reduce job-related accidents. Substance abuse is also linked to reduced productivity. Drug-screening tests are specifically excluded from the ADA's medical-examination requirement and may be required prior to extending an offer.

The legalization of drugs such as marijuana can present a significant challenge for HR practices, particularly when state laws differ from federal laws. In states where marijuana is legal, HR practitioners must navigate accommodating employees who use marijuana legally while still adhering to federal regulations that classify marijuana as an illegal substance and the need to keep workers safe. This can complicate drug-testing policies, workplace safety standards, and hiring decisions. HR practitioners should develop clear policies that comply with both state and federal laws and stay informed about legal changes at both the state and federal levels.

Negligent Hiring

Negligent hiring occurs when an employer knew or should have known about an applicant's prior history that endangered customers, employees, vendors, or others with whom the employee comes in contact. Employers can prevent negligent-hiring lawsuits by carefully checking references and running background checks for all candidates. Once an employer finds out about such a history, the employer is obligated to safeguard others who come in contact with the individual during the workday by taking whatever action is necessary to maintain a safe work environment.

To defend themselves against claims of negligent hiring, employers can demonstrate that they exercised due diligence in the hiring process by taking the following steps:

- Conducting reference checks with previous employers
- Obtaining reports from the Departments of Motor Vehicles in the states where the applicant has lived or worked
- Verifying the validity of the applicant's Social Security number
- Conducting criminal record checks
- Verifying the validity of any government-issued licenses, such as a medical or engineering license issued by a state
- Conducting drug-screening tests

Negotiations and Employment Offers

The stage of employment offers in the talent acquisition lifecycle follows the recruitment, screening, and interviewing processes. At this stage, the employer formally extends a job offer to the selected candidate, detailing the terms of employment. This process involves creating offer letters and negotiating salary and benefits.

Negotiations

One of the goals of the selection process is to collect information from candidates about their expectations for cash compensation, benefits, and other terms and conditions of employment that may be appropriate to the position. When it's time to make an offer, these expectations are incorporated into the decision-making process of crafting the offer. Prior to making the offer, any required approvals are obtained, along with approval for any "wiggle room" should the candidate come back with a request for a higher salary or increased benefits.

It is becoming unlawful in some states for employers to ask about salary history. Asking about salary history can perpetuate systemic discrimination, as employment offers based on past discriminatory practices only further unequal pay. Regardless of whether you live in a state with salary history bans, it is an HR best practice to have a plan in place for offering and negotiating pay. This includes establishing pay ranges based on market data for each role, and making employment offers within that range. Wage banding is discussed in greater detail in Chapter 6, "Total Rewards."

The behavioral sciences can help understand why asking about salary history has the potential to perpetuate systemic discrimination. In one study, participants spun a wheel to select a number between 0 and 100. They were then asked to adjust that number to reflect how many African countries were in the United Nations. Those who spun a high number gave high estimates, and those who spun a low number gave lower estimates, an indication that the participants were using their original number as the anchoring point for their decision. *Anchoring bias* occurs when a candidate (or recruiter) makes a decision from an anchoring point. When the initial anchor figure is set high, the final negotiated salary is often higher as well. Having market-based wage ranges and a strong compensation philosophy will help organizations avoid overpaying for talent or perpetuating pay disparities due to anchoring bias.

Senior HR leaders should also ensure that recruiters have the proper amount of authority in negotiating salaries so that the recruiters can make autonomous decisions in a timely fashion to avoid losing critical talent.

Finally, some organizations offer recruiting bonuses that are calculated as a percentage of the new hire's base pay. This can be a powerful incentive to get critical positions filled quickly. In these cases, however, proper checks and balances should exist to avoid a recruiter offering higher salaries to receive a higher bonus. In this case, salary ranges should be set and approved prior to the final offer being made.

Once the verbal negotiations are complete, the written offer can be completed.

Offer Letters

Offer letters communicate the basic details of the position, including title, salary, start date, and benefits. The offer letter should be prepared immediately upon acceptance of the verbal offer by the candidate. The standard offer letter should be reviewed by the corporate attorney to ensure that its provisions don't compromise the organization and that it contains the terms of the offer as well as any contingencies that apply, such as a medical exam, a background check, or proof of the right to work in the United States. The salary offer should be stated in an hourly or monthly amount. The offer should state clearly that the organization is an at-will employer and that only the terms and conditions of the offer contained in the offer letter are valid. Finally, there should be a reasonable time frame for returning a signed acceptance of the offer.

Care should be taken to ensure that any promises of benefits or special conditions agreed on by the hiring manager are included in the offer letter so there is no ambiguity about the complete offer.

Employment Contracts

Employment relationships in many states are subject to the common law concept of *employment-at-will,* meaning that the relationship can be ended at any time by either party with or without a reason. An *employment agreement or contract* is essentially the opposite of at-will employment, meaning that employment can only be terminated in accordance with the clauses of the contract, usually defined as "cause." As a result, few employees today work under employment contracts. In most cases, the relationship is defined in an offer letter that is composed after negotiations are complete.

An employment contract binds both parties to the agreements contained in the contract. Contracts are generally reserved for senior-level managers and professionals such as doctors and teachers, and they can cover a wide range of topics. Any areas of the employment relationship not specifically covered in the contract are subject to common law. Standard clauses seen in employment contracts include the following:

Terms and Conditions of Employment This clause covers the start date and duration of the contract and, if the contract is for a set period of time, includes any automatic extension agreements.

Scope of Duties General and specific duties and responsibilities are covered by this clause. The duties can be part of the contract, or the job description may be incorporated into the agreement as an addendum. Expectations for performance are included here as well.

Compensation The compensation package is described in this clause, which includes the base salary, any bonus and incentive agreements, auto or telephone allowance, company car, or other agreements.

Benefits and Expense Reimbursements Items covered by this clause include disability and health insurance benefits and retirement plans. The extent of and conditions for expense reimbursements are also described here.

Noncompete Agreements Noncompete agreements are contracts between employers and employees that restrict the employee's ability to work for competing businesses or start a competing business for a specified period after leaving the employer. The enforceability of noncompete agreements varies by jurisdiction, with some states imposing strict limitations or outright bans on their use, particularly to ensure they do not unfairly restrict workers' ability to find new employment and maintain their livelihoods.

Nonsolicitation Agreements This clause sets forth agreements that limit the employee's ability to solicit customers, vendors, and employees during the course of the contract and for an agreed-on period of time after the contract ends.

Nondisclosure Agreements Employment nondisclosure agreements (NDAs) are contracts that prohibit employees from disclosing confidential information about their employer's business, operations, or proprietary data. They are often used to protect trade secrets and maintain competitive advantages. The enforceability of NDAs, particularly in the context of sexual harassment claims, has been subject to increased scrutiny and legislative changes. In addition to individual state limitations to NDAs, the federal Speak Out Act of 2022 limits the use of NDAs and non-disparagement clauses that aim to prevent individuals from disclosing allegations of sexual misconduct.

Advice of Counsel A clause advising the employee to seek legal counsel prior to signing the contract is often included.

Disability or Death The employer can include a clause that states what happens to the agreement in the event of the disability or death of the employee.

Termination Clause The termination clause sets forth conditions that would lead to a termination for cause, such as inability to perform, neglecting the duties of the position, misconduct, violations of company policy, or other egregious acts.

Change of Control A change of control clause protects the employee's job and compensation in the event of a reorganization, an acquisition, or a merger, for a specified period of time.

Candidates Not Selected

Another area rich with opportunity for HR improvement exists in handling candidates who have not been selected for hire. Strategic HR pros know that *how* candidates are notified that they have not been selected can leave only one of two impressions—positive or negative. For this reason, it is an HR best practice to notify the "no" candidates as soon as possible in a professional manner. This can be in accordance with how far the candidate has progressed through the process. For example, an email to a candidate whose résumé was received but who a company declined to interview would be reasonable. However, for a candidate who got through the entire interview process but was not selected, a personal phone call from the recruiter would be more appropriate.

Additionally, in a tight labor market, an organization may make an offer to a candidate who accepts and then—for a variety of reasons—decides to renege on the acceptance, leaving HR to make the offer to the next most qualified person. If the next qualified candidate was treated rudely, or ignored for a period of time, they may be unmotivated to accept the offer, leaving HR to begin the process anew.

Post-Offer Employment Activities

When the offer has been accepted, the transition from candidate to employee begins. At this stage, employees form their first impressions about what it will be like to work in the organization. During this time, employers can take steps to begin the relationship positively by including employees in special events that may be scheduled prior to their first day, and providing them with information that will help them become productive more quickly and begin assimilating into the work group.

Relocation Practices

In some circumstances, employers may be willing to pay the costs of relocating an employee or an applicant. When that occurs, HR may manage the process. Elements of relocation packages that can be negotiated include a company-paid trip for the spouse and family to see the area and look for a new home, assistance with selling the old and/or purchasing the new home, payment of moving expenses, assistance with a job search for the spouse in the new area, and a guarantee of the sale price of the old house if it doesn't sell.

Relocation is an activity that lends itself to outsourcing. Some organizations contract with moving companies that include relocation assistance as part of the moving package, and there are also professional organizations that manage the entire process for the organization and the family. These companies can provide property-management services, home inspections, real estate attorneys or title companies, home appraisals, moving companies, and, in some cases, corporate living situations for short-term job assignments. This can be a cost-effective solution that saves time for in-house staff.

Immigration Processes

In 2003, enforcement responsibility for the Immigration and Nationality Act (INA) of 1952 and its amendments was transferred to the U.S. Citizenship and Immigration Services (USCIS), an agency of the Department of Homeland Security. The INA and its amendments control immigration policy for the United States established by the following:

INA of 1952 and Amendment of 1965 The purpose of the INA was to simplify the multiple laws that previously governed U.S. immigration policy. As established by previous legislation, immigration quotas continued to be set on the basis of national origin.

Following the trend of equal opportunity established by the Civil Rights Act of 1964, the 1965 amendment eliminated national origin, race, and ancestry as bars to immigration and changed the allocation of immigrant visas to a first-come, first-served basis. The amendment also established seven immigration categories with the goals of reunifying families and giving preference to those with specialty skills that were needed in the United States.

Immigration Reform and Control Act (IRCA) of 1986 IRCA was enacted in 1986 to address illegal immigration into the United States. The law applied to businesses with four or more employees and made it illegal to knowingly hire or continue to employ individuals who weren't legally authorized to work in the United States. Unfair immigration-related employment practices were defined as discrimination on the basis of national origin or citizenship status.

Employers are required to complete Form I-9 for all new hires within the first 3 days of employment and to review documents provided by the employee that establish identity or employment authorization or both from lists of acceptable documents on the Form I-9. IRCA requires employers to maintain I-9 files for 3 years from the date of hire or 1 year after the date of termination, whichever is later, and allows, but doesn't require, employers to copy documents presented for employment eligibility for purposes of complying with these requirements. The act also provides that employers complying in good faith with these requirements have an affirmative defense to inadvertently hiring an unauthorized alien. Substantial fines for violations of both the hiring and recordkeeping requirements were provided in the law. In 2023, increased fines took effect. Paperwork violations (including failure to complete or retain forms) may result in a penalty of $252 to $2,507 (as of April 2023) for each violation. In addition, for penalties assessed for missing or incomplete I-9 forms, IRCA established fines for unauthorized employees.

U.S. immigration law is enforced by the Department of Homeland Security (DHS). It is considered a criminal act to bring undocumented immigrants into the United States, transport them within the country, harbor them, encourage them to enter the U.S. unlawfully, engage in conspiracy, aid, or abet such activities, and knowingly hire undocumented immigrants. In addition to fines, the penalties range from 5 to 20 years imprisonment.

Until 2005, IRCA required employers to store Form I-9 on one of three types of media: paper, microfilm, or microfiche. Passage of HR 4306, which was signed into law by President George W. Bush, allows employers to store Form I-9 in PDF files or other electronic formats.

E-Verify E-Verify is a free service offered through the USCIS. It's a tool that helps employers comply with IRCA's requirement that employers must verify the identity and employment eligibility of new employees. The employer accesses E-Verify through the Internet, inputs basic information gleaned from the Form I-9, and receives a near-instant "employment authorized" or "tentative nonconfirmation" (TNC) reply from the website. The employer then prints the results. A TNC result gives the employee more information about the mismatch and a statement of that person's rights and responsibilities under the law. It's important to note that employers may not terminate employees for the initial TNC; it's only when they receive a final nonconfirmation that employers may terminate under E-Verify.

To get started in the program, employers must first enroll their company, sign a memorandum of understanding (MOU) reviewing their obligations and acknowledging their understanding of the terms of enrollment, and commit to using E-Verify for every new employee at the affected hiring site. Under federal law, employers may designate the use of E-Verify to certain locations, although this may be restricted under some state laws.

Electronic Storage of Records

Technology has influenced many HR practices, not the least of which is records retention. Before deciding to electronically store records, an HR professional must consider the specific regulatory requirements of the law(s) governing record retention, security, access, and legibility. A good example of the considerations for the electronic storage of records is given by the USCIS related to storing the Form I-9 electronically:

Instructions from the U.S. Citizen and Immigration Services

Employers may use a paper system, an electronic system, or a combination of paper and electronic systems to store Form I-9 records. An electronic storage system must:

- Establish reasonable controls to ensure the system's integrity, accuracy, and reliability;
- Establish reasonable controls designed to prevent and detect the unauthorized or accidental creation of, addition to, alteration of, deletion of, or deterioration of an electronically completed or stored Form I-9, including the electronic signature, if used;
- Have an inspection and quality assurance program that regularly evaluates the system and includes periodic checks of electronically stored Form I-9, including the electronic signature, if used;
- Include an indexing system that allows users to identify and retrieve records maintained in the system; and
- Have the ability to reproduce legible and readable paper copies.[1]

TIP

The USCIS provides several webinars designed to educate employers and employees about the E-Verify process. Visit their home page at `https://www.uscis.gov/portal/site/uscis` and follow the instructions to these free webinars.

[1] M-274 Handbook for Employers `https://www.uscis.gov/i-9-central/form-i-9-resources/handbook-for-employers-m-274`

Immigration Act of 1990 The Immigration Act of 1990 made several changes to IRCA, including adding the requirement that a prevailing wage be paid to H-1B immigrants to ensure that U.S. citizens didn't lose jobs to lower-paid immigrant workers. The act also restricted to 65,000 annually the number of immigrants allowed under the H-1B category and created additional categories for employment visas, as shown in Table 4.2. In 1996, the number and types of documents to prove identity and eligibility to work were reduced.

Illegal Immigration Reform and Immigrant Responsibility Act (IIRIRA) of 1996 This act reduced the number and types of documents allowable to prove identity, employment eligibility, or both in the hiring process and established pilot programs for verification of employment eligibility.

NOTE Visit www.uscis.gov and select the Legal Resources tab to view the full text of INA and its amendments.

TABLE 4.2 Employment visas

Visa	Classification
	Visas for Temporary Workers
H-1B	Specialty occupations, DoD workers, fashion models
H-1C	Nurses going to work for up to 3 years in health professional shortage areas
H-2A	Temporary agricultural worker
H-2B	Temporary worker: skilled and unskilled
H-3	Trainee
J-1	Visas for exchange visitors Visas for intracompany transfers
L-1A	Executive, managerial
L-1B	Specialized knowledge
L-2	Spouse or child of L-1
	Visas for Workers with Extraordinary Abilities
O-1	Extraordinary ability in sciences, arts, education, business, or athletics

TABLE 4.2 Employment visas *(continued)*

Visa	Classification
	Visas for Athletes and Entertainers
P-1	Individual or team athletes
P-1	Entertainment groups
P-2	Artists and entertainers in reciprocal exchange programs
P-3	Artists and entertainers in culturally unique programs
	Visas for Religious Workers
R-1	Religious workers
	Visas for NAFTA Workers
TN	Trade visas for Canadians and Mexicans

Employee Onboarding, Orientation, and Integration Programs

Once a new employee starts work, the processes of onboarding, orientation, and employee integration begin. While often used interchangeably, these three terms are distinct. *Onboarding* typically refers to the entire process of integrating a new employee into the organization, which includes *orientation* as well as broader aspects such as training, setting expectations, and providing resources for success. Orientation, on the other hand, specifically focuses on introducing new hires to the company policies, procedures, culture, and facilities during their initial days or weeks. *Employee integration* encompasses both onboarding and orientation but extends beyond to fostering connections between new employees and existing team members, facilitating socialization, and ensuring ongoing support for their adaptation and success within the organization. Note that the term "integration" is becoming more widely used that its predecessor, assimilation, (including in HRCI's exam content outline) in terms of diversity, equity, and inclusion (DEI) efforts. This is because the term integration emphasizes the value of diversity and inclusion rather than expecting individuals to conform to a dominant culture through assimilation.

Formal onboarding and orientation programs consist of two elements: a general introduction to the organization as a whole and a job-specific orientation. HR often is responsible for providing the organizational orientation, including information about the mission, goals, and values, and for answering general questions. The job-specific orientation is conducted or overseen by the hiring manager and provides information specific to the department and position, sets performance expectations, and ensures that the new hire knows where to go for assistance when needed. These programs are an important part of a new hire's introduction to the organization. In many organizations, daily events move so quickly that new employees are sometimes left to fend for themselves without understanding what they're supposed to do or how to get help when they need it. The onboarding and orientation programs help ensure that new employees have the support they need to be successful. HR helps to bridge the gap between the more administrative orientation activities to the more robust introduction that make up the activities of onboarding.

Employee Integration

Some studies show that new employees make the choice to stay or leave their company within the first 6 months of employment. This means that the early days of the job have a significant impact on employee retention. During the first 90 days of employment, employee integration activities encompass various components aimed at ensuring a smooth transition and fostering a sense of belonging. These may include introductions to key team members and stakeholders to facilitate networking and relationship-building. Regular check-ins with managers provide opportunities for feedback, clarification, and addressing any concerns. Encouraging participation in team meetings, collaborative projects, and social activities further promotes integration by fostering camaraderie and teamwork. Providing access to resources, support systems, and mentorship programs also plays a vital role in helping new employees establish themselves in their new role.

As with any successful HR program, scheduled follow-up to measure successful entry is an important component of the onboarding process. The most effective activities take place over an extended period of time with regularly scheduled follow-ups that provide opportunities to check in with the employee and provide support as needed.

Summary

Identifying, attracting, and employing talent requires several key human resource competencies. These competencies include workforce planning, the ability to recruit and select qualified employees, and management of the activities within the talent acquisition lifecycle. These competencies enable HR professionals to support organizational results within the domain of workforce planning and talent acquisition, ensuring alignment between organizational goals and the skills and capabilities of the workforce.

Identifying candidates who not only have the best KSAOs for the job but whose personal goals, ambitions, and qualities also complement the needs of the organization requires HR professionals to be keenly aware of the organization's strategic direction. Providing opportunities to all qualified candidates opens up the labor pool available to the organization and includes candidates with a great deal to offer who might not have been considered in the past.

An effective hiring process begins with using sources that produce a pool of candidates with diverse backgrounds who have the required KSAOs, continues with screening the candidates with a fair and equitable process designed to find the best match for the organization, and concludes by welcoming them with orientation programs that assist them in becoming productive members of the team.

Pre-offer activities involve crafting comprehensive job descriptions, sourcing candidates through various channels, conducting initial screenings and interviews, and assessing candidates' skills and cultural fit. Post-offer activities include extending job offers, conducting background checks and assessments, finalizing employment contracts, and facilitating the onboarding process to ensure a smooth transition for new hires into their roles within the organization. These activities collectively ensure that the talent acquisition process is thorough and efficient, and results in the successful integration of new employees into the company.

Exam Essentials

Understand the differences between workforce planning and the talent acquisition lifecycle. Workforce planning involves forecasting future personnel needs, aligning skills with organizational goals, and optimizing staffing levels. The talent acquisition lifecycle focuses on the recruitment, selection, and onboarding of individuals to fulfill immediate staffing needs. While workforce planning takes a strategic, long-term perspective, talent acquisition focuses on the tactical execution of hiring processes to meet current demands.

Be able to identify recruitment methods. Depending on the level of experience and skill being sought, there are a variety of methods to consider in the recruiting process. HR professionals must understand which methods will produce the candidates who are most appropriate to fill positions at different levels.

Be able to establish and implement selection procedures. Effective selection procedures help ensure that candidates selected for the organization meet all the job requirements. Interviewing, testing, realistic job previews, and assessment centers help organizations determine whether the candidate is the right fit for the job. Reference checks ensure that the candidate has performed successfully in previous positions.

Be able to conduct post-hire activities. HR activities conducted during the post-hire phase have implications for the long-term success of new hires. It's important to understand the ramifications of employment offers and ensure that the new employee has all the necessary information to be successful. An effective orientation will make new employees feel welcome, introduce them to the company, and provide information on company policies.

Review Questions

You can find the answers in Appendix A.

1. The marketing director needs to hire a replacement for the marketing coordinator, who is being promoted. The position has changed quite a bit since the last time the job was advertised, and the director is looking to HR to assist in redefining the job requirements so the recruiting process can begin. Which of the following would *not* be used in determining the job requirements?
   A. Job competencies
   B. Job description
   C. Job specifications
   D. Candidate profile

2. Which of the following is *not* a BFOQ?
   A. A synagogue hiring a new rabbi requires that the rabbi be Jewish.
   B. A lingerie catalog hires only female models.
   C. A retail store in a predominantly Asian neighborhood advertises for Asian clerks.
   D. A swimming club requires that the men's changing-room attendant be male.

3. The court case that identified adverse impact as an unlawful employment practice was which of the following?
   A. *Griggs v. Duke Power Co.*
   B. *Albemarle Paper v. Moody*
   C. *Washington v. Davis*
   D. *Taxman v. School Board of Piscataway*

4. To determine the numbers and types of jobs necessary to realize business goals, HR must assess the KSAOs available within the organization during a staffing needs analysis. What other factor is necessary to complete the assessment?
   A. The KSAOs needed to achieve future goals
   B. The tasks, duties, and responsibilities for the work
   C. The KSAOs available in the local labor market
   D. The organization's core competencies

5. Your New Orleans plant has an opening for a controller, and four candidates have been selected for interviews. Jack, the son of a plant employee, worked as an accountant for 2 years to put himself through the Wharton Business School and recently earned his MBA. Richard is a CPA with 8 years of experience in a public accounting firm. Susan also has a CPA and has worked as an accounting manager in the corporate office of a large corporation in the same industry. Jane does not have a CPA or MBA but has worked as controller of a smaller local competitor for 8 years. After interviewing all four candidates, the

general manager told you that he wants to hire Jack because he shows promise. You know from previous conversation with the general manager (GM) that he also worked his way through college. Which of the following biases could be influencing the GM's decision?

A. Knowledge-of-predictor

B. Halo effect

C. Similar-to-me

D. Gut feeling

6. Which of the following is an HR best practice when notifying candidates that they have not been selected for a job?

A. A standard email sent to all candidates not selected.

B. Personal phone calls to all those rejected for hire.

C. A hybrid approach depending on how far the candidate made it through the process.

D. It is not necessary to notify candidates that have not been selected for hire.

7. An employee applied for a current job opening in another department. Her supervisor is reluctant to make the recommendation. When pressed, you discovered that it was because the employee was particularly talented in her current role, and the manager did not want to have to replace her. How should you address the issue?

A. Allow the employee to go through the application process just like all other candidates.

B. Promote the employee if she is truly qualified.

C. Respect the manager's concern and do not promote the employee.

D. Discipline the supervisor for holding an employee back.

8. Which of the following is *not* required by IRCA?

A. That an I-9 form be completed for all new hires within 3 days of hire

B. That employers comply with IRCA in good faith

C. That I-9 forms be maintained for all employees

D. That copies of documents presented for employment eligibility be maintained

9. In a self-audit of your employee's I-9 forms, several errors were found. These errors included incomplete sections, questionable documents accepted for verification, and over-documentation. Of the following corrective and prevention strategies, which should you recommend to your employer?

A. Training for employees

B. Recertification of all I-9 forms

C. Enrollment in E-Verify

D. Requesting updated documents from affected employees

10. Electronic storage of records must include specific controls to ensure which of the following?
    A. Online retrievability on demand
    B. No unauthorized access
    C. Ease of use
    D. Collaboration with an HRIS
11. When is job bidding an appropriate HR activity? (Choose all that apply.)
    A. For highly competitive jobs
    B. When the company wants to promote from within
    C. To create a pipeline of future candidates for a specific role
    D. To measure interest in various roles
12. Which of the following is a requirement of the Uniform Guidelines on employee selection procedures?
    A. Any selection tool that results in discrimination based on a protected class characteristic is unlawful.
    B. All selection tools must be job-related and valid predictors of future success.
    C. Application forms must be the same for all employment classifications within the organization.
    D. Internet recruiting efforts are excluded from applicant-tracking requirements.
13. Within the first 90 days of his employment, a security guard physically assaulted an alleged shoplifter. Upon investigation, it was found that he had been previously convicted of a violent crime, but the employer failed to conduct a background check. This is an example of which of the following?
    A. A violation of the Privacy Act of 1974
    B. Negligent hiring
    C. Failure to report
    D. A criminal act
14. What is the primary purpose of conducting a skills inventory?
    A. To analyze jobs for core competencies
    B. To develop a legally compliant workforce plan
    C. To identify skills redundancies in a merger or acquisition
    D. To assess talent to use in a gap analysis
15. Professionals, craft workers, and laborers/helpers have what in common?
    A. They are all job categories on the EEO-1 report.
    B. They are all classifications for defining exempt workers.
    C. They are all examples of types of labor unions.
    D. They are all examples of protected-class individuals.

16. Which of the following definitions is correct for the term *job bidding*?
   A. An internal job announcement
   B. Allowing contractors to submit requests for proposals
   C. The means by which internal employees can express interest in a job prior to it becoming available
   D. Ranking job applicants based on their comparative qualifications

17. Which of the following interview questions is unlawful?
   A. Are you willing to relocate?
   B. Are you a U.S. citizen?
   C. Tell me about a time you disagreed with your boss about a course of action.
   D. Any job offer made will be contingent on a medical exam. Are you willing to undergo one if we offer you the job?

18. Which of the following statements best describes a contingent job offer?
   A. A job offer that is unconditional and guaranteed
   B. A job offer that is subject to successful completion of background checks or drug tests
   C. A job offer that is open-ended with no specified start date
   D. A job offer that is contingent upon the candidate's acceptance of a lower salary than originally discussed

19. Which of the following best describes talent pools?
   A. Talent pools refer to groups of individuals with diverse skills and expertise who are actively seeking employment opportunities.
   B. Talent pools are exclusive networks of high-performing employees within an organization identified for promotion and career advancement.
   C. Talent pools encompass a database of passive candidates who possess specialized skills and are open to new job opportunities.
   D. Talent pools consist of individuals identified as potential candidates for future job openings based on their skills and qualifications.

20. The employment contracts for senior leaders include a clause that reads "Employee's stock options vest immediately upon acquisition of the company by another entity." This is the best example of which of the following types of employment contract clauses?
   A. Golden parachute
   B. Change of control
   C. Noncompete
   D. Benefits

Chapter 5

PHR | PHRi Exam: Learning and Development

PHR AND PHRi RESPONSIBILITIES:

CONTRIBUTING TO THE ORGANIZATION'S LEARNING AND DEVELOPMENT ACTIVITIES BY IMPLEMENTING AND EVALUATING PROGRAMS, PROVIDING INTERNAL CONSULTATION, AND PROVIDING DATA.

- ✓ **3.1 Implement and evaluate career development and training programs, including providing resources and guidance on professional growth and development opportunities (for example: career pathing, management training, mentorship, coaching, learning development plan)**
- ✓ **3.2 Contribute to succession planning discussions with management by understanding and providing relevant data (for example: compensation, performance, turnover, exit surveys, attrition, evaluations, skills assessments, skills development resources)**
- ✓ **3.3 Administer learning and development programs designed to achieve desired outcomes by the organization (for example: compliance, safety, benefits, HR systems and security, diversity, equity, and inclusion [DEI])**

Learning and Development (L&D) is the functional area of human resources that seeks to affect two types of behaviors: that of the employee and that of the company. This is so that the organization can achieve its goals through engaged and productive employees. This chapter looks at ways that organizations implement the changes necessary to accomplish their missions and the strategies they use to align employees with the vision, mission, and goals developed by their leaders. It includes a review of learning and development activities that support positive organizational and employee outcomes.

The PHR and PHRi (PHR/i) exams share the same responsibilities listed in the opening objectives. L&D activities are often driven by what the employer values, what they exist to "do," as well as by external forces such as customer needs or regulatory demands. Every organization makes determinations about these issues, whether consciously, as part of an organizational development (OD) process, or unconsciously, as a result of the way its people operate on a day-to-day basis. Effective organizations are those in which values and beliefs are shared at all levels and are reflected in the behavior of individuals throughout the organization.

Organizational Development

As introduced in Chapter 2, "Shared Competencies," organizational development (OD) is a systematic process aimed at improving organizational effectiveness and facilitating change within a company. It encompasses various strategies and techniques designed to enhance the organization's structure, culture, processes, and people. An *intervention* is a structured activity or set of activities designed to improve an organization's functioning. These activities can target individuals, groups, or the entire organization and are aimed at addressing specific problems, enhancing performance, or facilitating change.

OD interventions are developed by diagnosing organizational issues followed by intervention design and implementation, and then evaluation of outcomes. Examples of these planned interventions include the following activities:

- **Leadership Development Programs:** Initiatives aimed at developing leadership skills and competencies among key personnel to drive organizational change and strategic initiatives effectively.
- **Change Management Processes:** Strategies and frameworks designed to manage and facilitate transitions within the organization, such as mergers, acquisitions, restructuring, or technological advancements.

- **Performance Management Systems:** Tools and processes for setting goals, assessing performance, providing feedback, and aligning individual and team objectives with organizational goals.
- **Organizational Culture Initiatives:** Efforts to define, shape, and reinforce the values, beliefs, and behaviors that characterize the organization's culture, fostering alignment with strategic objectives.
- **Communication Strategies:** Plans and mechanisms for effectively communicating the organization's vision, goals, and initiatives to employees, stakeholders, and external partners, fostering alignment and engagement.
- **Process Improvement Initiatives:** Methodologies such as Lean Six Sigma, McKinsey 7S, or total quality management aimed at streamlining operations, enhancing efficiency, and driving continuous improvement throughout the organization.
- **Knowledge Management Systems:** Tools and practices for capturing, sharing, and leveraging organizational knowledge and expertise to support decision making and innovation.

PHR/i candidates should focus on the operational aspects of implementing these interventions. This means taking steps to translate strategic goals into practical actions, which usually involves enhancing efficiency and productivity.

Learning and Development Programs

HR professionals are responsible for developing and implementing several different types of training programs in the workplace. The exams specifically mention the following types of programs that successful candidates will be familiar with:

Compliance Training These programs ensure that employees understand and adhere to laws, regulations, and internal policies relevant to their roles, mitigating legal and financial risks for the organization. Examples include harassment prevention and environmental training (waste management, air resources, etc.).

Safety Training These are initiatives aimed at educating employees on workplace hazards, emergency procedures, and best practices to prevent accidents and injuries.

Benefits Training These are programs that provide employees with information and guidance on available employee benefits such as health insurance, retirement plans, and wellness programs.

HR Programs and Policies Training This training familiarizes employees with organizational HR policies, procedures, and practices, ensuring consistency and fairness in HR-related decision-making processes. Examples include code of conduct or training on the employee handbook.

Cybersecurity This is training that educates employees on best practices for safeguarding sensitive data, such as customer information and intellectual property, from unauthorized access or breaches.

Diversity, Equity, and Inclusion (DEI) Training DEI programs promote awareness, understanding, and respect for diverse perspectives and backgrounds, fostering a culture of inclusivity, fairness, and belonging within the workplace.

Career Development

At the heart of the practice of HR are several foundational knowledge components that should be understood regardless of which exam you have chosen to sit for. In the functional area of Learning and Development, Chapter 2, provided an in-depth review of two specific areas that are part of all six exams: career development and succession planning. For PHR/i candidates, it is helpful to look at these topics from an operational perspective.

By investing in career development initiatives, organizations can cultivate a pipeline of talented individuals with the skills, knowledge, and experience necessary to fill key leadership roles. This is the process of *succession planning*. Career development programs provide employees with opportunities for growth, skill enhancement, and advancement within the organization, thereby fostering a culture of internal talent mobility. As employees progress in their careers and acquire new competencies, they become better positioned to step into leadership roles when vacancies arise. Career development initiatives help organizations retain top talent by demonstrating a commitment to employee growth and advancement, reducing turnover and mitigating the risk of critical skill gaps.

Upskilling refers to the process of acquiring new skills or enhancing existing ones to adapt to changes in job roles, technologies, or industry trends. It involves providing employees with training and development opportunities that enable them to perform their current roles more effectively or prepare them for future responsibilities within the organization. Upskilling initiatives focus on building competencies that align with evolving job requirements, such as digital literacy, data analysis, or project management skills, to enhance employee performance, productivity, and career growth prospects.

Reskilling involves retraining employees to transition into entirely new roles or functions within the organization or in response to shifts in industry demands or technological advancements. Reskilling initiatives aim to equip employees with the skills and knowledge needed to thrive in different job roles or industries, often requiring significant changes in job responsibilities or career paths. Reskilling programs may focus on teaching employees new technical skills, soft skills, or domain-specific knowledge to enable successful career transitions and address emerging talent needs within the organization. Overall, both upskilling and reskilling play important roles in supporting employee development, organizational agility, and market competitiveness.

HR teams must be proficient at analyzing workforce data comprehensively and translating it into actionable insights for career development and succession plans. This entails not only understanding the current skill sets and performance levels of employees but also forecasting future talent needs based on organizational goals and growth projections. HR teams must adeptly utilize HRISs (human resources information systems) and other data analytics tools to gather, organize, and interpret relevant workforce metrics. Effective succession planning requires HR professionals to identify high-potential employees, assess their readiness for advancement, and develop targeted talent development initiatives to groom them for future leadership roles.

Skill development can be pursued through a variety of resources tailored to individual learning preferences and goals. Online courses and e-learning platforms offer flexible options, enabling self-paced learning on a wide range of topics. Books and industry publications provide in-depth knowledge and insights, serving as valuable self-study resources. Workshops, seminars, and webinars offer interactive learning experiences facilitated by experts, while mentoring and coaching provide personalized guidance and support. On-the-job training, shadowing, and professional certifications offer practical experience and industry recognition. Networking within professional associations provides opportunities for knowledge sharing and skill exchange. Many organizations take a partnership approach to employee development, and this requires robust training program management.

Employee Training Programs

Training in the context of learning and development refers to the systematic process of improving employees' skills, knowledge, and competencies to enhance their job performance and, thus, organizational results. It is a form of an individual intervention. Training is an effective tool for improving productivity and increasing operational efficiency, but it isn't the answer to every organizational problem. Training can solve problems related to employee skills or knowledge about a specific process, but it can't solve problems caused by structural or system issues. Before developing a training program, it's important to find out what is causing the problem and whether training is the appropriate solution.

For example, if customer service representatives are expected to handle an average of 20 calls per hour and they're handling an average of 12, it's important to find out why. One possibility is that the CSRs aren't familiar enough with the products to answer the questions easily, so they must look up answers in a manual. Another possibility is that the call volume has tripled since the call center phone system was installed and it can no longer handle the load, so it's frequently offline. The first possibility can be resolved with training, but the second can't.

Training may take place at one of the following three levels:

Organizational *Organizational-level training* may encompass the entire organization or a single division or department. At this level, training is focused on preparing for future needs. Analyzing indicators that suggest a decline in the effectiveness of organizational operations can indicate the need for a training intervention. Some indicators that training is needed could include an increase in the number of accidents, a change in strategic direction, or the addition of a new product line. Metrics indicating a negative trend, such as a decline in employee satisfaction or productivity measures, are indicators that training is needed at this level.

Task *Task-level training* involves processes performed in a single job category. The need for training at this level may be indicated by low productivity for a single process or poor-quality results.

Individual *Individual-level training* involves a review of performance by individual employees and can be indicated by poor performance reviews or requests for assistance by the employee.

Employee training programs have many facets and approaches. The following sections will explore special issues with training decentralized teams, adult learning processes, learning and development programs, instructional design models, artificial intelligence, and learning management systems.

Decentralized Team Training

A *decentralized team* is a group of individuals who work remotely or across different locations, collaborating and communicating virtually to achieve common goals and objectives. Managing the performance of decentralized teams requires a strategic approach to ensure alignment with organizational goals and effective collaboration among team members. Communication plays a crucial role in keeping team members informed, engaged, and accountable despite physical distance. Setting clear goals and expectations, establishing regular check-ins, and providing timely feedback are essential for maintaining performance standards. Leveraging technology tools for project management, communication, and performance tracking can streamline workflows and facilitate seamless collaboration across distributed teams. A learning management system (LMS) supports the management of decentralized teams' performance in several ways:

- **Centralized Learning Hub:** An LMS serves as a centralized platform where decentralized team members can access learning resources, training materials, and performance support tools from anywhere, at any time. This ensures consistent access to essential information and resources, regardless of geographic location.
- **Training and Development:** LMS platforms enable organizations to deliver training and development programs to decentralized teams efficiently. Through the LMS, team members can access e-learning courses, webinars, and virtual training sessions tailored to

their roles and learning needs. This helps ensure that team members receive consistent training and development opportunities, regardless of their physical location.

- **Performance Tracking and Reporting:** LMS platforms offer robust tracking and reporting features that allow managers to monitor the performance and progress of decentralized team members. Managers can track completion rates, assess quiz scores, and gather feedback on training activities to evaluate individual and team performance effectively. This data can inform performance reviews, identify areas for improvement, and support decision making related to training and development initiatives.
- **Collaboration and Communication:** Many LMS platforms include built-in communication and collaboration tools that facilitate interaction and engagement among decentralized team members. Features such as discussion forums, chat functionalities, and social learning capabilities enable team members to share knowledge, ask questions, and collaborate on projects in real time, regardless of their physical location.

Adult Learning Processes and Learning Styles

HR practitioners must have a foundational understanding of how adults learn as they approach the task of training design and development. The concept that adult learning processes were different from those of children was developed in the United States by Eduard Lindeman during the 1920s. Lindeman first promoted the idea that, for adults, the methods of learning were more important than what was being taught. His belief was that the most effective learning for adults took place in small groups where knowledge could be shared based on the life experience of the participants. Malcolm Knowles expanded on Lindeman's theories in the 1970s when he identified characteristics that set adult learning apart from the way children learn.

The work of Lindeman and Knowles is the basis for the study of how adults learn known as *andragogy*. The definition of andragogy evolved as researchers sought to further define adult learning; today it has come to mean education in which the learner participates in decisions about what will be taught and how it will be delivered. This approach is in contrast to *pedagogy*, the study of how children learn, which is defined as education in which the teacher decides what will be taught and how it will be delivered.

Much of Knowles's work centered on identifying characteristics of adult learning that would make the process more productive for learners. Knowles promoted the idea that, with maturity, people grow into new ways of learning, described by the following five characteristics, which form the basis of andragogy today:

Self-Concept An individual's self-concept moves from dependency on others to autonomy and self-direction.

Experience An individual builds a wealth of knowledge that grows with each new experience. This information reserve can then be drawn on for further learning.

Readiness to Learn Individuals become increasingly interested in the relevance of information to specific needs and how directly it applies to their current situations.

Orientation to Learning The ability to apply information immediately to solve current problems is increasingly important to learners.

Motivation to Learn The motivation to learn is based more on personal needs and desires than on expectations of others.

When designing training, you must consider adult learning styles, which answer the question, "How do I learn?" There are generally considered to be three types of learners:

Auditory *Auditory learners* process information by hearing. Individuals who are auditory learners will, for example, recite information out loud several times to memorize it.

Visual *Visual learners* depend on their visual processing of information. Often described as "thinking in pictures," these learners prefer visual tools such as outlines and graphs.

Tactile/Kinesthetic *Tactile/kinesthetic learners* are physical learners; they rely on their sense of touch for memory recall. These individuals are recognizable in training as the ones who periodically get up to stand in the back of the room or tap their fingers against the table during lectures.

Because all learning styles are represented in the workforce, it's important to incorporate elements of each style when designing training. Other factors to consider include the following:

- These styles are often innate; you can train employees to use multiple styles, but their default method of learning will often yield the best results.
- Trainers often unintentionally discriminate. They design training to their own personal learning style instead of accounting for the blended needs of their audience.
- The study of these categories of learning styles continues to evolve, via the use of music, logic, videos, virtual reality, pictures, and simulation.

TIP

Several websites offer free or low-cost tools to inventory your personal learning characteristics. Go online to discover your learning style, and then use the results to create your study plan for the PHR/i exams.

These basic characteristics of adult learners are important concepts with implications beyond traditional training and development. Learning is, of course, the point of training, so understanding the best ways to provide information in work situations can enhance productivity and job satisfaction for the workforce.

Instructional Design Models

Although development programs address long-term organizational needs, training programs are designed to address short-term needs. Training activities are more technical in nature and include such topics as new-hire orientation, safety, and skill development, among others. This section will examine the ADDIE model in depth and then will explore several other models.

The ADDIE Model

The design and development of training programs follows an instructional design model known as the *ADDIE model*. ADDIE is an acronym that describes the five elements of instructional design:

- Analysis
- Design
- Development
- Implementation
- Evaluation

The ADDIE model is discussed here in the context of training at the task level, but the principles of the model can be used to develop training programs at the organizational or individual level as well.

Training needs are often identified by managers who notice a problem in their departments and determine that training is needed to correct it. This determination may be based on a drop in the production rate, installation of new machinery or equipment, or the addition of a new line of business. Once the need for training has been identified, a needs assessment determines whether training will solve the problem and, if it will, proposes possible solutions.

Analysis

Figure 5.1 demonstrates how a needs assessment model can be used in assessing training needs. Using the model, the following process will provide the information to determine what type of training is necessary to solve the problem:

1. Identify the goal. The needs assessment begins by identifying the desired outcome. In the preceding example, the customer service manager determined that the CSRs should handle an average of 20 calls per hour, which is the desired outcome. The desired outcome forms the basis for several other steps in the analysis process, including what data is collected, the identification of instructional goals, and development of solutions.

2. Gather and analyze data. Once you know the desired outcome, you can begin to collect relevant information that will be used to determine the cause of the problem. Information may be gathered in a number of ways from a variety of sources:

Review documents. Many types of documents can be used to gather information about training needs. These include measures of organizational effectiveness such as production records and records of customer complaints, a review of the human resource succession plan to determine what training is needed to prepare individuals for future needs based on skills inventories and performance-appraisal forms, and an analysis of the organizational climate based on HR metrics such as turnover rates and the results of exit interviews.

FIGURE 5.1 Training needs assessment model

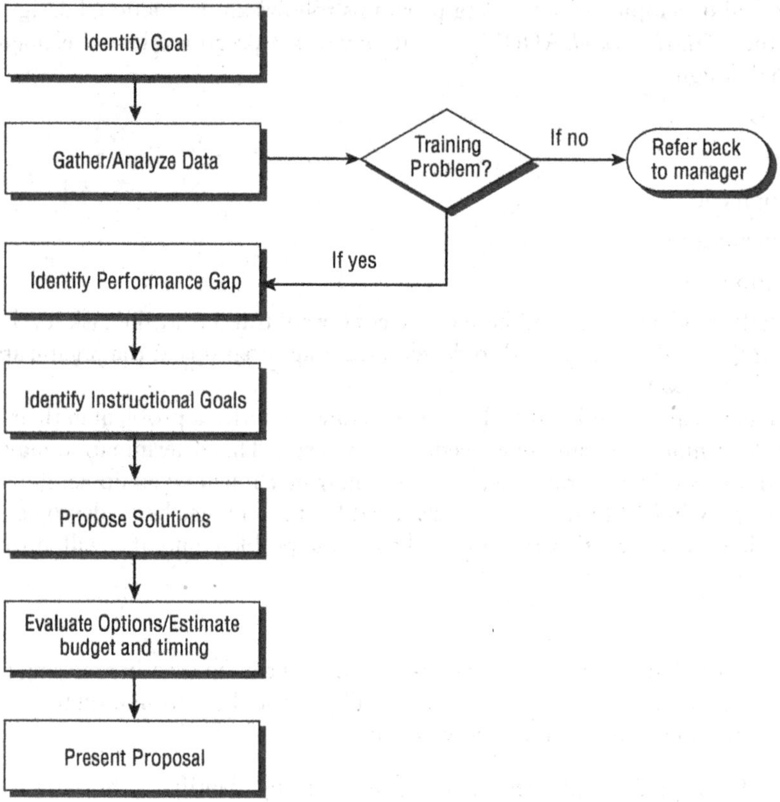

Access ISO standards. Industries such as healthcare, manufacturing, and human resources develop standards and best practices to guide organizational decision making. The ISO standards are internationally recognized guidelines and specifications developed by the International Organization for Standardization (ISO) to ensure quality, safety, efficiency, and interoperability of products, services, and systems across various industries.

Review labor law. Compliance with various labor laws often involves the training of supervisors and workers to the standards. For example, in establishing an affirmative defense against a sexual harassment claim, employers must demonstrate not only that they had a written policy, but that employees and supervisors were properly trained to the requirements. Understanding which labor laws apply to an employer is a necessary component to establishing both short- and long-term training needs.

Ask employees. Training often is a function of reaction: reacting to changing market demands, poor performance, or the demands of legal compliance. While all three of those examples are necessary to analyze when assessing training needs, it is also helpful to ask your employees what types of training or development opportunities would be most beneficial. Clearly defining the outcome is necessary in order to ensure the most relevant response from employees. When the data has been gathered and analyzed, a determination can be made as to whether training is the appropriate solution. If it is, the needs analysis continues; if not, L&D can report the results of the analysis to the requesting manager with a recommendation for an appropriate solution.

3. Identify the performance gap. Once all the data has been gathered, it's possible to compare where the organization is to where it wants to be. At this stage, the L&D professional begins to have a sense of the type of training that will be required.

4. Identify instructional goals. The performance gap is the starting point for identifying the corrections that need to be put into place.

5. Propose solutions. At this stage in the needs assessment, all possible means for filling the gap should be identified and considered to find the solution that best meets the organization's needs.

6. Evaluate options and estimate the budget impact and training timeline. Once a comprehensive list of possible solutions is available, it's possible to conduct a cost–benefit analysis to estimate the cost of implementing each of them and the benefits that will result from the training. It's important to include both direct and indirect costs associated with the program in the estimated budget. This includes the cost of the trainer, facility, preparation of materials, use of equipment, transportation, meals and lodging, wages and salaries of the participants for the time they spend training and in traveling to the training, lost production time due to the training, and incidental office support. It's also important to consider potential savings from increased productivity, reduced errors, higher product quality, and other similar gains that will result from the training and, finally, what it will cost the organization if the training doesn't occur.

At the same time, an estimate of the time required to implement the solution can be made.

7. Present findings. The result of the needs assessment is a proposal that describes the desired outcome, the current situation, and the gap between the two. The proposal should include as many alternative solutions as is feasible, with an estimate of the cost and time needed to implement each of them and L&D's recommended solution. Where possible, use infographics, charts, and graphs to illustrate data points and trends.

During the assessment phase, a key consideration is whether the program will be created internally, whether a prepackaged program will be used, or whether the process will be outsourced. These decisions are based on a variety of factors unique to every organization and include the size of the organization, the training expertise and availability of in-house staff, the uniqueness of the subject matter, and the availability of prepackaged programs on the topic. For example, sexual-harassment training may be best conducted by a trainer specializing in the subject matter who is able to answer in-depth legal questions and "what-if" scenarios. Conversely, a training program that is specific to a proprietary manufacturing process may be better developed in-house.

Design

When the appropriate decision makers concur that training is the appropriate solution for the problem, the design phase begins. During this phase of a training project, the program begins to take shape. The data gathered during the needs analysis phase will be useful in this stage as well:

1. Compile a task inventory. To complete the design process, the trainer must know what tasks are required for the job in question. A *task inventory* lists all tasks included in the job. Each task description should contain an action verb, an object, and a function; for example, "Answer phone to assist customers."

The inventory can be compiled from information collected during the needs-assessment process, or additional information can be acquired during the design phase. The inventory may also be gleaned from a job description if it was written as a result of a job analysis.

2. Identify the target audience. Knowing who will be attending the training will be of great use in designing a program that will keep the audience interested. Preparing a training program about the proper completion of expense reports for a group of middle managers from the accounting department will look very different from the same presentation to the salesforce.

In identifying the audience, it's important to keep in mind the three learning styles that impact an individual's ability to learn:

- Visual learners retain information better when they can see or read it.
- Auditory learners retain information more easily when they hear it.
- Kinesthetic learners retain information best when they're able to have a hands-on experience during training.

Incorporating elements of all three learning styles in a training program helps ensure that all individuals attending the program will benefit from the information presented.

3. Develop training objectives. *Training objectives* are statements that describe a measurable outcome of the training and are developed based on the target audience and task inventory. Objectives help the L&D professional during the development process and during implementation communicate to employees what they will learn. They're also useful during the evaluation phase to determine whether the training was successful.

A useful training objective is a precise description of what is to be accomplished in normal job circumstances. For example, a training program for carpenters may include a session on how to build straight walls. The objective begins with a description of a normal job situation, uses an action verb to describe a measurable behavior, describes the conditions under which the behavior will occur, and finally describes the criteria that will be used to measure the results. Here is an example of an objective that includes all these elements:

> Using the company's sales software, employees will be able to independently produce quarterly revenue reports, accurately compiling and submitting them within the specified deadline, while demonstrating a decrease in errors by at least 20 percent compared to previous reporting periods.

This objective leaves no doubt about what is to be accomplished and includes the basis for determining whether the training was successful.

4. Develop the course content. Based on the training objectives, the trainer can begin to design the course, identifying what material should be included to best prepare the attendees to take the information back to their jobs and begin using it immediately.

An important consideration for this aspect of training design is the learning curve associated with various subjects. A *learning curve* is a graphical representation of the rate of learning over time. Let's look at some examples of various learning curves:

> **Negatively Accelerating Learning Curve** A *negatively accelerating learning curve* is characterized by rapid increases in learning at the beginning that taper off as the learner becomes more familiar with the process or task. Negative learning curves are representative of routine tasks, such as operating a cash register. Figure 5.2 provides an example of this learning curve.

FIGURE 5.2 Negatively accelerating learning curve

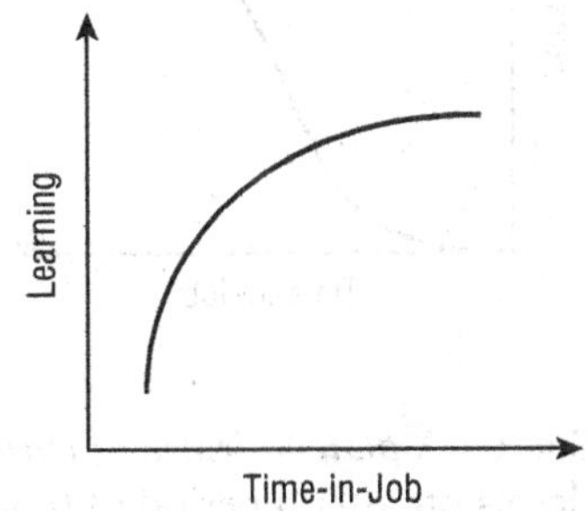

Positively Accelerating Learning Curve A *positively accelerating learning curve* is characterized by a slow start in learning that increases as the learner masters different aspects of the process or task. Positive learning curves are representative of tasks that are complex, such as a junior accountant learning to use an accounting software program. The accountant must first know basic accounting practices in order to become proficient in using the program. Figure 5.3 shows a positive learning curve.

FIGURE 5.3 Positively accelerating learning curve

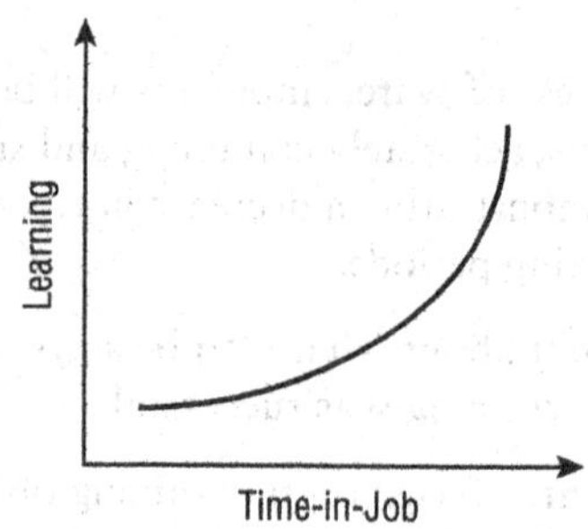

S-Shaped Learning Curve The *S-shaped learning curve* is a combination of positive and negative learning curves. It begins with a slow learning process that accelerates over time and then slows again. This learning pattern can be found in software-conversion projects. Learners must understand how the new system works before they're able to become as proficient at it as they were with the older system. Figure 5.4 is an example of an S-shaped learning curve.

FIGURE 5.4 S-shaped learning curve

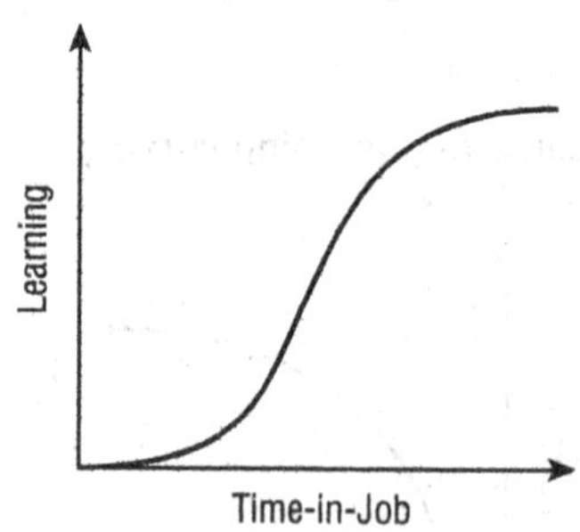

Plateau Learning Curve A *plateau learning curve* begins with a rapid increase in knowledge that levels off after a period of time, and no additional progress occurs for an extended period of time. A plateau curve might occur when an employee performs a task irregularly, not often enough to become proficient. Figure 5.5 shows a plateau learning curve.

FIGURE 5.5 Plateau learning curve

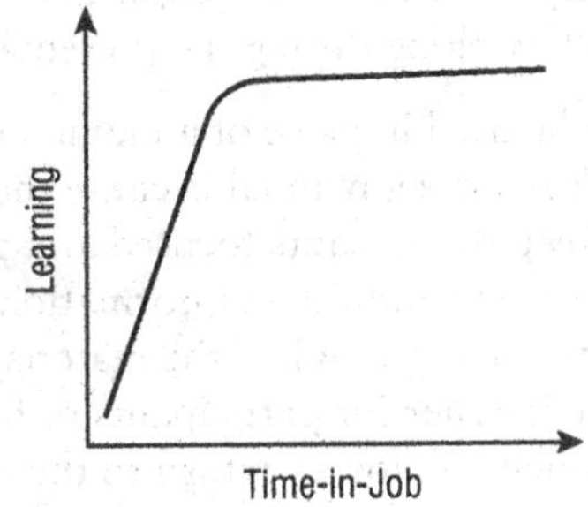

5. Develop evaluation criteria. Now is the time to develop the evaluation criteria for the program. The initial evaluation will be based on whether the trainees are able to perform the task described by the objective within the parameters that it sets forth. The real evaluation of training effectiveness is whether the trainees are able to maintain the level of proficiency that was developed during the training and improve operating results.

Development

During the training development phase, the program design is translated into the presentation format. The program developer creates a strategy for the presentation, deciding on the materials, instructional techniques, and program-delivery methods that will be used. The trainer may conduct a pilot presentation during this phase to work out the kinks and, if necessary, will revise the program based on the results of the pilot.

Training Materials

One of the activities occurring during the development phase of the training process is the collection of appropriate training materials. It's often tempting to use work created by others, particularly if the material is perfectly suited to the topic of the training. The two federal laws protecting the rights of writers, artists, and inventors with regard to unauthorized use of their original works, the Copyright Act of 1976 and the U.S. Patent Act, are discussed in Appendix C, "Federal Employment Legislation and Case Law."

Aside from considerations related to the use of copyrighted material, training materials created in the development phase should be appropriate to the subject matter and the needs of the participants. Some types of materials to consider include the following:

Leader Guide When more than one trainer will be presenting the training sessions, a leader guide ensures consistency in the presentations. These guides may provide notes to assist the trainer in presenting the material, timing information, and questions for use in facilitating discussion during the session. The guide provides a basic road map for the presentation.

Manuals Manuals can provide a reference to assist in reinforcing the information covered during the training session when participants return to their jobs. In addition to an agenda or a schedule, they can contain handouts and copies of slides for note-taking purposes as participants follow along during the presentation.

Handouts Handouts may be used in place of a manual or included with the manual. For presentations that don't require a manual because they're relatively straightforward, a handout can help keep participants focused and provide a place to take notes. In addition, handouts can provide additional information that isn't covered during the presentation but is related to the topic. When the material being covered is technical in nature, a handout can make it easier for participants to follow along and may also be used as a handy reference when employees return to their jobs.

Implementation

Implementation is the phase of training where all the preceding work comes together for the presentation. The trainer or facilitator sets up a program schedule, creates the agenda, and notifies participants about the training. At this time, it may be necessary to conduct "train the trainer" sessions to ensure that those who will implement the trainings are themselves fully trained to proceed.

The process begins with selection of the facility, setting the schedule and the trainers or facilitators:

Facility The facility selected for the training will depend on the type of training to be conducted, the number of participants attending, and the amount budgeted for the program. Although individual-level training may best be conducted at the employee's workstation, training for larger groups of people is best conducted away from the distractions of the workstation. A conference room at the worksite may provide an adequate training facility if the size of the group is small (or the room is large enough). It may be necessary for a variety of reasons to conduct the training off-site. Although the cost will be greater to rent a facility, the reduction of distractions may result in a more effective training experience with longer-lasting results.

Passive training that requires little more of participants than listening requires the least amount of space. More space is required for situations in which participants will be taking notes or practicing work activities. Figure 5.6 through Figure 5.11 depict some of the more common seating styles for trainings and the types of training for which each is most appropriate. Other factors such as lighting, temperature and background noise should also be considered to ensure the comfort of the participants and to minimize distractions from the learning content.

FIGURE 5.6 Theater-style seating

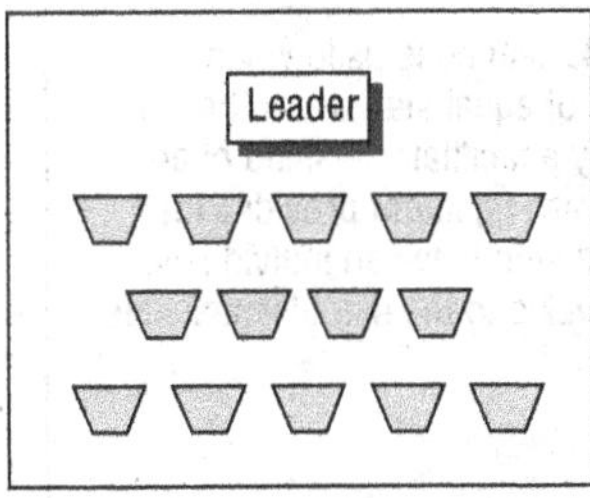

Theater-style seating is best for training when lectures, films, or video presentations are used. This seating style accommodates the largest number of people in any space.

FIGURE 5.7 Classroom-style seating

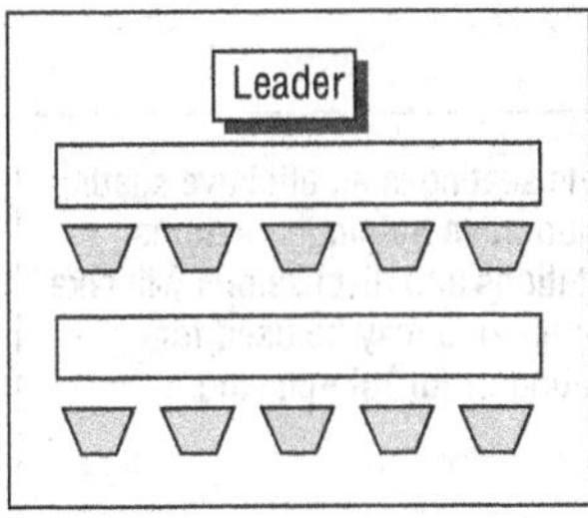

Classroom-style seating is best for training situations when participants will be listening to presentations, using manuals or handouts, and taking notes.

FIGURE 5.8 Banquet-style seating

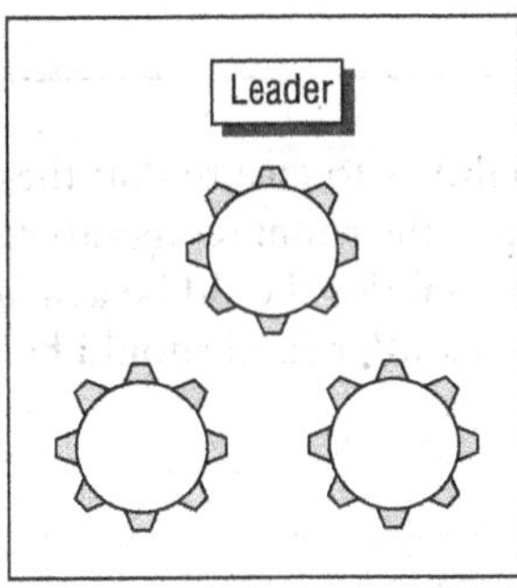

Banquet-style seating is best for training situations in which participants will be taking part in small group discussions and interacting with each other in addition to participating in activities as a single group.

FIGURE 5.9 Chevron-style seating

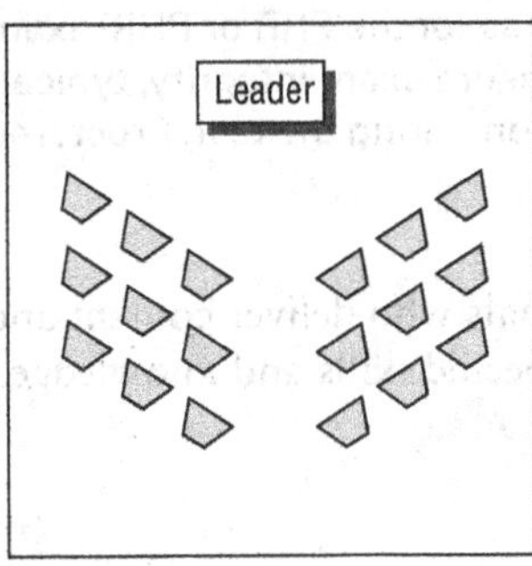

The chevron arrangement is appropriate for training situations in which participants will be interacting with the instructor and each other. This seating style is able to accommodate larger groups than some other seating styles. Useful for situations in which participants will be engaged in several activities: lectures, films, or video presentations, in addition to interacting with others in the room. Chevron-style seating can be used with tables or without, depending on the particular training and space available.

FIGURE 5.10 Conference-style seating

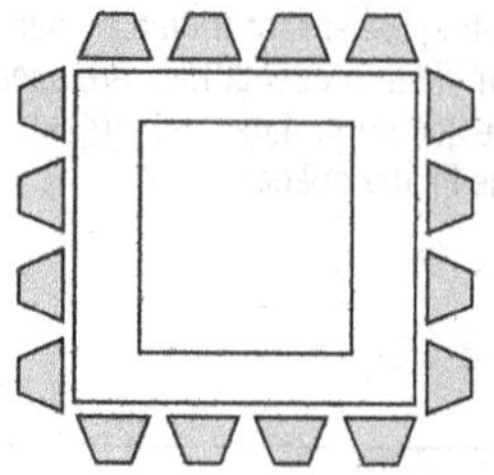

Conference-style seating is used when participants are of equal status and the training is led by a facilitator instead of an instructor. This arrangement provides for maximum interaction between individuals, but is not conducive to the use of visual aids.

FIGURE 5.11 U-shaped-style seating

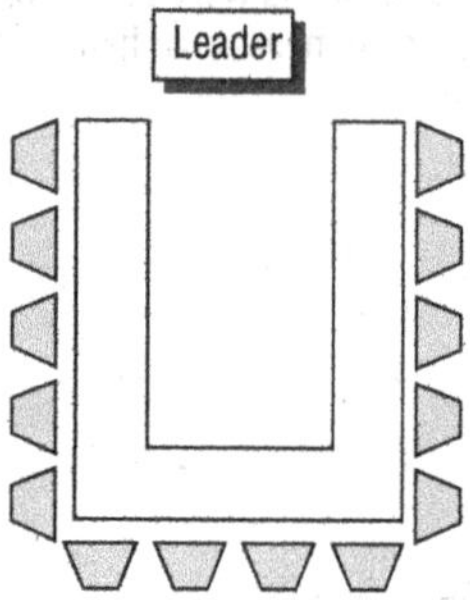

U-shaped-style seating is an effective seating style for collaborative training situations when presentations and discussions will take place. The center area may be used for additional seating or for role-playing.

Another very important step in preparing the facility is to ensure that the physical environment is conducive to learning. For example, the room temperature should be comfortable for most people, sufficient restroom facilities should be available to accommodate the number of participants, and beverages and/or food should be available as appropriate.

> **NOTE** Live training involves real-time interaction with instructors and peers, offering immediate feedback and the opportunity for dynamic discussions between the instructor, students, and other participants. Proctored training or certification testing, such as for the PHR or PHRi exam, provides a monitored environment to ensure exam integrity, typically with stricter controls and limited interaction during the test. Proctored training can be live or virtual.

Trainers and Facilitators Trainers are professionals who deliver content and instruction to individuals or groups to develop specific skills and knowledge. Trainers may be selected based on their mastery of the subject matter or for their ability and skill in training. This decision will be based largely on the nature of the training being conducted.

Facilitators are individuals who guide groups through processes to ensure effective collaboration and problem-solving. Unlike trainers, who primarily focus on delivering content and teaching specific skills, facilitators emphasize creating an environment that encourages participation, communication, and collective decision making among group members.

Schedule The training schedule is affected by many factors, including the feasibility of shutting down operations entirely for the length of the training session so that all employees are trained at the same time or whether it's more cost-effective to conduct multiple sessions in order to maintain operations. Sessions may need to be broken into segments and scheduled over a period of days or weeks to accommodate operational needs.

The selection of program-delivery mechanisms and instructional methods for various types of training needs are related to the size of the group, type of training needed, and geographic location of the participants.

Evaluation

Training evaluation occurs both before and after the training takes place and is based on criteria established in the assessment phase. The ultimate goal of the training is to improve performance on the job. This is known as *transfer of training*, and it takes place when learning occurs away from the regular work environment and must then be applied to the real job situation.

It's obviously important that the investment made in training employees provides a return in increased productivity, quality, or safety (whatever the subject of the training) on the job. A failure of training to transfer to the job can occur when the new skill isn't applied in the work environment and therefore isn't reinforced. A technique that can overcome this problem is the development of an action plan to be implemented after training. This approach requires trainees to visualize and describe how they plan to apply the training when they're back on the job so they're more likely to use their new skills. An effective evaluation will include provisions for measuring job performance for a period of time after the training has been completed to ensure that the new skills have been transferred to the job.

Formative Evaluation

Formative evaluation is a process used in the design phase of training. It involves testing or previewing the content prior to final delivery to ensure that it will result in the desired behaviors. Designed primarily to elicit feedback from participants, it's a useful tool when used to modify design elements and content prior to the actual delivery. Formative evaluations are designed to identify what the participants want, know, and need. Examples of strategies used in the formative evaluation process include the following:

Needs Assessment This is a review of who needs the program, what elements must be addressed, and the best method of delivering the message. Asking potential participants for their wants and needs will help to ensure a program designed toward effective transfer of training.

Asking People There are many methods for gathering information from people, including observations; interviews with employees, supervisors, or subject matter experts (SMEs); attitude surveys; questionnaires; focus groups; and advisory committees. See Chapter 2 for more information on these techniques.

Analyzing Jobs In some cases, it may be necessary to conduct a full job analysis to determine where training is needed.

Pilot Test Pilot tests are used once the training design and content have been developed. They involve a focus group of participants used to evaluate the relevance of the content and delivery methods to the stated training objectives, followed up by their feedback and influence on the final delivery.

Pretest A pretest can be used to measure participant knowledge prior to the design of the training. In addition to content-specific questions, it should also ask for feedback related to "the muddiest point"—the content that seems most unclear to the end user. Other options for testing employee knowledge include assessment centers, knowledge tests to measure what people know, and practical tests to determine whether they're able to apply what they know.

Summative Evaluation

A common model for summative training evaluation was developed by Donald Kirkpatrick. He proposed four levels of evaluation for training programs: reaction, learning, behavior, and results. Measurements at each level are based on the objectives developed during the design phase:

Reaction The *reaction evaluation method* measures the initial reaction of the participants. This is most commonly determined by a survey completed by participants at the end of the training. Although this level of evaluation doesn't measure the organization impact, it does provide feedback for the trainer in terms of the presentation of the information.

Learning The *learning evaluation method* uses a test to measure whether the participants learned the information that was presented. Although this level of evaluation provides more information about the effectiveness of the training, it still doesn't provide feedback about the application of the information on the job.

In some cases, learning evaluation uses an experimental design known as the *pretest/posttest comparison*:

1. A group of employees is selected for training.
2. The employees are randomly assigned to two different groups.
3. An identical pretest is administered to both groups of employees.
4. One group receives the training, also known as a *treatment*.
5. An identical posttest is administered to both groups of employees.
6. The results are compared to see whether the training resulted in improved performance.

Behavior The behavior evaluation method attempts to measure the behavioral changes that occurred as a direct result of the training. It is often viewed as an attempt to measure the successful application of the new knowledge. This category includes the introduction of new processes or systems that help trainees apply the knowledge.

Results The results evaluation method measures the impact training had on the initial training targets. Because training initiatives are often looked at as investments in future results, many organizations focus this level of training evaluation solely on the final outcomes. However, HR can support positive outcomes by tracking shorter-term milestones as predictors of results. In this way, HR may intervene and adapt where necessary.

The pretest/posttest comparison is appropriate when an organization wants to isolate the impact of training on productivity. To make a legitimate comparison, all other factors that could affect performance must be equalized. For example, all employees in the group should have similar KSAs, be using similar equipment, and have access to similar resources. If other factors are dissimilar, it isn't possible to isolate the training impact on performance. Dr. Kirkpatrick's family has continued his legacy by continually refining his original work to remain relevant. You can visit the website at `www.kirkpatrickpartners.com` to learn more about this training evaluation standard.

Other Instructional Design Models

While ADDIE continues to be used in many organizations today, there are a few other more project-oriented instructional design tools. They include the following:

Agile The Agile (align, get set, iterate and implement, leverage, and evaluate) methodology is used to accomplish "content chunking," a concept that seeks to break up large amounts of training content into more manageable modules. Whereas the ADDIE model is applied to entire training programs, the Agile model will be used repeatedly to build out training content in silos, rather than once in a whole piece.

Scrum The Scrum instructional design model, rooted in Agile principles, guides the development of learning solutions through collaboration and flexibility. Key to this model is the idea that the development process should be *iterative*, which means developing and refining a product or solution through a series of incremental cycles or iterations. Teams engage in sprint planning to define objectives, identify content needs, and prioritize tasks for the upcoming sprint. Daily stand-up meetings facilitate progress check-ins and adjustments. At the end of each sprint, a review session gathers stakeholder feedback and refines plans for subsequent iterations. Ongoing backlog refinement ensures tasks align with evolving needs. The iterative approach allows for incremental development, enabling rapid prototyping, testing, and refinement to meet learner objectives.

SAM The Successive Approximation Model (SAM) is an instructional design technique that relies on repetition and collaboration. Designers engage in a collaborative cyclical design process that begins with analyzing the training needs and gathering information, designing the project plan and brainstorming for input, and then developing the content with real-time changes as identified.

Instructional Methods

You can choose from a variety of instructional methods when designing a training program, and selecting the appropriate one for a given situation can add to the success of the training.

Passive Training Methods

Passive training methods are those in which the learner listens to and absorbs information. These methods are instructor-focused and require little or no active participation from the learner:

Lecture *Lectures* are used to inform and to answer questions, often in combination with other training methods such as demonstrations.

Presentation A *presentation* provides the same information to a group of people at one time.

Conference *Conferences* are generally a combination of lecture or presentation with question-and-answer sessions involving the participants.

Active Training Methods

Active training methods are those in which the learning experience focuses on the learner:

Facilitation *Facilitation* is a moderated learning situation led by a facilitator who leads a group to share ideas and solve problems. Facilitators generally have skills in moderating group discussions and may be experts in the subject of discussion.

Case Study A *case study* reproduces a realistic situation that provides learners with the opportunity to analyze the circumstances as though they were encountered in the course of business. Case studies let learners investigate, study, and analyze the situation and then discuss possible solutions with the group. Solutions are developed and presented to fellow learners.

Simulation *Simulation training* is an interactive training method that provides the learner with opportunities to try new skills or practice procedures in a setting that doesn't endanger the inexperienced trainee, coworkers, or the public.

Vestibule *Vestibule training* is a form of the simulation method. It allows inexperienced workers to become familiar with and gain experience using equipment that either is hazardous or requires a level of speed that can be attained only with practice. Vestibule training is commonly used to train equipment operators in the construction industry and to help retail clerks gain speed at the checkout counter.

Socratic Seminar *Socratic seminars* are based on the method of instruction used by the Greek philosopher Socrates in which ideas are examined in a question-and-answer format. A question may be posed by the seminar leader at the beginning of the seminar and discussed by participants to gain a full understanding of the topic.

Experiential Training Methods

Experiential training methods provide experience in real-time situations:

Demonstration The *demonstration* method of training can be used as part of an on-the-job training program or combined with a lecture program. The method involves the trainer explaining the process or operation, demonstrating it on the equipment, and then having the learner perform it under the guidance of the trainer.

One-on-One In *one-on-one training*, an inexperienced worker is paired with an experienced supervisor or coworker who uses a variety of techniques to provide the worker with the information and hands-on experience necessary to do the job.

Performance *Performance-based training (PBT)* is most often used to correct performance problems in highly technical or hazardous professions. The trainee is provided with opportunities to practice and demonstrate the necessary skill or knowledge until the required level of proficiency is mastered.

Program Delivery Mechanisms

Devising suitable delivery methods for training programs is subject to a number of factors, including what information is to be covered, who will be attending the training, the experience level of the participants, the availability of technology, and so on:

Classroom Classroom training provides the same content to a group of employees in a classroom setting. It's effective for small groups when providing the same information to everyone in the group.

Self-Study A program of self-study is directed entirely by the learner, who determines what, when, and where learning will occur. It may be based on a defined program and involve a trainer or mentor, but it's controlled by the learner.

Programmed Instruction *Programmed instruction*, also referred to as *self-paced training*, is the forerunner of computer-based training (CBT). In this method, the learner progresses from lesson to lesson in a predesigned course of instruction as mastery of the objectives is attained. This method allows learners to progress at their own rate. Programmed instruction is effective for disseminating facts and concepts, refreshing previously learned skills, or expanding a learner's knowledge in a field that is already familiar.

Virtual Training (VT) Deciding whether to conduct training in a classroom setting through the use of virtual tools or use the tried and true on-the-job training (OJT) is one of the first steps taken in training design. In response to the advance of technology and the generational preferences of the emerging workforce, virtual learning is evolving into a viable method for training delivery.

The virtual classroom has grown in importance in many areas, not the least of which has been in the application of training. As one technique in the category of electronic learning (e-learning), virtual classrooms or virtual reality systems are gaining in popularity despite their expense. Other e-learning tools include web-based training (WBT), CBT, self-directed learning (SDL), mobile learning (m-learning), videoconferencing, simulation, multimedia and social networking sites, and discussion boards. These techniques can be *synchronous* (occurring at the same time with the instructor) or *asynchronous* (self-paced), depending on the content, the training goals, and an analysis of training barriers.

Real World Scenario

Mixed Reality Methods

Mixed reality (MR) is another method being used by employers to enhance their training methods. Microsoft has been at the forefront of this technology with their HoloLens 2, which integrates MR into various industries for training and operational improvements.

For example, in healthcare, the HoloLens 2 allows medical professionals to connect with remote experts and access 3D patient data, enhancing the quality of care and training efficiency. This technology provides holographic instructions that guide users through complex procedures, which has significantly reduced training time and improved skill acquisition.

See more at `www.microsoft.com/en-us/hololens`.

Other companies are contributing in this space as well. The Meta Quest 3, for example, features groundbreaking Meta Reality technology and high-fidelity color passthrough, allowing users to seamlessly blend virtual elements with their physical environment. This enhanced capability enables businesses to create lifelike training scenarios that improve skill acquisition and efficiency. Learn more about this emerging technology at `www.xrtoday.com/mixed-reality/luminous-ports-vr-training-on-meta-quest-3-amid-1m-fundraiser`.

E-learning encompasses several types of electronically based training delivery systems that are generally cost-effective, self-directed methods for training employees:

Electronic Performance Support Systems An electronic performance support system (EPSS) is a training tool integrated in the computer system used by employees on the job. It allows instant access to information that helps them complete tasks more effectively.

Computer-Based Training *Computer-based training (CBT)* is an interactive training method that combines elements of the lecture, demonstration, one-on-one, and simulation methods, thus allowing the learner to have a real-world learning experience. Well-designed CBT programs ensure consistency of training across a company that is geographically dispersed. CBT is based on the programmed instruction method.

Distance Learning Sometimes referred to as a *virtual classroom*, this is similar to lectures and allows simultaneous training to occur in geographically dispersed multiple locations. *Distance learning* provides participants with the ability to communicate with presenters and participants at other locations.

Microlearning Microlearning is characterized by short bursts of information, mostly in the form of online videos. This method is a highly efficient way to deliver narrowly tailored content to users. It is also more easily updated, as shorter videos have less to edit/refine than longer, mixed-content series.

Blended Learning Blended learning uses multiple delivery methods to enhance the learning experience. The term is currently used to describe different ways of combining delivery methods, such as multiple web-based learning methods, a combination of instructor-led delivery with some form of technology, or combining learning technology with the performance of actual job tasks.

Online Bulletin Boards Online bulletin boards allow trainees to post questions and share information with one another. They may be supervised or facilitated by a leader who is knowledgeable in the subject matter and acts as a resource for the participants.

The Association for Talent Development (ATD) reports that U.S. companies spend billions of dollars on self-paced e-learning. For the human resource professional, this means the ability to demonstrate the return on investment for e-learning initiatives such as VT is a critical stage in the development of strategic training solutions.

Artificial Intelligence in Training

AI, or artificial intelligence, refers to the simulation of human intelligence processes by machines, typically characterized by the ability to learn from data, recognize patterns, make decisions, and solve problems autonomously. HR teams can leverage AI to enhance learning and development activities in several ways. AI-powered personalized learning paths can be tailored to individual employee needs by analyzing performance data, skills gaps, and learning preferences. This ensures that employees receive relevant training aligned with their roles and career aspirations.

AI-driven adaptive learning platforms are also able to dynamically adjust content delivery and difficulty levels based on individual learner progress, maximizing engagement and knowledge retention. AI-powered chatbots and virtual assistants provide instant support to employees, answering questions, offering guidance, and facilitating on-the-job learning opportunities in real time. These virtual assistants can streamline administrative tasks, freeing up HR professionals to focus on more strategic initiatives.

Using AI tools such as Microsoft Copilot, HR departments will be able to create and refine training materials based on existing content, discussions, and other resources. With time, AI is going to impact all areas of the ADDIE and other instructional design models.

AI analytics provide valuable insights into learning effectiveness, identifying trends, patterns, and areas for improvement in training programs. By analyzing learner behaviors, performance metrics, and feedback, HR teams can continuously optimize learning experiences, enhance training outcomes, and drive organizational success.

Learning Management Systems

It can sometimes be difficult to convince senior management of the benefits of training. As with any other HR initiative, it's important to demonstrate how a training program will add value to the bottom line. As part of the Workforce Innovation and Opportunity Act (WIOA), the federal government will fund some training programs that are managed by state workforce agencies. Some states use these funds to reimburse training costs to employers who want to hire, retain, or upgrade the skills of employees. In Maine, for example, key WOIA initiatives include enhancing adult education and literacy programs, offering grant opportunities for workforce development, and improving digital literacy among job seekers to meet modern economic demands.

A *learning management system (LMS)* is computer-based software that administers, tracks, and reports employee training and development activities. An LMS helps to streamline the administration of employee training programs. The components included in an LMS depend on organization size and the complexity of training needs. These systems can be used to automatically enroll students in required courses (such as safety training required by OSHA) and notify managers when employees don't attend. The programs can provide managers with access to approve training requested by employees and to identify skill-development needs in their departments or for individual employees. An LMS can maintain curriculum for required (or optional) courses and provide access on an individual, functional, or organizational basis. Other administrative functions performed by LMS programs include course calendars, facility assignments, pre- and post-testing, and report generation. An LMS can also include self-service functions that eliminate tedious administrative chores from daily HR tasks, such as registering employees, notifying participants, obtaining approvals, and maintaining waitlists. Table 5.1 summarizes the functions available in an LMS system.

TABLE 5.1 LMS system functions

HR tasks	Training tasks	User benefits
Streamline process (automate recordkeeping, notices, and reminders)	Manage resources: facilities, instructors, and equipment	Employees: self-registration, web access, online learning
Automatic enrollment for mandated courses	Manage course calendar	Managers: Approve employee requests, access to online assessment tools, plan department trainings
Verify qualifications	Self-registration	
Manage waiting lists	Web-based delivery	
Generate reports	Deliver/score tests, including pre- and posttests; score and record coursework	

An LMS is capable of managing the organization's learning tasks in a wide range of situations, from tracking attendance, maintaining training calendars, and generating reports to delivering web-based content to participants, administering and scoring tests, and providing planning tools for managers.

Learning and Performance Management Systems

Integrating training and career development with an LMS is possible by using *learning and performance management systems (LPMSs)*. These systems incorporate functions for managing performance (including 360-degree assessments, self-evaluations, succession planning, and manager feedback) and track individual rewards. These functions improve a manager's ability to assess performance, assign training to address areas of improvement, and prepare employees for the next level in their career growth.

Organizations that develop their own content often use *learning content management systems (LCMSs)* to create, deliver, and modify course content. These systems allow trainers to develop content, often in a module format so that a single module can be used in multiple training courses. For example, a geographically dispersed organization may create an orientation program with different modules for corporate information, employee benefit options, expense reporting, and other information common to employees throughout the organization, along with modules for each geographic location. This allows an HR professional in a regional office to provide a customized orientation that includes information specific to that office along with relevant information about the corporation at large.

Summary

Learning and development (L&D) address organizational challenges with such programs as learning organizations, total quality management, and management by objectives that are designed to align the workforce with the leaders and the organization strategy. These programs must fit in with the culture and strategy of the organization to be successful.

Employee-development programs prepare talented individuals to accept positions of greater responsibility and authority in the organization and aid the retention of individuals who are key to its long-term success. This includes succession planning to meet future needs and challenges.

Training is an important aspect of L&D. The ADDIE, Agile, and SAM models are used to develop training programs that address the needs of the organization and of individuals in the organization.

HR practitioners play a key role consulting with managers and employees on all intervention activities, and apply their understanding of adult learning principles to engage the workforce.

Exam Essentials

Understand and be able to describe organizational development intervention strategies. OD interventions address strategic objectives through a series of interventions. Built on a strong change management and knowledge management foundation, HR contributes to techno-structural, human process, and human resource management interventions to achieve desired results.

Understand and be able to describe instructional design models. The ADDIE, SAM, Scrum, and Agile models are instructional design tools used for creating training programs. The ADDIE model is distinct in that it applies to building training content as a whole, whereas Agile, Scrum, and SAM chunk training into smaller units for easier consumption and revision. AI continues to evolve as an important feature of instructional design and training delivery.

Be able to identify the four types of training evaluation. The four types of evaluation are reaction, which measures immediate feedback; learning, which measures what was learned through testing; behavior, which measures job performance six months or more after training; and results, which measures whether the training had a positive impact on the bottom line.

Understand the role of career pathing and succession plans. Career pathing initiatives within learning and development programs provide employees with clear pathways for skill development and advancement, aligning their professional growth with organizational goals and succession planning strategies. By identifying high-potential employees and offering targeted learning opportunities, organizations can groom future leaders from within, ensuring a seamless transition of talent and promoting long-term organizational continuity.

Be able to leverage the capabilities of learning management systems (LMSs). Leveraging the diverse capabilities and features offered by LMSs includes understanding the various functionalities of these platforms, such as centralized content management, course delivery, assessment and tracking, collaboration tools, and reporting capabilities.

Review Questions

You can find the answers in Appendix A.

1. Which of the following statements best describes artificial intelligence (AI)?
   - A. AI refers to the implementation of human-like robots in the workplace to perform various tasks autonomously.
   - B. AI involves the use of computer algorithms to simulate human intelligence processes, such as learning from data and making decisions.
   - C. AI focuses on enhancing workplace productivity solely through the automation of manual tasks without human intervention.
   - D. AI primarily relies on human input and oversight to guide machines in performing complex operations effectively.

2. Which of the following best describes the Scrum training model?
   - A. A traditional hierarchical approach to project management focused on rigid planning and execution
   - B. An iterative and adaptive framework derived from Agile principles, emphasizing collaboration and flexibility
   - C. A linear instructional design model that emphasizes sequential steps and predefined outcomes
   - D. A specialized training program for project managers that focuses on project efficiencies and deliverables

3. In the evaluation phase, the _________ evaluation method focuses on how well the training resulted in learning new skills and competencies.
   - A. Reaction
   - B. Learning
   - C. Behavior
   - D. Results

4. Upskilling is learning that is focused on _________, whereas reskilling is a type of training that focuses on _________.
   - A. Improving current skills; transitioning to a new role
   - B. Learning new technologies; mastering soft skills
   - C. Enhancing leadership abilities; developing technical expertise
   - D. Career advancement; personal development

5. A(n) _________ learning curve begins slowly, with smaller learning increments, but increases in pace and with larger increments as learning continues.
   - A. Positively accelerating
   - B. Negatively accelerating
   - C. S-shaped
   - D. Plateau

6. Which of the following best describes the difference between asynchronous and synchronous training?
   - **A.** Asynchronous training involves real-time interaction between instructors and learners, whereas synchronous training allows learners to access materials at their own pace.
   - **B.** Asynchronous training allows learners to access materials at their own pace, whereas synchronous training involves real-time interaction between instructors and learners.
   - **C.** Asynchronous training focuses on group discussions and collaborative activities, whereas synchronous training provides individualized learning experiences.
   - **D.** Asynchronous training emphasizes self-directed learning, whereas synchronous training emphasizes instructor-led sessions with fixed schedules.
7. Which of the following skill development resources would be most useful for a high potential employee being groomed for a leadership role?
   - **A.** Leadership workshops and seminars
   - **B.** Job shadowing
   - **C.** Mentoring and coaching
   - **D.** Professional networking
8. Which of the following is a primary purpose of analyzing feedback from exit surveys for HR and L&D professionals?
   - **A.** Identifying current employees' training needs
   - **B.** Evaluating employee performance metrics
   - **C.** Identifying trends and patterns related to training and career development
   - **D.** Assessing organizational profitability
9. An employer uses short bursts of content delivered via video to train employees on new product designs. This is the *best* example of which of the following instructional design models?
   - **A.** ADDIE
   - **B.** SAM
   - **C.** Agile
   - **D.** Virtual
10. Mentoring involves which of the following?
    - **A.** Someone who monitors an employee's performance in doing their job
    - **B.** Someone whose goal is to develop an employee in a particular area
    - **C.** Someone who takes a personal interest in an individual's career and who guides and sponsors the individual
    - **D.** Someone who provides training in areas of interest to an employee

11. Melissa recently facilitated companywide diversity training through a series of webinars. Prior to designing the training, she surveyed a sampling of employees to identify their experiences in the organization related to harassment, promotion opportunities, and equitable treatment. This is an example of which of the following?

 A. Summative evaluation
 B. Knowledge banking
 C. Attitude assessment
 D. Formative evaluation

12. Wine Cellar Barrels recently became aware of several negative reviews online related to the company's customer service. Management has tasked HR with designing a strategic training initiative to address the interpersonal skills of the call center staff. Using the ADDIE model, HR's first step should be which of the following?

 A. Design the training.
 B. Conduct a needs assessment.
 C. Identify training participants.
 D. Schedule the training.

13. As the HR Generalist for a large manufacturing organization, you have been tasked with understanding how current wage rates are affecting employee performance. Which of the following surveys should you design and administer?

 A. Market wage surveys
 B. Employee satisfaction surveys
 C. Compensation surveys
 D. Exit surveys

14. How can chatbots influence employee learning and development?(Choose all that apply.)

 A. Chatbots provide instant access to learning resources and information, facilitating continuous learning and development on demand.
 B. Chatbots offer personalized learning experiences by providing tailored recommendations, quizzes, and feedback based on individual learning preferences and performance.
 C. Chatbots can replace human trainers and instructors, delivering all learning content autonomously.
 D. Chatbots can only provide basic information and are not capable of supporting complex learning needs or interactive learning experiences.

15. Participants in a training program are asked to log into a website at their convenience, watch a video lecture, and take a quiz. This is an example of which of the following types of training?

 A. Vestibule
 B. Mobile learning
 C. Asynchronous
 D. The Delphi technique

16. Which of the following types of evaluations are designed to identify what the participants want, know, and need?

A. Reaction summaries

B. Formative evaluations

C. Summative evaluations

D. Trainer evaluations

17. Which of the following best describes the primary difference between operational HR and strategic HR?

A. Operational HR focuses on day-to-day tasks and administrative functions, whereas strategic HR emphasizes long-term planning and alignment with organizational goals.

B. Operational HR primarily deals with employee relations and conflict resolution, whereas strategic HR focuses on recruitment and talent management.

C. Operational HR involves compliance with labor laws and regulations, whereas strategic HR involves performance management and employee development.

D. Operational HR focuses on payroll and benefits administration, whereas strategic HR focuses on organizational culture and change management.

18. Calculate the training cost per employee using the following data: $2,000 for the training design and facilitator; $2,500 for the facility; 20 full-time employees (40 hours per week) and 10 part-time employees (20 hours per week).

A. $75

B. $150

C. $180

D. $300

19. A training session involved asking a group of participants to answer questions related to how Aflac Insurance used a duck to successfully launch its brand. This was an example of which of the following types of training?

A. Vestibule

B. Facilitation

C. Case study

D. Socratic seminar

20. In which of the following ways does an LMS support the learning and development of decentralized teams? (Choose all that apply.)

A. By serving as a centralized platform for accessing learning resources and training materials from anywhere, at any time

B. By enabling efficient delivery of training and development programs tailored to the roles and learning needs of decentralized team members

C. By offering robust tracking and reporting features to monitor the performance and progress of decentralized team members

D. By facilitating collaboration and communication among decentralized team members through built-in communication and collaboration tools

Chapter 6

PHR | PHRi Exam: Total Rewards

PHR RESPONSIBILITIES:

IMPLEMENTING, PROMOTING, AND MANAGING COMPENSATION AND BENEFIT PROGRAMS THAT ATTRACT AND RETAIN TALENT WHILE COMPLYING WITH FEDERAL LAWS.

- ✓ **4.1 Manage and communicate total rewards programs to foster employee engagement and enhance employee experience (for example: compensation, payroll, recognition programs, incentives)**
- ✓ **4.2 Implement and promote awareness of non-monetary rewards (for example: paid volunteer time, tuition assistance, workplace amenities, and employee recognition programs)**
- ✓ **4.3 Implement benefit programs (for example: workplace amenities, flexible scheduling, remote/ hybrid options)**
- ✓ **4.4 Monitor and sustain US federally compliant compensation and benefit programs (for example: pay equity, benchmarking, salary bands, status changes, and life events)**

PHRi RESPONSIBILITIES:

IMPLEMENTING, PROMOTING, AND MANAGING COMPENSATION AND BENEFIT PROGRAMS THAT ATTRACT AND RETAIN TALENT WHILE COMPLYING WITH LOCAL LAWS.

- ✓ **4.2 Implement and promote awareness of non-monetary rewards (for example: workplace amenities, flexible scheduling, remote/hybrid options)**
- ✓ **4.3 Understand and administer benefit and leave programs (for example: health plans, retirement plans, employee assistance plans, paid time-off, other insurance)**
- ✓ **4.4 Monitor and sustain compensation and benefit programs (for example: pay equity, benchmarking, salary bands, status changes, and life events)**

The Total Rewards function of the PHR/i exam accounts for 15 percent of exam content. In terms of total weight, that equates to about 14 out of 90 scored questions that you will see related to this subject on exam day. Although this may not seem to be much, it is impossible to anticipate what those 14 questions will be about, so it is critical you are thoroughly prepared in two primary areas: employee compensation and employee benefits.

Total Rewards is the functional area where there is the most significant differences between the PHR and the PHRi exams. The main differences include:

- **Jurisdiction:** PHR focuses on compliance with federal laws within the United States, whereas PHRi focuses on compliance with local laws internationally.
- **Legal Compliance:** PHR covers compliance with U.S. federal laws regarding compensation, benefits, and related areas. In contrast, PHRi covers compliance with local laws, which can vary significantly by country or region.
- **Benefit and Leave Programs:** While both exams cover benefit programs, PHR includes understanding and administering benefit and leave programs specific to U.S. regulations. PHRi, on the other hand, encompasses a broader understanding of international benefit and leave programs.
- **Non-monetary Rewards:** Both exams address implementing and promoting awareness of non-monetary rewards, but the examples provided differ slightly based on cultural and regional norms.
- **Scope of Responsibilities:** While the core responsibilities related to compensation, benefits, and employee engagement are similar in both exams, the specifics may vary to accommodate the differences in legal frameworks and cultural contexts between the U.S. and international locations.

Total Rewards Defined

At the broadest level, *Total Rewards* can be described as an exchange of payment from an employer for the services provided by its employees. In today's economy a competitive Total Rewards program is vital to attracting, retaining, and motivating employees. In many organizations, compensation and benefits costs are the single largest operating expense and therefore an extremely important component of the HR program. A Total Rewards package includes all forms of rewards, which are generally categorized into one of two components: monetary and non-monetary compensation. Let's look now at what goes into each of these components:

Monetary Compensation Monetary compensation includes any costs the organization incurs for the benefit of employees, such as all forms of cash compensation, 401(k) matching, medical care premiums, pension plans, and paid time off. Other kinds of rewards include benefits that support the organization's culture such as stock options, employee stock ownership programs (ESOPs), and incentive plans.

Non-monetary Compensation It's important to recognize that just as monetary rewards are a critical component of a global Total Rewards program, so are non-monetary rewards. This chapter focuses primarily on tangible rewards, but providing an environment that supports intrinsic and extrinsic non-monetary rewards is a very important part of the Total Rewards package.

An *intrinsic reward is* one that encourages individual employee self-esteem, such as satisfaction from challenging and exciting assignments. An *extrinsic reward* is one in which esteem is achieved from others, such as fulfillment from working with a talented team of peers. The relationship employees have with their supervisors, recognition of accomplishments, development and career opportunities, and teamwork are a few examples of non-monetary rewards. Non-monetary rewards also include nontraditional work-life balance benefits such as telecommuting, on-site childcare, and flex time.

Other terms used throughout this chapter are direct and indirect compensation:

Direct Compensation *Direct compensation* includes payments made to employees that are associated with wages and salaries. This includes base pay, variable compensation, and pay for performance.

Indirect Compensation *Indirect compensation* consists of any employee payments not associated with wages and salaries. This includes fringe benefits such as vacation, sick, and holiday pay; insurance premiums paid on behalf of employees; leaves of absence; 401(k) or other pension plans; and government-mandated benefits such as Social Security or Family and Medical Leave Act (FMLA) and other benefits.

The mix of components included in a Total Rewards package is unique to the compensation and benefits philosophy, strategic direction, and culture of each organization. Ultimately, the goal of a Total Rewards package is to maximize the return on investment (ROI) of resources spent on employee rewards.

For PHR/i candidates, it is important to focus on implementing, promoting, and managing legally (or locally for the PHRi) compliant compensation and benefits programs.

Compensation

Deciding how best to compensate employees for the work they do is based on various factors, including internal value (the importance of jobs relative to each other), external value (economic factors, such as supply and demand), and the knowledge, skills, and abilities (KSAs) individual employees demonstrate on the job.

Organizations must be aware of a variety of external factors when developing programs and administering compensation, including economics, the labor market, competition in the product market, and other pressures such as those related to tax and accounting requirements and government legislation and regulations:

Economic Factors The ability of an organization to find qualified employees is affected by a number of economic factors at the local, national, and global levels, including economic growth, inflation, interest rates, unemployment, and the comparative cost of living. These factors influence the *cost of labor*, or the cost to attract and retain individuals with the skills needed by the organization to achieve its goals. Organizations recruiting employees with a particular skill set create a competitive environment for individuals with those skills, resulting in an increase in the cost of labor. For example, when two large companies in the same metropolitan area are hiring large numbers of experienced manufacturing technicians, the supply of individuals with this skill set is in demand, and the availability of qualified individuals decreases. This combination of increased demand and decreased availability raises the competitive compensation rate for this skill set, thereby increasing the cost of labor.

With the increasingly competitive global economy, many industries are constantly assessing how to increase quality, accelerate time to market, and improve productivity. This increased intensity has resulted in a creative approach to organizing and redesigning work that, in turn, affects the skill sets needed by the organization and the cost to employ individuals with those skills.

Labor Market Organizations may need to revise their compensation programs to meet the demands of changing labor markets. The *labor market* is made up of any sources from which an organization recruits new employees; a single organization may find itself recruiting from several different labor markets, depending on the availability of skills for different positions. Ultimately, the combination of supply and demand for a certain skill set in the labor market impacts what the employers competing for those skills must pay to individuals who possess them. For example, the quit rate by industry post-COVID was greatest in hospitality and retail. From a forecasting perspective, HR professionals in these industries should be brainstorming on how to recruit for and retain talented personnel, or upskilling and reskilling existing talent, and these strategies should be included in a Total Rewards review.

Labor markets vary by region and industry. Urban areas provide a greater pool of candidates with a wider set of skills from which to select. Because there are more businesses in urban areas competing for this pool of candidates, urban environments may be more competitive, leading to an increase in the cost of labor. As a result, the cost of labor for a single skill set may vary widely between the areas in which an organization operates. To offset these differences, many companies use regional pay structures to reflect the market conditions of the different areas in which they have business locations. For example, a company that is headquartered in the southeast may have a different pay structure for their regional offices in New York City and in the Silicon Valley in California to reflect the higher cost of labor in those areas.

Over the years, the way people look at pay has changed because of the increased mobility of the workforce, the shift from a manufacturing economy to a knowledge-based economy, and fluctuating economic conditions. During the technology boom of the late 1990s, job hopping and generous compensation packages were prevalent, particularly for individuals with sought-after technological skills. Organizations recruited at a national level and were willing to relocate candidates because the labor market was so competitive. When the technology bubble burst and the unemployment rate increased, organizations were able to recruit for many positions locally, reducing the cost of labor. As the economy improved, competition for talented employees again led to increased labor costs. As this cycle repeats over time, newer trends have also emerged. For example, the rise of remote work, accelerated by the COVID-19 pandemic, has significantly impacted compensation strategies. Companies are now able to access a global talent pool, leading to more diverse and distributed teams. This shift has caused organizations to rethink their compensation models, often incorporating location-based pay adjustments. Additionally, the emphasis on work-life balance and flexible work arrangements has become a headliner in attracting and retaining talent. As remote work becomes more permanent, companies are finding innovative ways to offer competitive compensation packages that reflect the evolving expectations of the modern workforce. HR professionals must be aware of changing economic factors that impact the labor market and adjust compensation strategies in their organizations to maintain their competitive edge in the labor market.

New Business Models The COVID-19 pandemic catalyzed a significant rise in independent contractors as traditional employment structures underwent substantial shifts. Faced with economic uncertainty and remote work opportunities, many individuals turned to freelancing and gig work to maintain income streams. The flexibility offered by independent contracting became increasingly appealing, allowing workers to adapt to changing circumstances and balance personal responsibilities amidst lockdowns and restrictions. As companies embraced remote collaboration and outsourced tasks, the demand for independent contractors surged across various sectors, from digital services to delivery and transportation. This trend reflects a broader societal shift toward a more decentralized and agile workforce in the wake of the pandemic's impact on traditional employment models.

For example, companies such as Uber and DoorDash rely on a similar business model where they act as brokers between service providers (drivers or delivery people) and consumers (riders or customers). They take a percentage of each transaction facilitated through their platform as their revenue.

One major concern of gig and other freelance work is the often precarious nature of income for workers in these sectors. While gig workers enjoy flexibility, they often lack stable wages, benefits like health insurance, and employment protections afforded to traditional employees. Additionally, the algorithmic nature of platforms like Uber and DoorDash can lead to unpredictable earnings and arbitrary deactivations, leaving workers vulnerable to exploitation and financial instability.

The gig economy has been subject to much debate regarding labor rights, worker protections, benefits offering, and the broader implications for the economy and the future of work, and also impacts HR budgets. Jobs can no longer be budgeted in the traditional way based on annual pay, benefits, and burden. Pricing the work as projects or by busy seasons are now factors HR must consider.

Note that minimum wage and overtime requirements only apply to employees, not independent contractors. Rules such as those issued by President Biden's administration sought to clarify that individuals that are "economically dependent" upon a company must be considered employees; this is determined by the IRS's definition of control:

- **Behavioral:** Does the company control or have the right to control what the worker does and how the worker does their job?
- **Financial:** Are the business aspects of the worker's job controlled by the payer? (These include things like how worker is paid, whether expenses are reimbursed, who provides tools/supplies, and so on.)
- **Type of Relationship:** Are there written contracts or employee type benefits (for example, pension plan, insurance, vacation pay, and so on)? Will the relationship continue, and is the work performed a key aspect of the business?

Misclassifying workers is a costly mistake for employers, so HR must be up-to-date on these definitions and apply the knowledge by auditing their workforce and then advising executive management on any changes that should be made.

NOTE

The Biden administration's rule regarding gig workers in 2024 replaced a previous ruling by the Trump administration. Lawmakers planned to fight Biden's lawmaking, making the status unpredictable. For the exams, focus on understanding the context behind the regulations rather than the specific requirements, as it is subject to change based on states' rights, union contracts, and presidential administrations. These issues go beyond the law and impact organizational results (recruiting and retention) and employee well-being (livable wages, flexibility).

Product Market Competition Competitive product markets place financial pressure on an organization and challenge its ability to attract and retain qualified employees. Increased competition creates pressure to do everything faster, better, and cheaper. These added pressures place a strain on the employee population. In a climate epitomized by strong competition between organizations accompanied by a decrease in demand, issues related to the financial health of an organization will likely surface. Repercussions of these pressures for employees can include wage freezes, which may result in skipping a merit-review process, eliminating promotions, and/or not paying incentives. In a strong economy, increased competition can mean growth for the organization because of increasing demand, resulting in increased financial rewards for employees. HR professionals must be aware of the implications of changes in the competitive environment to ensure that the programs they propose are in line with these pressures.

Tax and Accounting Several external factors affect compensation and benefit decisions, including regulations by many state and federal agencies. These include the Securities and Exchange Commission (SEC), the Financial Accounting Standards Board (FASB), and the IRS. These agencies affect compensation and benefits issues through the enforcement of federal tax legislation, such as Social Security and Medicare taxes, pension regulation, and enforcement of rules about some benefit programs. When an organization wants to make changes to compensation or benefit programs, it may want to find out how the IRS will view the changes for tax purposes before it makes them. In some situations, it may be beneficial to request a *private letter ruling* from the IRS before the changes are made. These rulings apply only to the specific taxpayer and circumstances included in the request and are used to find out what the tax implications of a complex or unusual financial transaction will be.

In addition to tax regulations, the DOL has established strict rules regarding minimum wage, overtime, and compensable time for employees, so PHR candidates must be well versed in up-to-date laws regarding compensation and benefits practices (these are discussed in Appendix C).

Types of Compensation

Compensation comes in many forms. The topic of this section is all forms of direct compensation, from base pay to differentials, variable-pay plans, and commissions and bonuses. The backbone of a compensation program is base pay—the salary or hourly wage paid to employees for the work they do.

Base Pay

Whether paid as a salary or as an hourly wage, *base pay* is the amount of compensation that the employer and the employee agree will be paid for the performance of particular job duties. Base pay both reflects the internal value of jobs while striving to recognize their external market value.

HR professionals take a variety of factors into consideration when making base-pay determinations: The KSAs that employees bring to the job, previous earnings, and internal equity are all part of the decision-making process. Once an employee is hired, changes in base pay may be based on various factors, including performance in the job, seniority, and increased skills.

Ideally, base pay is evaluated on an annual basis. When employees take on new roles and responsibilities, base pay can increase through the promotion process. Other changes in base pay can occur as the result of demotions or changes in job duties. Other times, pay is increased to align with cost-of-living adjustments.

When determining a new hire's base pay, the length and type of previous experience are key factors to consider. Years of experience in a certain profession, a certain industry, or total experience may be relevant to the job. Depth of experience versus time spent in a single role may also be relevant to a certain position. How well the new hire will perform in the job is an unknown variable and will be taken into account once the employee begins work.

The federal government establishes a minimum wage that must be paid to employees. As of 2024, the federal minimum wage continues to be $7.25. There are several prevailing wage requirements for federal contractors that require higher-than-minimum pay. Most states have their own minimum wage standards, and where an employee is subject to both state and federal minimum wage laws, employers are required to pay the higher of the two wages.

Tipped employees are defined as workers who receive at least $30 per month in tips. An employer is only required to pay these workers $2.13 per hour in direct wages, provided that the tips (when combined with direct wages) meet the minimum wage standard of $7.25 per hour.

To remain as current as possible for your exam day, bookmark the following web page for reference on these issues: `https://www.dol.gov/general/topic/wages`.

Compensation Philosophy

The company's compensation philosophy drives the type of compensation program that is used. These are categorized as either performance-based or seniority-based programs.

Performance-Based Compensation

Performance-based pay programs, which may include merit increases or promotions, are based on how well individual employees perform against the company's process for measuring performance. The performance ratings earned by employees determine the eligible range of increase for the review period.

Differentiating pay based on performance means the base salaries of employees in the same classification or salary range may vary from one another. When using a performance-based compensation system, it's important to keep accurate records that justify the reasons for disparity in salaries between employees in the same positions. This documentation will be useful in defending against claims of unfair pay practices should they occur.

Seniority-Based Compensation

Organizations that use *seniority-based compensation* systems make pay decisions based on the length of time employees have been in a position and on years of related experience. A seniority-based compensation system is representative of an entitlement compensation philosophy where employees feel "entitled to" certain pay or benefits based on length of service as opposed to individual performance.

A good example of seniority-based compensation is an organization with a union representing its workers. In a union context, long- and short-term compensation decisions are the result of negotiations between the union and the employer. Because of this, they aren't necessarily driven by an organization's compensation philosophy. In a union environment, annual increases are typically determined by seniority.

Pay Differentials

Some organizations use pay differentials to encourage employees to perform work that is uncomfortable, out of the ordinary, inconvenient, or hazardous. Pay differentials serve as incentives for employees to work on tough assignments or to be available to respond at inconvenient times. A *pay differential* provides additional pay for work that is considered beyond the minimum requirements of the job. For example, multinational employers who require employees to travel and work in potentially dangerous parts of the world may use hazard pay to make those jobs more attractive to employees.

Examples of pay differentials include overtime, shift pay, on-call pay, call-back pay, reporting pay, hazard pay, and geographic pay.

Overtime

Although the Fair Labor Standards Act (FLSA) requires payment only for overtime exceeding 40 hours in a week, some states have overtime laws that exceed federal requirements, and employees are paid at the more generous state rate. Federal law allows employers to require unlimited overtime as long as employees are paid at the required wage rate. It isn't common practice to pay overtime to exempt employees, but doing so isn't prohibited by the FLSA; however, doing so by definition requires employees to keep track of their hours. Requiring exempt employees to keep track of their time isn't prohibited by the FLSA as long as it doesn't result in a reduction of their pay based on the quality or quantity of work produced. Wage and hour law violations remain among the top charges filed with the DOL, meaning that complying with the FLSA is complex. PHR candidates should study Appendix C to fully understand the intricacies of this foundational labor law.

It's important for employers to take a leadership position in managing overtime costs. To prevent abuse, it's ideal for overtime work to be approved in advance. Employers may also want to develop a process or policy when scheduling overtime work for large groups of employees, such as scheduling employees for overtime based on their skill sets, seniority, or shift, depending on the needs of the employer. Overtime is an area that is commonly cut when employers face financial and/or economic challenges.

Shift Differentials

The days and hours of a typical workweek vary by industry—the most common work schedule is one in which employees work Monday through Friday. A *shift* is any scheduled block of time during the work week when employees perform job-related duties. Shifts have a specific start and end time and are most applicable to nonexempt employees but can also affect exempt employees. Typically, there are three commonly recognized shifts: the day shift, with hours from 8 a.m. to 4 p.m.; the evening, or *swing shift*, with hours from 4 p.m. to 12 a.m.; and the *graveyard shift*, with hours from 12 a.m. to 8 a.m. Shift work is necessary in industries with 24-hour operations, such as hospitals, airlines, law enforcement, and some manufacturing operations. Many employers define the shifts in accordance with their needs, so these are just standard examples.

In some cases, employers pay more than what is required by the state or federal government for shifts or other time spent at work, such as paying employees for rest or meal periods. Compensating employees in excess of FLSA requirements typically reflects common practice in an industry or market segment. Employers may decide to pay for these items in order to maintain a competitive advantage to more effectively attract, motivate, and retain employees.

A *shift premium* is additional compensation provided for employees who work other than the day shift. Shift premiums may be paid as a percentage of base pay or may be factored into the hourly rate. For example, in high-tech manufacturing, it's common to pay a 10 percent shift premium for shifts that overlap 6 p.m. to midnight and 15 percent for shifts that overlap the midnight to 6 a.m. time period. Although it's most common for nonexempt employees to be paid shift premiums, they may also be paid to exempt employees.

Shift-premium calculations can be a little tricky. Here's an example: Laura works as a nonexempt manufacturing technician at MonoCorp, working an 8-hour shift, 5 days a week, resulting in a 40-hour workweek; she makes $10 an hour. Laura also works some hours on the second shift, from 4 p.m. to midnight, Monday through Friday. The second shift at MonoCorp pays a 10 percent shift premium. Table 6.1 illustrates the base pay and overtime costs for Laura's work.

TABLE 6.1 Laura's schedule: hours worked

Day	Shift/scheduled hours	Overtime
Monday	8	0
Tuesday	8	2
Wednesday	8	0
Thursday	8	2
Friday	8	2
Total hours worked	40	6

As you can see, Laura worked a full 40-hour week and put in 6 hours of overtime. Table 6.2 illustrates Laura's pay based on her $10/hour salary and her 10 percent shift premium.

TABLE 6.2 Laura's pay schedule

Category	Hours	Pay
Regular	40	$400
Overtime at 1.5 times regular rate	6	$90
Subtotal	46	$490
Shift Premium @ 10 percent		$9
Total		$499

On-Call Pay

Although the FLSA establishes minimum requirements for on-call time, employers may decide to provide *on-call pay* that is more generous. Employees who are required to respond to work-related issues on short notice, typically emergencies, and who must be available via pager, telephone, or email, may be paid an hourly or daily premium. In certain professions, being on call is part of the job, and on-call premiums aren't paid.

Call-Back Pay

Some companies may provide *call-back pay* to employees who are called to work before or after their scheduled hours. Nonexempt employees who are called into the facility or who work from home are paid their regular rate of pay and any other applicable premiums.

Reporting Pay

When an employee is called into work and there is no work available, the employer may be required by state law or employment agreements to pay for a minimum number of hours of work. This is called a *reporting premium* and ensures the employee receives compensation for showing up for their regular shift or when called to the worksite.

Hazard Pay

Hazard pay is additional pay for dangerous and/or extremely uncomfortable working conditions. Hazard pay may be needed to attract candidates to jobs that require contact with hazardous elements such as radiation, chemicals, or extreme conditions. Firefighters commonly receive hazard pay, because they deal with extreme conditions and physically demanding duties. Examples of other professions that may receive hazard pay include medical positions that work with infectious diseases, police officers, and federal employees who are posted to assignments in countries that are considered dangerous because of wars and/or active hostilities. Although certain jobs may have risks, they may not provide a hazard pay premium, and their compensation is instead reflective of the labor market. FLSA doesn't require hazard pay, but it does require employers who provide hazard pay to factor it into overtime calculations.

Geographic Pay

Organizations use *geographic pay* to ensure that employees in different locations are paid at rates competitive in the labor market for specific jobs and locations. Geographic structures are put into place to make sure the employees are paid competitively and aligned with the organization's compensation philosophy. It's common to find nonexempt pay structures that vary by city and/or state because of the local cost of labor.

Exempt structures may be adjusted by region to reflect regional labor markets. Having an exempt salary structure specific to the Northeast, Pacific Northwest, or Southeast may be appropriate for some labor markets. As an example, if a manufacturing organization is headquartered in the Silicon Valley in Northern California and has manufacturing plants in San Francisco, St. Louis, and Boston, it would be appropriate to have a salary structure specific to each location.

Variable Compensation

Increasingly, organizations are designing compensation programs that include individual or group incentives as a significant component of the total compensation package. According to several salary surveys, almost two-thirds of U.S. companies include some sort of variable compensation in the pay packages offered to employees. Known as *variable compensation, incentive pay*, or *pay for performance*, these programs reward employees for individual and/or organizational results. When aligned with the organization's compensation philosophy, this form of compensation can help shape or change employee behavior or organizational culture by rewarding behaviors that are valued by the organization. An effective variable-pay program motivates employees to achieve business objectives by providing a line of sight between desired performance and the reward.

Another reason incentive pay has become a key component of compensation packages is that the broad spreading of merit dollars may not always reinforce performance. Merit budgets have become smaller, on average, which can make it difficult to provide meaningful rewards that differentiate between levels of performance. Providing meaningful rewards to employees through the merit process, given the average merit budget, requires many employees to be passed over for annual merit increases so the dollars can be spent on top performers.

Once an organization determines the type of employee performance or behavior it wants to encourage, an appropriate incentive plan can be selected. Whether the incentive plan is based on individual or group performance, or on some type of special incentive, depends on the organization's specific needs.

Individual Incentives

Individual incentives reward employees who achieve set goals and objectives and can be powerful tools for motivating individual performance. Incentives are prospective in that they state specific objectives that need to be achieved over designated periods of time and include payout targets stated either as a percentage of base pay or as a flat dollar amount.

Successful incentive-plan programs have three critical phases:

Plan Design Plan design should be kept simple and should make it as easy and convenient as possible for employees to understand and recall performance goals (for instance, an employee or group needs to increase production by 10 percent or decrease defective parts by 5 percent). Complicated incentive plans tend to create confusion and distrust and may not produce the desired results.

Research on incentive programs has found that a minimum bonus target of 10 percent is required to influence and change behavior. Bonus targets of less than 10 percent of base pay may not provide sufficient motivation for employees to put forward the effort or spend the additional time to achieve the plan objectives and as a result may not produce the desired results.

Review Process Typically, bonus review and payment corresponds to the end of the organization's fiscal year. In some cases, incentives may be paid more frequently if employees have a direct influence on revenue generation. As with most compensation programs, the *ability to pay* (the company affordability factor) is critical to any incentive program. Many bonus-based incentive programs define desired financial metrics that must be achieved before incentives are paid.

Communication and Implementation Individual incentive-plan objectives are ideally communicated before or at the beginning of the review period. For example, annual, calendar-based plans are usually communicated in January. Targets for incentive plans are commonly part of an offer package but can be modified as needed. When bonus targets are modified, whether they're increased or decreased, great care should be taken in communicating the rationale. Legal counsel and/or local HR representatives should be involved in making these changes to ensure legal compliance with state and local law, particularly in global environments when modifying bonus targets may require new employment contracts.

Communication of an incentive-plan program is key to ensuring that employees understand the metrics of the plan. As part of a communication strategy, some organizations may choose to create and publish a plan document that describes the incentive program in detail.

Organization or Group Incentives

Organization incentives or *group incentives* have many of the same characteristics as individual incentives. A sure step to a successful organization or group incentive plan is that the plan objectives align with the organization's compensation philosophy. Organization or group incentives are commonly used to increase productivity, foster teamwork, and share financial rewards with employees. Benefits that are common to all group incentives include increased awareness of and commitment to company goals. As the name implies, group incentives aren't used to reward individual performance. There are several types of group incentives, including the following:

Gainsharing *Gainsharing* programs involve employees and managers in improving the organization's productivity and sharing the benefits of success. The key components of gainsharing include the following:

- Employees and management work together to review organizational performance.
- When measurable improvements are achieved, employees and managers share the success.
- The organization and the employees share the financial gains.

Some of the organizational benefits derived from gainsharing include the following:

- Teamwork, sharing knowledge, and cooperation
- Increased motivation
- Employee focus on and commitment to organizational goals
- Greater employee acceptance of new methods, technology, and market changes
- Perceived fairness of pay, which results in increased productivity at all levels

Improshare *Improshare* was developed in the 1970s by Mitchell Fein. It's differentiated from other group incentive plans because a key part of the program is the establishment of a baseline for organization productivity and a baseline for productivity costs. The difference between the baseline productivity and the new output is used to calculate the group's or organization's performance.

Scanlon Plan The *Scanlon plan* is one of the earliest pay-for-performance plans. In the 1930s, Joseph Scanlon created his plan to increase productivity and decrease costs through employee involvement. Employees receive a portion of cost savings achieved through productivity gains and cost savings. This type of group incentive requires the disclosure of financial information and productivity metrics to employees. Scanlon plans are administered by committees that are representative of the employee population.

Profit Sharing Very similar to the Scanlon plan, profit sharing is an incentive-based program that shares company profits. Profit-sharing plans are typically qualified plans found across many industries and available to employees at all levels, from individual contributors to senior management. Profit-sharing plans distribute pretax dollars to eligible employees, typically based on a percentage of an employee's base salary. Distribution of profit-sharing dollars typically occurs annually, after the close of the fiscal year. The set formula for a profit-sharing plan defines individual contributions and distributions. It's typical for the plan to have a vesting schedule, described in the plan document. The document details when and how distributions occur and what happens at milestone events, such as employee termination, leave of absence, death, retirement, and so on. Because most profit-sharing plans are a form of defined-contribution plan, they're covered by regulations of the Employee Retirement Income Security Act (ERISA).

Employee Stock Ownership Plans (ESOPs) An *employee stock ownership plan (ESOP)* is a tax-qualified, defined-contribution plan that allows employees to own shares in a company. An employer sets up a tax-deductible trust that accepts tax-deductible contributions made by the company. Employee eligibility can be based on a formula that may include base salary, length of service, or other factors. At the time of termination, retirement, or death, employees are able to receive the vested portion of their ESOP, which becomes taxable at the time funds are distributed.

Employee Stock Purchase Plans (ESPPs) ESPPs allow employees to use after-tax payroll deductions to purchase company stock at a discounted price. Typically, there is an offering period in which the employee deductions are accumulated until the purchase date, when the money is used to purchase company stock at a discounted rate of up to 15 percent. These types of benefits programs serve a culture of employee ownership, help develop employee loyalty, and can provide a direct line of sight from employee inputs to rewards.

Special Incentives

In some cases, an organization may decide to provide incentive plans to address specific circumstances. For example, as part of an acquisition, the acquiring company may want to make sure specific executives or other key employees from the company being acquired stay with the new organization long enough to ensure a smooth transition. A financial incentive, often referred to as a *retention bonus*, is one way to do this. Retention bonuses are generally structured so that the full bonus is paid if the employee remains with the company through a certain date, but the entire amount is forfeited if the employee leaves before that date. Retention bonuses are also used in situations when an organization is closing its doors. Some employees, such as an accounting manager, will be needed to complete final tasks, and a retention bonus can be used to make sure those employees don't accept new jobs until the necessary tasks are completed.

Special incentive plans can also be included as part of executive compensation packages to reward top executives for achieving established financial goals, such as a percentage of increased sales, a predetermined stock price increase, and other performance goals established by a board of directors.

Commissions and Sales Bonuses

Commissions provide incentives to sales employees by paying them a percentage of the sale price for products and services sold to a customer. Commissions may serve as the entire cash compensation package, or they may be used in combination with a base salary. When sales employees receive a base salary, it's usually a portion of their target cash compensation. The incentive or variable component is intended to drive sales objectives. Compensation for sales employees paid on a commission-only basis must meet at least the minimum wage.

An alternative to a commission plan is a sales bonus plan, in which a percentage of base pay compensates the employee for sales targets achieved. The difference between commission and bonus plans is the method of calculation, and this has many implications for the design of sales compensation programs. For example, Joaquin sells new cars and has an annual quota of 100 cars. For every car Joaquin sells over 100, he receives a bonus of 1 percent of his base salary.

When performance targets are clearly communicated, commissions and bonuses are an excellent way to motivate sales employees to perform desired behaviors and achieve desired results.

Bonus Plans

A *bonus* is additional compensation for performance above and beyond expectations and is paid in addition to an employee's base salary or hourly rate. Unlike incentive plans communicated when an assignment is made and conditional upon successfully completing the assignment, most bonuses are considered discretionary. This means the bonus is optionally offered and isn't based on established objectives. An example of a *bonus plan* is the holiday bonus that some organizations distribute at the end of the year. It's up to the employer to decide whether a bonus will be paid each year, which employees are eligible to participate, and how much each individual receives. Another example is a spot-bonus plan, which provides an immediate reward for outstanding performance, such as an employee who makes sure a critical customer proposal is completed in time to make the delivery cutoff schedule. Bonuses also take the form of a sales-performance bonus paid to salespeople who exceed their quotas, employee-referral bonuses paid to employees who refer candidates hired for open positions, patent awards, employee-of-the-month rewards, and so on.

Traditional Pay Structures

Traditional pay programs have existed relatively unchanged for more than 50 years. The way an organization develops pay structures and uses them to administer pay on a day-to-day basis is known as *salary administration*, *compensation administration*, or *pay administration*. Figure 6.1 represents the steps in this process.

Salary Structure Development

A salary structure provides an organized, systematic way of identifying base pay for employees in different jobs throughout the organization. The structure consists of a specified number of salary grades with a range of compensation attached to each. Developing a salary structure requires an analysis of both internal equity and external labor market conditions obtained through the job-pricing process. Jobs are grouped using the data collected during job evaluation and pricing. During the pricing process, job descriptions are matched to comparable benchmark positions that provide a market range for each.

FIGURE 6.1 Salary administration

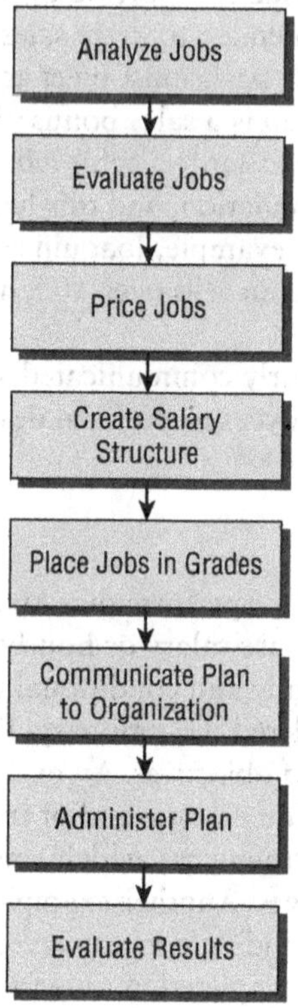

In most cases, the market median or 50th percentile is used as the data-comparison point for each job. There may be times when an organization decides to use a higher point of comparison for some jobs (highly skilled positions that are in short supply in the labor market, for example) or for all jobs (if the compensation philosophy is to lead the market). Jobs are grouped according to the data points established by the survey. These groups of jobs with similar market levels provide the basis for determining the number of job grades to include in the structure.

Using the grouped jobs as a starting point, mid-points are established for each job grade. The *mid-point progression*, or difference between the mid-points of consecutive grades, is generally narrower for lower grades and increases for higher grades. Typically, the mid-point progression ranges from 12 percent to 15 percent at lower grades to 25 percent at higher grades. Once grades are established, a pay range is developed for each grade.

A *pay range* (also known as a *salary range*) is the spread between the minimum and maximum pay for the job grade. Ranges can be stated as an hourly amount for workers paid on an hourly basis or a monthly, semimonthly, biweekly, or annual amount for salaried workers. The spread of traditional pay ranges is typically narrow and varies depending on level. At entry-level grades, ranges are the narrowest based on the assumption that employees in those grades will gain the KSAs and progress to higher job grades. At the highest grades, the spread is quite wide to provide salary progression for highly valued employees who remain in positions for longer periods of time. The spread for entry-level job grades usually begins at 15 percent and can go as high as 25–30 percent for the highest job grades. The spread is calculated based on the mid-point established by the market.

For example, the pay grade for a group of midlevel professional positions might have an 18 percent spread. At a mid-point of $50,000, the minimum would be 82 percent of the mid-point, or $41,000, and the maximum would be 118 percent of the mid-point, or $59,000.

Placing Jobs in Grades

Initially, jobs are placed in pay grades based on the grouping done to develop the grades. If market data was collected only for benchmark positions, the rest of the jobs will need to be placed in the ranges based on internal equity with the benchmark positions. At this point, the placements are reviewed with senior management to ensure they make sense in the context of the organization's strategic direction. By providing a chart or spreadsheet that shows the jobs in each job grade by business unit, executives can determine whether changes are necessary. Once agreement is reached, the structure is finalized and communicated to employees.

Real World Scenario

Comparable Worth

Comparable worth, or *pay equity*, describes the concept of minimizing pay disparities between jobs traditionally held by women, such as teachers, with higher-paying jobs traditionally held by men, such as carpenters. This concept suggests that jobs with similar duties and responsibilities requiring similar levels of knowledge, skill, and ability should be paid similarly. Comparable worth doesn't reflect supply and demand in the labor market because it's about the inherent value of the job's content to society. The issue is complex because value is a subjective measure and how jobs are valued often depends on who is valuing them. Those opposed to this concept argue that the price of a particular job in the labor market is based on the supply and demand for its skills and that social engineering isn't an appropriate role for business.

Comparable worth can be seen in the case of the state of Minnesota's pay equity efforts in the 1980s. The state conducted a comprehensive job evaluation study comparing male-dominated jobs, like highway maintenance workers, to female-dominated jobs, such as clerical workers. Despite differences in job content, they found that the skills, responsibilities, and effort required were comparable. As a result, Minnesota adjusted salaries to ensure that female-dominated jobs were paid equitably in relation to male-dominated jobs, addressing systemic pay disparities and promoting gender pay equity within the state workforce.

Communicating the Structure

The goal of the communication plan is to have buy-in at all levels of the organization so that the salary structure accomplishes what it needs to do: provide a fair and equitable structure for making pay decisions. To do this, communication about the pay structure takes place at two levels: employee and manager. Employees need to understand how the structure was developed so they feel fairly compensated for their work and have a line of sight from their performance to their compensation. Explaining how the structure was created should alleviate any concerns about political influence or favoritism in the decision-making process.

Managers need to understand how the salary structure can be used to influence behavior in a way that encourages employees to accomplish their goals and objectives. They need to be well versed in how the structure works so they can effectively explain pay decisions to employees.

Administering the Compensation Plan

Once a pay structure is created, managers must have the tools they need to administer pay for their work units. Compiling a salary-administration handbook helps managers throughout the organization apply the system consistently. A typical handbook contains the following kinds of information:

- The organization's compensation philosophy
- The roles played by HR, line managers, and executives in salary administration
- Basic information about pay increases
- A description of how salaries or wages for new hires are determined

If variable compensation is part of the compensation mix, information about bonuses and other incentives is included as well.

Range Placement

Up to this point, the pay-structure discussion has concentrated on jobs, not on the employees in the jobs. The focus now turns to using the pay structure to make decisions for individual employees. One of the key factors to consider when making individual pay decisions is the employee's place in the pay range. Table 6.3 illustrates how ranges are used to make individual pay decisions.

TABLE 6.3 Using ranges in pay decisions

Placement	Use for...
Minimum	Entry-level employees Employees new to the organization or the position Employees performing below standard
Mid-point	Fully proficient employees
Maximum	Employees highly valued by the organization based on technical skill level, company-specific experience, and/or consistently outstanding level of performance

When changes are made to an existing salary structure, pay for some employees may fall outside the new range. Pay that falls below the minimum of the salary range is referred to as a *green circle* rate of pay. Employees may also be green-circled because their experience and/or skills don't meet the requirements of the position or as a result of performance issues. Conversely, *red circle* pay refers to employees whose pay falls above the maximum of the salary range. This may occur when an employee is demoted without a corresponding decrease to base pay, because of a transfer or for some other unusual circumstance.

Wage Compression

Wage compression occurs when new employees are hired at a rate of pay greater than that earned by incumbent employees for similar skills, education, and experience. These situations are usually the most challenging during high-growth economic times or when there is high demand for certain skill sets. Compression may also occur if the organization's pay practices, merit increases, and promotional budgets aren't in line with the market. One way to reduce compression is to provide salary adjustments for the incumbent population.

Compa-ratios

A *compa-ratio* is a simple formula used to compare employee salaries. It is calculated as a percentage by taking the employee's base pay and comparing it to the mid-point of the pay range. This measure is commonly used for comparison against a group of employees and is especially useful when providing recommendations for pay increases for promotions, merit increases, and so on.

Here's the formula for finding the compa-ratio:

$$Base\ Salary \div Midpoint\ of\ Salary\ Range \times 100$$

Here's an example of a compa-ratio in action:

$$120{,}000\ base\ salary \div 100{,}000\ midpoint \times 100$$

$$= 120$$

A compa-ratio of 100 percent indicates that the base pay equals the mid-point of the salary range. For example, say an HR manager, Elena, is evaluating the new base pay for Joseph, an executive who is about to be promoted to the next pay grade. Elena determines that incumbents in the new position have an average compa-ratio of about 110 percent. Because Joseph is entering this level for the first time, a compa-ratio of less than 100 percent may be most appropriate for him.

Increases to Base Pay

Base pay can be increased for a variety of reasons: cost-of-living adjustments, annual reviews, and promotions are some of the most common.

Cost-of-Living Adjustments (COLAs)

Cost-of-living adjustments (COLAs) are generally used during periods of high inflation to reduce the effects of wage compression. These adjustments happen more often in public sector jobs than in the private sector, which generally relies on survey data to maintain compensation at a level that is competitive with the appropriate labor market, whether at the local or the national level. Many employers tie the percentage of increase to the Consumer Price Index (CPI) recommendations.

Annual Reviews

Calculating increases for annual reviews can be simple or complex. In a seniority-based compensation system where increases are based on time in the job, the calculation is relatively simple—the most common methods use a fixed dollar amount or percentage of base pay. In a performance-based system, where *merit increases* are based on demonstrated performance, the calculation is usually more complex.

Merit programs are often aligned with a performance-management system. When this is the case, an annual performance rating is the key determining factor for the amount of a merit increase. Reviews may be conducted on an employee's anniversary date or during a *focal review* period when all employees are reviewed at the same time.

A merit matrix is commonly developed by HR as a tool for managers to use in planning increases for their work units. A merit matrix combines a performance rating with the employee's position in the salary range to recommend the amount of increase. The matrix shown in Table 6.4 demonstrates that in addition to differentiating employees based on performance, it's important to differentiate based on their positions in the salary range. For example, employees at the mid-point of the salary range are considered to be fully trained and able to perform all job duties. Employees on the low end of the salary range who are moving up the learning curve quickly may warrant a higher merit increase than an employee at the mid-point or maximum of the salary range.

TABLE 6.4 Merit increase matrix, assuming 5 percent annual merit budget

Performance/position in range	Minimum	Mid-point	Maximum
Exceeds expectations	8–10 percent	6–8 percent	3–6 percent
Meets expectations	5–7 percent	4–6 percent	0 percent
Doesn't meet expectations	0 percent	0 percent	0 percent

There are several things to consider before giving a merit-based salary increase:

Employee's Position in the Salary Range Before providing a merit increase, consider the employee's current salary and where it fits into the range for the job title. For example, Tanya and Maurice are both customer service representatives. They perform the same job equally well. Tanya is at the high end of the salary range, and Maurice is on the low end. In order to keep Tanya and Maurice within the same range, Maurice, with his salary on the low end, should receive a higher merit increase than Tanya. Typically, the mid-point of the salary range is the ideal place in the salary range for a fully trained, solidly performing employee.

Tenure in Position (Hire Date/Date of Last Promotion) It's important to consider how long an employee has held a job, the amount of time since the employee's last promotion, and the date of the last increase. For example, an employee who was recently promoted may still be learning a position and not performing all job requirements at a fully qualified level. The impact of this situation on the amount of increase would be to reduce the amount of the award so that the employee's salary is between the low and mid-points of the salary range. This would reflect the level of performance being delivered.

Skill Set and Performance Compared to Peer Group HR managers and supervisors should be aware of the marketable skills and current compensation of an employee relative to the employee's peers. Employees have access to market data via the Internet, and many are very aware of their worth in the marketplace. From the employer's perspective, this places employees at risk for recruitment by competitors if they believe their pay is substandard.

In addition to merit matrices, some organizations require managers to use some sort of forced-distribution calculation when awarding merit increases. This helps to manage the salary increase budget and forces managers to differentiate between varying levels of performance by employees in their work units. To reward outstanding performers with a meaningful increase, increases for poor performers are minimal or nonexistent. This approach is designed to send a message to employees in both categories.

Managers should understand how to connect merit increases to performance and explain the connection between the two to employees. When it's unclear, employees can begin to view merit increases as COLAs. Connecting the two will help managers avoid an atmosphere of entitlement in their work units.

Promotions

Promotions occur when employees are moved into new positions with different duties and greater responsibilities or when they develop a level of experience and skill enabling them to assume added responsibilities in their current positions. Typically, a promotion is accompanied by a change in title and salary level. In organizations with traditional pay structures, this also means an increase in salary grade.

When determining how much of an increase to provide for a promotion, several factors are considered. These include how long the employee has been in the current position, how recently a merit increase was awarded, whether the new position is in the same area of the organization or a different one, and where the new salary will place the employee in the new salary range. Generally speaking, an increase of 10–15 percent is provided for promotions.

Nontraditional Pay Structures

In the more than 50 years that traditional pay structures have been used, significant changes in the way businesses operate have taken place, and many compensation professionals think that traditional, job-based systems don't serve current employer needs. Some organizations may strongly consider skill sets as determining factors for pay decisions, awarding increases to employees who possess skills that are critical to the organization's success. Other organizations may provide additional compensation for the development and acquisition of new skills. An example of this can commonly be found in manufacturing environments, where an entry-level operator who acquires additional skills for the position receives additional compensation for these skills. One method for doing this is competency-based compensation.

Although traditional pay programs focus on job requirements, a *competency-based compensation* program bases salaries on demonstrated skills and knowledge. Competency-based pay programs place responsibility for advancement on each employee: The greater the level of competence, the higher the level of pay that is available. The underlying concept for organizations is that as employees gain competence in their jobs, fewer employees are needed to achieve organizational goals, and employers can afford to pay them more.

As the information and knowledge economies replaced the industrial economy, many organizations found the bureaucracy of traditional pay programs an impediment to the rapid changes necessary for responding to changing market conditions. Instead of conducting a job analysis and evaluation so that a new job description can be created each time an employee's duties change, competency-based programs encourage employees to hone their current KSAs and develop new ones, rewarding them for their increased abilities instead of for specific job duties that may change over time.

Competency profiles replace job descriptions in these programs. A competency profile consists of 10–12 key competencies identified by those who know the job requirements best—in most cases, job incumbents who are performing at a high level. A career ladder then identifies specific levels of competency required at various stages (usually three or four, beginning at entry level and advancing to a senior, highly skilled level). The profile describes the level of fully functional competence expected from employees at each stage and the corresponding pay for each level. Competency profiles include technical skills specific to individual jobs and softer skills identified as valuable to the organization, such as communication skills, teamwork, or adaptability. Because competency-based compensation doesn't reward performance in the way traditional programs do, it's often combined with cash incentive programs to reward desired performance.

Competency-based compensation is used most effectively with broadband salary ranges to maximize flexibility as employees attain greater levels of competence in current KSAs or add new ones. Range levels are generally tied to the different stages of the competency profile.

This type of pay program communicates organizational focus to employees by selecting competencies that support strategic goals. For example, creating competencies that reward teamwork will help to change the culture from highly competitive to one that is more team-based by rewarding those employees who work effectively in teams. Clearly defined competencies help employees see that increased competence results in higher compensation and places responsibility for advancement on individual employees.

Traditional salary structures don't support the needs of competency-based pay, so some organizations have used broadbanding in conjunction with this pay program. *Broadbanding* splits positions in the company into just a few specific pay ranges. Each range includes a variety of jobs. For example, a broadband classification structure may have four levels, such as individual contributor, manager, director, and VP. All jobs in the company fit into one of the four classifications. Broadbanding helps organizations remain flat and facilitates lateral career movement. In contrast, narrowbanding or traditional pay classifications have many levels and are organized in a hierarchical and vertical fashion. Narrowbanding may not facilitate lateral movement and can create an employee focus on the organizational structure rather than job responsibilities. One benefit of broadbanding is that it can lead to greater collaboration by limiting employee focus on hierarchical differences between jobs.

Payroll

In many organizations, payroll is administered as a function of the finance department, but in others it's an HR responsibility. Although an in-depth knowledge of payroll systems and administration isn't required for the PHR/i exams, candidates should have basic knowledge of payroll activities and how they interact with HR responsibilities.

NOTE

Employers are not required under federal law to give former employees their final paycheck immediately. They can process the final paycheck in accordance with their regular payroll processing schedule. However, many states require that an employee's final paycheck be delivered on their last day of work, or within a certain number of days.

Payroll Systems

Whether an organization employs one person or hundreds of thousands, a payroll system must meet some basic requirements:

- It must accurately calculate payments that are due to employees.
- It must accurately calculate statutory and voluntary deductions.
- It must track payroll tax payments owed to federal and state agencies.
- It must provide accurate reports of payroll costs to management.
- It must provide security for payroll information.

In a small organization with a few employees, all of these requirements may be met with a manual system in which a qualified bookkeeper manually calculates the payments that are due to employees, uses federal and state tax publications to look up withholding information, and prepares checks. This process can be streamlined with the addition of an off-the-shelf accounting software program that makes the calculations, prints the checks, and tracks tax payments owed to federal and state agencies. As organizations grow, manual systems are no longer feasible and may be replaced by a service bureau, which performs the necessary calculations, prints the checks or deposits them electronically, and submits payroll tax payments on behalf of the organization. Very large organizations may develop proprietary software designed to handle their specific needs.

Because payroll systems collect some of the same information that is entered into human resource information systems (HRISs), HR managers can benefit from systems that are able to interact and share information to reduce or eliminate the double entry of information into separate systems.

Payroll Administration

Payroll administration is the function in the company that is responsible for calculating employee earnings and deductions and maintaining records of those payments. Administering payroll is one of the most visible functions performed in any organization because it affects every employee from the CEO to the most junior assistant. Not only is it visible to everyone, but a payroll error has the potential to profoundly affect an employee's life, if only until the error can be corrected.

Employee Earnings

The payroll department is responsible for preparing employee paychecks and ensuring that earnings are calculated correctly. To calculate nonexempt earnings, the payroll department must know the employee's base pay rate, shift differentials, tips, and bonuses; how many hours the employee worked during the pay period; and whether any paid leave was used. With this information, the *gross pay*, or earnings before taxes, can be calculated.

To calculate earnings for exempt employees, payroll needs to know the base salary, any bonus amounts, and any paid leave used during the pay period.

Statutory Deductions

Before employees receive their paychecks, various deductions are made from the gross earnings. These deductions include the following:

- Social Security
- Medicare
- Federal income tax
- State income tax
- Unemployment insurance (in some states)
- Disability insurance (in some states)
- Other state and local taxes

These amounts are withheld from employee earnings. Employers match the amount of Social Security and Medicare taxes that are withheld from employees. These amounts, along with the federal income tax withheld, are remitted to the IRS at regular intervals. Failure to remit taxes on time results in substantial penalties for employers. State and local taxes are remitted separately to the appropriate government agency according to payment schedules established by each agency.

At the end of each calendar quarter, reports of gross payroll and withheld taxes are filed with the federal, state, and local taxing authorities. These reports reconcile the amount of tax withheld to the amounts deposited during the quarter. At the end of the year, W-2 forms are prepared for each employee and submitted to federal and state tax agencies.

Federal law in the United States mandates that payroll taxes must be withheld and paid for remote workers, just as they are for on-site employees. Employers are required to withhold federal income tax, Social Security, and Medicare taxes from employees' wages, regardless of their work location. Additionally, employers must also contribute their share of Social Security and Medicare taxes.

When it comes to state payroll taxes, the rules can be more complex, as they vary depending on the states involved. Employers must consider the state where the remote worker resides and the state where the company is based. Some states have reciprocal agreements that simplify tax withholding for employees who live in one state and work in another, but it is important for employers to comply with both federal and applicable state tax laws to ensure proper payroll tax withholding and reporting.

In terms of global remote workers or expatriates, the United States has *totalization agreements* with several countries to avoid double taxation on social security. These agreements determine which country's social security system the employee and employer will contribute to, preventing the employee from having to pay into both systems.

Voluntary Deductions

A number of other deductions may be made from an employee's paycheck. These include medical, dental, and other health benefit contributions; 401(k) contributions; union dues; and, in some cases, contributions to charities designated by employees.

Involuntary Deductions

From time to time, employers may be required by a court order or tax levy to withhold additional funds from employee paychecks. These withholdings are known as *wage garnishments* and are issued to satisfy a debt owed by the employee. Garnishments may come in the form of a court order (for example, an order to pay child support or another debt) or from a government agency such as the IRS or other taxing authority to collect unpaid back taxes. Wage garnishments aren't voluntary, and employers have no discretion as to whether to honor them.

The Federal Wage Garnishment Law is found in Title III of the Consumer Credit Protection Act (CCPA) of 1968 and applies to all employers and employees. Employers are required to withhold funds from an employee's paycheck and send the money to an entity designated in the court order or levy document.

Title III of the CCPA protects employees in three ways:

- Prohibits employers from terminating employees whose wages are garnished for any one debt, even if the employer receives multiple garnishment orders for the same debt
- Sets limits on the amount that can be garnished in any single week
- Defines how disposable earnings are to be calculated for garnishment withholdings

The law doesn't protect employees from termination if the employer receives garnishments for more than one debt.

Disposable earnings are what is left in an employee's paycheck after all legally mandated deductions have been made, such as federal and state income tax, Social Security, state and local taxes, disability insurance, and so on. Title III provides separate garnishment calculation methods for debt garnishments and child-support orders:

Debt Garnishment Calculations Title III defines two methods for calculating the maximum weekly garnishment. The first method allows garnishment of up to 25 percent of disposable earnings. Disposable earnings are the amount of earnings left after legally required deductions have been made. The second method is calculated by multiplying the federal minimum wage ($7.25 per hour as of 2024) by 30 ($217.50). The total is subtracted from the disposable earnings. Any disposable earnings that exceed that amount must be sent directly to the recipient designated in the order and not to the employee.

The maximum amount of garnishment allowed is the lesser of those two calculations.

Child-Support Garnishment Calculations Title III allows child-support garnishments of up to 50 percent of an employee's disposable earnings if the employee is currently supporting a spouse or child and up to 60 percent if not. Earnings include:

- Commissions
- Discretionary and nondiscretionary bonuses
- Profit sharing
- Referral and sign-on bonuses
- Moving or relocation incentive payments
- Attendance, safety, and cash service awards
- Retroactive merit increases
- Payment for working during a holiday
- Workers' compensation payments for wage replacement, whether paid periodically or in a lump sum
- Termination pay (e.g., payment of last wages, as well as any outstanding accrued benefits)
- Severance pay

If support payments are more than 12 weeks in arrears, wages may be garnished an additional 5 percent. There are no restrictions on child-support garnishments.

Personal Responsibility and Work Opportunity Reconciliation Act of 1996

This legislation requires employers to report all new hires within 20 days of their hire date to the State Department of New Hires. The law requires only that employers forward the W-4 form to the state, but some states have developed their own forms for this purpose. As a side benefit for employers, the new hire reporting database has reduced and prevented fraudulent or erroneous unemployment payments that would otherwise be charged to the employer's unemployment insurance account. The database also cross-checks against workers compensation claims, which has reduced fraud and errors in those programs as well.

Payroll-Related Information

The data collected throughout the lifecycle of the employee's tenure with the organization must be adequately accounted for and managed. This data generation begins at the time of hire when basic information is gathered, such as tax withholdings, and continues with pay adjustments to account for benefits enrollment, wage increases, or exceptions such as garnishments. It ends at the time of termination when accrued benefits are calculated, health insurance and retirement benefits are rolled over or cancelled, and final wages are paid to the employee.

Outsourcing Compensation

Many organizations are turning to outsourcing groups to help navigate the complexities of managing the various components of compensation and benefits plans. In fact, one of the most common outsourced HR functions is that of processing payroll. The services offered by various companies include payroll, COBRA administration, quarterly reporting, tax filings, and HR expertise in other functions. Outsourcing payroll is a strategic decision that allows the internal talent to focus on the core competencies required for successful operations. However, managing the vendors is still an important function of HR, because the hiring company typically retains liability in the case of errors or omissions in compliance.

Finding the right provider(s) is the first step toward effectively managing the outsourcing process. Clearly defining expectations and needs, clarifying the frequency of contact, and agreeing on set deliverables are all methods of effective vendor management.

Benefits

Employee benefit programs are an integral part of a company's total compensation plan and represent a significant cost to employers. Of equal importance to compensation in the Total Rewards mix, employee benefit programs are varied and designed to meet specific employee needs. There are two basic types of benefit programs: those that are legally mandated and those that are voluntary. The purpose of this section is to explore how HR professionals, working with senior management, can determine the mix of benefits that will attract and retain the type of employees needed by the organization to achieve its goals.

When most employees think about their benefit packages, they think of medical and dental insurance, vacation and sick leave, and the retirement plan; however, employers provide many other benefits that employees often overlook. These include non-monetary benefits such as the location of their facilities, the length of the daily commute for employees, "dress down" days, and monetary benefits such as paid volunteer time or tuition assistance. These are all factors taken into consideration by candidates when determining whether to accept an offer. However, without specific effort on the part of employers, employees are often unaware of the value of the benefits provided for them because they rarely consider these costs when they think about their total income. Decisions about these facets of the employment relationship in each company can either help or hurt the efforts of the organization to attract and retain employees.

NOTE

The Human Resource Certification Institutes (HRCIs) glossary of terms has at least four separate entries related to the term "benefits." Though slightly redundant, this is a useful way to understand the term through the filter of exam content:

- **Benefit Programs:** Workers' entitlements in addition to base salary. Examples include health insurance, life insurance, disability pay, retirement pension, and so on.
- **Benefits:** Compensation that the employee receives in addition to base salary. Examples include health insurance, company housing, company meals, clothing allowance, pensions, and gym memberships.
- **Employee/Employer Benefits:** Payments or allowances that organizations give to their employees (e.g., medical insurance, Social Security taxes, pension contributions, education reimbursement, and car or clothing allowance).
- **Healthcare Benefits:** Company-sponsored medical plans that help employees pay for the cost of doctor visits, hospitalization, surgeries, and so on.

Two main categories of benefits may be offered: involuntary and voluntary.

Involuntary Benefits

The first involuntary, or legally mandated, employee benefits were introduced as part of President Franklin Delano Roosevelt's (FDR's) New Deal programs during the mid-1930s to aid the millions of Americans who lost their jobs and were unable to find work during the Great Depression. Unemployment reached 25 percent at the low point of the Depression, leaving many families destitute, homeless, and living in shantytowns throughout the nation. In response to this economic crisis, when FDR was elected in 1932, he set about creating protections for American workers to provide a safety net during economic downturns.

Once again, keep in mind that legal requirements in your state may differ in some respects from the federal requirements. For the PHR examination, you must be familiar with the *federal* requirements. They include Social Security, Medicare, unemployment insurance, family and medical leave (eligibility based on number of employees in the organization and individual hours worked), workers' compensation, and COBRA benefit continuation. All of these are discussed in great detail in Appendix C.

It is also worth noting that many states are exploring (and adopting) paid sick leave requirements. New York, for example, passed the Earned Sick Time Act, which requires that workers earn one hour of paid sick time for every 30 hours worked. For PHR exam preparation purposes, you don't need to know or understand the specifics of state laws—the exam is based on federal acts. You do need to understand that when there are competing laws between the federal and state government, you generally must comply with the law that gives the greatest benefit to the employee.

NOTE

Understanding unemployment rates is important because it is a measure of an employer's ability to attract qualified workers. Higher rates mean there are more individuals looking for work; lower rates mean a tighter labor market. As referenced earlier, the highest rate of unemployment in the United States occurred in 1933 at 25 percent. For perspective, compare this to other unemployment highs of 11 percent in the '80s, 7 percent in the '90s, 9.9 percent in the first decade of the 2000s, and the most recent high of 3.8 percent in 2023. Find the full list at `https://www.thebalancemoney.com/unemployment-rate-by-year-3305506`.

Voluntary Benefits

The kinds of benefits that organizations may voluntarily provide are significantly more complicated. Table 6.5 provides some examples of voluntary benefits.

TABLE 6.5 Voluntary employee benefits

Types of benefits	Benefit details
Deferred compensation	Qualified pension plans Nonqualified pension plans
Health and welfare benefits	Dental insurance Vision insurance Life insurance AD&D insurance Short-/long-term disability insurance Long-term care insurance
Work-life balance	Vacation leave Sick leave Paid time off Paid holidays Childcare Fitness Elder care

TABLE 6.5 Voluntary employee benefits *(continued)*

Types of benefits	Benefit details
Other voluntary benefits	Employee assistance plans Relocation assistance Tuition reimbursement On-site schooling Student loan help Flexible spending accounts Cafeteria plan Adoption assistance Section 529 plans Commute assistance

Employers attract qualified candidates with different types of skills by offering cash compensation that leads or matches the labor market for those skills. They can also use the mix of their benefit packages to attract and retain segments of the labor market with characteristics that align to their particular business values and goals. For example, an organization interested in attracting employees focused on maintaining a high level of knowledge in their chosen fields may offer a generous educational reimbursement benefit and provide training opportunities as a way of attracting and retaining those employees.

Making decisions about the voluntary benefit package that is most appropriate for a particular organization's workforce requires consideration of many factors: demographics, industry standards, local area practices, the financial situation of the company, and the organizational culture, among them. A needs assessment provides insight into which benefits are most attractive to the organization's current workforce and provides a starting point for evaluating options. There are many choices, and finding the right mix can significantly affect an employer's ability to attract and retain employees with the desired qualifications. For example, Amazon has a Career Choice program that will reimburse a portion of employee tuition and fees to train them in high-demand fields such as nursing, tech, and machining. Participants can use the program to advance their career with Amazon but are not required to. Amazon noted that participants in this program have one fourth of the attrition rate for nonparticipants. The benefit to Amazon is that it allows for workforce planning because they have data related to employees who will be exiting the company within the four years or so that the benefit is available.

Voluntary benefits programs also need to address the lifestyle needs of all employees, not just some. LinkedIn, for example, heard from employees without kids who were frustrated that they did not get the same benefit from the paid parental leave policy as their coworkers with children. In response, LinkedIn has a personalized benefit offering where employees can choose their perks, up to an annual allowance. Employees can spend this on lifestyle perks, including dog walking and massages. LinkedIn is an excellent case study in creative benefits management; you can take a deeper look here: `https://perkupapp.com/post/the-linkedin-employee-benefits-that-employees-love`.

To aid in understanding the discussion of benefits in this section, candidates for the PHR/i exams should be familiar with the following list of terms:

Defined Benefit A *defined-benefit plan* is a traditional pension plan in which the employer provides a specific benefit upon retirement. The funds in these plans aren't accounted for individually.

Defined Contribution A *defined-contribution plan* is an individual plan in which the amount of funds contributed is known but the amount of the benefit that is eventually paid out isn't known because it depends on the investment returns that are earned. The funds are accounted for in individual accounts for each participant.

Nonforfeitable A *nonforfeitable claim* is one that exists because of a participant's service. Nonforfeitable claims are unconditional and legally enforceable.

Party in Interest A *party in interest* may be a fiduciary, a person, or an entity providing services to the plan, an employer, or employee organization; a person who owns 50 percent or more of the business; relatives of any of the above; or corporations that are involved with the plan in any of these functions.

Plan Administrator The *plan administrator* is the person designated by the plan sponsor to manage the plan.

Plan Sponsor The *plan sponsor* is the entity that establishes the plan. This may be a single employer, a labor organization, or in the case of a multiemployer plan, a group representing the parties that established the plan.

Qualified Plan A *qualified plan* meets ERISA requirements and provides tax advantages for both employees and employers. To be classified as a qualified plan, a pension plan can't provide additional benefits for officers, shareholders, executives, supervisors, or other highly compensated employees—all employees in the organization must be eligible for all plan benefits.

Nonqualified Plan A *nonqualified retirement plan* is one in which the benefits exceed the limitations of qualified plans or don't meet other IRS requirements for favorable tax treatment. These plans aren't required to include all employees, so they may provide additional benefits to officers, shareholders, executives, supervisors, or other highly compensated employees.

Voluntary benefits fall into four main categories: deferred compensation, health and welfare benefits, and non-monetary rewards. Although there are no federal laws requiring employers to provide any of these (with the exception of the mandates of the Affordable Care Act covered in Appendix C), some federal laws regulate pensions or benefits when employers choose to include them in their Total Rewards packages.

Deferred Compensation Benefits

Deferred compensation is a type of employee pension that is tax-deferred, such as individual retirement accounts (IRAs), 401(k) programs, or traditional employer pension plans. HRCI defines deferred compensation programs as those that "allow an employee to contribute a portion of income over time to be paid as a lump sum at retirement when the employee's income tax rate will be lower." This employee benefit was first offered in the late 19th century by business owners who wanted to reward long-term employees. Early pension plans were defined-benefit plans with all funds being provided by the employers. The payments owed to retirees weren't set aside specifically for them but were made from business operating funds. As a result, a company that went out of business was no longer able to make the pension payments, and employees didn't receive the benefits that had been promised to them. To encourage businesses to provide pension benefits, in 1935 the Social Security Administration (SSA) allowed employers who provided pension plans to deduct the full amount of the payments they made to employees, but there were no laws to govern how the plans operated or to require that the funds to pay pensions be set aside to ensure their availability for retirees. In 1958, Congress made its first attempt to exert some control over private pension plans when it passed the Welfare and Pension Plans Disclosure Act (WPDA) requiring the administrators of health insurance, pension, and supplemental unemployment insurance plans to file descriptions of the plans and annual financial reports with the DOL.

As the number of pension plans provided for employees by American businesses grew, some companies found ways to obtain tax benefits from pension plans while denying benefits to employees. There were no requirements for communicating information to plan participants, so many employees were unaware of eligibility requirements. There was also little oversight of the ways the plans were operated. Vesting schedules were inadequate, and many long-term employees found themselves ineligible to receive pension benefits as a result. There were no established standards to ensure the viability of plans to pay promised benefits. The result of this was that many employees found themselves without pensions when they were ready to retire. Furthermore, some businesses set lengthy vesting schedules to obtain tax benefits but terminated long-term employees just before they vested in the plan.

Qualified Deferred Compensation Plans

A qualified deferred compensation plan is one that meets all Employee Retirement Income Security Act (ERISA) requirements and protects employees from loss of benefits due to employer mismanagement of pension funds. Within the broad description of a qualified plan, employers have a number of options to choose from when designing a plan that meets the needs of their particular workforce:

Defined-Benefit Plans HRCI defines a *defined-benefit plan* as "a retirement plan that tells participants exactly how much money they will receive on a specific later date (usually the day they retire)." A defined-benefit plan is based on a formula. The formula looks at two factors: salary and length of service with the company. In most traditional defined-benefit plans, the retirement benefit is based on the salary earned during the last 5 to 10 years of earnings, but it may also be based on career average earnings, a flat dollar amount for each year of service, or a unit benefit plan in which the benefit payment is based on a percentage of earnings multiplied by the years of service.

Real World Scenario

Retirement Before ERISA

In 1963, nearly 7,000 employees of the Studebaker Corporation lost all or most of their pension benefits because of a plant closure in Indiana. More than 4,000 of these employees had served an average of more than 22 years with the company and, at the time of the plant's closure, were an average of 52 years old. The pension fund failed largely because there was no legal precedent requiring organizations to set aside adequate funds with which to pay retirement benefits; plans at that time were still being funded from current operating funds in the Studebaker Corporation.

Although the failure of the Studebaker Corporation fund wasn't unique, the large number of workers deprived of benefits focused national attention on the problem and led eventually to the passage of the Employee Retirement Income Security Act (ERISA). ERISA increased reporting requirements, required that pension funds be separated from the operating funds of the business, established vesting schedules for plan participants, required employers to provide summary plan descriptions of the plans to employees, and set minimum standards for fund management.

In these plans, the company is committed to pay a specified benefit amount when an employee retires. How much the company must accrue each year may fluctuate based on the return earned on the invested funds. If the funds are invested in high-growth investments, the company will need to transfer less cash from its operating funds to the pension trust. But if the return earned on the investment drops, the company may have to play catch-up with larger-than-anticipated transfers of cash to maintain the viability of the plan. During the stock-market boom of the late 1990s, many companies didn't need to transfer large sums to fund their pension accounts, but when the stock market dropped, much of the value of the pension funds was lost. This required larger transfers to be made to maintain availability of the pension funds for employees. In defined-benefit plans, employers take the risk for paying out the promised benefit at retirement.

Cash-Balance Plans *Cash-balance plans (CBPs)* have become increasingly popular since they were approved by the IRS in 1985. According to the DOL, CBPs work as follows:

> "When a participant becomes entitled to receive benefits under a cash balance plan, the benefits that are received are defined in terms of an account balance. For example, assume that a participant has an account balance of $100,000 when he or she reaches age 65. If the participant decides to retire at that time, he or she would have the right to an annuity based on that account balance. Such an annuity might be approximately $8500 per year for life. In many cash balance plans, however, the

> participant could instead choose (with consent from his or her spouse) to take a lump sum benefit equal to the $100,000 account balance."

It is easy to understand CBP's by thinking of it as an individual employee savings account in which the employer makes deposits based on a defined formula.

For employees, the benefit of the CBP is that it's portable. CBPs also have higher contribution limits, which can be attractive for employees who are behind on retirement savings.

Defined-Contribution Plans A defined-contribution plan relies on contributions from employees and employers to fund IRAs. In these plans, the amount of the contribution is fixed, but the amount of the benefit available upon retirement can vary based on the type of investments made and the returns earned on them. In these plans, the employee takes the risk for having funds available at retirement. There are several types of defined-contribution plans:

Profit-Sharing Plans Also known as *discretionary contributions*, *profit-sharing plans* allow employers to contribute deferred compensation based on a percentage of company earnings each year. The percentage of the contribution may vary from year to year, and the company may elect to make no contributions in some years. This is an employer-only contribution plan. As of 2024, contribution limits are the lesser of 100 percent of compensation, up to $69,000. These contributions have favorable tax implications, so employers benefit. And, because the contributions may vary from year to year, profit-sharing plans work well for companies with erratic profit levels. Employees benefit as they gain retirement savings, and participant loans are allowed.

Money-Purchase Plans A *money-purchase plan* uses a fixed percentage of employee earnings to defer compensation. This type of plan works well for organizations with relatively stable earnings from year to year because the percentage is fixed, and once established, contributions must be made every year. The contribution limits are the same as the limits for profit-sharing plans.

Target-Benefit Plans A *target-benefit plan* is a hybrid plan with similarities to a defined-benefit plan and a money-purchase plan. Instead of using a fixed percentage of employee salaries to determine annual contribution amounts, actuarial formulas calculate the contribution amount needed to reach a predetermined benefit amount at retirement. Because this amount takes into consideration the current age of each employee, different amounts will be contributed for employees with equal compensation packages. As with other deferred-contribution plans, the amounts are distributed to individual employee accounts, and the contribution limits are the same as the limits for profit-sharing plans.

401(k) Plans A common type of deferred compensation is the 401(k) plan, established by the Revenue Act of 1978. A 401(k) plan allows for contributions from both employees and employers. Employees may defer part of their pay before taxes up to predetermined limits. Employers may make contributions as well; the limits for these are the same as those for profit-sharing plans. Plans similar to the 401(k) are available for nonprofit workers [403(b) plans] and for public employees (457 plans). Any earnings or losses that accrue in the account impact the funds available for retirement, and employees are ultimately responsible for ensuring that the funds are properly managed and available for use when they're ready to retire.

One requirement of 401(k) plans is that they may not provide greater benefits to highly compensated employees (HCEs) than other employees. An HCE is defined as a plan participant who is either an owner with more than 5 percent equity, or a worker who received compensation in excess of $155,000 or more during the 12-month period immediately preceding the plan year (the lookback year), and at the company's discretion, is one of the top-paid 20 percent of employees. If you are an HCE, the U.S. government limits contributions to your retirement plan. Each year, an actual deferral percentage (ADP) test must be conducted to ensure that the plan is within limits set by IRS regulations. When the ADP test indicates that HCE participants are realizing greater benefits from the plan than non-HCE participants, the company must take action to correct this or lose the tax benefits of the plan. To correct the problem, a company may refund the excess contributions to HCE participants, which will increase their taxable income for the prior year, or the company may increase matching contributions to non-HCE employees in order to pass the test. Another option to correct imbalances is to aggregate the plan with other plans sponsored by the employer, if available.

Nonqualified Deferred Compensation

Nonqualified deferred-compensation plans aren't protected by ERISA and are generally made available only to a limited number of employees at the executive level. Known as *top-hat plans*, these benefits provide retirement funds that supplement qualified retirement benefits and aren't subject to ERISA discrimination testing requirements. These plans allow highly compensated employees to defer income in excess of limits placed on qualified plans. Two types of nonqualified plans are as follows:

Grantor or Rabbi Trusts Commonly known as *rabbi trusts, grantor trusts* are nonqualified deferred-compensation plans established to provide retirement income for officers, directors, and HCEs. The funds are unsecured and therefore subject to claims made by the organization's creditors. Benefits are taxable as ordinary income at the time they're paid to beneficiaries.

Excess Deferral Plans An excess deferral plan allows the organization to make contributions to a nonqualified plan in order to reduce the impact of discrimination testing on HCEs. This is done by making up the difference between what the executive could have contributed to the plan and what was actually allowed because of limits required by the qualified plan.

Health and Welfare Benefits

Health and welfare benefits have come to be expected by most American workers. The benefits that fall into this category are described in this section.

Medical Insurance

The cost of medical insurance is substantial for employers and employees. The costs can be controlled to a certain extent by the type of plan selected. These are some plans to consider:

Health Maintenance Organizations (HMOs) HMOs are a type of managed-care plan that focuses on preventive care and controlling health costs. HMOs generally use a *gatekeeper*, most often the patient's primary care physician (PCP), to determine whether the patient need to be seen by a specialist.

Preferred Provider Organizations (PPOs) PPOs use a network of healthcare providers for patient services and don't require patients to be referred by a primary care physician. Employees who use healthcare services within the network make copayments. Out-of-network providers may be used, but the insured will have to pay the difference between the fees negotiated by the plan and those charged by the provider.

Point-of-Service (POS) Plans A POS plan is a hybrid between an HMO and a PPO where the employee gets to choose which service to use each time they see a provider. POS plans include network physicians but allow for referrals outside the network. Like HMOs, these plans require employees to select a primary care physician (PCP) from doctors in the network. The PCP generally refers employees to specialists in the network when needed, but like PPOs, an employee may see specialists outside the network as well. When employees see physicians outside the network, they must submit reimbursement claims to the insurance company themselves. Payment is covered by the plan, but when the employee sees a care provider outside the POS network, the employee usually pays a higher percentage of the cost than for in-network physicians.

Exclusive Provider Organizations (EPOs) An EPO consists of a network and includes a hospital. Unlike physicians who participate in a PPO, EPO physicians may see only those patients who are part of the EPO. Patients in an EPO may see only those healthcare providers in the network; they receive no reimbursement for healthcare obtained outside the network.

Physician Hospital Organizations (PHOs) In a PHO, physicians join with a hospital and together rely on the PHO structure to develop and market their services and to negotiate and sign contracts. PHOs are unique in that they contract directly with employer organizations to provide services.

Fee-for-Service (FFS) Plans An FFS plan is typically the most expensive to employers and employees because it places no restrictions on the doctors or hospitals available to the patient. These plans require patients to pay for services out-of-pocket and submit claims to be reimbursed for expenses.

In managed-care settings, providers often determine premiums based on the costs incurred by the group during the current coverage period. The costs are analyzed by type, and premiums for the following period are adjusted based on this *experience rating*. Experience rating affects premiums by adjusting them based on an individual or group's past claim history, leading to higher premiums for those with more claims and lower premiums for those with fewer claims. Some organizations have implemented wellness programs to improve the experience rating and lower premiums.

Most carriers use a standard coordination of benefits (COB) process when an employee is also covered as a dependent on another plan, such as that of a spouse or parent. When this occurs, the employee's primary coverage pays according to the plan benefits. The secondary coverage will then pay up to 100 percent of the allowable expenses, including deductibles and copayments for the claim. The secondary plan will pay only up to the amount it would have paid as the primary carrier, so the total insurance payout may still be less than 100 percent of the claim.

Other Health Benefits

In addition to medical insurance benefits, many companies offer other health-related benefit options. These include dental, vision, and prescription coverage insurance, among others:

Dental Insurance Employers may choose dental insurance plans to provide varying levels of coverage for preventive or restoration work such as fillings, major restoration work such as bridges, and orthodontia.

Vision Insurance One of the lowest-cost benefits available, vision insurance provides employees with reduced costs for eye examinations and contact lenses or glasses.

Prescription Coverage Even though most medical plans include some form of coverage for prescription drugs, these plans are also offered separately. The cost of the plans is managed by controlling the amount of the required copayment and requiring the use of generic drugs instead of name brands.

Life Insurance Many insurance companies bundle basic life insurance with medical or dental insurance for a very low rate and offer supplemental insurance for employees who are willing to pay an additional premium for the coverage.

It's important to keep in mind that the IRS views group life insurance in excess of $50,000 as *imputed income* (any indirect compensation paid on behalf of employees) when the premiums are paid by employers. This means that there are no tax consequences if the total amount of life insurance policies do not exceed $50,000. The imputed cost of coverage beyond the threshold must be included in income calculations and is subject to Social Security and Medicare taxes. The calculation of imputed income for group life insurance is based on a table provided by the IRS. The table assigns a small amount per month for each $1,000 of coverage that exceeds $50,000 based on an employee's age. The amounts range from $.05 for employees who are under age 25 to $2.06 per month for employees age 70 and older.

NOTE You can find a complete guide for employers on imputed income and fringe benefits at `https://www.irs.gov/pub/irs-pdf/p15b.pdf`.

Accidental Death and Dismemberment (AD&D) Insurance AD&D insurance can provide insurance for employees and their dependents in the event of an accident that results in the death of the covered person or the loss of a bodily function. AD&D doesn't pay benefits in the event of death due to an illness.

Short- and Long-Term Disability Insurance Disability insurance protects employees from income loss because of disability caused by illness or accident. Disability protection generally begins with sick leave provided by employers. When employees exhaust their sick leave, they may become eligible for short-term disability insurance, which can be in effect for anywhere between 3 and 6 months. Employees still disabled when short-term disability ends become eligible for long-term disability coverage, which can last for anywhere from 2 years until age 65.

Because these benefits are so common, businesses seeking to use them as recruiting and retention tools must find some way to differentiate their plans from those of their competitors. This need must be balanced with the skyrocketing cost of medical insurance and its impact on the bottom line. Companies looking for a way to increase the attractiveness of their benefit packages may want to reduce or eliminate the employee contribution toward premiums for themselves or for their families or include coverage for domestic partners in the package. A *domestic partnership* is a legal or personal relationship between two people who aren't legally married or in a legally recognized civil union. State and local governments vary in how they view and recognize domestic partnerships.

Health Benefit Cost Management

Regardless of the health plan selected, it's crucial for HR professionals to manage the cost of benefits by selecting the most cost-effective method for funding those benefits. There are several choices, and determining the most appropriate choice for a particular organization depends on factors such as the size of the organization and claim history.

One common funding method for smaller organizations is to purchase insurance coverage for the plan. The organization pays premiums for all participants in the plan, and the insurance company manages payment to the service provider and manages claims issues. In this funding method, the insurer assumes the risk for any unusual claims that may result in claim costs exceeding premiums received. Insurers keep track of the claim history and adjust premiums in subsequent years to recover any losses.

In larger organizations, it may make sense to self-fund the insurance plan. A *self-funded plan* or *captive plan* is one in which the employer creates a claim fund and pays all claims through it. Self-funded plans must conduct annual discrimination tests to ensure that HCEs aren't using the plan disproportionately to non-HCEs. In this case, the employer assumes the risk for unusual claims that may exceed the amount budgeted for the plan.

Another option is for organizations to implement a *partially self-funded plan*. These plans use *stop-loss insurance* to prevent a single catastrophic claim from devastating the claim fund. The employer agrees on a preset maximum coverage amount that will be paid from the claim fund for each participant before the insurance company begins to pay the claim.

Self-funded organizations may decide to contract with an insurance company to manage and pay claims, which is known as an *administrative services only (ASO) plan.* A third-party administrator (TPA), which provides claim-management services only and isn't part of an insurance company, may also be used for self-funded plans.

To take advantage of economies of scale, smaller employers may form *health purchasing alliances (HPAs)* with other employers in the geographic area. The HPA negotiates and contracts for the plans on behalf of all members of the group.

Non-monetary Rewards

PHR/i responsibility specifically calls out several non-monetary rewards, which are a form of non-cash payments usually delivered as a perk or a benefit. Non-monetary rewards enhance an employer total compensation package and are designed to attract and retain a qualified workforce.

Work-Life Benefits

Work-life benefits help employees manage the conflict between work demands and family responsibilities and develop a healthful balance for the many areas of their lives. Some of the benefits in this category include time-off programs, wellness benefits, and assistance with childcare or eldercare needs.

Vacation Pay Vacation pay is generally earned as employees complete time on the job. Many companies require employees to work a specific period of time, usually 3 to 6 months, before they're eligible to use any accumulated vacation pay. Some companies allow employees to accumulate vacation pay year-to-year; others have a "use it or lose it" policy, although some state laws prohibit companies from forcing employees to forfeit time off that has been earned. In those cases, companies may decide to pay employees for the leave that would otherwise be forfeited.

Most vacation-pay policies require employees to schedule time off in advance and obtain approval from their supervisors before scheduling vacations.

Sick Pay Sick pay is provided for employees to use when they're ill or when they need to care for a sick child or other family member. Some states such as California are now mandating sick time, so HR practitioners must stay up-to-date on how state requirements may differ from the voluntary nature of sick pay at the federal level.

Holiday Pay Many companies provide paid time off for a variety of national holidays, including New Year's Day, Presidents' Day, Martin Luther King, Jr.'s birthday, Memorial Day, Juneteenth, Independence Day, Labor Day, Columbus Day, Veterans Day, Thanksgiving, and Christmas.

Paid Time Off (PTO) Many companies have combined all forms of time off into a single PTO bank that employees can use as they see fit to handle illnesses, personal needs, vacations, and other matters. This provides greater flexibility for employees but can add to employer costs because of the way state laws view vacation and sick pay. Vacation pay is usually viewed as earned leave, meaning that employees must be paid for the leave if they don't use it (for example, if they resign from the company). Sick leave is usually viewed differently, and employees aren't compensated for sick time they don't use. Because PTO combines the two, it's viewed as earned leave, and employees must be compensated for all leave they have earned but not used.

Unlimited Paid Time Off Unlimited time-off programs have received a lot of recent attention thanks in large part to high-profile companies such as Netflix and Virgin Airlines adopting unlimited vacation time for their employees. While still very few employers offer unlimited time-off benefits, it is an emerging trend for which HR practitioners should be prepared. Often combining both vacation and sick pay, employers with unlimited time-off policies have the advantage of not having to track accruals as well as the positive employee morale that is associated with such programs. The expectation is that trusted employees will manage their time effectively and not take time off that will negatively impact the business. The downside to these programs is that some jobs cannot be structured to allow employees to miss days, making these programs difficult to apply consistently and with precise fairness. Defining just what "unlimited" means can also back employers into a corner when complying with medical and other leave policies or collective bargaining agreements.

Sabbaticals and Leaves of Absence In educational institutions, sabbaticals are a long-standing benefit provided for educators in which, after working for a specified period of time, they receive a year off with pay to pursue further education, conduct research, or write books in their field of study. Some companies have adopted this benefit for long-term employees to encourage professional development.

Jury Duty Pay Employers are required to provide time off for employees who are called to jury duty, although most states don't require employees to be paid for this time. Many employers pay the difference between the employee's regular earnings and the amount they're paid for performing jury duty.

Bereavement Leave Most companies allow employees time off with pay to attend funeral services for close relatives.

Parental Leave Some companies provide paid leave for parents of newborns or newly adopted children. These can be run concurrently with the benefits of the Family Medical Leave Act (FMLA); many employers offer more generous paid or unpaid time off on top of the protected time offered by the FMLA.

Volunteer Time Off (VTO) Another growing trend in time off benefits is allowing employees to take paid or unpaid time off to volunteer. Volunteer work has evolved beyond physical locations, and many individuals now participate online or over the phone. The Association of Corporate Citizenship Professionals surveyed members in 2023 and found more than 60 percent reported a rise in participation in employee volunteer activities, counteracting recent declines. This increase reflects a concerted effort to enhance engagement and align corporate values with those of employees through volunteerism. To increase participation, employers are diversifying volunteer options, including more group volunteering opportunities (59 percent), emphasizing in-person volunteering (48 percent), and expanding individual volunteering options (35 percent). Volunteer time-off policies are able to attract socially conscious and committed employees as well as increase their loyalty over the long term, and can be easily absorbed into the administration practices of existing time-off systems.

Tuition Reimbursement

Workplace tuition reimbursement programs offer employees the chance to pursue further education while working, with the company covering part or all of the tuition costs. These programs aid in talent attraction and retention while improving the skills of the workforce and supporting career pathing and succession planning.

In today's economy, some employers also offer student loan forgiveness as part of their benefits package, alleviating the burden of educational debt for employees. Section 2206 of the CARES Act allows employers to provide tax-free payments of up to $5,250 per year to their employees' federal student loans, without the payments being subject to federal income tax for the employee. This relief is in effect until 2025 but it may be extended or made permanent, so it is necessary to keep an eye on this.

Workplace Amenities

Employers are becoming increasingly creative in finding ways to differentiate themselves to attract and retain diverse talent. Workplace amenities are one way to do this. These amenities encompass a wide range of offerings, often designed to enhance employee convenience, well-being, and productivity. Additionally, employers are using enhanced workplace amenities such as on-site gyms, gourmet cafeterias, and relaxation spaces to entice remote workers back to the office. For instance, Google has revamped its office spaces to include amenities like massage rooms, fitness centers, and free meals to encourage employees to return to in-person work.

There can be a perception of inequity when remote workers lack access to the amenities available to their in-office counterparts. HR can offset this inequity by offering equivalent benefits to remote workers, such as stipends for home office equipment, wellness programs, and meal delivery services.

Employee Recognition

Employee recognition programs are initiatives implemented by organizations to acknowledge and reward employees for their contributions, achievements, and performance. These programs aim to boost employee morale, motivation, and engagement by publicly recognizing and appreciating their efforts and contributions to the organization's success. Here are examples of workplace recognition programs:

- **Employee of the Month:** Recognizing one outstanding employee each month for their exceptional performance, attitude, or contributions to the team. Employee-of-the-month programs are still a common practice, but HR teams should be aware that these programs can sometimes create unhealthy competition and resentment among employees, undermining teamwork and morale. As one CEO put it, recognizing one employee can send a message to others that they are not important.

- **Spot Awards:** Providing on-the-spot recognition or rewards to employees who demonstrate exemplary behavior, problem-solving skills, or customer service.
- **Peer-to-Peer Recognition:** Encouraging employees to recognize and appreciate their colleagues' contributions through a peer-recognition program, such as a "kudos" board or online platform.
- **Longevity Awards:** Celebrating employees' years of service with the organization by awarding milestone gifts, certificates, or special events to commemorate their dedication and loyalty.
- **Digital Badges:** Issuing digital badges or credentials to employees for completing training programs, acquiring new skills, or achieving certifications, which they can display on their profiles or résumés to showcase their accomplishments.
- **Team Recognition Events:** Organizing team-building activities, outings, or special events to recognize and celebrate collective achievements and milestones reached by departments or project teams.
- **Personalized Thank-You Notes:** Providing handwritten thank-you notes or personalized messages from managers or leadership to acknowledge and appreciate individual contributions and efforts.
- **Employee Appreciation Days:** Designating special days or events throughout the year to show appreciation for employees, such as Employee Appreciation Week or National Employee Appreciation Day, with activities, treats, or small gifts.

Wellness Benefits

Some employers have developed *health and wellness programs* to prevent employee illnesses and to lower healthcare costs. As with any program proposal, it's essential that HR professionals show management how the company will benefit from the program, how much it will cost, and what return the company can expect on its investment. Being able to provide specific costs and savings demonstrates HR's ability to develop programs that serve the long-term strategic goals of the business. Table 6.6 illustrates some of the benefits and costs to consider in analyzing the advantages of a wellness program for the company.

TABLE 6.6 Costs and benefits of wellness programs

Benefits	Costs
Increased productivity	Program implementation
Reduced turnover	Ongoing vendor costs
Reduced medical costs	Administrative costs
Reduced absenteeism Enhanced ability to attract top-quality employees Reduced workers compensation premiums	Liability issues

A typical wellness program must be voluntary for employees and includes a physical screening to assess each employee's current fitness level and needs. The program may include nutrition counseling; education programs for weight control, smoking cessation, and stress reduction; and a program of physical exercise. Other programs could include education about substance abuse, spinal care, and prenatal care, depending on the needs of the particular employee population. Health and wellness programs can take many forms, depending on the budget of the employer, the needs of the employees, and the availability of services in the local area.

Employees like wellness programs because they provide convenient opportunities to make healthful lifestyle choices that result in more energy and less stress, both on and off the job.

The size of the budget available for a wellness program will obviously dictate how the program is offered. Some large companies provide fitness centers on-site, along with employee cafeterias that serve healthful meals. Smaller organizations may engage a wellness vendor to provide the educational piece of the program and offer employees subsidies for gym memberships or develop walking or sports programs for employee participation.

An important consideration for programs that include on-site fitness centers will be to analyze the total costs, including not only the space and equipment but also fitness personnel and liability for injuries suffered while an employee is working out. Recommendations for on-site programs should therefore include an assessment of the possible risks involved as part of the cost analysis.

Eldercare

Eldercare support is generally provided in the form of resources made available to employees so that they can find suitable programs for elderly parents requiring ongoing care.

Flexible Spending Accounts

FSAs were authorized by the Revenue Act of 1978. Also known as *Section 125 plans*, they allow employees to set aside pretax funds for medical expenses they plan to incur during the calendar year. Employees should be cautioned to be conservative when projecting the amounts they plan to spend during the year because any funds left in the FSA after all expenses for the year have been paid will be forfeited and may be used by the employer to pay the administrative costs of the plan. For employers, a downside to offering an FSA account is that employees may be reimbursed for expenses before the funds have been withheld from their paychecks. If they leave the company before the funds have been withheld, they aren't required to reimburse the company for those expenses.

Expenses that may be included for reimbursement are the costs of any copayments and deductibles from medical, dental, or vision-care plans and other medical expenses approved by the IRS for reimbursement. Other allowable expenses include acupuncture treatments, orthodontia, psychiatric care, wheelchairs, physical therapy, Braille books and magazines, and a variety of other medical expenses. Some expenses that aren't included are monthly premiums, memberships to fitness clubs or gyms, babysitting, elective cosmetic surgery, weight-loss programs, and nonprescription drugs. To receive reimbursement for covered expenses, employees must provide receipts for expenditures.

A similar *dependent-care account* is authorized by Section 129. Employees may set aside a maximum of $5,000 to be used to care for dependent children or elders. To obtain reimbursement for dependent-care expenses, employees must provide an itemized statement of charges from the caregiver. Unlike the FSA for medical expenses, employees may not be reimbursed for expenses in excess of the amounts that have been withheld from their paychecks.

For employees to use either of these accounts, they must sign up at the beginning of the year, at the time they join the company, or during an open enrollment period. Once the contribution amount has been set for the year, it may be changed only if a qualifying event occurs, such as the birth or adoption of a dependent, death, divorce, or a change in employment status for the employee or the employee's spouse.

The IRS requires employers to conduct annual discrimination tests to ensure that FSA plans are being used consistently. Two types of tests are used to determine this: eligibility tests and utilization tests such as the key-employee-concentration test and dependent-care test. A plan that doesn't pass the test may lose its favorable tax treatment.

There are no federal laws requiring employers to offer any of these benefits; when they're offered, amendments to ERISA, COBRA, HIPAA, and the Mental Health Parity Act (MHPA) of 1996 have implications for administering them.

Cafeteria Plans

Large employers with diverse employee populations may offer cafeteria plans with a wide variety of benefit options in response to various needs of different employee groups. At the beginning of each plan year, employees select the benefits that best meet their needs. For example, a parent with young children may select dependent coverage as a benefit to cover daycare needs. Once children no longer need daycare, another benefit, such as 401(k) matching, may be selected.

Employee Assistance Programs (EAP)

An EAP is sponsored by the employer as a benefit. EAPs are often as advantageous for employers as they are for employees because they're generally a low-cost benefit that provides a resource for employees with problems that aren't work-related and can't be solved in the work context. In some cases, this assistance allows people who might not otherwise be able to remain employed to stay on the job.

EAPs offer a variety of counseling services for problems ranging from alcohol and drug abuse to legal assistance or financial counseling. Many EAPs are a source for outplacement counseling during a layoff, and some programs offer on-site smoking cessation. During times of crisis, such as after the death of an employee or an incident of workplace violence, the EAP can be a resource for employees to come to grips with their feelings so that they're able to continue with their jobs.

EAP services are most often provided through a third party to ensure the confidentiality of employee information, but some employers have in-house programs with counselors on staff. Smaller businesses may join together in a consortium and jointly contract with an EAP to lower costs.

Communicating Compensation and Benefits Programs

Taking the time to develop a compensation philosophy, participate in salary surveys, and develop new compensation programs doesn't help the organization unless results and objectives are clearly communicated to employees and managers.

For example, when rolling out the annual merit-increase process, it's important to have timely, effective, and frequent communication geared toward both management and employee populations. Management typically receives different or additional information designed to facilitate their role as evaluators. Sharing salary survey results with management continues the dialogue about attracting, retaining, and motivating talent through existing or new programs. Furthermore, training management in corporate policies and compensation philosophies allows them to properly respond to employees when questions arise. Emotions can run high when employees have questions about their pay or benefits, so it's important that frontline supervisors have the information necessary to meet employee needs. Answering questions about deductions, understanding leave policies, and justifying pay rates are all examples of information that can be shared through systematic management training.

Communicating compensation programs or philosophy involves a series of written communications, many of which are mandatory. There are several required written communications for employee benefits under ERISA and other regulations include:

- **Summary Plan Description (SPD):** A document required by ERISA that provides participants with a comprehensive overview of their retirement or health benefit plan, including details on plan benefits, rights, obligations, and procedures for claiming benefits.
- **Summary of Material Modifications (SMM):** Describes changes to the plan or information in the SPD.
- **Summary Annual Report (SAR):** Provides a summary of the plan's financial status, based on the Form 5500 annual report.
- **Notice of Privacy Practices:** Required for health plans under the Health Insurance Portability and Accountability Act (HIPAA), detailing how personal health information is protected.
- **Initial COBRA Notice:** Informs employees of their rights to continue health coverage under the Consolidated Omnibus Budget Reconciliation Act (COBRA).
- **Qualified Default Investment Alternative (QDIA) Notice:** For retirement plans, informing participants about default investment options if they do not make investment choices.
- **401(k) Safe Harbor Notice:** Details the plan provisions if the employer's 401(k) plan uses a safe harbor design to meet certain nondiscrimination tests.

- **Newborns and Mothers' Health Protection Act (NMHPA) Notice:** Describes protections for hospital stays following childbirth.
- **Medicare Part D Creditable Coverage Notice:** For health plans that provide prescription drug coverage, informing participants if the coverage is as good as or better than Medicare Part D.

Updating the company intranet, the employee handbook, and plan documents are a few other examples of written information that serve as great resources for employees.

Employee self-service options are gaining in popularity. These interactive, online services allow employees to gather relevant data based on their specific needs. Forms requests, online benefits enrollment, and access to payroll data are all examples of the convenience of robust self-service programs for employees. Benefits for employers also exist through the use of self-service programs. Time is saved by allowing employees to update their own personal information; reports such as benefit-utilization reviews can be gathered, wage statements including the value of employee benefits can be generated and communicated, and surveys and polls can be conducted to identify the needs of the real-time workforce.

Ultimately, communication of compensation programs should be simple, and the alignment to compensation philosophy should be visible. Compliance with various federal laws should also be audited on a regular basis for risk management purposes.

PHRi Only

There are three main areas of difference between the PHR and the PHRi exams. These include various norms related to preferences of non-monetary rewards, leave programs, and differences in monitoring issues related to the administration of compensation and benefits programs.

Local vs. Federal Regulations

PHRi candidates will be asked questions focused on local regulations and norms. The primary differences between U.S. labor laws and local norms in compensation and benefits often lie in the level of regulation, entitlements, and cultural expectations. International norms regarding compensation and benefits can vary significantly depending on the country, regional agreements, and cultural factors. While some principles, such as nondiscrimination and fair wages, are widely recognized and promoted by international organizations like the International Labour Organization (ILO), specific regulations and practices differ from one country to another.

In many European countries, for example, there are strong labor laws mandating minimum wages, generous vacation time, and extensive social benefits such as healthcare coverage and parental leave that go beyond U.S. requirements. Nordic countries are known for their comprehensive social welfare systems, including universal healthcare and robust unemployment benefits.

In contrast, emerging economies may have less stringent regulations and fewer social protections. In some countries, informal employment is prevalent, and workers may lack access to basic benefits such as healthcare or retirement savings.

International norms can also be influenced by regional agreements and conventions. For instance, the European Union sets certain labor standards and regulations that member states must adhere to, promoting consistency across member countries.

While there are common principles guiding compensation and benefits on an international scale, the specific implementation and extent of these norms vary widely across countries and regions due to historical, legal, cultural, economic, social, and political factors. This is likely to be represented on the exams by a strong focus on U.S. federally complaint compensation and benefits programs on the PHR, and general best or regional practices on the PHRi.

Benefits and Leave Preferences

The differences in employee benefits such as health plans, retirement, employee assistance plans, paid time off, and other insurance between the United States and other countries reflect diverse cultural, economic, and regulatory environments. The PHRi exam content outline identifies several key areas for review; these are covered next.

Health Plans In the United States, employers typically provide health insurance as part of employee benefits, with significant employee contributions. In contrast, many countries like the UK, Canada, and Germany have national health services or mandatory health insurance schemes funded by taxes or social security contributions, reducing the burden on employers and employees.

Retirement The United States relies heavily on employer-sponsored retirement plans like 401(k)s, where employees contribute a portion of their salary, often matched by the employer. In countries like Germany, retirement benefits are primarily funded through a public pension system, where contributions are made by both employers and employees into a national scheme.

Employee Assistance Plans (EAPs) EAPs in the United States are common and offer services such as mental health counseling, legal assistance, and financial advice. In countries like Sweden, employee assistance is often integrated into broader workplace wellness programs, supported by a strong emphasis on work-life balance and employee well-being.

Paid Time Off (PTO) The United States does not mandate paid vacation days, and the average PTO provided by employers is relatively low compared to other countries. For example, France mandates at least five weeks of paid vacation, and Sweden requires a minimum of 25 paid vacation days per year.

Other Insurance In the United States, additional insurances such as life, disability, and dental insurance are often part of an employee benefits package. In contrast, countries like Japan provide extensive social insurance systems that cover a range of benefits, including health, unemployment, and pension insurance, funded through employer and employee contributions to a national system.

These differences highlight how the approach to employee benefits varies widely, influenced by national policies, cultural attitudes toward work, and economic structures.

Summary

Compensation and benefits packages are a key factor in virtually every organization's quest to attract and retain employees who are best qualified to achieve its goals. The Total Rewards package is guided by the corporate mission and goals and reflects its organizational culture. The culture in particular impacts the intrinsic and extrinsic rewards that employees derive from their work. Total Rewards philosophy drives the organization's ability to attract, retain, and motivate its employees to meet strategic objectives.

HR practitioners must apply their knowledge of budgeting and accounting principles to their employer's compensation programs. This includes conducting market research on salaries in order to build wage structures that can be used to inform decision making. Skilled practitioners are also able to administer legally compliant payroll practices.

The first mandatory benefits, Social Security, Medicare, and unemployment insurance, were developed to provide a safety net for American workers. More recent benefits such as FMLA and COBRA require employers to actively participate in and administer programs.

The mix of voluntary benefits chosen by an organization can help it attract and retain employees with particular characteristics. For example, a generous educational reimbursement benefit will help the company attract employees who are committed to continuous learning and skill development.

Exam Essentials

Be aware of the components of compensation. Base pay is the foundation of an employer's compensation program because it reflects the value placed on individual jobs by the organization. Differentials such as overtime and hazard pay motivate employees to spend longer hours at work or to accept assignments that may be unpleasant or hazardous. Incentive pay motivates and rewards employees when they achieve corporate goals.

Understand how HR interacts with payroll systems. Whether HR interacts with or administers payroll, HR professionals are involved in ensuring that changes to employee pay and deductions are accurate.

Be able to communicate the compensation and benefits program to employees. An effective communication program informs employees about the Total Rewards package so they're able to take advantage of benefits that are offered and have an understanding of the full cost to the employer of providing the different programs.

Be aware of the wide variety of benefits that are available. With an awareness of the various and sometimes unusual benefits that are available, employers are able to develop a benefit mix that meets the needs of employees at the lowest cost to net profits.

Be aware of mandatory benefits. Mandatory employee benefits are determined by Congress and affect employers with varying minimum numbers of employees. Social Security, Medicare, unemployment insurance, FMLA leave, and COBRA continuation benefits are required by statute.

Understand how voluntary benefits influence employees. Voluntary benefits fall into four categories: deferred compensation, health and welfare, work-life balance, and other benefits. Some benefits, such as medical insurance and paid time off, have come to be expected by employees, whereas others will attract and retain different types of employees with different needs.

Review Questions

You can find the answers in Appendix A.

1. What impact does a gig economy have on an employer's compensation plan?
   A. Gig workers usually have a higher base pay.
   B. HR must budget compensation costs differently.
   C. HR must ensure they are not discriminating against gig workers.
   D. Gig workers may still be entitled to mandated benefits.
2. The employer you work for has a marketing specialist who is an independent contractor. She is required to work three days a week, from 8:00 a.m. to 5:00 p.m. You have advised your employer that she is improperly classified and should be hired as an employee. Which IRS factor are you most likely basing this on?
   A. Behavioral
   B. Financial
   C. Type of relationship
   D. None; her classification is legally compliant.
3. Which of the following is an example of an intrinsic reward?
   A. Recognition of accomplishments
   B. The satisfaction of a job well done
   C. A great supervisor
   D. An exciting assignment
4. A Total Rewards philosophy can help achieve an organization's strategic goals by doing which of the following?
   A. Attracting and retaining employees with the necessary KSAs
   B. Establishing a pecking order for jobs in the organization
   C. Positioning the company to lead the competition for employees
   D. Maintaining an entitlement culture
5. An entitlement culture is appropriate for a business that needs what type of workforce?
   A. One that continues to show productivity increases over time
   B. One that has a line of sight to retirement
   C. One that is highly competitive in completing daily assignments
   D. One that has a skill set that's in high demand

6. A company that wants to reduce the cost of its unemployment insurance should do which of the following? (Choose all that apply.)
   A. Aggressively fight unjustified claims for unemployment
   B. Establish an effective performance-management program
   C. Consistently terminate employees who violate company policy
   D. Invest in employee retention strategies
7. An unlimited time-off plan has which of the following advantages for the employer?
   A. Employers are better able to schedule workflow.
   B. The employer does not have to worry about timecards.
   C. The employer is better able to achieve work-life balance goals.
   D. The employer does not have to track time-off accruals.
8. The state in which you practice HR requires a higher minimum wage than the federal government. Your employer only wants to pay the federal minimum wage. What should you do?
   A. Make all employees exempt from overtime to reduce hourly wages.
   B. Conduct market research and create wage bands so your employer can see what their competitors are paying.
   C. Tell your employer that paying the federal minimum wage would be unlawful and that the company is required to pay the state minimum wage.
   D. Agree to pay the federal minimum wage rate, but gradually increase employee pay to the state minimum.
9. What is the primary purpose of paying employees commission?
   A. To keep employee wages variable
   B. To reward employees who work harder than others
   C. To keep labor costs low
   D. To incentivize employees to behave in a certain way
10. A summary plan description is *not* required for which of the following? (Choose all that apply.)
    A. Defined-contribution plans
    B. Defined-benefit plans
    C. Flexible spending accounts (FSAs)
    D. Group health insurance
11. Which of the following expenses may generally not be used against a flexible spending account?
    A. Gym membership
    B. Durable medical equipment
    C. Acupuncture
    D. Psychiatric care

12. ESOPs, ESPPs, and profit-sharing are all examples of which of the following?
    - **A.** Deferred compensation
    - **B.** Gainsharing strategies
    - **C.** Group incentives
    - **D.** Sales bonus options

13. When several workers at a nuclear power plant call in sick with the flu, the manager calls James and asks him to come in three hours early. James will be paid a premium on top of his normal pay rate for these hours. This is an example of what?
    - **A.** On-call pay
    - **B.** Call-back pay
    - **C.** Reporting pay
    - **D.** Hazard pay

14. Cost-of-living adjustments are generally tied to which economic factor?
    - **A.** Consumer price index
    - **B.** Social Security index
    - **C.** Employment cost index
    - **D.** Producer price index

15. In a merit matrix, where would be the best position to place a fully trained employee who is meeting performance expectations and who has been with the company for about three years?
    - **A.** The minimum for the range
    - **B.** The mid-point of the range
    - **C.** The maximum point for the range
    - **D.** Somewhere between the mid-point and maximum

16. Prescription coverage is an example of what type of employee benefit?
    - **A.** Deferred compensation
    - **B.** Perquisites
    - **C.** Health and welfare
    - **D.** Long-term care insurance

17. Which of the following is *not* an example of a voluntary benefit?
    - **A.** Medicare
    - **B.** Vision insurance
    - **C.** Qualified pension plan
    - **D.** Sick pay

18. Which of the following would be the best choice of a profit-sharing plan if the employer wishes to improve organizational productivity through shared management and employee efforts?

    A. Employee stock purchase plan

    B. Bonuses

    C. Gainsharing

    D. Improshare

19. Job fulfillment from working with a talented peer group is an example of which of the following types of compensation?

    A. Monetary

    B. Intrinsic

    C. Extrinsic

    D. Total Rewards

20. Earnings before taxes are most commonly referred to as which of the following?

    A. Gross pay

    B. Net pay

    C. Employee burden

    D. Wages, salaries, and tips

Chapter 7

PHR | PHRi Exam: Employee Engagement

PHR AND PHRi RESPONSIBILITIES:

DEVELOPING, COMMUNICATING, AND ENHANCING EMPLOYEE ENGAGEMENT INITIATIVES TO SUPPORT OPTIMAL EMPLOYEE PERFORMANCE MANAGEMENT ACTIVITIES THROUGHOUT THE EMPLOYEE LIFECYCLE.

✓ 5.1 Measure and advise on functional effectiveness at each stage of the employee lifecycle and identify alternate approaches as needed (for example: hiring, onboarding, performance management, retention, exit process, alumni program)

✓ 5.2 Support the implementation and communication of organizational programs to enhance employee participation and engagement (for example: surveys, focus groups, welfare/wellness activities, employee resource groups [ERG], action plans from feedback)

✓ 5.3 Support the organization's performance management strategy by completing appropriate steps in order to achieve organizational goals and objectives (for example: employee reviews, promotions, recognition programs)

✓ 5.4 Support performance and employment activities (for example: coaching, performance improvement plans, corrective actions, involuntary separations, job eliminations, reductions in force [RIF], offboarding)

PHRi RESPONSIBILITIES:

✓ 5.1 Measure and advise on functional effectiveness at each stage of the employee lifecycle (for example: hiring, onboarding, performance management, retention, exit process, alumni program) and identify alternate approaches as needed

The 2024 exam content updates created two new functional areas for the PHR and PHRi exams. These included Employee and Labor Relations and Employee Engagement. Perhaps even more interesting is that both of these new functional areas now account for the highest amount of exam content, with Employee and Labor Relations making up 20 percent of exam content and Employee Engagement—the focus of this chapter—17 percent. The addition of these functional areas and the carrying weight suggests that both are important for the modern-day HR practitioner.

Note that there is a small variation in objective 5.1 between the PHR and the PHRi. While the bulk of the content is identical, PHRi candidates are also tasked with being able to identify alternate approaches to manage engagement at all stages of the employment lifecycle.

Employee Engagement Defined

Employee engagement is the emotional and psychological commitment an employee has toward their organization, which influences their willingness to contribute to organizational success. The study of employee engagement by industrial-organizational psychologists has been an area of interest for several decades, with its roots tracing back to the 1990s when the concept began to gain prominence as distinct from related constructs like job satisfaction and organizational commitment. In other words, employee engagement is a unique phenomenon that can be measured separately from an employee's satisfaction with their work, and their loyalty to the company.

According to `Wellbale.com`,[1] there are three levels of employee engagement, and they include:

- **An engaged worker:** an employee who is fully invested in the work. These employees feel aligned with the company purpose, passionate about their job and connected to their coworkers.
- **A disengaged worker:** the "quiet quitter," those who do the minimum amount of work required of them, often feeling a high degree of dissatisfaction with the company or their job.

---

[1] Why Employee Engagement Is Beneficial to Employers, `https://www.wellable.co/blog/employee-engagement-statistics-you-should-know/#h-why-employee-engagement-is-beneficial-to-employers`.

- **An actively disengaged worker:** one who may actively sabotage the employer or their peers, exhibiting *counterproductive work behaviors* such as a negative attitude, below-standard performance, and resistance to authority or rules.

These definitions are significant because they set the stage for the impact of engagement on organizational results. Research has found that organizations with highly engaged employees experience positive outcomes, including:

- Increased productivity
- Lower turnover
- Enhanced customer service
- Lower workplace injuries
- High employee morale

Conversely, organizations with a disengaged workforce experience the opposite effect, with higher turnover, lower morale, and even lower profit margins. Gallup leads research in the field of engagement by tracking metrics each year. Unfortunately, as of early 2024, U.S. engagement levels have reached an 11-year low:

> Last year, Gallup found U.S. employees were increasingly detached from their employers, with the workforce reporting less role clarity, lower satisfaction with their organizations and less connection to their companies' mission or purpose. Employees were also less likely to feel someone at work cares about them.[2]

Real World Scenario

The Positive and Negative Impacts of Engagement

Gong, a revenue operations and intelligence company, is an excellent example of how a strong focus on employee engagement can drive organizational success. At Gong, 87 percent of employees consider it a great place to work, a significantly higher percentage than the industry average of 57 percent. This high level of employee satisfaction and engagement is linked to their recognition by Forrester as the Q4 2023 leader for B2B revenue in their market. Gong's emphasis on creating a positive and supportive work environment has translated into tangible business outcomes, reinforcing the connection between employee engagement and overall company performance.[3]

---

[2] U.S. Engagement Hits 11-Year Low, `https://www.gallup.com/workplace/643286/engagement-hits-11-year-low.aspx`.

[3] Forrester Wave, `www.gong.io/blog/gong-recognized-as-the-leader-conversation-intelligence-forrester-wave-2023`.

The Disconnect Over Return-to-Office Policies

In contrast, many organizations are currently facing challenges with employee engagement due to rigid return-to-office mandates. Despite a significant preference for flexible work arrangements among employees, 7 out of 10 companies worldwide are enforcing office mandates. This disconnect between employees' desire for flexibility and senior leadership's push for in-office presence is leading to decreased engagement, higher turnover rates, and difficulty in retaining talent. Employees who feel their preferences and needs are ignored are more likely to disengage, impacting their productivity and overall morale.

So, what leads to employee disengagement? More than half of all respondents to a survey by `Wellable.com` reported complacent leadership as the top reason they are disengaged, and only 9 percent of employees believe their leadership is committed to culture initiatives.[4] Other reports note that the number one reason employees leave an organization is lack of recognition. While the research is somewhat inconsistent, it is most important to understand why employees leave your organization and create engagement initiatives that address those specific challenges.

Company culture is closely related to employee engagement as a positive, inclusive, and supportive culture creates and supports higher levels of engagement by making employees feel valued and connected to their work and organization. HR has opportunities throughout the employee lifecycle to influence the development and support of a culture that drives engagement.

The Workplace Value Proposition

The workplace value proposition (WVP) is a system of integrated rewards and support mechanisms that align with employees' diverse needs and preferences that include not just traditional compensation and benefits, but also career development opportunities, work-life balance initiatives, recognition programs, and a positive organizational culture to drive engagement and performance. The evolution from Total Rewards to the WVP in the context of employee engagement reflects a shift from traditional, transactional elements to a more holistic, dynamic approach. The WVP serves as the connective tissue that aligns broader workforce needs with organizational goals. In short, the WVP is a system designed to increase employee engagement.

In practice, many companies acknowledge the importance of a WVP but struggle to implement it effectively. This is often due to a lack of alignment between organizational goals and employee expectations, as well as difficulties in consistently delivering the promised benefits and work environment. This misalignment can lead to unmet expectations and a disconnect between leadership and the workforce. To succeed, a comprehensive strategy that integrates traditional rewards with engagement initiatives throughout the lifecycle of the employee is the task at hand for HR and other organizational leaders.

---

[4] Employee Engagement Statistics for 2024, `www.wellable.co/blog/employee-engagement-statistics-you-should-know/#h-1-two-thirds-of-employees-are-disengaged-at-work`.

Engagement and the Employee Lifecycle

Exam objective 5.1 launches the area of employee engagement by tasking PHR/i candidates to "measure and advise on functional effectiveness at each stage of the employee lifecycle . . ." *Functional effectiveness* is the ability of an organization, team, or individual to achieve desired outcomes efficiently and effectively through optimal use of resources and processes. Achieving functional effectiveness and enhancing employee engagement involves several key strategies throughout each stage of the employee lifecycle:

Hiring Evaluating key metrics such as time-to-hire, quality of hire, and candidate experience through surveys and performance assessments helps to improve increased engagement at the time of hire. This data is used to identify areas for improvement and recommend alternate approaches, such as optimizing job descriptions, enhancing the interview process, and leveraging technology for better candidate screening.

PHRi candidates can take an alternate approach where appropriate by tailoring recruitment strategies to local markets and norms, and by leveraging technology for remote recruitment and hiring.

Comprehensive Onboarding A thorough onboarding process ensures new employees are well integrated into the organization, understand their roles, and are familiar with company culture and values. Considering that most new hires choose to stay or leave within the first 6 months of employment, this is a critical time to engage the team member.

PHRi candidates should consider providing onboarding materials and support in multiple languages to accommodate non-native speakers and ensure that inclusive practices are not subsumed by employer acclimatization practices.

Continuous Training and Development Providing ongoing learning opportunities helps employees develop new skills and stay engaged with their work. This includes formal training programs, workshops, and access to online learning platforms. An investment in an employee's career goals and developing their skills shows employees that the company cares about them, and the cost of retaining untrained, disengaged workers is far higher than the potential risk of losing well-trained, motivated employees. Many leaders struggle with the issue of investing in employee development and high levels of turnover. This choice is illustrated in Figure 7.1.

Some countries may experience skill gaps in critical areas due to the emigration of their skilled workforce (sometimes called "brain drain"). Companies in source countries may need to invest more in training and development programs to bridge these gaps and create a sustainable talent pipeline.

FIGURE 7.1 The value of investing in training

Monetary Rewards Monetary rewards can improve engagement by providing immediate motivation and recognition for performance, but they are limited in fostering long-term commitment and intrinsic motivation. Overreliance on financial incentives may overlook the importance of non-monetary factors such as job satisfaction, professional development, and workplace culture.[5] Monetary rewards also cannot improve ethical behavior or change the nature of the job, so engagement initiatives need to go beyond financial rewards.

Many cultures have values and priorities that go beyond monetary rewards as well. Understanding and respecting cultural nuances can enhance the effectiveness of both monetary and non-monetary rewards programs. Alternative approaches include personalizing rewards that cater to individual and cultural preferences, such as titles, additional vacation days, or paid time off to volunteer.

Thoughtful Offboarding A structured offboarding process ensures that departing employees leave on good terms, providing valuable feedback and maintaining positive relationships. This can include exit interviews, knowledge transfer sessions, and offering support for their future endeavors, which helps sustain a positive organizational culture and engagement among remaining employees. Establishing and maintaining an alumni network creates opportunities for former employees to possibly return in the future.

On an international scale, the use of local languages and culturally sensitive questions help to ensure open feedback. PHRi candidates must also ensure that the offboarding process complies with local labor laws and cultural practices. This might include different notice periods, severance packages, and legal documentation requirements.

---

[5] What Monetary Rewards Can and Cannot Do: How to Show Employees the Money, `https://www.sciencedirect.com/science/article/abs/pii/S0007681312001632`.

Employee Involvement

Employee involvement is the active participation and engagement of employees in decision-making processes, problem-solving, and organizational improvement initiatives, creating a sense of ownership and commitment to the company's success. Encouraging employees to participate in decision-making processes and giving them ownership over their work can lead to higher engagement levels. This requires that employers are proactively gathering employee feedback, and then taking action on what they find.

Employee surveys are a systematic method for collecting feedback from employees using structured questionnaires. They can cover a wide range of topics, such as job satisfaction, engagement, and organizational culture, and where possible, should be conducted anonymously to encourage honest responses. Surveys provide quantitative data that can be analyzed to identify trends and areas for improvement.

Focus groups involve a small, diverse group of employees who are brought together to discuss specific topics or issues in a facilitated setting. This method allows for in-depth qualitative feedback and can uncover detailed insights, perspectives, and suggestions that might not emerge from surveys alone. Focus groups encourage open dialogue and can provide a deeper understanding of employee concerns and ideas. For employers with unions, it is important to distinguish employee focus groups with unauthorized collective bargaining. Note that focus groups only represent a small, cross-section of employee opinions and ideas.

NOTE Methods for quantitative and qualitative analysis are covered in Chapter 2, "Shared Competencies."

Employee resource groups (ERGs) are voluntary, employee-led groups that provide a platform for employees to share their experiences and feedback related to specific interests or identities, such as cultural background, gender, or professional development. Feedback from ERGs can offer valuable insights into the needs and challenges of various employee segments and inform targeted initiatives for improvement.

It is not enough for employers to simply collect employee feedback; they must take steps to take action on what is discovered. Employers can create action plans and respond to employee feedback by first analyzing the collected data to identify key themes and areas needing improvement. Next, they should prioritize these issues based on their impact on employee satisfaction and organizational performance. Employers can then set specific, measurable goals and develop targeted initiatives to address the identified concerns, such as enhancing communication channels, providing additional training opportunities, or improving workplace conditions. Regularly updating employees on the progress of these initiatives and involving them in the implementation process supports a culture of transparency and continuous improvement. Establishing a feedback loop where employees can see how their input leads to tangible changes will reinforce their engagement and trust in the organization.

Key to employee engagement is creating a psychologically safe work environment so that employees are willing to speak up and candidly share their experiences.

Psychological Safety

Psychological safety in the workplace is a condition where employees feel safe to take risks, express their ideas, and voice their concerns without fear of negative consequences such as ridicule, punishment, or ostracism.

The impact of psychological safety on employee engagement is significant. When employees feel psychologically safe, they are more likely to be engaged, contribute and collaborate creatively, and participate actively in their roles. This environment of trust and openness not only enhances individual and team performance but also leads to higher job satisfaction, lower turnover rates, and a more positive organizational culture.

Google is well known for their work on psychological safety, most notably for Project Aristotle, a comprehensive study conducted on its teams. This study found that psychological safety was the most critical factor in determining high-performing teams. In practice, Google fosters psychological safety by encouraging open communication and the free exchange of ideas, and their leader's model inclusive behavior to ensure all perspectives are heard.

A more recent example of a study on psychological safety in the workplace is the Wiley Workplace Intelligence report, which highlights significant gaps in levels of psychological safety between employees and executives. The study found that executives are 43 percent more likely to feel safe taking risks at work compared to individual contributors. This disparity underscores the importance of creating a culture where all employees, regardless of their position, feel comfortable expressing their ideas and concerns without fear of negative repercussions.[6]

Additionally, research from HR Executive in 2023 emphasizes that psychological safety not only improves mental and physical well-being but also enhances productivity, creativity, and teamwork. The study suggests that when employees feel safe to take risks and voice their opinions, it leads to better problem-solving, decision making, and overall team performance.[7]

HR programs such as regular employee feedback sessions, inclusive leadership training, and mental health support initiatives contribute to creating a psychologically safe workplace. Implementing team-building activities and diversity and inclusion programs also helps build trust and respect among employees.

Engaging Early- to Mid-Career Professionals

Much has been studied about the young professional and their demographic preferences regarding the workplace. For example, by 2028, 58 percent of the workforce will be millennials and Gen Z, and according to a survey reported by the British Council, the majority of them prefer remote work.[8] Other important data about these early- to mid-career professionals to consider when designing engagement initiatives is shown in Table 7.1.

---

[6] `https://newsroom.wiley.com/press-releases/press-release-details/2023/New-Wiley-Survey-Reveals-Gaps-in-Levels-of-Psychological-Safety-Between-Employees-and-Executives/default.aspx`.

[7] `https://hrexecutive.com/psychological-safety-a-driver-of-workplace-dynamics-and-wellbeing`.

[8] The Future of Employee Engagement: Current Trends and Tomorrow's Insights, `https://corporate.britishcouncil.org/insights/future-employee-engagement-current-trends-and-tomorrows-insights`.

TABLE 7.1 Key features of millennials and Gen Z

Millennials (Born 1981–1996)	Gen Z (Born 1997–2012)
Are tech savvy and comfortable with digital communication.	Are digital natives, having grown up with smartphones and social media.
Likely to prioritize experiences over material goods.	Many show an entrepreneurial spirit and desire for independence.
Emphasize the importance of work-life balance.	Likely to value authenticity and transparency, as consumers and employees.
Known for having strong values and being socially conscious.	Place a high priority on mental health and well-being.
Value opportunities for career development.	Value diversity and inclusiveness on a local and a global scale.

HR can engage younger workers by tailoring benefits to their stage of life. Consider tuition reimbursement for early career professionals or family benefits for employees starting families. Other options include implementing flexible work arrangements, offering continuous learning and development opportunities, and supporting a culture of transparency and inclusivity. Leveraging digital tools for communication and collaboration can resonate well with these tech-savvy and socially conscious generations.

Performance Management

While Chapter 2 covers the operational and strategic performance management initiatives, the PHR/i exams place significant weight on performance management and its effect on engagement. Objectives 5.3 focuses on career growth, such as reviews and promotions, whereas 5.4 focuses on performance improvement, including the disciplinary and separation processes.

Career Growth

Employees at different stages of their careers have different objectives when it comes to managing their career path. Career stage significantly affects engagement levels as employees' priorities and needs evolve over time. For example:

- Early-career employees are generally more engaged when they are provided with opportunities for learning, development, and career advancement. They value mentorship, training programs, and challenging assignments that help them build their skills and experiences.

- For mid-career employees, engagement is often tied to career progression, job stability, and work-life balance. They seek roles that offer leadership opportunities, recognition, and the ability to influence organizational outcomes. Employers that provide clear career paths, performance incentives, and support for work-life integration can maintain high engagement levels among mid-career professionals.
- Late-career employees may prioritize job security, legacy building, and flexible work arrangements. Their engagement levels are influenced by factors such as the respect and value they receive from the organization, opportunities to mentor younger colleagues, and the flexibility to balance work with other life commitments as they approach retirement. Organizations that recognize the contributions of late-career employees and offer phased retirement options or part-time work can keep this group engaged.

Specific HR programs that support career growth at all stages that are covered on the exam include the following:

Employee Reviews Employee reviews influence employee engagement by offering structured opportunities for feedback, recognition, and development. Regular and constructive performance reviews provide employees with a clear understanding of their strengths and areas for improvement, aligning their efforts with organizational goals and personal career goals, thus boosting engagement. Reviews also serve as a platform for recognizing achievements, which, when authentic and thoughtful, can improve an employee's sense of accomplishment and motivation, key features of an engaged worker.

The goal-setting and career development discussions during reviews help employees see a clear path for growth, making them more invested in their roles and, when done properly, help employees see a clear line of sight between their work efforts and organizational results.

Promotions A benefit of a structured career path is that employers are able to engage in replacement and succession planning. When an employee is identified for a future role, the employer can plan for the appropriate training and development so that they are prepared for the opportunity when it becomes available. If the employee knows that there is a growth path available, they are less likely to leave the company.

In addition, promotions can significantly increase employee engagement by recognizing and rewarding individual contributions, which boosts morale and motivation. When employees see clear opportunities for advancement based on merit, they are more likely to be engaged and committed to their work. Organizations benefit from a motivated workforce that is more likely to innovate and perform at higher levels, which in turn supports business results.

Recognition Recognition can increase employee engagement by making employees feel valued and appreciated for their contributions. Consistent recognition creates a positive work environment and strengthens the emotional connection employees have with their organization, leading to increased loyalty and productivity. Personalizing employee recognition is a best practice and can be achieved by tailoring rewards to individual preferences and acknowledging specific achievements. Outsourcing recognition programs to specialized firms can add value by ensuring consistent, professional implementation and leveraging expertise to create impactful, customized recognition strategies that enhance employee engagement.

Performance Improvement

The Gallup poll referenced in the earlier section on engagement notes that engagement levels have reached an 11-year low. In fact, the survey found that 30 percent of employees are engaged, 50 percent are not engaged, and 20 percent are actively disengaged.

As shown in Figure 7.2, this means that 70 percent of employees are disconnected from their work.[9] This means that there will be levels of underperformance that will need to be addressed in ways that go beyond discipline and termination. These include positive and more formal channels of performance management.

FIGURE 7.2 Levels of engagement

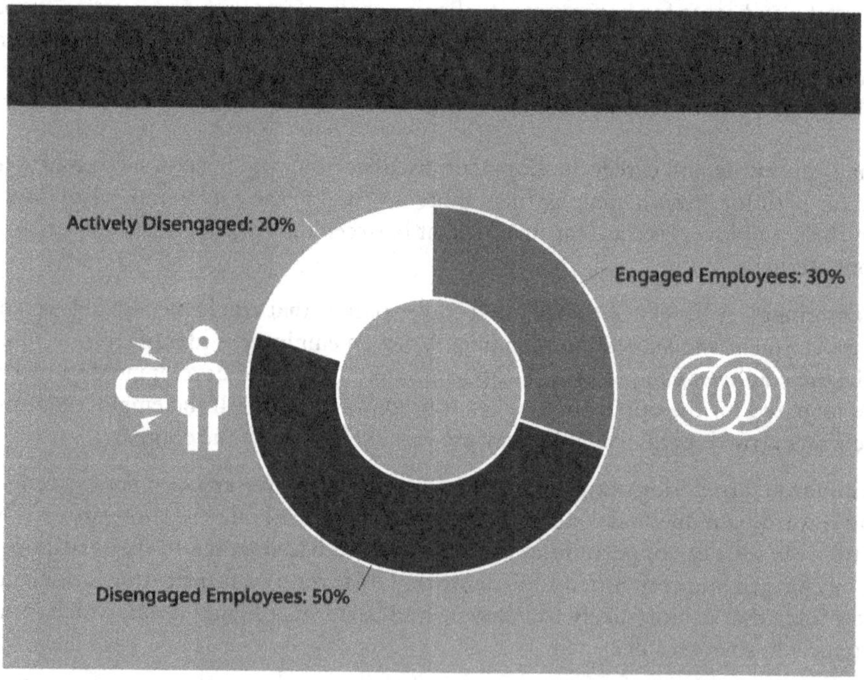

[9] In New Workplace, U.S. Employee Engagement Stagnates, `https://www.gallup.com/workplace/608675/new-workplace-employee-engagement-stagnates.aspx?version`.

Constructive Performance Improvement Techniques

While formal discipline and termination continue to be viable options, HR provides value to their organizations when they are able to use alternative approaches that constructively build a productive and engaged workforce. These options include:

Coaching Coaching involves providing personalized guidance and support to employees to help them develop their skills and improve their performance. Through regular one-on-one sessions, coaches can identify strengths and areas for improvement, set achievable goals, and offer constructive feedback. This personalized attention helps employees feel valued and supported, enhancing their engagement and commitment to their roles.

Positive Discipline Positive discipline is a constructive approach to addressing performance issues that focuses on encouraging good behavior and improving performance rather than punishing mistakes. It involves clear communication of expectations, consistent and fair application of rules, and providing opportunities for employees to learn and grow from their mistakes. This approach helps build trust and respect between employees and management, which in turn, increases engagement.

Performance Improvement Plans (PIPs) Performance improvement plans (PIPs) are structured plans that outline specific steps an employee needs to take to improve their performance. PIPs typically include clear performance goals, a timeline for achieving these goals, and the resources and support available to the employee. By providing a clear path to improvement and regular feedback, PIPs can help employees understand where they need to improve and how to get there, leading to increased engagement and better performance outcomes.

Job Redesign Job redesign involves restructuring job roles and responsibilities to better align with employees' strengths and interests, and to meet organizational goals more effectively. This can include adjusting tasks, workflows, and work environments to enhance job satisfaction and productivity. By involving employees in the redesign process and ensuring their roles are meaningful and engaging, organizations can boost employee morale, reduce turnover, and improve overall performance.

Disciplinary Performance Improvement Techniques

Unfortunately, it is not always possible to engage a worker through the performance improvement strategies just discussed, and it becomes necessary to take a more formal approach of consequences. The exam content outline specifically notes taking corrective actions that can lead to terminations.

Corrective action is a process of identifying and addressing performance issues or behavioral problems in order to bring an employee's performance up to organizational standards and prevent recurrence. This is often done through progressive discipline strategies that start with a verbal warning and escalates all the way up through termination. *Involuntary terminations* are when an employee is involuntarily separated from their job, also known as "being fired." *Constructive discharge* occurs when an employee resigns due to an employer creating a work environment so intolerable that a reasonable person would feel compelled to quit. This is considered a form of harassment and is unlawful.

Progressive discipline policies and involuntary terminations carry risks such as potential legal challenges, especially if the procedures are not followed consistently or are perceived as unfair, leading to claims of wrongful termination or discrimination. These actions can also negatively impact employee morale and trust within the organization, potentially causing decreased productivity and increased turnover among remaining staff. Progressive discipline can erode the doctrine of employment at will. Wrongful termination claims often result in significant financial awards for the plaintiffs. In the United States, the median settlement for wrongful termination lawsuits can range from $40,000 to $100,000, with some cases resulting in multimillion-dollar awards depending on the circumstances and the severity of the employer's misconduct.

Employers can avoid the erosion of at-will employment, wrongful termination claims, and constructive discharge claims by implementing clear, consistent policies and procedures for performance management and terminations, and thoroughly documenting employment actions. Employers (including HR and organizational leaders) should model respectful and inclusive communication, especially when addressing performance issues. Training managers on lawful termination practices and effective communication can also help mitigate these risks. Additionally, providing avenues for employees to voice concerns and addressing issues promptly and fairly can prevent misunderstandings and potential legal disputes.

Layoffs and Reductions in Force

Employee separations can occur for nonperformance-related reasons as well. *Job elimination* involves the removal of specific roles or positions within an organization due to various factors such as technological advancements, organizational restructuring, or strategic shifts in business focus. The most common types of job elimination are layoffs and a reduction in force (RIF).

Layoffs *Layoffs* refer to the involuntary termination of employees due to business reasons such as economic downturns, restructuring, or cost-cutting measures. Unlike performance-based terminations, layoffs are usually related to the employer's financial health or strategic decisions and are often implemented to reduce labor costs or reallocate resources. Affected employees may receive severance packages and support services such as outplacement assistance to help them transition to new employment opportunities.

Reduction in Force (RIF) *Reductions in force (RIFs)* involve the permanent elimination of positions within an organization due to budget cuts, organizational restructuring, or other economic factors. RIFs are typically more comprehensive and permanent than layoffs, as they result in a long-term decrease in the workforce. Employees affected by RIFs may be provided with severance benefits, reemployment assistance, and other support services to mitigate the impact of their job loss.

Layoffs and RIFs have a significant impact on employee engagement, primarily by increasing job insecurity and reducing morale among remaining employees. When layoffs occur, employees often feel uncertain about their own job stability, which can lead to increased stress and anxiety. This atmosphere of uncertainty can diminish trust in the organization and its leadership, as employees may feel that the company does not value their contributions or care about their well-being. Layoffs can disrupt team dynamics and increase workloads for remaining employees, leading to burnout and further disengagement.

Reductions in force (RIFs) can have a similar impact on employee engagement as layoffs, but the effects may be more profound due to the often permanent nature of RIFs. The announcement of RIFs can create a climate of fear and insecurity, leading to decreased motivation and productivity among the remaining workforce. Employees may experience a sense of loss and grief for their colleagues who were let go, which can negatively affect team cohesion and morale. The perceived lack of job security and potential for increased workload can further erode trust in management and reduce overall engagement and commitment to the organization.

During job eliminations, HR can provide emotional support through counseling services and career transition assistance, such as outplacement services, to help affected employees cope and find new opportunities. Working toward rebuilding morale among remaining employees through professional development opportunities, workload management, and a supportive workplace culture can mitigate the negative impacts on engagement and productivity.

Summary

The impact of employee engagement on positive workplace outcomes should not be underestimated. Engagement levels are at a decade low, and HR plays a vital role in creating and maintaining a positive workplace culture that creates a psychologically safe workplace where employees feel empowered to perform at their best.

The workplace value proposition helps differentiate HR programs from the transactional—such as compensation, rewards and traditional discipline—to the more transformational, such as recognition and positive discipline strategies.

HR also supports efforts to engage employees throughout the employee lifecycle, and at all stages of career development, from early career to those transitioning into retirement. This requires awareness of performance management strategies that drive engagement and align individual efforts with organizational results.

Exam Essentials

Understand the principles and importance of defining employee engagement to enhance organizational performance. Defining employee engagement involves identifying its key components and understanding its role in driving productivity, retention, and overall organizational success. By clearly articulating what engagement means, HR can implement targeted strategies to boost employee motivation and commitment, leading to enhanced performance and competitive advantage.

Develop and implement strategies to create and maintain psychological safety within teams. Creating psychological safety is key to building a culture of trust and open communication, where team members feel comfortable sharing ideas and concerns without fear. This feedback allows HR to structure meaningful programs that support engagement initiatives.

Understand the components and benefits of a strong workplace value proposition in engaging employees. A strong workplace value proposition (WVP) goes beyond the transactional components of competitive compensation, benefits. A WVP focuses on the holistic elements that truly affect employee engagement levels such as a positive work environment and career opportunities.

Explain how effective performance management practices contribute to higher employee engagement. Effective performance management affects levels of employee engagement at all stages of the employee lifecycle. Providing feedback to those who have been identified for promotion, as well as managing engagement through performance improvement needs and downsizing, are ways that HR teams provide value to their organizations.

Review Questions

You can find the answers in Appendix A.

1. The degree to which an employee is fully invested in their work is the best definition of which of the following?
   - **A.** Job satisfaction
   - **B.** Organizational commitment
   - **C.** Job characteristics
   - **D.** Employee engagement
2. Which of the following statements is true about the study of employee engagement?
   - **A.** It has been an area of interest since the early 2000s.
   - **B.** It is a concept that is synonymous with job satisfaction and organizational commitment.
   - **C.** It began to gain prominence in the 1990s and is considered distinct from job satisfaction and organizational commitment.
   - **D.** It cannot be measured separately from an employee's satisfaction with their work.
3. Which of the following types of rewards best demonstrates the workplace value proposition? (Choose all that apply.)
   - **A.** Base wages
   - **B.** Career development
   - **C.** Mental health benefits
   - **D.** Company culture
4. Which of the following is the primary reason employees feel disengaged from their work?
   - **A.** Lack of competitive salary
   - **B.** Poor management and leadership
   - **C.** Inadequate office facilities
   - **D.** Limited access to technology
5. Which of the following statements best demonstrates an actively disengaged employee?
   - **A.** Frequently complains to coworkers about their boss
   - **B.** Has a pattern of absences on Mondays or Fridays
   - **C.** Behaves in a hostile and bullying manner to others
   - **D.** Regularly finds ways to undermine their coworkers

6. Which of the following best defines the concept of functional effectiveness within the employee lifecycle?
   A. The ability of an organization to ensure that its employees are contributing to the achievement of business goals at each stage of their employment
   B. The complete set of benefits and opportunities an organization offers to attract, retain, and motivate employees
   C. The emotional and psychological commitment an employee has toward their organization
   D. The level of contentment employees feel with their job roles, which can be influenced by factors such as work environment, compensation, and personal growth opportunities

7. How is company culture related to employee engagement?
   A. Company culture influences employee engagement by setting the tone for work expectations and social interactions.
   B. A positive company culture facilitates higher employee engagement by creating a supportive and motivating work environment.
   C. Employee engagement can shape company culture by encouraging practices that align with employee values and preferences.
   D. Company culture has a limited effect on employee engagement, which is more influenced by individual job roles and responsibilities.

8. Which of the following engagement measures should HR take to address an employee who is actively disengaged from their work?
   A. Discipline the employee for counterproductive work behaviors.
   B. Upskill the supervisor so they can properly coach the employee to better performance.
   C. Place the employee on a PIP.
   D. Monitor the employee for signs of sabotage.

9. How do employee reviews influence employee engagement? (Choose all that apply.)
   A. By offering opportunities for social interactions and team bonding
   B. By providing structured feedback and recognition of accomplishments
   C. By establishing goals for career development
   D. By emphasizing underperformance for improvement

10. In which of the following ways can HR ensure that promotions are aligned with organizational results?
    A. By promoting employees based on their tenure within the company
    B. By setting clear performance metrics that link individual achievements to organizational goals
    C. By rotating employees through different departments to broaden their skill sets
    D. By conducting random selection for promotions to ensure fairness

11. What is psychological safety in the workplace?
   A. The absence of physical hazards and ensuring a safe working environment
   B. The state where employees feel secure about their job stability and future within the company
   C. The belief that one will not be punished or humiliated for speaking up with ideas, questions, concerns, or mistakes
   D. The provision of mental health resources and counseling services to employees

12. An employee is afraid to speak up about a potential issue because their manager often dismisses or criticizes their concerns harshly. This is the best example of which of the following workplace concerns?
   A. Lack of employee engagement
   B. Lack of psychological safety
   C. A toxic work environment
   D. Workplace harassment

13. Which of the following is a benefit of high employee engagement in the workplace?
   A. Increased employee satisfaction with pay
   B. Higher levels of innovation and productivity
   C. Enhanced ethical behaviors of employees
   D. Improved job characteristics and tasks

14. Which of the following is a method of a constructive performance technique? (Choose all that apply.)
   A. Coaching
   B. Performance improvement plans
   C. Job redesign
   D. Organizational restructuring

15. Which of the following is a challenge of progressive discipline policies? (Choose all that apply.)
   A. They can be time-consuming for managers to implement consistently.
   B. They may lead to legal challenges if not applied uniformly.
   C. They often result in immediate termination without prior warnings.
   D. They do not provide employees with opportunities to correct their behavior.

16. Which stage of the employee lifecycle is most likely to increase employee engagement through feedback and transparent communication?
   A. Hiring
   B. Onboarding
   C. Performance management
   D. Separation

17. Which of the following best describes how an alumni group affects employee engagement?
    - **A.** It provides current employees with additional networking opportunities within the organization.
    - **B.** It fosters a sense of belonging and long-term connection to the organization, even after employees have left.
    - **C.** It offers financial benefits to former employees, encouraging them to maintain positive relationships.
    - **D.** It serves as a tool for evaluating the reasons behind employee turnover.

18. What is an HR best practice to help support remaining employee engagement after a companywide layoff?
    - **A.** Reducing remaining employees' workloads to prevent burnout
    - **B.** Providing transparent communication and support to address concerns and rebuild trust
    - **C.** Offering financial incentives to remaining employees to boost morale
    - **D.** Implementing a flexible work schedule to accommodate employees' personal needs

19. What is the main difference between a layoff and a reduction in force?
    - **A.** Layoffs are generally temporary, whereas reductions in force are permanent.
    - **B.** Layoffs are due to employee performance issues, whereas reductions in force are due to financial reasons.
    - **C.** Layoffs involve rehiring employees after a certain period, whereas reductions in force do not guarantee reemployment.
    - **D.** Layoffs typically affect only a few employees, whereas reductions in force impact the entire organization.

20. What is the primary purpose behind a performance improvement plan?
    - **A.** To document an employee's past performance issues for legal purposes
    - **B.** To identify areas where employees can be reassigned to different roles
    - **C.** To evaluate employees for potential promotions within the organization
    - **D.** To structure goals for performance improvement

Chapter 8

PHR | PHRi Exam: Employee and Labor Relations

PHR AND PHRi RESPONSIBILITIES:

MANAGE, MONITOR, AND/OR PROMOTE LEGALLY COMPLIANT PROGRAMS AND POLICIES THAT IMPACT THE EMPLOYEE EXPERIENCE.

- ✓ **6.1 Understand and apply knowledge of programs, US federal laws, and regulations to promote outreach, diversity, equity, and inclusion (DEI) (for example: affirmative action, employee resource groups [ERG], community outreach, corporate social responsibility [CSR])**
- ✓ **6.2 Support workplace programs related to US federal health, safety, security, and privacy laws and regulations (for example: OSHA, workers' compensation, emergency response, workplace violence, substance abuse, legal postings, documentation, investigations)**
- ✓ **6.3 Provide interpretation and ensure compliance to organizational policies and procedures (for example: employee handbook, SOPs, time and attendance, expenses)**
- ✓ **6.4 Process and support the resolution of employee complaints, concerns, or conflicts and escalate as needed (for example: investigate, document, initiate, recommend solutions, abide by grievance and ADR [alternative dispute resolution] procedures)**
- ✓ **6.5 Promote techniques and tools for facilitating positive employee and labor relations with knowledge of US federal laws affecting union and nonunion workplaces (for example: anti-discrimination policies, harassment)**

PHRi RESPONSIBILITIES:

- ✓ 6.1 Understand and apply knowledge of programs, applicable laws, and regulations to promote outreach, diversity, equity, and inclusion (DEI) (for example: corporate social responsibility [CSR])
- ✓ 6.2 Support workplace programs relative to health, safety, security, and privacy laws and regulations
- ✓ 6.5 Promote techniques and tools for facilitating positive employee and labor relations with knowledge of applicable laws affecting union and nonunion workplaces (for example: anti-discrimination policies, harassment)

The 2024 exam content updates created the new functional area of Employee and Labor Relations. This new content accounts for the largest amount of content covered on the PHR and PHRi exams. This functional area is also where there is the greatest distinction between the PHR and the PHRi, mainly in the area of federally compliant labor laws.

Appendix C, "Federal Employment Legislation and Case Law," covers most of the labor laws referenced in this functional area in great detail, and while PHR candidates should study that appendix thoroughly, this is an area that PHRi candidates can ignore (unless, of course, the information is relevant to their jobs).

Employee and Labor Relations Defined

Employee and labor relations (ELR) is the management of interactions and conflicts (the relationship) between employers and employees, including union negotiations, to maintain a positive and legally compliant workplace environment.

Over the last century, employee and labor relations in HR have evolved from basic labor rights and unionization efforts to a comprehensive focus on employee engagement, conflict resolution, and strategic alignment with organizational goals. Early 20th century efforts centered on improving working conditions and establishing labor laws, such as minimum wage and limitations on child labor. Midcentury saw the rise of unions and collective bargaining, as well as emphasis on safe workplaces through the passage of laws like the Occupational Safety and Health Act (OSHA). In recent decades, the emphasis has shifted toward fostering positive workplace cultures, reflecting broader societal changes and the increasing importance of "people" in the context of organizational success. These trends are all represented in the PHR and PHRi exam objectives.

Employee and Labor Relations Programs

Several factors help shape how an HR department is organized, and the ways in which the department is able to prioritize employee and labor relations programs. These variables include the following:

Organizational Size and Structure Organizational size affects the structure of an HR department by determining the extent of specialization and the number of dedicated roles within the team. Larger organizations require more structured and formalized ELR activities, including specialized teams for conflict resolution, compliance, and union negotiations, whereas smaller organizations may handle these activities more informally and with less segmentation. Additionally, a decentralized structure may require more specialized regional and other knowledge than structures that are more centralized.

Industry and Sector The industry and sector in which an organization operates influence the HR department's structure by dictating the need for specific expertise and compliance requirements. In highly regulated industries, ELR activities focus heavily on ensuring legal compliance and managing union relations, whereas service-oriented sectors prioritize employee engagement and customer-facing skills development. One area of opportunity for HR teams is to advocate for positive employee relations activities regardless of which industry they represent.

Company Culture and Values Company culture and values shape the structure of an HR department by emphasizing roles and functions that align with the organization's core principles and behavioral expectations. In organizations with a culture of innovation, ELR activities concentrate on fostering a supportive environment for creativity and development, whereas in companies with strong union presence, ELR efforts focus on maintaining cooperative labor relations and effective conflict resolution.

Geographic Dispersion Geographic dispersion affects the structure of an HR department by necessitating regional or local HR offices to manage diverse labor laws and cultural differences. In globally dispersed organizations, ELR activities must be tailored to address region-specific employment issues, legal compliance, and localized employee engagement strategies, whereas centrally located organizations can maintain more uniform ELR practices across the board.

Technological Adoption Technological adoption influences the structure of an HR department by determining the extent to which processes are automated and streamlined, potentially reducing the need for larger HR teams. In highly tech-integrated organizations, ELR activities leverage advanced HR technologies for efficient conflict resolution, data-driven decision making, and enhanced employee communication, whereas less tech-savvy organizations rely more on manual processes and personal interactions to manage employee and labor relations.

Strategic Organizational Goals Strategic organizational goals influence the structure of an HR department by prioritizing functions that align with the company's long-term objectives and growth plans. When focused on expansion, ELR activities emphasize recruitment, talent acquisition, and integration, whereas during restructuring or downsizing, ELR efforts concentrate on change management, employee support, and conflict resolution.

Workforce Demographics Workforce demographics impact the structure of an HR department by necessitating roles that address the specific needs and characteristics of the employee population. For a diverse workforce, ELR activities focus on diversity, equity, and inclusion (DEI) initiatives, cultural competency training, and tailored conflict resolution, whereas a predominantly younger workforce might drive efforts toward career development, engagement, and technology-driven communication strategies.

Union Presence Union presence influences the structure of an HR department by requiring specialized roles dedicated to managing labor relations and collective bargaining processes. In unionized environments, ELR activities focus on negotiating and maintaining collective bargaining agreements, handling grievances, and fostering collaborative relationships with union representatives, whereas non-unionized workplaces concentrate more on direct employee relations, engagement, and conflict resolution.

While these variables are highly diverse, they each require a set of shared HR competencies for successful performance. These include:

- **Business Acumen:** Understanding the organization's operations, strategy, and financial metrics to align HR practices with business goals
- **Conflict Management:** Effectively addressing and resolving workplace disputes to maintain a positive and productive work environment using coaching and other human relations techniques
- **Relationship Building and Management:** Developing and maintaining strong interpersonal relationships within the organization to enhance collaboration and share positive outcomes
- **Cultural Intelligence:** Recognizing and respecting diverse cultural backgrounds and adapting HR practices to accommodate cultural differences
- **Data Analytics:** Being able to collect, interpret, and present data in a meaningful way that supports organizational decision making
- **Negotiations:** Skillfully negotiating employment terms, collective bargaining agreements, and resolving conflicts between parties
- **Communication:** Clearly and effectively conveying information, expectations, and feedback across all levels of the organization; includes active listening to engage in constructive problem-solving

Diversity, Equity and Inclusion and Affirmative Action

DEI through the lens of ELR focuses on creating a fair, respectful, and inclusive workplace where all employees feel valued and empowered. ELR and HR professionals play an important role in developing and implementing policies that promote equal opportunities, address systemic biases, and ensure compliance with antidiscrimination laws. They also facilitate open dialogue and conflict resolution, helping to bridge cultural differences. By prioritizing DEI, ELR efforts contribute to a positive organizational culture. DEI is covered extensively in Chapter 2, "Shared Competencies."

Affirmative action is a policy framework aimed at promoting DEI by actively seeking to remedy historical and systemic inequalities faced by underrepresented groups in areas such as education and employment. It involves measures to improve opportunities for historically marginalized populations, including targeted recruitment, training programs, and consideration of diversity in hiring and admissions decisions.

Affirmative action is not about granting unearned advantages or setting quotas; in fact, quotas are explicitly unlawful. Affirmative action programs are intended to level the playing field to ensure that all individuals have a fair chance to succeed based on their merits while considering the context of unequal opportunities historically afforded to different groups.

Affirmative action programs are typically required in the following scenarios:

- **Federal Contractors:** Companies that do business with the federal government and meet specific contract value thresholds are required to develop and maintain affirmative action plans. The Office of Federal Contract Compliance Programs (OFCCP) enforces these requirements under Executive Order 11246.
- **Legal Settlements and Court Orders:** Organizations may be required to implement affirmative action programs as part of legal settlements or court orders to remedy past discrimination.

Some organizations voluntarily adopt affirmative action programs to promote workplace diversity and inclusion, even if not legally required. This often aligns with corporate social responsibility goals and public commitments to diversity.

An affirmative action plan (AAP) typically includes several key components designed to promote diversity and ensure equal employment opportunities. These components are:

- **Organizational Profile:** A snapshot of the company's workforce that outlines job classifications and workforce demographics, helping identify areas where diversity can be improved
- **Job Group Analysis:** Grouping job titles with similar duties, responsibilities, and compensation, then analyzing the composition of these groups to identify underrepresentation of women and minorities
- **Availability Analysis:** Determining the availability of qualified women and minorities for each job group, using internal and external labor market data to set benchmarks for expected diversity
- **Comparison of Incumbency to Availability:** Comparing the current workforce composition to the availability data to identify gaps where women and minorities are underrepresented
- **Placement Goals:** Establishing specific, measurable goals to address the identified gaps and increase the representation of women and minorities in the workforce
- **Action-Oriented Programs:** Developing strategies and initiatives aimed at achieving the placement goals, such as targeted recruitment efforts, training programs, and career development opportunities for underrepresented groups

- **Internal Audit and Reporting System:** Implementing mechanisms to regularly monitor and report on the progress of the AAP, ensuring compliance and accountability within the organization
- **Responsibility for Implementation:** Assigning specific individuals or teams within the organization to oversee and ensure the effective implementation of the AAP

For more detailed information, refer to resources from the U.S. Department of Labor or the Office of Federal Contract Compliance.

Real World Scenario

Labor-Management DEI Cooperatives (Co-Ops)

The collaboration between the United Auto Workers (UAW) and major automotive companies like Ford, GM, and Stellantis is an excellent example of how unions and organizations can come together to promote DEI. In recent collective bargaining agreements, the UAW has successfully negotiated for comprehensive DEI initiatives, including commitments to increase the hiring and promotion of women and minority employees, implement bias training programs, and establish diversity committees to oversee progress. This partnership aims to create a more inclusive workplace and ensure fair treatment for all employees, reflecting the evolving priorities in labor relations and corporate responsibility.

Corporate Social Responsibility

Corporate social responsibility (CSR) is the commitment of a business to contribute positively to society and the environment through ethical practices, sustainable initiatives, and community engagement, beyond its financial and operational objectives. The term "CSR" was first used in a modern context in the early 1950s, highlighted by Howard Bowen's 1953 publication "Social Responsibilities of the Businessman," which is considered one of the foundational works in CSR literature. Bowen argued that businesses have an obligation to pursue policies and make decisions that align with societal values and objectives, laying the groundwork for contemporary CSR practices.

The *triple bottom line (TBL)* is another framework that is related to CSR in that it broadens a business's focus beyond financial performance to include social and environmental impacts. Coined by John Elkington in 1994, TBL suggests that companies should commit to measuring their success not just by profit, but also by how they impact people (social responsibility) and the planet (environmental sustainability). This approach encourages businesses to pursue sustainable practices that balance economic growth with ecological and community well-being, often referred to as the three Ps: Profit, People, and Planet. Implementing TBL can lead to more comprehensive corporate strategies that promote long-term sustainability and ethical accountability.

U.S. and international HR teams are often responsible for *community outreach*, which is connecting and creating positive relationships between businesses and the communities in which they operate. This engagement can take various forms, characterized by the following key concepts:

Philanthropy *Philanthropy* in CSR refers to businesses making charitable donations to support social causes, community projects, and nonprofit organizations. This can include financial contributions, donating goods and services, or providing grants to initiatives that align with the company's values and mission. Philanthropy aims to create a positive social impact and demonstrates the company's commitment to giving back to society.

Microsoft is well-known for its extensive corporate philanthropy program, which includes donating $3.2 billion in technology to over 300,000 nonprofits worldwide, benefiting more than 1.2 billion people. The company also matches employee donations up to $15,000 at a 1:1 ratio and offers volunteer grants, providing $25 per hour volunteered without a minimum required number of hours.[1]

Volunteerism *Volunteerism* in CSR involves encouraging and enabling employees to volunteer their time and skills to support community service projects and nonprofit organizations. This can include company-organized volunteer events, paid time off for volunteer work, and initiatives that leverage employees' professional expertise to benefit the community. Volunteerism fosters a sense of purpose among employees and strengthens the company's relationship with the community.

In a post-pandemic world, virtual volunteer opportunities have become an attractive and sustainable option for employees, with 51 percent of volunteer hours being virtual in 2023, compared to 23 percent before the pandemic. For example, in HR, many professionals can help others with interview skills, résumé building, mentoring, and professional skill development. Sixty percent of companies offer rewards, such as making donations to the nonprofit of choice in exchange for employee volunteer hours.[2] Many times, these donations are tax-deductible for the employer and increase employee engagement.

Partnerships *Partnerships* in CSR involve collaborating with local organizations, nonprofits, government agencies, and other businesses to address social and environmental issues. These partnerships can enhance the effectiveness of CSR initiatives by combining resources, expertise, and networks to achieve shared goals. Successful CSR partnerships are built on mutual trust, aligned objectives, and a commitment to creating sustainable and impactful outcomes for the community.

---

[1] Double the Donation, Corporate Philanthropy Examples: 14 Companies Doing It Right, `https://doublethedonation.com/corporate-philanthropy-examples`.

[2] New Benevity Report Reveals a Surge in Corporate Volunteerism, `https://benevity.com/press-releases/2024-state-of-corporate-volunteering`.

Many partnerships are made with a *nongovernmental organization (NGO)*, which is a nonprofit, voluntary group that operates independently of government control. NGOs are typically organized on local, national, or international levels to address social, political, environmental, or humanitarian issues. They are driven by people with a common interest and often rely on donations, membership dues, and grants to fund their operations. NGOs work in various sectors, including human rights, health, education, and environmental conservation, aiming to effect change through advocacy, service provision, and grassroots organizing. Their independence from government influence allows them to address issues that may be overlooked or inadequately addressed by the public sector.

Workplace Safety

The general duty clause is a provision in the Occupational Safety and Health Act of 1970 that requires employers to provide a workplace free from recognized hazards that are likely to cause death or serious physical harm to employees. This clause serves as a catch-all provision to address hazards for which there are no specific OSHA standards.

OSHA and other safety-related regulations are covered in Appendix C, and PHRi candidates will not be tested on this act. However, the general duty clause is a good example of the obligation that an employer has when it comes to worker safety and health. The exam specifically notes areas of responsibility in workers' compensation, workplace violence, substance abuse at work, and documentation; these are covered next.

Workers' Compensation Insurance

Employers are responsible for providing workers' compensation insurance to protect employees who suffer work-related injuries or illnesses. This insurance ensures that employees receive necessary medical care and compensation for lost wages.

An *injury* is typically the result of a specific incident or accident, such as a fall, cut, or burn, and occurs suddenly. It is generally easy to identify the exact moment or cause of an injury. Conversely, an *illness* often develops over time and can be due to exposure to harmful conditions or substances, such as chemicals, repetitive stress, or pathogens, resulting in conditions like respiratory disorders, repetitive strain injuries, or infections. Illnesses may have multiple contributing factors and a gradual onset, making them harder to pinpoint to a specific event.

Workers' compensation is mandated by federal law but enforced at state level. It was designed as a no-fault system, meaning that even if the employee did not follow safety procedures and was injured as a result, they are still covered by the insurance. The no-fault system also supports employee reporting of injuries as they will be less worried about retaliation. Large employers often choose to *self-insure*, meaning that an employer assumes the financial risk for providing workers' compensation benefits to its employees rather than purchasing insurance from a third-party carrier. Workers' compensation is *experience-rated*, meaning that the premiums an employer pays are adjusted based on the employer's claims history, with higher rates for those with more frequent or severe claims and lower rates for those with fewer or less severe claims. In the case where an employer is uninsurable due to a high volume of incidents, they may be required to participate in a state-assigned risk pool or state fund, which provides coverage to high-risk employers who cannot obtain insurance in the regular market.

Workplace Violence

Workplace violence is any act or threat of physical violence, harassment, intimidation, or other disruptive behavior that occurs at work. It ranges from threats and verbal abuse to physical assaults and even homicide. Workplace violence can affect and involve employees, clients, customers, and visitors.

Violent events can occur in settings beyond traditional office environments, often requiring specific strategies and training to manage and prevent such incidents effectively. Consider the following examples:

- A physical altercation broke out between two artists' entourages backstage at a major music festival, leading to several injuries and requiring intervention from security and law enforcement.
- A retail employee in New York was trampled to death by a stampede of people rushing into the store for Black Friday deals.
- A bus driver in London was attacked by a passenger refusing to wear a mask during the COVID-19 pandemic.

While workplace violence prevention is not currently a requirement under OSHA, failing to implement preventive measures and policies to mitigate risks could become a violation under the general duty clause.

Intimate partner violence (IPV) in the workplace involves employees experiencing physical, emotional, or psychological abuse from a partner that affects their work life. Statistics show that between 21 and 60 percent of IPV victims lose their jobs due to the abuse[3] (it varies by state), and IPV has significant economic impacts, costing an estimated $3.6 trillion over victims' lifetimes due to medical expenses, lost productivity, and other related costs.[4] Addressing IPV in the workplace ensures the safety and well-being of employees and maintains a productive work environment. Victims of IPV often disclose the abuse to their managers or coworkers, and so employees would benefit from training, policy development, and programs such as counseling and *EAPs (employee assistance programs)* to offer support and avoid escalation into a workplace violence incident.

---

[3] National Coalition Against Domestic Violence, Domestic Violence Statistics, `https://ncadv.org/statistics`.

[4] Workplace Interventions for IPV: A Systematic Review, `https://www.ncbi.nlm.nih.gov/pmc/articles/PMC7176402`.

HR can take several other steps to reduce any workplace violence incidents, including the following:

Develop a comprehensive workplace violence prevention policy. Clearly define what constitutes workplace violence, establish zero-tolerance policies, and outline the procedures for reporting and responding to incidents.

Enhance security measures. Implement security measures such as access controls, surveillance cameras, and emergency response protocols to protect employees.

Establish a reporting system. Create a confidential and accessible reporting system for employees to report incidents or threats of violence without fear of retaliation.

Conduct risk assessments. Regularly assess the workplace for potential risks and vulnerabilities related to violence, and take proactive measures to mitigate these risks.

Create a positive work environment. Promote a culture of respect, inclusivity, and open communication to reduce tension and conflict among employees.

Substance Abuse

Substance abuse in the workplace refers to the use of alcohol, drugs, or other substances by employees during work hours or in a manner that affects their job performance and safety. Substance abuse in the workplace costs American employers approximately $81 billion annually due to decreased productivity, absenteeism, turnover, and healthcare costs. Employers spend an average of $8,817 per employee with an untreated substance use disorder (SUD) each year.[5] Addressing substance misuse can lead to significant savings, with employers potentially saving over $8,500 for each employee in recovery, as these workers typically have fewer absences and lower healthcare costs compared to those with untreated SUDs. In addition to outlawed substances, employees are also prohibited from borrowing and using someone else's prescription medication.

Similar to workplace violence prevention, employers can address substance abuse by implementing clear policies, providing education and training, offering support programs such as EAPs, and ensuring a safe and healthy work environment through regular monitoring and support initiatives.

Many states have legalized the use of medical marijuana, causing some confusion over how employers should handle those with medical cards. Employers can address this by developing clear policies that balance compliance with state laws. Here are some key steps employers can take:

Update drug policies. Revise workplace drug policies to address the use of legal marijuana explicitly. Clearly define prohibited behaviors, such as use during work hours or impairment while on the job. Ensure the policy is communicated to all employees and is included in the employee handbook.

---

[5] National Safety Council, Substance Use Costs Your Workplace More Than You Think, `https://www.nsc.org/safety-first/substance-use-costs-your-workplace-more-than-you-t`.

Focus on impairment. Rather than solely testing for marijuana use, which can detect past use but not current impairment, consider policies that focus on impairment. Train supervisors to recognize signs of impairment and establish procedures for handling suspected impairment cases.

Comply with state laws. Understand and comply with the specific marijuana laws in your state. Some states protect employees from discrimination based on their legal use of marijuana, whereas others allow employers to enforce zero-tolerance policies.

Manage safety-sensitive positions. For positions that are safety-sensitive, such as operating heavy machinery or driving, maintain strict no-use policies to ensure workplace safety. Regularly review these policies to align with any changes in state and federal regulations.

Provide support. Offer support through employee assistance programs (EAPs) for employees who may struggle with substance use. Ensure that employees are aware of these resources and encourage their use.

Consult legal experts. Regularly consult with legal experts to stay updated on evolving marijuana legislation and its implications for workplace policies. This ensures that your policies remain compliant and legally defensible.

Note that companies who are subject to federal government employment rules (such as contractors) must still treat marijuana as an illegal substance as part of the Drug Free Workplace Act.

Drug-Testing Programs

There are several factors to take into account when a company decides to implement a drug-testing program. First, the program must be implemented in a fair and consistent manner to avoid charges of discrimination. Next, the company must decide what type of testing will be done:

Preemployment Testing Lawful only after an offer of employment has been made. Before beginning a testing program, the employer must decide which applicants will be tested. This decision may be based on the type of work done in different jobs; for example, a company may decide to test all employees who operate machinery. The test must be conducted fairly and consistently on all applicants for the designated jobs.

Random Drug Testing Done on an arbitrary, unscheduled basis. To make the testing truly random and reduce the risk of legal challenges, employers may want to use a computer program that randomly selects employees. Random drug testing should be implemented with legal counsel to avoid violating privacy rights unnecessarily.

Scheduled Drug Testing Can be useful when monitoring the rehabilitation progress of employees but has limited value because employees who may be currently using drugs are generally able to stop long enough before the test to clear their systems of the drugs.

Reasonable-Suspicion Drug Testing Can be used any time there has been an accident in which an employee's actions contributed to the cause of the accident in the workplace or when a supervisor suspects, based on behavior, that an employee is under the influence of drugs.

Regardless of the substance abuse testing schedule that is used, it's important to keep in mind that implementation must be fair and equitable to avoid charges of discrimination. If employers choose to test specific job categories, then all employees in those categories must be subjected to the testing process. If random testing is used, all employees in the selected category must be included in the selection group.

HR professionals must also keep in mind that, under the ADA, current users of illegal drugs are specifically excluded from protection, while current abusers of alcohol aren't automatically denied protection. Regardless, employers may take adverse action if the behavior negatively affects an employee's ability to do the job. Entering recovery is a trigger for protection under the ADA for both groups.

Return-to-Work Programs

Whether the absence was the result of a work-related illness or injury or another cause, a return-to-work (RTW) policy can reduce the risk of re-injury. Some organizations develop a comprehensive policy that includes accident reporting procedures, definitions of various terms, types of leaves covered by the RTW program, and administrative procedures in their procedures, whereas others develop separate policies and procedures for different aspects. Organizations will develop policies tailored to their specific needs, but all should include a clear statement of compliance with specific legal requirements of Family and Medical Leave Act (FMLA) medical certifications, workers' compensation, or other laws that may apply. The procedure should answer basic questions for supervisors and employees, such as the following:

- What is the goal or objective of the RTW program?
- Who is eligible?
- Are there policy or procedure differences between a work-related medical leave of absence (MLOA) and a non-work-related MLOA?
- What is the impact of an MLOA on employee compensation and benefits?
- Under what conditions will the organization accommodate modified work assignments that allow employees to transition back to work before they have recovered completely?
- What are the employee's responsibilities with regard to the leave and RTW?
- What are the employer's responsibilities with regard to the leave and RTW?
- What are the responsibilities of the HR department with regard to the leave and RTW?
- What type of medical release does the organization require prior to accepting workers back on the job?

Once the previous questions have been adequately addressed, designing the elements of an RTW process becomes necessary. Examples include the following:

Modified Duty Assignment Because many injured workers are quite willing and able to perform some but not all of the essential duties of a job, modifying specific tasks or functions may be necessary to allow an employee to return to work. In fact, workers' compensation studies have shown that employees who are offered modified/light-duty assignments return to full duty more quickly than injured workers who incur lost time. This translates into a lower overall injury cost and allows the employee to get back into the routine of work much more quickly. Modified duty may include eliminating essential functions or creating a short-term job for the employee until they're able to return to full duty.

Having accurate job descriptions is necessary to engage in this process, as the employee and doctor will use them to return the employee to work with the proper restrictions.

Reasonable Accommodations Reasonable accommodation is similar to modified duty, with two very major distinctions. Modified duty is typically a short-term option used for injured workers who are expected to be able to return to full duty, and an employer need not create a light-duty position for a "non-occupationally injured employee" as part of reasonable accommodation efforts. The process of identifying reasonable accommodation includes discussing options such as a reduced schedule, additional unpaid time off, and reassignment to a vacant position for which the disabled individual is qualified. It very well could also be modifying the essential functions of the job if that action wouldn't impose undue hardship on the employer.

Independent Medical Exam (IME) Fit-for-duty exams are effective tools to use to determine if an employee is capable of returning to work without causing harm to themselves or others. These types of exams allow for an impartial review of the injured employee's medical status. For employers, IMEs can help to prevent fraud and deal with excessive extensions of time off due to lack of a proper diagnosis or treatment. For employees, these types of exams are helpful when there are conflicting reports of their needs or an employee doesn't agree with a doctor's findings.

A clear, legally compliant RTW policy mitigates the risk of inadvertent errors by managers and helps ensure that all employees are treated equitably when returning from medical leaves. In addition, requiring a medical release prior to an employee's return reduces the risk of re-injury.

Documentation

Several types of documentation and legal postings are required to ensure compliance with regulatory standards and to maintain a safe work environment.

For example, employers are required to maintain comprehensive written safety policies outlining the organization's commitment to safety and health. These must include detailed procedures for handling various safety and health scenarios, including emergency response plans (covered in Chapter 2). Employers also must document the safety training provided to employees, including dates, attendees, and topics covered, as well as incident reports and any investigative reports that outline the cause of incidents and corrective actions taken. Audits are another area of required documentation and should include regular safety inspections and audit reports, including findings, corrective actions, and maintenance logs for safety equipment and machinery.

Safety is not the only area where documentation is required. In fact, there are documentation requirements for every function of human resources, and they include:

Employment Records

- **Applications and Résumés:** Documentation of all job applications and résumés received during the hiring process
- **Employment Contracts:** Copies of contracts or offer letters detailing the terms and conditions of employment
- **Job Descriptions:** Detailed descriptions of roles and responsibilities for each position within the company

Payroll Records

- **Time Sheets:** Records of hours worked by employees, including overtime
- **Payroll Registers:** Documentation of wages paid, including deductions and net pay
- **Tax Forms:** Copies of tax forms such as W-2s and 1099s, along with records of tax withholdings and filings

Performance Records

- **Performance Reviews:** Documentation of employee performance evaluations, goals, and feedback
- **Disciplinary Actions:** Records of any disciplinary actions taken, including warnings, suspensions, and terminations
- **Awards and Recognitions:** Documentation of any awards, recognitions, or promotions given to employees

Benefits Records

- **Enrollment Forms:** Documentation of employee enrollment in benefit programs such as health insurance, retirement plans, and other benefits
- **Claims Records:** Records of claims made by employees for benefits such as health insurance, disability, and workers' compensation
- **COBRA Notices:** Documentation of COBRA notices provided to employees upon termination or change in benefits status

Training Records

- **Training Schedules:** Records of training sessions provided, including dates, topics, and attendance
- **Certificates:** Copies of certificates or proof of completion for training programs
- **Continuing Education:** Documentation of ongoing professional development and continuing education activities

Leave Records

- **Leave Requests:** Documentation of requests for leave, including vacation, sick leave, and family medical leave
- **Approval Notices:** Records of leave approvals or denials
- **Leave Balances:** Updated records of leave balances for each employee

Compliance Records

- **EEO Reports:** Equal Employment Opportunity (EEO) reports documenting compliance with antidiscrimination laws
- **Immigration Forms:** Copies of I-9 forms and supporting documents verifying employment eligibility
- **Audit Records:** Documentation of any internal or external audits conducted, along with findings and corrective actions

Due Diligence

- **Relevant Records:** Any records that may be requested as part of a legal dispute or that would be necessary to disclose as part of a merger, acquisition, or other proceeding

In addition to maintaining thorough documentation and compliance records, employers must update several state and federal postings annually. These include federal labor law posters for the Fair Labor Standards Act (FLSA), Occupational Safety and Health Act (OSHA), Family and Medical Leave Act (FMLA), and Equal Employment Opportunity (EEO). Additionally, state-specific notices for minimum wage laws, unemployment insurance, workers' compensation, and state antidiscrimination laws must be displayed. Employers also need to post employee rights under the National Labor Relations Act (NLRA) and emergency contact details. These postings must be placed in visible locations accessible to all employees to ensure compliance and inform workers of their rights and responsibilities.

NOTE

Workplace safety and health, emergency response, and conducting investigations are closely related to enterprise risk management. All are covered in more detail in Chapter 2.

Company Policies, Procedures, and Rules

In employee and labor relations, policies, procedures, and rules are used to maintain a structured and compliant workplace. These documents provide clear guidelines on expected behaviors, operational procedures, and employee rights, which help prevent misunderstandings, ensure fairness, and enhance overall organizational efficiency. Key components include:

- **Policies:** Policies are overarching guidelines established by an organization to govern decisions and ensure consistent, fair treatment of employees while complying with legal requirements.
- **Procedures:** Procedures are detailed, step-by-step instructions that outline the specific methods and processes to be followed in order to achieve compliance with policies and accomplish particular tasks.
- **Rules:** Rules are specific, mandatory directives that define acceptable and unacceptable behaviors and actions within the workplace, often with clearly stated consequences for violations.

Policies, procedures, and rules are usually communicated through the employee handbook and standard operating procedures:

Handbook The employee handbook is a comprehensive document that outlines the company's policies, procedures, benefits, and behavioral expectations. It serves as a reference for employees to understand their rights and responsibilities. Examples include policies on workplace behavior and anti-harassment, which define acceptable conduct and the procedure for reporting and handling harassment complaints; attendance and leave policies that detail expectations for attendance, procedures for requesting time off, and rules for tardiness or absenteeism; and expense reimbursement procedures that explain how employees can claim work-related expenses and the rules governing allowable expenses.

Standard Operating Procedures (SOPs) SOPs are detailed, written instructions that describe the step-by-step processes for performing specific tasks. They ensure consistency, efficiency, and safety in daily operations.

At an organizational level, *ISO standards*, developed by the International Organization for Standardization, provide guidelines and best practices for various aspects of organizational management, including human resources. These standards can be used in ELR to ensure consistent, fair, and effective HR practices across an organization. For instance, ISO 30414 provides guidelines on human capital reporting, helping organizations measure and report on key HR metrics such as employee turnover, absenteeism, and diversity. Another example is ISO 45001, which focuses on occupational health and safety management systems, aiming to reduce workplace risks and create safer working environments. Other types of ISO standards include ISO 9001 for quality management systems, which ensures products and services consistently meet customer and regulatory requirements, and ISO 14001 for environmental management systems, which helps organizations minimize their environmental impact and improve sustainability practices. Employers who want to get certified in ISO standards must first demonstrate understanding of the relevant standards, conduct a gap analysis, implement necessary changes, and undergo a successful audit by an accredited certification body. The benefits of ISO certification include improved efficiency, enhanced reputation, increased customer satisfaction and effective risk management.

Employee Complaints

Employee complaints are expressions of dissatisfaction or concerns raised by employees regarding various aspects of their work environment or conditions. These complaints can relate to problems with the physical and mental work environment, including safety hazards, employee and management behaviors, lack of necessary equipment, or uncomfortable working conditions. In a union environment, complaints are also called *grievances,* and they may also involve unfair treatment, poor communication, lack of support, or inappropriate behavior from supervisors or managers. Other complaints relate to interpersonal conflicts, such as bullying, harassment, or discrimination.

Concerns about excessive workload, unclear job responsibilities, or lack of recognition for efforts and contributions are common, as are complaints regarding unfair wages, inadequate benefits, or discrepancies in pay and promotion practices. Issues related to work hours, overtime, lack of flexibility, or insufficient leave policies can also lead to dissatisfaction.

Employers may handle employee complaints by establishing a company hotline, which allows employees to report issues confidentially and anonymously. HR can act as a mediator to uncover the root issues and work through the conflict to achieve a satisfying conclusion. When HR is not trusted or part of the issue, outside resources should be retained.

Alternative Dispute Methods

Alternative dispute resolution (ADR) refers to a range of processes that help parties resolve conflicts without resorting to litigation. Common ADR methods include mediation and arbitration. ADR is often faster, less formal, and less expensive than traditional court proceedings. It emphasizes collaborative solutions and can preserve relationships by promoting mutual understanding and agreement. *Mediation* involves a neutral third-party facilitating discussions, while *arbitration* involves a binding decision from an arbitrator.

Arbitration agreements are often part of the onboarding paperwork for new employees. These agreements require employees to resolve any future disputes through arbitration rather than in court. To ensure compliance and understanding, HR explains the terms and significance of the agreement, emphasizing that signing is a condition of employment. The agreements aim to streamline conflict resolution and minimize litigation costs. However, it is essential that employees understand their rights and the implications of arbitration, as these agreements often face scrutiny and legal challenges regarding fairness and enforceability.

A notable example of a challenge to an arbitration agreement is the case of *Epic Systems Corp. v. Lewis* (2018). In this case, employees argued that their arbitration agreements, which waived their rights to participate in class or collective actions, violated the National Labor Relations Act (NLRA). The Supreme Court ultimately ruled that such agreements are enforceable under the Federal Arbitration Act (FAA), allowing employers to require individual arbitration and preventing employees from pursuing group claims in court. This decision underscored the legal tension between arbitration agreements and employee rights to collective action.

Workplace Investigations

In some cases, HR may need to conduct an investigation in cases of employee misconduct, harassment, discrimination, or violations of company policies. Table 8.1 shows the difference between internal versus external investigations.

TABLE 8.1 Internal vs. external investigations

Aspect	Internal investigation	External investigation
Familiarity	Investigators are familiar with company culture, policies, and personnel, which can speed up the investigation process.	External investigators bring objectivity and are perceived as unbiased, which can enhance credibility.
Cost	Generally lower cost since it uses existing resources.	Can be more thorough and bring specialized expertise, which may uncover issues that internal teams might miss.
Control	Company retains more control over the investigation process and can ensure alignment with internal policies.	Reduces potential conflicts of interest and can provide a fresh perspective on issues.
Confidentiality	Perception of lack of confidentiality or bias.	Perceived as more impartial by employees, which can increase trust in the investigation outcome.

Investigations are covered thoroughly in Chapter 2. However, investigation best practices include maintaining confidentiality, conducting thorough and impartial interviews with all parties involved, documenting findings, and advising leaders on potential solutions and any associated risks.

Several federal labor laws require investigations as part of compliance to ensure fair treatment and a safe work environment. Key laws include:

Title VII of the Civil Rights Act of 1964 Requires investigations into complaints of discrimination based on race, color, religion, sex, or national origin. Employers must investigate and address any allegations to avoid liability for workplace discrimination.

Americans with Disabilities Act (ADA) Mandates investigations into complaints of discrimination based on disability, ensuring that employees with disabilities receive reasonable accommodations where appropriate.

Occupational Safety and Health Act (OSHA) Requires employers to investigate workplace accidents, injuries, and safety complaints to maintain a safe work environment and comply with safety standards.

Fair Labor Standards Act (FLSA) Involves investigations into wage and hour complaints, including issues related to minimum wage, overtime pay, and child labor laws.

Family and Medical Leave Act (FMLA) Requires investigations into complaints related to employees' rights to take unpaid, job-protected leave for specified family and medical reasons.

Workplace Incivility and Counterproductive Work Behaviors

Workplace incivility refers to rude, discourteous behavior and lack of respect that negatively impacts the work environment. This behavior can include condescending comments, ignoring colleagues, or other forms of disrespect. The cost of workplace incivility is significant, as it can lead to decreased employee morale, lower productivity, increased turnover, and even physical and mental health issues for affected employees. According to the Society for Human Resource Management (SHRM)'s new Civility Index, over half of U.S. workers believe American society is uncivil. These behaviors not only erode workplace culture but also contribute to a toxic environment that undermines organizational success.

The Civility Index provides insights into the prevalence of incivility and its effects on businesses. Organizations with high levels of incivility face increased costs associated with employee disengagement, absenteeism, and the need for conflict resolution interventions. Additionally, the reputational damage can hinder talent attraction and retention, further impacting the bottom line. Find out more about this tool and the findings at `www.shrm.org`.

Counterproductive work behaviors (CWBs) are actions by employees that harm or intend to harm organizations and their members. These behaviors can range from minor acts, such as wasting time or taking excessive breaks, to more severe actions, like theft, sabotage, or workplace aggression. CWBs are typically categorized into two main types: interpersonal deviance (e.g., harassment, bullying) and organizational deviance (e.g., vandalism, fraud).

Similar to workplace incivility, the impact of CWBs on organizations is substantial, leading to decreased productivity, increased costs, and a negative workplace atmosphere, not to mention potential legal liability.

HR can enhance workplace civility and reduce CWBs by implementing clear policies that define acceptable behavior and consequences for violations, and by ensuring these policies are well communicated and enforced. Offering regular training programs focused on effective communication, conflict resolution, and stress management equips employees with the necessary skills to interact respectfully. Promoting a positive work culture through recognition programs and encouraging open communication can help maintain a respectful and productive work environment. Employers should also take steps to actively investigate complaints and address grievances in a transparent and timely manner.

Positive Employee and Labor Relations Strategies

SHRM is a professional association that provides resources, education, and advocacy to support the development and management of human resources. A quick search under their topic of "employee relations" found these top topics:[6]

- 7 Tips for Successfully Hiring Talent with Developmental Disabilities
- How Corporate Philanthropy Can Boost Employee Retention and Engagement
- 6 ways to Help Your Employee During Tax Season
- How to Conduct a Workplace Investigation
- Encouraging Generation Z and Baby Boomers to Work Together
- Meeting Mental Health Needs Across Generations

The common theme among these bullet points is the employer's responsibility to implement strategies that enhance employee well-being and engagement. These topics contribute to *positive employer relations strategies*, which are the effective and proactive management of interactions between employers and employees.

The exam content outline shares similarities with the topics from SHRM, in that there are specific themes that should be understood in the context of positive employer relations strategies. Tools and techniques to achieve this include the following:

- **Open Communication Channels:** Establish clear and consistent methods for communication, such as regular meetings, suggestion boxes, and open-door policies.
- **Antidiscrimination and Zero Tolerance Policies:** Implement and enforce strict antidiscrimination policies and zero tolerance for harassment.
- **Feedback Systems:** Create regular feedback loops through surveys, performance reviews, and one-on-one meetings. Create action plans and follow-up items.

---

[6] Society for Human Resource Management, `https://www.shrm.org/topics-tools/topics/employee-relations#sortCriteria=relevancy%2C%40ytlikecount%20descending`.

- **Union-Management Collaboration:** For unionized environments, build a cooperative relationship with union representatives to address employee issues and negotiate contracts effectively.
- **Intergenerational Initiatives:** Develop programs that encourage collaboration and understanding between different age groups within the workforce.
- **Participative Management Techniques:** Involve employees in decision-making processes to build trust, increase engagement, and reduce uncertainty.

NOTE

Exam objective 6.5 for both the PHR and PHRi exams notes either knowledge of U.S. federal laws or applicable laws, respectively. These are covered extensively in Appendix C. PHRi candidates will not be tested on US federal laws.

Summary

Employee and labor relations (ELR) are defined by the processes and practices that HR professionals use to manage relationships between employees and the organization. ELR involves ensuring compliance with labor laws, which protect workers' rights and outline employer obligations. This includes adhering to regulations such as the Fair Labor Standards Act, the Occupational Safety and Health Act, and the National Labor Relations Act, which mandate fair treatment and workplace safety.

HR teams are responsible for building effective ELR programs to support a positive work environment. These programs should focus on clear communication, fair dispute resolution, and consistent enforcement of policies. Behavioral issues, such as counterproductive work behaviors (CWBs) and abusive conduct, undermine workplace harmony and productivity. Other issues such as workplace violence and substance abuse put employees at risk. Addressing these issues promptly and effectively through investigations and taking prompt action is a necessary component of successful ELR management.

HR professionals can use positive ELR strategies to create a healthy workplace by promoting open communication, recognizing and rewarding positive behavior, and providing training and development opportunities. Encouraging employee engagement and involvement in decision making can also help build trust and commitment.

Exam Essentials

Understand the principles and importance of defining employee and labor relations to enhance organizational performance. Defining employee and labor relations involves identifying its key components and understanding its role in driving productivity, retention, and overall organizational success. By clearly articulating what these relationships entail, HR can structure its department functions to align ELR activities with organizational results.

Develop and implement strategies to support workplace safety programs. Effectively managing health and safety risks require HR to understand the environment and related hazards in which employees are asked to perform. Factors to consider include substance abuse, workers' compensation insurance and preventing workplace violence.

Explain how positive employee relations strategies contribute to higher employee engagement. Positive employee relations strategies affects levels of employee engagement at all stages of the employee lifecycle. Providing and asking for feedback and other employee involvement strategies are ways HR can improve engagement.

Review Questions

You can find the answers in Appendix A.

1. Which of the following is a key purpose of employee and labor relations?
   A. To improve communication between employees and management
   B. To reduce employee training costs
   C. To enhance the company's social media presence
   D. To improve benefits for employees

2. Which of the following factors related to hiring are most likely to influence employee and labor relations programs? (Choose all that apply).
   A. Workforce demographics
   B. Strategic goals
   C. Geographic locations
   D. Company culture and values

3. What is the primary goal of affirmative action in the workplace?
   A. To defend against charges of unlawful harassment
   B. To ensure equal opportunity for employment and advancement for underrepresented groups
   C. To build inclusive practices through diversity initiatives
   D. To create hiring quotas of minority groups to increase diversity

4. Which of the following actions is typically part of an affirmative action plan?
   A. Mandating a certain percentage of underrepresented hires, such as 20 percent women in leadership.
   B. Hiring a chief diversity officer to repair past discriminatory practices
   C. Complying with private employer reporting requirements to federal and state agencies
   D. Conducting workforce analysis to identify underrepresentation

5. Which of the following are classified as a workplace disease? (Choose all that apply.)
   A. Hearing loss
   B. Carpal tunnel syndrome
   C. A broken arm
   D. Occupational burnout

6. How should an employer handle employees with a medical marijuana card in states that allow medical marijuana use?
   A. Enforce a strict no-tolerance policy for any marijuana use as it is unlawful at the federal level.
   B. Require mandatory drug testing for all employees in safety sensitive positions.
   C. Focus on impairment and ensure employees are not under the influence while performing job duties.
   D. Exempt covered employees from the employer's substance abuse policy.
7. Which of the following is an example of a participative management technique?
   A. Managers setting goals and asking for employee input on how to achieve them
   B. Employees being encouraged to take part in decision-making processes through regular team meetings
   C. Supervisors implementing an open-door policy for employees to share suggestions and concerns
   D. Managers providing detailed instructions for tasks and expecting employees to follow them
8. What is the main difference between a complaint and a grievance in the workplace?
   A. A complaint is informal, whereas a grievance follows a formal process.
   B. A grievance is always related to legal issues, whereas a complaint is not.
   C. A complaint is voiced by an individual, whereas a grievance is filed by a group.
   D. There is no main difference; they are used interchangeably.
9. What is the primary difference between arbitration and mediation in alternative dispute resolution?
   A. Arbitration involves a neutral third party who facilitates discussions, whereas mediation results in a binding decision.
   B. Mediation is voluntary, whereas arbitration is always mandated by law.
   C. In arbitration, a neutral third party makes a binding decision, whereas in mediation, the parties work toward a mutually agreed solution.
   D. Mediation is only used for workplace disputes, whereas arbitration is used for all types of disputes.
10. Which of the following labor laws require that employers have a written employee handbook?
    A. Americans with Disabilities Act.
    B. Fair Labor Standards Act.
    C. Title VII of the Civil Rights Act of 1964.
    D. An employee handbook is not required by any labor law.

11. What is the primary difference between counterproductive work behavior and workplace harassment?

    A. Counterproductive work behavior involves actions that harm the organization, whereas workplace harassment involves actions that create a hostile or abusive environment for specific individuals.

    B. Counterproductive work behavior is always illegal, whereas workplace harassment is not always against the law.

    C. Counterproductive work behavior includes only physical actions, whereas workplace harassment includes only verbal actions.

    D. Counterproductive work behavior is always intentional, whereas workplace harassment can be unintentional.

12. Which of the following is a key feature of mediation as an alternative dispute resolution method?

    A. The mediator imposes a binding decision on the parties.

    B. The process is informal and focuses on facilitating mutual agreement.

    C. It involves a formal trial with a judge.

    D. Only legal issues can be addressed through mediation.

13. Which of the following is the best example of a work rule?

    A. Employees must adhere to a professional dress code.

    B. The company has zero tolerance for workplace harassment.

    C. Employees are required to clock in and out for lunch and meal breaks.

    D. Employees should submit their expense reports by logging in to the company intranet, clicking on the tab labeled Expense Reports, and following the instructions from there.

14. An injury is caused by a ________ whereas an illness is caused by ________.

    A. Sudden event; prolonged exposure

    B. Medical condition; physical trauma

    C. Psychological factor; environmental hazard

    D. Chronic condition; acute incident

15. Which of the following best describes the components of the triple bottom line?

    A. Profit, Quality, Customer Satisfaction

    B. People, Profit, Planet

    C. Productivity, Sustainability, Revenue

    D. Performance, Ethics, Efficiency

16. Which of the following statements is true regarding workers' compensation insurance?

    A. Workers' compensation insurance is optional for employers in most states.

    B. Workers' compensation insurance only covers injuries that occur on the employer's premises.

C. Workers' compensation insurance provides medical benefits and wage replacement to employees injured in the course of employment.

D. Workers' compensation insurance covers injuries that occur during an employee's regular commute.

17. Which of the following is an example of corporate social responsibility? (Choose all that apply.)

A. A company implements a comprehensive recycling program to reduce its environmental footprint and actively promotes it among employees and customers.

B. A corporation donates a percentage of its profits to local charities and sponsors community development projects.

C. An organization provides employees with paid volunteer days to contribute to social causes and supports their participation in community service activities.

D. A business increases its advertising budget to reach underrepresented individuals in the labor force.

18. Which of the following is a best practice when designing programs to prevent workplace violence?

A. Implementing a zero-tolerance policy for any form of workplace aggression

B. Conducting regular employee training on conflict resolution and recognizing signs of potential violence

C. Installing security cameras in all areas of the workplace

D. Encouraging employees to handle conflicts independently without involving management

19. What are the main differences between diversity programs and affirmative action programs?

A. Diversity programs focus on improving workplace culture, whereas affirmative action programs aim to correct historical inequalities.

B. Affirmative action programs are mandated by law, whereas diversity programs are typically voluntary initiatives.

C. Diversity programs require specific compliance requirements, whereas affirmative action programs do not.

D. Affirmative action programs solely focus on gender diversity, whereas diversity programs encompass a broader range of attributes.

20. In what way does the competency of business acumen influence an HR practitioner's ability to manage ELR programs?

A. Business acumen helps negotiate collective bargaining agreements.

B. Business acumen influences the ability to build strong relationships.

C. Business acumen supports the ability to manage conflicts effectively.

D. Business acumen informs the alignment of HR strategies with strategic objectives.

Chapter 9

PHR | PHRi Exam: HR Information Management

PHR AND PHRi RESPONSIBILITIES:

TOOLS, TECHNOLOGY, AND SYSTEMS THAT EFFICIENTLY OPTIMIZE THE ORGANIZATION'S ACCESS TO ITS HUMAN RESOURCE DATA.

- ✓ **7.1 Utilize and manage HR database content and technologies (for example: HRIS, maintain personnel data, employee status changes, salary changes)**
- ✓ **7.2 Assess and communicate information obtained from HR databases (for example: generate reports, data analytics, identify trends)**
- ✓ **7.3 Promote and maintain security best practices (for example: system access and permissions, front end user support, compliance, data integrity and data accuracy)**

Human resource information management (HRIM) is the systematic handling of all information related to an organization's human resources. Accounting for 10 percent of the PHR/i exams, this content area covers topics including data collection, storage, and utilization to support various HR functions such as recruitment, training, performance evaluation, and employee relations. Effective HRIM ensures that accurate and timely information is available for reporting to leadership to aid in decision making.

HR Information Management

An effective HRIM approach combines both proactive and reactive elements. This requires a focus on managing digital risks through prevention efforts, education and response. Proactive systems allow for strategic foresight and preparation, whereas reactive systems ensure that the organization can address immediate issues efficiently.

HR Workflow

In the course of a single day, thousands of data points are generated within a busy HR department. Figure 9.1 shows a typical day in the life of HR data generation. This requires that HR information management practices be fully integrated with department and organization operations, and technology can help make this happen.

HR technology has significantly improved the operational efficiencies of an HR department. Automating tasks such as time-keeping, payroll, and benefits administration has freed up HR professionals to focus on more human-centered HR tasks, such as problem solving and engagement. Integration with other management programs such as enterprise resource, customer service management, and messaging programs such as Teams or Slack also reduces redundancies and can enhance communication.

Employee self-service (ESS) portals allow employees to access their digital employment record and make time-off requests, update addresses, and select benefits during open enrollment, all with automated support using reference guides, FAQs, and chatbots.

FIGURE 9.1 Day in the Life

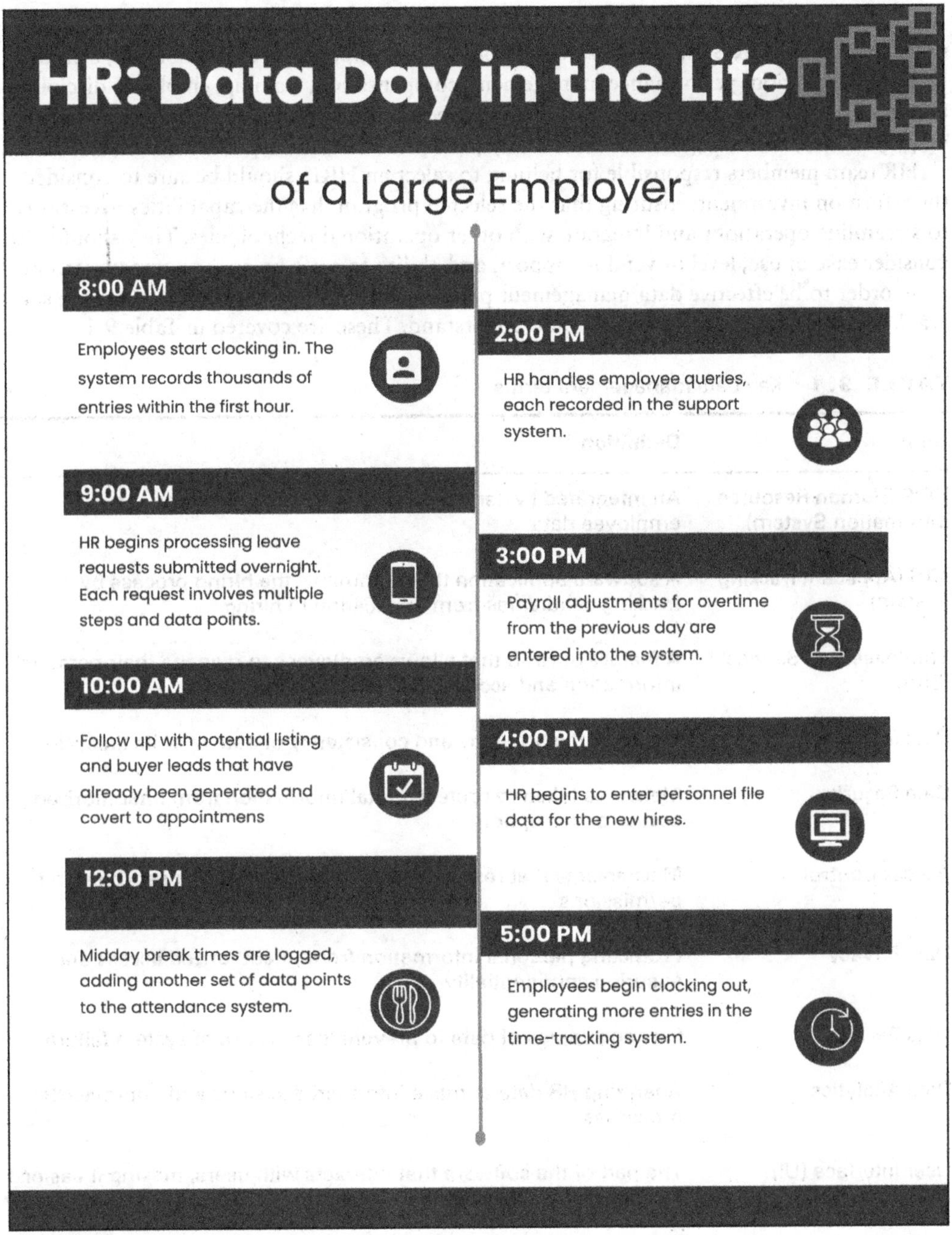

Human Resource Information Systems

A *human resource information system (HRIS)* serves many purposes in HR information management. An HRIS is a database with modules that support all aspects of HR, including recruiting, selection, performance management, compensation, training, employee discipline, and more. A major feature of an HRIS is its ability to both organize and secure sensitive employee data, decreasing the need for bulky personnel files and paper recordkeeping.

HR team members responsible for helping to select an HRIS should be sure to consider the return on investment, ensuring that the selected program has the capabilities necessary to streamline operations and integrate with other operational technologies. They should also consider ease of use, level of vendor support, and ability to scale up as the company grows.

In order to be effective data management partners within the organization, there are several key terms an HR practitioner should understand. These are covered in Table 9.1.

TABLE 9.1 Key data management terms

Term	Definition
HRIS (Human Resource Information System)	An integrated system used to gather, store, and manage employee data
ATS (Applicant Tracking System)	A software application that automates the hiring process by tracking candidates from application to hiring
Employee Self-Service (ESS)	A feature of HRIS that allows employees to manage their personal information and access HR-related services
Data Integrity	Ensuring the accuracy and consistency of data over its lifecycle
Data Security	Measures taken to protect digital information from unauthorized access or corruption
Access Control	Mechanisms that restrict access to data based on user roles and permissions
Data Privacy	Protecting personal information from unauthorized access and ensuring confidentiality
Data Backup	Creating copies of data to prevent loss in case of system failure
Data Analytics	Analyzing HR data to make informed decisions and improve HR processes
User Interface (UI)	The part of the software that interacts with users, making it easier for them to use the system
Data Migration	The process of transferring data from one system to another

Term	Definition
Integration	Combining different systems and software to work together seamlessly
Audit Trail	A record of changes made to data, used for security and compliance purposes
Multifactor authentication	An electronic authentication method requiring two or more pieces of evidence (or factors) to gain system access
Firewalls	A part of a computer system or network that is designed to block unauthorized access while permitting outward communication
Tiered permission	A security approach that organizes and restricts access to systems into different layers based on the user's role, function, or level of privilege

Data Analytics

Data analytics in the workplace involves analyzing data to inform decision making and improve business processes and performance.

Within an HR department, there are several methods for analyzing data. Each method helps HR professionals understand different aspects of employee and organizational performance.

- ***Descriptive analytics*** involves looking at past and present data to identify trends and patterns. This method uses *data aggregation*, which means summarizing employee information from various sources. Additionally, *data visualization* tools like charts, graphs, and dashboards are used to display trends such as turnover rates and average tenure.
- ***Predictive analytics*** uses historical data to predict future events. For example, regression analysis can predict employee turnover or performance based on different factors. Machine learning algorithms are also used to forecast hiring needs or identify potential high performers.
- ***Prescriptive analytics*** goes a step further by providing recommendations for actions to achieve desired outcomes. This can include optimization models to determine the best resource allocation for staffing or scenario analysis to evaluate different strategies for employee development and retention.
- ***Diagnostic analytics*** looks at data to understand why certain events happened. This involves root cause analysis, which investigates the reasons behind high employee turnover. Correlation analysis can also be used to identify relationships between employee engagement and productivity.

- ***Qualitative analysis*** focuses on understanding the underlying reasons, opinions, and motivations of employees. Methods such as interviews and focus groups gather in-depth insights on employee satisfaction.
- ***Thematic analysis*** helps identify common themes from employee survey feedback.
- ***Quantitative analysis*** uses numerical data to identify patterns and measure outcomes. Statistical analysis applies tests to employee performance data, while trend analysis monitors changes in metrics like absenteeism rates over time.
- ***Sentiment analysis*** analyzes textual data to determine the emotional tone of employee communications. Text mining techniques analyze open-ended survey responses to gauge employee sentiment, and natural language processing (NLP) algorithms interpret and classify emotions in written feedback.

By utilizing analytics such as turnover rates, performance, employee sentiments and recruitment efficiency to make data-driven decisions, HR is best positioned to act as an operational business partner with other company leaders.

Trend Analysis

Trend analysis in HR involves examining historical data to identify patterns and trends over time. Key trends that should be analyzed include employee turnover rates, absenteeism, engagement levels, performance metrics, and safety incidents. By analyzing these trends, HR can uncover underlying issues and develop strategies to address them.

For instance, a rising turnover rate might indicate dissatisfaction or issues within the workplace, prompting a review of employee engagement initiatives or compensation packages. Tracking absenteeism can help identify areas where workplace conditions or employee health initiatives need improvement. Analyzing performance metrics over time can highlight the effectiveness of training programs and identify high performers for future leadership roles. Monitoring safety incidents can lead to enhanced safety protocols and training, reducing workplace accidents.

Google is known for its data-driven approach to managing its workforce. The company frequently conducts trend analysis to improve various aspects of HR, including employee engagement, productivity, and retention. Google tracks employee turnover rates across different departments, job roles, and tenure (time in position) groups and regularly conducts surveys to measure employee engagement and job satisfaction. From this, the company can create targeted engagement initiatives or enhance their employee support offerings to improve job satisfaction, work/life balance and ultimately, retention.

Data Storytelling and Reporting

As discussed earlier, with the thousands of data points HR collects every day, it becomes important that HR can communicate the findings from analytics in a way that is easily understood and actionable. Traditional data reports using software programs such as Microsoft Excel or databases such as Salesforce are useful; however, the amount of data that is available can make it very difficult to interpret and communicate in meaningful ways.

Data storytelling involves presenting data insights in a compelling and easily understandable narrative format to inform and engage the audience. This can be done using simple best practices to organize data into a coherent narrative:

- **Clarity and Simplicity:** Present data in a clear, concise, and easy-to-understand manner, focusing on the main points.
- **Accuracy:** Ensure all data is accurate, reliable, and up-to-date.
- **Relevance:** Include only relevant data that supports decision making.
- **Consistency:** Use consistent formats, terminology, and scales across reports.
- **Visualization:** Utilize charts, graphs, and other visual aids to enhance understanding.
- **Timeliness:** Provide reports in a timely manner to ensure information is actionable.
- **Audience Focus:** Tailor reports to meet the needs and knowledge level of the intended audience.
- **Security and Confidentiality:** Protect sensitive data and ensure reports comply with privacy regulations.
- **Actionable Insights:** Highlight key insights and recommendations to guide decision making.
- **Continuous Improvement:** Regularly review and refine reporting processes for better outcomes.

Records Management: The Lifecycle

Every employment-related activity in the scope of human resources receives or generates a record. The specific retention, storage, and destruction of these records make up the *records lifecycle*.

Personnel files are where the bulk of records related to the employee are kept. It's important to remember that any document retained in writing can be subpoenaed in a dispute, so care must be taken to ensure that employee rights are protected and risk to the company is effectively managed. Confidential records such as medical documents (doctor's notes, workers compensation claims, etc.) should be kept separate from the main personnel record, as should Form I-9. This is primarily because this information should not be readily accessible to others, nor should it be used to make employment-related decisions, such as compensation or eligibility for promotion or training.

Establishing the Policy

An effective records-management policy should be focused on defining controls. This includes controlling the creation, access, legibility, retrieval, use, retention, and destruction of each record.

A records-retention policy should include a description of the employment documents covered by the policy (defining what is a record), a control system for limiting access and ensuring availability upon demand or need (description of maintenance or use), and a schedule for retention and eventual destruction by record type.

An HR professional should have a firm understanding of the laws and applications related to developing and implementing a records-retention process. In addition to being a best practice, records retention is required by several federal laws. For example, the Civil Rights Act of 1964 requires that employers with at least 15 employees must retain applications and other personnel records relating to hires, rehires, tests used in employment, promotion, transfers, demotions, selection for training, layoff, recall, terminations, and discharge for one year from making the records or taking the personnel actions. See Table 9.2 for more examples of the types of records that are generated by the functional area of HR.

TABLE 9.2 Types of records generated by HR

Functional area of HR	Examples of types of records created or received	Laws or rules governing recordkeeping or retention requirements
Equal Employment	Medical certifications, training selection procedures, applicant tracking, Affirmative Action Plans/results	FMLA ADA ADEA EPA CRA 1964 VEVRAA Uniformed Services Employment and Reemployment Rights Act (USERRA)
Staffing	Applications, pre-employment test results, selection notes, EEO-1 reports, I-9 forms, job postings, reference check information, credit reports, basic employee data	IRCA CRA 1964 ADA UGESP FCRA Federal Unemployment Tax Act (FUTA)
Compensation and Benefits	Payroll records, tax records, benefits administration records, summary plan descriptions, leave of absence (LOA) records, copies of employee notices describing benefits, records of insurance premium payments	Employee Retirement Income Security Act (ERISA) HIPAA FMLA PDA Fair Labor Standards Act (FLSA) IRS tax code
Training and Development	Participant records, description of tools used in training	OSHA ADA

Functional area of HR	Examples of types of records created or received	Laws or rules governing recordkeeping or retention requirements
Employee Relations	Performance reviews, adverse employment actions, investigative reports	CRA 1964 ADA ADEA
Risk Management	Workplace injury and illness records, records of exposure to hazardous material	OSHA

Proper Disposal

The Federal Trade Commission (FTC) issued a disposal rule related to the destruction of consumer information. This rule covers employment records related to sensitive personal information (Social Security numbers, medical history), consumer credit, references, and background searches. It directs affected companies to destroy covered records in a manner that protects against "unauthorized access to or use of the information." The FTC describes the following as acceptable methods for compliance. Employers may:

- Burn, pulverize, or shred papers containing consumer report information so that the information cannot be read or reconstructed.
- Destroy or erase electronic files or media containing consumer report information so that the information cannot be read or reconstructed.
- Conduct due diligence and hire a document destruction contractor to dispose of material specifically identified as consumer report information consistent with the rule.
- Conduct regular training to ensure data protection.

You can find the final rule in its entirety on the FTC's website at `https://www.ftc.gov/os/2004/11/041118disposalfrn.pdf`.

Electronic Storage

Technology has influenced many HR practices, not the least of which is records retention. Before deciding to electronically store records, an HR professional must consider the specific regulatory requirements of the law(s) governing record retention, security, access, and legibility.

A good example of the considerations for the electronic storage of records is given by the U.S. Citizen and Immigration Services (USCIS) related to storing Form I-9 electronically. The following is an excerpt from the USCIS website (`https://www.uscis.gov/i-9-central/form-i-9-resources/handbook-for-employers-m-274/100-retaining-form-i-9/101-form-i-9-and-storage-systems`):

You may retain Form I-9 using either a paper or electronic system, or a combination of both. If you complete a paper Form I-9, you may scan and upload the original signed form, correction or update, and retain it electronically. You may destroy the original paper form after you have securely stored it in an electronic format. Any electronic system you use to generate Form I-9 or retain completed Form I-9 must include:

- Reasonable controls to ensure the system's integrity, accuracy, and reliability;
- Reasonable controls designed to prevent and detect the unauthorized or accidental creation of, addition to, alteration of, deletion of, or deterioration of an electronically completed or stored Form I-9, including the electronic signature, if used;
- An inspection and quality assurance program that regularly evaluates the system and includes periodic checks of electronically stored Form I-9, including the electronic signature, if used;
- An indexing system that allows users to identify and retrieve records maintained in the system; and
- The ability to reproduce legible and readable paper copies.

Data Privacy and Security

HRIS and other operational technology come with risks, including data security vulnerabilities, potential for data breaches, and compliance issues. Ensuring proper access controls, regular system updates, and comprehensive employee training can help to mitigate these risks. Risk mitigation of vulnerabilities can be achieved in several ways:

Systems Access and Permissions Ensure that sensitive employee data is protected by controlling who can access and modify information based on their role within the organization. This helps prevent unauthorized access and potential data breaches, maintaining the confidentiality and security of HR data.

Front-End User Support Select software that provides user-friendly interfaces and support tools that help employees and managers navigate the system efficiently. This support includes tutorials, help desks, and automated assistance, which enhance the user experience and promote effective system utilization.

Compliance HR systems can help organizations adhere to legal and regulatory requirements by automating compliance tracking and reporting. This is done by ensuring that all HR processes are documented and aligned with current labor laws.

Data Integrity HR technology can help to maintain data integrity by implementing regular data validation checks and audits to ensure the consistency and reliability of stored information. This prevents data corruption and ensures that HR decisions are based on accurate and trustworthy data.

Data Accuracy Systems should improve data accuracy by reducing manual data entry errors through automated processes and real-time data updates. This ensures that HR records are accurate, current, and thus, credible.

Data Controls Programs such as an HRIS should have controls in place to verify employee identity and control access. Firewalls, multifactor authentication, and tiered permissions all help to manage technology risks from unauthorized access from internal or external individuals.

Real World Scenario

The Yahoo Data Breach

Yahoo, once a leading Internet services company, experienced one of the largest data breaches in history. In 2013 and 2014, the company was targeted in two major cyberattacks, compromising the data of all 3 billion user accounts. There was a potential ethical breach as well, as the company did not reveal the hacking publicly until 2016.

The breaches were the result of multiple security weaknesses, including the use of easily discoverable passwords. Hackers were able to exploit these weak passwords, which were often simple, reused across multiple sites, and lacked complexity. This allowed the attackers to gain unauthorized access to Yahoo's user database, obtaining sensitive information such as names, email addresses, dates of birth, and hashed passwords.

There were severe consequences for Yahoo and its users. Personal information was exposed, leading to potential identity theft and other forms of cybercrime. The company faced significant financial losses, legal repercussions, and a damaged reputation. Yahoo's valuation was reduced, affecting its acquisition deal with Verizon Communications, which was finalized at a lower price due to the incident.

Yahoo's experience highlights the importance of strong password practices. Organizations should enforce strict password policies, employ advanced techniques for password storage, and implement multifactor authentication (MFA) to add an extra layer of security.

The most common mistakes made with password generation include:

- **Using Easily Guessable Passwords:** Choosing simple passwords such as "password," "123456," or "qwerty" makes it easy for attackers to guess.
- **Reusing Passwords across Multiple Accounts:** Using the same password for different accounts increases vulnerability if one account is compromised.

- **Creating Short Passwords:** Short passwords are easier to crack through brute-force attacks compared to longer passwords.
- **Not Including a Mix of Characters:** Failing to use a combination of uppercase and lowercase letters, numbers, and special characters weakens password strength.
- **Using Personal Information:** Incorporating easily obtainable personal information, such as names, birth dates, or phone numbers, makes passwords more susceptible to targeted attacks.
- **Failing to Update Passwords Regularly:** Keeping the same password for extended periods increases the risk of it being compromised without the user's knowledge.
- **Ignoring Two-Factor Authentication (2FA):** Enabling 2FA when available adds an additional layer of security, which could otherwise protect the user even if the password is compromised.
- **Writing Passwords Down:** Storing passwords in easily accessible places, such as sticky notes or unencrypted files, exposes them to unauthorized access.

Helping employees avoid these mistakes by training them and setting minimum password requirements can significantly improve password security and protect sensitive information from unauthorized access.

Laws such as the General Data Protection Regulation (GDPR) in the European Union and the Health Insurance Portability and Accountability Act (HIPAA) in the United States guides employers on best practices when it comes to data security, requiring that sensitive employee and customer personal or financial information be properly stored, secured, and destroyed. The GDPR requires that employees have access to their own data, and HIPAA guards the confidentiality of employee records, specifically medical information. Employees should be properly trained on best data management practices. Both of these laws are covered in more detail in Appendix C.

Summary

HR Information Management was created as part of the Human Resource Certification Institute (HRCIs) 2024 exam content update, but these functional issues have been developing in the workplace for decades. Because technology (its merits and challenges) evolves so rapidly, HR needs to stay up-to-date on how to support company best practices to leverage the benefits and minimize the risks of technologies in the workplace.

Operationally, HR technology such as human resource information systems (HRISs) can greatly enhance department efficiencies. These systems can handle functions such as payroll, benefits administration, recruitment, and performance management. Accurate data entry and maintenance practices ensure that employee records are up-to-date and reliable, and the ability to generate and interpret reports and dashboards using storytelling and other data visualization techniques brings information to life, allowing for deeper understanding and application. Employee self-service portals, which allow employees to access and manage their own HR information, are also an important aspect of HR information management, as is accurate, accessible, and protected reporting and recordkeeping.

Data analysis helps HR professionals improve decision making and build HR programs that support organizational results, and the ability to communicate the data in a compelling, actionable way through reporting and storytelling is an important competency of an HR professional.

Data privacy and security is another area of understanding in the domain of HR Information Management. Understanding data protection regulations such as GDPR and HIPAA is necessary for ensuring compliance. Developing a plan for responding to data breaches, including notification procedures and mitigation strategies, is also supported by HR's efforts. This includes training employees on data privacy and security best practices helps safeguard against potential breaches.

Exam Essentials

Understand how to manage and utilize HR data effectively. Leveraging HR technology allows for streamlined HR operations such as payroll, benefits administration, recruitment, and performance management. This requires accurate data entry and maintenance of employee records and generating and interpreting reports and dashboards for informed decision making.

Analyze HR data to improve decision making and strategic planning. Descriptive analytics involves summarizing historical data to identify trends and patterns, whereas predictive analytics uses this data to forecast future HR needs and challenges. Prescriptive analytics goes further by providing recommendations based on data analysis to enhance HR practices. It is important to understand both quantitative analysis, which deals with numerical data, and qualitative analysis, which involves thematic analysis of non-numerical data.

Efficiently manage HR records to ensure compliance and accessibility. Effective document storage and retrieval involve organizing and storing HR records for easy access and retrieval. Understanding legal requirements for record retention and developing compliant policies and familiarity with digital tools and systems helps HR know how to maintain accurate and secure HR records.

Protect sensitive HR data from unauthorized access and breaches. Understanding data protection regulations such as GDPR and HIPAA helps to govern data privacy. Implementing and managing access controls ensures only authorized personnel can access sensitive data, while encryption and secure storage methods protect this information. This includes developing a plan for responding to data breaches, including notification procedures and mitigation strategies, and training employees on data privacy and security best practices.

Review Questions

You can find the answers in Appendix A.

1. Which of the following best describes the primary function of a human resource information system (HRIS)?
   - A. Managing financial transactions and payroll processing
   - B. Storing and organizing employee data and facilitating HR processes
   - C. Storing training records delivering training
   - D. Complying with recordkeeping laws and guidelines
2. When selecting an HRIS, which of the following are key considerations? (Choose all that apply.)
   - A. The need to be section 508 compliant
   - B. The system's ability to integrate with existing software and applications
   - C. The cost of implementation
   - D. How data is stored
3. In a large organization, employees must use their unique ID cards to enter secure areas of the building. Once inside, they log into their workstations using a two-factor authentication process that requires both a password and a fingerprint scan. The software they use is designed to be user-friendly, ensuring they can easily access the information they need without compromising security. Which of the following does this scenario best describe? (Choose all that apply.)
   - A. Access control
   - B. HR control
   - C. Interface
   - D. Phishing
4. Which of the following is a requirement of the General Data Protection Regulation (GDPR) in the workplace?
   - A. Collecting personal data only with written consent from employees
   - B. Providing individuals with the right to access their personal data
   - C. Limiting access to confidential medical records
   - D. Installing firewalls to guard sensitive employee data
5. Which of the following is a requirement under HIPAA laws for protecting employees' health information in the workplace?
   - A. Employers must keep medical files separate for general personnel records.
   - B. Employers must store all health records in physical, locked cabinets only.
   - C. Employers must ensure that any electronic transmission of health information is encrypted and secure.
   - D. Employers must report all health information breaches directly to the Department of Labor.

6. After analyzing employee turnover data and identifying key factors contributing to resignations, the HR department recommends implementing a flexible work schedule and enhancing professional development programs to retain talent. This is an example of what type of data analytics?
   - A. Descriptive
   - B. Qualitative
   - C. Predictive
   - D. Prescriptive
7. After collecting employee satisfaction survey responses and summarizing the results to identify common themes and areas of concern, the HR department uses this analysis to understand overall employee morale. This is an example of what type of data analytics?
   - A. Descriptive
   - B. Prescriptive
   - C. Predictive
   - D. Quantitative
8. Which of the following best describes a scenario where workforce analytics solves an organizational problem?
   - A. The HR department conducts exit interviews to understand why employees are leaving the company.
   - B. The HR department surveys employees to measure job satisfaction and morale.
   - C. The HR department analyzes employee turnover data to identify factors contributing to high attrition rates and implements targeted retention strategies.
   - D. The HR department organizes team-building activities to improve workplace culture.
9. Which of the following is a key consideration for user support in the design of organizational databases?
   - A. Ensuring the database has a complex query structure to leverage reporting capabilities
   - B. Implementing front-end interfaces that allow easy navigation and access to data for non-technical users
   - C. Limiting access to the database to only IT professionals to maintain data security
   - D. Prioritizing backend database optimization over front-end features
10. Which of the following best describes a phishing scheme in the workplace?
    - A. An employee receives an email from their IT department with a link to update their password, but the link directs them to a fake website designed to steal their credentials.
    - B. An employee installs a new software update to improve their computer's performance and security and it contains a harmful virus that infects the entire system.
    - C. An employee is followed into a nonsecure building and their password, written on a sticky note on their computer, is stolen.
    - D. An employee uses a non-company-approved VPN to securely access the corporate network from home, and hackers gain access.

11. Which of the following is a best practice when it comes to establishing a records management policy in the workplace?
    - **A.** Allowing each department to create their own individual records management procedures
    - **B.** Retaining all records for at least 10 years
    - **C.** Implementing a standardized policy
    - **D.** Storing all records digitally

12. Which of the following data analytics findings best represents a thematic statement?
    - **A.** "Over the past year, employees who participated in the company's wellness program had an average of 2.5 fewer sick days compared to those who did not participate."
    - **B.** "There is a strong positive correlation (r = 0.78) between employee engagement scores and their productivity levels, suggesting that more engaged employees tend to be more productive."
    - **C.** "Based on our analysis, implementing flexible work hours could reduce employee turnover by 15% over the next year, as it aligns with the preferences of our high-performing staff."
    - **D.** "Analysis of employee feedback reveals a desire for professional development opportunities, indicating that providing more training and growth prospects could improve overall job satisfaction and retention."

13. As the HR manager of a large, multinational tech company, you are responsible for managing HR data throughout the employee lifecycle. This includes collecting and securely storing employee information during recruitment, updating records during employment, and ensuring proper handling of data during offboarding. Recently, your company implemented a new HR software system to streamline these processes. What is the most important step to take to ensure proper management of HR data throughout the employee lifecycle?
    - **A.** Regularly back up all employee data to prevent data loss.
    - **B.** Focus on data protection during the recruitment stage, as this is when most sensitive data is collected.
    - **C.** Periodically review and update data protection policies to ensure compliance with changing regulations.
    - **D.** Decentralize the system to comply with regional and local recordkeeping requirements.

14. Which of the following statements best describes the concept of data integrity?
    - **A.** Ensuring that all employee records are accurate, complete, and up-to-date
    - **B.** Properly disposing of records in compliance with state and federal regulations
    - **C.** Making sure that employee records are stored securely
    - **D.** Conducting regular audits to effectively manage risks

15. The company you work for has surveyed employees and discovered a high rate of employee dissatisfaction. There is a question about the accuracy of the survey results. What steps should HR take next?

    A. Ignore the survey results as they might lack data integrity.

    B. Conduct a follow-up survey to verify the accuracy of the initial findings and gather more detailed feedback.

    C. Report findings to senior leaders and request advice for next steps.

    D. Move forward with the findings as data is usually fairly objective.

16. In a mid-sized financial services firm, the HR department discovers that an employee inadvertently sent a spreadsheet containing sensitive personal information, including Social Security numbers and bank account details of all employees, to an external contractor via an unsecured email. The email was meant to contain only anonymized survey results for an employee satisfaction study, but due to a copy-paste error, the confidential data was included. The breach is discovered a week later when the contractor alerts the HR department about the unexpected sensitive information in the email. What is the first step the HR team should take to mitigate this data breach?

    A. Notify the affected employees about the data breach and advise them on protective measures.

    B. Contact the contractor to request the immediate deletion of the sensitive data from their systems.

    C. Conduct an internal audit to determine how the breach occurred and identify vulnerabilities.

    D. Review and update the company's data protection policies and procedures.

17. Why is it important to conduct trend analysis as an HR professional?

    A. To help make hiring decisions that are legally defensible

    B. To understand and predict workforce patterns

    C. To evaluate the effectiveness of HR programs

    D. To analyze workforce training needs

18. Which of the following statements about employee turnover best demonstrates the clarity aspect of data storytelling?

    A. "Employee turnover has been rising, and this is causing some issues."

    B. "The number of employees leaving the company has increased over the past year."

    C. "Employee turnover has increased by 15% over the last six months, primarily due to lack of career growth opportunities."

    D. "We've seen a rise in the number of people quitting their jobs recently."

19. Which of the following describes a compliant method for destroying consumer and employee records after the retention period has expired? (Choose all that apply.)
   - A. Shredding
   - B. Permanently deleting
   - C. Burning
   - D. Hiring a document destruction contractor

20. Which of the following statements is/are true regarding the storage of Form I-9? (Choose all that apply.)
   - A. You are required to store Form I-9 with an employee's other personnel records.
   - B. Form I-9s can be stored without any access restrictions as long as they are in a secure location.
   - C. Form I-9s may be stored electronically provided they are secure and accessible.
   - D. You may destroy the original paper form after you have securely stored it in an electronic format.

Chapter 10

SPHR | SPHRi Exam: Leadership and Strategy

SPHR/i RESPONSIBILITIES:

LEADING THE HR FUNCTION BY DEVELOPING HR STRATEGY, CONTRIBUTING TO ORGANIZATIONAL STRATEGY, INFLUENCING PEOPLE MANAGEMENT PRACTICES, AND MONITORING RISK.

- ✓ **1.1 Contribute to the development of the organizational strategy and planning (for example: vision, mission, values, ethical conduct, future business opportunities)**
- ✓ **1.2 Develop, execute, and lead HR strategies that are aligned to the organization's strategic plan (for example: HR initiatives, plans, budgets, business plans, service delivery plans, workforce requirements)**
- ✓ **1.3 Analyze and assess internal and external factors that impact operations and people management to decide on the best available risk management strategy (for example: human capital risk analysis, business continuity, response planning, geopolitical environment scanning, mental health)**
- ✓ **1.4 Interpret and use business metrics to assess and drive achievement of strategic goals and objectives (for example: key performance indicators [KPIs], financial statements, budgets)**
- ✓ **1.5 Use credible and relevant information to make decisions and recommendations (for example: salary data, management trends, published surveys and studies, legal/regulatory analysis)**

✓ 1.6 Develop and manage workplace practices that are aligned with the organization's vision, mission, values, sustainability, corporate social responsibility (CSR), ethics, and anti-corruption, to shape and reinforce organizational culture

✓ 1.7 Develop and evaluate strategies and workplace practices to promote diversity, equity, and inclusion (DEI)

✓ 1.8 Identify and analyze HR metrics to inform strategic actions within the organization (for example: develop new metrics, predictive analytics, business intelligence, turnover rates, cost per hire, employment statistics, return on investment [ROI], pay equity analysis)

✓ 1.9 Design, implement, and facilitate effective change strategies to align organizational performance with the organization's strategic goals (for example: change leadership, change management)

✓ 1.10 Advise and influence organizational behavior and outcomes through effective relationships with key stakeholders

✓ 1.11 Ensure alignment of HR strategies across the organization (for example: across geographic locations/sites, across business units)

✓ 1.12 Evaluate the applicability of US federal laws and regulations to organizational strategy and/or complex HR strategies and make recommendations based on findings (for example: policies, programs, practices, business expansion/reduction, concerted activity)

SPHRi RESPONSIBILITIES:

THE SPHRi RESPONSIBILITIES ARE THE SAME AS THOSE FOR THE SPHR, EXCEPT FOR 1.12.

✓ 1.12 Apply and evaluate the applicability of local labor laws, regulations, and, guidance to organizational strategy/ or complex HR strategies to adhere to legal and ethical requirements

Developing the human resource professionals of today into robust business partners is more important than ever. Not only does competing in the 21st century require increased levels of adaptability, but the pace of change demands highly agile, competent professionals with a senior-level understanding of the business framework within which we conduct our craft.

The acronym *VUCA* has become a mantra, defining the environment in which HR practitioners must operate. Circumstances tend to be volatile, subject to changing needs and priorities at any given moment. HR practitioners operate with high degrees of uncertainty, especially when managing risk and anticipating the effects of regulatory mandates and management trends. Navigating complex situations is often the norm, with HR having to respond to the chaotic dictates of the unplannable. And senior leaders must become adept at maneuvering the ambiguous, making decisions based on fact and reason, but the obscure as well.

The functional area of Leadership and Strategy is especially grounded in these principles. This is evidenced by the Human Resource Certification Institute (HRCIs) assertion that senior HR leaders are responsible for "leading the HR function by developing HR strategy, contributing to organizational strategy, influencing people management practices and monitoring risk." Exam content related to this domain makes up 33 percent of the SPHR/i, so it is well worth a deep dive into the related concepts.

Corporate Strategy

Corporate strategy is a business approach that guides a company in achieving its long-term goals. It does this by integrating organizational design, strategic planning, and understanding the competitive landscape. It involves structuring the organization effectively, setting strategic objectives, and analyzing market conditions to ensure the company remains competitive and successful.

Alignment is a word that is important to understand in the context of leadership and strategy. It means properly positioning the tasks, priorities, or goals in relation to each other to achieve a favorable outcome. Specifically, the SPHR/i exam calls upon senior leaders to align HR plans and programs with business strategy and results. In this sense, it is not enough to simply have a plan. HR is responsible for achieving the goals that cascade down from the organization's mission, vision, and values. For example, if the company's mission is to provide the "best customer service experience in the world," HR's strategic plan may include elements of employee training and development that support this mission. This often includes designing organizational interventions that execute goals through change management efforts.

HR teams are also responsible to ensure that HR strategies are aligned across the organization, whether geographically dispersed companies or across business units. Traditional business units are those that are sorted by functions, such as Production, Accounting, or Human Resources. Achieving alignment is done by developing and applying consistent policies and practices, implementing unified training programs, and facilitating effective communication channels. HR also uses data and analytics to monitor departmental or regional compliance and performance, making sure that all parts of the organization are working toward the same goals. HR teams are responsible for collaborating with leadership to adapt strategies as needed to address regional or departmental differences where appropriate.

At a macro level, HR must design, implement, and evaluate their policies and programs within the structural framework of the business. This is explored next.

Organizational Structures

Keeping a large group of people with different perspectives and assignments moving in the same direction is a challenge for organizations. *Organizational structures* were designed to provide a framework that keeps information flowing to departments and the employees who need it to do their jobs. In some cases, organizations may use different structures in different business units. For example, the vice president of sales in a functional organization would report to the CEO, but a sales organization may be organized with a geographic or product structure for the most efficient management of the sales operation. The general types of structures are as follows:

Functional Structure The *functional organization structure* is represented by the traditional pyramid-shape organization chart with which most people are familiar. It's a hierarchical structure in which communication moves from the top down and from the bottom up. These structures are more formal and rigid than some other structures and are appropriate for businesses with a single product line where specialization is an advantage. In this structure, each functional area reports to the CEO. Functional organizations are generally very centralized.

Product-Based Structure A *product-based organization structure*, also known as a *customer-oriented structure*, is organized by product line and is appropriate when the company has well-defined product lines that are clearly separate from each other. In this structure, each product line reports to the CEO; these structures lend themselves to either centralized or decentralized decision-making processes.

Geographic Structure In a *geographic organization structure*, executives of regional areas are responsible for all the business functions in their assigned region; the regional executives report to the CEO. Structuring an organization in this way is appropriate when there are common requirements in the region that are different from the requirements in other regions. Geographic structures are decentralized, with most decisions being made at the local level.

Divisional Structure A *divisional organization structure* has characteristics similar to that of the geographic structure, but the divisions may be based on criteria other than geography, such as the market or industry. Like the geographic structure, divisional structures are characterized by decentralized decision making.

Matrix Structure In a *matrix organization structure*, employees report to two managers. Generally, one manager is responsible for a product line and the other has functional responsibility. For example, the VP of marketing and the production manager for a specific product would both supervise the marketing coordinator who is creating collateral for the product. A matrix organization is advantageous because it encourages communication and cooperation; it requires a high level of trust and communication from employees at all levels to ensure that contradictory instructions are minimized.

Seamless Organization A *seamless organization* is one in which the traditional hierarchies don't exist—it's a horizontal organization connected by networks instead of separated by the boundaries that characterize other organization structures. The purpose of this structure is to enhance communication and creativity. Seamless organizations wouldn't be possible without the technology that allows employees to connect with each other via email and the Internet from anywhere in the world. This technology enables employees to meet with coworkers who have specialized knowledge without the expense of traveling.

Strategic Planning

Global competition requires business leaders to use many tools to give them an advantageous position in the marketplace. One such tool is known as *strategic planning*. Broadly defined, strategic planning is a systematic way of setting the direction for an organization and developing tactics and operational plans to ensure its success. HRCI defines strategic planning as "the process of defining a company's direction for the future in 4 stages: analysis, development, implementation and evaluation." Strategic planning is a dynamic process—it's not something an organization does one time to produce an attractively bound booklet that sits on the shelf gathering dust. By its very nature, strategic planning requires that organizations constantly revisit the plan to make sure it's still viable in the face of changes within the organization and in the marketplace.

Because strategic planning has been a popular topic for business writers, consultants, and academicians during the past decade, there are a number of planning models from which to choose.

The specific model selected for use in an organization will depend on the structure and culture of that organization. The elements of all the models fall into four very broad categories: environmental scanning, strategy formulation, strategy implementation, and strategy evaluation.

You should be aware of how all these elements contribute to the strategic planning process.

NOTE The steps are described here in a logical sequence. In real life, the process may not occur in a straight-line progression; if new information that will affect results is uncovered at any stage, previous steps may be revisited so that the information can be incorporated into the plans and goals.

Planning to Plan

Very often, a strategic planning initiative is led by a consultant experienced in the process. This is helpful for many reasons, not least of which is that during the course of determining the future of the organization, disagreements about the long-term direction of the company may surface, and these are more readily resolved with a neutral third party who is better able to facilitate a resolution and move the process forward than someone with a vested interest in the outcome. When a consultant is used, the preplanning process is generally part of the service they provide.

The *preplan* includes decisions about who will be invited to participate and at what stages in the process, a time frame for completing the plan, and a determination of the tools to be used in collecting data for the plan. Spending this additional time at the beginning of the process can prevent costly errors or omissions from being made and can assist in making the resulting strategic plan more accurate and meaningful.

The result of this stage should be an agreement about the process to be followed, a list of those who will be involved at various stages in the process and the type of information they will be asked to provide, the timeline for completing the plan, and a list of the planning tools to be used in gathering information to be used in the planning process.

Let's begin by defining the terms that will be used to discuss the strategic planning process:

- A *strategy* uses the strengths of a business to its competitive advantage in the marketplace.
- A *goal* describes the direction the business will take and what it will achieve. Goals are set at the corporate and business-unit levels of the organization.
- An *objective* is a specific description of the practical steps that will be taken to achieve the business goals. Objectives are set at the functional level of the organization.

To effectively determine the future direction of a company, it's necessary to know what is going on within the organization, industry, and marketplace and to know what the technology developments will mean for operations. Beginning the strategic planning process with this information can help to focus management on a plan that will avoid pitfalls and take advantage of existing opportunities.

Environmental Scanning Concepts

To develop a strategic plan and set the future direction of a company or develop HR programs to support its growth, leaders need to know what is going on in the organization, in the industry, and in the marketplace, and they need to know how developments will affect operations. An *environmental scan* provides the framework for collecting information about factors relevant to the decision-making process and can help management make decisions that take advantage of existing opportunities and avoid pitfalls. There are two elements to the scanning process: internal assessment and external assessment.

Conducting a comprehensive environmental scan can be a challenge; a great deal of information is available from many sources, and finding the information that is relevant to the specific business can be time-consuming. In addition to the information available from industry associations, government agencies, and trade organizations, customers and suppliers are excellent sources of information for a specific business. Many business-focused cable television channels present in-depth program segments on pertinent topics such as unemployment and inflation (among others), and business publications also provide in-depth examination of some topics. A wealth of information is available—the challenge comes in finding what is most appropriate for a specific organization's needs.

A number of tools are available for use in the scanning process. Let's take a look at some that are commonly used:

SWOT Analysis A *SWOT analysis* looks at the strengths, weaknesses, opportunities, and threats that are facing the organization. Strengths and weaknesses are internal factors that can be controlled by the organization; opportunities and threats are external factors that may impact an organization's plans:

Strengths Strengths are internal factors that will support the organization's plans. These can include people, such as a workforce that is highly trained in a unique skill not available to other businesses in the market. Machinery and equipment can be a strength; for example, when a recent upgrade of manufacturing equipment allows the company to produce more high-quality products at a lower cost. Developments in technology, such as a state-of-the-art order-processing system, and other factors that give the organization an edge in the marketplace are also considered strengths that contribute to organizational success.

Weaknesses Weaknesses are also internal factors, but these represent obstacles to the organization. Weaknesses can include workforce issues such as poorly trained workers, old machinery or equipment that is inefficient and costly to operate, outdated technology, and any other factors that make it difficult for an organization to achieve its goals.

Opportunities Opportunities are external factors that will aid the organization in the marketplace. These can include a wide variety of circumstances such as economic upswings, demand for the product, or a competitor whose product quality has declined.

Threats External factors that the organization must overcome or turn to an advantage are threats to its ability to achieve success. These can include strong product competition, economic problems, low unemployment rates, and other factors that make it more difficult for the organization to compete.

PESTLE Analysis A *PESTLE analysis* scans the external environment to identify opportunities and threats as part of the SWOT analysis. PESTLE is an acronym for political, economic, social, technological, legal, and environmental factors. PESTLE is discussed in more detail in the "External Assessment" section, later in this chapter.

Porter's 5 Forces *Porter's 5 Forces* is an analytical tool created by Michael E. Porter, a professor at Harvard Business School who has written extensively on business planning and strategy. In his book *Competitive Strategy: Techniques for Analyzing Industries and Competitors* (Free Press, 2008), he described five forces that are found in all industries. These forces include new competitors, suppliers, buyers, alternative products available to consumers, and the type and level of competition in the industry. The importance of these factors in strategic planning is discussed more fully in the "External Assessment" section.

Internal Assessment

Leaders need a firm grasp of the talent and resources currently available in the organization. Here are areas to consider in an assessment of strengths and weaknesses:

- Credibility of executive team
- Market penetration
- Strength of management team
- Customer service reputation
- Organization culture
- Market share
- Workforce diversity
- Customer loyalty
- Current product quality
- Level of sales
- Time to market
- Employee loyalty

- State of technology
- Turnover rate

The areas to be reviewed depend to a certain extent on the nature of the business but should include an assessment of performance in every function of the business.

This information can be collected in a number of ways: questionnaires, qualitative analyses, focus groups, surveys (of customers, suppliers, and employees), and stakeholder interviews.

External Assessment

Scanning the external environment presents more challenges than does an internal assessment because the vast amounts of information available must be sought in a wide variety of locations. Tools such as the PESTLE analysis and Porter's 5 Forces analysis can assist in narrowing down what kind of information needs to be collected. The PESTLE analysis provides a guide for collecting information related to the general business environment:

Political The political force in the PESTLE acronym refers to the impact of government policies, regulations, and political stability on businesses. It encompasses factors such as tax policies, trade regulations, labor laws, and government stability, which can significantly influence a company's operations, market access, and strategic decisions.

For multinational corporations, consideration must be given to political situations in each country of operation, including the stability of the government in some countries, restrictive trade policies, and the friendliness of the government to foreign investment.

All countries and businesses are now faced as well with the threat of terrorism that has negatively impacted sales in the travel industry; however, products related to security have a wider market in this situation.

Economic The most obvious example of economic concerns has to do with the strength of the economy—can customers afford the organization's products? The unemployment rate is a key factor here, along with interest rates, inflation, and changes in fiscal policy.

Another economic factor employers must consider is the cost of living in the locations where they operate. For example, California state passed a law designed to increase the minimum wage for fast-food workers to $20.00 per hour in 2024. The cost of living in the epicenter of the tech industry—the Silicon Valley—is so high that the U.S. Department of Housing and Urban Development (HUD) classified single people in San Francisco who earn less than $104,400 as low income.

For investment and expansion purposes, the stock market impacts the ability of a business to raise capital, and the price of real estate can add to the cost of purchasing or leasing new facilities. The strength of the U.S. dollar, exchange rates, and the rate of inflation must be considered when creating a long-term strategy.

Social The demographics of the target market must be considered in long-term planning as well. If an organization's products are targeted at young adults, for example, and that population is static or decreasing, the organization must either change its products or find new markets for them. For multinational corporations, analyzing the social factors of widely diverse markets around the world can prove challenging, but it's essential to ensure that the long-term planning will result in a strategy that increases the success of the business.

Technological The rate of change in technology varies in different industries, as does the cost of purchasing new technology. Technology affects the level of automation in an organization, and that impacts the overall cost of products. In 2015, the fast-food giant McDonald's announced that it would begin rolling out self-service kiosks in more than 14,000 restaurants from which their customers may place their order. McDonald's combined this with a digital locator that will allow for table service by their employees, and the development of an app that will allow patrons to both order and pay from their mobile device. Restaurants such as Panera, Olive Garden, and Wendy's have followed suit. From cell phones to handheld computers and robotics on production lines, advances in technology affect how work is done and must be considered in the environmental scanning process.

Legal The legal force in the PESTLE acronym refers to the influence of laws and regulations on businesses. It encompasses various aspects such as employment laws, health and safety regulations, consumer protection laws, and industry-specific regulations, which businesses must comply with to operate ethically and avoid legal risks and penalties. Understanding and adapting to the legal landscape is crucial for organizations to ensure their operations are conducted within the boundaries of the law and to mitigate potential legal challenges. For example, the Families First Coronavirus Response Act (FFCRA) is a federal law that HR must understand, as it requires employers to provide employees with paid sick leave or expanded family and medical leave for specified reasons related to COVID-19.

Environmental The environmental aspect pertains to the impact of ecological factors on businesses. It includes considerations such as climate change, environmental regulations, sustainability practices, and natural resource availability. Organizations must assess their environmental impact, adapt to changing environmental regulations, and implement sustainable practices to mitigate risks, enhance reputation, and ensure long-term viability in a rapidly changing environmental landscape.

Although the PESTLE analysis provides a guide for scanning the general business environment, Porter's 5 Forces analysis hones in on issues specific to the industry in which the organization operates. It's critical to understand these industry-specific factors and address them during the planning process. The following questions gather the information necessary to conduct the analysis:

How likely is it that new competition will enter the market? A market with great demand for a product that is inexpensive to produce and requires little initial investment will encourage new competition. This puts pressure on the organization to maintain a competitive price or to differentiate its product on some basis to maintain market share.

How reliant is the organization on its suppliers? When an organization produces a product requiring a unique part that can be obtained from only one supplier, the organization may find itself at the mercy of the supplier should it decide to raise the price of the part, discontinue it, or change it substantially.

How diverse is the organization's customer base? A company reliant on one or only a few customers or a single target market may find itself being pressured to lower prices, particularly if the product is easy to obtain from other sources.

Are comparable replacement products available to customers at a reasonable cost? A serious threat to the organization's customer base will be present if a product is generic and similar products made by competitors are easy to obtain at a comparable or lower price.

What is the level of competition in the marketplace? The level of competition in the market will, to a certain extent, limit the strategies available to an organization wanting to enter that market. A market dominated by one or two large competitors holding the bulk of the market share presents quite a different challenge than a new, untapped market with a few small competitors.

Strategy Formulation

Having scanned both the internal and external environments and gathered data relevant to the strategic planning process, the executive team is ready to create the vision, mission, and core value statements, which guide the organization over the long term. Once these long-term guidelines have been established, corporate goals are developed to provide direction during the implementation phase:

Vision Statement A *vision statement* should inspire the organization and inform customers and shareholders, describing what will carry the organization into the future and what it will accomplish. HRCI notes that a vision statement is a "declaration of what an organization wants to become."

Mission Statement The *mission statement* gets a bit more specific, describing where the organization is in the present. Specifically, HRCI notes that a mission statement is "a short description of the main purpose of an organization, which does not change (unlike strategy and business practices, which can change frequently)."

Core Competencies During the formulation of a strategic plan, organizations often identify their *core competencies*: the parts of their operations that they do best and that set them apart from the competition. Here also HRCI provides direction by defining core competencies as "the skills or knowledge that an organization needs to do its work." Many organizations believe that focusing on these core competencies makes it possible to expand their revenue streams. Competencies can be related to the technology used in operations, customer relationship management, product characteristics, manufacturing processes, knowledge management, organization culture, or combinations of these or other organizational aspects that work together synergistically and are difficult for others to replicate. When core competencies are identified, organizations can focus their strategy on ways to build related products or services instead of moving into unrelated areas. In many companies, HR becomes a core competency when it is embedded in operations rather than a segregated business unit. This involves HR leading change, fostering teamwork, developing staff, and contributing to organizational decision making and strategic planning.

Corporate Core Values Statement A statement of *core values* is a way for the executive team to communicate their standards for how the organization will conduct business. Core values are "the basis upon which the employees of an organization make decisions, plan strategies and interact with others" (HRCI). The values chosen for this purpose should be those that will be true regardless of changes in product lines or business processes. A question to ask in selecting an organization's values is whether the value would hold true if the organization changed its focus entirely and began doing business in a completely different way. Values such as integrity, excellence, teamwork, customer service, and mutual respect are some of those that remain constant regardless of changes in business operations.

These beliefs about the organization are usually reflected in its culture. When identifying corporate values, it's important to look not only at what the management team would like to see in the way of behaviors in the organization but also at the values being demonstrated in the course of business each day. When there are discrepancies between the stated, formal values and the informal values demonstrated by the workforce, the strategic plan can include goals designed to align the two.

Goal Setting

Once the vision, mission statements and values are defined, corporate goals are needed to describe how the organization will perform in the mid to long term planning horizons. Effective corporate goals follow the SMART model:

Specific The goal should be descriptive enough to guide business-unit managers in developing action plans that will accomplish the goal.

Measurable The goal must include a method for determining when it has been met.

Action-Oriented Goals must describe the actions that will be taken.

Realistic The goal must be high enough to challenge the organization or individual but not so high that it's unachievable.

Time-Based Goals must include a time frame for completion.

HR strategies and goals must align across organizations to ensure consistency and effectiveness in managing human capital. For instance, multinational companies operating in different geographic locations must weigh the benefits of adapting HR policies to comply with local labor laws and social mores (decentralized) with the need to maintain global standards to foster a cohesive corporate culture. Similarly, within a single organization, HR strategies need to be tailored to the unique needs of different business units, such as sales, marketing, or R&D, to optimize talent acquisition, development, and retention strategies that align with each unit's objectives and requirements.

Strategy Implementation

The strategy implementation phase further defines the corporate goals for implementation at the business-unit and functional levels of the organization, where most of the short-range activities are developed, including:

Tactical Goals Specific objectives that guide daily operations and support the broader strategic goals, such as reducing customer complaints by 20 percent within 6 months.

Action Plans Detailed steps and initiatives to achieve the tactical goals, like implementing a new customer service training program.

Performance Targets Quantifiable outcomes set to measure progress and success—for example, achieving a 95 percent customer satisfaction rate.

Milestones Key checkpoints that mark significant stages in the implementation process, such as completing the rollout of the training program within 3 months.

Strategy implementation may also drive organizational interventions to help prepare the environment for the "new" normal. This often requires that HR professionals act as change agents, helping their teams adapt to both short- and long-term initiatives.

Additionally, it may be necessary to build a *business case* to persuade executive management to take action. A business case takes into account the findings from the internal and external assessments, company goals, and current and desired future states, and it then clearly defines the risk of taking/not taking the proposed action. Most often, a business case serves as an analytical justification for taking a prescribed action.

Real World Scenario

Wright Sisters, Inc. Strategic Plan

Wright Sisters, Inc. (WSI) is a fictional company with 3,000 employees that has been recently challenged by the appearance of a new manufacturing plant in the small Midwestern city where it's located. The unexpected impact of this seemingly small change in the external environment has made senior management and the board of directors realize how unprepared they are to respond rapidly to changes in their business sector. They've decided to be proactive and implement a strategic planning process to discover what other unexpected changes could be lurking in the future.

Over the years, there have been many changes in the market for WSI's products, both technological and demographic. Because WSI has always maintained strong relationships with the hardware stores that distribute its products, WSI has been able to meet the changing needs of its customer base.

As a result of the strategic planning process, the WSI board has settled on the following statement of their vision for the company:

> Bringing the joy of gardening to new generations of gardeners.

To accomplish this vision, WSI has developed a mission to guide its operations over the next 5 years:

> We are the home-gardening source. The quality of our products allows busy families to enjoy gardening together. Our gardening education programs grow "gardeners for life" by teaching adults and children to make gardening easier and more enjoyable.

Based on the company's history and its vision and mission statements, the board created a corporate value statement to set expectations for how employees and managers interact:

> WSI values integrity and excellence in its products and its people. We treat ourselves, our customers, and our suppliers with dignity and respect. We believe in and encourage new ideas to make our products better and help our business grow, and we acknowledge and reward those who present these ideas. We are accountable for our actions, and when mistakes occur, we focus on preventing future errors and moving forward. We are passionate about achieving our goals, and we are passionate about gardening.

As a result of the environmental scan, the WSI board learned that one of its underutilized strengths is the popularity of "Ask Lydia," a gardening column written by one of its founders, Lydia Wright. Because of this, they have decided to capitalize on Lydia Wright's knowledge of and passion for gardening. To do this, they have developed the following corporate goal:

> Within three years, create a nationally recognized gardening education program based on the "Ask Lydia" columns.

In order to accomplish this midrange goal, the marketing department has developed a short-range tactical goal and action plan:

> Tactical goal: Increase the number of newsletter subscribers in which "Ask Lydia" appears by 25 percent by the end of the fiscal year.

The marketing action plan looks like this:

1. Identify new online users.
2. Create a social media campaign.

3. Identify affiliates.
4. Draw up contracts.
5. Submit weekly columns.

With the goals in place, the marketing department is now able to develop a budget and implement the plan.

Strategy Evaluation

The ability of a company to accomplish its mission and conduct business in accordance with its core values largely depends on the behavior modeled by upper management. Employees are quickly able to observe any disconnect between what the employer says and what the employer does. Reinforcing values through corporate behavior is accomplished by modeling value-based behavior, communicating successful missions (celebrating success), and coaching employees using the mission, vision, and values as performance benchmarks. These activities help the organization achieve positive outcomes while reinforcing its strategic plan.

Evaluating the strategy tells the planners whether the organization is achieving the desired goals and moving the strategy forward. This stage is important because if the action plans aren't working or if conditions in the marketplace change, the organization must be prepared to respond immediately and adjust the tactical goals and action plans. In some cases, the corporate goal may need to be revisited and adjusted to adapt to the change in conditions.

Once the action plans, including the methods for evaluation, are developed, it's possible to determine how many and what kind of resources will be required to implement the strategy. The plan may require additional employees, funds to outsource some components of the plan, or the purchase of new technology or new equipment; if so, these elements determine how much cash is required to achieve the desired goal. At this point, those involved in the planning process have the information necessary to compare the cost of achieving the goals against the potential benefits before committing resources to implement the strategy.

Business Plans

Similar to a strategic plan, a business plan serves as a road map to achieving organizational objectives. A business plan is a documented series of actionable steps with clearly defined ends, ways, and means, that meets established criteria by the company leadership and that enables the company's business model to remain viable—in short, for the company to remain competitive in their market. It encompasses market analysis, operational strategies, financial projections, and risk assessments, providing a comprehensive guide for decision making and resource allocation. A business plan serves as a communication tool, conveying the value proposition and potential of the business venture to stakeholders such as investors, partners, and employees. The three main components of a business plan are:

Executive Summary This section provides an overview of the entire business plan, summarizing key points such as the business concept, target market, unique value proposition, financial projections, and the team's qualifications. It serves as a concise introduction to the business idea and its potential for success, typically spanning one to two pages.

Business Description and Market Analysis This component delves into the details of the business, including its mission, vision, and objectives. It outlines the products or services offered, the target market, and the competitive landscape. Additionally, it includes a thorough analysis of the industry, market trends, customer needs, and potential opportunities and threats. Market research findings and SWOT (strengths, weaknesses, opportunities, threats) analysis are often included to provide a comprehensive understanding of the business environment.

Operational Plan and Financial Projections This section outlines how the business will be operated on a day-to-day basis, detailing key operational processes, milestones, and timelines. It covers aspects such as production or service delivery, marketing and sales strategies, distribution channels, and staffing requirements. This section of the business plan is likely to include financial projections, such as income statements, cash flow statements, and balance sheets, to forecast the financial performance of the business over a specified period, typically 3 to 5 years. Financial assumptions and break-even analysis may also be included to justify the projected numbers and demonstrate the feasibility of the business venture.

Both business plans and strategic plans are important for organizational success, and they differ in scope, focus, time horizon, level of detail, and purpose. Business plans focus on specific ventures or projects within the organization and have a shorter time horizon, whereas strategic plans encompass the entire organization and set its long-term direction and priorities.

Human Capital Management Plans

> You don't build a business. You build people, and then people build the business.
>
> *Zig Ziglar*

Strategic plans are important to identify opportunities and guide business actions, but as a general rule, they cannot be achieved without people. A *human capital management plan (HCMP)* is a comprehensive strategy outlining how an organization will attract, develop, retain, and manage its workforce to achieve its business objectives effectively.

HCMPs support a business's strategic plan by aligning the organization's workforce with its overall objectives and goals in several ways, all of which are performed within HR programs. These include:

Talent Acquisition and Recruitment An effective HCMP ensures that the business attracts and hires the right talent needed to execute its strategic initiatives. By identifying the required skills and competencies, the plan helps in recruiting individuals who can contribute to the achievement of strategic objectives.

Employee Development and Training The HCMP includes strategies for employee development and training programs that enhance the skills and capabilities of the workforce. This ensures that employees are equipped to meet the evolving demands of the business and contribute effectively to strategic goals.

Performance Management Through performance management systems integrated into the HCMP, businesses can set clear performance expectations aligned with strategic objectives. Regular performance evaluations provide feedback to employees, identify areas for improvement, and recognize achievements that contribute to strategic outcomes.

Succession Planning A well-defined HCMP includes succession planning strategies to identify and develop future leaders within the organization. By grooming talent from within, businesses can ensure continuity in leadership and maintain momentum in achieving long-term strategic goals.

Employee Engagement and Retention Engaged and motivated employees are more likely to contribute positively to the business's strategic objectives. The HCMP incorporates initiatives to foster a positive work environment, promote employee engagement, and retain top talent, thereby supporting the sustained execution of the strategic plan.

Knowledge Capital *Knowledge capital* refers to the intangible assets within an organization that come from the collective knowledge, expertise, skills, and capabilities of its workforce. It encompasses not only the explicit knowledge documented in manuals, databases, and systems but also the tacit knowledge embedded in the minds of employees through experience, learning, and collaboration. From a market competitiveness position, knowledge capital can make a company more attractive to buyers by showcasing its intellectual assets, including specialized skills, innovative processes, and expertise, thereby enhancing its perceived value and potential for future growth and profitability. This capital can be leveraged in the same way as other, more tangible resources, if properly accounted for within an HCMP.

Workforce Analytics and Metrics HCMPs utilize workforce analytics and metrics to track *key performance indicators (KPIs)* related to employee productivity, satisfaction, turnover rates, and other relevant metrics. This data-driven approach enables businesses to make informed decisions and adjustments to their strategic plan based on the performance and capabilities of their workforce.

A properly crafted HCMP allows the organization to adapt quickly to changes in the business environment or shifts in strategic priorities. This flexibility ensures that the workforce remains agile and responsive to emerging opportunities and challenges, supporting the overall resilience of the business strategy. In essence, a well-crafted HCMP serves as a strategic multiplier, ensuring that the organization's most valuable asset—its people—are effectively leveraged to drive the successful execution of its strategic initiatives.

Service Delivery Plans

An HR service delivery plan is a strategic document that outlines how HR services will be delivered within an organization. It defines the structure, processes, and resources required to effectively meet the needs of employees and the organization as a whole. HR service delivery plans are designed to ensure that HR functions align with organizational objectives, support employee needs, and contribute to overall business success. They provide a framework for delivering high-quality HR services efficiently and consistently across the organization. Several key features must be taken into account when designing HR service delivery, and these are covered next.

Service Delivery Models

HR service delivery models encompass various approaches that dictate how human resource functions are structured and administered within an organization:

- **Centralized:** HR services are delivered from a single, centralized location or department within the organization, offering consistency and standardization.
- **Decentralized:** HR services are dispersed across various departments or locations within the organization, allowing for tailored support but potentially leading to inconsistency.
- **Shared Services:** HR services are consolidated into a centralized unit that serves multiple departments or locations, promoting efficiency and cost-effectiveness while maintaining some degree of customization.

Service Level Agreements

Service level agreements (SLAs) are formal agreements between HR and internal stakeholders or departments that define the level of service expected, including response times, quality standards, and performance metrics. They outline the scope of services, responsibilities of both parties, and consequences for not meeting agreed-upon standards, fostering accountability and transparency in HR service delivery.

Technology Platforms

Technology platforms refer to the software systems and tools used to facilitate HR service delivery, such as human resources information systems (HRISs), applicant-tracking systems (ATSs), and learning management systems (LMSs). These platforms streamline processes, automate tasks, and enhance data management, enabling HR to deliver services more efficiently and effectively.

Staffing Requirements

Staffing requirements specify the personnel needed to deliver HR services effectively, including roles, responsibilities, and skill sets. They consider factors such as workload, expertise, and availability to ensure that HR teams have the capacity and capabilities to meet the organization's needs. Staffing requirements may also include considerations for training and development to enhance HR service delivery capabilities.

Strategic Management

As organizations developed and grew ever larger, the need for controlling large numbers of workers in geographically diverse locations presented a challenge for business owners, who responded by creating bureaucracies to ensure that operations were conducted in accordance with the direction set by senior management. These bureaucracies, developed by American businesspeople in the mid-19th century, enabled the dominance of American products throughout the world for 100 years and were emulated by businesses in other countries. As long as the demand for products was greater than the number of products available, this model, in which business dictated what it would produce to the customer, worked extremely well.

When business conditions changed and customers became more demanding, this "one size fits all" approach was not as successful. Japanese manufacturers gave customers an alternative, and customers responded by purchasing those companies' products. American businesses, because of their bureaucratic methods, were slow to respond. The need for constant innovation to satisfy changing customer needs was a difficult transition, and it continues to affect American business.

It's up to management to ensure that the strategies and plans developed to meet changing customer needs are implemented and accomplished. Four basic management functions are used for this purpose: planning, organizing, directing, and controlling. These functions ensure that organization resources are used in the best way to achieve corporate goals. The planning function has been covered extensively; let's talk briefly now about the other functions.

Organizing Managers are responsible for providing a structure within which employees are able to complete their work. Many factors must be considered, including what work needs to be done, how employees interact and with whom, the decision-making process in the organization, and how work is delegated. Issues to be considered in developing an organization structure are whether management is centralized or decentralized, the nature of the functions, and the span of control for each manager.

A *centralized organization* is one in which the decision-making authority is concentrated at higher levels in the organization; in a *decentralized organization*, the decision-making authority is delegated to lower levels.

Business functions are classified as either *line functions*, such as operations and sales, which make decisions about operating needs, or *staff functions*, such as human resources and finance, which don't make operating decisions but do advise line managers.

Finally, *span of control* refers to the number of employees that one manager can directly supervise. Depending on the nature and complexity of the task, this number varies. Managers responsible for very complex tasks requiring closer supervision are able to supervise fewer employees than managers responsible for those performing less complex tasks.

Directing Managers must establish relationships with the employees they supervise to encourage and support them in accomplishing their goals. Management style contributes to the development of these relationships.

Controlling This function is used by managers to ensure that the strategies, tactics, and plans developed during the planning process are implemented. As discussed earlier in "Strategy Evaluation," this is an ongoing process. In addition to evaluating individual goals and action plans as described in that section, management must have a "big picture" view of overall progress.

There are several areas under the umbrella of strategic HR management; these are covered next.

Enterprise Human Resource Management

Enterprise human resource management (EHRM) refers to the strategic approach of managing all aspects of human resources across an entire organization or enterprise. Unlike traditional HR management, which may focus on individual departments or functions, EHRM takes a holistic view, considering the workforce as a unified entity with interconnected needs and goals.

EHRM involves aligning HR practices and processes with the overall strategic objectives of the organization, ensuring that human capital is effectively leveraged to drive business success. This includes activities such as talent acquisition, performance management, learning and development, compensation and benefits, workforce planning, and employee relations.

Key features of enterprise human resource management may include the use of integrated HRISs or enterprise resource planning (ERP) systems to streamline HR processes and facilitate data-driven decision making. EHRM emphasizes collaboration and communication across different departments and functions to optimize workforce effectiveness and support organizational agility and innovation.

Strategic Relationships

If the purpose of business strategy is to plot the course for organizational success, what is meant by a *strategic relationship*? For HR professionals, strategic relationships are those that advance the contribution of the HR function toward achieving organization goals. Strategic relationships reflect the business plan and are important enough to make any strategic-planning tool succeed or fail. Strategic relationships are built between individuals defined as *stakeholders*, who are the employees, the management hierarchy, the shareholders, and the community. In addition, these relationships create a subculture of the very identity of the brand—both internally from the perspective of the management team and their employees and externally, driven by the forces of the business climate.

It could be argued that the success of any strategic or business planning outcomes depends on the quality of the internal and external relationships:

Internal Relationships Internal relationships that move HR toward the accomplishment of organization goals are built over time as the HR function establishes its credibility with the executive team, management, employees, and vendors. Credibility is established when the HR function provides solutions to organization workforce problems at all levels. Often identified through an organizational chart, the relationships that exist within the corporate framework reflect both personal and professional connections. The ability of individuals to work with each other helps create the culture that drives business outcomes and often is the target of HR efforts defined under the function of employee and management relations. Communication, goal-setting, and project-management skills are representative of the types of behaviors that can be addressed through strategic employee relations activities.

These labor-management relationships are at the core of many of HR's responsibilities, because HR defines the structure from which management takes employment-related action. The following are examples of the HR activities that define these relationships:

- Creating policies, procedures, and rules
- Complying with legal and regulatory directives
- Analyzing jobs from which job descriptions and performance metrics are developed
- Employing strategic HCMPs to ensure that the workforce has the appropriate skill set to achieve the corporate objectives identified through the strategic planning process

External Relationships and Data Sources A network of individuals whose work influences or intersects with an organization's goals brings long-range benefits to HR professionals. Frequently, the ease with which you can obtain information about the best service providers, find employees with critical skills, or build partnerships that add value to human resource programs and influence the bottom line is enhanced when relationships are established before they're needed.

Note that senior HR leaders are often plugged into external sources for information that may be used to inform decision making throughout the organization. For this reason, the ability to discern what is credible or incredible becomes a sought-after skill. For example, the Internet has available a multitude of sites with salary data that may be used by HR to build pay scales. These sites range from the formal, published salary surveys to user self-reports. Sites that allow users to self-report (such as `http://Glassdoor.com`) contain data that may—or may not—be scientifically credible. Another example of external sources for information is the study of employee engagement. Much has been written about this management trend because increased employee engagement is positively correlated with desired outcomes such as retention and productivity. From a psychological perspective, employee engagement refers to the level of investment an employee has in the job tasks—not their level of commitment to the organization. This distinction is important in that if companies expect human resources to increase employee engagement, the HR plan will address job tasks, not necessarily the organizational culture as a whole. HR leaders must be able to evaluate the credibility of surveys, management trends, and even legal analysis *before* recommending their companies base decisions on it. At a minimum, HR should be sure that the intervention being recommended is a valid predictor of the desired outcome.

In addition, identifying reliable, high-quality service providers for organization workforce needs, such as recruiting agencies, benefit brokers, and others with expertise in areas of importance to the organization, ensures the availability of services when they're required.

Risk Management

Exam objective 1.3 charges senior HR leaders to understand the internal and external factors that impact operations based on risk. While covered in detail in Chapter 2, "Shared Competencies," the SPHR/i exam objectives specifically cover the following:

Human Capital Risk Analysis This involves assessing potential risks related to the workforce, such as talent shortages, turnover rates, skill gaps, and succession planning challenges. It aims to identify vulnerabilities and develop strategies to mitigate these risks, ensuring the organization has the necessary human resources to achieve its objectives.

Business Continuity Business continuity refers to the ability of an organization to maintain essential functions and operations during and after disruptive events, such as natural disasters, pandemics, or cyberattacks. It involves developing plans and protocols to ensure critical processes can continue with minimal interruption, safeguarding against financial loss and reputational damage.

Response Planning Response planning involves developing strategies and protocols to address and mitigate risks when they materialize. It includes establishing clear roles and responsibilities, communication channels, and escalation procedures to facilitate a coordinated and effective response to emergencies, crises, or unexpected events.

Geopolitical Environment Scanning Geopolitical environment scanning involves monitoring and analyzing political, economic, social, and cultural factors in various regions or countries where the organization operates. By assessing geopolitical risks, such as regulatory changes, trade tensions, or instability, HR can anticipate potential impacts on workforce management, supply chains, and business operations.

Mental Health Mental health risk management involves promoting employee well-being and addressing psychological risks in the workplace. This includes providing support resources, raising awareness, reducing stigma, and implementing policies and programs to foster a mentally healthy work environment, ultimately enhancing employee resilience, productivity, and retention.

Concerted Activity Concerted protected activity in HR management refers to actions taken by employees, either individually or collectively, to address workplace issues or improve working conditions, which are legally protected under labor laws. Legal issues surrounding concerted protected activity primarily revolve around ensuring that employees' rights to engage in collective action, such as union organizing, discussing wages, or addressing workplace grievances, are upheld. Employers must navigate laws such as the National Labor Relations Act (NLRA), which protects employees' rights to engage in concerted activities for their mutual aid or protection. Violations of these rights can lead to legal disputes, unfair labor practice charges, and potential financial penalties. Employers must tread carefully to avoid infringing upon employees' rights while maintaining the integrity and productivity of the workplace.

SPHRi Local Laws and Regulations

Global HR leaders face the complex task of ensuring compliance with local laws and regulations in multiple jurisdictions, each with its own unique legal landscape. Failure to adhere to these laws can result in legal liabilities, financial penalties, reputational damage, and even operational disruptions.

To navigate these challenges, global HR leaders must first conduct comprehensive research and analysis to understand the legal requirements in each country or region where their organization operates. This includes labor laws, employment regulations, tax codes, immigration policies, and data protection laws.

Establishing strong relationships with local legal experts or law firms is a useful way to stay current on regional variances. These experts can provide guidance on compliance matters, interpretation of laws, and legal processes. Global consultants can be a valuable resource as well.

Regular audits and reviews of HR policies and practices across all locations help identify any gaps or areas of concern, allowing for prompt corrective action. By prioritizing compliance and staying vigilant about legal developments in each jurisdiction, global HR leaders can uphold ethical standards, protect their organization's interests, and connect with global stakeholders within and outside of the organization.

Change Management

Implementing new business strategies often requires significant changes within an organization, ranging from shifts in processes and procedures to alterations in organizational culture and employee roles. The process of managing these changes effectively is known as change management.

HR plays an important role in change management by facilitating organizational transitions and ensuring employee engagement. HR professionals act as champions of change, guiding employees through the process, addressing concerns, and promoting a positive culture. They develop communication strategies, provide training, and manage resistance to foster acceptance and commitment to change. HR oversees the alignment of talent with new business strategies, ensuring that skills and competencies match evolving organizational needs.

Change agents also play an important role in change management efforts by serving as enthusiastic advocates and influencers within the organization. These individuals possess credibility, leadership, and a deep understanding of the proposed changes. Champions effectively communicate the benefits of the change, address concerns, and rally support from their peers. They act as role models, demonstrating commitment and resilience throughout the transition process. By leveraging their influence and expertise, champions help overcome resistance, motivate employees, and drive momentum toward successful implementation.

Chapter 2 has an in-depth review of the various change management theories and models.

Project Management

Project management (PM) describes the process of initiating, planning, executing, controlling, and closing an assignment that is temporary in nature. It is described by HRCI as a methodical approach to planning projects that includes goals, timetables, deliverables, and procedures. The assignment may involve designing a new software program, constructing a building, implementing a new marketing strategy, or doing any other activity that isn't part of the ongoing operations of a business. The Project Management Institute (`https://www.pmi.org/about/what-is-a-project`), describes a five-stage process group model as follows:

Initiation During the initiation phase, project requests are evaluated and selected for implementation. Those who will be affected by the project—the *stakeholders* such as the project manager, sponsor, team members, customers, and others—meet to discuss the proposed project. Once a project is selected, the sponsor creates a project charter to sanction the project and commit resources to its completion. The charter also identifies the goals and appoints the project manager.

Planning The planning phase is led by the project manager (PM) and lays out how the project will be accomplished. The plan describes the deliverables, budget, and scope of the project and then develops specific activities and identifies the *knowledge, skills, and abilities* (KSAs) required to execute the activities. Finally, a timeline for completing the project is created.

Executing During this phase, the project plan is implemented. A project team is created, and other resources are acquired. Activities identified in the planning phase are completed during this time, and the PM manages the timeline, conducts status meetings, and disseminates information to the sponsor and other stakeholders as needed.

Controlling The PM keeps the project on course and on budget by comparing accomplishments to the original plan and making course corrections as needed. As the project progresses, stakeholders may request changes to the original scope, and the PM will review and incorporate them into the project as appropriate.

Closing The closing phase is the point at which the sponsor/customer acknowledges achievement of the project goals. The PM collects information from stakeholders to improve future projects, stores documentation of project activities, and releases resources for use in other projects or activities.

For HR professionals, the ability to manage projects is critical to success. The following list shows how HR projects can occur in any of the functional areas:

- **Leadership and Strategy:** Integrating the cultures of two organizations after a merger
- **Talent Planning and Acquisition:** Developing a new-hire socialization program
- **Learning and Development:** Creating a career-development program
- **Total Rewards:** Developing a stock option program
- **Employee Relations and Engagement:** Developing an employee handbook

Each of these activities is a short-term assignment that will result in a program that will become part of the organization operations when it's complete, but the process of designing the program isn't an ongoing operation.

Diversity, Equity, and Inclusion (DEI)

Diversity, equity and inclusion is also covered in great detail in Chapter 2 as it is an important function of human resource professionals at all stages of their careers. Senior HR leaders should be aware of the general concepts, and also pay special attention to championing DEI as a strategic initiative tied directly to organizational results. This requires that DEI is addressed within the strategic planning process, has the support of executive leadership, and is properly resourced and evaluated for success. The positive effects of undertaking robust DEI efforts can be argued using data. For example, in their annual (2024) report, Forbes reported that 47 percent of black workers and 49 percent of Hispanic workers report quitting their jobs after witnessing discrimination.[1] With this data, HR can lead the effort to decrease discriminatory practices not only to lower turnover, but also to effectively manage risk.

Evidence-Based Decision Making

In the world of HR leadership, every day is packed with decisions. From selecting the best recruitment channels to making decisions about the HR budget, leaders are increasingly being called upon to engage in creative but evidenced-based decisions.

Evidence-based decision making involves using objective, verifiable evidence to inform and justify decisions rather than relying solely on intuition, tradition, or personal opinion. It entails systematically gathering, analyzing, and evaluating relevant data, research, and best practices to determine the most effective course of action in a given situation. By prioritizing evidence over assumptions, biases, or anecdotal experiences, organizations can enhance decision quality, mitigate risks, and achieve better organizational and HR outcomes. This evidence can come from many sources, including the ones noted on the exam content outline of salary data, management trends, and published surveys and studies.

Salary Data In evidence-based HR decision making, leveraging salary data provides valuable insights into market trends, competitive compensation packages, and internal equity. By analyzing salary benchmarks, HR professionals can ensure fair and competitive pay structures that attract and retain top talent while aligning with organizational goals and budgets. This data-driven approach empowers HR leaders to make informed decisions about salary adjustments, promotions, and recruitment strategies. Incorporating compensation strategies into HR decisions allows for the alignment of salary data with broader organizational objectives, such as incentivizing desired behaviors or attracting quality candidates.

Data Trends Various types of data trends, such as market trends, customer behavior patterns, and workforce analytics, inform business decision making. For instance, analyzing turnover rates and employee engagement survey data helps HR leaders identify retention trends and address underlying issues to improve employee satisfaction and reduce turnover costs. Additionally, tracking recruitment metrics like time-to-fill and sourcing effectiveness assists in optimizing hiring strategies and allocating resources effectively to attract top talent.

Published Studies and Surveys Published studies and surveys offer valuable insights for business decision making, encompassing market research, consumer preferences, and workforce trends. In HR decision making, leveraging studies on workplace diversity and inclusion aids in developing strategies to foster a more inclusive culture, enhancing employee engagement and innovation. Similarly, internal surveys on employee satisfaction and well-being provide critical data to shape policies and initiatives that prioritize employee wellness, leading to higher retention rates and improved productivity.

---

[1] `https://www.forbes.com/advisor/business/hr-statistics-trends.`

Real World Scenario

Decision-Making Fatigue

The struggle is real. HR and other leaders often suffer from decision-making fatigue due to the vast number of choices they must make every day. Decision-making fatigue refers to the deteriorating quality of decisions made by an individual after a prolonged period of decision making. As individuals make more choices throughout the day, their mental resources become depleted, leading to poorer judgment, increased impulsivity, and a greater likelihood of making suboptimal decisions. In some cases, individuals will avoid making decisions altogether.

Three strategies HR professionals can employ to mitigate decision-making fatigue are as follows:

Implementing Decision Support Tools HR professionals can introduce decision support tools, such as decision trees, checklists, or software solutions, to streamline and simplify decision-making processes. These tools can help organize information, guide decision makers through complex choices, and reduce cognitive load, thereby mitigating decision-making fatigue. See the following Figure 10.1 for an example of a matrix to support decision making.

FIGURE 10.1 The pugh matrix

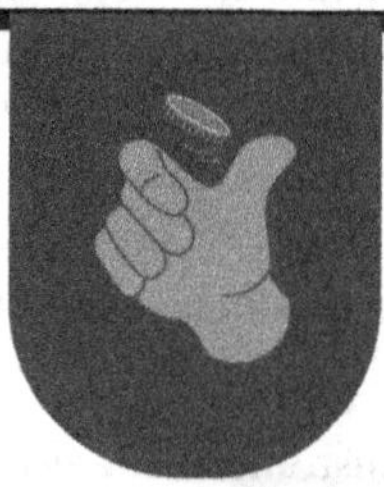

Decision-Making

Selecting a Candidate for a Job Position

Criteria	Candidate A	Candidate B	Candidate C
Relevant Skills	4	5	3
Cultural Fit	2	4	5
Potential for Growth	4	3	3
Availability	5	3	4
Compensation Requirements	4	3	5
Total	**19**	**18**	**20**

Key Notes: The Pugh decision matrix, devised by Stuart Pugh, aids in selecting the best option among alternatives by evaluating them against predefined criteria. Criteria are chosen and each choice rated against the criteria. Optionally, weights can be assigned to criteria. Analysis of scores helps identify the most favorable alternative. This structured approach mitigates biases and subjectivity, commonly employed in engineering, design, project management, and business decision-making processes.

Prioritizing and Delegating Decisions HR professionals can prioritize decisions based on their impact and urgency, focusing on high-priority tasks while delegating less critical decisions to appropriate team members. Delegating decisions not only distributes the decision-making workload but also empowers employees and fosters a sense of ownership and accountability.

Promoting Structured Breaks and Rest Periods HR professionals can advocate for structured breaks and rest periods between decision-making tasks to allow employees to recharge and replenish their cognitive resources. Encouraging regular breaks, providing opportunities for relaxation or physical activity, and fostering a supportive work environment that values work-life balance can help mitigate decision-making fatigue and enhance overall well-being.

Educating other leaders on the importance of self-care, time management, and delegation can help mitigate decision-making fatigue across the organization and help teams feel supported.

Business Metrics

Interpreting and utilizing business metrics is essential for organizations to assess and drive the achievement of strategy goals and objectives effectively. Business metrics provide quantifiable measures of performance across various aspects of the organization, offering valuable insights into the success or shortcomings of strategic initiatives. This section reviews the need for comprehensive legal analysis, the use of business intelligence, and budgets.

Legal Analysis

It is unclear from the exam content outline alone just how much specific labor law will be covered on the SPHR exam. The 2024 outline describes the labor law responsibility of HR leaders as how they apply to "organizational strategy and/or complex HR strategies," and notes specific examples of policies, programs, practices, business expansion/reduction, and concerted activity. While these topics are discussed in the next section, it is recommended that you rigorously study Appendix C, which covers the major legislation related to all domains of human resources.

Leadership and Strategy responsibility 1.12 is the only area of distinction between the SPHR and SPHRi exams, as SPHRi candidates are charged with being able to "apply and evaluate the applicability of local labor laws, regulations, and guidance to organizational strategy/or complex HR strategies to adhere to legal and ethical requirements." This suggests that SPHRi candidates do not need to be as familiar with U.S. federal labor law as do SPHR candidates.

Employment Policies and Practices

Employment policies are essential for organizational structure but carry legal implications that demand careful attention. Chief among these are antidiscrimination laws, which require policies to ensure fair treatment regardless of protected characteristics. Harassment policies are also an area of risk that must be managed, with the goal to prevent and address workplace harassment while upholding a culture of respect and inclusivity. Privacy concerns arise regarding monitoring employee communications and digital activities, requiring policies and practices that balance organizational interests with employee privacy rights and legal regulations. In general, employment policies must adhere to labor laws governing wages, hours, benefits, and workplace safety. By crafting clear, comprehensive policies that align with legal requirements and foster a fair, respectful workplace culture, employers can mitigate legal risks, promote employee trust, and ensure organizational success.

Senior HR leaders can mitigate legal risks by implementing compliant training programs to educate employees on antidiscrimination and harassment policies. They should regularly review and update employment policies to ensure compliance with evolving laws and regulations, and audit organizational practices to ensure compliance and remedy issues where necessary. Fostering a culture of transparency and accountability can encourage early reporting and swift resolution of potential legal issues.

Employers must navigate labor laws such as the Fair Labor Standards Act (FLSA) to ensure compliance with minimum wage, overtime pay, and child labor provisions. Additionally, they must adhere to the Family and Medical Leave Act (FMLA) regarding unpaid leave for qualified medical and family reasons, as well as Title VII of the Civil Rights Act to prevent discrimination based on race, color, religion, sex, or national origin. Other important laws include the Americans with Disabilities Act (ADA) governing accommodation for individuals with disabilities and the Occupational Safety and Health Act (OSHA) ensuring safe and healthy working conditions.

Business Expansion and Reduction

Expanding or reducing a business can trigger various legal considerations that require careful navigation to mitigate risks and ensure compliance. When expanding, businesses must adhere to regulations governing new markets, such as licensing requirements, zoning laws, and tax obligations. Additionally, international expansions introduce complexities related to foreign laws, trade regulations, and intellectual property protection.

Conversely, during periods of contraction or downsizing, businesses must comply with employment laws governing layoffs, severance pay, and worker retraining programs. Mishandling these processes can result in costly lawsuits for wrongful termination or violation of labor laws.

To manage legal risks during expansion or reduction, businesses should conduct thorough due diligence, seeking legal counsel to identify and address regulatory requirements and potential liabilities. Clear communication with employees about changes in employment status, benefits, and rights is important to maintain trust and minimize legal disputes.

Senior leaders are responsible for championing and in some cases, designing proactive risk management strategies, such as implementing fair and transparent selection criteria for layoffs and documenting the decision-making process. These activities can help mitigate legal exposure and uphold ethical standards throughout the expansion or reduction process.

Employers must consider the Worker Adjustment and Retraining Notification (WARN) Act, which requires advance notice of mass layoffs or plant closings affecting a certain number of employees. Additionally, they must adhere to the Older Workers Benefit Protection Act (OWBPA) when offering severance packages to older workers, as well as the Consolidated Omnibus Budget Reconciliation Act (COBRA) providing continuation of health coverage after job loss. Other critical laws include the Foreign Corrupt Practices Act (FCPA) when expanding internationally and the Employee Retirement Income Security Act (ERISA) regarding pension and retirement plans during business changes.

Business Intelligence

Business intelligence (BI) refers to the use of technology, processes, and strategies to analyze data and provide actionable insights that support decision making and drive business performance. It involves collecting, organizing, and transforming raw data into meaningful information, which can then be used to identify trends, patterns, and opportunities, as well as to monitor key performance indicators (KPIs) and track progress toward organizational goals.

BI encompasses a range of methodologies, tools, and technologies, including data visualization, reporting, dashboards, data mining, and predictive analytics. These capabilities enable organizations to gain a deeper understanding of their operations, customers, and markets, allowing them to make informed decisions, optimize processes, and drive innovation. The various concepts tied to business intelligence are covered next.

Key Performance Indicators (KPIs)

To interpret business metrics effectively, organizations must first identify *key performance indicators* (KPIs) aligned with their strategic objectives. These KPIs may include financial metrics such as revenue growth, profitability, and return on investment, as well as nonfinancial metrics like customer satisfaction, employee engagement, and operational efficiency.

Once KPIs are established, organizations can use business metrics to monitor progress, identify trends, and pinpoint areas for improvement. Regular analysis of metrics enables informed decision making, allowing leaders to allocate resources, adjust strategies, and prioritize initiatives based on performance data.

Predictive Analytics

Predictive analytics has emerged as a powerful business metric, enabling organizations to harness the vast amount of data available to make informed decisions and anticipate future outcomes. By analyzing historical data and identifying patterns, trends, and correlations, predictive analytics can forecast various business metrics, such as sales, customer behavior, employee performance, and market trends. This proactive approach allows organizations to anticipate potential challenges, identify opportunities for growth, optimize resource allocation, and mitigate risks.

Predictive analytics in HR involves analyzing historical HR data to forecast future trends and outcomes related to workforce management, talent acquisition, and employee performance. By leveraging predictive analytics, HR professionals can make data-driven decisions, anticipate staffing needs, identify high-potential candidates, and develop strategies to enhance employee engagement and retention. More on this important topic covered in Chapter 14, "HR Information Management, Safety, and Security."

Pay Equity Analysis

Pay equity analysis involves evaluating compensation practices within an organization to ensure fairness and eliminate gender, racial, or other biases in pay. Its purpose is to identify and rectify any disparities in compensation for employees performing similar work or with similar qualifications. The process typically involves collecting and analyzing data on employee demographics, job roles, and compensation levels to identify any unexplained pay gaps, followed by implementing corrective measures such as adjusting salaries or addressing underlying systemic issues to achieve equitable compensation practices.

Financial Statements

From an HR leader's perspective, interpreting *financial statements* provides critical insights into the organization's financial health and performance. By analyzing metrics such as revenue, expenses, and profit margins, HR leaders can understand the financial implications of human capital investments, such as recruitment, training, and compensation. Additionally, examining financial statements allows HR leaders to align HR strategies with broader organizational goals, ensuring that HR initiatives contribute to the organization's financial sustainability and long-term growth. Features of financial statements that senior HR professionals should understand include the following:

- ***Income Statement* (Profit-and-Loss Statement):** Provides a summary of revenues, expenses, and net income over a specific period. Understanding this statement helps HR professionals comprehend the organization's financial performance and profitability.
- ***Balance Sheet*:** Presents the organization's financial position at a specific point in time, showcasing assets, liabilities, and equity. HR professionals should understand this statement to assess the organization's liquidity, solvency, and overall financial health.
- ***Cash Flow Statement*:** Details the organization's cash inflows and outflows during a specific period, categorizing activities into operating, investing, and financing activities. HR professionals can use this statement to assess the organization's ability to generate cash and manage liquidity effectively.
- ***Financial Ratios*:** These metrics provide insights into various aspects of financial performance, such as profitability, liquidity, efficiency, and solvency. Senior HR professionals should understand key financial ratios relevant to their organization's industry and strategic objectives to assess performance and make informed decisions.

Here are three significant financial ratios that senior HR leaders should understand:

- ***Return on Investment*** **(ROI):** Measures the profitability of HR initiatives by comparing the net profit generated to the initial investment cost, enabling HR leaders to assess the effectiveness of programs like training, recruitment, or employee engagement.
- ***Labor Cost Ratio*:** Calculates the proportion of total expenses attributed to labor costs, providing insights into workforce management efficiency and cost containment strategies.
- ***Revenue per Employee*:** Determines the revenue generated per employee, indicating productivity levels and efficiency of human capital utilization within the organization. Understanding this ratio helps HR leaders assess workforce productivity and identify opportunities for improvement.

Other common accounting terms can be found in Table 10.1.

TABLE 10.1 Common accounting terms

Term	Definition/description
Accrued expense	Expenses, such as vacation leave, that have been incurred but not yet paid
Accounts payable	Money owed by the business to its suppliers
Accounts receivable	Money owed to the business by customers
Assets	Tangible or intangible items of value owned by the business
Audited financial statements	Financial statements that have been examined by an independent auditor (not affiliated with the company) to determine whether they fairly represent the financial condition of the business
Budget	A projection of revenue and expenses used to control actual expenses
Cost of goods sold	Money spent on supplies and labor to produce goods or services
Equity	Value of the business to owners after all liabilities have been paid
Expense	Money spent to operate the business
Generally accepted accounting principles (GAAP)	Standards established by the Financial Accounting Standards Board (FASB) for recording financial transactions
Gross profit	Sales revenue less cost of goods sold

TABLE 10.1 Common accounting terms *(continued)*

Term	Definition/description
Liability	Money owed by the business to others, such as lenders or the government (for payroll taxes withheld), or to employees (for unused vacation time)
Net profit	Gross profit less operating expenses
Profit	Money earned by the business after all expenses have been paid
Retained earnings	Net profits that aren't distributed to owners but remain in the business as equity
Revenue	Money received from customers for products or services

By comprehending these key features of financial statements, senior HR professionals can effectively collaborate with finance and executive teams to align HR strategies with organizational goals, optimize resource allocation, and drive sustainable growth.

Budgets

The budgeting process determines how many and what kind of resources will be required to accomplish goals and objectives generated by the strategic plan. Whether the plan requires additional employees, funds to outsource elements of the plan, new technology, or new equipment, these elements determine how much cash is needed to achieve the goal. There are two basic ways to create a budget; the first is based on historical budget information, and the second is known as *zero-based budgeting (ZBB)*:

Budgets Based on Historic Information A historic budget bases the current budget on the prior year's budget. Past budgets and expenditures are reviewed and the new budget is based on the historical trends. In some cases, the amounts in the budget are increased by a flat percentage rate, based on inflation or anticipated salary increases. This method assumes that operationally, nothing will change from the last budget.

Zero-Based Budgeting (ZBB) The concept behind ZBB is very simple: Assume you're starting from scratch, and then determine what is needed to achieve the goals. How many people will be required? How much will you need to spend on outsourcing? What will be the cost of new technology or equipment? Unlike the historic budget process, ZBB requires that the need for each expenditure be justified in terms of the new goals and action plans.

As part of a zero-based budget planning process, HR examines all the programs offered to employees to determine whether they're still adding value to the organization. Programs that no longer add value are dropped and replaced with those that do add value or, if cost cutting is required, are dropped and not replaced.

Regardless of the way in which the budget is developed, it can be created from the top down, from the bottom up, or with a combination approach:

Top-Down Budgeting The *top-down budget* is created by senior management and imposed on the organization. Managers with operating responsibility have little input on how much money they will have to achieve their goals. This process is advantageous to senior management because they have complete control of how and where the money is spent. The disadvantage is that those creating the budget are generally far removed from actual operations and may not have full knowledge of what will be needed to achieve the goals they establish. This method often results in political battles as mid- and lower-level managers lobby senior management for additional funds for their particular departments.

Bottom-Up Budgeting The *bottom-up budget* includes all managers with budget responsibility in the budget-creation process. Managers with direct operating responsibility for achieving goals develop a budget based on their knowledge of operating costs and provide the information to senior managers, who have a view of the big picture for the organization. One advantage of this process is the commitment of operating managers to a budget they helped to create. Disadvantages include the amount of time required, the lack of awareness of the organization's big picture on the part of operating managers, and initial budget requests that may be unrealistic.

Parallel Budgeting A *parallel budget* includes elements of both the top-down and bottom-up approaches: Senior management provides broad guidelines for operating managers to follow in creating budgets for individual departments. This approach gives operating managers a context for developing individual budgets that are more realistic.

Monitoring budget performance allows HR leaders to identify opportunities for cost savings, efficiency improvements, and strategic investments in human capital development. Key features of an HR budget include:

- **Labor Costs:** Labor costs encompass salaries, wages, benefits, and related expenses associated with employees. This category typically forms the largest portion of the HR budget.
- **Training and Development:** Budget allocations for training programs, workshops, certifications, and other initiatives aimed at enhancing employee skills and capabilities.
- **Recruitment Expenses:** Funds earmarked for recruiting activities such as advertising, job fairs, recruitment agency fees, and applicant tracking systems to attract and hire new talent.

- **Employee Benefits:** Budgetary provisions for employee benefits such as healthcare, retirement plans, paid time off, and other perks offered to attract and retain talent.
- **HR Technology and Systems:** Budget allocations for HR software, tools, and systems to streamline HR processes, manage employee data, and enhance operational efficiency.

Summary

The leadership role of senior-level human resource professionals is directly tied in with business strategy. HR professionals functioning as business partners require a deeper view of business operations, including the components of how businesses are structured and practices are managed. This requires working knowledge of change management and project management in order to execute business goals.

Leading the strategic planning process is an essential competency for HR leaders. Scanning the internal and external environment is a data-gathering effort that will be used to inform many business practices. Understanding key elements of budgeting and accounting is also an important consideration when planning a business strategy. Metrics designed to evaluate interventions such as key performance indicators and other workforce measures are the foundation of evidence-based decisions.

HR plans, business plans, and human capital management plans should cascade down from business strategy and be aligned with the company's mission, vision, and values. From these plans, decisions may be made about how to deliver HR programs. This includes managing change when business must be done differently and developing important relationships to achieve strategic goals and objectives.

Exam Essentials

Understand different business structures. HR professionals must understand the purpose of different structures and how they drive business and human resource outcomes. Understanding the unique needs of each structure allows HR to be more effective in managing risk and making recommendations on elements such as workflow and growth.

Understand the strategic planning process. The strategic planning process consists of four broad elements: scanning the environment; formulating the corporate strategy with the vision, mission, values, and corporate goals; implementing the strategy with tactical goals, action plans, and budgets to accomplish organization goals; and evaluating the strategy to ensure that it can be adjusted to accommodate changes in the organization or the external environment.

Apply environmental scanning tools. Evaluating internal strengths and weaknesses and external opportunities and threats (SWOT), as well as the political, economic, social, technological, legal, and environmental (PESTLE) factors are used to evaluate the climate in which an organization will build a strategy to compete.

Be able to describe and design a human capital management plan. HR creates an HCMP to describe how it will contribute to achieving the organization's strategic plan. The HCMP clearly describes the strategic direction for the HR function, states the desired results to be achieved, states the objectives for achieving the results, creates action plans, and describes how the goals will be communicated and measured.

Understand HR data analytics and how it is used in HR practice. Evidence provides a means for quantifying HR programs and activities to justify and direct organizational decision making. The best data is that which provides relevant predictive or historical information to management and adds value to the decision-making process.

Review Questions

You can find the answers in Appendix A.

1. HR participates in the strategic planning process by doing which of the following?
   A. Formulating the strategy
   B. Scanning the environment
   C. Providing expertise
   D. Identifying strategic goals

2. What is a statement that describes what an organization does that is different from others?
   A. Values statement
   B. Corporate goal
   C. Vision statement
   D. Mission statement

3. What is the purpose of an HR budget? (Choose all that apply.)
   A. To determine the resources required for HR operations
   B. To gain approval for business lines of credit
   C. To properly fund the goals in the company's strategic plan
   D. To comply with reporting requirements to company shareholders

4. Salaries, payroll taxes, and benefits are all examples of which of the following HR activities?
   A. Conducting a business impact measure
   B. Creating an HR budget
   C. Creating a compensation strategy
   D. Analyzing the cost of recruiting

5. Based on an analysis of the industry and labor market trends, a VP of human resources has determined that the best course of action for her company is to change from a narrow to a broadband salary structure. The current structure has been in place for more than 15 years, and the VP is anticipating strong resistance to making the change. Which of the following tools should the VP use to convince the executive team to make the change?
   A. Calculate the return on investment.
   B. Build a business case.
   C. Calculate the cost–benefit analysis.
   D. Conduct a SWOT analysis.

6. Which of the following is *not* an appropriate use of an HRIS?
   A. Tracking applicant data for the EEO-1
   B. Tracking time and attendance
   C. Tracking employee expense reports
   D. Maintaining employee records

7. The best way for HR to contribute to the development of an organization's strategic plan using internal business operational factors is to do which of the following?
   A. Interpret and apply internal operational information such as the relationships between departments.
   B. Scan the legal and regulatory environment.
   C. Analyze industry changes.
   D. Stay informed of technological development.

8. Which of the following is another term for a profit-and-loss statement?
   A. Income statement
   B. Statement of cash flow
   C. Balance sheet
   D. Fiscal year summary

9. Which of the following organizational structures would be *most* effective for a company with three distinct commodities for sale?
   A. Functional structure
   B. Product-based structure
   C. Divisional structure
   D. Flat-line structure

10. The retail chain for which you work is dependent upon low-wage workers to staff their entry-level positions. For this reason, there is high turnover. This is the best example of which of the following SWOT elements?
    A. Strength
    B. Weakness
    C. Opportunity
    D. Threat

11. The cost of living in the Silicon Valley of California has made it difficult for educational institutions to recruit teachers. This is because teachers cannot typically afford the housing costs in the areas where the schools are located. This is the best example of which element of a SWOT audit?
    A. Strength
    B. Weakness
    C. Opportunity
    D. Threat

12. Being granted a U.S. patent for an invention protects against which of Porter's 5 Forces of competition?
    A. Barrier to entry
    B. Threat of substitutes
    C. Bargaining power of customers
    D. Bargaining power of suppliers

13. Which of the following best describes the purpose of a pay equity analysis?
    A. Analyzing compliance with the Fair Labor Standards Act
    B. Evaluating the competitiveness of employer compensation programs
    C. Assessing employee satisfaction with workplace benefits
    D. Ensuring fairness and eliminating biases in compensation practices

14. Total liabilities + equity is most likely to be reflected in which of the following?
    A. Assets on a balance sheet
    B. Cash flow
    C. Forecasted budget
    D. Income statement

15. What is the purpose of the Generally Accepted Accounting Principles (GAAP)?
    A. To create the body of knowledge for accounting professionals
    B. To guide the competencies required of certified public accountants
    C. To establish consequences for accounting professionals who behave in an unlawful manner
    D. To create checks and balances within accounting departments

16. You are the director of HR responsible for building the Learning and Development budget for the new fiscal year. You decide to take whatever you spent in this fiscal year and add 10 percent. This is an example of which budgeting technique?
    A. Zero-based
    B. Historic
    C. Top down
    D. Parallel

17. The corporate office in which you work is located in Peoria, Illinois. The company has distribution centers located on the East and the West coasts, and each location has its own budget, balance sheet, and profit-and-loss statements. This is an example of what type of structure?
    A. Regional
    B. Bureaucratic
    C. Decentralized
    D. Centralized

18. The advisement role of the accounting department is best reflected by which of the following?
    A. Line management
    B. Staff functions
    C. Span of control
    D. Controlling

19. In which stage of project management are the plan deliverables and timelines most likely to be established?

   A. Implementation
   B. Evaluation
   C. Initiation
   D. Planning

20. What are the ways a human capital management plan may be effective? (Choose all that apply.)

   A. If it aligns with the company's strategic plans
   B. If it properly forecasts the talent necessary to achieve company goals
   C. If it creates a competitive advantage for organizations
   D. If it orients human assets toward achieving strategic objectives.

Chapter

11

SPHR | SPHRi Exam: Workforce Planning and Talent Acquisition

SPHR AND SPHRi RESPONSIBILITIES:

FORECASTING ORGANIZATIONAL TALENT NEEDS AND DEVELOP STRATEGIES TO ATTRACT AND ENGAGE NEW TALENT.

✓ **2.1 Evaluate and forecast organizational needs throughout business cycles to develop or revise workforce plans (for example: corporate restructuring, divestitures, workforce expansion, or reduction)**

✓ **2.2 Develop, monitor, and assess recruitment strategies to attract talent (for example: labor market analysis, salary expectations, selection processes, sourcing, employee value proposition [EVP] and employer branding)**

✓ **2.3 Develop and evaluate strategies for onboarding new employees and managing cultural integrations (for example: new employee orientation, onboarding, restructuring, global expansion, mergers and acquisitions [M&A], joint ventures)**

For SPHR and SPHRi (SPHR/i) candidates, the functional area of Workforce Planning and Talent Acquisition makes up 17 percent of exam content related to a senior leader's ability to "forecast organizational talent needs and develop strategies to attract and engage new talent." It centers around the need for HR to align talent availability with organizational needs—having the right people in the right jobs and at the right time to execute business strategies.

Workforce Planning and Talent Acquisition Defined

From a senior human resource leader's perspective, workforce planning and talent acquisition are strategic processes aimed at ensuring that the organization has the right people, with the right skills, in the right positions, at the right time. Workforce planning involves forecasting future workforce needs based on organizational goals, analyzing current workforce capabilities, and identifying any gaps. Talent acquisition focuses on attracting, sourcing, and hiring top talent to fill those gaps, aligning recruitment efforts with the organization's strategic objectives. Together, these processes enable HR leaders to proactively address talent challenges, optimize resource allocation, and drive organizational success through a strong, capable workforce.

Strategic Analysis

Strategic analysis in workforce planning involves assessing current and future organizational needs, analyzing internal capabilities and external trends, and identifying gaps between supply and demand for talent. It informs decision-making processes to align workforce strategies with organizational goals, ensuring effective resource allocation and sustainable growth.

Chapter 2, "Shared Competencies," includes a robust discussion of both quantitative and qualitative analysis methods. For purposes of the SPHR/i and workforce planning, it is important to understand three main types of analysis:

Supply Analysis Internally, skills inventories are a useful tool to use when conducting a supply analysis. Skills inventories are typically described by the Human Resource Certification Institute (HRCIs) as a "listing of the capabilities, experiences, and goals of current employees as a tool for meeting the organization's human resource goals and objectives." Other factors to consider include the current cost of labor plus burden, and the capacity for in-house training. This step also requires an extensive analysis of the labor market for current skills and trending labor shortages.

Demand Analysis Focused on the future, a demand analysis seeks to identify needs based on organizational strategy.

Gap Analysis HRCI describes a gap analysis as being used by organizations to "compare its actual performance with its potential performance." In strategic analysis, a gap analysis identifies the missing KSAs between supply and demand of labor.

Once HR has collected and sorted the data, they are ready to present their findings and recommend solutions.

Workforce Goals and Objectives

During a company's strategic planning process, organization leaders make decisions about how to achieve business goals and objectives that provide a competitive advantage, improve the level of business performance, and add value for its stakeholders. In some cases, this requires the company to restructure some part of its business. An SPHR/i-level candidate must be able to understand and apply transition techniques for the following business restructures:

Reengineering The goal of reengineering is to realign operations in a way that adds value to customers. For workforce planning, this may mean eliminating jobs in some areas and adding jobs in others. Twenty-first century reengineering may also include a heavy dose of automation. For example, a McKinsey & Company report found that nursing assistants spend about two-thirds of their time collecting health information. By adopting data collection technology, this time may be reduced, allowing time for more patient interaction and care. View the full potential of automating jobs at `www.mckinsey.com/capabilities/mckinsey-digital/our-insights/where-machines-could-replace-humans-and-where-they-cant-yet`.

Corporate Restructuring Corporate restructuring looks at individual units in the organization to reduce or eliminate redundancy or bureaucratic processes in order to reduce costs and increase production. For workforce planning, this means reducing the workforce or reassigning employees to new jobs.

Offshoring/Outsourcing In most cases, *offshoring* or outsourcing decisions result in a workforce reduction or transfer of employees to other jobs. When employees are acquired by an outsource provider, they're terminated from the organization and hired by the new company.

One thing is certain: HR professionals must be ready to respond rapidly to changes in business workforce requirements with a road map that produces employees who possess the talent needed by the business to achieve its goals. This road map is built on the jobs that need to be performed and the individuals who will perform those jobs.

Labor Market Analysis

Conditions in the labor market affect the ability of an organization to hire the qualified individuals it needs. A labor market analysis looks at various economic indicators and other factors that impact the availability of those individuals:

Economic Indicators A variety of economic measures are used in labor market analysis. The Bureau of Labor Statistics (BLS) collects data from employers throughout the United States and makes this information available on its website. Some of the measures useful in analyzing the labor market are the unemployment rate, occupational outlook, demographics, and wages by area and occupation. The BLS's Job Openings and Labor Turnover Survey (JOLTS) is published to produce data on job openings, hires, and separations. You can find updated data each year at `www.bls.gov/jlt/home.htm`.

Industry Activity Another important factor to consider in a labor market analysis is the industry situation. Are new competitors entering the market? Is an existing competitor ramping up to produce a new product? Is a competitor losing market share and laying off employees? Activity within an industry affects an organization's ability to obtain qualified individuals to fill job openings. With the rise of e-commerce, many companies are having to rethink their strategies. For example, Walmart now offers free grocery pick-up for customers who place their orders online. Walmart has a competitive advantage over Amazon in that Walmart has a store within 15 miles of 90 percent of Americans, something Amazon does not. From a talent planning perspective, Walmart will have to consider having employees bring the groceries out to the customer, or even begin to hire delivery drivers to offer delivery services if Amazon continues to gain market share.

Labor Market Categories Depending on specific job requirements, the labor market most often falls into one of three broad categories:

Geography This labor market can be local, regional, national, or international and contains individuals with a wide variety of technical and professional skills and levels of education. Selection of the geographic labor market depends on the availability of candidates with the necessary skills for the position. For example, the pool of candidates for an entry-level customer service representative opening could be quite large in the local labor market, whereas obtaining a sufficient pool of candidates to fill an open CEO position could require looking at the national or international labor market.

Technical/Professional Skills This labor market contains individuals with expertise in a specific skill or discipline, such as accounting or information technology. These skills are often transferable between industries and can expand the available pool of candidates for openings.

Education This labor market includes individuals with similar levels of education. In some professions, such as teaching, medicine, or science, an advanced degree may be required to fill a position.

A useful labor market analysis for a particular organization includes data that is relevant to the needs of the organization and the types of employees and skills it's seeking to hire.

Strategic Workforce Planning

The goal of strategic workforce planning is to ensure that qualified employees are available when the organization needs them. An effective workforce planning process includes the following:

- Forecasting business needs
- Assessing employee skill
- Building plans that bridge the gap between business needs and available talent
- Embedding ways to engage to retain employees

HRCI defines *human capital* as the "employees' knowledge, talent and skills that add to the value of the organization." In strategic planning, the term *human capital management* is a staffing-planning approach that views individuals as assets to be used in achieving business outcomes. In this way, employees are resources that must have a strategic, planned-for use in order to not be wasted. This is most often organized through a human capital management plan.

Human Capital Management Plans

During the strategic planning process, HR, along with all other business functions, develops tactical goals and action plans designed to meet the needs of the organization. Forecasting is related to having a deep-level understanding of the organization's current and future staffing needs. This is often done by building a *human capital management plan (HCMP)*.

Also known as a strategic HR plan, an HCMP answers four key questions:

- Where are we now?
- Where do we want to be?
- How will we get there?
- How will we know when we arrive?

To be effective and credible, the HCMP must align with the corporate strategy and goals and help achieve the desired business results. So, the answer to the question "Where do we want to be?" is based on the human capital requirements of the goals in the organization's strategic plan. From there, the HCMP lays out the HR contribution to those goals. The most impactful HCMP is as critical as any marketing plan or R&D road map—something that creates a competitive advantage for the organization.

The specific requirements of an HCMP will differ in various organizations, but some common components need to be addressed, as described in Table 11.1.

TABLE 11.1 Human capital management plan

Component	Description
HR statement of strategic direction	The HR team gathers information from the organization's strategic plan, external sources (such as labor market demographics), and internal sources (other functional areas of the organization), and so on, to clearly understand the workforce requirements for organization goals, what resources are available to achieve those goals, and the timing of deliverables.
Desired results or goals	Broadly stated, what will the HR function contribute to the organization's strategic goals? For example, "Attract and retain skilled workers to assemble the new product line."
Objectives	What, specifically, will HR do to achieve its goals? For example, "Reduce time to hire."
Action plans	Identify the steps to be taken to achieve the objectives. For example, "Hire contract recruiter with expertise in sourcing candidates with required skills."
Communication plan	If necessary to achieve the objective, describe how HR will notify the organization of changes. For example, "Conduct workshop for production supervisors on hiring for retention."
Measurement	The means used to measure success of the HCMP coincide with other measures used by the organization. For example, if the technical workforce in the production department needs to be increased to accommodate a new product line, a hiring target of *x* number of employees can be used. For other types of objectives, metrics such as retention rate, ROI, and so on may be more appropriate.

Information developed during the HCMP is necessary for creating the HR function budget. As with any functional area budget, some standard expense items are under the control of the head of the HR functions, such as the following:

- Salaries
- Payroll taxes

- Benefits
- Equipment and supplies
- Repairs and maintenance
- Training and development (for HR team)
- Travel
- Professional services
- Outsourced services (human resource information systems [HRISs], payroll, and so on)

The budget may also include expenses that are allocated from budgets created in other functional areas, such as the following:

- Liability insurance (often managed by the accounting or finance function)
- Software (often purchased through the IT function)
- Computer hardware (often purchased through the IT function)

In some organizations, the HR function creates budget items that are then allocated to other functional business units, such as the following:

- Training and development
- Employee awards
- Performance increases
- Temporary replacements
- Recruiting fees

Positioning HR as a strategic partner also requires scrutiny of current HR practices with an eye toward streamlining them to increase organizational productivity and to provide better service to internal customers. This could mean replacing the HR department head count with outsourced services, implementing an employee self-service system, or implementing an HRIS that provides managers with access to information about their direct reports. These and similar process changes can reduce HR department costs and free professionals to spend more time on other organization issues.

Human Capital Projections

The "human" in human resources refers to the people getting the work done on behalf of the organization. *Human capital projecting* is a budgetary activity in which HR attempts to measure the value of these resources. These projections take into account the elements of the HCMP, creating depth by identifying the current competencies of the existing internal workforce. Further creating the competitive advantage, the process analyzes the skill set of the current employees and matches it to the skill sets necessary to accomplish the strategic objectives. From here, the gap is documented, and a plan is created to develop the competencies necessary to meet performance targets. These projections take into account the following:

- The necessary skill set of the workforce to achieve both short- and long-term objectives as communicated through the strategic plan

- The current skill set of the workforce, measured through skills inventories/assessments and the performance management system
- The creation of a plan to address any deficiencies
- The decision to build or buy/develop the talent in-house or hire from the external labor force
- The cost of implementation
- The return on the investment in the human resource

One example of a strategic consideration related to human capital management is the national unemployment rate. It's often a great moment to "buy" talent from outside the organization in times of high unemployment, because the surplus of available labor and knowledge resources allows companies to compete at far less cost than in a healthy economic climate. Although it may seem at first glance that freezing hiring in times of economic stress is a good strategy, HR must make the argument for hiring when the right conditions exist, calculate the ROI, and align the hiring behavior with the organizational objectives.

Many state and local resources are available to help employers make strategic hiring decisions. Analyzing the labor market using these resources can yield data such as the availability of training reimbursement dollars from government agencies, the unemployment rate, cost of living, wage data, the skill set of the labor force population in the area, and hiring support, such as through state unemployment agencies.

Another example of a strategic need is that of global staffing. While there are other exams that deal with multinational corporations and operating on an international scale, U.S. employers are increasingly seeking talent from global sources. Conversely, an interesting trend that is emerging is that of international companies scooping up U.S. workers for remote roles, further increasing competition for talent. This grew even more rapidly in response to the rise in the interest and availability in remote roles post-pandemic. It is primarily due to the idea that employers want to attract and hire the best talent in order to compete in their industries, regardless of where they were born. A strategy of global sourcing for talent will require changes in all functional areas of HR. From a staffing perspective, the use of technology and virtual interviewing skills and the management of employment visas—become part of the process. On a compensation level, immigration-related perks such as housing may become necessary. Cultural awareness for both the new hires and existing employees through diversity initiatives would also be useful for this staffing strategy to be successful.

Finally, with the shift of U.S. labor output from manufacturing to service, it has become necessary to measure knowledge and mind competencies rather than only the objective, such as physical output. This requires a shift in the way employers structure jobs, upskill or reskill workers, and measure results.

The Impact of the Business Lifecycle

Talent forecasting is much more than guesswork. In this way, the business lifecycle may help inform decisions.

The *business cycle* refers to the stages a company goes through from infancy (startup), to growth, through maturity and then decline. Holistically, how a company does business is significantly influenced by HR behaviors at each stage. From a talent acquisition perspective, it is narrower in focus.

The ability of HR to forecast staffing needs at each stage of the business lifecycle is imperative. For example, companies needing costly talent during the infancy stage may need HR to create Total Rewards packages that include equity compensation at the expense of higher base pay, for example. By adding a vesting component, HR may also use this same approach to increase retention as the company works to survive the early years.

It is also possible for an organization to need multiple staffing strategies at once. For example, in 2023 Amazon completed the first phase of their second headquarters (HQ2) in Northern Virginia, generating an estimated 50,000 new jobs. Prior to this, Amazon threatened to move their Seattle operations in response to a proposed tax of $275 per employee per year to address affordable housing. For a company with 45,000 employees at the Seattle location, this would have prompted the need for simultaneous termination and talent acquisition strategies. They most likely considered a separation strategy of a *reduction in force*, defined by HRCI as a type of temporary or permanent layoff due to lack of funding or change in work requirements. It may also have resulted in HR offering *relocation services* for qualified employees willing to move to a new location. Relocation services can include offering pre-departure orientation, home finding, tax and legal advice, and other country-specific support. Many staffing strategies are driven by two types of organizational changes: workforce expansion and workforce reduction.

Workforce Expansion

An organization may decide to expand its workforce in order to accomplish business objectives. For example, if the strategic plan calls for increasing sales by 15 percent, leaders may determine that achieving that goal requires increasing the salesforce.

A company choosing to grow by starting a *greenfield operation* (defined by HRCI as a "new business facility built in a new location") will most likely need to staff it from the ground up. Conversely, a *brownfield operation* is the "reuse of land previously used for industry or manufacturing."

A *merger and acquisition (M&A)* involves one company purchasing another, or two companies combining to form a new entity. It aims to leverage strengths, expand market share, or acquire new capabilities and in some cases, acquire new talent. For example, one trend to watch is that within the cannabis industry. As regulations of the industry become less restrictive, many large corporations in industries such as food and pharmaceuticals may take action by acquiring the smaller, independent entities that grow, process, or sell cannabis. *Due diligence* will be an important element to these mergers and acquisitions. HRCI defines due diligence as "the gathering and analysis of important information related to a business acquisition or merger, such as assets and liabilities, contracts, and benefit plans." Additionally, risk management enters the picture as a need to review past tax and legal history as well as banking records. Although the gathering of data is certainly important, many senior leaders may also be called upon to help interpret the data and analyze risk, making recommendations in the process for the longer term.

M&As can occur through stock purchases, asset acquisitions, or other financial transactions, reshaping industries and markets. One example of a merger and acquisition that reshaped a business landscape is the acquisition of WhatsApp by Facebook in 2014. This deal, valued at $19 billion, allowed Facebook to expand its reach in the messaging app market and solidify its position as a dominant player in the social media and communication industry.

HR senior leaders play an important role in managing employee integration during M&As by implementing several key strategies:

- **Communication:** Maintain transparent communication with employees regarding the M&A process, including timelines, changes, and expectations.
- **Cultural Integration:** Assess and address cultural differences between the merging entities to foster a cohesive organizational culture.
- **Talent Assessment:** Evaluate talent from both organizations to identify key performers, address skill gaps, and ensure retention of critical employees.
- **Leadership Development:** Develop and support leaders to effectively manage teams through the transition and promote alignment with the new company direction.
- **Change Management:** Implement change management strategies to minimize disruption, manage resistance, and facilitate a smooth transition for employees.
- **Employee Support:** Provide resources, support, and avenues for employees to voice concerns, ask questions, and navigate changes effectively.
- **Performance Management:** Establish clear performance expectations and metrics aligned with the new organizational goals, providing feedback and recognition to motivate employees.

By focusing on these areas, HR senior leaders can facilitate a successful integration process, mitigate risks, and maximize the potential benefits of the M&A for both the organization and its employees.

A *joint venture* is a strategic partnership between two or more companies to collaborate on a specific project or venture. Each party contributes resources, expertise, and capital to achieve mutual goals and share risks and rewards. Joint ventures allow companies to leverage each other's strengths and expand into new markets or ventures collectively.

Integration in joint ventures presents unique challenges, including aligning different organizational cultures, structures, and management styles. Negotiating decision-making processes, resource allocation, and governance mechanisms becomes crucial. Additionally, managing expectations, addressing power dynamics, and ensuring effective communication among partners are paramount. Balancing autonomy with collaboration and navigating potential conflicts require careful attention to foster successful integration and partnership longevity.

Workforce Reduction

Whether necessitated by a restructuring, a merger, or an acquisition, or in response to a loss of market share, reducing labor costs is a painful result of some business decisions. There are many examples of workforce reductions in the business environment, including the job losses that occurred during the dot.com bust of 2000–2001 and the many tech sector layoffs in the mid-2000s, to the more recent post-COVID turmoil in the hospitality industry.

Other companies are choosing to downsize due to factors other than poor organizational performance or external market forces such as a global pandemic. Consider McDonald's, the popular hamburger restaurant, who restructured their corporate offices resulting in layoffs at all levels of the business. This was an effort to cut more than $500 million in general and administrative expenses. McDonald's was also one of the first restaurants to implement self-serve kiosks as part of a broader trend in the fast-food industry to reduce labor costs, especially in response to rising minimum wages. McDonald's began installing self-serve kiosks in 2015, and this trend has accelerated with recent minimum wage increases, including the $20 per hour minimum wage for fast-food workers in California, which took effect in April 2024. This has led to increased adoption of kiosks to offset higher labor costs, potentially impacting job numbers through layoffs.

Divestitures are another element that will dictate the talent needs of an organization. In some cases, a parent company may not have the proper resources necessary to take the business unit to the next level, so selling it off or "divesting" from it makes the most sense. In other cases, a business unit may be consuming a disproportionate amount of company resources—time, labor, and financial—making a divestiture the best way to free up these resources and bolster cash flow. As with mergers and acquisitions, retention of key talent is HR's priority throughout the event. This goal can be accomplished through typical retention efforts, but it may be necessary to narrowly focus the efforts on accountability. This may include a management development program to actively engage managers in the retention process. As many HR pros already know, managers may be the most influential link to whether an employee stays or leaves.

A *severance* package may be used as a risk management tool to help employers avoid employment discrimination claims. Defined by HRCI as "an additional payment (other than salary) given to an employee when employment termination occurs," a severance package may also help to reward separating workers for years of service and offset lost employee wages due to other downsizing events.

Strategic Recruiting and Selection

Strategic recruitment and selection is a proactive approach employed by organizations to attract, identify, and hire top talent in alignment with their long-term goals and objectives. It involves a systematic process of sourcing candidates, assessing their suitability through various means such as interviews, tests, and simulations, and ultimately selecting the most qualified individuals who possess the required skills and experience and align with the company's culture and values. By strategically planning recruitment efforts, organizations can anticipate their future workforce needs, identify potential skill gaps, and develop tailored recruitment strategies to address these gaps effectively. This is the primary purpose of workforce planning.

The focus of strategic selection extends beyond the mere filling of vacant positions; it includes building talent pipelines from internal and external sources for current staffing needs, future staffing needs through upskilling and reskilling, and preparing leaders. Senior leaders must also nurture relationships with potential candidates, and continuously refine recruitment strategies based on market trends and organizational needs. These approaches involve leveraging various recruitment channels such as job boards, social media platforms, employee referrals, and partnerships with educational institutions or industry associations to cast a wide net and attract a diverse pool of candidates.

Building the Employer Brand

Phrases such as "employer of choice" and "best places to work" are designed to communicate to potential employees (and others) the *employer brand*. HRCI defines the employer brand as "the image the employer presents to its employees, stakeholders and customers." Branding is a form of labor market positioning that communicates a message about what it is like to work for the employer. Employer branding is essential and ongoing, meaning that what the employer does in their marketplaces at any given time—not just when recruiting—has a significant impact on its reputation. For this reason, the brand messaging should be positive and honest, highlighting an employer's corporate responsibility and how they behave toward employees. Often, the brand is not only communicated by the employer; many employees via word of mouth and through social media are telling a story about what the employer values. Consider the transportation company Uber, when a video of their then CEO went viral of him berating a driver for asking questions about the future of the company. Or the story of a Zappos employee spending more than nine hours on the phone with a customer—and the company supporting it. Consumers as well as passive job seekers take in this information, and both consciously and unconsciously develop judgments based on it.

Not only is the brand communicated through actions that affect employees, it also sends a message about what the employer values as an organization. For example, when a popular airline was fined over $1 million for leaving passengers stranded on the tarmac for more than three hours during the busy holiday travel season, the negative press fundamentally hurt the brand. Compare that to the perception of Virgin Airline's CEO Richard Branson, who is known for valuing his passengers (and employees). Which culture would most people prefer to work for?

Targeted messaging efforts may also be part of a senior leader's role. The reason for this is that not all individuals are looking for the same thing from an employer. By building applicant profiles, and then targeting messages through marketing efforts, the employer is most likely to achieve a stronger job and organizational fit by "hiring right."

An *employee value proposition (EVP)* is also part of the branding effort. HRCI defines an EVP as "the balance of benefits and rewards an employee receives in return for their performance on the job. In addition to compensation, intangible rewards may include development opportunities, challenging and meaningful work, or an attractive organizational culture." This may include tangibles such as pay and benefits and intangibles such as brand awareness and reputation. An example of providing an intangible benefit is the company Which Wich Superior Sandwiches (a *franchise* business model, defined by HRCI as a business that sells and receives ongoing payments for licenses to use a trademark, product, or service). The company hosts an annual event each summer where patrons and employees decorate sandwich bags with patriotic drawings. The finished bags are put on display and eventually filled with goodies and sent to active and veteran military service members. This event communicates to employees and customers some of what the company values. This effort would be attractive to individuals (customers, applicants, potential franchise owners) who share those same values.

Senior-level HR leaders must understand how the brand affects employees and other stakeholders while serving as advisers to management. Ways to manage the branding process are varied, but many experts agree that a significant portion of it occurs online. According to CareerBuilder, 64 percent of candidates said they research a company online and 37 percent said they will move on to another job opening if they can't find information on the company. Other more traditional ways to build the employer brand include participating in job fairs, presence at community events or sponsorships, and media advertising, even when not hiring for open positions. Other examples include hosting developmental workshops on college campuses, sponsoring local college sports teams, and building apprenticeship programs for difficult-to-fill roles. These activities help individuals become familiar with the brand, a form of continuous recruitment to the organization as opposed to recruitment for a specific job.

Actively managing the brand requires that the company first understands how the brand is perceived in the relevant markets. This is followed by taking an objective look at what the company says it values and what HR programs support those values. Where there is a gap, interventions may be designed to build programs or embed practices that support the company values and increase congruency. Lastly, transparency about where the company is currently and where they want to be is key. One Glassdoor survey discovered that 96 percent of job seekers say that it's important to work for a company that embraces transparency. Employees (and customers) are increasingly coming to value transparency as a driver of business outcomes. In this way, the employer brand may serve as an employee retention tool as well.

Job Analysis

Job analysis serves as the foundational step in strategic recruiting and selection processes by providing a comprehensive understanding of the specific requirements and responsibilities associated with a given role within an organization. Through job analysis, critical information such as essential skills, competencies, qualifications, and behavioral attributes are identified and documented. This detailed understanding enables recruiters and hiring managers to develop targeted recruitment strategies, including crafting job postings, determining suitable sourcing channels, and designing selection criteria aligned with the demands of the position. Job analysis facilitates the alignment of recruitment efforts with organizational goals and objectives, ensuring that the individuals selected possess the capabilities necessary to contribute effectively to the achievement of strategic objectives. When done correctly, job analysis enables organizations to attract, assess, and select candidates who are best suited to drive organizational success.

Operational and strategic job analysis methods in the workplace differ in their focus, scope, and purpose. Whereas PHR and PHRi candidates focus on operational job analysis methods and filling immediate job vacancies, SPHR and SPHRi senior leaders are responsible for overseeing the entire talent acquisition process.

Strategic job analysis methods take a broader and forward-thinking approach, aligning job roles and responsibilities with long-term organizational goals and objectives. Strategic methods, such as job analysis workshops, task inventories, and job documentation review, focus on forecasting future workforce needs, identifying emerging skill requirements, and adapting job roles to changes in technology or industry trends. By combining operational and strategic job analysis methods, organizations can ensure that their workforce remains aligned with both immediate operational needs and long-term strategic objectives.

Data Literacy

Utilizing data-driven insights and analytics to make informed hiring decisions is an important facet for senior HR leaders to consider. Data-driven insights and analytics increases the likelihood of selecting candidates who possess the requisite skills and demonstrate potential for long-term success and growth within the organization.

Internally, data analytics can provide valuable insights into the performance and behavior of current employees, helping to identify patterns of success and characteristics correlated with high performance. By analyzing metrics such as employee turnover rates, promotion trajectories, and performance evaluations, organizations can develop profiles of ideal candidates and tailor their recruitment efforts to target individuals who align closely with these profiles. Data analytics can help identify potential skill gaps within the existing workforce, allowing organizations to prioritize recruitment efforts in areas where specific talents are lacking, thus ensuring a more balanced and effective talent pool.

Externally, data insights enable organizations to gain a deeper understanding of the talent market landscape, including demographic trends, skill shortages, and emerging job roles. By leveraging external data sources such as labor market reports, industry surveys, and competitor analyses, organizations can anticipate future talent needs and proactively adjust their recruitment strategies accordingly. Data-driven insights can inform decisions regarding the most effective recruitment channels and messaging to reach and engage with potential candidates. For example, by analyzing the effectiveness of various recruitment platforms and marketing campaigns, organizations can allocate resources more efficiently and maximize their return on investment in recruitment efforts.

One prominent example of a company that leverages data analytics to create a recruiting strategy is Google. Google's human resources department, known as People Operations or "People Ops," extensively utilizes data analytics throughout the entire recruitment process. Google collects and then analyzes vast amounts of data from résumés, interview feedback, performance evaluations, and employee surveys to identify patterns and predictors of success.

Google employs sophisticated algorithms to assess the likelihood of a candidate's fit within the company culture and their potential for long-term success. For instance, they use data to identify specific traits or experiences that correlate with high performance in certain roles and then actively seek out candidates who possess these characteristics. Additionally, Google continuously monitors and evaluates the effectiveness of its recruitment strategies by analyzing metrics such as time-to-hire, candidate satisfaction, and retention rates.

By leveraging data analytics in this way, Google not only ensures that they attract top talent but also continuously refines and optimizes their recruiting processes to adapt to changing market conditions and organizational needs. This data-driven approach has played a significant role in Google's reputation as a leader in talent acquisition and employer branding.

Real World Scenario

Hilton Hotels' Transformation in Talent Acquisition Through AI

Hilton Hotels, a global leader in the hospitality industry, faced significant challenges in talent acquisition. The company struggled with lengthy hiring processes and difficulty in identifying top talent from a large pool of applicants. To overcome these issues, Hilton implemented artificial intelligence (AI) to help transform its recruitment strategy.

Hilton's traditional recruitment process involved manual résumé screenings, leading to prolonged hiring times, and they had difficulty in identifying the most suitable candidates from a large applicant pool. This was in part due to their inconsistent interview processes across different locations. To address these issues, Hilton integrated AI-driven tools into their recruitment process, which included:

- **AI-Powered Screening:** Hilton implemented AI tools to automate résumé screening. These tools used natural language processing (NLP) to scan résumés for relevant keywords and qualifications, significantly reducing the initial screening time.
- **Chatbots for Initial Engagement:** AI-powered chatbots were introduced to engage with candidates at the initial stages. These chatbots answered frequently asked questions, scheduled interviews, and provided updates on application status, creating a sense of a connected candidate experience.

- **Predictive Analytics:** Hilton used predictive analytics to identify candidates who were more likely to succeed in their roles. By analyzing historical data and performance metrics, the AI tools helped to shortlist candidates who matched the company's success profiles.

The implementation of AI in Hilton's talent acquisition process led to significant improvements. The AI tools reduced the time taken to fill positions by 75 percent, and the use of chatbots and automated processes provided a more engaging and responsive experience for candidates. The use of predictive analytics helped in identifying high-potential candidates, leading to better hiring decisions and improved employee performance over time.

Sources:

`https://www.forbes.com/sites/neilsahota/2024/03/06/ai-in-hospitality-elevating-the-hotel-guest-experience-through-innovation`

`https://www.hospitalitynet.org/opinion/4122644.html`

Managing Salary Expectations

The holiday season of 2018 was anticipated to be record-breaking for online retailers. This presented a challenge for airlines needing to keep pilots in the air to deliver packages across the globe. In response, freight companies such as FedEx Corporation offered retirement-age pilots bonuses of up to $100,000 to stay on through the holiday season. This is one example of how companies are using their Total Rewards programs to respond to the critical skill shortages happening on an international scale.

Strategically, the short-term solution of FedEx is a single response to a much larger talent shortage issue throughout many professions, including IT, nursing, and trucking. A blended approach using Total Rewards to improve retention, along with other workforce planning strategies such as partnering with universities and in-house training programs, are ways senior-level HR leaders can help their employers in a tight labor market. Competitively, this may mean that employers will need to pay above the 50th percentile of market wages and then manage issues such as *pay compression* within their employee wage bands. Pay compression occurs when incumbent pay rates do not keep up with market conditions.

Developmental rewards may also be part of an overall strategy. Attracting candidates through policies such as tuition reimbursement for future education, paying off student loans, and offering paid volunteer time are all ways HR is using Total Rewards programs to attract (and keep) talent.

Retaining senior leaders is another area for SPHR/i candidates to have a general understanding of. Executive compensation levels have long been understood to be complex, with many boards expressing the need to understand and communicate how C-suite performance is linked to large, six-figure-and-above salaries. This not only has an internal impact but can affect the brand as well. The negative press received by the U.S. Department of Veterans

Affairs in response to executive bonuses of upward of $100 million amidst the scandal of patient care required a rapid revamp of the executive pay program. More often than not, senior-level HR professionals will need to influence the development of Total Rewards strategies that link executive pay to performance. HR may also be called upon to develop the "golden" strategies (such as golden handcuffs) described in Chapter 13, "Total Rewards," in order to retain executives.

Employee Integration

Employee integration is the systematic process of assimilating and orienting recently hired individuals into the organizational culture, roles, and processes to ensure their successful transition and contribution to the company. The behavioral sciences give us a view of the topic of employee integration, also called *employee socialization*. Integration occurs when new members learn the social and task expectations of their role. For companies that focus strictly on task orientation, the value of the social aspect gets lost or underutilized. It has long been understood that humans are social creatures, ones with emotions and a need to belong. Consider, for example, the last time you started a new job. What feelings existed? If you are like many, there was a mix of both excitement and anxiety. The socialization process can be a valuable time to help individuals navigate these feelings while also exposing them to the company mission, vision, values, and culture.

Senior HR leaders manage strategic employee integrations by aligning talent with organizational objectives. They develop comprehensive integration plans, incorporating cultural assimilation, role clarity, and performance expectations. Clear communication is prioritized, ensuring employees understand their roles and contributions. HR facilitates cross-functional collaboration, fostering teamwork and knowledge sharing. Senior leaders provide ongoing support, addressing challenges promptly and adjusting strategies as needed. They track progress against integration goals, leveraging data and feedback to refine processes. By proactively managing strategic employee integrations, HR leaders optimize talent utilization, enhance organizational effectiveness, and foster a cohesive, high-performing workforce poised for success.

Strategic considerations of onboarding new employees and managing cultural integrations include:

- **Alignment with Organizational Values:** Ensure that the onboarding process reflects the company's values, mission, and culture to instill a sense of belonging and purpose from the outset.
- **Customized Onboarding Plans:** Tailor onboarding programs to meet the needs of different roles, levels, and departments, providing relevant information and resources for each employee's success.
- **Cross-cultural Training:** Offer training programs to facilitate cultural understanding and integration, promoting collaboration and synergy among diverse teams.

- **Clear Communication Channels:** Establish open lines of communication to address questions, concerns, and feedback during the onboarding process, fostering transparency and trust.
- **Buddy/Mentor Programs:** Pair new employees with experienced colleagues or mentors to provide guidance, support, and integration into the company culture.
- **Continuous Feedback and Evaluation:** Regularly assess the effectiveness of onboarding and cultural integration initiatives, making adjustments based on feedback and outcomes to enhance future experiences.
- **Celebrating Diversity:** Embrace and celebrate diversity within the organization, recognizing the unique perspectives and contributions of employees from different backgrounds.

Integrating Virtual Teams

With the rise of hybrid and fully remote work, of special note are onboarding and engaging a workforce of virtual employees.

Challenges to integrating new virtual team members include communication barriers due to lack of face-to-face interaction, difficulty in establishing rapport and building relationships remotely, potential feelings of isolation or disconnection, varying time zones leading to scheduling conflicts, and navigating cultural differences without the benefit of in-person cues. Additionally, misalignment in expectations, unclear role definitions, and limited access to resources or support systems can hinder the seamless integration of virtual team members. Maintaining engagement, addressing technology issues, and fostering a sense of belonging in a virtual environment are also common challenges.

Since the use of technology is critical to the success of these work structures, videoconferencing may be a successful strategy to begin with face-to-face encounters. Other companies tackle engagement of remote or virtual workers through the use of boot-camp style events, where members are brought together for immersion sessions on topics ranging from company culture to performance expectations.

Other best practices for integrating virtual team members involve establishing clear communication channels from the start. This may involve creating a virtual directory with employee headshots, their title, and reporting structure to help new employees get a sense of the team. Technology is the main format used for several integration activities, including collaboration, regular check-ins, and fostering a sense of belonging through team-building activities.

Clarity can be elusive, yet it is a critical component to successful integration. Assigning clear roles and responsibilities, providing necessary resources, and setting realistic expectations are essential. Encouraging autonomy while promoting a culture of trust and accountability fosters productivity and engagement. Additionally, recognizing and celebrating achievements, addressing challenges promptly, and soliciting feedback ensure continuous improvement and team cohesion.

Real World Scenario

Rapid Response in Remote Work

In the week of March 13, 2020, Zoom experienced exponential growth as global lockdowns due to COVID-19 drove a massive shift to remote work and virtual meetings. Daily users surged from 10 million in December 2019 to over 200 million by March 2020. This increase was fueled by businesses, schools, and individuals turning to Zoom for videoconferencing, leading to a 20-fold user growth in just three months. This surge required Zoom to rapidly scale its operations and infrastructure, and to develop the ability to scale its talent acquisition strategies to handle the increased demand and maintain service quality. This in turn created a favorable competitive market position.

Source:

Adapted from Reuters. Zoom pulls in more than 200 million daily video users during worldwide lockdowns, April, 2020. `https://www.reuters.com`.

Global Integration

Global expansion necessitates workforce expansion to meet the demands of new markets, capitalize on emerging opportunities, and maintain competitiveness. As companies extend their operations internationally, they require a diverse talent pool with local expertise and cultural understanding.

Global expansion requires special efforts of senior HR leaders to culturally integrate the new team members. Three strategies for managing cultural integrations are as follows:

Cross-Cultural Training Implement comprehensive training programs to promote understanding and appreciation of diverse cultural norms, values, and communication styles among employees. This helps mitigate misunderstandings and fosters collaboration across multicultural teams.

Cultural Ambassadors Appoint individuals within the organization who possess cultural knowledge and sensitivity to serve as liaisons or ambassadors. They can facilitate communication, mediate conflicts, and provide guidance on navigating cultural nuances.

Integration Workshops and Events Organize workshops, team-building activities, and cultural events that encourage interaction and relationship-building among employees from different cultural backgrounds.

Challenges may arise from cultural differences, language barriers, and logistical complexities, so HR teams should evaluate the effectiveness of these programs and intervene where necessary. This effort should be ongoing. By investing in workforce expansion aligned with global growth strategies, companies can leverage local talent, enhance market responsiveness, and establish a strong international competitive presence.

Summary

Strategic workplace planning and talent acquisition is an important function for senior HR leaders that goes beyond the operational aspects of recruiting, selection, and onboarding. This functional area of HR helps organizations achieve sustainable growth and maintain competitiveness in their relevant market. By proactively identifying and developing talent with the potential to take on expanded roles and responsibilities, organizations can foster innovation, agility, and resilience.

The planning process begins with strategic analysis to understand the various factors that influence an organization's competitive position in the labor market. This entails a comprehensive evaluation of both internal and external factors to inform decision-making processes and ensure alignment with organizational objectives. From this, strategic goals are developed, and human capital management plans are created.

Workforce planning and talent acquisition activities take place throughout the stages of the business lifecycle, requiring creative interventions to meet the varying talent needs of each stage. These needs are shaped by many factors, including salary expectations, managing the employer brand, and integration needs driven by business strategy.

Exam Essentials

Lead the efforts of strategic workforce planning. The primary focus of a strategic workforce plan is that it is strictly tied to company goals and objectives. This requires the abilities of senior-level HR leaders to forecast labor needs and identify gaps, using a human capital management plan to outline action steps and metrics. This may also require the development of short-term replacement plans and longer-term succession planning.

Organize and implement the staffing process. While highly operational in nature, the recruiting and selection process is the means by which the strategic workforce plan is implemented. Senior leaders must take into account factors such as the current skill set of employees, the availability of talent in the labor market, the impact of wages on hiring and retention, as well as the current and proposed labor laws at both a federal and a state level. These and other factors are influenced by how a business and corresponding jobs are structured.

Communicate the employer brand. The employer brand continues to be a decisive force in attracting and retaining a talented workforce. HR may help the executive team objectively analyze the brand and how it is perceived, then build HR programs and policies to shape a healthy brand image in their relevant labor markets.

Manage employee integrations. Virtual teams, global expansion and structural strategies like mergers and acquisitions and joint ventures all have unique employee integration needs with solutions defined by senior HR leaders. Factors that must be considered include communication, role clarity, and creative engagement and retention approaches.

Review Questions

You can find the answers in Appendix A.

1. What is the primary objective of workforce planning?
   A. Maximizing short-term profits
   B. Identifying potential areas for cost-cutting
   C. Aligning human capital with organizational goals
   D. Minimizing employee turnover
2. Which of the following best describes the purpose of strategic talent planning? (Choose all that apply.)
   A. Avoiding laying off in one department while hiring in another
   B. Identifying potential areas for outsourcing
   C. Aligning talent management strategies with long-term organizational goals
   D. Implementing performance appraisal systems to evaluate employee productivity
3. Human capital projecting is a form of which of the following? (Choose all that apply.)
   A. Budgeting
   B. Planning
   C. Analyzing
   D. Sourcing
4. Which of the following is an external example of data used to make human capital projections?
   A. Skills inventories
   B. Regional salary information
   C. Availability of off-the-shelf training software
   D. The organization's core competencies
5. The corporate offices for which you direct human resources have decided to explore opening a plant in Sparks, Nevada. They have heard that companies such as Tesla and `Chewy.com` have opened centers there, and they want to identify whether this is a business strategy they should follow. They have asked you to put together an analysis of the labor market. Which of the following resources would be the best place to start?
   A. The local newspaper
   B. Nevada Chamber of Commerce
   C. Nevada Department of Employment and Training
   D. A real estate broker

6. The company you work for is in an industry with a national unemployment rate of less than 5 percent. Your company projects that you will need to begin hiring for skilled labor within the next six months. What strategies should you consider? (Choose all that apply.)
   A. Building a training program to promote from within
   B. Budgeting for engagement programs to retain key talent
   C. Redesign of jobs
   D. Reskilling employees where appropriate

7. Which of the following best describes the focus of employee integration?
   A. Educating the new hire about the social aspects of the workplace
   B. Having employees complete the required new hire paperwork
   C. Touring the facility and introducing the employee
   D. Helping the employee socialize in the first 90 days

8. Which of the following workforce planning activities serves as the foundation for all other human resource systems?
   A. Recruiting
   B. Job analysis
   C. Strategic planning
   D. Employee socialization

9. The company you work for prides itself on its mission to "grow the people that manufacture the most innovative products that make us money." Which of the following interview questions best predicts candidate success with this company?
   A. Tell us about a recent time you learned something new.
   B. What would your previous manager tell us about your work ethic?
   C. If you were an animal, what kind of animal would you be?
   D. Where do you professionally want to be in the next 5 years?

10. Which of the following best describes the role of data in strategic recruiting?
    A. Data is primarily used to randomly select candidates for interviews.
    B. Data helps recruiters make informed decisions based on historical trends and predictive analytics.
    C. Data is irrelevant in the recruitment process as it often leads to biased hiring decisions.
    D. Data is used to track the number of applications received for each job posting.

11. What is considered a best practice for achieving global integration in a joint venture?
    A. Implementing uniform HR policies across all partner countries
    B. Encouraging autonomy and independence among partner subsidiaries
    C. Embracing cultural diversity and fostering cross-cultural communication
    D. Maximizing communication and collaboration between partner organizations

12. Which one of the following is not a strategic recruitment activity?
    A. Labor market analysis
    B. The design of Total Rewards packages
    C. Employee referral programs
    D. Defining the employer brand
13. Which one of the following is not a human capital management activity?
    A. Analyzing the labor market
    B. Designing Total Rewards packages
    C. Freezing hiring
    D. Conducting skills inventories
14. In which of the following scenarios would the use of a severance package be appropriate? (Choose all that apply.)
    A. To offset lost income to employees due to company reductions in force
    B. To avoid a wrongful termination claim
    C. To reward a retiring worker for years of service
    D. When an employee is being laid off after several years of service
15. Analyzing the future hiring needs for an annual strategic plan is the best example of which of the following?
    A. HR budgeting
    B. Workforce planning
    C. Forecasting
    D. Data analytics
16. The large chocolate manufacturing plant in your town recently moved its operations to Mexico, leaving a large food-grade manufacturing plant sitting empty. The local paper announced that another chocolate factory will be purchasing the land and moving its operations there by the end of the year. This is the best example of which of the following?
    A. A brownfield operation
    B. A greenfield operation
    C. A workforce plan
    D. An acquisition
17. The large auto parts manufacturer for which you work has recently purchased land in an adjacent city and plans to build an additional warehouse. This is the best example of which of the following?
    A. A brownfield operation
    B. A greenfield operation
    C. A workforce plan
    D. An acquisition

18. Labor market analysis and defining the employer brand are activities of which of the following senior-level activities?

A. Benchmarking

B. Candidate sourcing

C. Strategic recruitment

D. Employee selection

19. Which of the following is the best example of the employer value proposition?

A. Competitive salary and benefits package

B. Access to professional development opportunities

C. Flexible work hours and remote work options

D. An inclusive company culture

20. The company you work for prides itself on its reputation for innovation, employee development, and commitment to corporate social responsibility initiatives. In its latest recruitment campaign on social media, the company highlights its work in underprivileged communities by partnering with local high schools to develop the skills needed for the future workforce. Which of the following is the company communicating in its recruiting posts?

A. Its diversity initiatives

B. Their desire to be an inclusive place of work

C. The employer brand

D. Corporate governance initiatives

Chapter 12

SPHR | SPHRi Exam: Talent Management

SPHR AND SPHRi RESPONSIBILITIES:

DEVELOPING AND DESIGNING TALENT MANAGEMENT PROGRAMS AND INITIATIVES THAT FOSTER AN ENGAGING AND HIGH PERFORMING WORKFORCE.

- ✓ **3.1 Evaluate the integration of diversity, equity, and inclusion (DEI) in the workplace culture and make recommendations based on findings**
- ✓ **3.2 Design, implement, and evaluate programs or processes in order to develop the workforce (for example: training and development, knowledge management, mode, timing)**
- ✓ **3.3 Analyze business needs to develop a succession plan for key roles (for example: identify talent, outline career progression, implement coaching and development) to promote business continuity**
- ✓ **3.4 Design and evaluate strategies for employee engagement, satisfaction, and retention (for example: mentoring and sponsorship, flexible work arrangements)**
- ✓ **3.5 Align team and individual performance goals to organizational measures of success**
- ✓ **3.6 Design and evaluate strategies and processes for performance management (for example: performance evaluation, performance improvement, feedback, coaching)**
- ✓ **3.7 Identify and implement strategies and processes for leadership development (for example: conflict resolution, mentoring, performance discussions, coaching, effective communication)**

- ✓ **3.8 Develop and evaluate employee career and growth opportunities (for example: assessing talent, developing career paths, managing job movement within the organization)**
- ✓ **3.9 Design policies and processes for the return of employees to the organization (for example: parental leave, expatriates returning to home country, employees returning from sabbaticals or layoffs)**
- ✓ **3.10 Create and evaluate labor strategies (for example: collective bargaining, grievance program, strategic alignment with labor, other union-related activities)**
- ✓ **3.11 Design and assess offboarding strategies, processes, and trends (for example: exit interviews, layoff strategies, alumni programs)**

Talent management is a holistic approach that uses HR programs in, according to the Human Resource Certification Institute (HRCI), "recruiting, integrating, and developing new workers, developing and keeping current workers, and attracting skilled workers." For purposes of the SPHR/i, the Talent Management exam content outline (ECO) notes that senior-level HR professionals are tasked with "Developing and designing talent management programs and initiatives that foster an engaging and high performing workforce."

The functional area of Talent Management was created as part of the 2024 updates. It combined three of the former content areas of Employee Relations, Engagement, and Learning and Development. Therefore, Talent Management makes up the second-largest amount of content on the SPHR/i exams, at 23 percent, second only to Leadership and Strategy.

A senior HR leadership team engages a high-performance workforce through talent management by implementing strategic initiatives aimed at attracting, developing, and retaining top talent. This involves aligning HR practices with the organization's goals and values, creating a culture of continuous learning and growth, and providing opportunities for employees to excel and advance in their careers through performance management and career development initiatives. By investing in talent development programs, performance management systems, and employee engagement initiatives, the HR leadership team creates an environment where employees feel valued, motivated, and empowered to contribute their best work, driving organizational success and competitive advantage.

Learning Organizations

Learning organizations are innovative environments in which knowledge is originated, obtained, and freely shared in response to environmental changes that affect the ability of the organization to compete. Defined by HRCI as promoting ongoing employee education and innovation, these organizations are focused on improving their competitiveness through continuous learning. The atmosphere in a learning organization is one in which employees are able to solve problems by experimenting with new methods that have been observed outside the organization or that have been experienced in other parts of the organization.

Talent management and the design of learning organizations are closely related in that both focus on maximizing the potential of employees to drive organizational success. Talent management encompasses strategies for attracting, developing, and retaining top talent within an organization, while the design of learning organizations involves creating a culture and infrastructure that support continuous learning, skill development, and knowledge sharing among employees. By integrating talent management practices with the principles of learning organization design, organizations can create environments where employees are empowered to grow. This alignment ensures that talent development efforts are aligned with organizational goals and that learning is embedded within the ecosystem of the organization's culture and operations.

Peter Senge, author of *The Fifth Discipline: The Art & Practice of the Learning Organization* (Crown Business, revised edition, 2006), identifies five disciplines, or guiding principles, that enable organizations to increase their ability to realize desired results, cultivate new ways of thinking, expand on individual ideas, and encourage continuous lifelong learning in the organization. These disciplines are as follows:

Systems Thinking *Systems thinking* describes the ability of individuals and organizations to recognize patterns and to project how changes will impact them.

Personal Mastery *Personal mastery* describes a high level of expertise in an individual's chosen field and a commitment to lifelong learning.

Mental Models *Mental models* refer to the deep-seated beliefs that color perceptions and can affect how individuals see the world around them and react to it.

Building a Shared Vision Stretching beyond the corporate vision statement and building a *shared vision* encourages the organization to plan for a future that inspires commitment on the part of all individuals in the organization.

Team Learning *Team learning*, as defined by Senge, refers to the ability of a team to share and build on their ideas without holding anything back.

Workforce Development

Once an environment has been created that encourages employee development and growth, HR teams are tasked with designing systems that develop the workforce. Workforce development refers to systematic efforts aimed at enhancing the skills, productivity, and employability of the workforce. This includes activities such as training, education, mentoring, and career development initiatives designed to meet both individual and organizational needs.

SPHR/i exam objective 3.2 tasks senior HR professionals to "design, implement and evaluate programs or processes in order to develop the workforce." These include concepts related to training and development, knowledge management, mode and timing; these are covered next.

Integrated Learning and Development

Several learning and development (L&D) activities occur within the context of an integrated talent management program. As with many other HR functions, the first step is to conduct a *needs assessment* or analysis. Usually defined as a process, a needs analysis assesses "the present situation to determine the steps necessary to reach a desired future goal" (HRCI). The process begins by identifying an organization's strategic goals and is followed by an analysis of the individual, group, or organizational competencies that will be necessary to achieve those goals. Those first two steps will drive the third, which is conducting a gap analysis to compare current state to desired future state, and then design an appropriate intervention plan to bridge the gap.

A needs analysis may be narrow in scope, such as with a training needs or skills assessment, or broader in scope, such as analyzing future business needs that will drive the decision of whether to "build" talent through training and development programs or "buy" talent through acquisition efforts. Both examples require integration of efforts with other HR structures because, as noted in *Chief Learning Officer* magazine, "If talent management involves employee recruitment, development and management—from the time they are identified as candidates until they leave the company—learning becomes a vital thread that binds this entire system" (*Chief Learning Officer*, "What Is Learning's Role in Talent Management?," 2017).

L&D integration is also highly dependent on the needs of the organization. For example, does your company need employees who are innovative and highly skilled at problem-solving? Does the company structure call for individuals who are able to work independently, such as within a virtual environment? These are examples of what can be discovered using an individual needs assessment to identify what type of training or development activities may be necessary to build an employee up for success within the organization. Additionally, there appears to be a shift away from a development strategy that focuses solely on high-potential employees. True talent management involves all employees in the process, from the CEO down to the newest hire.

As a reminder, a training needs assessment and an individual assessment are both tools that should (in the context of supporting business needs) cascade down from the organizational needs identified through the strategic planning process.

Strategic Alignment

As discussed in Chapter 10, "Leadership and Strategy," HR is responsible for collaborating with company leadership to clearly define and communicate the organization's mission, vision, and values to all employees. By ensuring that these core principles are well understood and integrated into the company culture, HR sets the stage for aligning talent management practices throughout the employee lifecycle. Examples of alignment within the lifecycle framework include the following:

- Alignment starts with the recruitment and selection processes. By seeking candidates whose skills, experiences, and personal values align with those of the organization, HR helps to build a workforce that is committed to advancing the company's goals.
- When managing employee performance, it's important to set performance goals and Total Rewards programs that are in line with the company's strategic objectives and that provide regular feedback and recognition to employees who demonstrate behaviors consistent with its values. In this way, culture is determined by what behaviors are rewarded, and what behaviors are incompatible with the organization's values.

- HR facilitates learning and development programs that reinforce the company's mission, vision, and values. By offering learning opportunities that promote new skill development, upskilling, and reskilling, HR helps employees contribute directly to achieving organizational results.
- Managing the separation process in accordance with the company's mission, vision, and values leaves the door open for separating employees to boomerang. A *boomerang employee* is someone who returns to work for a company where they had previously been employed and left in good standing. Boomerang employees can bring several benefits to a company. They often possess institutional knowledge and understanding of the company's culture, which can reduce the time and resources needed for onboarding. In addition, they may have gained new skills or experiences during their time away, which they can bring back to contribute to the organization. Companies increasingly view boomerang employees as valuable assets and may even implement strategies to encourage their return, such as maintaining positive relationships with former employees and maintaining alumni networks.

Training as an Intervention Strategy

When training is selected as a strategic intervention, it is usually because the company has identified a skills gap in the workforce. When aligned with a company's strategic goals, training can support powerful strategic outcomes. The fast-food restaurant chain McDonald's is one example of this. The company partners with local colleges to offer voluntary, free English language classes specifically to prepare current employees for customer-facing roles. Part of a larger "Archways to Opportunity" program, McDonald's pays employees to attend the classes. The return-on-investment of this program is significant when the following program outcomes are considered:

- The program improves customer service and removes language barriers to productivity.
- The program increases employee loyalty and thus retention in a typically high turnover industry.
- The program communicates a commitment to a diverse workforce.
- The program builds skills that result in greater lifetime earnings' potential for the individual, which in turn impacts the communities where they do business.
- The program allows for greater connection with others, which in turn builds stronger relationships, a fundamental human relations activity.

The design and development of training programs will need to take into consideration several factors. In the McDonald's example, the company used a *blended learning* (a method that combines face-to-face teaching with online learning) approach where classes were offered both in person and virtually. This was important, as so much of language learning is dependent on interaction with others. The classes were offered off-site and over a period of 8 to 22 weeks to ensure employees had the support system and proper environment to reinforce the learning. The content was built around work interactions, with titles such as "shift basics" or "shift conversations." McDonald's also designed content for managers around delivering performance feedback. This increased the relevance and applicability of the training content to their jobs.

As you can see by this example, training as part of a larger L&D intervention program can support a company's mission, vision, and values while at the same time providing practical support to the achievement of business goals. The McDonald's scenario also demonstrates the impact of mode and timing on learning outcomes.

In the context of training programs, *mode* refers to the method or format through which the training is delivered. It essentially describes the way in which the training content is presented to the participants. Common modes of training include:

- **In-Person Training:** This involves face-to-face interaction between the trainer and the participants in a physical setting, such as a classroom or conference room.
- **Online Training:** Also known as e-learning or virtual training, this mode utilizes digital platforms and technologies to deliver training content over the Internet. Participants can access the training materials remotely, often at their own pace and convenience.
- **Blended Learning:** This mode combines elements of both in-person and online training. It typically involves a mix of traditional classroom instruction and digital learning components, offering participants flexibility while still incorporating some level of face-to-face interaction.
- **On-the-Job Training:** In this mode, employees learn by performing tasks and duties within their actual work environment, often under the guidance of a more experienced colleague or supervisor.
- **Self-Directed Learning:** This mode empowers individuals to take control of their own learning process. Participants independently seek out and engage with learning materials, resources, and activities according to their own interests and goals.
- **Synchronous vs. Asynchronous***:* These terms refer to whether the training occurs in real time or can be accessed at any time. Synchronous training involves live interaction between the instructor and participants, whereas asynchronous training allows participants to access materials and complete activities at their own pace.

The choice of mode depends on various factors, such as the nature of the content, the preferences and needs of the participants, logistical considerations, and available resources. Different modes may be used alone or in combination to create effective and engaging training programs.

In instructional design, *timing* refers to the strategic allocation of time for learning activities. It involves pacing, sequencing, and duration to optimize learning effectiveness. Pacing ensures learners can absorb content without feeling rushed, while sequencing organizes material in a logical order. Duration balances engagement and practice time, avoiding unnecessary repetition. Effective timing supports engagement, retention, and learning objectives, considering content complexity and learner abilities. Adjustments are based on feedback and evaluation.

For many organizations, identifying training and development needs is included as part of performance management strategies.

Performance Management Strategies

The operational aspect of a robust performance management system is detailed in Chapter 2, "Shared Competencies." This knowledge is important because it serves as a foundation for building strategies that support organizational outcomes. This is the role of senior HR leaders within the domain of performance management.

Strategic performance management takes a macro approach to directing organizational and individual performance toward common objectives. It requires that employees have a clear line of sight between their individual efforts and organizational results.

Strategic performance management also requires a framework for measuring, monitoring, and driving employee performance through activities that go beyond the traditional annual reviews. Strategic performance management is a continuous evaluation and support of employee performance, enabling leaders to closely monitor progress and provide timely feedback. This cultivates employee engagement and loyalty through personalized development plans connected to organizational objectives. Following are the key components of strategic performance management that are likely to be on the exams:

Performance Evaluation Performance evaluation is a systematic process of assessing an employee's job performance against predetermined criteria and standards. It typically involves gathering feedback, analyzing data, and providing employees with constructive feedback on their strengths and areas for improvement. Performance evaluations are often conducted periodically, such as annually or semi-annually, and serve as a basis for decisions related to promotions, compensation, training, and development.

Performance Improvement Performance improvement refers to the process of enhancing an employee's job performance to meet or exceed established goals and expectations. This process involves identifying areas where performance is lacking or could be enhanced, developing action plans to address deficiencies, providing necessary resources and support, and monitoring progress over time. Performance improvement efforts aim to maximize employee potential, productivity, and overall effectiveness within the organization.

Feedback Feedback is information provided to an individual or a group regarding their performance or behavior. It can take various forms, including constructive criticism, praise, suggestions for improvement, and performance evaluations. Effective feedback is timely, specific, and actionable, focusing on both strengths and areas for development. It plays an important role in fostering employee growth, learning, and motivation, as well as improving communication and collaboration within teams and organizations.

Coaching Coaching involves providing guidance, support, and feedback to help individuals improve their skills, achieve their goals, and maximize their potential. Unlike traditional training or instruction, coaching focuses on facilitating self-awareness, problem-solving, and personal development. Coaches work collaboratively with employees to identify strengths, weaknesses, and areas for growth; set achievable goals; and develop action plans to overcome obstacles. Coaching can occur one-on-one or in group settings and is often used to enhance leadership skills, performance, and career development.

Strategic performance management also involves identifying high-potential employees. This allows leaders to create succession plans to generate a pipeline of future leaders.

Succession Planning

Succession planning has both operational and strategic components, and thus, it is covered in more detail in Chapter 2. Specific to the SPHR/i exams, however, is the use of succession plans to promote business continuity.

NOTE

Key person insurance covers individuals within a company whose absence or loss would have a significant impact on the business's operations and financial stability. These key leads can include top executives such as CEOs, CFOs, and COOs, as well as key employees with specialized skills or knowledge critical to the company's success, such as technical experts, top salespersons, or key project managers. These positions should be further supported with succession plans.

Business continuity is the capability of an organization to maintain essential operations and functions during and after a disruptive event such as a natural disaster, cybersecurity attack, or loss of key leaders. Using succession plans to support continued operations begins by identifying and nurturing talented individuals within the company who have the potential to fill key positions in the future. Through succession planning, critical knowledge and skills are systematically transferred from experienced employees to potential successors, documenting essential expertise within the organization. This readiness instills confidence in stakeholders, and increases employee engagement and loyalty by offering professional development and growth opportunities within the organization.

A significant feature of learning, development, and succession plans is a strong focus on knowledge transfer, and this requires that a company has a fully developed knowledge management process.

Career pathing plays an important role in succession plans, as this activity is tied to identifying replacements for attrition events such as promotion or retirement. Career pathing is the strategic process of mapping individual career development to future organizational need and involves goal-setting, skill enhancement, and advancement opportunities.

A career management budget for an HR leader includes provisions for various initiatives such as professional development programs, training workshops, leadership coaching, and mentorship programs. It aims to nurture talent from recruitment through to career progression, ensuring employees have access to opportunities for skill enhancement, career guidance, and leadership cultivation. Funds may be allocated for career counseling services, certification programs, and educational assistance to support employees in achieving their career goals. By investing in such initiatives, HR leaders support a culture of continuous learning and development and demonstrates the organization's commitment to the growth and success of its workforce.

Knowledge Management

During the course of business each day, organizations generate data (such as sales figures) and review it to glean useful information (such as trends). Individual employees then interpret the information based on past experiences with similar circumstances and draw conclusions that are used to move the organization forward. These conclusions are referred to as *knowledge*. Although data and information can be easily replicated by other employees with the right skills, the knowledge that comes from past experiences isn't always so easily repeated. The process of attempting to retain this ability is known as *knowledge management (KM)*. This term generally encompasses activities related to the creation, retention, and distribution of organizational knowledge. For the purposes of the exams, knowledge management focuses the organizing of information to improve business performance at an individual and an organizational level.

Much of the knowledge that an individual acquires over time in an organization disappears when that person leaves the company. Whether because of layoffs, outsourcing, or the retirement of key employees, the loss of critical knowledge negatively impacts organizations.

Real World Scenario

Using KM to Solve Administrative Problems

Over time, an experienced executive assistant (EA) learns shortcuts and details that enhance an executive's ability to operate more effectively by eliminating administrative concerns. Some of these details are personal preferences for individual executives, but many are useful for any executive in an organization, such as which IT support person is best at long-distance troubleshooting, or out-of-town businesses that can provide quality services in an emergency, such as printing presentation materials on short notice if they aren't delivered on time.

Sharing this information among EAs usually occurs on an ad hoc basis, but this requires that individuals with specific knowledge be available when an emergency occurs. A better solution for long-term benefits is the creation of a knowledge management database or manual that the EAs update as they learn new information that can help executives achieve organization goals and objectives.

Executives benefit because they're able to accomplish more, and the EAs benefit because they save time, whether it's locating the best travel deals, identifying restaurants that provide appropriate venues for client meetings, finding the coworker who can be counted on to solve urgent problems, or handling other administrative details that allow the executives they support to be more effective in their jobs.

Knowledge Management Systems

Some business functions lend themselves to the use of a *knowledge management system (KMS)*. These systems support and collect the creation, capture, storage, and dissemination of organizational knowledge and information. The goal of a KMS is to provide employees with easy access to information that has been collected from various sources, verified for accuracy, and organized for retrieval to answer questions or solve problems. An example of an effective KM program with which many people have had some experience is customer relationship management (CRM). Customers often complain about the frustration they experience when calling a customer support or help line and having to repeat all the details of a problem with a product to each new customer service representative (CSR) who comes on the line. An effective KMS has each CSR enter facts about customer problems into a database so that, when the customer calls back, the next CSR to answer the call knows everything that has already transpired between the customer and the company. The customer doesn't need to repeat information, and the CSR can avoid going back to step one in the problem-solving process.

Knowledge as Capital

The knowledge of employees represents a valuable form of capital that organizations can strategically harness to gain a competitive advantage in their respective markets. Organizations can leverage the knowledge of their employees by implementing knowledge management systems and practices that facilitate the capture, sharing, and application of expertise and insights across the organization. This enables them to innovate more rapidly, make better-informed decisions, and adapt more effectively to changing market conditions. This knowledge can include *explicit knowledge*, such as documents, reports, and databases, or *tacit knowledge*—the unwritten, informal knowledge and expertise, generally gained through experience and engagement, and passed down through informal channels such as conversations, shared circumstances, and observations. Key components of knowledge management in the workplace may include:

- **Capture:** Identifying and documenting processes and procedures within the organization through various means such as interviews, reference guides, and knowledge-sharing sessions.
- **Organize:** Structuring and categorizing knowledge assets in a way that makes them easy to find and retrieve when needed. This may involve the use of hierarchical classification systems (taxonomies), databases, and other information management systems.
- **Share:** Facilitating the exchange of knowledge and expertise among employees through collaboration platforms, forums, mentorship programs, and other channels.
- **Store:** Establishing knowledge bases where captured knowledge can be stored securely and accessed by authorized users.
- **Apply:** Encouraging employees to apply the knowledge they have acquired in their day-to-day work activities and decision-making processes.

TIP

Acronyms are a great way to store and recall information. For example, COSSA can be used to learn and remember the components of a robust knowledge-sharing program: capture, organize, share, store, and application. Adding a clever little phrase by substituting the acronym COSSA for "'cause I" can enhance retention, such as "I need to retain this knowledge COSSA want to pass this test!" To retain the vast amount of dry material in these exams, it's smart to vary your approach to prevent the content from blending together.

Knowledge Management Tools

Organizations use different methods to retain and institutionalize knowledge so that it's easily accessible for improving processes and increasing profits. These methods can be categorized in one of the following ways:

Expert Registers An expert register or directory collects the names and areas of expertise of employees and is made available to all employees, who are then able to contact internal experts to discuss problems and find solutions.

Best-Practice Standards The term *best practice* is often used to describe methods or practices that have been demonstrated to produce desired results over a period of time. In the KM context, best practices are those that have been used in an organization by one group of employees to achieve particular results and are codified for distribution to other employees in similar jobs or groups throughout the organization with the idea that the results will be duplicated. Best practices also exist at an industry level, such as human resources, with a *body of knowledge* used for practitioner reference. The HR Certification Institute's™ Guide to the Human Resource Body of Knowledge™ (HRBoK), for example, describes both knowledge and competencies for practicing HR in the 21st century.

After-Action Evaluations An after-action evaluation is sometimes referred to as a *postmortem* and is a review conducted at the end of a project or other group endeavor. The purpose of the evaluation is to share in the group what worked, what didn't work, and what knowledge can be retained for use in future projects.

Communities of Practice A *community of practice (CoP)* is an informal means of learning what works well in environments characterized by open communication and trust. CoPs may be spontaneous and self-organized or sponsored by the organization. In either case, they consist of people with common work interests or needs who are willing to share experiences and expertise with coworkers. These groups benefit individuals by enhancing skills, satisfaction, and productivity; benefit the work group with increased trust and learning opportunities; and benefit the organization with improvements in sales, improved product development, reduced time-to-market lead times, and, ultimately, improved market share because of improved customer satisfaction.

Technology Solutions The information technology (IT) group can play a large role in facilitating KM initiatives. As the organization function for communication infrastructure, IT implements database management and other IT tools that encourage knowledge sharing among employees. These include self-service support functions such as a frequently asked questions (FAQs) page, video tutorials, chatbots, and user or employee forums. KM tools such as these are often organized within a centralized knowledge base, categorized around product-, process-, or company-centric content.

Leadership Development

In the context of workforce development, empowering leaders within organizations to acquire the necessary skills, knowledge, and competencies necessary to effectively lead teams directly drives results. This is because effective leadership leads to more engaged employees, and highly engaged workers are innovative, creative problem solvers. There are several competencies necessary for effective leadership. The SPHR/i exam content outline specifies the following:

Conflict Resolution Conflict resolution in leadership involves the ability to address and manage disagreements or disputes among team members or within the organization. Leaders proficient in conflict resolution can identify the root causes of conflicts, facilitate constructive dialogue, and negotiate solutions that satisfy all parties involved.

William Ury is a renowned negotiation expert, author, and co-founder of the Harvard Program on Negotiation, recognized for his influential work in the field of conflict resolution and negotiation theory. In his YouTube video titled "The Walk from No to Yes" (`https://www.youtube.com/watch?v=Hc6yi_FtoNo`), Ury notes that in conflict, leaders should seek hospitality over hostility. It can be beneficial to use outside resources such as Ury to train leaders in conflict management for many reasons. External perspectives offer fresh insights, diverse strategies, and impartial guidance, and bring a level of credibility and practical methods to resolve conflicts in the workplace.

Senior HR leaders are responsible for ensuring that a code of conduct is in place, enforced, and modeled by managers to help keep minor disagreements from escalating into full-blown conflict.

Mentoring Mentoring in leadership refers to the practice of guiding and advising individuals to help them develop their skills, knowledge, and career paths. Effective mentors provide support, encouragement, and feedback to their mentees, helping them navigate challenges, set goals, and realize their potential. Mentoring fosters professional growth, builds relationships, and contributes to the overall success of both the mentor and the mentee.

Three research-backed methods for mentoring include:

Structured Mentorship Programs: Implementing formalized mentoring programs that provide clear guidelines, objectives, and expectations for both mentors and mentees. Research shows that structured programs lead to more successful mentoring relationships, increased knowledge transfer, and greater overall satisfaction for participants.

Peer Mentoring: Facilitating mentoring relationships between peers within the organization, where individuals with similar levels of experience or expertise support one another's development. Studies indicate that peer mentoring can foster a sense of camaraderie, promote knowledge sharing, and offer unique perspectives that traditional hierarchical mentoring may not provide.

Mentoring Training and Support: Providing training and ongoing support for mentors to enhance their mentoring skills, communication abilities, and cultural competence. Research suggests that mentor training programs result in more effective mentoring relationships, improved mentee outcomes, and greater satisfaction among both mentors and mentees.

TIP

Google Scholar is an excellent resource to find peer-reviewed and other academic research on important HR topics. Go to `https://scholar.google.com` and type your query in the search bar, select Articles or Case Law, and run the search. Not only is this a useful study tool, but it can also help on the job when crafting workforce strategies.

Employee Sponsorships Similar to mentorships are *employee sponsorships*. Sponsorship programs facilitate connections between leaders and high-potential employees to expedite their career growth. They involve executives advocating for individuals, especially those from underrepresented backgrounds, unlike high-potential programs focused on grooming leaders. Sponsors actively support their protégés' advancement, leveraging their influence and providing mentorship. This commitment helps counteract biases and inequalities, fostering a more inclusive workplace. When sponsorship programs are a strategic initiative, it can drive diversity in leadership across organizations and begin to close equality gaps. This means they must have executive support and be properly resourced.

Leadership Coaching Coaching in leadership entails guiding individuals or teams to improve their skills, achieve their goals, and overcome challenges. Effective coaches establish trust, provide guidance, and empower their coaches to explore their potential and find solutions independently. Through active listening, asking powerful questions, and offering support, coaches help individuals develop self-awareness, build confidence, and maximize their performance.

The primary difference between coaching and mentoring lies in their focus and structure. Coaching typically focuses on short-term skill development, performance improvement, or specific goals. It often involves a structured process where the coach helps the individual identify challenges, develop action plans, and achieve desired outcomes. Mentoring, on the other hand, tends to focus on long-term career development, guidance, and overall personal growth. Coaching relationships are often formal and structured, with defined objectives, timelines, and expectations. Coaches may use specific techniques, tools, and assessments to guide the coaching process and measure progress. Mentoring relationships are typically more informal and flexible, based on mutual trust and rapport between the mentor and mentee. Both seek to support individuals in their development.

Effective Communication Communication is often considered the most important leadership competency because it serves as the foundation for all other leadership skills and activities. Here's why:

Alignment Effective communication aligns individual efforts with organizational objectives, fostering a sense of purpose and direction among team members.

Collaboration Leaders who communicate effectively can facilitate brainstorming, problem-solving, and decision-making processes, leading to innovative solutions and better outcomes.

Engagement Leaders who communicate regularly and transparently build trust, boost morale, and inspire commitment among their team members.

Change Management Leaders who communicate clearly and consistently can manage resistance, alleviate fears, and guide their teams through transitions successfully.

Relationship Building Communication is fundamental to building strong relationships with employees and other key stakeholders. Leaders who listen actively, provide feedback, and communicate with empathy can establish rapport and foster positive working relationships.

A *leadership pipeline* refers to a systematic approach for identifying, developing, and promoting individuals with leadership potential to fill key roles and succession positions at various levels within the organization. This requires that strategic HR professionals engage in professional development for these individuals to ready them for promotion. One challenge to this is the lack of resource allocation by organizations for leadership development professionals. In "The Leadership Development Benchmark Report 2024" by LEADx,[1] it was reported that in 2024, there was one leadership development professional for every 267 managers. In 2023, that ratio was one leadership development professional for every 89 people managers, an alarming trend in the wrong direction. In a best-case scenario, HR is able to take on the role of leadership coach. More often, however, there is no formal leadership development program at all, or executives believe that they will be able to hire

[1] https://leadx.org/the-leadx-leadership-development-benchmark-report.

the leaders when it becomes necessary, but this is simply not true. HR can help buffer this challenge by communicating the value of leadership development professionals and training, a concept the LEADx report calls "proof of impact."

Using tools such as Donald Kirkpatrick's levels of training evaluation helps to communicate the value of development activities:

- **Level 1 - Reaction:** Conducting participant satisfaction surveys after a leadership training workshop to gather feedback on the program's content, delivery, and overall experience. Questions might include rating the relevance of the material, the effectiveness of the facilitator, and whether participants feel more confident in their leadership skills after the training.
- **Level 2 - Learning:** Administering pre- and post-training assessments to measure the increase in knowledge and skills acquired during the leadership development program. This could involve testing participants on leadership concepts, techniques, or best practices covered in the training to assess their learning progress.
- **Level 3 - Behavior:** Implementing 360-degree feedback assessments to evaluate changes in leadership behavior and effectiveness following the development program. Colleagues, direct reports, and supervisors provide input on observable changes in the leader's actions, such as improved communication, decision making, or team collaboration.
- **Level 4 - Results:** Analyzing key performance indicators (KPIs) or organizational metrics to assess the impact of leadership development efforts on business outcomes. This could involve measuring changes in employee engagement scores, productivity levels, turnover rates, or financial performance attributable to improvements in leadership effectiveness resulting from the development program.

Discover more about Kirkpatrick's evaluation standards at `https://www.kirkpatrickpartners.com`.

Another way to measure the effectiveness of leadership development programs is to calculate the return on investment (ROI). ROI evaluates the financial gains against the costs incurred. It quantifies the impact of leadership programs on organizational performance, such as increased productivity, revenue growth, and employee retention. ROI analysis provides quantifiable insights into the effectiveness and value of leadership development initiatives, showing that not only do these initiatives produce results, but also that they may self-fund.

For instance, suppose a company invests $50,000 in a leadership development program. Over the following year, they observe a 20 percent increase in employee productivity, resulting in an additional $200,000 in revenue. Calculating the ROI: (($200,000 – $50,000) / $50,000) × 100 = 300% (net investment divided by the cost of the investment, multiplied by 100). This indicates a substantial return on investment.

As demonstrated in the LEADx study, the impact and influence of organizational leaders cannot be understated. Strong (or poor) leadership affects productivity, results, quality, safety, customer satisfaction, and employee engagement.

Employee Engagement

Employee engagement is the degree of emotional, physical, and mental investment a team member has with their job and the company. In the behavioral sciences, engagement is closely related to the concept of job satisfaction. For SPHR/i candidates, strategic engagement considers the need to align workforce initiatives with organizational goals, ensuring that they reflect the company's values, culture, and priorities. Factors for engagement also include specific needs driven by globalization, artificial intelligence (AI), and remote/hybrid work structures.

Senior HR leaders can engage a globalized workforce by implementing inclusive policies and practices that respect cultural diversity and developing global leaders in cultural intelligence. HR should also look for ways to provide opportunities for cross-cultural collaboration and learning and leveraging technology to facilitate remote work and communication across geographical boundaries and time zones. Diversity, equity, and inclusion (DEI) is covered in detail in Chapter 2.

Another use for technology to improve employee engagement is the use of AI. AI can impact employee engagement by personalizing experiences using data-driven insights, enabling predictive analytics for identifying and addressing potential issues, automating routine tasks to free up time for meaningful work, and facilitating real-time feedback.

Engagement and Remote Work

Since the pandemic of 2020, remote and hybrid work has significantly increased. Predictions show that by 2025, some 32.6 million Americans will work remote, and 93 percent of employers plan to continue conducting job interviews remotely.[2] These statistics demonstrate that it is important for HR to, where possible, structure jobs in ways that allow for flexible scheduling and fully remote or hybrid work to widen the applicant pool. And while HR does not need to be technology experts, they should build the digital competencies necessary to ensure that they can effectively leverage technology to streamline processes to organizational success. Figure 12.1 shows other key remote work statistics from Forbes Advisor.

Not all roles can be designed to work from home (WFH). General labor positions such as those found in construction, client-facing roles such as retail associates, and emergency response positions such as EMTs all require a physical presence. Employees are increasingly being recalled back from remote positions from companies such as Starbucks, General Motors, and Disney. The primary reason cited by many organizations is the need to rebuild an office culture. Considered through a strategic lens, reasons could also include the need to optimize empty office space and create opportunities for employees to build relationships, thus fostering retention. Conversely, many employees enjoy the benefits that working from home can bring, so a hybrid model where employees are required to be in office 3 or 4 days a week is a productive solution.

[2] `www.forbes.com/advisor/business/remote-work-statistics`.

FIGURE 12.1 Remote work statistics

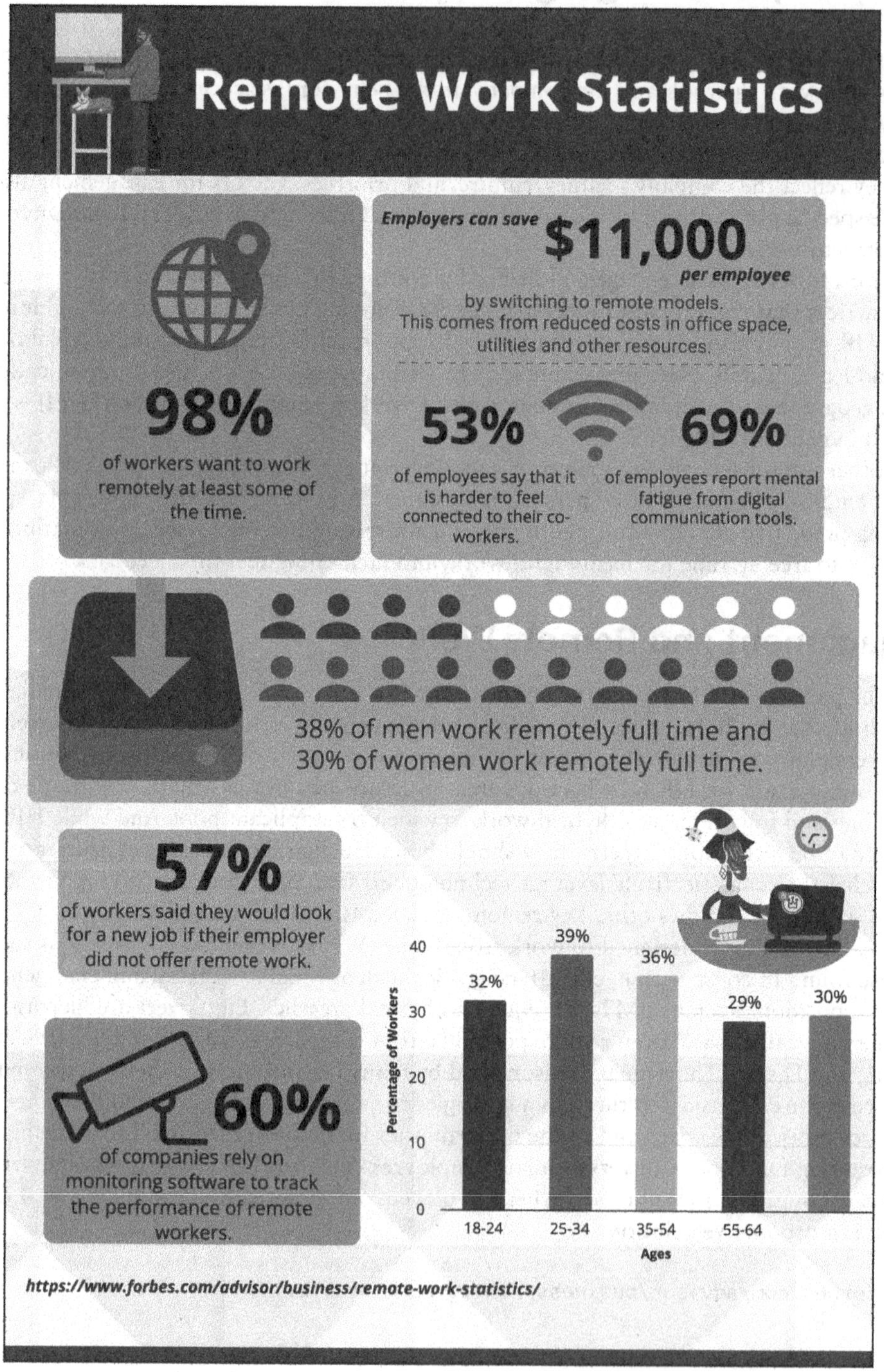

HR plays an important role by educating senior leaders on the value of hybrid work structures to the company and employee. These advantages are shown in Figure 12.2 and described as follows:

FIGURE 12.2 Advantages of hybrid work structure

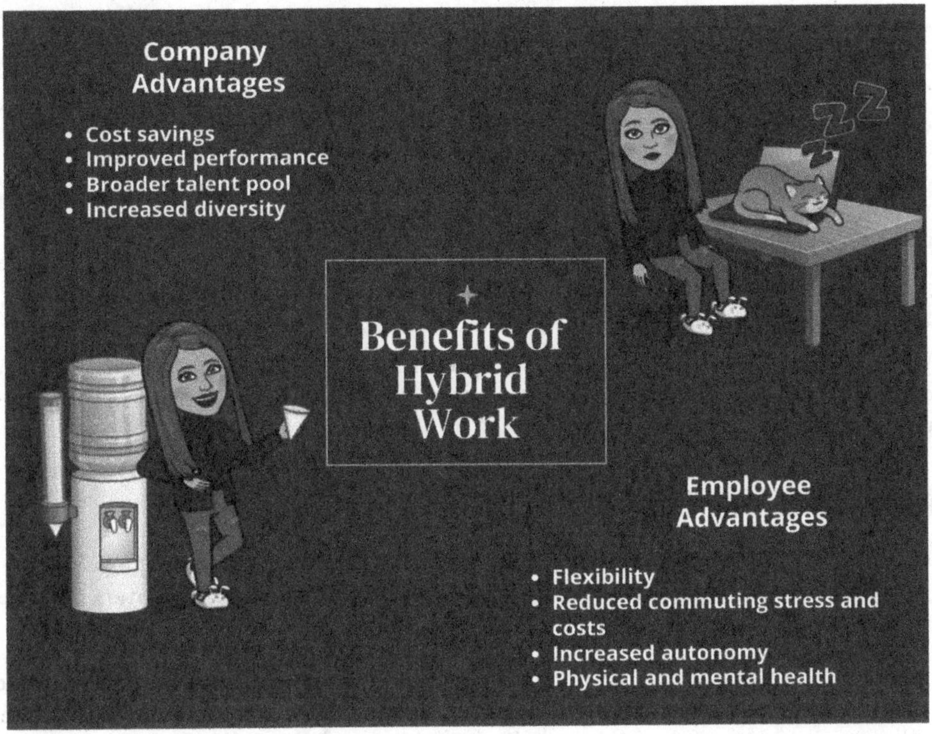

Benefits to the company:

- **Cost Savings:** Reduced office space requirements, lower utility bills, and decreased spending on office supplies and equipment.
- **Increased Performance:** Flexible work (not telework) significantly increases work engagement, which leads to better performance.[3]
- **Broader Talent Pool:** By offering hybrid work options, companies can attract talent from a wider geographic area.
- **Increased Diversity:** Hybrid work models have been shown to support women, women of color, the LGBTQ+ community, and individuals with disabilities.[4]

3* “”The Future of Work: Work Engagement and Job Performance in the Hybrid Workplace,” by M. Muzamil Naqshbandi, Ibrahim Kabir, Nurul Amirah Ishak, and Md. Zahidul Islam, https://www.emerald.com/insight/content/doi/10.1108/TLO-08-2022-0097/full/html.

4“Hybrid Work Models Are Empowering Women in Tech,” by Soulaima Gourani, www.forbes.com/sites/soulaimagourani/2024/03/05/breaking-barriers-hybrid-work-models-are-empowering-women-in-tech/?sh=2a919b986b75.

Benefits to Employees:

- **Flexibility:** Hybrid work provides employees with the flexibility to balance their professional responsibilities with personal commitments.
- **Reduced Commuting Stress and Costs:** Hybrid work arrangements typically involve fewer days commuting to the office, leading to reduced stress associated with transportation and lower expenses related to commuting, such as fuel costs, parking fees, or public transportation fares.
- **Increased Autonomy and Productivity:** Hybrid work empowers employees to take greater control over their work environment and schedule. With the ability to choose when and where they work, employees can optimize their productivity by capitalizing on their most productive times and creating a work environment that suits their preferences.
- **Improved Physical and Mental Health:** employees can make meals at home, substitute commuting time for exercise, and work with their pets around them, often improving moods and mental well-being.

As more and more companies recall employees from WFH situations, HR is responsible for crafting and implementing return-to-work strategies, which are also necessary for other circumstances. These are covered next.

Return-to-Work Strategies

Exam objective 3.9 discusses the responsibilities of senior HR leaders to design policies and processes for employees returning to work after a period of leave. Employers may need return-to-work strategies for various reasons, including:

Remote Work Transitions As organizations transition to remote work models or adopt hybrid work arrangements, employers may need strategies to support employees as they adjust to new ways of working, including providing technology training, establishing communication protocols, and promoting work-life balance.

Pandemics or Health Crises During events such as pandemics or health crises (i.e., COVID-19), employers may need strategies to safely reintegrate employees into the workplace after extended periods of remote work or furloughs, while minimizing the risk of virus transmission.

Sabbaticals Upon returning from sabbaticals, employees may need time to reacclimate to the work environment and catch up on industry developments. Companies can support their transition by offering reorientation sessions, access to updated training materials, and opportunities for knowledge sharing with colleagues.

Illness or Injury Employees who have been on medical leave due to illness or injury may require tailored return-to-work plans to ensure a smooth transition back into their roles, taking into account any accommodations or modifications needed to support their recovery and well-being.

Repatriation Returning expatriates may experience readjustment challenges as they reintegrate into the workplace, requiring support and guidance to navigate cultural shifts and reestablish professional networks. Employers can facilitate a smooth transition by providing orientation programs, mentorship, and resources to help returning expatriates acclimate to their roles and surroundings.

Parental Leave Employees returning to work after taking parental leave may benefit from strategies that facilitate their reintegration into the workplace, such as phased returns, flexible scheduling options, or access to childcare support services.

Workplace Accidents or Traumatic Events Following workplace accidents or traumatic events, employers may need strategies to support employees as they return to work, including providing counseling services, implementing safety measures, and addressing any concerns about returning to the scene of the incident.

Organizational Changes Significant organizational changes, such as mergers, acquisitions, restructurings, layoffs, or changes in leadership, can impact employees' roles, responsibilities, and work environments, necessitating return-to-work strategies to help employees navigate and adapt to these changes effectively.

Mental Health and Well-Being Employees experiencing mental health challenges or burnout may require return-to-work strategies that prioritize their well-being, such as providing access to mental health resources, offering flexible work arrangements, or implementing wellness initiatives.

In addition to employees returning to work, HR leaders are tasked with designing and assessing offboarding strategies, processes, and trends. An effective offboarding strategy involves conducting exit interviews, providing clear guidance on transition tasks, maintaining positive relationships, and offering support to departing employees. This ensures a smooth transition, preserves institutional knowledge, and upholds the organization's reputation as a supportive employer.

There are many benefits to helping separating employees feel supported during the offboarding process, including courting the boomerang worker referenced in an earlier section. Leveraging alumni connections can facilitate talent referrals and enhance employer branding, which in turn can attract top candidates beyond the alumni.

Many employers underestimate the value of an exit interview due to a perception that by the time an employe has decided to leave, it is too late to change their minds. Other employers do not trust the information gathered during an exit interview, perceiving it as either excessively negative or too generic to be of much use. However, there are several best practices that can increase the value of an exit interview. They include:

- **Preparing Thoughtful Questions:** Develop a set of open-ended questions that encourage departing employees to provide honest feedback about their experiences, reasons for leaving, and suggestions for improvement.
- **Ensuring Confidentiality:** Assure the departing employee that their feedback will remain confidential and create a comfortable environment where they feel safe expressing their thoughts and concerns without fear of retaliation.

- **Active Listening and Empathy:** Listen attentively to the departing employee's responses, demonstrate empathy, and validate their feelings. Avoid interrupting and show genuine interest in understanding their perspective.
- **Act on Feedback:** Use the insights gathered from exit interviews to identify trends, address systemic issues, and make meaningful changes to improve organizational processes, culture, and employee retention efforts. Follow up with departing employees if appropriate to inform them of any actions taken based on their feedback.

Another way to supplement or even replace exit interviews is to conduct periodic stay interviews to identify what current employees value, thus improving retention.

Real World Scenario

Using Exit Interviews to Solve Organizational Challenges

A regional retail chain appointed a store manager to oversee a team of 16 employees. After a year, only eight remained, with four resigning and four transferring. HR reviewed exit interviews of the four resigning employees and found a consistent narrative: The manager lacked essential leadership qualities, failing to foster team commitment, appreciation, and clear communication of goals. The interviews also highlighted a broader issue: The company's promotion criteria favored individuals with advanced degrees over managerial experience and people skills. In response, the executive team revised the promotion criteria to prioritize people and transferable experience skills and created a leadership development plan for the manager. The HR team also recognized the need to conduct stay interviews as the manager developed to improve the retention of the remaining and replacement workers.

Labor Relations

Labor relations, viewed through the lens of human resource management, refers to the relationship between employers and employees, often within the context of unions or collective bargaining. Central to a labor relations strategy is to create and maintain open communication channels between management and labor. HR professionals facilitate dialogue to address grievances, negotiate collective bargaining agreements, and convey organizational policies and objectives transparently.

Senior HR teams also help to ensure compliance with labor laws and regulations, such as the National Labor Relations Act (NLRA), Labor Management Relations Act (LMRA), and the Labor Management Reporting and Disclosure Act (LMRDA), all covered in Appendix C. These acts—enforced by the National Labor Relations Board (NLRB)—govern employer and union practices in areas such as wages, hours, and working conditions, to safeguard both employee rights and organizational interests. They also provide guidance to management on navigating labor-related legal issues and facilitate resolution when disputes arise.

Labor Unions

The history of American labor relations begins with the formation of the Knights of Labor in 1869. This organization was an advocate of the 8-hour workday when 12 or 14 hours per day was the norm. By the end of the 19th century, unions became powerful enough to threaten business profitability, and federal antitrust laws were used to hinder their growth. In reaction, Congress enacted labor legislation that supported union growth. The pendulum swung back and forth until the 1960s, when the political focus turned to civil rights legislation.

Although labor unions grew in importance for more than a century, there was a period in recent history where they have lost some of their appeal to working people. The headlines suggest that a union boom is recurring with employees at companies such as Starbucks, Amazon, Trader Joe's, and other retailers voting to unionize. However, the Bureau of Labor Statistics released its most recent union data for 2023 and it shows that union membership has remained flat at 10 percent—the same as in 2022, with the bulk of union membership remaining in the public sector workforce.[5]

Union Organization

At the initial stages of a union-organizing campaign, signs of union activity are difficult to detect. By the time management notices something unusual is taking place, the organizing process may already be well underway.

One early indication that an organizing campaign has begun is a noticeable change in employee behavior. For example, employees may begin to challenge management decisions using union terminology related to benefits or employee rights. The earliest signs of a union presence are characterized by sometimes subtle changes in workforce relationships. First-line supervisors, those closest to rank-and-file employees who are the target of organizing efforts, are the ones most likely to notice that something about those relationships is different. How these changes manifest themselves is different in every company, but some signs that raise concern include the following:

- Groups of employees begin to congregate in unlikely places, scattering or ending their conversation when a supervisor or another manager appears.
- Employee behavior during meal and rest periods changes noticeably; instead of "hanging out," some employees are obviously occupied with nonwork activity.
- Absenteeism increases significantly in a short period of time for no apparent reason.
- Groups of employees challenge supervisors or managers with questions about benefits and employment practices in an uncharacteristically antagonistic manner.
- Former employees or newcomers approach employees in the parking lot or at public entrances to the building.

[5] Bureau of Labor Statistics news release, `https://www.bls.gov/news.release/pdf/union2.pdf`.

- People are observed taking down license numbers on employee cars.
- Employees who normally hang out with one group of coworkers befriend others, jumping from one group to another during meal or rest periods.
- Union slogans in the form of graffiti begin to appear in locations where employees congregate.

As organizing activity intensifies, the union may instigate a confrontation with the employer by coaching one or a group of employees to defy instructions for reasons that are protected by the NLRA, such as refusing to work because they aren't paid enough to do a particular job. If the refusal is based on an activity protected by the NLRA, employees may not be fired and must be treated as lawful strikers.

The Organizing Process

The recognition process has seven basic elements, but not all of them occur in every situation. The process consists of authorization cards, a demand for recognition, a petition to the NLRB, an NLRB conference, a preelection hearing, a campaign, and finally the election.

Authorization Cards

The goal of the union during the organizing process is to obtain signed authorization cards from employees. An *authorization card* is the means by which the NLRB determines that there is sufficient support for a union to hold an election. The NLRB will hold an election if 30 percent of the eligible employees in the anticipated bargaining unit sign the authorization cards. In practice, the union would like to have far more signed cards before submitting a petition for an election—generally it would like to have signed cards from at least 50 percent of the eligible employees.

Demand for Recognition

When the union has a sufficient number of signed authorization cards, it's ready to approach the employer with a demand for recognition. This usually comes in the form of a letter to the employer in which the union claims to represent a majority of workers and demands to be recognized by the employer as the exclusive bargaining agent for employees. The demand may also be made in person when a union representative approaches any member of the management team, including a first-line supervisor, offering proof that a majority of employees want the union to represent them. It's crucial that whoever is approached doesn't respond in a way that could be construed as recognition by the union, politely referring the union to the HR department or a senior member of the management team.

Union representatives may also approach employers requesting a neutrality agreement or a card-check election. In a neutrality agreement, an employer agrees not to say or do anything in opposition to the union. A card-check election means that the employer agrees to recognize the union based on signed authorization cards. At a minimum, agreeing to either situation limits the employer's ability to resist unionization efforts. Agreeing to one of these alternatives may be interpreted as voluntary recognition of the union.

An employer may choose to recognize a union voluntarily under some circumstances, but this should be done only after conferring with legal counsel. One-way unions may seek voluntary recognition is to approach management with signed authorization cards to have management witness its majority status by accepting the cards. A number of NLRB cases have involved union claims that management has witnessed majority status by counting the authorization cards, so supervisors and management should be made aware of the consequences of handling the cards.

Petitioning the NLRB

If management refuses to grant voluntary recognition, the union files a petition for an election with the NLRB, along with evidence of employee interest in union representation. The NLRB reviews the petition to determine that it represents an appropriate level of interest in union representation and that signatures on the petition or authorization cards are valid.

NLRB Conference/Preelection Hearing Issues

When the NLRB is satisfied with the legitimacy of the petition, it schedules a conference with the employer and employee representatives. During the conference, an NLRB representative reviews any jurisdictional issues, the makeup of the bargaining unit, the eligibility of voters in the proposed unit, and the time and place of the election. If either party disputes issues related to the bargaining unit, legitimacy of the authorization cards, or timing of the election, a formal hearing is held by the NLRB to resolve those issues.

Bargaining Units

The makeup of the bargaining unit is a critical factor to both union and employer points of view. The union wants the unit to be as large as possible and include a majority of employees who are in favor of the union. Management, of course, wants to limit the size of the unit and include a majority of employees who choose to remain union-free.

The NLRA grants broad discretion for bargaining unit determinations to the NLRB. Guidance in the act is that "the unit appropriate for the purposes of collective bargaining shall be the employer unit, craft unit, plant unit, or subdivision thereof." Aside from that, the only specifics provided are that a bargaining unit may not consist of both professional and nonprofessional employees unless the professional employees vote to be included in the unit, and that individuals hired as guards to protect the employer's premises or property may not be included in a unit with other employees. The NLRB looks at several objective criteria to devise a bargaining unit that is appropriate for the individual situation, beginning with determining whether there is a "community of interest" in the unit—that is, that the interests of members of the unit are sufficiently similar to preclude disagreements during the bargaining process. The NLRB looks as well at factors such as how the employer administers its business (whether it uses standard policies across the entire company or diverse policies in different locations), geography (how far apart the locations are in the proposed unit), whether the unit is made up of employees involved in a major process of the company, whether employees are cross-trained or frequently transfer between locations, what unit the employees want to be part of, and any relevant collective bargaining history. Finally, the NLRB considers the extent to which employees are already organized, although the act makes it clear that this may not be the determining factor.

Bargaining units may consist of two or more employees in one employer location or employees in two or more locations of a single employer. If there is an employer industry association, the bargaining unit may include employees of two or more employers in several locations.

Some employees aren't eligible for inclusion in a bargaining unit. These include confidential employees, supervisors, and management personnel. The act also excludes independent contractors and some agricultural laborers from bargaining units.

Temporary Workers

In August 2000, the NLRB made a significant change to its previous rulings on the inclusion of temporary workers in an employer's bargaining unit in a case involving M. B. Sturgis, Inc. Sturgis is a gas hose manufacturer in Missouri that was the target of an organizing campaign. When the union petitioned for an election, Sturgis wanted to include the temp workers on its site in the bargaining unit, but the union didn't want them included. The NLRB reversed two long-standing positions in this case by deciding that the determining factor in this decision is whether a community of interest in wages, scheduling, and working conditions exists between the regular employees and the temp workers, and that a unit including temp workers isn't considered a multiemployer unit needing the consent of both employers.

Union Campaign Tactics

At their peak in 1953, unions represented 35.7 percent of the private sector workforce. According to the Bureau of Labor Statistics, unions represented only 10 percent of the private sector workforce in 2023. However, unions are far more prevalent in today's public sector. As unions struggle to maintain membership levels, they have had to reexamine their strategies for attracting new members.

As the economy in the United States moved from a manufacturing to an informational base, the workforce changed from predominantly blue-collar workers who were the traditional union members to white-collar workers who haven't traditionally been attracted by union membership. Although the strategies vary with each union, the general trend is to find ways of attracting white-collar workers to union membership. Once potential members indicate interest in unionizing their place of work, a number of methods are used to organize the employees:

Internet Many unions have sophisticated websites that provide information for employees who are interested in forming a union. The sites contain information on labor laws, information on unfair labor practices, advice on beginning a campaign, and opportunities for interested workers to contact union personnel.

Home Visits This tactic is most often used when the union is trying to gain initial supporters in the company. It provides an opportunity for organizers to have private conversations with potential inside organizers. Because home visits are expensive for the union and can be viewed as an unwanted invasion of privacy, they aren't widely used.

Inside Organizing The most effective organizing process occurs when one or more employees work from within the organization to build support for the union. Insiders can use their influence on coworkers, identify those most likely to respond to the effort, and encourage participation.

Salting *Salting* occurs when a union hires a person to apply for a job at an organization they have targeted. Once hired, the employee acts in much the same way as an inside organizer who was already employed by the company.

Meetings Union-organizing meetings bring together experienced organizers, inside organizers from the company, and employees who are undecided about supporting the organizing process. Meetings provide opportunities to communicate the benefits of membership and exert peer pressure on potential members.

Leafleting The goal of union leaflets is to point out the advantages the union will bring to the workforce and to counter information that management provides to employees about the benefits of remaining union-free. Leaflets are generally used when the organizing campaign is well underway.

Media Unions have developed expertise in getting their message out. When management commits an unfair labor practice (ULP) or takes any action the union perceives as unfavorable, the union will issue a press release that interprets the action in the most favorable way for the union. For example, in 1999, the Union of Needletrades, Industrial, & Textile Employees (UNITE) was conducting an organizing campaign at Loehmann's Department Store in New York City. With little more than a month before the scheduled NLRB election, the store fired one of the leaders of the organizing campaign. UNITE issued a press release that concentrated on the fact that the employee had an exemplary work record at the store and was a single mother. The union went on to allege that the store had spied on the employee during her lunch break in order to find a reason to fire her. The union used this as the basis for encouraging the public to boycott the store.

Picketing *Picketing* occurs when a group of employees patrols the entrance to a business in order to inform customers and the public about disputes or to prevent deliveries to a business that the union is trying to influence in some way. It can also occur to advise the public about ULPs the union believes the employer has committed. The NLRB recognizes three types of picketing:

> **Organizational Picketing:** *Organizational picketing* occurs when the union wants to attract employees to become members and authorize the union to represent them with the employer.
>
> **Recognitional Picketing:** *Recognitional picketing* occurs when the union wants the employer to recognize the union as the employees' representative for

collective bargaining purposes. The NLRA places a limit of 30 days on recognitional picketing, after which a petition for an election must be filed.

Informational or Publicity Picketing: *Informational* or *publicity picketing* is done to truthfully advise the public that an employer is a union-free workplace.

There are three instances when picketing is prohibited: when another union has been lawfully recognized as the bargaining representative for the organization; when a representation election has been held within the previous 12 months; and when a representation petition isn't filed within 30 days of the start of the picketing.

NLRB Elections

The purpose of an NLRB election is to determine whether a majority of employees in the unit desire to be represented by the union. During the time between the NLRB decision and election day, both management and the union present the case for their point of view to employees in the bargaining unit. The employer is required to post notices of the election in "conspicuous" locations frequented by employees in the bargaining unit. Within two days of the consent or direction to hold an election, the employer must provide to the union an *Excelsior list* in electronic format containing the full names, work locations, shifts, job classifications, and "available" contact information, including the personal emails and phone numbers of all employees in the proposed bargaining unit.

A preelection hearing will be scheduled within eight days from the date of service of the Notice of Hearing. The purpose of the hearing is to determine if a question of representation exists. The company must complete a Statement of Position form that identifies any issues they wish to raise at the hearing. The NLRB in their 2015 updates identified what must be addressed at the preelection hearing. These include:

- Jurisdiction
- Labor organization status
- Bars to elections
- Appropriate unit
- Multifacility and multiemployer issues
- Expanding and contracting unit issues
- Employee status (for instance, if the classification of independent contractors concerns more than 20 percent of the unit)
- Seasonal employees
- Inclusion of professional employees or guards with other employees
- Eligibility formulas
- Craft and healthcare employees

In 2023, the NLRB updated this list of issues . The focus now is on only those issues necessary to determine whether an election should be conducted, deferring other issues to the post-election stage if they do not need immediate resolution. This approach aims to reduce unnecessary litigation and streamline the process.[6]

The NLRB's 2015 rules specifically list the existence of a joint employer relationship as one of the issues that must be litigated at the preelection hearing. However, except for jurisdiction, the employer will waive these issues if not raised in the Statement of Position.

The regional director of the NLRB will schedule the election for the earliest date practicable. On the day of the election, neither the employer nor the union may conduct campaign activities in or around the polling area.

To be eligible to vote in the election, an employee must have worked during the pay period prior to the election and must be employed by the business on the day of the election. Employees who are sick, are on vacation, are on military leave, or have been temporarily laid off may vote subject to rules established by the NLRA. Economic strikers who have been replaced by bona fide permanent employees may vote in any election that takes place within 12 months of the beginning of the strike.

The NLRB representative counts the votes at the end of the voting period and provides the vote count to the parties at that time. If the union receives 50 percent plus one vote, the union is certified as the bargaining representative for the unit. In the event of a tie vote, the union isn't certified.

After a vote, the party that lost the election may file charges that the prevailing party interfered with the election results by committing ULPs. The party filing the charge must also include a written offer of proof in support of their claim, in addition to providing the names of any witnesses to the ULP. The NLRB will investigate the charges in accordance with its administrative procedures and, should they be justified, will take remedial action against the offending party.

Norma Rae

For those unfamiliar with the organizing process, the 1979 movie *Norma Rae* provides dramatic insight into the unionization of a garment factory in the South. Based on a true story, the movie follows the efforts of a union organizer from New York to build support for a union in a textile factory in a small southern town. The organizer begins by visiting the homes of some of the workers, distributing leaflets at the front gate of the factory, and enlisting the support of one of the workers who becomes the inside organizer. This insider lends credibility to the union representative by introducing him to coworkers, sponsoring organizing meetings, and obtaining signed union-authorization cards. In the course of the campaign, management commits several ULPs. One of the final scenes dramatizes the vote count: As the NLRB official observes, representatives for management and the union count each vote.

(Fields, Sally. *Norma Rae*. Film. Directed by Martin Ritt. Los Angeles: Twentieth Century Fox, 1979).

[6] https://worklaw.com/blog/new-nlrb-representation-election-rules-and-procedures.

Bars to Elections

The NLRA won't allow elections in some circumstances. The following are known as *election bars*:

Contract Bar Except in very limited circumstances, the NLRB won't direct an election while a bargaining unit is covered by a valid collective bargaining agreement.

Statutory Bar The NLRA prohibits an election in a bargaining unit that had a valid election during the preceding 12-month period.

Certification-Year Bar When the NLRB has certified a bargaining representative, an election won't be ordered for at least one year.

Blocking-Charge Bar An election petition will be barred when there is a pending ULP charge.

Voluntary-Recognition Bar If an employer has voluntarily recognized a union as the representative for a bargaining unit, an election will be barred for a reasonable period of time to allow the parties to negotiate a contract.

Prior-Petition Bar When a union petitioning for an election withdraws the petition prior to the election, then no elections will be approved for six months.

Strikes

The NLRA grants employees the right to organize, join unions, bargain collectively, and engage in other "concerted activities" for mutual aid or protection, as well as the right to refrain from doing so.

The NLRA also protects the right of employees to strike and identifies lawful versus unlawful strikes:

Lawful Strikes One type of lawful strike is an economic strike, in which the union stops working in an effort to obtain better pay, hours, or working conditions from the employer. In an economic strike, employers may hire permanent replacements for striking employees and aren't required to rehire the strikers if doing so means the replacement workers would be fired. If employees make an unconditional request to return to work, they may be recalled at a later time when openings occur.

The other type of lawful strike is one that occurs when the employer has committed an unfair labor practice and employees strike in protest. In this case, strikers may not be discharged or permanently replaced.

Unlawful Strikes Strikes can be characterized as unlawful for several reasons:

- Strikes are unlawful if they support union unfair labor practices.
- Strikes are unlawful if they violate a no-strike clause in the contract.
- Lawful strikes can become unlawful if the strikers engage in serious misconduct.

Unfair Labor Practices

An *unfair labor practice (ULP)* is an action by an employer or a union that restrains or coerces employees from exercising their rights to organize and bargain collectively. Congress has identified ULPs for both employers and unions.

Employer Unfair Labor Practices

Employers who attempt to restrain or otherwise interfere with the right of employees to organize and bargain collectively can, in a worst-case scenario, be ordered by the NLRB to bargain with a union even if an election didn't take place or if the union loses an election. For that reason, it's extremely important for employers to be certain that all supervisory personnel are aware of what constitutes an unfair labor practice. An acronym that is helpful in avoiding prohibited activity is *TIPS*: employers may not threaten, interrogate, promise, or spy on employees.

Employer ULPs defined by the NLRA are as follows:

Interfere with, Restrain, or Coerce Unionization Efforts Employers may not interfere in any way with attempts to unionize the workplace, including organizing activity, collective bargaining, or "concerted activity" engaged in by employees for mutual aid or protection. Interfering also includes inhibiting the free speech of employees who advocate unionization.

Dominate or Assist a Labor Organization Employers are precluded from forming company unions that are controlled by management and, therefore, don't allow employees an independent representative. Employers are also prohibited from showing favoritism to one union over another.

Discriminate Against Employees Employers may not discriminate against union members in any of the terms and conditions of employment. This includes taking disciplinary action against employees for participating in union activities.

Discriminate Against NLRB Activity Employers may not retaliate against employees who have filed charges or participated in an investigation conducted by the NLRB.

Refuse to Bargain in Good Faith Employers must bargain with a union once it has been designated by a majority of the employees and the union has made a demand to bargain.

Enter into a Hot-Cargo Agreement It's unlawful for employers and unions to enter into a *hot-cargo agreement* in which, at the union's request, employers stop doing business with another employer.

Union Unfair Labor Practices

The LMRA identified the following union actions that are considered ULPs:

Restrain and Coerce Employees Union conduct that interferes with an employee's right to choose a representative or to refrain from participating in organizing or collective bargaining activity is a ULP. The act identifies some of the coercive behavior that is unlawful, including assaults, threats of violence, and threats to interfere with continued employment. Unions are also held responsible for coercive acts committed by union members in the presence of union representatives if the representatives don't renounce the actions.

Restrain or Coerce Employers Unions may not refuse to bargain with representatives chosen by the employer to negotiate with the union, or fine or expel from the union a supervisor based on the way the supervisor applies the contract during the course of business. Unions may not insist that employers accept contract terms the union has negotiated with other bargaining units.

Require Employers to Discriminate Unions may not require the employer to terminate an employee for working to decertify the union or require employers to hire only union members or others of whom the union approves.

Refuse to Bargain in Good Faith Unions must meet and confer with employer representatives at reasonable times to negotiate the terms and conditions of the contract.

Engage in Prohibited Strikes and Boycotts Unions may not engage in hot-cargo actions or secondary boycotts. Hot-cargo actions refer to agreements between unions and employers where the employer agrees not to handle or deal with the products of another employer that the union considers unfair, whereas secondary boycotts involve unions attempting to influence an employer by exerting pressure on another employer or business, often by encouraging others to cease doing business with the targeted company.

Charge Excessive or Discriminatory Membership Fees Membership fees must be reasonable and in line with the members' wages and industry standards.

Featherbedding Unions may not require employers to pay for services that aren't rendered. For example, unions may not require employers to continue to pay employees to do jobs that have been rendered obsolete by changes in technology. An example of this is the fireman on a train who fed coal into the fire on a steam engine to keep the water hot enough to run the train. When diesel trains came along, the fireman was no longer needed to run the train. If a union insisted on keeping the firemen on the trains even though they weren't necessary, this was known as featherbedding.

Organizational and Recognitional Picketing Although sometimes organizational and recognitional picketing are done lawfully, there are three instances in which they're unlawful:

- When another union has been lawfully recognized as the bargaining representative for the organization
- When a representation election has been held within the previous 12 months
- When a representation petition isn't filed within 30 days of the start of the picketing

Consequences of Unfair Labor Practices

If, as the result of an investigation, an employer or a union has been found to have committed a ULP, the NLRB can order remedial actions to be taken. The NLRB goal is to eliminate the ULP and to undo the effects of the illegal action to the extent possible. One of the requirements is that the offending party post notices in the workplace advising employees that the ULP will be discontinued and describing the actions to be taken to correct the offense:

- The NLRB may require that the employer disband an employer- dominated union, reinstate employees to positions they held prior to the ULP, or engage in the collective bargaining process and sign a written agreement with the union.
- Unions may be required to agree to reinstatement of employees it caused to be terminated or rejected for employment, refund excessive dues with interest to members, or engage in the collective bargaining process and sign a written agreement with the employer.

Filing an Unfair Labor Practice Charge

ULP charges can be filed by an employee, an employer, or a union representative (the charging party) on a form available from the NLRB. Charges may be filed in person, by fax, or by mail at the regional office of the NLRB where the alleged violation occurred.

Once the case has been received by the NLRB, the charged party is notified, invited to submit a written statement of the facts and circumstances about the case, and advised that they have the right to counsel. The case is then assigned to a board agent for investigation.

The board agent conducts interviews with all parties to the action, as well as with any witnesses, and makes a recommendation to the regional director for the disposition of the case. At this stage, the charges may be dismissed if unwarranted or result in a complaint if valid. Depending on the nature and severity of the offense, the complaint may result in an informal or formal settlement agreement. An informal settlement agreement requires that the charged party will take specified actions to remedy the ULP and doesn't involve a board order or court decree. A formal settlement involves a complaint issued by the NLRB against the charged party and results in a board order or court hearing.

An administrative law judge (ALJ), who conducts a hearing on the evidence, reviews the record and issues a "decision and order" for charges that aren't settled. If a party isn't satisfied with the order of the ALJ, they may file an exception with the NLRB office in Washington, DC, which will issue a final order concurring with or amending the finding of the ALJ.

If the charged party isn't satisfied with the NLRB findings, an appeal can be filed with the U.S. Court of Appeals in the appropriate jurisdiction.

Contract Enforcement

Disagreements that arise during the course of negotiating a collective-bargaining agreement (CBA) may take many forms; some are easily resolved through the grievance process established in the CBA, and others may go to arbitration before they're resolved.

Grievance Procedure

When disagreements occur in a union environment, the grievance process described in the CBA provides the framework for resolving them. The framework describes the steps to be taken and the time frames in which actions must be implemented to either resolve or reply to the grievance. Many grievances can be resolved at the first step in the process with the immediate supervisor, grievant, and union steward working together. If resolution isn't possible at that level, a union official takes the dispute to the next level of company management, where the grievant generally doesn't attend but is represented by the union. If the dispute isn't resolved at the second level, a member of the union grievance committee meets with the next level of management in the company. Grievances that are serious enough to be unsolved at the highest management level in the process then go to a third party for resolution. Depending on the terms of the CBA, this may involve binding arbitration, as is the case in the majority of contracts, or it may use mediation or another form of alternative dispute resolution.

Binding Arbitration

Arbitration is one method of resolving disputes without litigation. In the union environment, binding arbitration is used to resolve conflicts without resorting to work stoppages. Compulsory arbitration is mandated by legal statute to resolve disputes in the public sector where labor strikes are prohibited.

Mediation

The process used to mediate disputes in a union environment is the same as it is in a non-union environment. With the aid of the mediator, the parties to the disagreement work to develop a solution that is acceptable to both of them.

Court Injunctions

Injunctions are sought when immediate action is needed to temporarily prevent something from occurring. One example of the use of injunctions in the collective-bargaining process is the national emergency strike. The Taft–Hartley Act empowers the president to seek an injunction to stop a strike or lockout for an 80-day cooling-off period.

Duty of Successor Employers

In the event that a company with CBAs is acquired by a new company, the new management may be required to maintain the union contract. Whether the NLRB will consider an acquiring owner to be a successor employer is based on the following factors:

- Substantial continuity in operations
- The number of employees assimilated into the new company
- Similarity of operations and products
- The agreement with the previous employer

Although the terms and conditions may be changed by the new employer, the changes are required to be made through the collective-bargaining process and can't be made unilaterally by the employer.

Union Decertification

Employees may petition the NLRB for *decertification* if they're dissatisfied with the union's performance. A decertification petition requires signatures of at least 30 percent of the employees before the NLRB will act on it. Employees may want to decertify the union for a variety of reasons, including poor performance by the union in its representation of the employees or the desire of the employees to be represented by a different union. Decertification may also occur because the employee relationship with management is a good one, and employees no longer feel the need for union representation. It's critical for HR professionals and management to understand that the employer may not encourage or support employees in the decertification process. Doing so constitutes a ULP and may well result in employees being compelled to continue to be represented by the union.

Union Deauthorization

Employees may want to maintain the union but remove a union security clause, such as union-shop, dues check-off, or maintenance of membership clause. The NLRB will approve *deauthorization* based on a petition by 30 percent or more of the members of the bargaining unit. As with decertification, employers must not participate in the effort to deauthorize the union, because doing so is considered to be a ULP.

Collective Bargaining

The NLRA imposes a duty to bargain in good faith on both employers and unions. Mandatory subjects for the bargaining process include wages, hours, terms and conditions of employment, the agreement itself, and any questions that arise from the agreement. Bad faith in the bargaining process is evidenced by a lack of concessions on issues, refusing to advance proposals to decision makers, stalling tactics, or withholding information that is important to the process. Evidence of bad faith by management in the bargaining process can also be evidenced by attempts to circumvent the union representative by going directly to employees with proposals before they have been presented to the union. Another indicator of bad faith bargaining by management occurs when unilateral changes are made to working conditions. An indication of bad faith by the union would be failing to notify management of the intent to renegotiate the contract within 60–90 days before it expires.

Collective-Bargaining Positions

Before discussing the components of collective bargaining, it's important to understand the different bargaining positions that can be taken and how each position affects the bargaining process. There are three basic approaches to negotiating:

Positional Bargaining *Positional bargaining* is a strategy represented by demands made by each side. During positional negotiations, each side views the object of the negotiation as something finite that must be shared, stakes out the position they believe is in their own interest, and concentrates on "winning" that position for their side. This makes the process an adversarial, competitive one. Also known as *hard bargaining* or *distributive bargaining*, positional bargaining is a zero-sum game; in order for one side to gain something, the other side must lose something.

Concession Bargaining *Ultra-concession* or *concession* bargaining occurs when a union gives back a previous gain or surrenders negotiations in exchange for member job security. This type of bargaining may be necessary when a union recognizes that an employer's position is economically justified, such as in the print news industry beginning in 2009. Concession bargaining is seen by some as eroding the relevance of union representation because it requires the union to give up past gains for its members instead of making new ones. Additionally, union contracts are often negotiated based on the conditions of a previous contract, so any erosion impacts future gains as well. In ultra-concession bargaining, the employer may use threats to the union, dealing in extremes in order to remain competitive. Consider, for example, the aftermath of the September 11, 2001 terrorist attacks. Hijackers took control of three airplanes and flew them into the Twin Towers and the Pentagon. The impact these events had on the airline industry was significant. Travel was down and the cost of jet fuel rose by double digits. One airline's response to the downturn was to demand that mechanics agree to a 24 percent pay cut under threat of the airline declaring bankruptcy. Under similar conditions, the unions at Delta Airlines agreed to a contract that netted more than $1 billion in annual savings for the company.

Principled Bargaining Principled bargaining as a negotiating strategy is characterized by parties who are more interested in solving a problem than they are in winning a position. In doing so, the parties remain open to looking at the problem in new ways, brainstorming for ideas, and often coming up with an agreement that solves the original problem in a way that wasn't originally contemplated by either side. The most common forms of principled bargaining are as follows:

Integrative Bargaining: In integrative bargaining, the parties look at all the issues and are able to make mutually agreeable trade-offs between those issues.

Interest-Based Bargaining: Interest-based bargaining is based on the concept that both sides in the negotiation have harmonious interests. In labor-management negotiations, for example, both labor and management have an equal interest in the continuing viability of the business—for management to earn profits and for labor to have continued employment.

Collective-Bargaining Strategies

In addition to collective-bargaining positions, HR professionals should be aware of the four basic negotiating strategies used in union environments:

Single-Unit Bargaining The most common strategy, *single-unit bargaining*, occurs when one union meets with one employer to bargain.

Parallel Bargaining In *parallel bargaining*, also known as *pattern bargaining*, *whipsawing*, or *leapfrogging*, the union negotiates with one employer at a time. After a contract has been reached with one employer, the union uses the gains made during the negotiation as a base for negotiating with the next employer.

Multiemployer Bargaining In *multiemployer bargaining*, the union negotiates with more than one employer in an industry or region at a time. This situation can occur when temporary workers are part of a client employer's bargaining unit and the union negotiates with both the temp agency and the client employer on employment issues.

Multi-Unit Bargaining *Multi-unit bargaining*, or *coordinated bargaining*, occurs when several unions represent different bargaining units in the company. An example of this occurs in the airline industry, when the employer negotiates with the unions representing pilots, flight attendants, and mechanics or other employee classes. This allows the employer to coordinate negotiations on mandatory and permissive bargaining subjects while allowing the unions to cooperate on issues that have similar meaning to their various members.

Collective-Bargaining Subjects

The subjects open for negotiation during the collective-bargaining process fall into four areas:

Mandatory Subjects The NLRA defines the subjects that are mandatory in the collective-bargaining process. These are wages, hours, other terms and conditions of employment, and the negotiation of the agreement and bargaining related to questions that arise from the agreement. Both parties must bargain on mandatory subjects, and unresolved issues on them are the only ones that may be the subject of a strike or lockout.

Illegal Subjects The NLRA also identifies topics that are unlawful for inclusion in a collective-bargaining agreement, including hot-cargo clauses and closed-shop security agreements.

Voluntary Subjects Voluntary or permissible subjects for negotiation would be any lawful topic other than those identified as mandatory by the NLRA. These generally include management rights, such as production scheduling, operations, and selecting supervisors.

Reserved-Rights Doctrine Management generally includes a clause in the contract that states that any rights not covered specifically in the agreement are the sole responsibility of management.

Remaining Union-Free

To remain union-free, employers can make truthful statements about the consequences of unionization in response to union claims—as long as the TIPS guideline is followed (do not Threaten, Interrogate, Promise, or Spy). The FOE acronym is also useful to help supervisors respond to organizing activities (supervisors should state only Facts, Opinions, and give specific Examples). Just as union organizers work to convince employees to join the union, management may communicate their reasons for opposing unionization. During any organizing campaign, an experienced labor attorney should review management statements about the union before they're disseminated. All members of the management team should be coached on unfair labor practices and how to avoid them, particularly first-line supervisors because they interact most frequently with rank-and-file employees. First-line supervisors also have more influence with their direct reports than any other member of management, and employers should use this relationship by providing them with the information they will need to effectively represent the management view to employees.

Finally, organizers understand that enthusiasm and support for the union peaks at a certain point and then support begins to dwindle. For that reason, unions like to schedule elections to coincide with the peak of interest, and they gear their organizing activities to that goal. If an employer can delay the election, the chances of prevailing against the union are improved.

Most employers prefer to operate in a union-free environment. An effective Employer Relations program and organization culture that treats employees with dignity and respect is more likely to remain union-free because employee needs are being met without a union. Characteristics of organizations that are less vulnerable to unionization attempts include the following:

- An open, inclusive work environment
- Clear communication about organization goals and successes
- Consistent, equitable application of organization policies, procedures, and work rules
- An established conflict-resolution or complaint process that provides an outlet for solving problems so that employees feel heard and appreciated
- Disciplinary procedures that include an impartial, complete review of facts prior to taking action, particularly for termination decisions

When employees are treated poorly, are overworked, are stressed about their jobs, and don't have management support, union promises of better pay and working conditions are attractive, and employees often turn to unions with the hope that the union will be able to improve their work situation. Unions also offer leadership opportunities as shop stewards and union officers for members who may otherwise not have those opportunities.

Nonunion Philosophy

A carefully worded statement of an employer's philosophy regarding unions can be a useful strategy to help avoid union-organizing activities. While employees have the right to organize, an employer also has the right to communicate its desire to maintain an environment of close management-employee relations. Many employers fear that if they discuss unions with their employees, the employees will be motivated to begin organizing. However, open communication about the factual limitations of unions serves to educate employees, enabling them to respond favorably to the employer if approached by a union. For example, it's prudent for the employer to remind employees that a union can't provide for them anything the employer doesn't agree to through the collective-bargaining process and that if they need or desire specific working conditions or benefits, the employer is open for discussion with the employees directly. A nonunion philosophy statement can't threaten retaliation or promise benefits, but it may discuss the employer's desire to avoid third-party relationships. A nonunion philosophy statement should be properly vetted by a labor attorney to ensure compliance with the NLRA.

Climate Assessments

The best opportunity to identify and respond to labor/management communication deficiencies is before the relationship deteriorates. Assessing the organizational climate through employee surveys, committees, and third-party facilitation can provide the information necessary to get in front of issues before they grow into large-scale morale problems—a climate ripe for promises by unions of better working conditions. Building trust through open and honest communication and problem-solving will help reduce the likelihood of successful union authorization.

Management Training

Managers need to be trained to recognize union organizing activities such as the following:

- Increased interest in policies and benefits
- Surge of complaints against managers
- Unusual/excessive grouping of employees, such as in the parking lot
- Excessive strangers or visitors on-site with no clear purpose
- Open talk about unions, or the use of union terms when discussing working conditions or policies

These are just some examples of behavioral indications that a union may be attempting to organize. Further training of managers should include enforcement of open-door policies, fair and proper treatment of employees, responsiveness to complaints, and what they can/can't do if they suspect union organizing.

Summary

Talent Management in the 2024 HRCI exam updates blended three functional areas: Employee Relations, Engagement, and Learning and Development. These are interrelated functions within talent management, each contributing to the development and retention of employees to achieve organizational goals. Effective employee relations create and maintain a positive workplace environment, which in turn enhances employee engagement. Learning and development initiatives provide opportunities for skill enhancement and career growth, further deepening employee engagement and strengthening employee relations. When a business is unionized, these functions are conducted within a framework of labor relations.

A learning organization is an entity that prioritizes continuous learning, adaptation, and innovation, where individuals at all levels are encouraged to acquire and share knowledge to improve organizational performance. To be effective, senior HR leaders must develop talent and build a skilled workforce that is integrated and aligned with current and future organizational needs. To develop a learning organization, it is often necessary to use training as an intervention strategy that develops targeted programs to address gaps between actual and desired performance. Training is used to enhance current performance, whereas development programs are strategically designed to address future roles. Knowledge management is a key feature of learning organizations as a means of organizing and leveraging information to drive competitiveness and business continuity in the event of lost talent.

Key to talent management is focusing on employee engagement initiatives, and leaders are major drivers of employee retention. Organizations must undertake leadership development programs to retain a qualified workforce and prepare for future needs.

Part of employee relations is the need to develop and manage return-to-work strategies to provide guidance on facilitating smooth transitions for employees returning from different types of leave.

When a third party is present in talent management, such as a labor union, labor relations strategies form a significant portion of a senior leader's job. This requires a practical understanding of topics such as union organizing, strikes, unfair labor practices, and collective bargaining.

Exam Essentials

Understand the relationship between individual and organizational performance. Learning organizations connect individual and organizational performance by creating a culture of continuous learning and development. This culture is built upon a symbiotic environment where success is interdependent. These environments encourage employees to acquire new skills, share knowledge, and innovate, leading to enhanced productivity, adaptability, and competitiveness.

Understand and be able to develop and evaluate training strategies. Learning and development programs tie together the elements needed to attract and retain key employees. To do this, senior-level HR professionals will be well versed in program basics such as modes of delivery, timing, and content development.

Be able to analyze business needs to align employee development programs with business goals. Developing career paths and succession plans for employees serves many purposes. It helps employers identify where succession plans will need to be built. It offers employees meaningful feedback on the gap between where they are and where they hope to be. The career pathing process also improves retention by helping employees see the bigger picture of their role at the company and how they can develop to contribute. Conducting needs assessments and budgeting for these activities are critical tools throughout this process.

Develop, integrate, and evaluate L&D activities that are designed to increase retention. Retention is a critical activity for human resource business partners. In fact, activities related to L&D activities run through all other HR functions. HR staff use L&D to ensure that new hires are properly onboarded and trained. L&D activities are focused on preparing a workforce to be ready for growth—both individually (through career development and coaching) and organizationally (through strategic interventions such as assessing talent and managing employee movement).

Understand the union organizing, collective bargaining, and grievance dispute processes. Managing labor relations requires a thorough understanding of the laws governing employee-labor relations. These laws cover the right of workers to form unions, mandatory and permissive bargaining subjects, and handling employee grievances. A senior HR leader should also be well versed in practices designed to remain union-free.

Review Questions

You can find the answers in Appendix A.

1. ____________ is (are) a critical component to an effective learning and development system.
   - A. Design of training
   - B. Mode of delivery
   - C. Integration with other business outcomes
   - D. Cost savings initiatives
2. Career management and planning are two L&D activities that *best* promote which of the following outcomes?
   - A. Business continuity
   - B. Retention
   - C. Return on investment
   - D. Employee training
3. Which of the following is most likely to appeal to early career professionals?
   - A. Comprehensive retirement plans with high matching contributions
   - B. Extensive health insurance coverage, including dental and vision
   - C. Generous unlimited PTO policies and parental leave options
   - D. Opportunities for professional development and career advancement
4. Which of the following best illustrates the difference between operational and strategic learning and development activities in the workplace?
   - A. Operational learning focuses on short-term skill acquisition, whereas strategic learning emphasizes long-term organizational growth.
   - B. Operational learning involves immediate training needs, whereas strategic learning addresses future workforce capabilities.
   - C. Operational learning targets individual employee performance, whereas strategic learning concentrates on overall company objectives.
   - D. Operational learning pertains to day-to-day tasks, whereas strategic learning concerns broader organizational vision and direction.
5. Which of the following best describes strategic career pathing?
   - A. Assigning employees to various projects based on their current skill sets
   - B. Providing opportunities for horizontal movement within the organization
   - C. Planning and guiding employees' career progression in alignment with organizational goals
   - D. Conducting periodic performance evaluations to determine promotion eligibility

6. Which of the following describe training modes of delivery? (Choose all that apply.)
   - A. Classrooms with live instructors
   - B. Self-paced online modules for a virtual team
   - C. Asynchronous learning to increase flexibility
   - D. Formative assessment methods for facilitation

7. Which of the following assessments gauges employee perceptions within the workplace? (Choose all that apply.)
   - A. Climate assessments
   - B. Exit interviews
   - C. Annual reviews
   - D. Employee surveys

8. Which of the following strategies is most effective for utilizing L&D activities to enhance employee retention?
   - A. Offering curated training sessions to address employee needs as they develop
   - B. Implementing mentorship programs for ongoing support
   - C. Maintaining flexible modes of delivery to accommodate remote teams
   - D. Providing off-the-shelf training materials for consistent knowledge transfer

9. Where is the natural starting point for succession planning?
   - A. Selecting employees for promotion
   - B. Setting business goals
   - C. Conducting performance reviews
   - D. Conducting job analysis

10. "At RetailMart, we prioritize direct relationships with our employees based on trust, fairness, and transparency. We seek to maintain a workplace that fosters open communication, mutual respect, and collaboration. We provide competitive wages, comprehensive benefits, and opportunities for career growth." This statement is the best example of which of the following?
    - A. Code of conduct
    - B. Employment at will
    - C. Union-free philosophy
    - D. Company values

11. The company that you work for has asked HR to build a training program to improve decision making at all levels of the organization. What should your HR team do first?
    - A. Conduct a needs analysis.
    - B. Research off-the-shelf options.
    - C. Hire a new trainer.
    - D. Determine the ROI of the intervention.

12. Which of the following would be the *most* likely reason a company has chosen training as an intervention strategy?

    A. There is a high turnover rate in certain departments.

    B. There is a lack of motivation within the workforce.

    C. There is a gap between worker skills and organizational needs.

    D. The employees do not have the proper resources to do their jobs.

13. Which of the following correctly describes one type of strike used by labor unions?

    A. A wildcat strike initiated by management without union approval

    B. A lockout strike where employers prevent employees from working during a labor dispute

    C. A sympathy strike where workers strike to support another group of striking workers

    D. A judicial strike where a court orders workers to cease work due to legal violations

14. Which of the following steps is typically involved in handling an employee grievance as a senior leader?

    A. Allow the junior team to handle the initial complaint and get involved only if it escalates.

    B. Stay informed of the grievance status and intervene as necessary.

    C. Conduct an investigation to gather information and understand the nature of the grievance.

    D. Notify union representatives to protect the employee rights.

15. Which of the following strategies is most effective for fostering communication and addressing employee concerns in the workplace?

    A. Implementing hierarchical structures to streamline decision-making processes

    B. Establishing anonymous suggestion boxes to encourage feedback from employees

    C. Holding monthly town hall meetings where management delivers updates without opportunities for employee input

    D. Maintaining an open-door environment where employees feel comfortable approaching leadership with their concerns and ideas

16. As the HR Generalist for a large manufacturing organization, you have been tasked with understanding how current wage rates are affecting employee performance. Which of the following surveys should you design and administer?

    A. Market wage surveys

    B. Exit interviews

    C. Stay interviews

    D. Satisfaction surveys

17. Which of the following are mandatory subjects when collective bargaining? (Choose all that apply.)
    A. Wages
    B. Video surveillance for security purposes
    C. Third-party vending machine pricing
    D. Employee background checks
18. In what ways are succession plans tied to talent acquisition?
    A. A replacement employee may need to be groomed into a new position.
    B. A succession plan may require the need for a new hire.
    C. A succession plan will fail if not properly integrated with the talent acquisition process.
    D. A succession plan must be tied to business needs.
19. Which of the following should be included in a career management budget? (Choose all that apply.)
    A. Employee salaries
    B. HR salaries
    C. Training costs
    D. Background screening costs
20. Which of the following is a primary purpose of analyzing feedback from exit surveys for HR and L&D professionals?
    A. Identifying current employees' training needs
    B. Evaluating employee performance metrics
    C. Identifying trends and patterns related to training and career development
    D. Assessing organizational profitability

SPHR | SPHRi Exam: Total Rewards

SPHR/I RESPONSIBILITIES:

CREATING EFFECTIVE COMPENSATION AND BENEFIT STRATEGIES TO ATTRACT, REWARD, AND RETAIN TALENT THAT ALIGNS TO THE ORGANIZATIONAL STRATEGY AND CULTURE.

✓ **4.1 Design the total rewards philosophy and communications strategy that balances the organizational and individual needs (for example: hourly, salary, expatriate and foreign nationals, executives, board members, contractors)**

✓ **4.2 Create and evaluate compensation strategies that attract, reward, and retain talent (for example: classification, direct, indirect, incentives, bonuses, equity, executive compensation)**

✓ **4.3 Create and evaluate benefit strategies that attract, reward, and retain talent (for example: health, welfare, retirement, work-life balance, wellness)**

✓ **4.4 Design and develop employee recognition programs (for example: non-monetary and monetary rewards, workplace amenities, service awards)**

The exam content related to Total Rewards for the SPHR and SPHRi exams accounts for 17 percent of the exams, up from 12 percent in 2018 and tied for content weight with the Workforce Planning and Talent Acquisition function. The Exam Content Outline (ECO) summarizes this function as the ability for a senior-level professional to create effective compensation and benefit strategies to attract, reward, and retain talent that are in alignment with company goals and culture.

Total Rewards Defined

Total Rewards is defined by HRCI as the "financial and non-financial benefits that the employee sees as valuable." Additionally, HRCI notes that total compensation reflects the complete pay package that is made up of both compensation and benefits. As with all areas of human resources, the compensation and benefits function of an organization can be understood as having administrative, operational, and strategic activities. The administrative and operational components are covered at length in Chapter 6, "PHR/PHRi Total Rewards," but they should not be undervalued by those seeking to pass the SPHR/i exams. The fundamentals serve to inform strategic decision making, and strategic decision making affects organizational competitiveness. Perhaps this is simply another way of stating the directive from the ECO that Total Rewards (TR) strategies must be built around "attracting, rewarding, and retaining talent." In order for organizations to compete, they must be able to attract qualified people, reward them through monetary and non-monetary rewards, and then keep them satisfied—in short, balancing a desired workforce with one that is affordable. This chapter is focused on the TR strategies that help organizations achieve that competitive advantage. It begins with a look at the ethical and legal responsibilities an HR professional has when administering compensation programs.

Fiduciary Responsibility

The dictionary defines *fiduciary responsibility* as one that requires confidence or trust. HRCI takes that definition further, describing it as a "legal duty to act solely in the interest of another person without benefit, profit, or conflict of interest unless expressly permitted to do so by the other person." HR professionals who have responsibility for advising, managing, and/or administering TR programs find themselves in a role that legally requires them to act in a way that inspires confidence and trust of both management and employees to be effective.

In a legal context, a fiduciary relationship has one of the highest, if not the highest, standards of care imposed on the individual acting on behalf of another individual or entity. In the context of compensation and benefits, this most often applies to activities related to pensions and other benefit programs. Although the legal standard may not be as high in other TR functions, such as establishing salary ranges, recommending salary offers, or establishing merit budgets, these activities require HR professionals to act ethically and with integrity on behalf of their organizations. To establish and maintain a high level of trust and confidence, care must be taken to avoid even the appearance of conflicts or favoritism.

An HR professional could breach this responsibility in three ways:

- **Acting in Your Own Self-Interest:** HR professionals must always act in the best interest of the entire organization, not simply their own or their department's interest.
- **Conflicting Duties:** In some situations, an HR professional may need to give equal priority to two responsibilities. For example, when placing an HR position into a salary range, responsibility to the HR team may need to increase the wage band to attract qualified talent. The conflicting responsibility is to ensure the integrity of the salary ranges across the organization as a whole, which may simply equate to transparency by seeking higher approval. Relying on market data to make these and similar decisions can help eliminate such conflicts.
- **Profiting from Your HR Role:** It may be tempting to take advantage of the unique access to surveys and other information HR is privy to, but doing so to ensure personal gain destroys the trust of management and employees in the HR function.

Those tasked to act as a fiduciary must be aware of these violations in all elements of compensation and benefits administration.

Total Rewards Philosophy and Communicating Compensation Strategies

The *Total Rewards philosophy* is a high-level mission statement used to guide the development and implementation of compensation and benefits programs that attract, motivate, and retain employees. Typically, HR works closely with the executive management team to develop and implement the organization's TR philosophy as it must be aligned to an organization's purpose in order to be effective.

During the development or revision of a TR philosophy, the HR management team facilitates the process by gathering input from and building consensus with key stakeholders such as members of the executive team, board of directors, or compensation committee. Creating a TR philosophy in this way provides an opportunity to look at the whole package offered to employees and analyze which combination of programs will best achieve the organization's hiring, retention, and performance objectives. In smaller organizations or new startups that may not take the time to proactively define a TR philosophy, one may develop organically over time as a result of compensation programs implemented to meet specific needs or accomplish organizational goals. The danger in relying on this type of de facto philosophy in the long term is that it isn't likely to provide a framework that supports organizationwide goals and objectives as the company grows. Instead, business units may develop compensation practices designed to satisfy their individual needs but that conflict with programs implemented by other units. Senior-level HR has probably seen this play out in random job title assignments or disjointed duties that make benchmarking to external sources more difficult. Finally, as with any other HR function, the *development* of the program is equally as important as the *evaluation* of the program. Identifying whether the TR philosophy is resulting in the desired outcomes requires a long-term focus and strategy. Specific to the SPHR/i exams is the design of a Total Rewards philosophy that balances organizational needs with the needs of the individuals in the following ways:

Hourly Workers Craft a rewards structure that emphasizes fair wages, overtime pay, and benefits to recognize their contribution and increase commitment. Include opportunities for skill development and career advancement to enhance job satisfaction and retention.

Salaried Workers Develop a rewards program that balances competitive salaries, bonuses, and comprehensive benefits to incentivize performance and career growth. Incorporate personalized recognition programs and flexible work arrangements to support work-life balance.

Expatriate and Foreign Nationals Design a rewards system offering relocation assistance, tax equalization, and cultural support to ensure seamless integration and global competitiveness. Provide family support services and language training to facilitate a smoother transition.

Board Members Implement a rewards strategy that combines appropriate compensation and equity incentives to align their interests with organizational goals and governance. Supplement this with periodic performance reviews and transparent communication to build trust and accountability.

Contractors Create a rewards approach that provides competitive rates and project-based incentives to attract skilled contractors while maintaining budget flexibility. Pay attention to expansion of minimum wage laws to gig workers. Complement this with recognition programs and consistent communication to create a sense of inclusion and partnership.

Trend analysis can be an excellent way to help organizations keep pace with emerging needs and cutting-edge practices, particularly in the domain of Total Rewards. Consider, for example, that the title of this functional area has changed three times in the last 15 or so years, from Total Rewards to Compensation and Benefits and now back to Total Rewards. What can this small piece of information tell us about this field of practice? For one, it tells us that the workplace and the workforce are ever-changing and that our reward practices must respond. The recent decision to revert back to the Total Rewards title alerts us to the idea that the practice of attracting, retaining, and rewarding employees is not only about items such as base pay or health insurance. The workforce of today demands innovation and value from their employment. This includes more flexibility, rapid career growth, and the ability to gain a sense of purpose and meaning from their work.

Employees today see rewards as going beyond traditional compensation and benefits programs, and their tenure behaviors reflect this. The Bureau of Labor Statistics reported that as of January 2022, the average employment tenure of all wage workers was about 4.1 years, unchanged from the median in 2020. While 2022 is the most current year for this figure, it remains fairly consistent in that since 2016, the average tenure of workers was 4.2 years. This means that for almost a decade, the average tenure of employees is less than 5 years. This data should change the focus of an employer's Total Rewards strategy from legacies, (jobs people retire from) and orient programs toward shorter-term retention, knowledge management, and succession planning.

Beyond the national statistics, it is important that you understand the average tenure rate of employees within your company, preferably sorted demographically and by department. Workforce analytics is one way that you can use technology to help predict employee movement. Surveying employees on what they believe to be the most valuable in their Total Rewards offerings is another example of the use of analytics to inform TR decision making. HR can support technological solutions that are relevant and effective in retaining talented workers.

In the following section, we explore the driving needs and potential solutions to the new workplace, structured in accordance with the SPHR/i exam content outline.

Competing in the Market

Fundamental to an organization's compensation philosophy is the decision to *lead the market, lag the market,* or *match the market*—meaning the median pay in the relevant external labor market. HRCI defines these terms as strategies:

- **Lead the Market:** A compensation strategy that is higher than the average pay rate
- **Lag the Market:** A compensation strategy that is lower than the average pay rate
- **Match the Market:** A compensation strategy that seeks to match the average pay rate

This decision has many implications, including pay equity, cost of labor, and the ability to attract and keep talented workers.

A survey collaboration by Deloitte and Empsight on Total Rewards found that most employers' goal is to be at market median (`www2.deloitte.com/us/en/pages/human-capital/articles/total-rewards-survey-initial-findings.html`). That may be fine for some industries in some geographic locations and for some positions. However, as mentioned in the introduction, the workforce of today is incredibly diverse, and as a result, different organizations have different priorities and values. This may be driven by the size of the employer as well. The same Deloitte survey found that of those employers who desired to be *above* market median for their compensation philosophy, one third of those were small employers (fewer than 500 employees).

The economic climate is another factor that employers use to inform their compensation philosophy. In strong economies, there may be lower levels of unemployment, meaning that employers may need to lead their industries in TR. Geography also plays a role. Some geographic locations have higher concentrations of certain types of skill sets, meaning an employer can afford to lag the labor market for certain jobs as there is a greater supply of workers in the area. The cost of living in many areas plays an important role in an employer's TR philosophy. For example, the housing market in the San Francisco Bay area is so costly that pay rates and other cash and non-cash offerings (transportation, housing allowances, flexible commute schedules) must track with this and other cost-of-living factors.

A philosophy is driven by much more than just market conditions; it must also be aligned with the business's core strategy.

Strategic Alignment

Strategic Total Rewards programs are built from very similar components as business strategy. Compensation experts must consider internal and external conditions as well as external opportunities and threats that affect their ability to use compensation to attract, reward, and retain talent. Companies should also consider their core values and the type of employer they wish to be (or be perceived as being). For example, companies with growth plans will need to conduct skills inventories and regularly audit incumbent pay rates for competitiveness. Where gaps in skills or shortages in labor markets exist, they will then need to make decisions about whether to attract and "buy" the talent from outside the organization or to invest in training programs to "build" the talent up from within.

Senior-level HR professionals will also need to be up-to-date on emerging pay laws. An example of this includes the Department of Labor's new factors test for unpaid internships that will make it easier for employers to access talent. In short, the factors must show that the unpaid intern is the "primary beneficiary" of the unpaid internship—not the employer. The factors include whether or not the job duties are tied to the intern's educational program, the degree of scheduling in alignment with the academic calendar, the length of the internship, the degree to which the internship supplements as opposed to replaces an existing job, and the extent to which the intern understands that the job is unpaid.

HR will also need to consider the systems that must be built to deliver pay and where a self-service system can be successfully implemented. This includes determining how pay will be calculated in accordance with performance goals as well as the regulatory requirements of the locations where they do business. Finally, a compensation philosophy that is aligned with strategy will need to consider how Total Rewards will be allocated.

Strategic Allocation

The reality for many employers is that compensation and benefits account for the largest expense on their profit-and-loss statements. Many employers rely on senior HR professionals to help them find ways to stabilize what has been an increasing cost of doing business for the last several years. For this reason, a major consideration of rewards allocation is affordability. As a general rule, organizations use a two-year planning horizon when budgeting how much in compensation they can afford to commit. From this, a forecast that includes pay increases, incentives, and other factors can be created.

The mix of TR components is an important consideration when deciding how to allocate organizational resources. Once an employer has decided what it can afford, it must then make a choice about what to allocate toward cash and non-cash rewards. For example, $1 per hour in base pay is taxable, whereas an additional $1 in health benefits is not. Note that the IRS does require that employers tax as earnings pay in lieu of benefits.

Employees at different stages of life will often value very different things; millennials may be seeking relief from student loan debt, young parents may prize childcare offerings, and older workers may more appreciate part-time work options that offer health benefits. A *conjoint analysis* is a statistical survey that asks participants to assign a value to presented options. It allows employers to interpret what trade-offs employees may be willing to make in their TR plans. There are a few key advantages to this type of analysis. One is that it allows employers to use the resulting data to offer a total compensation mix that is most valued by their specific workforce instead of trying to "guess" what employees would prefer or try to follow their competitors.

NOTE Senior-level HR professionals must prepare for the coming skills shortage that is partially due to the baby boomer generation reaching retirement age. The Transamerica Center for Retirement Studies reports that 10,000 baby boomers will turn 65 every day between 2011 to 2029, with 58 percent of them planning to continue working after they retire. This means the workplace will continue to have up to four generations at a time with unique monetary and non-monetary rewards needs. You can find more about this at `www.transamericacenter.org/retirement-research/retirement-survey/infographics/10000-baby-boomers`.

With an aging population exploring employment options past the age of retirement, the need for retiree savings may be a priority for your workgroup.

Real World Scenario

7 Ways Employers Can Enhance Their Total Rewards Packages

The Transamerica Institute released a press release of the findings from their annual retirement survey. In it, they noted that almost 7 in 10 employers either currently use or plan to use artificial intelligence (AI) to supplement their current workforce, but "Robotics and artificial intelligence may be revolutionizing the business world, but human workers are still critically needed." Many employers are feeling the pain of the prolonged labor crunch. Those with innovative and robust benefit offerings have an edge in the competition for talent. (`www.transamericacenter.org/retirement-research/retirement-survey/infographics/10000-baby-boomers`)

The Institute described seven total rewards strategies to help enhance employer competitiveness in the labor market:

1. Facilitate Professional Development.

   With emerging technologies like artificial intelligence transforming the workplace, keeping employees' skills up-to-date is more important than ever. However, only 44 percent of employers currently offer job training, and just 35 percent provide professional development programs. Employers should prioritize helping their workers stay relevant in an evolving job market.

2. Expand Alternative Work Arrangements.

   The pandemic proved that flexible work arrangements can be successful, and employees aren't keen on returning to the old ways. While many employers offer some form of alternative work arrangement, there's room for improvement. Currently, the most commonly offered options include:

   - Flexible work schedules (59 percent)
   - Ability to adjust hours as needed (54 percent)
   - Unpaid leave of absence (44 percent)
   - Hybrid work (43 percent)
   - On-site work options (38 percent)
   - Exclusive remote work (37 percent)
   - Switching between full-time and part-time (36 percent)

3. Support Caregivers in the Workplace.

   As the population ages and the cost of long-term care rises, many workers are responsible for caring for aging loved ones. Despite this, employer support remains limited. The most common forms of assistance are:

   - Unpaid leave of absence (39 percent)
   - Paid leave of absence (35 percent)
   - Online resources/tools (25 percent)
   - Referrals to backup care (23 percent)
   - Caregiving training for employees (23 percent)

4. Offer Phased or Flexible Retirement.

   With baby boomers retiring and Generation X not far behind, many older workers are looking for a gradual transition into retirement rather than stopping work abruptly. Unfortunately, only 35 percent of employers have a formal phased retirement program, and just 28 percent plan to implement one in the future. Most employers rely on informal methods to help older workers transition out.

5. Foster an Age-Friendly Work Environment.

   The multigenerational workforce includes four generations spanning over seven decades. While 87 percent of employers believe they are age-friendly, the survey tells a different story. Only 44 percent have a formal diversity, equity, and inclusion policy that specifically mentions age alongside other demographic characteristics.

6. Provide More Health, Welfare, and Retirement Benefits.

   Although many employers offer some benefits, they can do better. The most commonly provided benefits include:

   - Health insurance (64 percent)
   - 401(k) or similar plan (59 percent)
   - Life insurance (46 percent)
   - Employee assistance program (35 percent)
   - Workplace wellness program (35 percent)
   - Disability insurance (34 percent)

7. Enhance Retirement Benefits.

   The SECURE 2.0 Act of 2022 makes it easier and more affordable for employers to adopt retirement plans, with new provisions to enhance current 401(k) offerings. Yet, only 32 percent of plan sponsors are "very" familiar with the law, and just 2 percent of employers without retirement benefits have a similar level of awareness. Employers should take advantage of these opportunities to help workers better prepare for retirement.

   Source: Adapted from `https://transamericainstitute.org/docs/default-source/research/employers-benefit-offerings/workplace-transformations-employer-business-practices-and-benefit-offerings-press-release-march-2024.pdf`

One solution may be found in the behavioral sciences. The Department of Labor (DOL)'s Chief Evaluation Office has been testing various approaches to how behavioral sciences can influence positive outcomes for employees. In our retirement savings example, the DOL tested whether simple emails, or emails plus reminders, would have an effect on savings behaviors. For example, their research found that receiving an email reminding the employee to contribute doubled the number of workers who contributed. For those already contributing, it increased savings by an average of $3,000 per year.

NOTE For a full review of the DOL's program, go to `www.dol.gov` and search for **behavioral insights**.

Integrative Approach

An integrative approach as a TR best practice is used to help employers align their Total Rewards strategies to three needs: 1) achieve business goals, 2) meet the needs of a diverse workgroup, and 3) manage costs. The Deloitte survey referenced earlier noted that many employers *know* that they must transform their TR strategy and delivery but that they are uncertain how to do so. As a result, *cost* continues to be the primary factor driving the design of Total Rewards. A truly integrated approach, however, must expand its focus to include what people want, what people need, customization, and flexibility. Companies that wish to attract and retain scarce or unique talent will need to structure their TR systems to allow for rewards based on the value that the individual adds to the company while not overpaying for certain roles.

A holistic approach should also account for employee career goals. For example, many talented workers in fields such as science and technology do not wish to go into management yet still want the opportunity to optimize their status, title, and earnings. A dual-career structure is one method that can help. A dual-career ladder allows employees to choose a management path or a path with increasing recognition and rewards based on professional achievements such as leading research or being published.

Employers are increasingly becoming aware of the value that generous leave and other time-off policies can bring. Google, for example, increased its paid maternity leave benefit from 12 weeks to 18 weeks and reported a 50 percent decrease in the number of new mothers who quit (`https://qz.com/work/1293090/what-the-gates-foundation-learned-by-offering-52-weeks-of-paid-parental-leave`). In an industry where women in STEM (science, technology, engineering, and math) jobs experience significant barriers to success, this strategy is effective.

Flexible work arrangements are another element of an integrative TR approach. With more than 40 percent of the millennial generation reporting that they plan to leave their jobs after just two years, flexible work arrangements and other work-life balance initiatives may be a viable solution to retention problems.

Effectively pricing dual-career and other career path models and designing flexible work arrangements that still allow for productivity are dependent on many factors, including the need for job analysis and job pricing. This is the focus of the following sections.

Job Analysis

The process of building job families is generally a feature of the workforce planning function of HR. In the context of compensation, however, it is also reliant on the structural drivers of the function of business management. How a company is structured will drive how jobs are structured, which in turn will drive how jobs are compensated.

Building job families is a classification technique used to group jobs according to business units. Job families are organized by titles, usually from the senior level down to the entry level. This sorting requires analysis to determine what makes each job unique from the others, including levels of knowledge, skills, abilities, and other performance measures. Once this has been accomplished, the salary structures can be built. Options include the following:

- **Traditional:** Useful for larger, more bureaucratic organizations that are hierarchical in nature and where jobs are structured to allow for progression in both responsibility and pay. Narrow-graded structures may have 10 or more grades in a job family and are dependent on job evaluation to define each grade. Pay ranges are then attached to each grade.
- **Broad-banded:** Perhaps the most useful to organizations that desire maximum flexibility in deciding pay rates, broad-banding has a greater spread between high and low pay, in some cases between 70 and 100 percent. This allows employers to reward employees for reasons other than grading or other market-driven controls.
- **Broad-graded:** Useful in organizations that desire a blended approach, broad-graded structures reduce the number of grades from 10 or more down to 5 or 6. These employers also adopt a broader wage spread than traditional structures, usually of around 30 to 80 percent.

Job grading (also known as leveling) is a type of compensation structure that provides the basis for assigning pay ranges. Leveling is a relatively new job evaluation method that is helping HR evaluate jobs based on the knowledge and skills as well as the cultural behaviors that are necessary to perform the job. This assists in the creation of career and development plans. For example, entry-level IT professionals may be paid at the lower end of a pay grade, but if they add skills or knowledge, they can become eligible to move up the pay grade. Leveling uses comparable worth to determine the relative value of a job within an organization. Many employees believe that their jobs should be worth more to the organization than internal comparisons or external market value dictates. HR can help educate employees on the processes used to price jobs, including how job descriptions and salary ranges are developed.

As you can see, salary structures are dependent on factors other than market rates; salary structures are a place where employers may embed what they value. However, in order to build a coherent salary structure, HR must have completed the process of evaluating and pricing jobs.

Job Evaluation and Pricing

The purpose of job evaluation is to help employers determine the worth of jobs within an organization when compared to internal data. Job worth is based on the principle that some jobs are more valuable to an organization's effectiveness and thus its ability to compete. Although traditional evaluation methods focus mostly on internal criteria, many scholars agree that employers must include external market factors in the evaluation process. This external data is used to establish internal *salary ranges,* which identifies the lowest and highest wages paid to employees who work similar jobs. Job pricing is achieved by calculating the floor and ceiling in relation to the *salary mid-point*—the amount of money between the highest and lowest amount paid for a particular job. The mid-point is often used to forecast salary budgets in strategic planning as well.

Job evaluation methods can be quantitative, such as evaluating job content to identify responsibilities, or nonquantitative, such as ranking jobs in order of importance to the company's core competencies.

Choosing which job evaluation method to use is dependent on the goals of a compensation program. For a smaller business, the most important consideration may be ease of development and use. Larger corporations may be more interested in perceptions of equity. For still other companies, it may be more realistic to blend one or more methods in order to achieve organizational goals.

NOTE

If you are unfamiliar with benchmarking and salary surveys used in the job evaluation process, you can refresh your knowledge by reviewing these sections in Chapter 2, "Shared Competencies."

Collective Bargaining and Contract Costing

Decisions about how to structure job families are dependent on many of the variables that affect the structure of TR programs. One factor to this is the presence of a union and formal collective bargaining agreement that dictates a large part of how TR will be designed and implemented, sometimes over several years. In fact, wages and benefits are a mandatory subject when negotiating a collective bargaining agreement. A feature of bargaining is how pay will be structured.

For example, in a two-tiered system, the union may agree to pay less for new hires performing work for which more senior employees are paid a higher wage. In some cases, wages for new members can be as much as 30 percent lower than their senior peers. Or less senior employees may receive fewer benefits or fewer protections against layoffs. Debatable as discriminatory or unfair representation, they nevertheless exist in many industries, including manufacturing and auto.

Another compensation issue that relates to collective bargaining includes using lump sum payments for annual increases. Lump sum payments do not increase base wages, which are what is used to calculate overtime and pension benefits. For this reason, lump sum payments are often used in negotiations by employers wishing to keep labor costs steady.

Two-tiered wage systems and lump sum payments both contribute to the total cost of a labor contract. For that reason, it is important for senior leaders to understand how to estimate how much a negotiated labor contract is worth. To do so, experts advise that they first focus on data collection. This must include total hours worked by both union and nonunion members and cost of total compensation, including non-cash and other rewards. HR must also have access to forecasts for the term of the contract and an average breakdown of labor costs by worker classification. HR should be well versed in basic accounting and budgeting principles and should have access to company financials such as income statements, balance sheets, and any other contracts that influence profitability.

NOTE It is beyond the scope of the exams to cover in detail the methods used for total costing of a collective bargaining agreement. However, there are several detailed accounts available, such as ones provided at www.calpelra.org, that we recommend if you wish to be more familiar with the concept.

Motivating and Retaining Through Total Rewards

Many employers (and employees) believe that higher pay equals higher performance. The truth of the matter is that there is a limitation on what money can do. Monetary compensation can certainly help employees run through Maslow's Hierarchy of Needs (see Chapter 2 for a refresher of this and other theories of motivation). For example, base wages and cash incentives meet individuals' basic needs, allowing them to purchase food and shelter. It allows employees to go on vacation with family, or to make financial contributions to religious or community organizations, which are both social needs tied to belonging. Higher pay and incentives that are tied closely with status may also meet an employee's esteem needs, both on and off the job. One CEO of a cosmetics company was quoted as saying, "It took me a long time to learn that people do what you pay them to do, not what you ask them to do." However, this seems contrary to many of the 21st century claims that employees seek recognition, praise, and appreciation above all else.

NOTE There is an excellent TED talk on the topic of motivation and rewards by Dan Pink. The title of the 2009 video is "The Puzzle of Motivation." View it to learn about the candle problem and how it is related to the true impact of incentive pay on creative thinking and problem-solving. Find it at `https://www.ted.com/talks/dan_pink_on_motivation?language=en`.

Regardless, there are limitations to what wages and other monetary incentives can do. This has been a focus of the organizational behavior sciences over the last several years, resulting in empirical evidence related to the topic. Several of these findings are reviewed next.

Efficiency vs. Empathy Wages

There are two important terms to understand in this section. *Efficiency wages* are above-market pay rates used specifically to attract talent in a competitive market. *Empathy wages* refer to the effect the pay premiums have on employee behavior when tied to feelings of gratitude and loyalty. Studies show that the effect efficiency wages have on employee performance is dependent on whether employees feel gratitude for the premium. Researchers noted that "non-star" employees, those described as being economically disadvantaged and lower on the performance scale when compared to others, are more likely to be appreciative of the additional pay and, thus, motivated and loyal. Note that this does not mean they are poor performers or unable to do their jobs; they are simply rated lower when compared to others. In contrast, star performers are more likely to believe that they are deserving of the pay premium and thus feel less gratitude. This, in theory, means that the effect the pay premium has on driving high performer behaviors is less. When considered in the context of commission-based pay, this has very real implications for employers that are potentially overpaying for labor.

NOTE

The source of much of the content in the "Efficiency vs. Empathy Wages" section was a 2013 journal article published in *Research in Organizational Behavior* and written by James N. Baron. The title is "Empathy Wages? Gratitude and Gift Exchange in Employment Relationships." Check it out for more on this emerging topic: `www.sciencedirect.com/science/article/pii/S0191308513000087`.

Other Studies

The design of incentive programs also has significant influence on creating intrinsic motivation—that is, behavior that is driven from within. One scientific survey found that *publicizing* recognition as a work incentive is effective. They found that publicly recognizing an employee's efforts in a ceremony or online seems to increase the motivating value of the reward regardless of whether it was monetary or non-monetary. This is due in part to the social reinforcement that naturally occurs when behavior is made public. The study also found that the *scarcity* of rewards increased positive feelings in employees. The authors attributed this to the attachment of an emotional reaction individuals have when they "win" something that is limited to a certain amount. This is in contrast to base pay as a motivating reward, because all employees receive wages.

NOTE

For more on the findings related to publicity and scarcity of rewards, take a look at the original 2013 study published in the *Journal of Socio-Economics* titled "And the Winner Is . . . ? The Motivating Power of Employee Rewards" conducted by Susanne Neckermann and Bruno S. Frey. Find the report at `https://papers.ssrn.com/sol3/papers.cfm?abstract_id=2369372`.

Another consideration in this realm is employee need. Some reports have shown that the effect that pay has on the job attitudes of employee engagement, job satisfaction, and organizational commitment is limited. Once employees exceed a certain pay threshold relative to their baseline needs, the effect of higher pay on job attitudes decreases, eventually having little to no effect on employee performance.

Finally, the sciences remind us that in order for rewards to be effective as motivational tools, employers must take care to manage pay equity issues. Environments where employees receive different pay for individual efforts without clear reasons for doing so may create feelings of unfairness or jealousy. Unequal pay dispersion can also increase negative organizational citizenship behaviors, from lack of teamwork to the more serious effect of sabotage. At its worst, if the unequal pay is based on discriminatory reasons, employers may be found guilty of violating Civil Rights laws.

What does this all mean in terms of attracting and retaining talent? Remember that a compensation philosophy is tied to decisions about whether to lead, lag, or match market rates. In a highly competitive industry, it may be valuable for employers to increase base wages (lead their market) to retain the talent necessary to operate. Perhaps more significantly the reverse is also true: Paying more for the highly talented may not be enough to bind them to your company, leading you back to the concepts of the integrative pay practices and application of fundamental theories of motivation.

Best Practices

The organizational sciences also give us insights into how to create TR best practices that increase rather than decrease employee motivation. Researchers found that money and incentives:

- **Do not improve job-related knowledge, skills, or abilities (KSAs).** Unless the monetary incentive is invested in training and development activities, the money alone does not improve an employee's KSAs.
- **Do not necessarily improve the quality of jobs.** Plenty of research exists that shows that money is only part of the equation, that the 21st century workforce craves autonomy, meaning, recognition, and feedback in addition to work-life balance.
- **Cannot improve ethical behaviors.** There is the possibility that monetary incentives may actually increase unethical behavior in some employees. For example, the authors of a study that presented an article in *Science Direct* recounted a story at a large frozen vegetable production facility, where the company incentivized employees for every insect they found on the line. It was later discovered that employees were bringing *in* insects, placing them in the vegetables, then removing them to receive the incentive (www.sciencedirect.com/science/article/abs/pii/S0007681312001632).

  The authors of this study noted that there are five fundamental principles to consider when designing successful monetary reward systems. These include that an organization should do the following:

  - Define and measure performance accurately. This includes both what employees should and should not do.

- Make rewards contingent on performance. Ensure there is enough variance between performance levels to actually motivate behaviors.
- Reward employees in a timely manner. Provide regular, ongoing feedback and rewards rather than relying on an appraisal system.
- Maintain justice in the reward system. Consider the process used to determine pay (procedural justice) and for whom the rewards are available (distributive justice).
- Use both monetary and non-monetary rewards. Survey or conduct focus groups with your employees and then build reward systems that they value.

Equity Compensation

Equity (ownership in a business) is a valuable retention tool in many industries, particularly for the manager level and above. Most commonly understood to occur through stock options and grants (discussed in the upcoming sections), equity compensation is highly regulated. Equity as part of a total compensation package does tend to get a lot of negative attention. In many cases, this is because there is no clear link between reward and performance. For that reason, and in order to ensure the incentive is effective, senior leaders must take care to do the following:

- Understand the business strategy for which equity will be used to achieve.
- Define both short- and long-term performance measures to balance decision making.
- Create criteria for which to evaluate success and/or failure.
- Tie a portion of the reward to the adherence to company values and ethics.

Blockchain tokens as equity incentives is also an emerging trend being used to reward and retain employees. The Society for Human Resource Management (SHRM) stated the following about the ways employers are using blockchain technology to reward employees:

> They are being used like equity or phantom-equity awards, granted as compensation for past or future services.
>
> They may be subject to vesting based on continued service or achievement of performance targets, and acceleration of vesting can be triggered based on designated events, such as the occurrence of a change of control transaction, the termination of an employee without cause, or the achievement of technical milestones.
>
> If an employee quits, the employer has the right to repurchase any remaining restricted tokens that have not yet vested.
>
> Johnson Y., Rathjen K. (2018). Blockchain tokens as compensation treated like equity awards. Society for Human Resource Management.
>
> *Source:* `http://SHRM.org`

Senior-level HR professionals must stay up-to-date on this emerging issue, especially as it relates to how this and alternate currency is to be regulated.

Executive Compensation

As the complexity of managing organizations in a global environment increases, the need to attract and retain executives with the skills and talent to lead a company is even more critical for success. Executive compensation is a controversial subject for shareholders and, since the collapse of major corporations in the finance industry in 2008, is the focus of increasing scrutiny by federal and state regulators.

The responsibility for negotiating executive compensation packages belongs to the board of directors (BoD). The BoD is expected to negotiate with executive candidates and incumbents "at arm's length," meaning that the negotiations are conducted with objectivity and in the best interest of the company. Because executive candidates and incumbents are, almost by definition, skilled negotiators, the conventional wisdom is that they will push hard for packages that they view as competitive and in their own interests. Shareholders are increasingly active in challenging excessive compensation, particularly when executives receive massive compensation when business results are falling, or employees are being laid off in large numbers as the result of poor decisions made by executives.

There have been many suggestions about how to develop compensation packages in a way that attracts and retains qualified, talented executives while maintaining the objectivity necessary to satisfy shareholder concerns. Some that are being considered or implemented include the following:

- Reporting transparency of executive compensation packages in annual reports and SEC filings
- Board compensation committees that consist only of outside directors (those without paid positions in the company) and that establish internal guidelines for executive compensation
- Use of independent data on competitive executive pay practices in developing internal guidelines
- Linking executive pay to long-term business results instead of quarterly or annual results (performance-based pay)
- Tying a significant piece of total compensation to achievable stretch goals that include profit goals in addition to share price
- Shareholder approval of executive stock-option plans
- Inclusion of non-monetary performance goals, such as "green" goals, ethical behaviors, or community investment in the rewards package

A typical compensation package for an executive can include elements from five categories: base salary, bonuses or short-term incentives, long-term incentives, employee benefits, and executive perks.

The composition of packages for individual executives varies by industry and company culture, with some having more pay at risk than others. In an effort to motivate executive performance and address shareholder concerns, BoDs construct packages that place the majority of executive compensation at risk in the form of short- and long-term incentives. The main theory at play in the use of incentive pay for executives is that, because they will benefit personally from decisions that achieve positive results for the company, they're more likely to act in ways that benefit the company than in ways that benefit them personally. One way this connection is achieved is that the size of the executive bonus pool is usually related to the profitability of the company, which by definition ties executive pay to business results.

Federal legislation has also impacted executive pay. In 1993, the Omnibus Budget Reconciliation Act (OBRA) was an attempt to reduce executive compensation by limiting employer tax deductions for executive pay to $1 million annually. Employers were allowed to deduct only what was deemed reasonable compensation. The definition of who is considered a covered executive includes chief financial officers (CFOs), meaning the deductibility of their compensation is also subject to the $1 million limitation. Because of this limitation, HR should be familiar with other, non-cash methods for which to reward and retain senior-level employees.

Publicly traded companies must disclose the relationship between executive compensation and company performance under the Security and Exchange Commission's (SEC) new "pay-versus-performance" rule. 2024 is the second year these disclosures are required, and companies will need to add an additional year of data in their tables and disclose "compensation actually paid" compared to financial performance, as well as their approach to executive pay. While a deeper dive into these new regulations is not required for exam readiness, it might be useful for HR professionals working for public corporations. Find out more about this recent development at `www.debevoise.com/insights/publications/2023/12/2024-executive-compensation-to-do-list`.

Executive benefits often include benefits available to employees throughout the organization, such as flexible work schedules, deferred compensation, tuition-reimbursement programs, or health club memberships. In some cases, benefit levels for executives may be expanded; for example, a flexible work arrangement for an executive may provide reimbursement for travel between the corporate office and the family home in another state, while the benefit available to nonexecutive employees allows telecommuting several days each week.

One unique element of executive compensation is *perquisites*. Perquisites, often referred to as *perks*, are additional benefits that provide comfort and luxury to the work and/or personal environment, usually intended for senior management and executives. The following are some of the perks provided to executive employees:

- Stock options
- Personal/spouse travel expenses
- Personal use of company aircraft
- Tax preparation and financial counseling
- Tax payments for benefits

- Supplemental retirement plans
- Housing allowances
- Home security services
- Company cars/chauffeurs
- Life insurance above company plan
- Medical plans above worker coverage
- Annual physicals
- Interest-free loans
- Company-paid legal advice

This element of an executive compensation package is often the least transparent and an area of increased interest to shareholders and regulators. At the beginning of 2007, the SEC requirements for reporting executive perks were reduced from $50,000 to $10,000, forcing companies to provide detailed lists of perks received by their executives. In some cases, the resulting exposure of payments outraged stockholders and employees and embarrassed BoDs. As a result, there is a growing trend of eliminating or reducing the numbers and types of perks previously provided. For example, the Lockheed-Martin BoD eliminated perks, including club memberships and fees and company-paid financial counseling and tax services for executives, and adjusted executive salaries to reflect the cash value of the perks to maintain the value of their compensation packages.

Other benefits that can be found in executive compensation packages include the following:

Golden Parachute A *golden parachute* provides significant benefits to an executive whose employment is terminated, usually under specific conditions such as a change in control of the company. Benefits can include severance pay, bonuses, options, continuation of medical coverage, and other types of benefits.

Golden Handshake A *golden handshake* is most often used when a CEO takes a position that entails a high risk of termination due to restructuring or a change in direction, or sometimes as an incentive to retire early.

Golden Handcuffs *Golden handcuffs* are a form of retention pay designed to keep key employees from leaving a company. They can take the form of stock options that vest over a period of years or a written agreement to pay back bonuses or other types of compensation if the employee resigns within a specified period of time.

Golden Life Jacket A *golden life jacket* is sometimes offered to executives of a company being acquired, to ensure that they remain with the reorganized company.

Finally, senior-level HR professionals should work with other resources such as tax and legal experts to review existing executive employment contracts. These advisers will be able to provide feedback and make recommendations on how to enhance contracts and take advantage of tax considerations while still managing the risk of this compensation activity.

Stock Options

A *stock option* is the right to purchase an employer's stock at a certain price (the strike price), at a future date, within a specified period of time. Options provide an employee with an opportunity to purchase shares but don't require that the employee do so. The *grant price* or *strike price* of the stock is based on the market price at the time the options are issued. It's common to find stock options vesting over a three-to-five-year period as a retention tactic; they can be exercised for up to 10 years. Stock options are valuable only if the stock price rises over time, so their value to employees depends on the company's financial performance. Although stock option plans vary between companies, all plans must be operated within parameters established by the SEC or IRS.

There are two types of stock options: *incentive stock options* (ISOs) and *nonqualified stock options*. The difference between the option types is the tax treatment for the employer and employee:

Incentive, or Qualified, Stock Options ISOs are stock options that can be offered only to employees; consultants and external members of the BoD aren't eligible. The tax treatment for ISOs is often favorable for employees because they don't face taxes at the time the stock option is exercised—they don't have income to report until the stock is sold at a later date. When an ISO is sold, however, it's likely that capital gains taxes will be due and subject to the alternative minimum tax under certain conditions. Use of ISOs isn't as favorable to employers because the company receives a tax deduction only if certain conditions are met.

Nonqualified Options Nonqualified stock options can be used for consultants and external members of the BoD as well as for employees. The organization receives a tax deduction when the options are exercised, and employees pay tax on any gain they realize from the sale. Income from the stock is treated as compensation, and when the stock is sold there are further tax implications.

Two other types of stock ownership employers provide to employees are restricted stock and phantom stock:

Restricted Stock *Restricted stock* is common stock offered to employees, typically executives or employees who demonstrate outstanding performance. Restricted stocks are actual shares, not the option-to-buy shares, like stock options. Restricted stock usually follows a vesting schedule designed to reward retention. Employees may be motivated to stay with the organization to realize the full benefit of their restricted stock, which is why employees perceive these as golden handcuffs, or a financial benefit that will be lost if they leave the organization.

Phantom Stock *Phantom stock* is used in privately held companies to provide the benefits of employee ownership without granting stock. Organizations use phantom stock to motivate and retain employees without granting equity or sharing ownership in the company. Phantom stock can generate the kind of payoffs that stock options or restricted stock can yield. Executives and outside members of the BoD are the most common recipients of phantom stock. There is usually a vesting schedule based on length of service and performance (individual or company). Like common stock, phantom stock follows the company's market-price movements. A valuation formula determines the value of the stock. When the phantom stock yields a payout, the employer is eligible to receive a tax deduction for the amount paid.

Board of Directors/Outside Directors

The BoD is elected by shareholders to oversee the management of the corporation on behalf of its stockholders. Members of the BoD can be executives of the organization (known as *inside directors*) or external to the organization (known as *outside directors*).

Inside directors receive executive compensation packages consisting of stock options, benefits, and base pay, to which they're entitled based on their roles as corporate executives. Outside directors commonly receive cash for meeting fees and retainers.

Benefits Strategies

While HR professionals at all stages of their career have responsibility in benefits administration, there are a few key differences between operational and strategic management. Operational benefits administration handles daily tasks, like enrolling employees, managing compliance, and vendor coordination. It's tactical and focuses on immediate needs, and is the focus of the PHR/i. Strategic benefits administration involves long-term planning, aligning benefits with organizational goals. It includes designing competitive packages, analyzing market trends, and using data to optimize costs and improve talent retention. This is the focus of SPHRi candidates.

Senior HR should develop and evaluate benefit strategies focused on key areas such as health, welfare, retirement, work-life balance, and wellness. A comprehensive approach in these areas will position the company as an employer of choice, reinforcing the employer brand and help to attract and retain key talent. When aligned with organizational results, these strategies can partially or in-full pay for themselves through reduced absenteeism, improved utilization, increased productivity, and lower costs of turnover.

Summary

The role of Total Rewards and the resulting compensation and benefits programs have a significant effect on an employer's ability to compete for talent. Human resource professionals have a fiduciary responsibility to administer TR programs in accordance with the highest degree of ethics and regulatory compliance, but also to serve the needs of both the employer and employee.

HR is often tasked with the development of a Total Rewards philosophy that should be tied to a company's mission or purpose. Doing so allows employees to have a clear view of what the company values. A clear philosophy also demonstrates that the employer is committed to providing base pay, health, wellness, work-life balance, time off, and retirement benefits in addition to training and career pathing as part of an integrative system. This system is used to meet employee needs in order to attract, retain, and reward the desired workforce.

Building an integrative TR system requires employers to access both internal and external resources for data. Surveying employees, benchmarking jobs, and conducting salary surveys are all sources that should be used to build effective TR programs.

Senior-level professionals should also be familiar with basic accounting and budgeting principles. This knowledge is used for many HR tasks, including forecasting labor costs and costing out labor contracts. They also serve to inform decisions when building executive compensation packages that go beyond base wages and are compliant with tax implications. Understanding these basic principles and applying them to the operational activities of day-to-day human resource tasks help develop HR into true business partners.

Finally, the organizational sciences have made significant progress in helping us understand how Total Rewards can—and cannot—motivate workers. Findings include the threshold that base pay has on creating loyalty and commitment, as well as the influence of Total Rewards programs on employee job attitudes.

Exam Essentials

Be aware of the high degree of financial responsibility of senior-level human resource professionals. Understanding what it means to have fiduciary responsibility underscores all human resource activities but is especially significant in Total Rewards. Acting in one's own self-interest, navigating the presence of conflicting duties, and profiting from the level of decision-making authority are all ways HR may breach their fiduciary obligations.

Understand the importance of having a Total Rewards philosophy. A TR philosophy will serve as the basis for creating the entire TR system. Fundamental to this is the employer's decision to lead, lag, or match the labor markets in which they compete for talent. The philosophy is driven by both internal and external considerations that influence an organization's ability to attract, retain, and reward employees.

Align TR programs with organizational strategies using an integrative approach. Aligning pay and benefits programs goes beyond base wages and health insurance. Senior-level HR professionals will also need to be able to use their TR programs to respond to external factors such as changing market conditions, economic factors, and geographic factors. Internally, HR will need to deliver pay systems that have the proper mix of options to address the rising cost of TR, the diverse needs of the workgroup, and the skills shortage many industries are now experiencing.

Be familiar with job analysis, evaluation, and pricing activities. Fundamental to the building of formal pay structures is the ability to group jobs into families. Doing so allows HR to accurately benchmark jobs and access wage data to offer competitive pay. Job analysis is also helpful when designing TR programs that offer career growth as a reward for staying with a company.

Know basic budget and accounting principles. Particularly when HR is called on to calculate the cost of a collective bargaining agreement and the tax implications of executive compensation packages, understanding basic business financials will inform many TR-related decisions.

Have up-to-date, empirical knowledge of how TR serves to motivate employees. The organizational and other sciences have made important contributions in understanding the relationship between pay and performance and other motivational aspects of TR programs. Senior-level HR professionals should understand these principles and use them to create programs that meet the needs of the company and the workforce.

Be familiar with the use of equity compensation and the complexity of administering executive compensation programs. Historically, employers have used equity compensation as a major portion of executive compensation. In recent years, however, equity as a form of compensation is also increasing in popularity with industry startups. Therefore, it is important that HR has a competency-based, thorough understanding of this in practice.

Design other benefits programs that balance employee needs with increasing costs. The design of benefits programs that are strategically aligned with organizational goals, employee needs, and cost management should be the focus of senior-level HR activities. This includes creative problem-solving that helps manage risk while offering nontraditional benefits discussed throughout the entire TR structure.

Review Questions

You can find the answers in Appendix A.

1. Senior HR professionals are called upon to design TR systems that balance the need to find and retain qualified talent with which of the following?
   A. Complying with the Fair Labor Standards Act
   B. Meeting the needs of an older workforce
   C. Designing a TR program that is personalized to employee needs
   D. Providing health insurance for all employees

2. In which of the following scenarios has an HR professional breached their fiduciary responsibility? (Choose all that apply.)
   A. Selecting a benefits plan because it best fits their family of four
   B. Moving an open position to a higher salary grade to make it easier for their team to recruit
   C. Choosing an insurance broker because they give generous gifts during the holidays
   D. Delaying a response to a state agency about a personnel record

3. A travel agency has decided they will pay less than their competitors for reservation agents as there is an abundant supply in the labor market. This is an example of what TR philosophy?
   A. Lagging the market
   B. Leading the market
   C. Matching the market
   D. Leveraging the market

4. In strong economies, which of the following is likely true?
   A. Companies will need to pay more for labor.
   B. There are many talented workers from which to hire.
   C. There are high levels of unemployment.
   D. There are low levels of unemployment.

5. Which of the following is the fundamental factor for creating unpaid internships?
   A. The individual must be the primary beneficiary of the internship.
   B. The company may be the primary beneficiary of the internship.
   C. The company cannot benefit by having the intern do critical work.
   D. The intern must be in an active semester at school.

6. About what period of time should employers project their cost of Total Rewards programs?
   A. 6 months
   B. 1 year
   C. 2 years
   D. 5+ years

7. Which of the following is a best representation of an integrative approach to Total Rewards programs?
   A. Providing retiree benefits through pensions
   B. Not overpaying for talent
   C. Creating reasonable executive compensation packages
   D. Creating rewards that motivate

8. The school district for which you work has requested that your team upgrade the pay structures. Currently, the plan has 12 grades sorted by job families. The current grades are best represented by which of the following types of salary structures?
   A. Traditional
   B. Open system
   C. Broad-banded
   D. Broad-graded

9. What is the main purpose of evaluating and pricing jobs?
   A. To properly group jobs into families
   B. To determine job worth when compared to internal and external factors
   C. To advise senior executives on effective variable pay plans
   D. To build pay programs that are competitive with the external labor market

10. Which of the following would be a best practice when selecting salary surveys?
   A. Involving line managers in validating job responsibilities
   B. Asking senior leaders to participate in the job description comparisons
   C. Selecting a survey that is not cost-prohibitive
   D. Choosing a survey that requires purchasers to participate

11. Jamie is an "HR department of one" at a small tech company startup with fewer than 30 employees. She has been tasked to begin the job evaluation process in order to build competitive pay systems. Which of the following is most likely going to be a top priority for her choice of evaluation method?
   A. Ensuring the method is legally compliant
   B. Clear criteria to ensure equity
   C. Perceptions of distributive justice
   D. Ease of development and use

12. The collective bargaining process is underway and one wage proposal is to increase incumbent pay by 12 percent but create lower new hire wages for the contract period. This is an example of which wage system?
   A. Banding
   B. Grading
   C. Two-tiered
   D. Lump sum

13. Determining the cost of labor rates over a two-year planning horizon is a feature of which function?
   A. Job costing
   B. Forecasting
   C. Financing
   D. Accounting

14. The small business you work for has approximately 800 hours of employee unused vacation time. This is an example of which of the following?
   A. Accrued expenses
   B. Accounts payable
   C. Accounts receivable
   D. Expenses

15. You have reached the point in the job analysis process where you are reviewing the Accounting department roles and responsibilities. Which of the following principles should govern how you distribute the tasks and duties of each job within the department?
   A. Authority principle
   B. Ethical principles
   C. Good Manufacturing Practices (GMP)
   D. Generally Accepted Accounting Principles (GAAP)

16. What is the main advantage of using a zero-based budget methodology?
   A. It is relatively simple to build.
   B. It minimizes the impact a new budget can have on cash flow.
   C. It allows for gradual progression of expenses that are more easily absorbed.
   D. It allows for real-time financial adjustments to technological, economic, or other forces that influence operations.

17. "People want what they can't have" is an example of which incentive technique designed to increase employee motivation?
    A. Scarcity
    B. Efficiency
    C. Public recognition
    D. Socioeconomics

18. Which of the following occurs when an employee has enough money for which to meet their baseline needs?
    A. Base pay increases employee motivation.
    B. Base pay decreases employee motivation.
    C. Base pay has no effect on employee motivation.
    D. It depends on the employee.

19. What type of compensation are stock options?
    A. Holistic
    B. Intrinsic
    C. Executive
    D. Equity

20. Which of the following is often used to build an executive Total Rewards package? (Choose all that apply.)
    A. Base pay
    B. Equity
    C. Perks
    D. Golden handshakes

Chapter 14

SPHR | SPHRi Exam: HR Information Management, Safety, and Security

SPHR RESPONSIBILITIES:

IDENTIFYING THE TOOLS, TECHNOLOGY, AND SYSTEMS THAT ARE NEEDED TO REPORT ON THE ORGANIZATIONAL STRATEGY WHILE ALSO MONITORING EMPLOYEE SAFETY AND SECURITY.

- ✓ **5.1 Align HR data privacy and security processes to organizational data protection strategies (for example: cybersecurity, phishing emails, documentation, employee files)**
- ✓ **5.2 Evaluate employee safety and security strategies (for example: OSHA, HIPAA, emergency response plans, access control, contingency planning, crisis management)**
- ✓ **5.3 Lead, implement, and evaluate HR digitalization initiatives (for example: information, workflows, emerging technologies, gamification, employee self-service, social networking, and human resource information system [HRIS], risk management system)**

SPHRi RESPONSIBILITIES:

THE SPHRi EXAM RESPONSIBILITIES ARE THE SAME AS THOSE FOR THE SPHR, WITH ONE EXCEPTION.

- ✓ **5.2 Evaluate employee safety and security strategies (for example: emergency response plans, access control, contingency planning, crisis management)**

The SPHR and SPHRi exam content for HR Information Management, Safety, and Security has three main objectives, and makes up 10 percent of the exams. It is one of the new functional areas added to the content areas in 2024. While this function may be new to the exams, the responsibilities are really just an extension of the regular risk management practices of an HR team. This means that HR's focus should be on prevention and education when designing risk management practices that protect the following assets:

- **Physical Assets:** Tangible resources owned by a company, such as buildings, machinery, equipment, and inventory, used to produce goods and services. Physical assets might be at risk from natural disasters, theft, or vandalism.
- **Financial Assets:** Monetary resources, including cash, stocks, bonds, and other investments, that provide economic value to a company. Financial assets might be at risk due to market volatility, fraud, or poor investment decisions.
- **Knowledge Assets:** Intellectual resources, such as patents, trademarks, proprietary information, and employee expertise, that contribute to a company's innovation and competitive advantage. Knowledge assets can be at risk from data breaches, corporate espionage, or loss of key personnel.
- **Human Assets:** The workforce of a company, encompassing the skills, experience, and abilities of employees that do the work. Human assets might be at risk from injury, accidents, or lack of engagement.

NOTE The SPHRi responsibilities related to emergency response plans, contingency planning, and crisis management are covered in detail in Chapter 2, "Shared Competencies." Access controls are covered later in this chapter.

HR Digitization

Digitization in HR refers to the process of converting traditional HR processes and data into digital formats. This includes automating tasks such as payroll, recruitment, performance evaluations, and employee records management to improve overall HR operations.

Exam objective 5.3 tasks senior HR leaders to "Lead, implement, and evaluate HR digitalization initiatives." The exam content covers several specific ways that HR should be able to digitize the department workflows. These are explored next.

Digitizing HR Workflows

HR workflows can be digitized by implementing HR software and tools that automate and streamline various processes. This includes using applicant-tracking systems (ATSs) for recruitment, electronic onboarding systems to facilitate new hire orientation, and payroll software for automated salary processing. Performance management systems enable continuous feedback and evaluations, and employee self-service portals allow staff to update personal information, access pay slips, and request leave digitally. Learning management systems (LMSs) help automate training activities, and cloud-based document management systems can store and organize employee records securely. At the heart of an automated HR department is the human resource information system (HRIS).

Human Resource Information Systems

With the reams of paper generated during the course of an employment relationship, the advent of the *human resource information system (HRIS)* was a clear benefit for HR professionals. An HRIS serves two purposes: first, as a repository of information, and second, as an aid to the operational efficiencies of an HR department.

As a repository of information, the HRIS provides an electronic means of storing employment documents, thereby reducing the need to maintain physical files. In firms with multiple locations, both national and global, the ability for employees to access information through the company's intranet or via the Internet reduces delays in payroll-processing tasks and ensures instant access to the information for those with the authority and need to access it. For companies required to produce reports for the Equal Employment Opportunity Commission (EEOC) or the Office of Federal Contract Compliance Programs (OFCCP), electronic access to the data needed to compile reports has increased accuracy and reduced the time required to produce them.

As an effective decision-making tool, the HRIS provides access to the information needed to make strategic decisions, such as analyzing turnover trends, creating succession plans, and projecting staffing needs. The HRIS also allows human resources to streamline services, eliminating wasted or redundant efforts in the execution of the many administrative tasks of a high-functioning HR department.

Selecting an HRIS

As with any project, the first step in selecting an HRIS is to conduct a needs analysis and identify the following:

- What information will be converted to the HRIS, and how is it currently maintained? Table 14.1 lists some uses to consider for an HRIS.

- Will the system need to integrate or share data with other company systems?
- Who will have access to the information, and how many levels of access will be needed (for example, to view and change individual records, view, and change workgroup records, view payroll information, and so on)? Table 14.2 displays what a typical access hierarchy could look like.
- What kinds of reports will need to be produced based on the information?
- Will the HRIS be accessible via the intranet or the web? If so, what security will be in place to protect the privacy of employees and prevent identity theft?

TABLE 14.1 Uses for HRIS

Applicant tracking	COBRA administration
Automated benefit administration	EEO/AA reporting
Tracking recruitment efforts	Administering training programs
Eliminating duplication of data entry	Compensation administration
Tracking service awards	Tracking time and attendance
Sharing payroll information with the finance department	

TABLE 14.2 Typical HRIS access hierarchy

HR access (global information)	
Maintain employee records	Coordinate payroll administration
Administer employee benefits	Administer labor relations programs
Post jobs	Administer safety programs
Administer compensation plan	Administer employee relations
Administer FMLA leaves	Manage recruiting
Track attendance/vacation time	Complete EEO/AAP reports
Track applicants	Administer training programs
Manage relocations	

Payroll access (restricted information)	
View payroll information	Administer payroll
Management access (restricted to workgroup)	
View budget/forecast reports	Manage performance
View succession plans	Administer service awards
Track attendance/vacation time	View compensation
Manage training needs	View recruiting status
Change emergency contact, address, telephone numbers, and family status	Change payroll tax withholding
View company policies	View attendance/vacation tracking
View benefit enrollment information	Open enrollment benefit changes
Bid for internal job openings	Obtain and view paycheck stubs

Once this information has been collected, research can begin on the availability and cost of a system that fulfills the requirements. This analysis should include the purchase cost for the system with a comparison to the cost of continuing to use the current system.

Implementing an HRIS

Once the HRIS installation project has been approved, some practical considerations need to be worked into the implementation schedule. If the HRIS software vendor or a third party will be handling the implementation phase, the RFP should include information about this phase of the project. If the implementation is to be done with internal IT staff, it's important to establish a timeline that works for both departments and allows the organization's HR information needs to be met during this stage.

When implementation is complete and the system has been tested to ensure that it's functioning correctly, the new service can be rolled out to those who will be using it. If an employee self-service component is included, this means providing the necessary level of training for all employees.

HRIS Access Controls

Access controls in an HRIS are used to protect sensitive employee data and help companies stay in compliance with data security requirements. *Tiered access* is a hierarchical approach to managing user permissions in a system, where access rights are organized into levels or tiers based on the user's role within an organization. Each tier represents a different level of access, with higher tiers granting broader and more comprehensive permissions compared to lower tiers. Key features of tiered access include:

- **Hierarchical Structure:** Access levels are structured in a hierarchy, ensuring that users at higher tiers have access to more sensitive data and advanced functionalities, while those at lower tiers have restricted, role-specific access.
- **Role-Based Permissions:** Users are assigned to tiers based on their job roles and responsibilities. This ensures that they only have access to the information and tools necessary to perform their duties.
- **Security and Efficiency:** By limiting access based on tiers, the system enhances security, reducing the risk of unauthorized access and data breaches. It also improves operational efficiency by ensuring users have the appropriate tools without being overwhelmed by unnecessary features.
- **Scalability:** The tiered structure allows for easy scalability, enabling the addition of new roles and permissions as the organization grows or changes.

Here is a sample of an HR team's responsibilities in a tiered structure:

Tier 1: Employee Basic access level for general staff.

Permissions: View and update personal information, submit timesheets, request leave.

Tier 2: Supervisor Intermediate access level for team leaders.

Permissions: All Tier 1 permissions, approve/reject timesheets and leave requests, view team performance reports.

Tier 3: Manager Advanced access level for department managers.

Permissions: All Tier 2 permissions, manage team hiring/termination, access detailed performance data, approve salary changes, generate departmental reports.

Tier 4: HR Administrator Full access level for HR leaders and system administrators.

Permissions: All Tier 3 permissions, full access to all employee records, configure HRIS settings, create/modify roles, audit system logs.

Most HRISs also have the capability to offer ad hoc access, such as for payroll or training modules.

Applicant Tracking Systems

An *applicant-tracking system* (ATS) provides an automated method for keeping track of job applicants from the time they first apply to an organization to the point when the position is filled—and beyond, if the database is searched as new openings occur. These systems range from Microsoft Excel spreadsheets to sophisticated database systems that track applicant qualifications, are easily searchable based on different criteria, and provide reports that can be used for annual EEO-1 reports or Affirmative Action Plans (AAPs). Table 14.3 presents the types of information typically captured in an ATS.

TABLE 14.3 Typical ATS capabilities

Applicant information	Open positions	Recruiter needs
Résumé upload	List of open positions	Applicant contact information
Application upload	Job descriptions	Search by applicant information
Applicant profile	Hiring manager access	Search by qualifications
Applicant auto-response	Job posting	Information security
Comments		EEOC report information
Link résumé to profile		Report generator

Hiring Management Systems

If ATSs ease the administrative burden of the hiring process, *hiring management systems (HMSs)* take the technology to the next level. An HMS uses technology to carry the employer brand throughout the application process. It integrates with corporate recruiting websites to simplify the candidate's experience by moving data directly from candidate input to the database. This reduces errors and improves relationship management with faster response times. HMSs can prescreen by providing questions that will help candidates self-screen out of the process if they don't meet minimum qualifications, thus reducing the time recruiters spend reviewing résumés of unqualified candidates.

An HMS also provides additional recruiter support with templates to standardize candidate communication and facilitate communication between recruiters in large organizations. Most HMSs include customizable report writers that can be used to answer questions about specific jobs or the recruiting system in general.

Learning Management Systems

A *learning management system (LMS)* streamlines the administration of employee training programs. The components included in an LMS depend on organization size and the complexity of training needs. These systems can be used to automatically enroll students in required courses (such as safety training required by OSHA) and to notify managers when employees don't attend. The programs can provide managers with access to approve training requested by employees and to identify skill-development needs in their departments or for individual employees. An LMS can maintain curriculum for required (or optional) courses and provide access on an individual, functional, or organizational basis.

Other administrative functions performed by LMS programs include course calendars, facility assignments, pre- and post-testing, and report generation. An LMS can also include self-service functions that eliminate tedious administrative chores from daily HR tasks, such as registering employees, notifying participants, obtaining approvals, and maintaining wait-lists. Table 14.4 summarizes the functions available in an LMS system.

TABLE 14.4 LMS system functions

HR tasks	Training tasks	User benefits
Streamline process (automate recordkeeping, notices, and reminders)	Manage resources: facilities, instructors, and equipment	Employees: self-registration, web access, online learning
Automatic enrollment for mandated courses	Manage course calendar	Managers: approve employee requests, access to online assessment tools, plan department trainings
Verify qualifications	Self-registration	
Manage waiting lists	Web-based delivery	
Generate reports	Deliver/score tests, including pre- and post-tests; score and record course work	

An LMS is capable of managing the organization's learning tasks in a wide range of situations, from tracking attendance, maintaining training calendars, and generating reports to delivering web-based content to participants, administering and scoring tests, and providing planning tools for managers. This still requires HR input and oversight, such as in defining learning objectives and establishing reporting parameters.

Learning and performance management systems (LPMSs) that incorporate functions for managing performance (including 360-degree assessments, self-evaluations, succession planning, and manager feedback) and that track individual reward, are the next level of LMS. These functions improve a manager's ability to assess performance, assign training to address areas of improvement, and prepare employees for the next level in their career growth.

Organizations that develop their own content use learning content management systems (LCMSs) to create, deliver, and modify course content. These systems allow trainers to develop content, often in a module format so that a single module can be used in multiple training courses. For example, a geographically dispersed organization may create an orientation program with different modules for corporate information, employee benefit options, expense reporting, and other information common to employees throughout the organization, along with modules for each geographic location. This allows an HR professional in a regional office to provide a customized orientation that includes information specific to that office along with relevant information about the corporation at large.

Employee Self-Service

Employee self-service (ESS) allows employees to access their own records through an automated system. This could be through a company intranet, the Internet, a mobile device, an automated phone system, or a computer kiosk. Providing employees with the ability to access and make changes to routine information frees HR staff to perform other mission-critical functions and gives employees 24/7 access to their information. Self-service, cloud-based software such as Bamboo HR (`http://bamboohr.com`) can help reduce the administrative burden of HR activities such as new hire orientation by allowing employees to enter their data directly.

ESS systems are evolving as technical capability continues to improve and the workforce becomes increasingly knowledgeable about computer and web use. Access to information such as skills profiles, learning opportunities, and goal-setting guidelines empowers employees and their managers to take charge of their personal development and career planning and facilitates successful communication in these important relationships. Advances in ESS technology also reduce repetitive administrative HR tasks, freeing professionals to concentrate on other important tasks and projects.

Gamification

Gamification in the workplace involves integrating game-like elements, such as point systems, leaderboards, and digital badges and rewards, into non-game contexts to motivate and engage employees. In terms of efficacy, the statistics[1] speak for themselves:

- 89 percent of employees say gamification makes them feel more productive at work.
- Companies using gamification in their training programs have seen a 50 percent increase in productivity and a 60 percent improvement in employee engagement.
- Organizations using gamification improve engagement by 48 percent, increase employee performance by 34 percent, and see a 36 percent improvement in turnover rates.
- 72 percent of employees claim gamification inspires them to work harder, and 51 percent would participate in more training if it had game-like elements.

---

[1]Talent LMS The Key Gamification Survey at Work, `www.talentlms.com/blog/gamification-survey-results`.

- Companies with engaged employees have 41 percent lower absenteeism and 17 percent higher productivity.
- Gamified environments foster stronger collaboration and team cohesion, with 70 percent of Global 2000 (the world's largest public businesses) companies using gamification to boost engagement, retention, and revenues.
- The gamification market size is expected to grow from $9.1 billion in 2020 to $30.7 billion by 2025. Seventy percent of Global 2000 organizations will use gamification to boost engagement and productivity.

HR can incorporate more game-like elements into their employees' day by designing a points-based reward system where employees earn points for completing tasks, meeting deadlines, or contributing innovative ideas. These points can then be accumulated and exchanged for various rewards, such as gift cards, extra vacation days, or exclusive company merchandise. HR can help to implement leaderboards that showcase top performers in different categories, updated in real time, which can be accessed through a company portal or displayed on digital screens in communal areas. Other ideas include organizing team-based challenges and quests that align with company goals. For instance, employees can participate in a quarterly innovation challenge where teams work together to develop new solutions or improve existing processes, with winners receiving recognition and rewards. Regular feedback loops and instant recognition tools, such as digital badges and shout-outs on social media or internal communication platforms, can further motivate employees by acknowledging their efforts and achievements promptly.

Storytelling plays a role in gamification as well as in presenting data, making experiences more immersive and personalized. A narrative can be themed around the company's mission and values, making the journey engaging and relevant to the employees' work. By weaving these game-like elements into the daily work routine, HR can create a more dynamic and motivating environment that enhances employee engagement and productivity.

Outsourcing or using software for gamification can streamline the implementation process by providing specialized tools and platforms designed to integrate game-like elements into daily operations.

Challenges to gamification are related to creating an unhealthy competitive environment, or overemphasizing individual achievement over group success. Another challenge are the costs of developing and maintaining gamified systems, and thus should be properly addressed in the HR budget. Not all employees may respond positively to gamification; it is essential to customize approaches to meet diverse preferences and needs. Ensuring that gamification supports rather than detracts from work is key to its successful integration into HR practices.

Service Delivery and Technology

The impact of technology on business strategy cannot be understated. With the rapid evolution of digital tools, it is even more important for human resource professionals to understand both the risks and benefits of using technology to manage team members or drive service delivery. Consider the following tales of three different companies, in three different industries, using emerging technology in three highly unique ways:

- **Company 1:** A Wisconsin-based company began offering to implant rice-size microchips into their employees' hands. The RFID device is then used to access the building, log on to computers, and even buy snacks. A year later, more than half the company's employees had the devices implanted under their skin.
- **Company 2:** A financial institution in London installed heat- and motion-sensing devices at the desks of their investment bankers. Designed to record how long each employee is spending at their desks, the OccupEye may be used for workspace utilization reviews. Although the company noted that the devices were not intended to monitor individual performance (it is about space utilization), the union is "keeping an eye on the situation."
- **Company 3:** A San Francisco boutique burger outlet was the first to introduce a hamburger made entirely by robotics. The machine contains 20 computers and 350 sensors that are used to assemble custom burgers that are delivered on a conveyer belt in less than five minutes.

These and similar practices may seem inadvisable due to risks such as privacy, employee health, and the cost associated with untested robotic work processes. Yet companies such as Three Square Market, Barclays PLC, and Creator are broadening the boundaries of the use of technology at work. For this reason, it is up to HR to partner with their executive teams to find ways to mitigate the risk of technology, as opposed to simply saying "no."

Real World Scenario

Power Business Intelligence in HR

Microsoft developed Power BI as a business analytics tool. It enables users to visualize and analyze data with ease. Power BI offers several specific features that are particularly useful for HR departments and senior HR leaders:

- **Interactive Dashboards:** Power BI allows users to create interactive dashboards that can visualize key HR metrics, such as employee turnover, diversity statistics, and performance trends. These dashboards can be customized with various charts, graphs, and tables, providing a comprehensive view of the data at a glance.
- **Data Integration:** Power BI can integrate data from multiple sources, including HR management systems, payroll software, and external databases. This feature enables HR leaders to consolidate data from different systems into a single platform, making it easier to analyze and report on various HR metrics.
- **Data Modeling and Transformation:** The Power Query Editor in Power BI allows users to clean, transform, and model data. HR can use this feature to prepare data for analysis,

such as merging datasets, creating calculated columns, and filtering out unnecessary information.

- **Custom Visualizations:** Power BI offers a wide range of visualization options, including bar charts, pie charts, scatter plots, and heat maps. Users can also import custom visuals or create their own, allowing HR leaders to present data in the most effective and engaging way.
- **Natural Language Query:** With the Q&A feature, users can ask questions in natural language to quickly generate visualizations. For example, an HR leader might type "Show employee turnover by department" and Power BI will instantly create a relevant chart.
- **Real-Time Data:** Power BI supports real-time data updates, allowing HR leaders to monitor live data feeds and stay up-to-date with the latest HR metrics. This is particularly useful for tracking real-time KPIs, such as recruitment progress or employee engagement scores.

Using tools such as Power BI allows HR teams to present actionable insights that add value to organizational decision making.

Data Privacy

Aligning data privacy and security processes with organizational data protection strategies is important for several reasons. As with any part of business operations, alignment with strategy ensures that the company has the proper resources—people, financial and leadership commitment—to achieve what the company hopes to achieve. Data privacy in particular has significant impact when organizations get it wrong. Take, for example, the Equifax data breach of 2016. The event exposed personal information of 147 million people, including Social Security numbers, addresses, and credit card details. It resulted in severe financial and reputational damage, regulatory scrutiny, and legal actions against Equifax. Another example is the 2018 Marriott International data breach. Hackers accessed the reservation database, compromising personal details of approximately 500 million guests, including names, addresses, passport numbers, and credit card information. This breach led to significant financial losses, legal repercussions, and damaged customer trust.

To align data privacy and security processes with organizational data protection strategies, HR professionals must ensure that the company's practices adhere to established legal and regulatory requirements while supporting the broader goals of the organization.

Legal and Regulatory Requirements

While the SPHR and SPHRi exams have a slightly different focus in terms of labor laws, there are shared components to data security. The General Data Protection Regulation (GDPR) requires organizations to ensure data protection by obtaining clear consent, implementing data minimization, ensuring data accuracy, providing data access and deletion rights, reporting breaches within 72 hours, and appointing data protection officers for monitoring compliance. Penalties for noncompliance can be substantial. The GDPR applies to any organization, regardless of location, that processes the personal data of individuals residing in the European Union (EU). This includes multinational companies offering goods or services to EU residents or monitoring their behavior within the EU.

Date Governance and Security Policies

Data governance is the framework of policies, procedures, and standards that an organization uses to manage its data assets effectively. It ensures data quality, consistency, security, and usability by defining roles, responsibilities, and processes for data management across the organization.

Senior HR leaders are responsible for establishing comprehensive data privacy and security policies that reflect the organization's data protection strategies. These policies should cover the multiple facets of data protection in the workplace. including the following:

Data Privacy Policy This policy should outline how the organization collects, uses, stores, and protects personal data of employees and other stakeholders. It should include details on consent, data subject rights, data retention, and data-sharing practices.

Data Security Policy This policy should define the measures and protocols in place to safeguard sensitive information from unauthorized access, breaches, and other security threats. It should cover aspects such as encryption, access controls, secure data handling, and regular security audits.

Incident Response Policy This policy should provide a clear plan for responding to data breaches and security incidents. It should detail the steps for identifying, reporting, managing, and mitigating incidents, including communication protocols and responsibilities of the incident response team.

Bring Your Own Device Policy (BYOD) This policy should outline the guidelines and requirements for employees who use their personal devices for work purposes. It should include details on device eligibility, security requirements, data access and usage, monitoring and compliance, incident reporting, and protocols for termination of employment.

These policies help establish a comprehensive framework for data protection to ensure that the organization meets legal requirements and effectively safeguards its sensitive information.

Real World Scenario

Sample Bring Your Own Device (BYOD) Policy

Purpose:

To outline the guidelines and requirements for employees who use their personal devices for work purposes, ensuring the security and privacy of organizational data.

Scope:

This policy applies to all employees, contractors, and affiliates who use their personal devices to access organizational systems, networks, and data.

Policy:

- **Device Eligibility:** Only devices that meet the organization's security standards are eligible for BYOD. This includes up-to-date operating systems, antivirus software, and the ability to support required security applications.
- **Security Requirements:** All personal devices must have password protection, encryption, and the ability to be remotely wiped in case of loss or theft. Employees must install and maintain approved security software and updates.
- **Data Access and Usage:** Employees are only allowed to access, store, and process organizational data using approved applications and systems. Personal use of the device must not interfere with the security and integrity of organizational data.
- **Monitoring and Compliance:** The organization reserves the right to monitor and audit devices used under the BYOD policy to ensure compliance. Employees must agree to regular compliance checks and cooperate with IT support for security configurations.
- **Incident Reporting:** Employees must immediately report any loss, theft, or potential data breach involving their personal device to the IT department. Quick reporting is crucial for initiating protective measures such as remote wiping.
- **Termination of Employment:** Upon termination of employment, employees must ensure all organizational data is removed from their personal devices. The organization may perform a remote wipe to ensure compliance.
- **Legal and Privacy Considerations:** Employees must comply with all relevant data protection laws and organizational privacy policies. Personal data on BYOD devices will be respected, but organizational data security takes precedence.

Responsibilities:

Employees are responsible for the security and maintenance of their personal devices. The IT department is responsible for providing support, conducting audits, and managing security configurations.

Enforcement:

Noncompliance with the BYOD policy may result in disciplinary action, including revocation of BYOD privileges or termination of employment.

Review and Updates:

This policy will be reviewed annually and updated as necessary to reflect changes in technology, legal requirements, and organizational needs.

Data Protection Technology and Tools

Data protection technology and tools can be leveraged to safeguard sensitive information from unauthorized access, breaches, and other security threats. These technologies ensure the confidentiality, integrity, and availability of data by implementing encryption, access controls, intrusion detection, and other security measures. While it is important for HR leaders to partner with IT for the practical aspects of data security, there are several key terms and protocols that they should be aware of:

Multifactor Authentication (MFA) MFA adds an extra layer of security by requiring employees to provide two or more forms of verification before accessing HR systems. For instance, when an HR manager logs into the payroll system, they first enter their username and password. Next, they must provide a second form of authentication, such as a code sent to their mobile phone or a fingerprint scan. This additional step ensures that even if a password is compromised, unauthorized access is prevented.

Data Encryption Data encryption transforms sensitive information into a secure format that can only be decoded with the correct encryption key. For example, when an HR professional sends an email containing an employee's performance review, the email content and attachments are encrypted. This ensures that even if the email is intercepted, the information remains unreadable without the decryption key. Additionally, encryption is applied to stored data in HR databases, protecting it from unauthorized access.

Data Masking Data masking involves hiding original data with modified content while maintaining the data's usability. In an HR context, data masking can be used to protect sensitive information such as Social Security numbers, salary details, and medical records during development, testing, or when sharing data with third parties. For example, when an HR system is undergoing testing, data masking can replace actual employee details with fictitious yet realistic data.

Data Loss Prevention (DLP) DLP tools and strategies are designed to prevent the unauthorized sharing or leakage of sensitive data. For example, DLP software monitors outgoing emails and file transfers for sensitive information such as Social Security numbers, financial data, or confidential HR documents. If an unauthorized attempt to share or export sensitive data is detected, the DLP system automatically blocks the action and alerts the IT security team. This ensures that sensitive employee information does not leave the organization's secure environment, whether intentionally or accidentally.

Access Control Access control mechanisms restrict access to data based on user roles and permissions. In an HR context, this means that only authorized personnel, such as HR managers and payroll specialists, have access to certain types of sensitive information. For instance, an HR assistant might have access to general employee contact information but not to salary details or performance reviews. Access control systems enforce these restrictions by requiring user authentication and verifying permissions before granting access to specific data or systems.

Endpoint Security Endpoint security measures protect devices such as computers, smartphones, and tablets that connect to the organization's network. For example, HR staff often use laptops and mobile devices to access employee records and other sensitive information. Endpoint security solutions, such as antivirus software, firewalls, and mobile device management (MDM) systems, ensure these devices are protected from malware, unauthorized access, and other security threats. These tools can also enforce security policies, such as requiring strong passwords and encrypting data stored on devices.

User Training and Awareness *Social engineering* is the manipulation of individuals into divulging confidential information or performing actions that compromise security through deceptive tactics. The three most common types of social engineering are *phishing*, where attackers use deceptive emails or messages to steal sensitive information; *pretexting*, where they create a fabricated scenario to trick individuals into providing data; and *baiting*, where they entice victims with promises or items to obtain their personal information. HR departments should conduct regular training sessions to teach staff how to recognize social engineering attempts, the use of strong passwords, and securely handle sensitive information.

Firewalls Firewalls are security systems that monitor and control incoming and outgoing network traffic based on predetermined security rules. In an HR context, firewalls can protect the network by blocking unauthorized access to sensitive data. For example, firewalls can be configured to prevent employees from accessing certain websites by blocking specific URLs, IP addresses, or types of content based on predetermined security rules and policies.

Secure Socket Layer (SSL) SSL is a protocol for establishing encrypted links between networked computers, ensuring that data transmitted over the Internet remains secure. In an HR context, consider the transfer of payroll over a network. SSL encrypts the data during transmission, making it unreadable to anyone who intercepts it.

Intrusion Detection Systems (IDSs) IDSs are tools that monitor networks for suspicious activity and potential breaches. In HR, IDSs can detect unauthorized attempts to access sensitive employee information and alert the IT security team to take immediate action. For instance, if an unusual pattern of data access is detected from an employee's account, the IDS can flag this activity, allowing the security team to investigate and respond swiftly.

Summary

HR information management is the process of collecting, storing, managing, and utilizing employee data to streamline HR operations. It involves HR digitization to transform traditional HR processes and workflows into digital formats to improve efficiency, accuracy, and accessibility, making sure to protect sensitive employee information. HR service delivery models are increasingly shaped by technology, which enhances efficiency and accessibility through tools like self-service portals, automated workflows, and data analytics, transforming how HR services are provided and managed.

Benchmark HR technology is the human resource information system (HRIS). The HRIS manages functions such as employee data management, payroll and benefits administration, and recruitment tracking. It streamlines performance management, time and attendance recording, and training and development programs. The HRIS can also help ensure compliance with labor laws, provide reporting and analytics for data-driven decisions, and offer employee self-service portals for personal information updates and requests. Another HR technology is the applicant-tracking system (ATS), which automates the recruitment process by managing job postings, tracking candidate applications, and facilitating the screening and selection of potential employees. A learning management system (LMS) facilitates employee training and development by organizing, delivering, and tracking educational courses, resources, and progress.

Data security and privacy in HR are other important considerations, with technology playing a prominent role in protecting sensitive employee information through encryption, access controls, and compliance with legal and regulatory standards.

Exam Essentials

Understand the principles of HR information management. HR information management involves collecting, storing, and managing employee data efficiently. It encompasses maintaining accurate records, ensuring data integrity, and using information systems to streamline HR processes, improve decision making, and enhance overall organizational effectiveness.

Be able to communicate the benefits of HR workflow digitization. Digitization of HR workflows transforms manual HR processes into automated, electronic ones. It improves efficiency, reduces errors, and provides real-time access to information, ultimately enhancing HR productivity and employee experience.

Develop an understanding of the use of HR technology. HR technology, including HRISs, ATSs, and LMSs, streamlines HR functions. HRISs manages employee data, ATSs optimize recruitment, and LMSs facilitate training and development. These also enhance efficiency, accuracy, and compliance, supporting strategic HR management.

Understand basic principles of data privacy and security techniques. Data privacy and security in HR involve protecting sensitive employee information from unauthorized access and breaches. This includes implementing encryption, access controls, and compliance with regulations like GDPR. Ensuring data privacy is crucial for maintaining trust and legal compliance.

Review Questions

You can find the answers in Appendix A.

1. Which of the following best describes the concept of social engineering in the context of cybersecurity?
   - A. The process of designing and implementing complex encryption algorithms to protect data
   - B. The application of business continuity strategies to effectively manage cyber-risks
   - C. The development of sophisticated hardware to enhance network security
   - D. The use of psychological manipulation to deceive individuals into divulging confidential information
2. Which of the following best describes a phishing scheme?
   - A. A type of attack where cybercriminals send fraudulent emails that appear to be from legitimate sources to trick individuals into revealing personal information
   - B. Malicious software designed to damage, disrupt, or gain unauthorized access to computer systems
   - C. Unauthorized access to computer systems or networks, often by exploiting vulnerabilities
   - D. The physical theft of computer hardware to gain access to sensitive data
3. You are the HR manager at an organization with 300 employees. You have a generalist and a safety specialist reporting to you. As part of the annual strategic planning session, all managers have been asked to present options to increase efficiencies within their departments and to decrease department expenses by 5 percent over the next 3 years. Which of the following should you recommend?
   - A. Adopting E-Verify to streamline Form I-9 processing time
   - B. Laying off the safety specialist and training department managers to be responsible for employee safety
   - C. Introducing an HR software system for automating administrative tasks and employee self-service
   - D. Hiring additional HR staff to manage workload more effectively
4. Your HR department is reviewing and updating its data management policies to enhance data security. Which of the following policies should be prioritized to achieve these goals?
   - A. Implementing a data retention policy to regularly delete outdated employee records
   - B. Hiring a company to professionally destroy outdated records
   - C. Prohibiting access to specific IP addresses to limit exposure to hackers
   - D. Increasing data backups to protect against loss of data

5. Your company is considering implementing a bring your own device (BYOD) policy to allow employees to use their personal devices for work purposes. To ensure data security and protect sensitive HR information, which of the following measures should be prioritized?

   A. Requiring employees to install mobile device management software on their personal devices

   B. Implementing strong encryption for all data accessed or stored on personal devices

   C. Prohibiting the use of personal devices for work

   D. Requiring employees to share their device passwords with the IT department for monitoring

6. Your organization is exploring the use of artificial intelligence (AI) to enhance workplace efficiency and productivity. Which of the following applications of AI should be prioritized to achieve these goals? (Choose all that apply.)

   A. Implementing AI-driven chatbots to handle routine HR inquiries

   B. Using AI algorithms to generate employee performance reviews

   C. Integrating AI tools to understand threats to employee retention

   D. Deploying AI systems to monitor employee activities and productivity in real time

7. Your HR department is looking to digitize its workflow to improve efficiency and reduce manual processes. Which of the following strategies should be prioritized to best achieve these goals?

   A. Implementing an employee self-service portal for managing personal information and benefits

   B. Contracting with a third-party record storage specialist group

   C. Conducting recruitment and onboarding processes using an applicant tracking system

   D. Decentralizing HR services

8. Your company is debating whether to adopt a centralized or decentralized HR structure. With the ongoing digitization of workflows, the decision has significant implications for efficiency and control. In this context, which of the following statements best supports the adoption of a centralized HR structure?

   A. Centralized HR allows for consistent implementation of policies and streamlined digital workflows across the entire organization.

   B. Decentralized HR enables each department to implement its own digital workflows tailored to specific needs, leading to better employee satisfaction.

   C. Centralized HR reduces the need for digital tools, as all processes can be handled manually at the headquarters.

   D. Decentralized HR ensures faster decision making at the local level, without reliance on centralized digital systems.

9. Your company is developing a new DEI strategy to foster a more inclusive workplace. Considering the impact of digitization on DEI initiatives, which of the following approaches should be prioritized to effectively leverage technology in supporting this strategy?
   - A. Using AI-driven recruitment tools that have been audited for compliance with antidiscrimination laws
   - B. Relying on traditional recruitment methods to maintain a personal touch in the hiring process
   - C. Implementing a uniform training program for all employees
   - D. Utilizing digital platforms to offer customized DEI training programs that cater to diverse learning styles and needs

10. To ensure the success of a remote-first business strategy, which of the following technological investments should be prioritized?
    - A. Investing in high-quality videoconferencing tools to facilitate effective communication and collaboration
    - B. Requiring all employees to work from the office at least one day a week to maintain team cohesion
    - C. Implementing a monitoring system to track employees' work hours and activity
    - D. Focusing on in-person team-building events to strengthen team relationships

11. Which of the following technology strategies can best guard against identity theft in the workplace? (Choose all that apply.)
    - A. Data encryption
    - B. Multifactor authentication (MFA)
    - C. Endpoint security
    - D. Data masking

12. Your company's HR department has experienced a recent increase in phishing attempts targeting employee data. To effectively combat these threats, which of the following actions should be prioritized?
    - A. Updating all HR software to the latest versions
    - B. Conducting phishing simulation exercises for HR staff
    - C. Implementing a VPN for remote access to HR systems
    - D. Increasing physical security measures in the HR office

13. Which of the following is the most effective strategy for preventing social engineering attacks in the workplace?
    - A. Implementing strong password policies
    - B. Providing regular employee training on recognizing and responding to social engineering attempts
    - C. Installing advanced antivirus software on all company devices
    - D. Limiting access to sensitive information based on job roles

14. Which of the following is a disadvantage to shifting HR systems to a cloud-based platform?
   - **A.** Dependence on Internet connectivity for access
   - **B.** Reduced data backup and recovery options
   - **C.** Challenges integrating with other software
   - **D.** Reduced physical storage options

15. Your company is adopting a new cloud-based HR management system to handle employee records, payroll, and benefits. To ensure the security of sensitive HR data stored in the cloud, which of the following practices should be implemented first?
   - **A.** Regular employee training on data security policies
   - **B.** Establishing strong password policies and regular password changes
   - **C.** Conducting a thorough security assessment of the cloud service provider
   - **D.** Implementing multifactor authentication for system access

16. To ensure the highest level of data protection and compliance with data privacy regulations, which of the following practices should be prioritized?
   - **A.** Using biometric authentication for system access
   - **B.** Training employees on existing access controls
   - **C.** Allowing employees to access their own records only from company devices
   - **D.** Implementing role-based access controls

17. When selecting an HRIS, which of the following criteria is most important to ensure the system effectively supports the company's HR needs? (Choose all that apply.)
   - **A.** Popularity of the vendor in the market
   - **B.** Integration capabilities with existing software
   - **C.** Presence of advanced reporting features
   - **D.** Availability of 24/7 customer support

18. A small startup that you work for recently received a large grant to help bring a new, innovative product to market. This will require the hiring of at least 25 new employees for the ramp-up, and an additional 50 over the next 18 months. Which of the following digital tools should you recommend to senior leaders to streamline the process and stay within budget? (Choose all that apply.)
   - **A.** Invest in a robust HRIS.
   - **B.** Enroll the company in E-Verify.
   - **C.** Purchase an applicant-tracking system.
   - **D.** Develop ESS capabilities.

19. Which of the following HRIS access controls would be appropriate for a team member that is responsible to track expenses within the HR budget?

A. Global information

B. Payroll access

C. Unlimited access

D. Management access

20. Which of the following HRIS access controls should be granted to a team member whose primary role is to oversee the process of performance reviews?

A. Tier 1

B. Tier 2

C. Tier 3

D. Tier 4

Appendix A

Answers to Review Questions

Chapter 2: PHR | PHRi and SPHR | SPHRi Exams: Shared Competencies

1. B. The mission describes what the company does today, the vision outlines what it aims to achieve in the future, and values represent the principles guiding its actions, so option B is correct. The mission focuses on the present purpose, the vision on future aspirations, and values on the core principles and ethics.

2. B. The unemployment rate represents the percentage of people in the labor force who are actively looking for jobs but cannot find employment.

3. B, D. Surveys are a common tool in quantitative analysis as they collect numerical data from a large sample size. The results can be statistically analyzed to identify patterns, trends, and correlations. Statistical review involves analyzing numerical data using statistical methods and tools, which is a hallmark of quantitative analysis. It includes techniques like regression analysis, hypothesis testing, and descriptive statistics. Options A and C are examples of qualitative analysis.

4. D. Concurrent validity is demonstrated when a new test is validated by comparing its results with existing performance metrics at the same time. Criterion validity (option A) assesses how well one measure predicts an outcome based on another measure. Construct validity (option B) evaluates how well a test measures the theoretical construct it intends to measure. Predictive validity (option C) refers to the extent to which a test predicts future performance. In this case, the test is used to predict current sales performance, not future performance, making concurrent validity the more accurate type of validity being demonstrated.

5. B. Workplace reengineering involves fundamentally rethinking and redesigning business processes to achieve significant improvements in critical aspects such as cost, quality, service, and speed. Implementing a new employee recognition program to boost morale (option A) is an example of an HR initiative aimed at improving employee satisfaction, not reengineering. Organizing team-building activities (option C) is an example of fostering a positive workplace culture, not reengineering. Offering flexible work hours (option D) is an example of implementing flexible work policies.

6. A, C. Organizational design involves creating an organizational structure that supports the company's strategic goals and enables efficient workflow and communication. Successful organizational development initiatives often result in higher employee morale, better engagement, and enhanced performance by addressing issues like leadership, communication, and work processes.

7. C. Vroom's theory suggests that employees are motivated when they believe their effort will lead to effective performance and subsequently to desirable rewards. Maslow's hierarchy of needs (option A) suggests that individuals are motivated by a hierarchy of needs, starting with basic physiological needs and progressing through safety, social belonging, esteem, and self-actualization. Herzberg's two-factor theory (option B) differentiates between hygiene factors, which can prevent dissatisfaction, and motivators, which can drive job satisfaction.

Equity theory (option D) is based on the principle of fairness and posits that employees are motivated when they perceive that they are treated equitably in comparison to others.

8. D. According to Herzberg's two-factor theory, recognition is considered a motivator. Motivators are factors that lead to job satisfaction and encourage employees to work harder. These factors are related to the content of the job itself and include aspects like achievement, recognition, responsibility, and opportunities for growth. Salary, policies, and working conditions are all considered hygiene factors in Herzberg's two-factor theory.

9. B, C. The SAM model emphasizes iterative development by using rapid prototyping and multiple iterations. The Agile model is characterized by its iterative and incremental approach. It involves breaking the project into small cycles (sprints) and continuously developing, testing, and refining the instructional materials based on stakeholder feedback and changing requirements. This iterative process allows for flexibility and continuous improvement.

10. C. The selection ratio for women is calculated 16 / 45, or 35 percent. The selection ratio for men is 27 / 60, or 45 percent. 35 percent divided by 45 percent equals 78 percent, which is less than 80 percent (4/5ths), so there is evidence of adverse impact in this example.

11. B. Training cost per employee is calculated by dividing the total of all associated training costs by the number of full-time equivalent employees. The proper calculation is $4,500 divided by 25 full-time equivalent employees. The full-time equivalent (FTE) calculation is based on a 40-hour workweek. Part-time workers are calculated by summing the total hours worked and divided by 40.

12. C. The primary purpose of job evaluation is to determine the relative value of jobs within an organization so that they can be placed in appropriate pay bands or grades. Job analysis is the process used to create job descriptions (option A), not job evaluation. Identifying physical and mental health requirements (option B) is related to job analysis and ensuring that employees meet the necessary conditions for a role. Comparing jobs to external market conditions (option D) is part of a market pricing or benchmarking process, which involves looking at compensation data from similar positions outside the organization.

13. B. Kaoru Ishikawa, a Japanese organizational theorist and professor, is credited with developing the fishbone diagram, also known as the cause-and-effect diagram or Ishikawa diagram. This tool is used to identify and analyze the root causes of a problem or effect in quality management. Joseph Juran (option A) is well-known for his work in quality management and the Juran Trilogy, which consists of quality planning, quality control, and quality improvement. W. Edwards Deming (option C) is renowned for his contributions to quality control and management, particularly through his Plan-Do-Check-Act (PDCA) cycle and his 14 Points for Management. Frederick Winslow Taylor (option D) is known for his principles of scientific management and his work in improving industrial efficiency through time and motion studies.

14. D. A process-control chart (option D), also known as a control chart, is used to monitor and control a process over time by plotting data points and identifying any variations or trends. It is well suited for studying and analyzing production times, as it helps in understanding process performance and detecting any deviations from the norm. A check sheet (option A) is primarily used for data collection and recording, allowing for easy counting and analysis

of occurrences or defects. The cause-and-effect diagram (option B), also known as the fishbone diagram or Ishikawa diagram, is used to identify and analyze the root causes of problems. It is not suited for measuring and analyzing production times directly. Stratification charts (option C) are used to separate data gathered from various sources so patterns can be observed. Although useful in identifying patterns, it is not specifically tailored for production time studies.

15. B. Job enrichment involves enhancing a job by adding more meaningful tasks and responsibilities that allow for personal growth and development, thereby increasing job depth. Job enlargement, on the other hand, increases the number of tasks an employee performs but typically at the same level of difficulty, thus increasing job breadth.

16. B. Autonomy refers to the degree to which a job provides an employee with the freedom, independence, and discretion to schedule their work and determine the procedures in carrying it out. Feedback (option A) refers to the degree to which carrying out the work activities required by a job results in the employee receiving direct and clear information about their performance effectiveness. Task significance (option C) refers to the degree to which a job has a substantial impact on the lives or work of other people, whether inside or outside the organization. Ethics (option D) are not a feature of the job characteristics model.

17. C. Corporate social responsibility (CSR) is about the responsibility of a corporation to operate in a manner that benefits society and the environment, while balancing the interests of various stakeholders, including shareholders, employees, customers, and the community.

18. B. Quid pro quo harassment occurs when job benefits, such as promotions or raises, are contingent upon the employee submitting to sexual advances or other forms of harassment, leveraging a power differential between the harasser and the victim. Hostile workplace harassment refers to conduct that creates an intimidating, hostile, or offensive work environment through unwelcome comments, actions, or behaviors, regardless of the power dynamics involved.

19. B. Mitigation involves taking steps to reduce the severity or likelihood of a risk. In this case, machine guards are installed to decrease the risk of injury to workers by providing a physical barrier between them and the hazardous parts of the equipment.

20. A, B, D. The CEO should be consulted because they have a comprehensive understanding of the organization's strategic goals and overall operations. The IT department is critical in developing a business continuity plan because they manage the technology infrastructure that supports business operations. Local first responders, such as fire departments, police, and emergency medical services, should be consulted to understand their response protocols and how they can assist during a business disruption. While employees' insights and cooperation are valuable for implementing the continuity plan, they are not typically consulted in the initial planning stages.

Chapter 3: PHR | PHRi Exam: Business Management

1. C. The general business environment refers to the external factors that influence the operations and performance of businesses. Economic conditions, social trends, and technological advancements are all examples of external factors that businesses must consider. Organizational culture is an internal factor that pertains to the values, beliefs, and behaviors.

2. B. Adapting recruitment strategies to comply with local regulations on diversity and inclusion directly addresses the impact of sociopolitical forces on HR practices. This ensures that the company adheres to legal requirements and cultural expectations regarding workforce diversity, promoting inclusivity and minimizing legal risks in diverse global contexts. Option A reflects a technological force, option C a cultural force, and option D an economic factor.

3. C. A stakeholder is one with a vested interest in the organization's outcomes, which can include employees, customers, suppliers, investors, and the community.

4. B. A human resources center of excellence (COE) is a specialized team within the HR department that focuses on developing and implementing best practices and strategies in specific areas of HR. Option A is incorrect as it describes a shared service model. Option C is incorrect as it describes an external consulting firm, which provides HR services externally. Option D is incorrect as it describes a cross-functional team tasked with improving organizational effectiveness and efficiency.

5. B. The strategic role of HR involves aligning HR practices with organizational goals, setting long-term objectives, and developing initiatives to drive organizational success. Conversely, the operational role focuses on executing HR policies and procedures to address immediate needs and ensure day-to-day HR functions run smoothly.

6. A. HR audits, including that of hiring practices related to diversity, are designed to help identify potential or real problems. This creates the opportunity for organizations to design preventive measures or correct existing issues prior to the need for attorneys, or in advance of an audit of compliance.

7. C. An HR audit examines HR policies and procedures for compliance and to determine whether the department is successfully meeting the organization's needs. This includes analyzing the employer handbook to ensure it is current with ever-changing labor laws. D. To ensure that employees are properly classified under workers' compensation codes

8. C. In a matrix structure, HR staff members report to both functional managers (such as HR department heads) and project managers, allowing for collaboration across different projects and functional areas. Option A is incorrect as it describes a traditional hierarchical structure where HR functions are divided based on specific job roles within the department. Option B is incorrect as it describes a flat organizational structure where HR professionals report directly to the CEO, which is not characteristic of a matrix structure. Option D is incorrect because it describes a decentralized structure where HR functions are outsourced.

9. D. Risk transfer involves shifting the financial burden of potential losses to another party, such as an insurance provider. Seeking proposals for employment practices liability insurance (EPLI) is a clear example of transferring the risk to an insurance company, as they would provide coverage for any liabilities arising from employment practices issues. Option A is incorrect as avoidance involves eliminating the risk entirely by not engaging in the activity that poses the risk. Option B is incorrect because acceptance involves acknowledging the risk and its potential consequences without taking any action to mitigate or transfer it. Option C is incorrect because mitigation involves taking actions to reduce the severity or impact of the risk.

10. A. An HR service culture influences employee engagement by implementing strategies such as open communication, recognition programs, and career development opportunities. This fosters a positive work environment where employees feel valued and motivated, ultimately leading to higher levels of engagement. Option B is incorrect as productivity may be influenced by various factors such as efficient processes, resource allocation, and management practices. Option C is incorrect as quality standards and practices are established by organizational policies and procedures rather than HR programs directly. Option D is incorrect as legal compliance is a broader organizational responsibility that involves adherence to laws and regulations governing employment practices, which may extend beyond the scope of HR functions.

11. C. Mentorship relationships focus on personal and professional development rather than on conveying behavioral expectations. Written policies are commonly used by organizations to communicate expected standards of behavior to employees. HR behavior modeling involves HR professionals demonstrating desired behaviors to employees, thereby serving as role models for proper conduct. An employee handbook contains information on company policies, procedures, and guidelines, including expected standards of behavior.

12. D. Documenting the vendor's failures and presenting evidence to senior management is the most proactive and transparent approach. This approach allows for informed decision making by senior management, who can then consider options such as renegotiating terms with the vendor or terminating the contract if necessary. It prioritizes the company's interests and ensures accountability in vendor management. Option A is incorrect because without holding the vendor accountable for their failures, there is no guarantee that their performance will improve over time, risking the company's ability to meet its recruitment needs efficiently. Option B is incorrect as confronting the vendor directly is a reactive approach that lacks a strategic plan for addressing the underlying issues and may not effectively resolve the problem in the long term. Option C is incorrect as it undermines trust and accountability within the organization and may lead to additional complications if the new vendors also fail to meet expectations.

13. A, B, C, D. An HR audit allows an employer to assess how well their current HR practices are serving the strategic objectives of the organization, identify risk exposure, assess the knowledge of the current workforce, and measure employee engagement levels. By examining various HR processes and procedures, such as recruitment, training, performance management, risk and compensation, employers can determine whether these practices contribute to the overall goals of the company.

14. D. A cybersecurity audit examines various aspects of an organization's cybersecurity framework, such as network security, access controls, encryption mechanisms, and incident response procedures, to identify potential vulnerabilities and risks to confidentiality. Option A is incorrect as a behavioral training audit primarily focuses on evaluating the effectiveness of training programs aimed at improving employee behavior and performance. Option B is incorrect as a phishing vulnerability audit assesses an organization's susceptibility to phishing attacks, focusing on technical vulnerabilities in email systems and user awareness levels. Option C is incorrect because a compliance audit verifies whether an organization is adhering to relevant laws, regulations, and industry standards.

15. A. An HR budget reflects how many and what types of resources are necessary to accomplish a goal. The addition of employees, costs to train, and the purchase of new equipment are all examples of items that require cash to achieve strategic goals.

16. A. Shareholders are individuals or entities who own shares of stock in the company, giving them a direct financial stake and ownership interest. Stakeholders are individuals or entities such as employees, customers, suppliers, communities, and the environment that are impacted by the company's activities and decisions, regardless of share ownership.

17. D. Services are intangible and often involve a certain level of customization to meet specific needs or requirements. Examples of services include consulting, maintenance, repair, and training. Goods are tangible items that can be manufactured, stored, and sold to customers. Goods have physical attributes and can be touched or seen. Examples of goods include clothing, electronics, food items, and automobiles.

18. B. Employee relations encompasses various activities aimed at fostering positive relationships between employees and the organization. This includes initiatives such as recognition programs to acknowledge employee contributions, conflict resolution processes to address disputes effectively, and employee assistance programs to support employees in times of need.

19. B. Mitigation involves taking proactive measures to reduce the likelihood or impact of identified risks, including implementing regular safety inspections and providing comprehensive training on hazard identification, and emergency procedures are proactive steps aimed at minimizing workplace accidents. Option A is incorrect as avoidance involves eliminating or completely avoiding exposure to a particular risk. Option C is incorrect because transferring risk involves shifting the financial burden or responsibility of managing a risk to another party, such as through insurance or outsourcing. Option D is incorrect as acceptance involves acknowledging the existence of a risk but choosing not to take any action to mitigate it.

20. B. Creating an HR budget takes into account standard expense items associated with having employees. They include salaries, taxes, benefits, training, travel, and equipment costs, to name a few. A compensation strategy (option C) defines pay equity both internally and externally. The cost of recruiting (option D) is a measurement of HR activities return on investment and can be a measurement of business impact (option A).

Chapter 4: PHR | PHRi Exam: Workforce Planning and Talent Acquisition

1. D. The candidate profile is developed after the job requirements have been determined, beginning with the job description and developing the competencies (broad requirements of the position) and the specifications necessary for successful performance. Job competencies (option A) identify skills and qualities beyond tasks and responsibilities specific to the position that help determine how well a candidate will fit into the work group, such as team orientation versus individual contribution or ability to learn new skills quickly. The job description (option B) provides the tasks and responsibilities that must be accomplished. Job specifications (option C) define the job-specific KSAOs that will be needed for success in the position.

2. C. According to the EEOC, there are no circumstances where race or color are a bona fide occupational qualification BFOQ. Option A is incorrect because Title VII specifically allows religious organizations to give preference to members of the religion. Options B and D are incorrect because Title VII specifically allows sex as a BFOQ if it is "reasonably necessary" for business operations.

3. A. *Griggs* identified adverse impact to mean that discrimination need not be intentional to exist; *Albemarle Paper* (option B) extended the concept to require that tests must be validated in accordance with the EEOC Uniform Guidelines for Employee Selection Procedures. *Washington* (option C) determined that employment tests resulting in adverse impact are acceptable if they predict future success on the job. *Taxman* (option D) found that employment decisions made on the basis of race are discriminatory.

4. A. A staffing needs analysis begins with an assessment of the KSAOs needed to achieve future goals along with those that are currently available within the organization. Although the tasks, duties, and responsibilities (option B) are used to determine what the KSAOs are, it is possible for individuals with the same or similar KSAOs to perform different jobs, so they are not used in a needs analysis. KSAOs available in the local labor market (option C) will be used to develop the recruiting strategy and plan but are not relevant to the staffing needs analysis. The organization's core competencies (option D) are factors that make the organization unique but are not generally part of the staffing needs analysis.

5. C. The GM could be influenced by his similar experience working his way through college. Knowledge-of-predictor bias (option A) is a factor when the interviewer knows that a candidate scored particularly high or low on an assessment test. The halo effect (option B) occurs when interviewers allow one positive characteristic to overshadow other, less positive attributes. The gut feeling bias (option D) occurs when interviewers rely on intuition to make hiring decisions.

6. C. Having a solid system in place to notify all candidates not selected is an HR best practice. A standard email may be appropriate for some, whereas a personal phone call—particularly for those who received interviews—leaves a positive impression and potential for future sourcing. Standard practices such as those listed in option A may not be appropriate or sufficient for all candidates, and option B is not practical. Option D is not true; it is

important to communicate with all candidates in some form to protect the employer brand and establish a candidate pipeline for future positions.

7. A. Allowing the employee to proceed through the application process is the best answer in this scenario. Not only does it give her the opportunity to compete, but it allows HR to work with the existing manager to develop a timely replacement plan. Option B is incorrect as other applicants should also be given a chance, option C does not support employee growth and can lead to low morale, and option D, discipline, should be a last resort after training, education, and support.

8. D. IRCA allows, but does not require, employers to make copies of documents presented for employment eligibility. Form I-9 must be completed within the first 72 hours of employment. Employers who make a good faith effort to comply with IRCA have an affirmative defense to inadvertently hiring an unauthorized alien. IRCA requires that I-9 forms be maintained and available for audit by the USCIS for 3 years from date of hire or 1 year after the date of termination.

9. C. E-Verify is an online system that allows employers to electronically verify the employment eligibility of newly hired employees by comparing information from their Form I-9 to data from the U.S. Department of Homeland Security and Social Security Administration records. By using E-Verify, employers can identify and rectify errors in I-9 forms in real time, ensuring compliance with immigration laws and regulations. Option A is incorrect as training should be part of a comprehensive approach to compliance, but it may not be sufficient to correct the errors already identified. Option B is incorrect as recertification involves reviewing and updating all I-9 forms in the employer's records, which may not be practical or necessary for all errors identified. Recertification may also pose challenges if employees are no longer with the company or if the errors are minor and do not warrant full recertification. Option D is incorrect because it may not address other types of errors such as incomplete sections or over-documentation.

10. B. Although the decision to store employment records online is influenced by all of these factors, the ability to limit access is a strong element of labor law and privacy compliance.

11. A, B, C, D. Job bidding may serve many purposes, including supporting a company that desires to promote from within. It is also helpful for highly competitive jobs in order to give employees the opportunity to notify HR of their interest. This also gives HR an instant applicant pool from which to draw from for future openings, as well as identifying employees who are interested in various roles within the company.

12. B. Any tool used to select employees must be job-related and a valid predictor of success on the job. If a selection tool results in discrimination against an individual who is a member of a protected class, the criteria used must be shown to be job-related and valid. For example, a bona fide occupational qualification occurs when religion, sex, or national origin is "reasonably necessary to the normal operation" of the business.

13. B. Negligent hiring occurs when an employer knows or should have known about an applicant's prior history that endangered customers, employees, vendors, or others with whom the employee comes into contact. Options A, C, and D are incorrect because while this behavior may be classified as a criminal act, it is not a violation of employee privacy but rather a

function of workplace violence that may have been prevented through proper screening at the time of hire.

14. D. During strategic workforce planning, skills inventories are used as part of the gap analysis process. It is a tool that identifies the current skill set of the workforce, which is then compared to the skills necessary to execute strategy. Any gaps will need to be planned for accordingly.

15. A. The EEO-1 report requires employers to group jobs into job categories based on average skill level, knowledge, and responsibility. Option B is incorrect as exempt workers are defined by professional, executive, and administrative exemption criteria, and option D is incorrect as these are not examples of the protected class groups under federal law. Option C is not true.

16. C. Job bidding allows internal candidates to express interest in a job prior to it becoming available. It gives employees the opportunity to develop the skills necessary to successfully compete for the position once it becomes available. Option A is incorrect as a job posting is an internal job announcement. Option B is incorrect as requests for proposal (RFPs) are typically used to allow outside vendors to bid on project work, and option D is incorrect since the ranking of job applicants is a function of the selection process used to identify the most qualified individual for the job.

17. B. Any inquiries into an applicant's citizen status must be specific to the requirements of the job. In this example, it is not necessary for the employer to know specifically whether the applicant is a U.S. citizen, but rather, whether the applicant is authorized to work in the United States. The other options are lawful provided that they are asked of all applicants.

18. B. A contingent job offer is one that is conditional or dependent on certain criteria being met before it becomes final and binding. One common condition for contingent job offers is the successful completion of background checks or drug tests. Option A is incorrect as it describes a noncontingent or unconditional job offer. Option C is incorrect because the absence of a specified start date does not necessarily make an offer contingent; instead, it may indicate that details about the start date are still being negotiated or finalized. Option D is incorrect because it describes a condition related to salary negotiation rather than the typical conditions associated with contingent job offers.

19. C. Talent pools commonly refer to databases or networks of passive candidates who possess specific skills, qualifications, or experience relevant to an organization's needs. These individuals may not be actively seeking employment but are open to new opportunities if presented with the right offer. Option A is incorrect because talent pools typically consist of passive candidates rather than actively seeking individuals. While individuals actively seeking employment may be part of a talent pool, the primary focus is on identifying and engaging with passive candidates who may not be actively searching for jobs but possess desirable skills and qualifications. Option B is incorrect as it describes succession planning or talent management practices within organizations rather than external talent pools. Option D is incorrect because it describes a common use of talent pools rather than the definition of talent pools themselves.

20. B. A change of control clause outlines the terms and conditions that apply to an employee's stock options or other benefits in the event of a change in ownership or control of the company. Option A is incorrect as golden parachute clauses are designed to provide generous severance packages or financial benefits to executives or key employees in the event of termination following a change in control, such as a merger or an acquisition. Option C is incorrect as a noncompete clause restricts an employee's ability to work for a competitor or start a competing business for a certain period after leaving the company. Option D is incorrect because, although it does relate to employee benefits, specifically stock options, it is more specifically categorized as a change of control clause rather than a general benefits clause.

Chapter 5: PHR | PHRi Exam: Learning and Development

1. B. Artificial intelligence (AI) is the use of computer algorithms to mimic human cognitive functions like learning, reasoning, and decision making. Option A is incorrect because AI encompasses a broader range of technologies beyond just robots, including software applications that do not have physical form. Option C is too narrow and misleading. While AI can automate manual tasks, its scope includes a wide array of functions such as data analysis, predictive modeling, and more, often with some degree of human oversight. Option D is incorrect because, while human oversight can be part of AI implementation, AI's defining feature is its ability to perform tasks that typically require human intelligence, including autonomously.

2. B. Scrum emphasizes collaboration, flexibility, and iterative development to manage complex projects effectively. It involves breaking down work into manageable chunks called sprints, allowing for rapid iteration, continuous improvement, and close collaboration among team members.

3. B. The learning evaluation method focuses on how well the training resulted in learning new skills. The reaction evaluation method (option A) focuses on participant reactions. The behavior evaluation method (option C) measures on-the-job behavior changes as a result of training, and the results evaluation method (option D) measures organizational results. Of the four methods, the results evaluation method is considered the most valuable for the organization.

4. A. Upskilling involves improving existing skills or acquiring new ones relevant to an individual's current or new role, enabling them to perform their job more effectively or advance within their current career path. Reskilling focuses on acquiring entirely new skills or knowledge to transition into a different role or field, often necessitated by changes in job requirements, technological advancements, or industry shifts.

5. A. The positively accelerating learning curve begins with smaller increments but increases in pace and size as learning continues. The negatively accelerating curve (option B) begins with larger increments that decrease as learning continues. The S-shaped learning curve (option C) is a combination of the positively and negatively accelerating learning curves, whereas a plateau (option D) occurs when no learning seems to take place.

6. B. In asynchronous training, learners have the flexibility to access learning materials, such as prerecorded lectures, online modules, or reading assignments, at their convenience. They can progress through the content at their own pace, without the need for real-time interaction with instructors or peers. Synchronous training involves real-time interaction between instructors and learners, typically through live lectures, virtual classrooms, or webinars. Learners participate in scheduled sessions where they can ask questions, engage in discussions, and receive immediate feedback from instructors or peers.

7. C. Mentoring and coaching provide personalized guidance, feedback, and support tailored to the individual's development needs and career goals. Through mentorship and coaching relationships with experienced leaders, the employee can gain valuable insights, learn best practices, and develop leadership skills necessary for success in their future leadership role. Option A is incorrect because they may not provide the personalized guidance and support necessary for individualized development tailored to the employee's specific needs and career goals. Option B is incorrect as job shadowing may not offer the structured guidance and feedback needed for comprehensive skill development and preparation for a leadership role. Option D is incorrect because it may not directly contribute to the development of leadership skills or provide the organizational insights necessary for success.

8. C. By identifying trends and patterns related to training and career development, organizations can pinpoint areas for improvement in their learning and development programs. This includes recognizing common themes such as inadequate training resources, limited growth opportunities, or mismatches between employee expectations and organizational culture. Option A is incorrect because exit surveys are specifically designed to gather feedback from departing employees. Option B is incorrect because exit surveys focus on gathering feedback on various aspects of the employee experience, not employee performance. Option D is incorrect because exit surveys are focused on individual employee experiences, not organizational performance.

9. C. The Agile model of instructional design is characterized by "chunking" training content (and projects) into smaller, more manageable pieces. Agile is most likely to result in training content delivered in multiple modules as opposed to ADDIE (option A), which is more linear than short-cycled. SAM (option B) is also cyclical, but it's more useful for smaller design projects that do not require complicated technical elements such as video. Virtual training is a mode of delivery, not an instructional design model (option D).

10. C. A mentor is someone who takes a personal interest in an employee's career and who guides and sponsors them. Although a supervisor may be a mentor, mentors are usually individuals who are outside the chain of command and may even be from outside the organization. The functions in options A, B, and D are not generally performed by mentors.

11. D. Formative evaluation is a technique used prior to the commencement and during the design phase of training. It is used to gather data that will be used in training to ensure that the objectives are met and that the training meets the needs of the workgroup. This is different from summative evaluation (option A), which occurs after the training has taken place. Knowledge banking (option B) and an attitude assessment (option C) are not used in the evaluation of training.

12. B. The ADDIE model is a process that begins with an analysis of the specific training needs. In this example, management may believe that the negative reviews are the result of a lack of training, but until a thorough needs analysis is conducted—including the gathering of relevant data—it is not possible to create specific training objectives that will result in the desired outcomes. While training design (option A), participant identification (option C), and scheduling (option D) are components of training, they do not launch the ADDIE model.

13. B. Employee satisfaction surveys are designed to gauge employees' perceptions and attitudes toward various aspects of their job and work environment, including compensation. By analyzing responses to employee satisfaction surveys, the HR Generalist can identify any dissatisfaction or concerns related to wage rates that may be affecting employee performance indirectly. Options A and C are incorrect because wage surveys, also called compensation surveys, collect data on wage rates within a broad market or industry, focusing on external benchmarks rather than internal impacts on employee performance. Option D is incorrect as exit surveys are administered to departing employees to gather feedback on their reasons for leaving the organization, not necessarily on the impact of wages on individual performance.

14. A, B. Chatbots can influence employee learning and development by providing instant access to learning resources and information. They serve as virtual assistants that employees can interact with to quickly retrieve relevant learning materials, such as training modules, manuals, videos, or articles. By analyzing user interactions and preferences, chatbots can deliver tailored recommendations, quizzes, and feedback to individual learners. This personalization enhances engagement and effectiveness by providing content and activities that align with each learner's interests, goals, and skill levels, fostering a more impactful learning experience. Option C is incorrect because chatbots are not intended to replace human trainers and instructors entirely; human interaction remains valuable for addressing complex learning needs, providing mentorship, and facilitating interactive discussions and collaborative learning experiences. Option D is incorrect because modern chatbots continue to evolve and are capable of supporting a wide range of learning needs and interactive learning experiences beyond basic information retrieval.

15. C. Asynchronous training is self-paced training that typically occurs using computer-based tools. Although timelines for completion may be preestablished (such as specifying that all assignments must be submitted no later than 11:59 p.m. Sunday evening), participants typically are able to set their own schedule for when they engage in learning the material. Vestibule training is a form of OJT (option A), mobile learning (option B) is a type of e-learning that occurs typically through mobile devices, and the Delphi technique (option D) is a decision-making or forecasting activity that relies on a group of experts to reach a consensus.

16. B. Formative evaluations are designed to gather information prior to the design of training to measure the needs of the participants. This allows the designer to include content and exercises that will aid in the participant transfer of the training to the job. Summative evaluations (option C) are used after the training has taken place and often include a measure of participant reactions (option A) and trainer evaluations (option D).

17. A. Operational HR focuses on day-to-day tasks and administrative functions, whereas strategic HR emphasizes long-term planning and alignment with organizational goals. Operational HR deals with immediate concerns such as payroll, benefits administration, and employee relations, and strategic HR involves activities like workforce planning, talent management, and developing HR initiatives that support the organization's long-term objectives and competitive advantage.

18. C. Training cost per employee is calculated by dividing the total of all associated training costs by the number of full-time equivalent employees. The proper calculation is $4,500 divided by 25 full-time equivalent employees. Full-time equivalent employees in this example are the 20 employees who work 40 hours per week, and the equivalent of 5 employees who work 40 hours per week.

19. C. A case study allows participants to review real-world scenarios related to their topic of study. Practical application and transfer of training are typically more successful when participants can see how it's done in the work environment. Vestibule training (option A) occurs "on the job," facilitation (option B) uses an individual to create an interactive training experience, and a Socratic seminar (option D) is a type of training that welcomes opposing viewpoints in a problem-solving setting.

20. A, B, C, D. An LMS serves as a centralized platform where decentralized team members can access learning resources and training materials from anywhere, at any time. This ensures consistent access to essential information and resources, regardless of geographic location, enabling decentralized teams to engage in continuous learning and development. These platforms enable organizations to efficiently deliver training and development programs to decentralized teams and offer robust tracking and reporting features that allow managers to monitor the performance and progress of decentralized team members. LMS platforms include built-in communication and collaboration tools that facilitate interaction and engagement among decentralized team members.

Chapter 6: PHR | PHRi Exam: Total Rewards

1. B. With the rise of independent contractors creating a "gig" economy, HR must budget for labor differently. The employee burden will be different, and depending on the nature of the contractors, the labor costs may need to be calculated on a project basis. Option A is incorrect as gig workers do not necessarily have a higher base pay, and option C is incorrect as employers may not unlawfully discriminate against any worker. In option D, true independent contractors are not eligible for mandated benefits (such as Social Security) through an employer, although this is an emerging area of compliance.

2. A. Improperly classifying a worker as an independent contractor can be determined by several factors. Behavioral factors include the degree of control an employer has over when and the way a worker performs the work. Option B is incorrect because financial factors include

how the worker is paid and how expenses are reimbursed, and in option C, the type of relationship may be determined by the presence of written contracts or benefits. The entire relationship should be reviewed when making a determination of worker classification, so option D is also incorrect.

3. B. Intrinsic rewards are those in which esteem is achieved from within oneself. Options A, C, and D are examples of extrinsic rewards that come from external sources.

4. A. A Total Rewards philosophy helps determine what kind of employees will be attracted to the organization. Developing a philosophy to target employees with the KSAs needed by the organization can help advance the organization's mission. Option B is incorrect as the pecking order for jobs is based on the value of those jobs to the organization. Option C is incorrect because the philosophy defines leading the competition as a strategy; positioning the company to do so is a result of creating the compensation structure. Option D is incorrect as an entitlement culture is maintained by continuing to pay employees for time on the job instead of for performance.

5. A. An entitlement culture rewards longevity in the job. If increased productivity is a function of time on the job, an entitlement culture will encourage employees to stay with the company. Option B is incorrect because line of sight occurs when employees know that their performance impacts their pay. Option C is incorrect because a highly competitive workforce is more likely to exist in a pay-for-performance culture. Option D is not correct because a workforce with a highly desired skill set would be better served by a pay-for-performance culture.

6. A, B, C, D. Options A, B, and D are obviously correct. Although option C may seem counterintuitive to some because many employers are hesitant to terminate employees for policy violations, those terminated for cause generally aren't eligible for unemployment insurance. Because retaining an employee who is not contributing to the organization is a poor business decision, maintaining adequate records to demonstrate the reasons for termination provides the tools to fight claims that are unjustified.

7. D. From an employer perspective, unlimited time-off plans reduce the administrative burden of tracking accruals. Unlimited time off actually can make it more difficult to schedule workflow, so option A is incorrect. Managing timecards is irrelevant in this scenario, so option B is incorrect. Option C is an advantage to the employee, not the employer.

8. C. The correct choice in this situation is to tell the employer that paying less than the state minimum wage is illegal. However, you may back this statement up by creating wage bands to make the argument that paying within range will help the employer retain employees (option B). Options A and D are both unlawful.

9. D. Commission-based pay is a form of incentive designed to drive employee behaviors specifically related to selling products. While it does so by making a portion of employee pay at risk, commission plans may not result in an employee making less than minimum wage and is not the primary purpose of this type of incentive (option A). Commissions are not always a measure of employees who work hard, so option B is incorrect. In some cases, employees paid on commission are among the highest paid employees in the organization, so option C is untrue as well.

10. A, B, C. Summary plan descriptions are required only for group health plans, and not for defined-contribution plans, defined-benefit plans, or FSAs.

11. A. Gym memberships are not reimbursable under flexible spending accounts. Options B, C, and D—durable medical equipment, acupuncture, and psychiatric care—are all allowable expenses.

12. C. Group incentives share common elements, including the reward of individuals based on their collective efforts. Option B is incorrect as gainsharing, employee stock ownership plans, employee stock purchase plans, profit-sharing, and gainsharing are all examples of group incentives. Option A, deferred compensation, refers to tax-deferred retirement plans, and option D, a sales bonus, is a type of commission paid to workers.

13. B. Call-back pay is a premium paid to employees who are called to work before or after their scheduled hours. Option A, on-call pay, is provided to employees who are required to be regularly available to respond to work-related issues on short notice and who must be available via pager, telephone, or email. Option C, reporting pay, is given when a worker shows up to their job and there is no work to perform. Option D, hazard pay, is given for dangerous circumstances. While a worker at a nuclear facility may (or may not) be given hazard pay, in this instance the premium is being given for coming to work early, not for potential hazards.

14. A. Wage compression occurs when employer pay rates do not keep up with external market conditions and the economy as a whole. When the cost of living goes up, pay rates should be adjusted as well. For this reason, employers often tie pay increases to the consumer price index published by the Bureau of Labor Statistics (BLS).

15. B. For fully trained employees with satisfactory performance who have been with the company less than five years, the mid-point of the salary range is reasonable. Option A is incorrect because placing them below mid-point puts them at risk for leaving, and option C, paying above mid-point, may mean the employer is overpaying for performance. In option D, paying them somewhere in between mid-point and maximum would require more information.

16. C. Prescription medication coverage is an example of an employee health and welfare benefit.

17. A. Medicare is a type of involuntary benefit introduced by the Social Security Act of 1935. Along with retirement (Social Security), these mandated benefits are subsidized by a tax on both the employer and the employee called FICA (Federal Insurance Contributions Act). Vision, retirement, and sick pay (options B, C, and D) are all examples of voluntary benefits that employers may choose to offer their employees.

18. C. A key component of a gainsharing plan is the shared responsibility of outcomes between management and employees. Productivity is reviewed, new performance is measured, and both workgroups share in the gain. ESPPs, bonuses, and Improshare (options A, B, and D) all could be used but are not specifically grown around the concept of shared responsibility between management and employees.

19. B. Intrinsic rewards are driven by internal versus external factors. Job fulfillment based on work relationships, the opportunity to use strengths, and career growth are examples of non-monetary compensation. Option C, extrinsic rewards, are those rewards that are driven by external factors, usually in the form of monetary (option A) or benefit rewards (components of a Total Rewards system [option D]).

20. A. Gross pay is the amount paid to an employee based on several factors, including the employee's base pay rate, shift differentials, tips, and bonuses; how many hours the employee worked during the pay period; and whether any paid leave was used. It is the amount due to an employee before any mandatory or voluntary deductions are made. Once the deductions are taken out, employees receive their net pay (option B), the amount that is often referred to as "take-home pay." The burden rate is the amount of indirect costs of employment, such as workers' compensation insurance (option C), and wages, salaries, and tips (option D) is only one component of calculating gross pay.

Chapter 7: PHR | PHRi Exam: Employee Engagement

1. D. Employee engagement is defined as the emotional and psychological commitment an employee has toward their organization and work, reflecting their willingness to contribute to organizational success and indicating a high degree of investment in their tasks. Option A is incorrect as job satisfaction refers to how content an employee is with their job, including aspects like work conditions, salary, and work-life balance. Option B is incorrect as organizational commitment relates to an employee's loyalty to the organization and their desire to remain a part of it, which is different from being fully invested in the work they perform. Option C is incorrect because job characteristics refer to the aspects of a job that can influence an employee's attitudes and behaviors, such as task variety, autonomy, and feedback, but do not directly define the degree of investment in the work.

2. C. The concept of employee engagement started gaining attention from industrial-organizational psychologists in the 1990s. Unlike job satisfaction, which measures how content an employee is with their job, and organizational commitment, which reflects an employee's loyalty and intention to stay with the organization, employee engagement focuses on the emotional and psychological investment an employee has in their work.

3. A, B, C, D. The workplace value proposition (WVP) includes base wages, career development, mental health benefits, and company culture. These elements collectively demonstrate an organization's commitment to fair compensation, professional growth, employee well-being, and a supportive work environment, which in turn, support high levels of employee engagement.

4. B. Ineffective leadership can lead to a lack of clear direction, poor communication, and insufficient support, all of which contribute to employee dissatisfaction and disengagement. Option A is incorrect as employees often prioritize factors such as recognition, development

opportunities, and their relationship with management over salary alone. Option C is incorrect because the physical work environment does not typically have as significant an impact on engagement as interpersonal and leadership factors. Option D is incorrect because technological limitations are often seen as obstacles rather than fundamental reasons for a lack of engagement.

5. D. Actively disengaged employees are not just unhappy at work; they act out their unhappiness. Regularly undermining coworkers shows a deliberate effort to disrupt the workplace, which is a clear indicator of active disengagement. This behavior can lead to a toxic work environment and decreased team productivity. Options A and B are incorrect as they are more indicative of a disengaged worker than an actively disengaged worker. Option C is incorrect as it is more a sign of abusive conduct and bullying, behavioral issues that go beyond active disengagement.

6. A. Functional effectiveness emphasizes the importance of aligning employee contributions with business goals at every stage of employment. Option B is incorrect as it describes the workplace value proposition, and option C is incorrect because it defines employee engagement. Option D is incorrect as it describes job satisfaction, which is a measure of how happy employees are with their jobs.

7. B. A positive company culture creates an environment where employees feel valued, supported, and motivated, leading to higher levels of engagement. Option A is incorrect as company culture encompasses broader aspects that directly impact how engaged employees feel at work. Option C is incorrect because it is more accurate to say that company culture has a stronger and more immediate impact on employee engagement. Option D is incorrect as culture sets the overall environment in which job roles are performed.

8. C. A performance improvement plan (PIP) is designed to address specific issues related to an employee's performance and engagement. It sets clear expectations, provides support, and offers a structured path to improvement, which can help reengage the employee. Option A is incorrect as there is not enough information in the question to determine if discipline is the correct course of action. Option B is incorrect as upskilling supervisors may not provide the immediate support needed to address an actively disengaged employee. Option D is incorrect because monitoring for signs of sabotage assumes the worst about the employee and does not provide any proactive or supportive measures to address the disengagement.

9. B, C. Performance reviews are developmental tools when conducted properly and have a positive effect on employee engagement when an employee feels they are fair and balanced. Performance reviews include goal-setting and career development discussions, which help employees see a clear path for growth. Options A and D are incorrect as neither represents the functional effectiveness of using performance reviews to enhance employee engagement.

10. B. Setting clear performance metrics ensures that promotions are based on measurable achievements that directly contribute to organizational success. Option A is incorrect as promotions based on tenure may overlook high-performing employees who have an impact on organizational results. Option C is incorrect as skills' development is valuable but needs to be coupled with performance metrics that reflect organizational goals. Option D is incorrect because random selection does not consider an employee's performance or contribution to

organizational results. Fairness in promotions should be based on merit and alignment with organizational goals rather than randomness.

11. C. Psychological safety involves creating an environment where employees feel confident that they can voice their thoughts and take risks without fear of negative consequences, which fosters open communication, creativity, and collaboration. Option A is incorrect as it refers to physical safety, which is about creating a hazard-free work environment. Option B is partially incorrect because there is not necessarily a correlation between feelings of job security and feeling safe to speak up. Option D is incorrect as psychological safety is about the day-to-day interactions and the culture that allows employees to feel safe to speak up and be themselves, not so much about mental health resources.

12. B. Fear of speaking up due to harsh criticism indicates a lack of psychological safety, where employees do not feel safe to express their ideas or concerns without negative repercussions. Option A is incorrect because lack of employee engagement refers to employees not being emotionally or mentally invested in their work. Option C is incorrect as while a lack of psychological safety can contribute to a toxic work environment, the scenario is specifically focused on the fear of speaking up and being criticized, which directly pertains to psychological safety rather than the broader concept of toxicity in the workplace. Option D is incorrect because workplace harassment involves unwelcome behavior that is discriminatory, intimidating, or abusive.

13. B. High employee engagement is directly linked to higher levels of innovation and productivity. Engaged employees are more motivated and committed to their work, leading them to contribute new ideas and work more efficiently. Option A is incorrect as it does not directly influence satisfaction with pay. Option C is incorrect because ethical behavior is influenced by many factors, including organizational culture and leadership, rather than solely by employee engagement. Option D is incorrect because improved job characteristics and tasks are typically a result of job design and organizational policies.

14. A, B, C. Coaching is a constructive performance technique that involves guiding and supporting employees to improve their skills and performance. Performance improvement plans (PIPs) are structured plans that outline specific goals and actions for employees to improve their performance. Job redesign involves structuring job roles and tasks to improve efficiency and satisfaction, which in turn, can improve performance. Option D is incorrect as restructuring is typically a broader organizational strategy rather than a direct method for constructive performance improvement.

15. A, B. Progressive discipline policies require managers to document each step and ensure consistent application, which can be time-consuming and require significant effort to manage effectively, and if progressive discipline policies are not applied consistently and fairly across all employees, it can lead to perceptions of bias and potential legal challenges. Option C is incorrect as progressive discipline is actually designed to avoid immediate termination by providing a series of warnings and opportunities for improvement before considering termination. Option D is incorrect because these policies are specifically designed to give employees multiple opportunities to correct their behavior through a structured series of warnings and interventions.

16. C. The performance management stage involves regular feedback and transparent communication about performance, goals, and development. This continuous interaction is key to increasing and maintaining employee engagement. Option A is incorrect because the hiring stage is not primarily focused on ongoing feedback and transparent communication to increase engagement. Option B is incorrect as the onboarding stage is critical for acclimating new employees and setting expectations, but it is not as focused on continuous feedback and transparent communication as the performance management stage. Option D is incorrect because while feedback during exit interviews can provide valuable insights, it does not focus on increasing current employee engagement.

17. B. Alumni groups help maintain a relationship with former employees, fostering a sense of belonging and continued connection to the organization. This can positively affect current employee engagement by showing a commitment to long-term relationships. Option A is incorrect because alumni groups' primary purpose is to maintain connections with former employees, not to provide networking opportunities within the organization for current employees. Option C is incorrect as alumni groups do not provide financial benefits to former workers. Option D is incorrect because alumni groups are not used to understand employee turnover.

18. B. Transparent communication helps address remaining employees' concerns, rebuilds trust, and shows that the organization values and cares for its employees. Option A is incorrect as engagement involves more than just workload management; it includes addressing emotional and psychological needs. Option C is incorrect because sustainable engagement requires more than just monetary rewards. Option D is incorrect as a flexible work schedule does not directly address the broader issues of trust, communication, and engagement that are critical after a layoff.

19. A. Layoffs are often intended to be temporary, with the possibility that employees may be rehired when conditions improve. Reductions in force (RIFs), on the other hand, are permanent separations from the company due to reasons such as organizational restructuring or long-term financial difficulties. The other options are false.

20. D. The primary purpose of a performance improvement plan is to provide a clear and structured approach for employees to improve their performance. It outlines specific goals, expectations, and support mechanisms to help the employee achieve the desired performance standards. Option A is incorrect as the main goal of a PIP is to help the employee improve their performance. Option B is incorrect as a PIP is not designed for reassigning employees to different roles. Option C is incorrect as promotions are typically based on consistently high performance, whereas a PIP is used for underperformers.

Chapter 8: PHR | PHRi Exam: Employee and Labor Relations

1. A. Good communication helps to resolve conflicts, ensure that employee concerns are heard, and promote a positive work environment. Option B is incorrect because although cost management is important, employee relations are more concerned with fostering a positive

work environment and addressing issues related to employee satisfaction and management practices. Option C is incorrect because enhancing a company's social media presence is typically the responsibility of marketing or public relations, not employee and labor relations. Option D is incorrect because the focus of employee relations activities is on maintaining a balanced relationship between employees and management rather than directly influencing specific benefits.

2. A, B. Understanding the demographics such as age, gender, ethnicity, and educational background help in designing programs that cater to the diverse needs of employees. Strategic goals determine the skills and competencies required for achieving long-term objectives. Option C is incorrect as employee relations programs focus more on the internal dynamics of the workforce rather than external geographic factors. Option D is incorrect because employee and labor relations programs are more focused on compliance, diversity, and strategic alignment rather than cultural fit alone.

3. B. Affirmative action aims to create a level playing field for employment and advancement opportunities for historically marginalized or underrepresented groups. Option A is incorrect because defense against harassment charges is called establishing an affirmative defense, not affirmative action. Option C is incorrect because although inclusive practices and diversity initiatives are important, the specific goal of affirmative action is to address and rectify disparities in employment opportunities. Option D is incorrect because hiring quotas are unlawful.

4. D. Conducting workforce analysis to identify underrepresentation helps to pinpoint areas where certain groups may be underrepresented and develop strategies to address these disparities. Option A is incorrect because hiring quotas are unlawful, even if well intended. Option B is incorrect as hiring a chief diversity officer is not a typical action specific to an affirmative action plan, which focuses more on systematic analysis and equitable practices. Option C is incorrect because compliance with reporting requirements is a legal obligation for many employers but is not specifically an action outlined in an affirmative action plan, which is more focused on internal assessments and proactive measures.

5. A, B. Workplace diseases, also known as occupational diseases, are illnesses that result from conditions or activities related to one's job. These diseases can be caused by various factors such as exposure to harmful chemicals, repetitive motions, or stressful environments. Hearing loss can be a workplace disease caused by prolonged exposure to loud noise, and carpal tunnel syndrome is a workplace disease resulting from repetitive motion or strain over time. Option C is incorrect as a broken arm is typically classified as a workplace injury, not a disease, as it is usually caused by a specific incident. Option D is incorrect as occupational burnout was classified by the World Health Organization as a workplace phenomenon, but not a workplace disease.

6. C. Focusing on impairment allows employers to prioritize workplace safety and productivity by monitoring actual impairment rather than simply the use of medical marijuana. This respects employees' legal rights while ensuring a safe and effective workplace. Option A is incorrect as, while marijuana is still illegal at the federal level, enforcing a strict no-tolerance policy may not be practical or fair in states where medical marijuana use is legal. Option B is incorrect as employers should focus on whether the employee is impaired while performing job duties rather than the mere presence of marijuana in their system. Option D is incorrect as exempting employees with a medical marijuana card from the substance abuse policy could lead to inconsistent application of workplace rules and potentially compromise safety.

7. B. Participative management is a management style in which employees at all levels are actively involved in the decision-making process. Option A is incorrect because although this approach involves employees in the goal-setting process, it is not as comprehensive in encouraging continuous and active participation as regular team meetings. This approach is more directive than fully participative. Option C is incorrect since an open-door policy relies on employees taking the initiative to approach supervisors, rather than actively involving them in decision-making processes regularly. Option D is incorrect because this approach is more autocratic and directive and does not involve employees in decision making or encourage their participation.

8. D. In many workplace contexts, the terms "complaint" and "grievance" are used interchangeably to refer to concerns raised by employees about workplace issues, without a distinct difference in meaning.

9. C. In arbitration, the arbitrator listens to both parties and then makes a binding decision. In mediation, the mediator helps the parties discuss their issues and reach a mutually acceptable agreement.

10. D. No specific labor law requires employers to have a written employee handbook. However, having an employee handbook is considered a best practice as it helps communicate company policies, procedures, and expectations, which can aid in compliance with various labor laws and regulations. Options A and B are incorrect as the Americans with Disabilities Act (ADA) and Fair Labor Standards Act (FLSA) do not require employers to have a written employee handbook. Option C is incorrect as Title VII of the Civil Rights Act of 1964 prohibits employment discrimination based on race, color, religion, sex, or national origin. While it requires employers to prevent discrimination and may encourage clear communication of policies, it does not specifically mandate the existence of a written employee handbook.

11. A. Counterproductive work behavior (CWB) refers to actions by employees that negatively impact the organization, such as theft, sabotage, or wasting time. Workplace harassment, on the other hand, refers to behavior that targets specific individuals and creates a hostile, intimidating, or abusive work environment for them. Option B is incorrect because counterproductive work behaviors may be legal per se, but not proper, and could be physical but also verbal, as shown in option C. In option D, harassment that is substantiated would be determined to be intentional.

12. B. Mediation is characterized by its informal nature and its focus on helping the parties involved come to a mutual agreement. The mediator acts as a neutral facilitator to guide the parties towards a resolution that they both find acceptable. In options A and C, a mediator's decision may not be binding and does not involve a judge or court. In option D, issues related to employment are addressed, which could include neutral referrals to employer reference checks, back wages, or other employment elements.

13. A. Adhering to a professional dress code is a clear, concise, and specific work rule that sets an expectation for employee behavior regarding dress code, making it easy to understand and follow. Options B and C are incorrect as they are more consistent with policy statements designed around compliance, as opposed to a company-specific work rule. Option D is incorrect as it is a better example of a procedure to follow rather than a rule.

14. A. An injury is typically caused by a sudden event, such as a fall, cut, or impact, which results in immediate physical harm. An illness is generally caused by prolonged exposure to harmful conditions or substances, such as repetitive strain, exposure to toxic chemicals, or long-term stress, leading to health conditions that develop over time.

15. B. The triple bottom line framework focuses on three key components: People, Profit, and Planet. This approach emphasizes the importance of social responsibility (People), economic viability (Profit), and environmental sustainability (Planet), aiming to create a balanced and sustainable business model that considers the well-being of society and the environment alongside financial performance.

16. C. Workers' compensation insurance provides medical benefits and wage replacement to employees injured in the course of employment. The other choices are false.

17. A, B, C. Corporate social responsibility (CSR) involves taking care and giving back to society and the communities where business operate. This may include implementing comprehensive recycling programs, donating profits to local charities, sponsoring community projects, and providing employees with paid volunteer days to contribute to social causes (options A, B, C). Option D is incorrect as increasing an advertising budget primarily for recruitment purposes does not directly reflect CSR. CSR focuses more on ethical, social, and environmental contributions rather than growth or hiring strategies.

18. B. Regular training helps employees identify early warning signs of potential violence and equips them with skills to resolve conflicts peacefully, making it a proactive approach to preventing workplace violence. Option A is incorrect as a zero-tolerance policy is not sufficient on its own to prevent workplace violence. Policies need to be supported by training, communication, and proactive measures to be effective. Option C is incorrect as security cameras do not address the root causes of workplace violence or equip employees with the skills to prevent it. Option D is incorrect as encouraging employees to manage conflicts on their own can lead to unresolved issues and escalate tensions.

19. A. Diversity programs generally aim to create a more inclusive and positive workplace culture by embracing and valuing differences among employees. In contrast, affirmative action programs are designed to address and correct historical inequalities by ensuring equal opportunities for historically marginalized groups. Options B, C, and D are not true.

20. D. Business acumen as a competency helps an HR practitioner align HR strategies with the company's strategic objectives so that employee and labor relations programs support the overall success of the organization. Option A is incorrect as negotiating is more about complying with law and bargaining in good faith to achieve cooperative outcomes. Option B is incorrect as business acumen's influence extends beyond just relationship building to a more comprehensive strategic alignment. Option C is incorrect because effective conflict management is a component of ELR programs, but business acumen's broader impact involves strategic alignment rather than solely conflict management.

Chapter 9: PHR | PHRi Exam: HR Information Management

1. B. An HRIS is designed to manage employee data, streamline HR processes, and provide tools for managing payroll, benefits, recruitment, training, and performance management. Options A, C, and D are incorrect as the main focus of an HRIS is broader than payroll, learning management, or compliance.

2. B, C, D. Section 508 of the Rehabilitation Act requires that employers comply with digital accessibility requirements, which is not a primary consideration for an internal human resource information system. Integration ensures the HRIS can work seamlessly with other systems already in use, and total cost of ownership, including initial setup, training, maintenance, and upgrades, should be factored into the selection process, as long as the functionality meets the needs. Data storage considerations such as security, accessibility, and compliance are important to protect sensitive employee information.

3. A, C. The use of unique ID cards, two-factor authentication, and role-based access to sensitive data are all examples of access control mechanisms. The user-friendliness of the software refers to the user interface, which is the part of the system that users interact with directly. Option B is incorrect as HR control pertains to the management of human resources within an organization, not data management. Option D is incorrect because phishing involves deceptive attempts to obtain sensitive information by pretending to be a trustworthy entity.

4. B. Under the GDPR, individuals have the right to access their personal data. This means organizations must be prepared to provide individuals with a copy of their data upon request, ensuring transparency and giving individuals control over their personal information.

5. C. HIPAA requires that electronic protected health information (ePHI) be encrypted to protect it from unauthorized access. Encryption ensures that even if data is intercepted or accessed without permission, it cannot be read or used by unauthorized individuals. Option A is incorrect as the requirement to keep medical records separate from general personnel files is mandated by the Americans with Disabilities Act (ADA) and the Genetic Information Nondisclosure Act (GINA), not HIPAA. Option B is incorrect because HIPAA does require secure storage of health records, but it does not mandate that they must be stored in physical, locked cabinets only; electronic storage is allowed. Option D is incorrect because HIPAA requires covered entities to report breaches of unsecured protected health information to the affected individuals and the Department of Health and Human Services (HHS), but not to the Department of Labor.

6. D. Prescriptive analytics goes beyond the act of collecting and sorting through data to identify trends or predict outcomes. The key characteristic of prescriptive analytics is that a solution is "prescribed" or recommended based on the data analysis. Option A is incorrect as descriptive analytics involves summarizing historical data to identify trends and patterns and the focus of the question is on using the analysis to make recommendations. Option B is incorrect because qualitative analysis involves analyzing non-numerical data to understand

themes and patterns. Option C is incorrect because predictive analytics uses historical data to forecast future outcomes. While the scenario might include elements of prediction (e.g., identifying factors that lead to resignations), the primary focus is on prescribing specific actions to take, which is characteristic of prescriptive analytics.

7. A. Descriptive analytics involves summarizing historical data to identify trends and patterns. Option B is incorrect as prescriptive analytics goes beyond summarizing data to provide recommendations for future actions. Option C is incorrect as predictive analytics uses historical data to "predict" future outcomes or trends, not just understand or identify current sentiments. Option D is incorrect because quantitative analysis deals with numerical data.

8. C. The best answer is C, as by analyzing turnover data, the HR department can identify the root causes of high attrition and develop specific strategies to improve retention, directly addressing the problem using data-driven insights. Option A is incorrect as exit interviews do not involve the systematic use of workforce analytics to analyze data and implement solutions. It is a qualitative method rather than a data-driven approach. Option B is incorrect because employee surveys do not explicitly involve workforce analytics. Option D is incorrect because it also is not based on workforce analytics.

9. B. Front-end user support focuses on making databases accessible and user-friendly for all users, including those without technical expertise. An intuitive user interface ensures that users can easily navigate and access the data they need, improving efficiency and satisfaction. Option A is incorrect as complex queries can be a barrier for nontechnical users. Option C is incorrect because limiting access to IT professionals does not support the needs of nontechnical users who require access to the database for their work. Option D is incorrect because ignoring the user experience over backend functionality can lead to frustration and inefficiency, as users may struggle to navigate and use the database effectively.

10. A. Phishing is a scheme where cybercriminals send deceptive emails that appear to be from a legitimate source. The purpose is to trick the recipient into entering sensitive information, such as passwords, on a fake website, leading to credential theft. Options B, C, and D describe malware, nonsecure buildings, and hacking, respectively, which are different from phishing schemes.

11. C. Implementing a standardized policy is the best practice for records management. A standardized policy ensures that all departments follow consistent procedures for the retention, storage, and disposal of records. Option A is incorrect because this approach can lead to inconsistencies and confusion and increases the risk of noncompliance with legal and regulatory requirements. Option B is incorrect as labor laws vary in record retention requirements. Not keeping records long enough violates on-demand accessibility for future disputes, and retaining records too long is inefficient and opens the company to scrutiny beyond what is required by law.

12. D. Thematic analysis identifies recurring themes or patterns in qualitative data, such as text from surveys or interviews, to understand underlying meanings and insights. Option A represents quantitative findings, which involves the numerical analysis of data to uncover patterns, trends, and insights that can be measured and quantified. Option B is an example of correlation analysis, which examines the relationship between two or more variables to determine how they move in relation to each other, and option C represents predictive analysis, which uses historical data and statistical algorithms to forecast future outcomes.

13. C. Regularly reviewing and updating data protection policies helps maintain data integrity and security from recruitment to offboarding. Option A is incorrect because although regular backups are important for data security, they alone do not ensure proper management of HR data throughout the entire employee lifecycle. Policies and procedures must also be in place to address data integrity and compliance. Option B is incorrect because only focusing on the recruitment stage neglects the importance of managing and protecting data throughout the entire employee lifecycle. Option D is incorrect because decentralized data management can lead to inconsistencies, data silos, and potential security risks.

14. A. Data integrity involves maintaining the accuracy, completeness, and reliability of data over its lifecycle. Ensuring that employee records are accurate, complete, and up-to-date is essential for making informed decisions, maintaining trust, and complying with legal and regulatory requirements. Option B is incorrect as it describes compliance with data regulations, not data integrity. Option C is incorrect because data integrity is about the accuracy and reliability of the data itself, whereas secure storage pertains to data protection. Option D is not correct as regular audits do not specifically address data integrity; audits can help maintain data integrity by identifying and correcting issues, but the primary focus of audits is broader risk management, not only the accuracy of the data being stored.

15. B. When there is doubt about the accuracy of survey results, conducting a follow-up helps verify the initial findings, ensuring that the data is reliable before taking any action. Gathering more detailed feedback can provide a clearer understanding of the issues and help HR develop more effective solutions. Option A is incorrect because even if there are questions about data accuracy, completely disregarding the feedback could mean missing out on addressing significant underlying issues within the organization. Option C is incorrect as reporting the findings to senior leaders without verifying the accuracy can lead to misguided decisions based on potentially flawed data. Option D is incorrect because it's important to validate the survey results to ensure that any subsequent actions are based on accurate and reliable data.

16. B. The first priority in mitigating a data breach is to contain the breach and prevent any further unauthorized access or misuse of the sensitive data. By immediately contacting the contractor and requesting the deletion of the sensitive information, the HR team can limit the exposure of the data and reduce the potential harm to affected employees. Options A, C, and D are all important steps that come after containing the exposure.

17. B. Conducting trend analysis helps HR departments make informed strategic decisions that align with the organization's goals and improve overall workforce management. Trend analysis does not influence legally defensible hiring decisions, so option A is incorrect. Workforce analytics can evaluate the effectiveness of HR programs; however, trend analysis is smaller in scope, making C incorrect. Option D is incorrect because analyzing workforce training needs is a specific application within HR, but trend analysis encompasses a broader scope.

18. C. Option C best exemplifies the need for clarity in data storytelling in HR. It provides precise information about the percentage increase in turnover and identifies the primary reasons for this increase. Options A, B, and D are vague and lack specific details that improve message clarity.

19. A, B, C, D. All of the answers are correct. Shredding is a compliant method for destroying paper records, ensuring that the information is irretrievably destroyed and cannot be reconstructed or read. Permanently deleting electronic records involves using methods to ensure that data cannot be recovered, such as using secure deletion software or physical destruction of storage devices. Burning is a compliant method for destroying paper records, as it ensures that the information is completely destroyed and cannot be reconstructed or accessed. Hiring a professional document destruction contractor is a compliant method for securely destroying records. These contractors use certified methods to ensure that records are destroyed according to legal and regulatory requirements.

20. C, D. Employers are allowed to store Form I-9s electronically as long as the electronic system meets the security requirements, ensures the records are accurate, and makes them accessible for inspection by authorized officials. Option D is also true stating that you may destroy the original paper form after you have securely stored it in an electronic format. Once the Form I-9 is securely stored in an electronic format that meets regulatory standards, the original paper form can be destroyed. Option A is incorrect as it is generally recommended to store Form I-9s separately from personnel files to ensure they are easily accessible during an audit without exposing other sensitive employee information. Option B is incorrect as access to Form I-9s should be restricted to authorized personnel only.

Chapter 10: SPHR | SPHRi Exam: Leadership and Strategy

1. C. HR participates in the strategic planning process by providing expertise on attracting, retaining, and managing a qualified workforce. Organization strategies (option A) are formulated by the executive team. Each business function participates in the environmental-scanning process (option B), gathering information about its area of responsibility. Strategic goals (option D) are identified by the executive team during the strategy formulation phase.

2. D. The mission statement describes who the organization is, what it does, where it is going, and how it is different from others. The corporate values statement (option A) communicates the executive team's expectations for the way the organization conducts business. Corporate goals (option B) describe what the organization plans to achieve in the future. The vision statement (option C) is a short, inspirational statement of what the organization will accomplish in the future.

3. A, C. The purpose of an HR budget is to determine the resources required to operate the functions of human resources including recruiting, training, and safety initiatives. An HR budget also anticipates the resources necessary to achieve any HR-related tasks within the company's strategic plan (options A and C). It is not intended to gain approval for business lines of credit or to comply with reporting requirements to company shareholders (options B and D); a company's overall budget is most likely to be required in those scenarios, not the HR budget.

4. B. Creating an HR budget takes into account standard expense items associated with having employees. They include salaries, taxes, benefits, training, travel, and equipment costs, to name a few.

5. B. A business case lays out the desired result of an action or program, presents alternative solutions, describes possible risks from both implementing and not implementing the action, and defines the criteria used to measure success. Return on investment and a cost-benefit analysis may be included as part of the business case, and a SWOT analysis may have identified the need for a program or action.

6. C. A human resource information system is generally designed and used to house a virtual employee personnel file. It has two primary purposes: to store information and to aid in the operational efficiencies of an HR department. Expense reports would be more a function of accounting than of HR.

7. A. The ability to interpret and apply information related to internal sources allows HR to respond to specific elements of an organization's strategic plan. For example, understanding how an HRIS can integrate with an accounting database is one example of cross-functional strategic decisions. Options B, C, and D—scanning the legal and regulatory environment, analyzing industry changes, and staying abreast of technological advances—are all examples of external forces that impact a strategic plan.

8. A. An income statement, also referred to as a profit-and-loss statement, provides financial information about revenue and expenses in a set reporting period. The statement of cash flow (option B) communicates the ways in which monies came in and out of the organization, and the balance sheet (option C) is a thumbnail sketch of assets, liabilities, and equity at a certain time. The fiscal year summary (option D) is a report that provides an overview of an organization's financial activities and performance over a 12-month period.

9. B. A product-based structure is useful for an organization with multiple well-defined product lines. The structure and subsequent job responsibilities are divided by product line, rather than shared companywide. Option A is incorrect as the functional structure is the more traditional format where the organization is divided by departments such as production and sales. Option C is incorrect because a divisional structure groups the company based on market or industry, useful for decentralized divisions. Option D is incorrect as a flat-line structure is a different term for a seamless organization, one in which hierarchies do not exist.

10. B. Paying low wages resulting in high turnover is an internal weakness that affects an organization's ability to compete. Option A is incorrect as it's more likely a challenge for the business. Option C is incorrect because it's a circumstance that requires management and mitigation, not opportunity. Option D is incorrect as it's not an external factor but rather an internal challenge.

11. D. The economic climate, including cost of living, is an example of an external threat that affects an organization's ability to compete in its relevant market. Option A is incorrect because the high cost of living is not a competitive strength. Option B is incorrect; although the difficulty in recruiting teachers due to high living costs could be considered a weakness, it's not an internal factor but rather an external challenge. Option C is incorrect because the high cost of living doesn't present an opportunity for educational institutions; rather, it poses a challenge to overcome.

12. B. The threat of substitutes or replacements is a threat that obtaining a U.S. patent may mitigate. A design patent grants the inventor the exclusive rights to profit from their unique design. Option A is incorrect as patents protect against imitation rather than hindering new entrants to the market. Option C is incorrect because patents generally do not directly influence the bargaining power of customers. Option D is incorrect because patents are unlikely to affect the bargaining power of suppliers in most industries.

13. D. Pay equity analysis is primarily focused on examining and addressing any disparities or biases in how employees are compensated within an organization. This includes factors such as gender, race, or other demographics that may lead to unequal pay for individuals performing similar work or possessing similar qualifications.

14. A. A balance sheet reflects the company assets at any given time. This is identified by adding together both equity and liabilities, which must equal the company assets, thus the name "balance sheet." Option B is incorrect as cash flow does not directly incorporate the total liabilities and equity of a company. Option C is incorrect because forecasted budgets focus on projected income and expenses, but they do not directly represent the relationship between liabilities and equity. Option D is incorrect as the income statement reports revenues, expenses, and net income over a specific period, but it does not include information about the total liabilities and equity of a company.

15. D. The Generally Accepted Accounting Principles (GAAP) are standards developed by the Financial Accounting Standards Board (FASB) to create checks and balances for accounting professionals recording business transactions. This helps to prevent fraudulent recordkeeping and employees hiding theft, among other things.

16. B. A budget built on past spending is called a historic budget. Option A is incorrect as a zero-based budget is one that is built from scratch, evaluating each expense item independently, regardless of past expenditures. Option C is incorrect as a top-down budget entails setting the budget based on overall organizational goals and directives, with little input from lower levels of management or departments. Option D is incorrect as a parallel budget involves creating two sets of budgets simultaneously, typically comparing different scenarios or strategies, rather than simply adjusting previous spending.

17. C. The key in this question is not so much the locations but how the financial recordkeeping is held. Because each location has their own profit and loss statements, budgets, and so forth, it is the best example of a decentralized business structure.

18. B. The staff functions of organizations are those that do not generate revenue or otherwise produce the core goods and services. This includes accounting and finance.

19. D. The planning phase of project management will describe the deliverables, budget, and scope of the project.

20. A, B, C, D. A human capital management plan (HCMP) is a critical tool to help develop tactical action plans for the achievement of company goals. An HCMP is most effective when it aligns with the company strategy by leveraging human assets, properly forecasts the talent necessary to achieve goals, and supports the creation of a competitive advantage through the company's people.

Chapter 11: SPHR | SPHRi Exam: Workforce Planning and Talent Acquisition

1. C. Workforce planning aims to ensure that the organization has the right people, with the right skills, in the right positions, at the right time to achieve its strategic objectives. Aligning human capital with organizational goals is a primary objective of workforce planning as it enables the organization to effectively utilize its workforce to drive success and achieve long-term sustainability. Option A is incorrect as maximizing short-term profits is a business strategy more so than a workforce planning strategy. Option B is incorrect since the main goal of workforce planning is to ensure that the organization's human capital is aligned with its strategic objectives, which may actually increase labor costs versus cutting costs. Option D is incorrect because turnover is a function of many factors that go beyond workforce plans, and in some cases, such as business restructuring or divestitures, turnover may increase.

2. A, B, C. Strategic talent planning aims to optimize the allocation of resources across departments while minimizing disruptions such as layoffs and ensuring continuity in talent acquisition and retention strategies. It is also an opportunity for organizations to identify what business processes could or should be outsourced. Aligning talent management strategies with long-term organizational goals ensures that the organization's workforce is equipped with the skills and capabilities necessary to achieve its strategic objectives and sustain long-term success. Option D is not correct because the performance management process is a separate function of human resources that is not related to workforce planning.

3. A, B, C. Human capital projecting involves forecasting future workforce needs, including demographics, skill requirements, and labor market trends. By projecting future workforce needs and identifying potential talent gaps, organizations can develop comprehensive plans to address these needs and align their human capital strategies with broader organizational goals. This analysis helps organizations gain insights into their future talent needs and make informed decisions regarding recruitment, training, and talent development initiatives. Option D is incorrect because although human capital projecting informs sourcing strategies by identifying future talent needs, it is not itself a form of sourcing.

4. B. Salary data, along with other relevant labor market data such as demographic trends, unemployment rates, and competitor hiring trends, helps organizations understand the external labor market landscape and make informed decisions, including the labor costs to compete in various areas. Option A is incorrect as a skills inventory typically consists of internal data related to the skills and competencies of current employees within the organization. It is not an external source of data used for human capital projections. Option C is incorrect because the availability of off-the-shelf training software is an internal consideration related to the organization's learning and development initiatives. Option D is incorrect since the organization's core competencies are internal factors related to its unique strengths, capabilities, and areas of expertise.

5. C. Many states have their own departments that track workforce statistics. Companies may access unemployment rates, cost of living, competitive organizations, and much more that may then be used to begin to build a business case to present to the executive team. Option A is incorrect as the information found in newspapers may be limited and may not cover all relevant aspects needed for a thorough labor market analysis. Option B is incorrect as its resources may be more geared toward promoting local businesses and fostering economic growth rather than providing detailed labor market data. Option D is incorrect because their expertise is not directly related to labor market analysis.

6. A, B, C, D. Senior-level HR leaders are responsible for recruiting strategy. This includes applying creative solutions and designing intervention strategies that will influence the selection process. In many cases, the recruiting and selection process starts from within. This includes identifying employees who may be groomed for promotion through upskilling and reskilling, building engagement programs that retain key talent, and redesigning jobs for simplification so that there are less qualifications (and thus a larger labor pool) necessary to do the work.

7. D. Although all of the answers may occur as part of the new hire integration process, the focus is to help the employee acclimate and socialize within the early months of their job.

8. B. The job analysis process is fundamental not only to the talent planning and acquisition function, but to all other HR systems as well. Job analysis is fundamental to recruiting, writing interview questions for employee selection, crafting performance feedback, building wage structures, and completing hazard assessments in risk management, just to name a few. Option A is incorrect as recruiting is an operational activity that is heavily influenced by job analysis and strategic planning but does not inherently serve as the foundation for all other HR systems. Option C is incorrect as strategic planning does not directly address the specific requirements and responsibilities associated with individual job roles. Option D is incorrect because employee socialization focuses on onboarding and orientation processes rather than establishing the fundamental framework for HR systems.

9. A. By asking candidates to describe a recent learning experience, interviewers can assess their curiosity, willingness to learn, and adaptability, which are crucial qualities for success in an organization that values growth and innovation. Option B is incorrect as it does not directly relate to the company's mission of growing its people and fostering innovation. It focuses more on past performance rather than future potential and alignment with the company's values. Option C is incorrect as this question is often considered a "fun" or unconventional interview question but does not directly assess skills, experiences, or qualities relevant to the company's mission or job requirements. Option D is incorrect because although it may provide insights into a candidate's ambitions, it does not necessarily predict success within the company's culture or objectives.

10. B. By analyzing historical recruitment data and utilizing predictive analytics, recruiters can identify patterns, trends, and insights to inform their decision-making process. This allows recruiters to make more informed and strategic decisions regarding sourcing strategies, candidate selection, and recruitment tactics, ultimately improving the effectiveness of the recruitment process. Option A is incorrect because it misrepresents the role of data in strategic recruiting. Data is not used to randomly select candidates for interviews but rather to inform

and guide the recruitment process based on objective insights and analysis. Option C is incorrect as, although it is true that data-driven decisions must be made carefully to avoid bias, data itself is a valuable tool for promoting fairness and objectivity in the recruitment process when used appropriately. Option D is incorrect because it overlooks the broader role of data in strategic recruiting. While tracking the number of applications received is one aspect of data analysis in recruitment, data serves a much broader purpose in informing decision making, improving processes, and optimizing recruitment strategies.

11. C. Embracing cultural diversity and promoting cross-cultural communication are essential for building mutual understanding, trust, and collaboration among partners from different cultural backgrounds. By acknowledging and respecting cultural differences, joint ventures can create an inclusive and supportive environment. Option A is incorrect because implementing uniform HR policies may not be feasible or effective in a joint venture context where partners operate in different cultural, legal, and regulatory environments. Option B is incorrect because overemphasizing autonomy may lead to siloed operations, and option D is incorrect because simply maximizing communication without considering cultural differences and nuances may not lead to effective global integration.

12. C. Strategic staffing and recruitment achieves the mission and vision of the organization over an extended time period, where operational-level actions carry out tasks required for the organization to function day to day. Identifying recruitment sources such as employee referrals may prove to be valuable once the strategies have been defined. Conducting a labor market analysis allows HR to identify the availability of a qualified workforce for use in the achievement of strategic objectives. Total Rewards packages include conducting wage surveys and utilization reviews to understand compensation and benefits trends, designed to compete with internal and external market conditions. Defining the employer brand not only creates an employer identity, but helps to differentiate a company from their competition.

13. B. Human capital management is a talent planning and acquisition process that is tied to the strategic plan. Designing Total Rewards—while important—is not a typical part of the HCM planning process.

14. A, B, C, D. Employee severance packages are given to separating employees for several reasons. It helps to offset lost wages due to company layoffs or reductions in force. A severance package may be used as a risk management tool in which the employee accepts the payment in exchange for the right to sue. And it can serve as a reward for loyalty to exiting employees or to offset loss of income due to a company layoff.

15. C. Forecasting enables HR professionals to anticipate staffing needs, identify potential skill gaps, and develop strategies to address these challenges proactively, aligning the workforce with the organization's strategic objectives. Option A is incorrect as HR budgeting is more concerned with financial planning and resource allocation. Option B is incorrect as workforce planning encompasses a broader range of activities aimed at aligning the organization's human capital resources with its strategic goals and objectives. Option D is incorrect because data analytics involves the use of data analysis techniques to gain insights, identify patterns, and make informed decisions across various HR functions, not to forecast future workforce needs.

16. A. Brownfield operations involve revitalizing or repurposing abandoned or underutilized industrial properties, often requiring remediation of environmental contamination or infrastructure redevelopment. Option B is incorrect because a greenfield operation refers to the establishment of a new facility or operation on previously undeveloped or agricultural land. Option C is incorrect because a workforce plan typically involves strategic planning and forecasting of an organization's future workforce needs, including recruitment, training, and development initiatives. Option D is incorrect because an acquisition typically refers to the purchase of one company by another, resulting in the acquiring company gaining control over the acquired company's assets, operations, and workforce.

17. B. The best answer is that of a greenfield operation. The key to this answer is that the company is building a new business facility in a new location, which specifically refers to the growth strategy of a greenfield operation.

18. C. Strategic recruitment involves a comprehensive approach to attracting and hiring talent that aligns with the long-term goals of the organization. It includes labor market analysis to understand the availability of skills and talents in the market and defining the employer brand to attract the right candidates. Option A is incorrect because benchmarking is the process of comparing one's business processes and performance metrics to industry bests and best practices from other companies; it does not involve employer branding. Option B is incorrect because candidate sourcing focuses on finding suitable candidates through various channels such as job boards and social media and does not involve labor market analysis or branding. Option D is incorrect because employee selection does not encompass labor market analysis or defining the employer brand, which are broader, more strategic activities.

19. D. An employer value proposition (EVP) encompasses the unique set of benefits, rewards, and values that an organization offers to its employees in exchange for their skills, talents, and contributions. A company culture that is inclusive and supportive and that values employee well-being and growth is a powerful driver of employee engagement, satisfaction, and retention. It goes beyond tangible benefits like option A, salary and benefits package; option B, professional development; and option C, flexible and alternative remote work options.

20. C. By showcasing its work in underprivileged communities and its partnership with local high schools to develop future workforce skills, the company is communicating its employer brand—the unique set of values, culture, and attributes that define its identity as an employer. This recruitment campaign helps to attract candidates who align with the company's values and aspirations, strengthening its employer brand in the eyes of potential recruits. Option A is incorrect as the primary focus of the scenario is on highlighting the company's reputation corporate social responsibility initiatives, not diversity. Option B is incorrect because inclusivity is the act of welcoming all perspectives to the workforce, which is not being highlighted in the scenario. Option D is incorrect as corporate governance initiatives typically refer to policies and practices related to corporate decision making, compliance, and accountability, rather than recruitment campaigns or employer branding efforts.

Chapter 12: SPHR | SPHRi Exam: Talent Management

1. C. A company's learning and development system must seek to integrate with other human resource outcomes such as talent acquisition and align with other business outcomes such as workforce planning and goal achievement. Options A and B involve designing training initiatives, including factors such as mode and timing. Option D, cost savings, while important, cannot be fully understood until the full scope—including integration—has been mapped out.

2. A. Ensuring the business continues in an ever-changing competitive landscape is one major outcome of designing effective career progression and coaching activities. This is particularly true when the focus is on aligning employee development goals with business development goals through succession planning.

3. D. Individuals in the early stages of their career are often attracted by opportunities to develop new skills. Option A is incorrect as retirement benefits are generally more appealing to mid- or late-career professionals. Option B is incorrect because it might not be the top priority for early career professionals who are more focused on immediate career growth and opportunities. Option C is incorrect because early career professionals may prioritize opportunities for learning and advancement over family-focused benefits.

4. B. Operational learning activities are geared toward fulfilling the immediate training requirements of employees to perform their current roles effectively. These activities typically focus on enhancing specific skills or knowledge that are directly applicable to the tasks at hand. Strategic learning activities are designed to align with the long-term goals and objectives of the organization. This may involve initiatives such as leadership development programs, succession planning, or cross-functional training aimed at preparing employees for future roles and responsibilities within the company.

5. C. Strategic career pathing involves a proactive approach to managing employees' careers within the organization. This may involve identifying key competencies needed for future roles, offering training and development opportunities to build those competencies, and guiding employees on potential career paths within the company that align with company goals. Option A is incorrect as it describes project assignments based on existing skills, which may not necessarily encompass a strategic approach to career development. Option B is incorrect as horizontal movement within an organization involves lateral transfers or job rotations; strategic career pathing involves a more deliberate focus on vertical progression to fill future roles. Option D is incorrect because while performance evaluations may inform decisions about promotions or career advancements, strategic career pathing involves a more comprehensive and ongoing process of career development.

6. A, B, C. A training mode of delivery refers to the method or format used to deliver instructional content to learners, encompassing various approaches such as classrooms, self-paced online modules, and asynchronous options without the need to synchronize schedules with instructors or peers. Option D is incorrect as it is a form of needs assessment to determine training needs rather than a form of content delivery.

7. A, B, D. Measuring organizational climate provides valuable insights into employee satisfaction, engagement, and overall well-being, which in turn can inform strategies to improve productivity, retention, and organizational effectiveness. This can be done through climate assessments that specifically focus on gauging employee perceptions within the workplace, exit interviews to gather feedback from departing employees about their experiences within the organization, and employee surveys used to gather feedback from employees about various aspects of their work environment, including their perceptions, attitudes, and satisfaction levels. Option C is not correct as reviews are primarily focused on evaluating individual performance rather than providing a comprehensive assessment of workplace climate.

8. B. Mentorship programs provide employees with ongoing guidance, support, and opportunities for skill development and career advancement. This approach creates a sense of belonging, growth, and investment in the organization, which are key factors in increasing employee retention. Option A is incorrect because it may not directly correlate with enhancing retention unless these sessions are part of a broader strategy that includes ongoing support and career development. Option C is incorrect because it primarily addresses logistical concerns rather than directly impacting employee retention. Option D is incorrect because off-the-shelf training materials may offer consistency in knowledge transfer, but they often lack personalization and may not fully address the unique career pathing needs of employees.

9. D. As with so many HR activities, conducting a job analysis allows for the discovery of how a job may progress for an employee as they gain the required knowledge, skills, and other competencies to move within and outside of job families. Once identified, the skill set and professional goals of incumbents may be reviewed, career goals established, and the replacement needs/timelines identified. Option A is incorrect as it is difficult to select which employees are qualified for promotion without first clearly defining the job. Option B is incorrect as setting business goals is an activity separate from succession planning that is affected by other strategic variables. Option C is also a function separate from the succession planning process.

10. C. The provided statement emphasizes RetailMart's commitment to fostering direct relationships with employees without the involvement of labor unions. It underscores values such as trust, fairness, transparency, and open communication, and highlights competitive wages, benefits, and opportunities for career growth, supporting the objective of maintaining a positive work environment and employee satisfaction. Option A is incorrect as the example does not focus on specific behavioral guidelines or rules of conduct, the legal language of employment at-will, or a comprehensive statement of employer values, making options A, B and D incorrect.

11. A. Needs analysis may be done at an individual or an organizational level. Prior to any type of intervention strategy, it is useful for HR to gain a clear understanding of the degree of need. For example, leaders may be required to make more strategic decisions, whereas individual contributors may be required to make more task-level decisions. Some employees may be "better" at making decisions than others. Once collected, this data will help HR make decisions about how to design the program (modes of delivery, timing) and develop content.

12. C. Training as an intervention strategy is typically used by organizations that identify a skills gap. This may be part of an organizational, departmental, or individual needs assessment, or even an outcome of strategic planning.

13. C. A sympathy strike, also known as a sympathy action or secondary strike, occurs when workers strike in support of another group of workers who are already on strike. The goal is to increase pressure on the employer by disrupting operations and demonstrating solidarity with the original strikers. Option A is incorrect as a wildcat strike is initiated by workers without official authorization from their union leadership. Option B is incorrect because a lockout is an action taken by employers to prevent employees from working during a labor dispute and is initiated by employers rather than employees. Option D is incorrect because a judicial strike occurs when a court issues an injunction or order requiring workers to cease work due to legal violations, such as violating a no-strike clause in a collective bargaining agreement and is not initiated by the workers themselves, nor is it a common tactic used by labor unions.

14. B. As a senior leader, staying informed about the status of employee grievances is important to maintain a supportive and proactive approach to conflict resolution. While delegating initial handling to the junior team is common, senior leaders should be ready to intervene when necessary. Option A is incorrect as while relying on a junior team member's handling without any senior leadership oversight may risk mismanagement or inadequate resolution of the grievance. Option C is incorrect as senior leaders may oversee the investigation process, but they are not typically directly responsible for conducting it. Option D is incorrect as while involving union representatives may be appropriate in certain cases, it is not the primary responsibility of senior leaders in handling employee grievances outside of unionized environments.

15. D. Maintaining an open-door environment is an effective strategy for fostering communication and addressing employee concerns in the workplace. This approach encourages transparency, trust, and collaboration between employees and leadership. Option A is incorrect as strict hierarchical structures can create barriers to communication and discourage employees from voicing their concerns or ideas. Option B is incorrect because anonymous suggestion boxes do not provide opportunities for real-time communication and discussion. Option C is incorrect because monthly town hall meetings may lack opportunities for meaningful dialogue and employee input.

16. D. Employee satisfaction surveys are designed to gauge employees' perceptions and attitudes toward various aspects of their job and work environment, including compensation. By analyzing responses to employee satisfaction surveys, the HR Generalist can identify any dissatisfaction or concerns related to wage rates that may be affecting employee performance indirectly. Options A and C are incorrect because wage surveys, also called compensation surveys, collect data on wage rates within a broad market or industry, focusing on external benchmarks rather than internal impacts on employee performance. Option D is incorrect as exit surveys are administered to departing employees to gather feedback on their reasons for leaving the organization, not necessarily on the impact of wages on individual performance.

17. A, B, C, D. Wages and hours are clearly covered under an employer and union's duty to bargain. Other issues are often decided on a case-by-case basis through the judicial system,

up to and including the Supreme Court. Judicial rulings of mandatory subjects include video surveillance use around employee break areas; the price of food in vending machines, even if they are owned by a third party; and the use of background checks on union members.

18. B. A succession plan may unearth the fact that there is no current employee who is either ready for promotion or ready to be groomed for promotion into a new role. Therefore, the succession planning process may need to connect with the talent acquisition process to ensure a qualified person is in place and ready to go at the time of need.

19. A, B, C. Developing adequate resources for a successful career management program requires the inclusion of both hard and soft costs. This includes salaries and the cost of any training program or materials. Background screens are not typically used as part of the career management process, making option D incorrect.

20. C. By identifying trends and patterns related to training and career development, organizations can pinpoint areas for improvement in their learning and development programs. This includes recognizing common themes such as inadequate training resources, limited growth opportunities, or mismatches between employee expectations and organizational culture. Option A is incorrect because exit surveys are specifically designed to gather feedback from departing employees. Option B is incorrect because exit surveys focus on gathering feedback on various aspects of the employee experience, not employee performance. Option D is incorrect because exit surveys are focused on individual employee experiences, not organizational performance.

Chapter 13: SPHR | SPHRi Exam: Total Rewards

1. C. Total Rewards programs and strategies must be developed to align with two main goals: finding and retaining critical talent while also building programs that are affordable. Both factors impact an organization's ability to compete. Legal compliance, including complying with the Fair Labor Standards Act and demographics, are addressed within the design of TR programs.

2. A, B, C. People determined to have a fiduciary responsibility in an organization are held to the highest ethical standards. Breaching this responsibility includes acting in one's own self-interest, putting HR department needs above the integrity of pay systems, and profiting from the decision-making authority inherent in senior-level duties. Lying or delaying a request to a state agency about personnel records is unlawful and unethical, but not related to an HR professional's fiduciary responsibility.

3. A. Companies that choose to pay below-market rates for talent are lagging the relevant labor market in pay rates. This is often in response to a skill set that is abundant in a labor market, making it easier to find workers.

3. C. Implementing an HR software system can automate various administrative tasks, such as onboarding, benefits management, time tracking, and performance reviews. It enhances employee self-service, reduces manual workloads, and improves data accuracy. This approach can lead to significant efficiencies and cost savings across the HR department. Option A is incorrect because adopting E-Verify does not provide a comprehensive solution for increasing overall efficiency or significantly reducing department expenses over the next 3 years. Option B is incorrect as laying off staff might reduce immediate costs but could lead to long-term risks and inefficiencies. Option D is incorrect as it increases overall department expenses rather than decreasing them.

4. C. By blocking specific IP addresses known to be associated with hacking or other suspicious activities, the risk of unauthorized access and potential data breaches is reduced. Options A and B are incorrect as they do not directly address the security of existing data or prevent unauthorized access. Option D is incorrect because data backups address data integrity and availability rather than data security.

5. B. Strong encryption ensures that sensitive data is protected, even if a device is lost or stolen. Encryption makes it much harder for unauthorized individuals to access sensitive information stored on personal devices. Option A is incorrect as mobile device management (MDM) can enforce security policies, but without strong encryption, data may still be vulnerable. It may also be difficult to enforce such policies on personal devices and maintain morale. Option C is incorrect as this option contradicts the goal of implementing a BYOD policy. While it would ensure data security by not allowing personal devices, it doesn't align with the intent of the policy and doesn't provide a solution for securing data if BYOD is to be implemented. Option D is incorrect because it raises privacy concerns and could lead to resistance from employees, and it increases the risk of passwords being mishandled or misused.

6. A, C. Option A is correct because AI-driven chatbots can efficiently manage routine HR inquiries, such as questions about company policies, benefits, and leave balances. This automation frees up HR staff to focus on more complex and strategic tasks. Option C is correct as AI tools can analyze various data points, such as employee feedback, engagement surveys, and turnover rates, to identify potential threats to employee retention. Option B is incorrect because relying on AI to generate performance reviews can lead to inaccuracies and biases; human judgment is important to provide a comprehensive and fair evaluation. Option D is incorrect because real-time monitoring of employee activities using AI can raise privacy and ethical concerns, and it can lead to a lack of trust and a negative work environment; HR should weigh the impact of such software against the benefits.

7. A. An employee self-service portal allows employees to independently manage their personal information, benefits, and other HR-related tasks. This reduces the administrative workload on HR staff and minimizes errors, thus enhancing both quality and efficiency. Option B is incorrect because using a third-party record storage specialist does not directly contribute to digitizing the workflow or reducing manual processes. Option C is incorrect because an ATS addresses only a specific aspect of HR operations, and onboarding requires a more personal, human approach. Option D is incorrect as decentralizing HR services means distributing HR tasks and responsibilities across various departments or locations; digitizing and streamlining HR workflows requires a more centralized and integrated approach.

8. A. Centralized HR allows for the consistent implementation of policies and streamlined digital workflows across the entire organization, ensuring uniformity and efficiency. This approach leverages digital tools to automate and standardize HR processes, reducing redundancy and ensuring that all employees receive the same level of service and support. While decentralized HR might offer flexibility, it can lead to inconsistencies and inefficiencies that centralized HR aims to avoid. The other options do not adequately address the benefits of digital workflow integration in a centralized HR structure.

9. D. By using digital platforms, your company can offer personalized training that accommodates diverse learning styles and needs. This ensures that all employees can engage with and benefit from the DEI initiatives. Option A is incorrect because using AI-driven recruitment tools focuses too narrowly on the recruitment process and does not address the broader aspects of DEI strategy, such as training, development, and overall workplace culture. Option B is incorrect as traditional recruitment methods do not leverage the potential of technology and may fall short in creating a more inclusive hiring process. Option C is incorrect because a one-size-fits-all training program is unlikely to address the diverse needs of employees effectively.

10. A. In a remote-first strategy, maintaining clear and consistent communication is essential for team cohesion and productivity. Videoconferencing tools enable real-time interaction, virtual meetings, and collaborative work sessions, helping to bridge the gap created by physical distance. Options B and D are incorrect as they do not support the remote-first strategy outlined in the question, nor are they technological solutions. Option C is incorrect because there are several factors that should be considered before implementing productivity monitoring software.

11. A, C, D. Data encryption is a technology strategy that protects sensitive information by converting it into a coded format that is unreadable to unauthorized users. Endpoint security involves protecting devices such as computers, smartphones, and tablets that connect to the corporate network. By securing these endpoints, organizations can prevent unauthorized access, malware, and other threats. Data masking involves obscuring specific data within a database so that it is not accessible or readable by unauthorized users. Option B is incorrect because MFA helps prevent unauthorized access to systems and accounts, but it does not address the protection of data itself from being accessed or stolen, which is more effectively managed through the correct answer options.

12. B. Conducting phishing simulation exercises for HR staff should be prioritized because it directly addresses the threat of phishing by providing hands-on experience in recognizing and responding to such attacks. These exercises simulate real-world phishing attempts, allowing employees to practice identifying suspicious emails and taking appropriate actions without the risk of actual data compromise. While updating software, using a VPN, and increasing physical security are all important (options A, C, D), simulation exercises specifically target the human vulnerabilities that phishing and other social engineering tactics exploit.

13. B. Regular employee training on recognizing and responding to social engineering attempts is the most effective strategy because social engineering attacks exploit human behavior rather than technical vulnerabilities. By educating employees about common tactics used by social engineers and how to respond appropriately, organizations can significantly reduce the risk of successful attacks.

Appendix

B

PHR | PHRi and SPHR | SPHRi Case Studies

CASE STUDY

Case Study 1: Human Resources Role in Preventing Workplace Violence

By Hector Alvarez, CTM

President, Alvarez Associates, LLC (www.wvpexperts.com)

The threat of workplace violence is a growing concern for organizations of all sizes and has placed a significant burden on human resources (HR) professionals to help intervene and prevent incidents from occurring—a significant threat to a productive and harmonious work environment than the fear of being injured. Although there is a growing body of knowledge of the problem, no mandatory standards are in place to direct organizations on how to address this complex, multifaceted issue.

There are, however, two significant documents that every HR professional should be familiar with. The General Duty Clause, Section 5(a)(1), of the Occupational Safety and Health Act of 1970 states that employers are required to provide their employees with a place of employment that is "free from recognized hazards that are causing or are likely to cause death or serious harm." The second was updated in 2020, titled ASIS WVPI AA-2020 *Workplace Violence Prevention and Active Assailant- Prevention, Intervention, and Response*; it provides the framework for identifying and intervening to prevent acts of violence. What is not specifically addressed in either of these two provisions is exactly how an organization—and specifically HR professionals—should approach this challenging issue.

It is helpful to consider a real-world scenario. A high-tech firm in the greater San Francisco Bay area employed a husband and wife who worked in two different parts of the organization. Both people were stellar employees who received high marks from their respective supervisors. On a Monday morning the female employee, "Jane," went to HR and stated that she had been assaulted by her husband over the weekend and that she had the bruises to prove her story. She stated that she was granted a restraining order by the local police, but she did not want it to be an issue at the office. She merely wanted to let HR know "just in case" and didn't want anybody to find out about what had happened over the weekend.

This story highlights the types of challenges that anybody working in HR faces on a regular basis. The issues are complicated and the potential impact to the organization can be considerable. It's important to recognize that many of these issues are too complicated for one person or department to manage on their own. One of the main themes the ASIS standard stresses is to take a multidisciplinary approach to evaluating the seriousness and credibility of a threatening situation. The reality is that it's not that simple. Establishing an effective workplace violence prevention program requires building and maintaining a significant level of trust in people who work outside the realm of HR. In the scenario described here, the security staff discovered that the husband was apparently dating a woman who also worked at the company.

The one thing that every HR professional should know is that preventing workplace violence is as much an art as it is a science and requires organizationwide commitment. The OSHA and ASISstandards and guidelines provide a framework, but trust and ultimately intuition cannot be overemphasized. The reality is that violence is intimate and personal. It's of the upmost importance to recognize that preventing violence requires involvement and collaboration from teams across the organization. Legal personnel, security staff, individual businesses units, and senior management all have a role to play in identifying and preventing violence, and they certainly will each have an opinion on what the best course of action is. HR professionals often have the role of coordinating and balancing what may be competing goals and agendas.

In the scenario of the married couple who worked at the high-tech firm, the HR employee who Jane spoke to about the assault made the decision to respect her wishes and took no further action. As a result, even though security personnel had pertinent information, the HR employee was not made aware of the extramarital affair until after there was an intense and heated argument in the company breakroom that involved Jane, her husband, and the other woman. After the argument, Jane came to HR and loudly yelled, "Now what are you going to do?"

In the end, Jane filed a hostile work environment complaint with the Equal Employment Opportunity Commission, the husband was arrested and ultimately fired for job abandonment, and the other employee quit her job at the company. The moral of this story: Preventing violence is a complicated issue that requires the involvement of multiple parties. Don't try to do it alone. While HR should take a lead role in creating a collaborative environment that brings together the key stakeholders to evaluate the seriousness and credibility of a situation, every employee has a role to play in preventing violence in an organization.

Questions

1. How can human resources professionals balance the need for workplace confidentiality with the goal of preventing an act of violence?
2. Who in the organization is ultimately responsible for preventing acts of workplace violence?
3. When should human resources involve other business partners regarding concerns of inappropriate or concerning behavior?

Answers

1. Establishing trusted partnerships with key organizational players in the legal, security, risk management, and similar departments allows for timely communications regarding inappropriate or concerning behavior. Addressing potential issues early decreases the likelihood that they will escalate. Doing so can also help limit the number of people who must be involved; as issues become problems, it's much more difficult to maintain confidentiality.
2. Everybody in an organization has a role in preventing acts of violence. However, HR plays an extremely important role in helping create an organizational culture that encourages and supports employees being able to share their concerns. Not unlike the environment that supported the #MeToo movement, employees must feel that somebody is taking them seriously.
3. Employee relations issues can quickly transition from routine personnel matters to critical threats. Unfortunately, there is no clearly defined line indicating when to reach out for help from business partners. HR professionals should be mindful of the reality that they may not be in a position to see all the issues surrounding a person of concern. Frequent collaboration with key business partners can help close this information gap. Evaluating the seriousness and credibility of concerning behavior is a high-risk activity. Leveraging the collective resources of your organization can help minimize this risk.

CASE STUDY

Case Study 2: Military Veterans in the Workplace

By Stephen L. Christian, Lieutenant Colonel (retired);
former Director of Training for the U.S. Army Adjutant General School

Each year, approximately 180,000 military personnel make the transition from military service to civilian life and become veterans. For purposes of this case study, veterans are defined as those personnel separated from military service on favorable conditions. A military retiree is a veteran, who served at least 20 years in the military and has an approved retirement. The average age of a new military retiree is between 38 and 55 years old. The total number of veterans in the United States is 17.8 million in 2024 and is forecast to decrease over the next decade. Of note, only 2 million veterans are female, with most of those becoming veterans after September 11, 2001. Seventy-nine percent are white, 13 percent African American, 8.5 percent Hispanic, 2 percent Asian/Pacific Islander, and .8 percent Native American/Alaska Natives. The military strives to maintain representation of a diverse cross-section of America within its ranks. The greatest concentrations of veterans live in Texas, Florida, California, Pennsylvania, and North Carolina; however, every state has a population of veterans.

The bottom line is that there are employable, diverse veterans in every state; a potentially untapped resource of seasoned professionals ready to make a positive impact in the civilian workforce. Currently, veterans account for 5.4 percent of the U.S. labor force. See Figure B.1.

FIGURE B.1 Military by the numbers

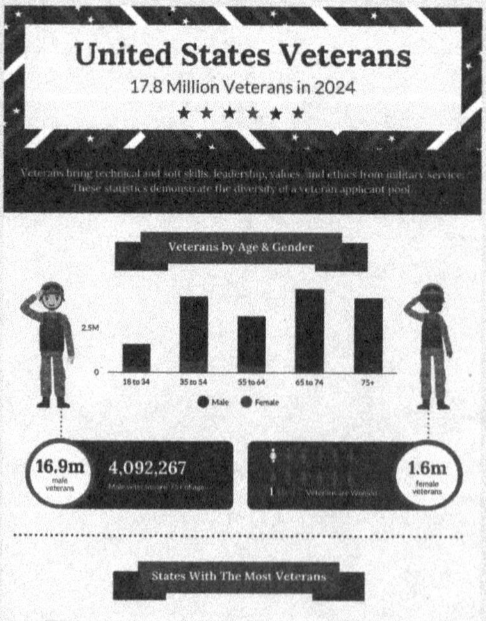

Source: With permission of Venngage Inc.

Veterans bring technical and soft skills, leadership, values, and ethics from military service. For example, the Army Values (Loyalty, Discipline, Respect, Selfless Service, Honesty, Integrity, and Personal Courage) and the Profession of Arms are engrained in behavior throughout a military career and are part of the veteran's mindset long after retirement. In fact, most military retirees seek a sense of purpose after retirement and desire to be part of a team, which makes them a great employment investment. The U.S. Department of Labor published an Employer Guide to Hiring Veterans, which is a fantastic resource for future employers to learn more about hiring veterans. Find it at `www.dol.gov/sites/dolgov/files/VETS/files/Employer-Guide-to-Hiring-Veterans-20231101.pdf`.

Now, we'll dig deeper into the human resources (HR) profession. Seventy-three percent of the HR professionals in the United States are women, with men filling just over a quarter of the civilian HR positions. There are more men working in Army civilian HR positions, with 60 percent women and 40 percent male. Of note, 50 percent of Army civilian HR professionals are veterans. There are over 37,000 Army HR military personnel serving in the U.S. Army Adjutant General's Corps, with approximately 54 percent male and 46 percent female. Given that there are more men working in Army HR compared to civilian HR, it can be beneficial to seek out veteran HR employees as a way to balance the civilian HR profession gender percentages.

Even though there are differences between military and civilian human resources, the same basic goals—taking care of people and providing managers with the information needed to make timely and accurate decisions—apply. Whether it be impacting warfighting readiness, or improving the bottom-line profit margin, the lines of effort and human resource objectives share similarities. The Army People Strategy (`https://people.army.mil`) signed by the Chief of Staff of the Army in 2019 puts "People First" and defines Army HR priorities as acquire, develop, employ, and retain talent, which are quite similar to the Human Resource Certification Institute's (HRCI) focus areas of recruitment, learning and development, employee relations, and employee retention. Overall, talent management is a critical enabler for success and employee satisfaction in both military and civilian HR arenas.

Unfortunately, there are challenges and gaps that must be overcome when transitioning from military to civilian employment. Terminology and language are often the biggest hurdle to cross. A veteran must be able to translate military service into civilian language to successfully communicate with future employers.

How do we bridge the gap between Army HR and civilian HR for our veterans to ease transition and improve organizational capacity? The Department of Army offers civilian credentialing programs for soldiers to earn a credential prior to retirement. For example, the Army offers Credentialing Opportunities Online (COOL) where a soldier can fund, prepare for, and earn a credential. HRCI's aPHR, PHR, and SPHR are prime examples of available offerings to help bridge the gap. In addition, the Army mandates participation in a transition assistance program prior to separation from the military to help prepare soldiers for civilian life.

Questions

1. Talent Management: What are some factors to consider when reviewing a veteran's résumé, interviewing a veteran, onboarding/training a veteran, and retaining a veteran in your organization?
2. Resource Management: As the HR Department Manager, complete a resource gap analysis for a new Veteran's Hiring Program. Use the DOTMLPF-p framework (Doctrine, Organization, Training, Materiel, Leadership, Personnel, Facilities, and Policy). Consider any facts and assumptions, and be prepared to request more information from corporate leadership. Using these areas or their civilian equivalents, conduct a capability gap analysis of an organization to determine potential areas of improvement to accomplish the organizational goals.
3. Military Terminology Translation: Match the following military terms to civilian terms.

Military term	Civilian term
Commander	Employees
Regulations	Objective/purpose
Service members	Senior manager
Chain of command	Business travel
Mission	Policy
Permanent change of station (PCS)	Career field
Temporary duty	Pay stub
Officer/Noncommissioned Evaluation Report (OER/ NCOER)	Executive levels
Military Occupational Specialty (MOS)	HR Department
Leave and Earnings Statement (LES)	Relocation
TRICARE	Current business conditions
Integrated Pay and Personnel System – Army (IPPS-A)	Performance appraisal
G1/S1	HR system/database
Operational environment (OE)	Decision making
Military Decision-Making Process (MDMP)	Health insurance

Answers

1. Realize that the veteran may subconsciously communicate in military terminology or use unfamiliar military acronyms. Expect a veteran to be early for events and often very direct with questions and answers. Expect veterans to search for a sense of purpose and teamwork, and to appreciate clear guidance and open communication from management.
2. Take inventory of your current resources and determine requirements for the new Veterans Hiring Program, objectives, and end state; determine the timeline (complete a plan of action and milestones [POA&M] for near- and long-term); and identify roles/responsibilities. Use the DOTMLPF-p framework for your assessment.
   - **Doctrine:** Does any language in the fundamental corporate guidance need to adjust for the new program?
   - **Organization:** Who will you report to? What internal/external offices/agencies will you coordinate with (up/down/in/out)? Adjust organization charts and points of contact.
   - **Training:** How will you educate the current workforce and future veteran hires on the new program?
   - **Material:** Do you have the automation and equipment needed to run the new program?
   - **Leadership:** Who will be the program manager? Can the position be filled internally or with a new hire? Set up a working group to brainstorm tasks. What additional information or guidance is needed from leadership?
   - **Personnel:** Develop and/or adjust position descriptions and conduct hiring/onboarding actions as needed. What knowledge, skills, and attributes/behaviors are you looking for?
   - **Facilities:** Do you have the space to conduct operations? Do you have the equipment and connectivity available to set up operations?
   - **Policy:** What existing policy (internal/external) and legal parameters must be considered? Review the Department of Labor publication for Employers on Hiring Veterans for information and benefits.
3. The following are the correct matches:
   - Commander – Senior manager
   - Regulations – Policy
   - Service members – Employees
   - Chain of command – Executive levels
   - Mission – Objective/purpose
   - Permanent change of stations (PCS) – Relocation

- Temporary duty – Business travel
- Officer/Noncommissioned Evaluation Report (OER/NCOER) – Performance appraisal
- Military Occupational Specialty (MOS) – Career field
- Leave and Earnings Statement (LES) – Pay stub
- TRICARE – Health insurance
- IPPS-A – HR system/database
- G1/S1 – HR Department
- Operational environment (OE) – Current business conditions
- MDMP – Decision making

Appendix C

Federal Employment Legislation and Case Law

The body of federal employment legislation and case law is extensive. This appendix provides a good introduction to this area of knowledge.

Affirmative Action Plans (AAPs)

All federal contractors and subcontractors who have at least 50 employees and designated monetary levels of government contracts or subcontracts must prepare and update annually two or three affirmative action plans (AAPs). Each AAP has specific requirements dictated by regulations. The three potential AAPs are as follows:

Executive Order 11246 AAP: Covers women and minorities and is required for each establishment, if a supply or services contractor (or subcontractor) has 50 or more employees and a government contract (or subcontract) of at least $50,000. Federally assisted construction contractors, however, do not prepare traditional EO 11246 but have 16 equal employment opportunity (EEO) and *affirmative action (AA)* specifications that they must meet and document.

Vietnam Era Veterans' Readjustment Assistance Action (VEVRAA) of 1974, as amended, 38 U.S.C. 4212 AAP: Covers protected veterans and is required for each establishment, if a government contractor (or subcontractor) has 50 or more employees and has a government contract (or subcontract) of at least $150,000. Federally assisted construction contractors must also prepare the same type of AAP. The categories of protected veterans are disabled veteran, recently separated veteran (three-year period), active duty wartime or campaign badge veteran, or an armed forces service medal veteran.

Section 503 of the Rehabilitation Act of 1973, as amended, 29 U.S.C. 793 AAP: Covers individuals with disabilities and is required for each establishment, if a government contractor (or subcontractor) has 50 or more employees and a government contract (or subcontract) of at least $50,000. Federally assisted construction contractors must also prepare the same type of AAP. The government allows the VEVRAA AAP and the Section 503 AAP to be combined into one if both are required.

The Office of Federal Contract Compliance Programs (OFCCP) in the U.S. Department of Labor constructs and enforces the affirmative action regulations. The OFCCP periodically will audit federal contractors and subcontractors on the contents of their AAPs and other regulatory requirements. Contractors and subcontractors are prohibited from discharging or otherwise discriminating against applicants or employees who inquire about, discuss, or disclose their compensation or that of others, subject to certain limitations.

Note that employers may not override an applicant's gender self-identification based on an employer's visual observation. Should an employee or applicant self-identify as nonbinary, the contractor must still include the individual in their AAP submission but may exclude that individual's data from the gender-based analyses that is part of the reporting requirements.

Executive Order 11246 AAP

The required components of an Executive Order 11246 AAP appear in Table C.1.

TABLE C.1 Required components of Executive Order 11246 AAP

AAP component	Description
Organizational profile	Employers choose the format that works best: organizational display (traditional organization chart) or workforce analysis (listing of job titles from lowest to highest paid).
Job group analysis	Places job titles with similar content, wages, and opportunities into job groups for analysis.
Placement of incumbents in job groups	Lists percentages of minorities and women employed in each job group.
Determining availability	Estimates the number of qualified minorities or women available for employment in a given job group, often within a specific geographic area.
Comparison of incumbency to availability	Compares the percentage of minorities and women in each job group with the availability for those job groups within a specific geographic area.
Placement goals	When the percentage of minorities or women employed in a particular job group is less than would reasonably be expected given their availability percentage in that particular job group, the contractor must establish a placement goal. Placement goals serve as objectives or targets reasonably attainable by means of applying every good-faith effort. Placement goals are not quotas or preferences.
Designation of responsibility	Assigns responsibility and accountability for the implementation of EEO and the affirmative action program to an official of the organization.
Identification of problem areas	Requires analysis of the total employment processes to determine whether and where impediments to equal opportunity exist.
Action-oriented programs	The contractor must develop and execute action-oriented programs designed to correct any problems identified and to attain established goals and objectives.
Internal audit and reporting system	The contractor must develop and implement an auditing system that periodically measures the effectiveness of its total affirmative action program.

VEVRAA AAP

The required components of the VEVRAA AAP include the following. Note that when the term *contractor* is used, it also applies to subcontractors.

Policy Statement The contractor's equal opportunity policy statement should be included in the AAP and be posted on the organization's bulletin board.

Review of Personnel Processes The contractor shall periodically review such processes and make any necessary modifications to ensure that its obligations are carried out. A description of the review and any modifications should be documented.

Physical and Mental Qualifications Provides for a schedule for the periodic review of all physical and mental job qualification standards to ensure that to the extent that qualification standards tend to screen out qualified disabled veterans, they are job-related for the position in question, and are consistent with business necessity.

Reasonable Accommodation to Physical and Mental Limitations Includes a statement that the contractor will make reasonable accommodation to the known physical or mental limitations of an otherwise qualified disabled veteran unless it can demonstrate that the accommodation would impose an undue hardship on the operation of the business.

Harassment Includes a statement about what the contractor has done to develop and implement procedures to ensure that its employees are not harassed because of their status as protected veterans.

External Dissemination of Policy, Outreach, and Positive Recruitment Includes listing the organization's outreach efforts, including sending written notification of the organization's EEO/AA policy to all subcontractors, vendors, and suppliers. Also requires the contractor to review, on an annual basis, the outreach and recruitment efforts it has taken over the previous 12 months to evaluate their effectiveness in identifying and recruiting qualified protected veterans. If not effective, the contractor shall identify and implement alternative efforts. These assessments are to be retained for a three-year period.

Internal Dissemination of Policy The contractor outlines its efforts to implement and disseminate its EEO/AA policy internally.

Audit and Reporting System The contractor describes and documents the audit and reporting system that it designed and implemented to measure the effectiveness of its affirmative action program, among other things.

Responsibility for Implementation The contractor documents which official of the organization has been assigned responsibility for implementation of the contractor's affirmative action program. Their identity should appear on all internal and external communications regarding the contractor's affirmative action program.

Training Describes the efforts made to train all personnel involved in the recruitment, screening, selection, promotion, disciplinary actions, and related processes on the contractor's commitments in the affirmative action program.

Other VEVRAA requirements not included in the AAP, but required by the regulations, include:

Data Collection Analysis Annual documentation, maintained for a three-year period, of the number of applicants who self-identified as protected veterans, the total number of job openings and the total number of jobs filled, the total number of applicants for all jobs, the number of applicants hired, and the number of protected veterans hired.

Hiring Benchmark The contractor shall either establish and document a hiring benchmark for protected veterans, based on specific criteria, or use the OFCCP-dictated hiring benchmark, which is 5.2 percent as of the time of publication (2024). The annual veteran hiring benchmark is updated every year. Stay up-to-date by scheduling an annual review at `www.dol.gov/agencies/ofccp/vevraa/hiring-benchmark` in March of each year to stay in compliance.

Section 503, Individuals with Disabilities AAP

Under Section 503 of the Rehabilitation Act of 1973, federal contractors are required to develop and maintain an Affirmative Action Program for individuals with disabilities. The required components of a Section 503 affirmative action program include:

- **Equal Opportunity Policy Statement:** A policy statement affirming the contractor's commitment to equal employment opportunity for individuals with disabilities and outlining the procedures for handling complaints of discrimination.
- **Review of Personnel Processes:** The contractor must periodically review its personnel processes to ensure that they provide for careful, thorough, and systematic consideration of the job qualifications of applicants and employees with disabilities.
- **Physical and Mental Qualifications:** The contractor must review all physical and mental job qualification standards to ensure that they are job-related and consistent with business necessity and safe performance of the job.
- **Reasonable Accommodation:** The contractor must ensure that reasonable accommodations are provided to qualified individuals with disabilities, unless providing such accommodation would cause undue hardship.
- **Harassment Prevention Statement:** The AAP must include a commitment to ensuring that employees are not harassed based on disability.
- **External Dissemination of Policy, Outreach, and Positive Recruitment:** The contractor must undertake appropriate outreach and positive recruitment activities to recruit individuals with disabilities.
- **Internal Dissemination of Policy:** The contractor must internally disseminate its equal opportunity policy to employees and applicants.
- **Audit and Reporting System:** The contractor must design and implement an audit and reporting system that measures the effectiveness of the AAP and indicates any need for remedial action.

- **Responsibility for Implementation:** The AAP must specify the responsibilities of individuals assigned to implement the program.
- **Training:** The contractor must provide training to all personnel involved in recruitment, hiring, and management to ensure they understand the AAP and their responsibilities.
- **Data Collection Analysis:** The contractor must collect and analyze data on applicants and hires to assess the effectiveness of its outreach and recruitment efforts.
- **Utilization Goals:** Contractors must establish a utilization goal of 7 percent for the employment of qualified individuals with disabilities within each job group of their workforce.
- **Invitation to Self-Identify:** The contractor must invite applicants and employees to voluntarily self-identify as individuals with disabilities at the pre-offer and post-offer stages of employment, and periodically thereafter.

Age Discrimination in Employment Act of 1967 (ADEA)

The purpose of the Age Discrimination in Employment Act (ADEA) is to "promote employment of older persons based on their ability rather than age; to prohibit arbitrary age discrimination in employment; to help employers and workers find ways of meeting problems arising from the impact of age on employment."

The ADEA prohibits discrimination against persons 40 years of age or older in employment activities, including hiring, job assignments, training, promotion, compensation, benefits, terminating, or any other privileges, terms, or conditions of employment. The ADEA applies to private businesses, unions, employment agencies, and state and local governments with more than 20 employees. As with Title VII, the ADEA provides for the following exceptions:

- Bona fide occupational qualifications (BFOQs) that are reasonably necessary to business operations
- The hiring of firefighters or police officers by state or local governments
- Retirement of employees age 65 or older who have been in executive positions for at least two years and are eligible for retirement benefits of at least $44,000 per year
- Retirement of tenured employees of institutions of higher education at age 70
- Discharge or discipline for just cause

Individuals who think they have been subjected to an unlawful employment practice must file charges with the Equal Employment Opportunity Commission (EEOC), which has federal enforcement responsibility for the ADEA, or with the state equal employment agency (if one exists for the location in which the incident occurred). Timely filing of charges is essential for complainants, since the EEOC will not investigate charges that are not made according to the guidelines.

Older Worker Benefit Protection Act Amendment to the ADEA

The Older Worker Benefit Protection Act (OWBPA) amended the ADEA in 1990 to include a prohibition on discrimination against older workers in all employee benefit plans unless any age-based reductions are justified by significant cost considerations. This amendment allows seniority systems as long as they do not require involuntary terminations of employees based on their age and extends ADEA protections to all employee benefits, as well as guidelines for legal severance agreements.

The OWBPA defines the conditions under which employees may waive their rights to make claims under the act. To be acceptable, waivers must include the following components:

- Waiver agreements must be written in a way that can be understood by the average employee.
- Waivers must refer specifically to the rights or claims available under the ADEA.
- Employees may not waive rights or claims for actions that occur subsequent to signing the waiver.
- Employees must receive consideration in exchange for the waiver in addition to anything to which they are already entitled.
- The waiver must advise employees of their right to consult an attorney prior to signing the document.
- In individual cases, employees must be given 21 days to consider the agreement before they are required to sign; when a group of employees is involved, employees age 40 and older must be given 45 days to consider their decision.
- Once the waiver is signed, employees may revoke the agreement within seven days.
- In cases of group terminations (such as a reduction in force or early retirement program), employees must be advised of the eligibility requirements for any exit incentive programs, any time limits for the programs, and a list of the job titles and ages of employees who have been selected or who are eligible for the program.

The federal agency responsible for enforcement of the OWBPA is the EEOC.

Americans with Disabilities Act of 1990 (ADA) and Amendments

The Americans with Disabilities Act (ADA) of 1990 was based in large part on the Rehabilitation Act of 1973 (discussed later in this appendix), and it extended protected class status to qualified persons with disabilities. Employment discrimination is covered by Title I of the act and identifies covered entities as employment agencies, labor unions, joint labor-management committees, and employers with 15 or more employees (including those who work on a part-time or temporary basis) for each working day in each of 20 weeks in the current or previous calendar year. Excluded from coverage are the federal government and 501(c) private membership clubs. The ADA prohibits discrimination in job application procedures; the hiring, advancement, or discharge of employees; employee compensation; job training; and other terms, conditions, and privileges of employment.

The ADA requires covered entities to make *reasonable accommodation* to develop employment opportunities for qualified persons with disabilities in two areas:

- Facilities should be accessible to persons with disabilities.
- Position requirements may be adjusted to accommodate qualified persons with disabilities.

The ADA allows that accommodations constituting an *undue hardship* to the business are not required and defines undue hardship as an accommodation that places an excessive burden on the employer. The act identifies the factors to be considered in determining whether an accommodation is an undue hardship by looking at the cost, the financial resources of the organization, the size of the organization, and other similar factors.

In 2008, Congress enacted the ADA Amendments Act of 2008, which took effect on January 1, 2009. According to language in the amendment, Congress took the action to clarify the intention of the original legislation, which was to make the definition of "disability" consistent with the way the courts had defined the term under the Rehabilitation Act of 1973. In fact, court interpretations under the ADA had "narrowed the broad scope of protection" originally intended. The amendment more clearly defined the intent of Congress in the following ways:

Broadly Defines "Disability" A disability is a physical or mental impairment that causes *substantial limitation* to one or more *major life activities* for an individual, a record of impairment for an individual, or an individual who is regarded as being impaired.

Defines "Major Life Activity" The amendment defines major life activities in two areas: general activities and major bodily functions. Table C.2 lists activities Congress cites in the law as examples but is not meant to be a complete list.

TABLE C.2 Major life activities

General activities	Major bodily functions
Caring for oneself, performing manual tasks, seeing, hearing, eating, sleeping, breathing, learning, reading, concentrating, thinking, communicating, working	Functions of the immune system; normal cell growth; and functions of the digestive, bowel, bladder, neurological, brain, respiratory, circulatory, endocrine, and reproductive systems

Ignores Mitigating Measures Congress directs that, except for "ordinary glasses or contact lenses," mitigating measures such as medication, prosthetics, hearing aids, mobility devices, and others may not be used to limit the definition of disability for an individual.

Clarifies the Definition of "Regarded As" This amendment requires that individuals who are able to demonstrate that they have been the subject of prohibited activities under the ADA, whether or not they actually have some type of impairment, are protected by its requirements.

Explicitly Authorizes the EEOC to Regulate Compliance The amendment mandates the EEOC to develop and implement regulations and guidance for employers to follow, specifying the inclusion of a definition for "substantially limits" that is consistent with the intent of Congress in the legislation.

Prohibits "Reverse Discrimination" Claims The amendment clearly states that individuals without disability may not use the ADA to file claims of discrimination when disabled individuals receive favorable employment actions.

A key element of ADA compliance is the requirement to engage in an interactive process with disabled individuals requesting a reasonable accommodation that will enable them to perform essential job functions.

Civil Rights Act of 1964 (Title VII)

Title VII of the Civil Rights Act of 1964 introduced the concepts of *protected classes* and *unlawful employment practices* to American businesses. Unlawful employment practices are those that have an adverse impact on members of a protected class, which is a group of people who share common characteristics and are protected from discriminatory practices. Title VII established the basis for two types of unlawful practices: disparate treatment and disparate impact. *Disparate treatment* happens when employers treat some candidates or employees differently, such as requiring women to take a driving test when they apply for a job but not requiring men to take the test when they apply for the same job. Practices that have a *disparate impact* on members of protected classes seem fair on their face but result in adverse impact on members of protected classes, such as requiring all candidates for firefighter positions to be a certain height. Although the requirement applies to all candidates equally, some Asian and female candidates who might otherwise qualify for the position might be eliminated because they are generally shorter than male candidates of other races.

The act identified five protected classes: race, color, religion, national origin, and sex. It also defined the following unlawful employment practices:

- Discriminatory recruiting, selection, or hiring actions
- Discriminatory compensation or benefit practices

- Discriminatory access to training or apprenticeship programs
- Discriminatory practices in any other terms or conditions of employment

Legitimate seniority, merit, and piece-rate payment systems are allowable under Title VII as long as they do not intentionally discriminate against protected classes.

Title VII allowed for limited exceptions to its requirements, some of which are listed here:

- Bona fide occupational qualifications (BFOQs) occur when religion, sex, or national origin is "reasonably necessary to the normal operation" of the business.
- Educational institutions were not originally subject to Title VII.
- Religious organizations may give preference to members of that religion.
- A potential employee who is unable to obtain, or loses, a national security clearance required for the position is not protected.
- Indian reservations may give preference to Indian applicants and employees living on or near the reservation.

Title VII created the Equal Employment Opportunity Commission (EEOC) with a mandate to promote equal employment opportunity, educate employers, provide technical assistance, and study and report on its activities to Congress and the American people. The EEOC is the enforcement agency for Title VII and other discrimination legislation.

Amendments to Title VII

Title VII was amended in 1972, 1978, and 1991 to clarify and expand its coverage.

Equal Employment Opportunity Act of 1972

Created in 1972, the Equal Employment Opportunity Act (EEOA) provides litigation authority to the EEOC in the event that an acceptable conciliation agreement cannot be reached. In those cases, the EEOC is empowered to sue nongovernmental entities, including employers, unions, and employment agencies.

The EEOA extended coverage of Title VII to entities that had been excluded in 1964:

- Educational institutions
- State and local governments
- The federal government

In addition, the EEOA reduced the number of employees needed to subject an employer to coverage by Title VII from 25 to 15 and required employers to keep records of the discovery of any unlawful employment practices and provide those records to the EEOC upon request.

The EEOA also provided administrative guidance for the processing of complaints by providing that employers be notified within 10 days of receipt of a charge by the EEOC and that findings be issued within 120 days of the charge being filed. The EEOC was empowered to sue employers, unions, and employment agencies in the event that an acceptable conciliation agreement could not be reached within 30 days of notice to the employer. The EEOA also provided protection from retaliatory employment actions against whistleblowers.

Pregnancy Discrimination Act of 1978

Congress amended Title VII with the Pregnancy Discrimination Act of 1978 to clarify that discrimination against women on the basis of pregnancy, childbirth, or any related medical condition is an unlawful employment practice. The act specified that pregnant employees should receive the same treatment and benefits as employees with any other short-term disability.

Pregnant Worker Fairness Act (PWFA)

The Pregnant Workers Fairness Act (PWFA) went into effect on June 27, 2023. It requires employers to provide reasonable accommodations to workers affected by pregnancy, childbirth, or related medical conditions, unless doing so would cause undue hardship to the employer. This includes modifications to work duties, schedules, and other job functions as needed to accommodate their health and well-being.

The key difference between the PDA and the PWFA is that the PDA prohibits discrimination based on pregnancy but doesn't require specific accommodations. In contrast, the PWFA mandates reasonable accommodations for pregnant workers, similar to those for disabilities under the ADA.

Civil Rights Act of 1991

The Civil Rights Act (CRA) of 1991 contained amendments that affected Title VII, the Age Discrimination in Employment Act (ADEA), and the Americans with Disabilities Act (ADA) in response to issues raised by the courts in several cases that were brought by employees based on Title VII.

The purpose of the Civil Rights Act (CRA) of 1991, as described in the act itself, is fourfold:

1. To provide appropriate remedies for intentional discrimination and unlawful harassment in the workplace
2. To codify the concepts of "business necessity" and "job relatedness" articulated by the Supreme Court in *Griggs v. Duke Power Co.* and in other Supreme Court decisions
3. To confirm statutory authority and provide statutory guidelines for the adjudication of disparate impact suits under Title VII of the Civil Rights Act of 1964
4. To respond to recent decisions of the Supreme Court by expanding the scope of relevant civil rights statutes in order to provide adequate protection to victims of discrimination

Amendments contained in the CRA affected Title VII, the ADEA, and the ADA. One of the issues addressed is that of disparate impact, first introduced by the *Griggs v. Duke Power Co.* case in 1971. Disparate impact occurs when an employment practice, which appears on its face to be fair, unintentionally discriminates against members of a protected class. The CRA places the burden of proof for discrimination complaints on the complainant when there is a job-related business necessity for employment actions. When an individual alleges multiple discriminatory acts, each practice in itself must be discriminatory unless the employer's decision-making process cannot be separated, in which case the individual may challenge the decision-making process itself. The CRA also provides additional relief for victims of intentional discrimination and harassment, codifies the concept of disparate impact, and addresses Supreme Court rulings over the previous few years that had weakened equal employment opportunity laws.

The CRA made the following changes to Title VII:

- Provided punitive damages when employers engage in discriminatory practices "with malice or with reckless indifference"
- Excluded back pay awards from compensatory damages
- Established a sliding scale for compensatory and punitive damages based on company size
- Provided that any party to a civil suit in which punitive or compensatory damages are sought may demand a jury trial
- Expanded Title VII to include congressional employees and some senior political appointees
- Required that the individual alleging that an unlawful employment practice is in use prove that it results in disparate impact to members of a protected class
- Provided that job relatedness and reasonable business necessity are defenses to disparate impact and that if a business can show that the practice does not result in disparate impact, it need not show the practice to be a business necessity
- Provided that business necessity is not a defense against an intentional discriminatory employment practice
- Established that if discrimination was a motivating factor in an employment practice it was unlawful even if other factors contributed to the practice
- Allowed that if the same employment decision would have been made whether or not an impermissible motivating factor was present, no damages would be awarded
- Expanded coverage to include foreign operations of American businesses unless compliance would constitute violation of the laws of the host country

Common Law Doctrines

Common law doctrines are the result of legal decisions made by judges in cases adjudicated over a period of centuries. A number of doctrines have implications for employment relationships, the most common of which is the concept of *employment at will.* Other common law issues that affect employment relationships are *respondeat superior*, constructive discharge, and defamation.

Employment at Will

In *Payne v. The Western & Atlantic Railroad Company* in 1884, Justice Ingersoll of the Tennessee Supreme Court defined employment at will in this way: ". . .either party may terminate the service, for any cause, good or bad, or without cause, and the other cannot complain in law." This definition allowed employers to change employment conditions, whether it was to hire, transfer, promote, or terminate an employee, at their sole discretion. It also allowed employees to leave a job at any time, with or without notice. In the absence of a legally enforceable employment contract, this definition was unaltered for more than 70 years.

Although there have always been exceptions to at-will employment based on employment contracts, beginning in 1959 the doctrine began to be eroded by both court decisions and statutes. This erosion resulted in several exceptions to the at-will concept, including public policy exceptions, the application of the doctrine of good faith and fair dealing to employment relationships, and the concepts of promissory estoppel and fraudulent misrepresentation.

Contract Exceptions

Employment-at-will intentions may be abrogated by contracts, either express or implied. An *express contract* can be a verbal or written agreement in which the parties state exactly what they agree to do. Employers have been known to express their gratitude for a job well done with promises of continued employment, such as "Keep doing that kind of work and you have a job for life" or "You'll have a job as long as we're in business." Statements such as these can invalidate the at-will doctrine.

An *implied contract* can be created by an employer's conduct and need not be specifically stated. For example, an employer's consistent application of a progressive discipline policy can create an implied contract that an employee will not be terminated without first going through the steps set forth by the policy. A disclaimer can offset the effects of an implied contract; however, there is little agreement in the courts as to what and how the disclaimer must be presented in order to maintain at-will status.

Statutory Exceptions

The at-will doctrine has been further eroded by legislation. At-will employment may not be used as a pretext for terminating employees for discriminatory reasons as set forth in equal opportunity legislation or other legislation designed to protect employee rights.

Public Policy Exceptions

Erosion of the doctrine of at-will employment began in 1959 when the California Court of Appeals heard *Petermann v. International Brotherhood of Teamsters*, in which Mr. Petermann, a business agent for the union, alleged that he was terminated for refusing to commit perjury on behalf of the union at a legislative hearing. The court held that it is "... obnoxious to the interest of state and contrary to public policy and sound morality to allow an employer to discharge any employee, whether the employment be for a designated or unspecified duration, on the ground that the employee declined to commit perjury, an act specifically enjoined by statute."

The public policy exception to employment at will was initially applied conservatively by the courts, but over time, its application has been expanded. In general, the public policy exception has been applied in four areas. The first is exemplified by the *Petermann* case—an employee who refuses to break the law on behalf of the employer can claim a public policy exception. The second application covers employees who report illegal acts of their employers (whistleblowers); the third covers employees who participate in activities supported by public policy, such as cooperating in a government investigation of wrongdoing by the employer. Finally, the public policy exception covers employees who are acting in accordance with legal statute, such as attending jury duty or filing a workers' compensation claim.

While the public policy exception to at-will employment originated in California, it has been adopted by many, although not all, states.

Duty of Good Faith and Fair Dealing

This tenet of common law provides that parties to a contract have an obligation to act in a fair and honest manner with each other to ensure that benefits of the contract may be realized. The application of this doctrine to at-will employment issues varies widely from state to state. The Texas Supreme Court, for example, has determined that there is no duty for good faith and fair dealing in employment contracts. On the other hand, the Alaska Supreme Court has determined that the duty is implied in at-will employment situations.

Promissory Estoppel

Promissory estoppel occurs when an employer entices an employee (or prospective employee) to take an action by promising a reward. The employee takes the action, but the employer does not follow through on the reward. For example, an employer promises a job to a candidate who resigns another position to accept the new one and then finds the offered position has been withdrawn. If a promise is clear, specific, and reasonable, and an employee acts on the promise, the employer may be required to follow through on the promised reward or pay equivalent damages.

Fraudulent Misrepresentation

Similar to promissory estoppel, fraudulent misrepresentation relates to promises or claims made by employers to entice candidates to join the company. An example of this might be a company that decides to close one of its locations in six months but, in the meantime, needs to hire a general manager to run the operation. If, when asked about the future of the company during the recruiting process, the company tells candidates that the plant will be expanded in the future and withholds its intention to close the plant, the company would be fraudulently misrepresenting the facts about the position.

Respondeat Superior

The Latin meaning of *respondeat superior* is "let the master answer." What this means is that an employer can be held liable for actions of its employees that occur within the scope and course of assigned duties or responsibilities in the course of their employment, regardless of whether the act is negligent or reckless. This concept has implications for many employment situations; one is sexual harassment, which will be discussed later in this appendix. Another could be an auto accident where a third party is injured when an employee hits another vehicle while driving an employer's delivery truck. *Respondeat superior* could also come into play if a manager promised additional vacation time to a candidate and the candidate accepted the position based on the promise. Even if the promise was not in writing and was outside the employer's normal vacation policy, and the manager made the promise without prior approval, the employer could be required to provide the benefit based on this doctrine.

Constructive Discharge

Constructive discharge occurs when an employer makes the workplace so hostile and inhospitable that an employee resigns. In many states, this gives the employee a cause of action against the employer. The legal standard that must be met varies widely between the states, with some requiring the employee to show that the employer intended to force the resignation, and others requiring the employee to show only that the conditions were sufficiently intolerable that a reasonable person would feel compelled to resign.

Defamation

Accusations of defamation in employment relationships most often occur during or after termination. Defamation is a communication that damages an individual's reputation in the community, preventing the person from obtaining employment or other benefits. When an employer, out of spite or with a vengeful intent, sets out to deliberately damage a former employee, the result is malicious defamation.

Concerns about defamation have caused many employers to stop giving meaningful references for former employees, in many cases responding to reference requests only with dates of employment and the individual's last title. Employers are generally protected by the concept of "qualified privilege" if the information provided is job-related, truthful, clear, and unequivocal. Obtaining written authorization prior to providing references and limiting responses to the information being requested without volunteering additional information can reduce the risks of being accused of defamation.

Copyright Act of 1976

The use of musical, literary, and other original works without permission of the owner of the copyright is prohibited under most circumstances. The copyright owner is the author of the work with two exceptions. The first is that an employer who hires employees to create original works as part of their normal job duties is the owner of the copyright because the employer paid for the work to be done. The second exception is that the copyright for work created by a freelance author, artist, or musician who has been commissioned to create the work by someone else is owned by the person who commissioned the work. These exceptions are known as *work-for-hire* exceptions.

For trainers who want to use the work of others during training sessions, two circumstances do not require permission. The first is related to works that are in the *public domain*. Copyrights protect original works for the life of the author plus 70 years; after that, the works may be used without permission. Works-for-hire are protected for the shorter of 95 years from the first year of publication or 120 years from the year of creation.

Other works in the public domain include those produced as part of the job duties of federal officials and those for which copyright protection has expired. Some works published without notice of copyright before January 1, 1978, or those published between then and March 1, 1989, are also considered to be in the public domain.

The second circumstance for use of published works without permission is known as the *fair use doctrine*. The act specifies that use of a work for the purposes of criticism, commentary, news reporting, or teaching (including multiple copies for classroom use, scholarship, or research) is not an infringement, depending on four factors:

- **The purpose and character of the use:** Is it to be used for a profit or for a nonprofit educational purpose?
- **The nature of the work itself:** Is it a work of fiction? Or is it based on facts? How much creativity did it require?
- **The amount of work:** How much of the work (one copy or 50?) or what portion (a paragraph or an entire chapter?) will be used?
- **The effect:** What effect will the use of the material have on the potential market value of the copyrighted work?

Permission for the use of copyright-protected material that is outside the fair use exceptions can generally be obtained by contacting the author or publisher of the work.

Davis–Bacon Act of 1931

The Davis–Bacon Act was the first federal legislation to regulate minimum wages. It requires that construction contractors and their subcontractors pay at least the prevailing wage for the local area in which they are operating if they receive federal funds. Employers with federal construction contracts of $2,000 or more must adhere to the Davis–Bacon Act.

Drug-Free Workplace Act of 1988

The Drug-Free Workplace Act of 1988 applies to businesses with federal contracts of $100,000 or more each year. Contractors subject to the act must take the following steps to be in compliance:

Develop and publish a written policy. Contractors must develop a written policy clearly stating that they provide a drug-free workplace and that illegal substance abuse isn't an acceptable practice in the workplace. The policy must clearly state what substances are covered and the consequences for violating the policy.

Establish an awareness program. The employer must develop a program to educate employees about the policy, communicate the dangers of drug abuse in the workplace, discuss the employer's policy, inform employees of the availability of counseling or other programs to reduce drug use, and notify employees of the penalties for violating the policy. The program can be delivered through a variety of media—seminars, brochures, videos, web-based training—whatever methods will most effectively communicate the information in the specific environment.

Notify employees about contract conditions. Employees must be made aware that a condition of their employment on a federal contract project is that they abide by the policy and inform the employer within five days if they're convicted of a criminal drug offense in the workplace.

Notify the contracting agency of violations. If an employee is convicted of a criminal drug offense in the workplace, the employer must notify the contracting agency within 10 days of being informed of the conviction by the employee.

Establish penalties for illegal drug convictions. The employer must have an established penalty for any employees convicted of relevant drug offenses. Within 30 days of notice by an employee of a conviction, the employer must take appropriate disciplinary action against the employee or require participation in an appropriate drug-rehabilitation program. Any penalties must be in accordance with requirements of the Rehabilitation Act of 1973.

Maintain a drug-free workplace. Contractors must make a good-faith effort to maintain a drug-free workplace in accordance with the act, or they're subject to penalties, including suspension of payments under the contract, suspension or termination of the contract, or exclusion from consideration from future contracts for a period of up to five years.

This act supersedes individual state laws.

EEO Survey

The EEO survey promotes equal employment opportunity by requiring employers to collect and report detailed workforce data on the representation of various demographic groups, such as race and gender. This data helps identify potential discrimination or disparities in hiring, promotions, wages and other employment practices. The EEOC and OFFCP worked together to develop the reporting form, known as the EEO-1 survey or report. It must be filed on or before September 30 of each year using employment data from one pay period in July, August, or September of the current survey year. All employers who meet the following criteria must complete the report:

- All federal contractors who are private employers and (a) are not exempt as provided by 41 CFR Section 60-1.5; (b) have 50 or more employees; *and* (i) are prime contractors or first-tier subcontractors, and have a contract, subcontract, or purchase order amounting to $50,000 or more, or (ii) serve as a depository of government funds in any amount, or (iii) are a financial institution that is an issuing and paying agent for U.S. Savings Bonds. Only those establishments located in the District of Columbia and the 50 states are required to submit. No reports should be filed for establishments in Puerto Rico, the Virgin Islands, or other American protectorates.
- All private employers who are subject to Title VII of the Civil Rights Act of 1964, as amended, with 100 or more employees.

Exceptions to the EEO-1 reporting requirements include:

- State and local governments
- Primary and secondary school systems
- Institutions of higher education
- Indian tribes
- Tax-exempt private membership clubs (other than labor organizations)

The preferred method for filing the EEO-1 survey is through the online filing application. Refer to the EEOC website at `www.eeoc.gov` for information on how to file the EEO-1 survey.

The "workforce snapshot period" is October 1 to December 31 (the fourth quarter of each year). In other words, each employer may choose any pay period during this three-month "workforce snapshot period" to count its full-time and part-time employees for the EEO-1 report. The deadline to file is generally early June, although the exact date may vary from year to year. Verify the deadline and file online at `www.eeocdata.org/eeo1`.

Report Types

Employers with operations at a single location or establishment complete a single form, whereas those who operate at more than one location or establishment must file employment data on multiple forms.

Headquarters Report All multiple-establishment employers must file a Headquarters Report, which is a report covering the principal or headquarters office.

Establishment Report Locations with 50 or more employees file a separate Establishment Report for each location employing 50 or more persons.

Locations with fewer than 50 employees may be reported on an Establishment Report or on an Establishment List. The Establishment List provides the name, address, and total number of employees for each location with fewer than 50 employees along with an employment data grid combining this data by race, sex, and job category.

Employees who work remotely and/or telework must be included in an employer's EEO-1 report(s) by the specific establishment to which the employees report. Under no circumstances should an employee's home address be reported on any EEO-1 Component 1 submission or report. According to the EEOC, "if a remote employee is not assigned to and does not report to any physical location on a permanent basis, the employee should be counted at the establishment to which the employee's manager reports or is assigned. If an employee does not report to an establishment and the employee's manager also does not report to an establishment, the employee (and their manager) should be included on the employer's 'Headquarters Report.'"

Consolidated Report Data from all the individual location reports and the headquarters report are combined on the Consolidated Report. The total number of employees on this report must be equal to data submitted on all the individual reports.

Parent corporations that own a majority interest in another corporation report data for employees at all locations, including those of the subsidiary establishments.

Race and Ethnicity Categories

Employers are required to report on seven categories of employees:

- Hispanic or Latino
- White
- Black or African American
- Native Hawaiian or Other Pacific Islander
- Asian
- American Indian or Alaska Native
- Two or More Races (not Hispanic or Latino)

Job Categories

The EEO-1 report requires employers to group jobs into job categories based on the average skill level, knowledge, and responsibility of positions within their organizations:

- Executive/senior-level officials and managers
- Midlevel officials and managers
- Professionals
- Technicians
- Sales workers
- Administrative support workers

- Craft workers
- Operatives
- Laborers and helpers
- Service workers

Data Reporting

Private employers and federal contractors with 100 or more employees, the EEO-1 report requires additional reporting components of employment data. These reports include:

Employee Report Total employees in the workforce snapshot for each job category and pay band

Pay Report W-2 Box 1 earnings for all employees identified in the workforce snapshot

Hours Worked Report Hours worked for all employees in the snapshot in their job category and pay band

The 12 pay bands are:

- $19,239 and under
- $19,240–$24,439
- $24,440–$30,679
- $30,680–$38,999
- $39,000–$49,919
- $49,920–$62,919
- $62,920–$80,079
- $80,080–$101,919
- $101,920–$128,959
- $128,960–$163,799
- $163,800–$207,999
- $208,000 and over

Employment Retirement Income Security Act of 1974 (ERISA)

The Employment Retirement Income Security Act (ERISA) was created by Congress to set standards for private pensions and some group welfare programs such as medical and life insurance.

ERISA requires organizations to file three types of reports: a summary plan description, an annual report, and reports to individual participants of their benefit rights.

Summary Plan Description (SPD)

A summary plan description (SPD) provides plan participants with information about the provisions, policies, and rules established by the plan and advises them on actions they can take in utilizing the plan. ERISA requires that the SPD include the name and other identifying information about plan sponsors, administrators, and trustees, along with any information related to collective bargaining agreements for the plan participants. The SPD must describe what eligibility requirements must be met for participating in the plan and for receiving benefits, as well as the circumstances under which participants would be disqualified or ineligible for participation or be denied benefits.

The SPD must also describe the financing source for the plan and the name of the organization providing benefits. Information on the end of the plan year and whether records are maintained on a calendar, plan, or fiscal year basis must be included in the description.

For health and welfare plans, the SPD must describe claim procedures, along with the name of the U.S. Department of Labor (DOL) office that will assist participants and beneficiaries with Health Insurance Portability and Accountability Act (HIPAA) claims. The SPD must also describe what remedies are available when claims are denied.

A new SPD reflecting all changes made must be prepared and distributed every five years unless no changes have occurred. Every 10 years, a new SPD must be distributed to participants whether or not changes have occurred.

Annual Reports

ERISA requires annual reports (Form 5500) to be filed for all employee benefit plans. The reports must include financial statements, the number of employees in the plan, and the names and addresses of the plan fiduciaries. ERISA mandates that any persons compensated by the plan (such as an accountant) during the preceding year be disclosed, along with the amount of compensation paid to each, the nature of the services rendered, and any relationship that exists between these parties and any party in interest to the plan. Information that is provided with regard to plan assets must be certified by the organization that holds the assets, whether it is the plan sponsor, an insurance company, or a bank.

The annual report must be summarized and distributed to plan participants. The summary annual report (SAR) provides participants with an overview of the plan's financial status and operations.

The annual reports must be audited by a CPA or other qualified public accountant, and any actuarial reports must be prepared by an enrolled actuary who has been licensed jointly by the Department of the Treasury and the Department of Labor to provide actuarial services for U.S. pension plans.

Once submitted, annual reports and other documents become public record and are made available in the DOL public document room. The DOL may also use this information to conduct research and analyze data.

Participant Benefit Rights Reports

Participants may request a report of the total benefits accrued on their behalf along with the amount of the benefit that is nonforfeitable. If there are no nonforfeitable amounts accrued at the time the report is requested, the earliest date that benefits will become nonforfeitable must be provided. Participants are entitled to receive the report no more than once per year.

ERISA records must be maintained for six years from the date they were due to be filed with the DOL. In addition to requiring the preparation of these reports, ERISA regulations stipulate that annual reports are to be filed with the DOL within 210 days of the end of the plan year. The DOL may reject reports that are incomplete or that contain qualified opinions from the CPA or actuary. Rejected plans must be resubmitted within 45 days, or the DOL can retain a CPA to audit the report on behalf of the participants. ERISA authorizes the DOL to bring civil actions on behalf of plan participants if necessary to resolve any issues.

In addition to the reporting requirements, ERISA sets minimum standards for employee participation or eligibility requirements, as well as vesting requirements for qualified pension plans.

Employee Participation

A participant is an employee who has met the eligibility requirements for the plan. The law sets minimum participation requirements as follows:

- When one year of service has been completed or the employee has reached the age of 21, whichever is later, unless the plan provides for 100 percent vesting after two years of service. In that case, the requirement changes to completion of two years of service or reaching age 21, whichever is later.
- Employees may not be excluded from the plan on the basis of age; that is, they may not be excluded because they have reached a specified age.
- When employees have met the minimum service and age requirements, they must become participants no later than the first day of the plan year after they meet the requirement, or six months after the requirements are met, whichever is earlier.

Vesting

Qualified plans must also meet minimum vesting standards. Vesting refers to the point at which employees own the contributions their employer has made to the pension plan whether or not they remain employed with the company. The vesting requirements established by ERISA refer only to funds that are contributed by the employer; any funds contributed by plan participants are owned by the employee. Employees are always 100 percent vested in their own money but must earn the right to be vested in the employer's contribution.

Vesting may be immediate or delayed. Immediate vesting occurs when employees are 100 percent, or fully, vested as soon as they meet the eligibility requirements of the plan. Delayed vesting occurs when participants must wait for a defined period of time prior to becoming fully vested. There are two types of delayed vesting:

- With *cliff vesting*, participants become 100 percent vested after a specified period of time. ERISA sets the maximum period at five years for qualified plans, which means that participants are zero percent vested until they have completed the five years of service, after which they are fully vested.
- *Graded vesting*, which is also referred to as graduated or gradual vesting, establishes a vesting schedule that provides for partial vesting each year for a specified number of years. A graded vesting schedule in a qualified plan must allow for at least 20 percent vesting after three years and 20 percent per year after that, with participants achieving full vesting after seven years of service. See Table C.3 for a graded vesting schedule that complies with ERISA requirements.

TABLE C.3 ERISA graded vesting schedule

Years of service	Percent vested
3	20 percent
4	40 percent
5	60 percent
6	80 percent
7	100 percent

Benefit Accrual Requirements

ERISA sets specific requirements for determining how much of an accrued benefit participants are entitled to receive if they leave the company prior to retirement. Plans must account for employee contributions to the plan separately from the funds contributed by the employer since the employees are entitled to all the funds contributed by them to the plan when they leave the company.

Form and Payment of Benefits

ERISA sets forth specific requirements for the payment of funds when participants either reach retirement age or leave the company. The act also provides guidance for employers to deal with qualified domestic relations orders (QDROs), which are legal orders issued by state courts or other state agencies to require pension payments to alternate payees. An alternate payee must be a spouse, former spouse, child, or other dependent of a plan participant.

ERISA also defines funding requirements for pension plans and sets standards for those who are responsible for safeguarding the funds until they are paid to employees. Finally, ERISA provides civil and criminal penalties for organizations that violate its provisions.

Funding

An enrolled actuary determines how much money is required to fund the accrued obligations of the plan, and ERISA requires that these funds be maintained in trust accounts separate from a business's operating funds. These amounts must be deposited on a quarterly basis; the final contribution must be made no later than eight and a half months after the end of the plan year.

Fiduciary Responsibility

For purposes of ERISA, a fiduciary is a person, corporation, or other legal entity that holds property or assets on behalf of, or in trust for, the pension fund. ERISA requires fiduciaries to operate pension funds in the best interests of the participants and their beneficiaries and at the lowest possible expense to them. All actions taken with regard to the plan assets must be in accord with the prudent person standard of care, a common law concept that requires all actions be undertaken with "the care, skill, prudence, and diligence. . .that a prudent [person] acting in like capacity" would use, as defined in ERISA itself.

Fiduciaries may be held personally liable for losses to the plan resulting from any breach of fiduciary responsibility that they commit and may be required to make restitution for the losses and be subject to legal action. They are not held liable for breaches of fiduciary responsibility that occur prior to the time they became fiduciaries.

ERISA specifically prohibits transactions between pension plans and parties in interest.

Safe Harbor Provisions

The safe harbor provisions under ERISA provide a framework that exempts certain fiduciaries from liability for investment decisions made by participants in individual account plans, such as 401(k) plans. These provisions allow plan sponsors to offer a selection of investment options and require them to provide participants with sufficient information to make informed investment choices. By following specific guidelines—such as offering a diverse range of investment options and providing clear communication—plan sponsors can limit their liability for participants' investment losses, as long as the decisions were made independently by the participants.

Administration and Enforcement

The Employee Benefits Security Administration (EBSA) conducts investigations of criminal violations of ERISA, including kickbacks, false statements, and embezzlement. Criminal penalties for willful violations of ERISA include fines beginning at $5,000 and imprisonment. The decision to seek criminal actions are based on the egregiousness and magnitude of the violation; the desirability and likelihood of incarceration as a deterrent and as a punishment; and whether the case involves a prior ERISA violator. Civil actions may be brought by plan participants or their beneficiaries, by fiduciaries, or by the DOL to recover benefits or damages or to force compliance with the law.

Amendments to ERISA

Amendments to ERISA include COBRA and HIPAA.

Consolidated Omnibus Budget Reconciliation Act of 1986 (COBRA)

Prior to 1986, employees who were laid off or resigned from their jobs lost any healthcare benefits that were provided as part of those jobs. ERISA was amended in 1986 by the Consolidated Omnibus Budget Reconciliation Act (COBRA), which requires businesses with 20 or more employees to provide health plan continuation coverage under certain circumstances. Employers who meet this requirement must continue benefits for those who leave the company or for their dependents when certain qualifying events occur.

Employers must notify employees of the availability of COBRA coverage when they enter the plan and again within 30 days of the occurrence of a qualifying event. Table C.4 shows the qualifying events that trigger COBRA, as well as the length of time coverage must be continued for each event.

TABLE C.4 COBRA qualifying events and coverage requirements

Qualifying event	Length of coverage
Employee death	36 months
Divorce or legal separation	36 months
Dependent child no longer covered	36 months
Reduction in hours	18 months
Reduction in hours when disabled[a]	29 months
Employee termination	18 months
Employee termination when disabled[a]	29 months
Eligibility for SSA benefits	18 months
Termination for gross misconduct	0 months

[a] An employee who is disabled within 60 days of a reduction in hours or a termination becomes eligible for an additional 11 months of COBRA coverage.

Employers may charge COBRA participants a maximum of 102 percent of the group premium for coverage and must include them in any open enrollment periods or other changes to the plans. Employers may discontinue COBRA coverage if payments are not received within 30 days of the time they are due.

Employees must notify the employer within 60 days of a divorce, a separation, or the loss of a child's dependent status. Employees who fail to provide this notice risk the loss of continued coverage.

Health Insurance Portability and Accountability Act of 1996 (HIPAA)

The Health Insurance Portability and Accountability Act (HIPAA) was another amendment to ERISA and prohibits discrimination on the basis of health status as evidenced by an individual's medical condition or history, claims experience, utilization of healthcare services, disability, or evidence of insurability. It also places limits on health insurance restrictions for preexisting conditions, which are defined as conditions for which treatment was given within six months of enrollment in the plan. Insurers may exclude those conditions from coverage for 12 months or, in the case of a late enrollment, for 18 months.

Insurers may discontinue an employer's group coverage only if the employer neglects to pay the premiums, obtained the policy through fraudulent or intentional misrepresentation, or does not comply with material provisions of the plan. Group coverage may also be discontinued if the insurer is no longer offering coverage in the employer's geographic area, if none of the plan participants reside in the plan's network area, or if the employer fails to renew a collective bargaining agreement or to comply with its provisions.

In April 2001, the Department of Health and Human Services (HHS) issued privacy regulations that were required by HIPAA. The regulations defined protected health information (PHI), patient information that must be kept private, including physical or mental conditions, information about healthcare given, and payments that have been made. Although these regulations were directed at covered entities that conduct business electronically, such as health plans, healthcare providers, and clearinghouses, they have had a significant impact on the way employers handle information related to employee health benefits. Many employers had to redesign forms for open enrollment periods and new hires, and update plan documents and company benefit policies to reflect the changes. The regulations have an impact on employers in other ways as well.

Although flexible spending accounts (FSAs) are exempt from other HIPAA requirements, they are considered group health plans for privacy reasons, so employers who sponsor FSAs must comply with the privacy requirements for them.

Employers who are self-insured or who have fully insured group health plans and receive protected health information are required to develop privacy policies that comply with the regulations, appoint a privacy official, and train employees to handle information appropriately.

Although the HIPAA regulations do not prevent employees from seeking assistance from HR for claim problems or other issues with the group health plan, they do require employees to provide the insurance provider or third-party administrator with an authorization to release information about the claim to the HR department. Note that in 2023, plans were announced to update HIPAA regulations for healthcare organizations to improve cybersecurity performance goals to protect patient privacy.

The regulations include stiff civil and criminal sanctions for violations; civil penalties of $137 per violation and up to $68,928 depending on the level of culpability. There are three levels of criminal penalties:

- A conviction for obtaining or disclosing PHI can result in one year in prison.
- Obtaining PHI under false pretenses can result in five years in prison.
- Obtaining or disclosing PHI with the intent of selling, transferring, or using it to obtain commercial advantage or personal gain can be punished with up to 10 years in prison.

Executive Orders

Executive orders (EOs) are presidential proclamations that, when published in the Federal Register, become law after 30 days. EOs have been used to ensure that equal employment opportunities are afforded by federal agencies and private businesses that contract or subcontract with those agencies. Certain executive orders relating to equal employment issues are enforced by the OFCCP.

Executive Order 11246, Amended by 11375, 13279, and 13672 Executive Order 11246, issued in 1965, prohibits federal contractors from discriminating based on race, color, religion, sex, or national origin. It also requires them to take affirmative action to ensure equal employment opportunities. The order was later amended by Executive Orders 11375 (adding sex discrimination), 13279 (providing religious exemptions), and 13672 (expanding protections to include sexual orientation and gender identity). These amendments strengthen the rules, ensuring fair treatment for all workers in businesses that work with the federal government.

Executive Order 11478, Amended by 13087, 13152, and 13672 Executive Order 11478, issued in 1969, requires the federal government to provide equal employment opportunities for all employees, regardless of race, color, religion, sex, national origin, or age. Amendments to the order expanded protections: Executive Order 13087 added sexual orientation, Executive Order 13152 included parental status, and Executive Order 13672 added gender identity. These changes ensure that federal employees are treated fairly and without discrimination, promoting a more inclusive workplace in the federal government.

Executive Order 12138 In 1979, with the implementation of EO 12138, the National Women's Business Enterprise policy was created. This EO also required federal contractors and subcontractors to take affirmative steps to promote and support women's business enterprises.

Executive Order 12989, Amended by 13286 and 13465 This order requires contractors with qualifying federal contracts to electronically verify employment authorization of: (1) all employees hired during the contract term, and (2) all employees performing work in the United States on contracts with a Federal Acquisition Regulation (FAR)

E-Verify clause. A federal contractor may be exempt from these clauses if any of the following apply:

- The contract is for fewer than 120 days.
- It is valued at less than $150,000, the simplified acquisition threshold.
- All work is performed outside the United States.
- It includes only commercially available off-the-shelf (COTS) items and related services.

Fair Credit Reporting Act of 1970 (FCRA)

The Fair Credit Reporting Act of 1970 (FCRA) was first enacted in 1970 and has been amended several times since then, most recently with the Fair and Accurate Credit Transactions (FACT) Act in 2003. Enforced by the Federal Trade Commission (FTC), the FCRA requires employers to take certain actions prior to the use of a consumer report or an investigative consumer report obtained through a consumer reporting agency (CRA) for use in making employment decisions.

Familiarity with three terms is valuable for understanding why these consumer protection laws are important for HR practitioners:

- A consumer reporting agency (CRA) is an individual, business, or nonprofit association that gathers information about individuals with the intent of supplying that information to a third party.
- A consumer report is a written document produced by a CRA containing information about an individual's character, reputation, lifestyle, or credit history for use by an employer in determining that person's suitability for employment.
- An investigative consumer report is a written document produced by a CRA for the same purpose as a consumer report but is based on information gathered through personal interviews with friends, coworkers, employers, and others who are acquainted with the individual.

The FCRA established the following four-step process for employers to follow when using CRAs to perform background investigations:

1. A clear and conspicuous disclosure that a consumer report may be obtained for employment purposes must be made in writing to the candidate before the report is acquired.
2. The candidate must provide written authorization for the employer to obtain the report.
3. Before taking an adverse action based in whole or in part on the credit report, either the employer must provide the candidate with a copy of the report and a copy of the FTC notice, "A Summary of Your Rights Under the Fair Credit Reporting Act," or, if the application was made by mail, telephone, computer, or similar means, the employer must notify the candidate within three business days that adverse action is being taken

based in whole or in part on the credit report. This notice must provide the name, address, and telephone number of the CRA and indicate that the CRA did not take the adverse action and cannot provide the reasons for the action to the candidate. If a candidate requests a copy of the report, the employer must provide it within three days, along with a copy of the FTC notice just described.

4. Candidates must be advised of their right to dispute the accuracy of information contained in the report.

When employers request investigative consumer reports on candidates, they must comply with the following additional steps:

- Provide written disclosure of its intent to the candidate within three days of requesting the report from a CRA.
- Include a summary of the candidate's FCRA rights with the written notice.
- Advise the candidate that they have a right to request information about the type and extent of the investigation.
- If requested, provide complete disclosure of the type and extent of the report within the later of five days of the request or receipt of the report.

The FCRA was amended in 2003 by the Fair and Accurate Credit Transactions (FACT) Act of 2003. Designed to improve the accuracy of consumer credit information, it gives consumers one free credit report per year. The act also requires disclosure to consumers who are subject to risk-based pricing (less favorable credit offers) or who are denied credit altogether because of a credit-related record.

FACT describes "reasonable measures" for destroying credit reports, depending on the medium:

- Paper documents must be shredded, pulverized, or burned in a way that prevents them from being reassembled.
- Electronic files or media must be erased in a way that prevents them from being reconstructed.
- Either type may be destroyed by an outside vendor once the employer has conducted due diligence research to ensure the vendor's methods are reliable.

Fair Labor Standards Act of 1938 (FLSA)

Enacted in 1938, the Fair Labor Standards Act (FLSA) today remains a major influence on basic compensation issues for businesses in the United States. FLSA regulations apply to workers who are not already covered by another law. For example, railroad and airline employers are subject to wage and hour requirements of the Railway Labor Act, so the FLSA does not apply to their employees.

There are two categories of employers subject to the requirements of the FLSA: enterprise and individual. Enterprise coverage applies to businesses employing at least two employees with at least $500,000 in annual sales and to hospitals, schools, and government agencies.

Individual coverage applies to organizations whose daily work involves interstate commerce. The FLSA defines interstate commerce so broadly that it includes those who have regular contact by telephone with out-of-state customers, vendors, or suppliers; on that basis, it covers virtually all employers in the United States.

The FLSA established requirements in five key areas to HRM:

- It introduced a minimum wage for all covered employees.
- It identified the circumstances in which overtime payments are required and set the overtime rate at one and one half times the regular hourly wage.
- It identified the criteria for determining what jobs are exempt from FLSA requirements.
- It placed limitations on working conditions for children to protect them from exploitation.
- It identified the information employers must keep about employees and related payroll transactions.

Minimum Wage

The FLSA regulates the federal minimum wage, which is set at $7.25 per hour as of 2024. The federal minimum wage for tipped employees is $2.13 per hour, however, the tipped minimum wage and amount of tips must reach at least $7.25; if not, the employer must make up the difference. Some states, such as Alaska, California, and New York, have set the minimum wage at a higher rate than the federal government; when this is the case, the state requirement supersedes the federal minimum wage. The DOL provides a useful map showing current minimum wage requirements by state at `www.dol.gov/whd/minwage/america.htm`.

Nonexempt employees must be paid at least the minimum wage for all compensable time. The FLSA defines compensable time as the time an employee works that is "suffered or permitted" by the employer. For example, a nonexempt employee who continues to work on an assignment after the end of the business day to finish a project or make corrections must be paid for that time.

Maximum Hours and Overtime

The FLSA defined the maximum workweek for nonexempt employees as 40 hours per week and required overtime to be paid for any compensable time that exceeds that maximum. The FLSA defined overtime for nonexempt workers as one and one half times the regular hourly wage rate for all compensable time worked that exceeds 40 hours in a workweek (also commonly known as time and a half).

Although double-time, or two times regular pay, is not required by the FLSA, it may be required by some states or may be part of a labor agreement.

While the FLSA does not require payment of overtime for exempt employees, it also does not prohibit overtime payments for them. Employers who choose to compensate exempt employees for hours worked exceeding the regular workweek are free to do so without risking the loss of exemption status. As long as overtime payments are in addition to the regular salary, exemption status is not affected. Exempt overtime can be paid at straight time, at time and a half, or as a bonus.

State or local government agencies may compensate employees with what is known as compensatory time off, or comp time, instead of cash payment for overtime worked. For example, a road maintenance worker employed by a city government may work 20 hours of overtime during a snowstorm. Instead of being paid time and a half for the overtime hours, the employee may receive 30 hours of additional paid time off (1.5 times 20 hours) to be used just as paid vacation or sick leave. From time to time, initiatives to expand comp time to private employers are presented in Congress, but at this time, the FLSA does not permit private employers to use comp time.

Overtime calculations are based on time actually worked during the week. For example, in a week with a paid holiday, full-time nonexempt employees will actually work 32 hours even though they are paid for 40 hours. If some employees then work 6 hours on Saturday, for a total of 38 actual hours worked during the week, those hours are paid at straight time, not time and a half (unless, of course, a state law or union contract requires otherwise). This requirement also applies when employees use paid vacation or sick leave or some other form of paid time off (PTO).

To accurately calculate overtime payments, it is necessary to understand the difference between compensable time—hours that must be paid to nonexempt employees—and non-compensable time. The FLSA defines several situations for which nonexempt employees must be paid, such as the time spent preparing for or cleaning up after a shift by dressing in or removing protective clothing. Other types of compensable time include the following.

Waiting Time

Time spent by nonexempt employees waiting for work is compensable if it meets the FLSA definition of engaged to wait, which means that employees have been asked to wait for an assignment. For example, a marketing director may ask an assistant to wait for the conclusion of a meeting in order to prepare a Microsoft PowerPoint presentation needed for a client meeting early the next morning. If the assistant reads a book while waiting for the meeting to end, that time is still compensable.

Time that is spent by an employee who is waiting to be engaged is not compensable. For example, time spent by an employee who arrives at work 15 minutes early and reads the newspaper until the beginning of a shift is not considered to be compensable.

On-Call Time

The FLSA does not require employees who are on call away from the worksite and are able to effectively use the time for their own purposes to be paid for time they spend waiting to be called. These employees may be required to provide the employer with contact information. If, however, the employer places other constraints on the employee's activities, the time could be considered compensable.

Employees who are required to remain at or close to the worksite while waiting for an assignment are entitled to on-call pay. For example, medical interns required to remain at the hospital are entitled to payment for all hours spent at the hospital waiting for patients to arrive.

Rest and Meal Periods

Although rest and meal periods are not required by the FLSA, if they are provided, that time is subject to its requirements. Commonly referred to as breaks, short periods of rest lasting less than 20 minutes are considered compensable time. Meal periods lasting 30 minutes or longer are not compensable time unless the employee is required to continue working while eating. For example, a receptionist who is required to remain at the desk during lunch to answer the telephone must be paid for that time.

Lectures, Meetings, and Training Programs

Nonexempt employees are not required to be paid to attend training events when all four of the following conditions are met:

- The event takes place outside normal work hours.
- It is voluntary.
- It is not job-related.
- No other work is performed during the event.

Travel Time

Regular commute time (the time normally spent commuting from home to the regular worksite) is not compensable. There are, however, some situations in which the FLSA requires that nonexempt employees receive payment for travel time.

Emergency Travel from Home to Work

Any time an employee is required to return to work for an emergency after working a full day, the employee must be compensated for travel time.

One-Day Off-Site Assignments

When nonexempt employees are given a one-day assignment at a different location than their regular worksite, the travel time may be considered compensable in certain circumstances. For example, if an employee drives to the off-site assignment, the travel time is compensable, but if they are a passenger in the car, the travel time is not compensable.

Travel Between Job Sites

Nonexempt employees (such as plumbers or electricians) who are required to drive to different worksites to perform their regular duties must also be paid for the driving time between worksites.

Travel Away from Home

Travel away from home is defined as travel that keeps employees away from their homes overnight. When nonexempt employees must travel overnight, the FLSA considers the travel time during regular work hours as compensable time. This includes time traveled on non-workdays (weekends, for example) when it occurs during the employee's regular work hours. The DOL excludes the time spent outside of working hours as a passenger on an airplane, train, boat, bus, or automobile from compensable time calculations. If the employee is driving or working while traveling, the time is compensable.

Exemption Status

The FLSA covers all employees except those identified in the law as exempt from the regulations. All other employees are considered nonexempt and must be paid in accordance with FLSA requirements.

Certain positions may be exempt from one or all of the FLSA requirements (minimum wage, overtime, or child labor). For example, police officers and firefighters employed by small departments of fewer than five employees are exempt from overtime requirements but not exempt from the minimum wage requirement. On the other hand, newspaper delivery jobs are exempt from the minimum wage, overtime, and child labor requirements.

The determination of exemption status is often misunderstood by both employers and employees. Employers often think that they will save money by designating jobs as exempt and paying incumbent employees a salary. Employees often see the designation of a job as exempt as a measure of status within the company. Neither of these perceptions is accurate, and jobs that do not meet the legal exemption requirements can have costly consequences for employers.

To assist employers in properly classifying positions, the DOL regulations include exemption tests to determine whether a job meets those requirements and is therefore exempt from FLSA regulations.

The U.S. Department of Labor announced a significant update to overtime and minimum wage exemptions in 2023. On July 1, 2024, the minimum salary threshold for exempt executive, administrative, and professional employees rose from $684 per week ($35,568 annually) to $844 per week ($43,888 annually). It will further increase to $1,128 per week ($58,656 annually) by January 1, 2025. The total annual compensation threshold for highly compensated employees will also rise from $107,432 to $132,964, and subsequently to $151,164.

Note that only a month after the final rule was adopted, legal challenges sought to invalidate or, at minimum, delay implementation. It is important that you are well versed in the status of the law *at the time of your testing*, so check for the most recent updates at www.dol.gov.

Executive Exemption

Employees who meet the salary basis requirement may be exempt as executives if they meet all of the following requirements:

- They have as their primary duty managing the enterprise, or managing a customarily recognized department or subdivision of the enterprise.
- They customarily and regularly direct the work of at least two other full-time employees.

- They have the authority to hire, fire, promote, and evaluate employees or to provide input regarding those actions that carry particular weight.
- Employees who own at least a 20 percent equity interest in the organization and who are actively engaged in management duties are also considered bona fide exempt executives.

Administrative Exemption

Employees who meet the salary basis requirement may qualify for the administrative exemption if they meet all of the following requirements:

- The primary duty is to perform office or nonmanual work directly related to management or general business operations.
- The primary duty requires discretion and independent judgment on significant matters.

Professional Exemption

The DOL identifies two types of professionals who may qualify for exemption:

- **Learned Professional Exemption:** Employees who meet the salary basis requirement may qualify for exemption as learned professionals if they also meet both of the following criteria:
  - The primary duty requires the use of this advanced knowledge for work that requires the consistent use of discretion and judgment.
  - They have advanced knowledge in a field of science or learning acquired through a prolonged course of intellectual instruction.
- **Creative Professional Exemption:** Employees who meet the salary basis requirement may qualify for exemption as creative professionals if the primary duty requires invention, imagination, originality, or talent in a recognized field of artistic or creative endeavor.

Highly Compensated Employee Exemption

Highly compensated employees may also be considered exempt. To meet this exemption requirement, employees must perform office or nonmanual work and, on a customary and regular basis, at least one of the duties listed earlier for the executive, administrative, or professional exemptions.

NOTE

The salary threshold for highly compensated employees (HCEs) under the U.S. Department of Labor's final 2024 rule was increased. As of July 1, 2024, the threshold is $132,964. It will further increase to $151,164 per year by January 1, 2025. Additionally, automatic updates to these thresholds will occur every three years beginning in 2027.

Computer Employee Exemption

Employees who meet the weekly salary requirement ($684) or who are paid at least $27.63 per hour may qualify for the computer employee exemption if they perform one of the following jobs:

- Computer systems analyst
- Computer programmer
- Software engineer
- Other similarly skilled jobs in the computer field

and if they perform one or more of the following primary duties as part of the job:

- Apply systems analysis techniques and procedures, including consulting with users, to determine hardware, software, or system functional specifications.
- Design, develop, document, analyze, create, test, or modify computer systems or programs, including prototypes, based on and related to user or system design specifications.
- Design, document, test, create, or modify computer programs related to machine operating systems.
- Perform a combination of the previously described duties, at a level requiring the same skill.

Outside Sales Exemption

Unlike the other exemptions, there is no salary requirement for outside sales personnel. To qualify for this exemption, employees must meet both of the following requirements:

- The primary duty of the position must be making sales or obtaining orders or contracts for services or for the use of facilities for which a consideration will be paid by the client or customer.
- The employee must be customarily and regularly engaged away from the employer's place of business.

Salary Deductions

There are certain circumstances where an employer may make deductions from the pay of an exempt employee. The DOL defines permissible salary deductions as the following:

- Absence for one or more full days for personal reasons other than sickness or disability
- Absence for one or more full days because of sickness or disability if the deduction is made in accordance with a bona fide plan, policy, or practice of providing compensation for salary lost due to illness
- To offset amounts employees receive for jury or witness fees or military pay

- For good-faith penalties imposed for safety rule infractions of major significance
- Good-faith, unpaid disciplinary suspensions of one or more full days for infractions of workplace conduct rules
- During the initial or terminal weeks of employment when employees work less than a full week
- Unpaid leave under the Family and Medical Leave Act

Employers who have an "actual practice" of improper deductions risk the loss of exemption status for all employees in the same job classification, not just for the affected employee. The loss of exemption status will be effective for the time during which the improper deductions were made.

Actual Practice

The DOL looks at a variety of factors to determine whether employers have an actual practice of improper deductions from exempt pay. These factors include the following:

- The number of improper deductions compared to the number of employee infractions warranting deductions
- The time period during which the improper deductions were made
- The number of employees affected
- The geographic location of the affected employees and managers responsible for the deductions

Safe Harbor

The DOL provides a safe harbor provision for payroll errors that could affect exemption status. The safe harbor applies if all of the following are met:

- There is a clearly communicated policy prohibiting improper deductions that includes a complaint mechanism for employees to use.
- The employer reimburses employees for improper deductions.
- The employer makes a good-faith commitment to comply in the future.

Employers who meet these criteria will not lose exemption status for the affected employees unless they willfully violate the policy by continuing to make improper deductions after receiving employee complaints.

Child Labor

The FLSA regulates the employment of workers under the age of 18. Children 16 years of age and up may work for an unlimited amount of hours. Children of any age may work for businesses owned entirely by their parents, unless they would be employed in mining, manufacturing, or other hazardous occupations. There are no restrictions on a youth 18 years of age or older.

Children 14 and 15 years of age can work in nonmanufacturing, non-mining, and non-hazardous jobs outside of school hours if they work the following hours:

- No more than 3 hours on a school day or 18 hours in a workweek
- No more than 8 hours on a non-school day or 40 hours in a non-school workweek

During the school year, youths between the ages of 14 and 15 can work between 7 a.m. and 7 p.m. During the summer months, June 1 through Labor Day, the workday can be extended to 9 p.m.

Recordkeeping

There are two common methods for reporting time worked: positive time reporting, in which employees record the actual hours they are at work along with vacation, sick, or other time off, and exception reporting, in which only changes to the regular work schedule are recorded, such as vacation, sick, or personal time. Although the DOL regulations accept either method, in general the positive time method is best for nonexempt employees because it leaves no doubt as to actual hours worked by the employee and protects both the employee and the employer if there is ever a question about overtime payments due. Exception reporting is more appropriate for exempt employees because their pay is not based on hours worked.

The FLSA does not prevent employers from tracking the work time of exempt employees. These records may be used for billing customers, for reviewing performance, or for other administrative purposes, but they may not be used to reduce pay based on the quality or quantity of work produced. Reducing the salary invalidates the exemption status and subjects the employee to all requirements of the FLSA.

The FLSA requires the maintenance of accurate records by all employers. The information that must be maintained includes the following:

- Personal information, including full name, Social Security number (SSN), home address, occupation, sex, and date of birth if younger than 19 years old
- The hour and day when the workweek begins
- The total hours worked each workday and each workweek
- The basis on which employee's wages are paid (e.g., "$15 per hour" or "$640 per week")
- The total daily or weekly straight-time earnings
- The regular hourly pay rate for any week, including overtime
- Total overtime pay for the workweek
- Deductions and additions to wages
- Total wages paid each pay period
- The pay period dates and payment date

These FLSA records are usually maintained by the payroll department. Records must be preserved for at least three years. They must include payroll records, collective bargaining agreements, and sales and purchase records.

Penalties and Recovery of Back Wages

It is not uncommon for an employer to make an inadvertent error in calculating employee pay. In most cases when that happens, the employer corrects the error as soon as the employee points it out or the employer catches the error in some other way. Although distressing for employees, employers who make a good-faith effort to rectify the error in a timely manner remain within FLSA requirements.

In other cases, employers intentionally violate FLSA regulations by either paying employees less than the minimum wage, not paying overtime, or misclassifying employees as exempt to avoid overtime costs. These and other employee complaints about wage payments are investigated by state or federal agencies. If the complaints are justified, the employers are required to pay retroactive overtime pay and penalties to the affected employees. The investigation of a complaint by a single employee at an organization can trigger a government audit of the employer's general pay practices and exemption classification of its other employees and may result in additional overtime payments or penalties to other employees if they are found to be misclassified.

Employees whose complaints are verified can recover back wages using one of the following four methods the FLSA provides. The least expensive cost to the employer requires payment of the back wages.

- The Wage and Hour Division of the DOL can supervise the payment of back wages.
- The DOL can file a lawsuit for the amount of back wages and liquidated damages equal to the back wages.
- Employees can file private lawsuits to recover the wages plus an equal amount of liquidated damages, attorney fees, and court costs.
- The DOL can file an injunction preventing an employer from unlawfully withholding minimum wage and overtime payments.

There is a two-year statute of limitations for back pay recovery unless the employer willfully violated the FLSA. In those cases, the statute extends to three years. Employers may not terminate or retaliate against employees who file FLSA complaints. Willful violators of the FLSA may face criminal prosecution and be fined up to $10,000; if convicted a second time, the violator may face imprisonment. A civil penalty of up to $1,100 per violation may be assessed against willful or repeat violators.

FLSA Amendments

The FLSA has been amended numerous times since 1938, most often to raise the minimum wage to a level consistent with changes in economic conditions. Two significant federal amendments have been added to the FLSA since 1938: the Portal to Portal Act and the Equal

Pay Act. Additionally, the Patient Protection and Affordable Care Act, commonly referred to as Obamacare, affected the FLSA requirements.

Portal to Portal Act (1947)

The Portal to Portal Act clarified what was considered to be compensable work time and established that employers are not required to pay for employee commute time. This act requires employers to pay nonexempt employees who perform regular work duties before or after their regular hours or for working during their lunch period.

Equal Pay Act (EPA) (1963)

The Equal Pay Act, the first antidiscrimination act to protect women, prohibits discrimination on the basis of sex. Equal pay for equal work applies to jobs with similar working conditions, skill, effort, and responsibilities. The Equal Pay Act applies to employers and employees covered by FLSA and is administered and enforced by the Equal Employment Opportunity Commission (EEOC). The EPA allows differences in pay when they are based on a bona fide seniority system, a merit system, a system that measures quantity or quality of production, or any other system that fairly measures factors other than sex. Prior to the EPA, the comparable worth standard was used by the U.S. government to make compensation decisions. When Congress passed the EPA, it deliberately rejected the comparable worth standard in favor of the equal pay standard.

The first act signed by former President Obama was the Lilly Ledbetter Fair Pay Act. The purpose of this act was to restore the protection against pay discrimination by clarifying that the 180-day statute of limitations for filing an equal-pay lawsuit resets with each new discriminatory paycheck.

Patient Protection and Affordable Care Act (PPACA) (2010)

In March 2010, President Barack Obama signed into law the Patient Protection and Affordable Care Act (PPACA). Largely intended as substantial healthcare reform, it included provisions for lactation accommodation in the workplace. The amendment requires that employers provide a reasonable break time for an employee to express breast milk for her nursing child for one year after the child's birth each time such employee has need to express the milk, and an appropriate place (other than a bathroom) that provides privacy.

There is some dispute as to whether this time must be paid, however. While the amendment states that the time need not be compensated, current FLSA language reads otherwise: "Rest periods of short duration, generally running from 5 minutes to about 20 minutes, are common in industry. They promote the efficiency of the employee and are customarily paid for as work time. It is immaterial with respect to compensability of such breaks whether the employee drinks coffee, smokes, goes to the rest room, etc." This is an excellent example of when existing employment practices must be considered when applying the law. For example, if an employer allows additional paid break time for employees who smoke (unprotected activity), it may be prudent for said employer to count lactation accommodation (protected activity) as paid time as well.

Family and Medical Leave Act of 1993 (FMLA)

In 1993, President Bill Clinton signed the Family and Medical Leave Act (FMLA), which was created to assist employees in balancing the needs of their families with the demands of their jobs. In creating the FMLA, Congress intended that employees should not have to choose between keeping their jobs and attending to seriously ill family members.

In addition to protecting employees from adverse employment actions and retaliation when they request leave under the FMLA, the act provides three benefits for eligible employees in covered organizations:

- Twelve weeks of unpaid leave within a 12-month period (26 months for military caregiver leave)
- Continuation of health benefits
- Reinstatement to the same position or an equivalent position at the end of the leave

Designation of FMLA Leave

Employers are responsible to designate leave requests as FMLA-qualified based on information received from employees or someone designated by employees to speak on their behalf. When the employee does not provide enough information for the employer to determine if the leave is for a reason protected by the FMLA, it is up to the employer to request additional information. The FMLA regulations do not require employees to specifically request FMLA leave, but they must provide enough information to allow the employer to determine if the request is protected by the FMLA. If leave is denied based on a lack of information, it is up to the employee to provide enough additional information for the employer to ascertain that the leave is protected by the FMLA.

The regulations allow employers to retroactively designate leave as FMLA-qualified, as long as sufficient notice is given to the employee and the retroactive designation does not cause harm or injury to the employee. The retroactive designation can be made by mutual agreement between the employee and employer. When an employer fails to appropriately designate that a leave is FMLA-qualified at the time of the employee's request, the employee may be entitled to any loss of compensation and benefits caused by the employer's failure. This can include monetary damages, reinstatement, promotion, or other suitable relief.

Failure to Designate in a Timely Manner

In 2008, the FMLA was amended by the National Defense Authorization Act (NDAA). One of the changes incorporated the Supreme Court ruling in *Ragsdale v. Wolverine Worldwide, Inc.*, a case that addressed what happens when an employer fails to designate a leave as FMLA-qualified in a timely manner. Prior to the *Ragsdale* case, some employees interpreted the regulations in a way that required employers to provide more than the 12 weeks of unpaid leave required by the FMLA. The regulations now state that, if an employer neglects to designate leave as FMLA, employees who are harmed may be entitled to restitution for their losses.

Waiver of Rights

Prior to the 2008 changes, the DOL required any settlement of past claims, even those mutually agreeable to both parties, to be approved by either the DOL or a court. The 2008 final rules amend this, allowing employers and employees who mutually agree on a resolution to settle past claims between them, avoiding costly and unnecessary litigation. However, the regulations do not permit employees to waive their future FMLA rights.

Substitution of Paid Leave

DOL regulations permit employees to request, or employers to require, the use of all accrued paid vacation, personal, family, medical, or sick leave concurrently with the FMLA leave. Eligible employees who do not qualify to take paid leave according to policies established by their employers are still entitled to the unpaid FMLA leave.

Perfect Attendance Awards

Employers may now deny perfect attendance awards to employees whose FMLA leave disqualifies them as long as employees who take non-FMLA leave are treated the same way.

Light-Duty Assignments

Under the Family and Medical Leave Act (FMLA), the final ruling on light-duty work assignments states that employers are not required to offer or provide light-duty assignments as an alternative to FMLA leave. Employees who cannot perform the essential functions of their original position due to a physical or mental condition are not entitled to restoration to a different, light-duty position under the FMLA. If an employee accepts a light-duty assignment, this does not count against their FMLA leave entitlement, and their right to job restoration is held in abeyance during the light-duty period. Note that the right to FMLA is absolute, meaning that an employee cannot be compelled to forfeit their leave for a light-duty assignment.

Recordkeeping Requirements

FMLA leave records must be kept in accordance with recordkeeping standards established by the Fair Labor Standards Act (FLSA) and may be maintained in employee personnel files. The FMLA does not require submission of FMLA leave records unless requested by the DOL, but they must be maintained and available for inspection, copying, or transcription by DOL representatives for no less than three years. The DOL may not require submission more than once during any 12-month period without a reasonable belief that a violation has occurred.

Employers Covered

The FMLA applies to all public agencies and schools, regardless of their size, and to private employers with 50 or more employees working within a 75-mile radius. The law provides detailed descriptions on how employers determine whether these requirements apply to them.

Fifty or More Employees

Employers must comply with the FMLA when they employ 50 or more employees for each working day during each of 20 or more calendar workweeks in the current or preceding year. The statute does not require the workweeks to be consecutive. Guidelines in the FMLA count the number of employees at a worksite as being determined by the number of employees on the payroll for that site.

Employers remain subject to FMLA rules until the number of employees on the payroll is less than 50 for 20 nonconsecutive weeks in the current and preceding calendar year. This means that if employers with 50 employees on the payroll for the first 20 weeks in 2025 reduce the number of employees for the rest of 2025 and remain at the reduced level throughout 2026, they must continue to comply with FMLA through the end of 2026.

Worksites within a 75-Mile Radius

The number of employees at each worksite is based on the employees who report to work at that site or, in the case of outside sales representatives or employees who telecommute, the location from which their work is assigned. This can be either a single place of business or a group of adjacent locations, such as a business park or campus.

A worksite may also consist of facilities that are not directly connected if they are in reasonable geographic proximity, are used for the same purpose, and share the same staff and equipment.

Employees such as construction workers or truck drivers who regularly work at sites away from the main business office are counted as employees in one of the three following ways:

- At the business site to which they report
- At the worksite that is their home base
- At the site from which their work is assigned

However, these employees may not be counted at a worksite where they may be temporarily deployed for the duration of a project.

Notice Obligations

Employers have two notice obligations for the FMLA: The first obligation is to inform employees of their FMLA rights and the second requires specific information to be provided in response to an FMLA leave request.

Informational Notice

Upon hire, employers must provide employees with a general informational notice in two formats. The DOL provides a poster (WH Publication 1420) explaining FMLA rights and responsibilities. Employers must post this information in an area frequented by employees.

Employers must also provide information about employee rights and responsibilities in the employee handbook, collective bargaining agreement (CBA), or other written documents. When an employer does not have a handbook or CBA, DOL provides Fact Sheet #28, a four-page summary of the FMLA that the employer may distribute to employees.

Notice in Response to Leave Request

Once an employee requests an FMLA leave, the final rules require employers to respond within five business days. At this time, employers must inform employees of their eligibility, rights, and responsibilities for an FMLA leave, and designate the leave as FMLA. The DOL provides two forms for this purpose: WH-381 and WH-382.

The eligibility, rights, and responsibilities notice (Form WH-381) informs employees of the following:

- The date of leave request, and beginning and ending dates of the leave
- The reason for the leave (birth or adoption of a child or serious health condition of employee or family member)
- Employee rights and responsibilities under the FMLA
- That employee contributions toward health insurance premiums continue and whether or not the employee will be required to reimburse the employer for premiums paid if the employee does not return to work after the leave
- Whether or not the employer will continue other benefits
- Whether or not the employee is eligible for an FMLA leave
- Whether or not the employee is designated as a *key employee* and therefore may not be restored to employment upon the end of the leave
- Whether or not the employer requires periodic reports on the employee's status and intention to return to work

The designation notice (Form WH-382) informs employees of the following:

- Whether or not the requested leave will be counted against their FMLA leave entitlement
- Whether or not a medical certification is required

- Whether or not the employer requires them to use their accrued paid leave for the unpaid FMLA leave; if not required, whether or not the employee chooses to substitute accrued paid leave for all or part of the FMLA leave
- Whether or not the employer requires a fitness-for-duty certificate prior to the employee's return to work

Employers are not required to use the DOL forms, but if a substitute form is used, it must include all information required by the regulations.

Employers may not revoke an employee's eligibility, once confirmed. Similarly, if an employer neglects to inform an employee that they are ineligible for FMLA leave prior to the date the leave begins, the employee is considered eligible to take the leave, and the employer may not deny it at that point.

Employees Eligible for FMLA

The FMLA also provides guidelines for determining which employees are eligible for leave. This includes employees who:

- Work for an employer that is subject to FMLA as described previously.
- Have been employed by the employer for at least 12 months, which need not be consecutive, but time worked prior to a break in service of seven or more years does not need to be counted unless the service break was to fulfill a military service obligation. Employees who received benefits or other compensation during any part of a week are counted as having been employed for that week.
- Worked at least 1,250 hours during the 12 months immediately preceding the leave, based on the FLSA standards for determining compensable hours of work. If accurate time records are not maintained, it is up to the employer to prove that the employee did not meet the requirement; if this is not possible, the law provides that the employee will be presumed to have met the requirement. The determination of whether an employee meets the requirement for 1,250 hours of work within the past 12 months is counted from the date the leave begins.

Key Employee Exception

An FMLA leave is available to all employees of covered organizations who meet the FMLA eligibility requirements. FMLA includes a provision that key employees may be denied reinstatement to the position they held or an equivalent position if the employer demonstrates that the reinstatement would cause "substantial and grievous economic injury" to its operations. A key employee is defined by FMLA as a salaried employee among the highest-paid 10 percent of employees at the worksite as defined previously. The law requires that the determination of which employees are the highest paid is calculated by taking the employee's year-to-date earnings (base salary, premium pay, incentive pay, and bonuses) and dividing the total earnings by the number of weeks worked. Whether an employee meets the definition of a key employee is to be determined at the time leave is requested. The employee must be advised of this status, either in person or by certified mail, as soon as possible. The employer must also explain why restoring the employee's job will cause substantial and grievous economic injury.

If the employee decides to take the leave after being informed of the implications of key employee status, the employee may still request reinstatement upon return to work. The employer must review the circumstances again and, if substantial and grievous economic injury would still occur under the circumstances at that time, notify the employee in writing, in person, or by certified mail that restoration is denied.

Key employees continue to be protected by the FMLA unless they notify their employer that they will not return to work, or until the employer denies reinstatement at the end of the leave.

Employee Notice Requirement

One FMLA requirement that caused difficulty for employers was an interpretation of previous rules that employees had up to two full days after an FMLA-qualifying event occurred to notify their employers of the need for FMLA leave. This made it difficult for employers to meet production schedules and ensure necessary coverage of critical work needs.

The 2008 final rules eliminated this language and clarified the timing of employee notices for two situations: foreseeable and unforeseeable leaves. In either case, employees must provide verbal notice so that the employer is aware of the need for FMLA-qualified leave, the expected timing and length of the leave, and information about the medical condition described in the upcoming section, "Reasons for FMLA Leave." Employees are not required to specifically request FMLA leave or mention FMLA for the first occurrence of a qualified event, but they are required to answer reasonable questions about the need for leave so that employers can determine whether the leave is qualified under the FMLA.

Foreseeable Leave

When the need for leave is foreseeable, FMLA rules require employees to notify their employers at least 30 days prior to the anticipated start date of leaves such as for the birth of a child, adoption, placement of a foster child, or planned medical treatment for a serious health condition. If the circumstances surrounding the planned leave change (such as a child is born earlier than expected), notice must be given as soon as practicable. This means as soon as both practical and possible, on the same day or the next business day. In these circumstances, a family member or someone else representing the employee may provide notice.

If the leave is foreseeable more than 30 days in advance and an employee fails to provide notice at least 30 days in advance without a reasonable excuse for delaying, the employer may delay FMLA coverage until 30 days after the date the employee provided notice.

If the need for FMLA leave is foreseeable less than 30 days in advance and the employee fails to notify the employer as soon as practicable, the employer may delay FMLA coverage of the leave. The amount of delay depends on the circumstances of each leave request and is evaluated on a case-by-case basis. Generally, the employer may delay the start of FMLA leave by the amount of delay in notice by the employee.

Unforeseeable Leave

At times, employees may be unable to notify their employers of the need for FMLA leave in advance. In these circumstances, the 2008 change to FMLA rules requires employees to provide notice in accordance with the usual and customary practice for calling in an absence unless unusual circumstances prevent the employee from doing so. An employee's representative, such as a spouse or another responsible person, may provide the notice if the employee is unable to do so. In emergencies when employees are unable to contact employers, they are permitted to supply the notice when they are able to use a telephone.

In order for employees to provide notice in accordance with the regulations, they must be aware of their responsibility to do so. The FMLA provides that proper posting of FMLA notice requirements by employers satisfies this requirement. Employers may waive FMLA notice requirements or their own rules on notice for employee leaves of absence at their discretion. In the absence of unusual circumstances, employers may choose not to waive their internal notice rules for employees who fail to follow those rules when requesting FMLA leaves, as long as those actions are consistent with practices regarding other leave requests. This is acceptable under the regulations as long as the actions do not discriminate against employees taking FMLA leave or violate the FMLA requirements described earlier.

Reasons for FMLA Leave

FMLA presents covered employers with a list of circumstances under which FMLA leave must be provided if requested by an eligible employee. Passage of the 2008 NDAA added care for military personnel and their families in some circumstances to existing circumstances that qualify for leave:

- **The Birth of a Child and Caring for the Infant:** FMLA leave is available to both fathers and mothers; however, if both parents work for the same employer, the combined total of the leave may not exceed the 12-week total. In addition, the leave must be completed within 12 months of the child's birth.
- **Placement of an Adopted or Foster Child with the Employee:** The same conditions that apply to the birth of a child apply here as well; in this case, the leave must be completed within 12 months of the child's placement.
- **To Provide Care for the Employee's Spouse, Son, Daughter, or Parent With a Serious Health Condition:** For purposes of FMLA leave, a spouse must be recognized as such by the state in which the employee resides.

A parent can be the biological parent of the employee or one who has legal standing *in loco parentis*, a Latin term that means "in place of the parent" and applies to those who care for a child on a daily basis. *In loco parentis* does not require either a biological or a legal relationship.

A son or daughter may be a biological child, adopted or foster child, stepchild, legal ward, or the child of someone acting *in loco parentis*. A child must also be younger than 18 years of age or, if older than 18, unable to care for themself because of a physical or mental disability. Under the FMLA, persons who are *in loco parentis* include those with day-to-day responsibilities to care for or financially support a child. Courts have indicated some factors to be considered in determining *in loco parentis* status:

- The age of the child
- The degree to which the child is dependent on the person
- The amount of financial support, if any, provided
- The extent to which duties commonly associated with parenthood are exercised

In a 2015 amendment to the definition of spouse, eligible employees in legal same-sex marriages are able to take FMLA leave to care for their spouse or family member, regardless of where they live. The 2015 change means that eligible employees, regardless of where they live, will be able to take:

- FMLA leave to care for their lawfully married same-sex spouse with a serious health condition
- Qualifying exigency leave due to their lawfully married same-sex spouse's covered military service
- Military caregiver leave for their lawfully married same-sex spouse
- FMLA leave to care for their stepchild (child of employee's same-sex spouse) regardless of whether the *in loco parentis* requirement of providing day-to-day care or financial support for the child is met
- FMLA leave to care for a stepparent who is a same-sex spouse of the employee's parent, regardless of whether the stepparent ever stood *in loco parentis* to the employee

Employers may require those employees requesting FMLA leave to provide reasonable documentation to support the family relationship with the person for whom they will be providing care.

Employees may qualify for FMLA leave for their own serious health condition, defined as an illness, injury, impairment, or a physical or mental condition that requires the following:

- Inpatient care or subsequent treatment related to inpatient care
- Continuing treatment by a healthcare provider because of a period of incapacity of more than three consecutive calendar days. Incapacity refers to an inability to work, attend school, or perform other daily activities as a result of the condition.
- Incapacity because of pregnancy or prenatal care
- Treatment for a serious, chronic health condition

FMLA time is available to employees who need to provide care for a covered service member with a serious injury or illness sustained while on active duty. In this situation, family members are eligible to take up to 26 weeks of leave in a 12-month period.

Additionally, FMLA-protected time is available to eligible employees for qualifying exigencies for families of members of the National Guard and Reserves. Qualifying exigencies include the following:

- Short-notice deployments
- Military events and related activities
- Child care and school activities
- Financial and legal arrangements
- Counseling
- Rest and recuperation
- Post-deployment activities
- Leave for other related purposes when agreed to by the employee and employer

Medical Certification Process

FMLA regulations allow employers to require medical certifications to verify requests for any qualified leave as long as the employee is notified of the requirements. The DOL provides the following forms for this purpose:

- WH-380-E (for employee's serious health condition)
- WH-380-F (for family member's serious health condition)
- WH-384 (for exigency leave for military families)
- WH-385 (for serious injury or illness to covered service member)

Employers should request initial certification within five business days of the employee's leave request. Additional certifications may be required at a later date to verify that the leave continues to be appropriate. Employers must provide at least 15 calendar days for the employee to submit the certification but may allow more time.

FMLA regulations require employees to provide "complete and sufficient" certification for the employer. If the certification does not meet the complete and sufficient standard, employers may request, in writing, the additional information needed to comply. A certification is not considered complete and sufficient if one or more of the entries on the form are not completed or if the information is vague, ambiguous, or nonresponsive. Employees must be allowed a minimum of seven days to return the form with the additional information. When employers request the certification or additional information, they must advise employees of the consequences for failing to provide adequate certification of the serious illness or injury. If employees do not return the certification or they fail to provide a complete and sufficient certification upon notice of deficiencies in what was submitted, FMLA regulations allow employers to deny the FMLA leave.

Employers are not required to use the DOL forms but may only request information that is directly related to the serious health condition necessitating the leave, including the following:

- Contact information for the healthcare provider.
- Approximate date the serious health condition began and an estimate of how long it will last.

- A description of the medical facts about the health condition, such as symptoms, diagnosis, hospitalization, doctor visits, prescribed medication, treatment referrals, or continuing treatments.
- For employees with serious health conditions, the certification must establish the inability to perform essential job functions, describe work restrictions, and indicate the length of the inability to perform job functions.
- For family members with serious health conditions, the certification must establish that the patient requires care, how often, and how long care will be necessary.
- Information that confirms the medical necessity for reduced or intermittent leave with estimated dates and length of treatment.

FMLA leave certifications may be complicated when workers' compensation, ADA, or employer-provided paid leave programs are used concurrently. FMLA regulations address certifications under these circumstances as follows:

- When FMLA runs concurrently with a workers' compensation leave, employers are prohibited from collecting information for workers' compensation purposes that exceeds what is allowed for FMLA purposes.
- Employers may require additional information in accordance with a paid leave or disability program but must advise employees that the additional information is required in conjunction with the paid-leave plan, not with the FMLA leave. Whatever information is collected may be used to evaluate continuation of the FMLA leave. Failure to provide the additional information does not affect continuation of the FMLA leave.
- When FMLA leave runs concurrently with ADA, employers may follow ADA procedures for collecting information. This information may be used to evaluate the claim for FMLA-protected leave.

Employees are responsible for providing their own medical certifications. If they choose to do so, they may provide employers with an authorization or release to obtain information directly from their healthcare providers, but employers may not require them to do so.

Types of FMLA Leave

FMLA provides for three types of leave: continuous, reduced leave, and intermittent. A *continuous FMLA leave* is one in which the employee is absent from work for an extended period of time. A reduced *FMLA leave schedule* is one in which the employee's regular work schedule is reduced for a period of time. This can mean a reduction in the hours worked each day or in the number of days worked during the week. An *intermittent FMLA leave* is one in which the employee is absent from work for multiple periods of time because of a single illness or injury. When utilizing intermittent leave, employees must make an effort to schedule the leave to avoid disruption of regular business operations. In addition, the employer may assign an employee requesting intermittent leave to a different position with equivalent pay and benefits in order to meet the employee's needs.

Calculating the FMLA Year

FMLA provides four possible methods for employers to use in calculating the FMLA year, the 12-month period during which employees may use the 12 weeks of leave. An FMLA year can be calculated as any of the following:

- The calendar year
- Any fixed 12-month period (such as the fiscal year or anniversary date)
- The 12-month period beginning when an FMLA leave begins
- A rolling 12-month period that is measured back from the date FMLA is used by an employee

Although the most difficult to administer, for many employers the rolling 12-month period is best. Other methods are more open to abuse of FMLA by some employees, resulting in the use of 24 weeks of leave by bridging two 12-month periods, allowing an employee to be on continuous FMLA leave for 24 weeks.

If an employer does not have a stated policy, the FMLA year must be calculated in the way that provides the most benefit to employees. Whichever method is selected, it must be used to calculate FMLA for all employees. Employers that decide to change the way they calculate the FMLA year must provide written notice to employees 60 days in advance of the change and obtain written acknowledgment of the change.

Tracking Reduced and Intermittent FMLA Leave

Although keeping track of the amount of FMLA used for a continuous leave is fairly straightforward, ensuring that accurate records of reduced and intermittent FMLA records are maintained can be a bit more difficult. In either case, only the amount of leave used may be deducted from the 12 weeks available to the employee. For example, an employee whose regular work schedule of 40 hours per week is reduced to 20 hours per week would be charged one-half week FMLA leave for each week that the employee works the reduced schedule.

For intermittent leave, employers may charge for leave in increments of not less than one hour. Employees should provide at least two days' notice of the need to utilize the intermittent leave whenever possible.

Ending FMLA Leave

FMLA leave ends when the employee has used the full 12 weeks of leave, the serious illness of the employee or family member ends, or, in some cases, when the family member or the employee dies. When one of these three circumstances occurs (other than the employee's own death), the employee may return to the same or an equivalent position with no loss of benefits. If the employee wants to continue the leave at that point, the company is under no obligation to grant it, unless there is a company policy in place to provide a longer leave.

Employers may require employees returning from FMLA leaves to provide a fitness-for-duty certification from their healthcare providers, attesting to their ability to return to work. If they choose to do so, employers may require the fitness-for-duty report to specify the employee's ability to perform the essential functions of the job. Employers that choose this type of certification must provide a job description or list of the employee's essential job functions with the designation notice provided to the employee. Similarly to medical certifications, employers may contact healthcare providers to clarify and authenticate information contained in the fitness-for-duty certificate, but they may not request information unrelated to the serious health condition that is the reason for the FMLA leave. Employees may be required to provide the fitness-for-duty certification prior to returning to work. Employees who neither provide the certificate nor request an extension of the leave are no longer entitled to reinstatement.

FMLA Implications for Employers

HR professionals need to ensure that supervisors and managers throughout their organizations are aware of the requirements for FMLA leaves and the consequences for noncompliance. FMLA requirements are complex and confusing, particularly when used in conjunction with workers' compensation or the ADA, and managers of other functional areas may not be aware of their obligations for FMLA requests.

There are some things employers can do to ensure that they comply with FMLA requirements. To start, review current leave practices to ensure that they comply with FMLA requirements and any state laws with more stringent requirements. FMLA leave policies should be included in the employee handbook; new hires must be advised of their rights to take leave under the act. It is important for HR professionals to work with supervisors and managers throughout the organization to ensure that they understand the implications for situations that may be subject to FMLA regulations and encourage them to talk to HR about potential FMLA leave situations. HR needs to take an active role in educating the management team about the interaction of FMLA, ADA, and workers' compensation requirements. Before an FMLA situation occurs, a documentation procedure and policy should be developed, and HR should take an active role in ensuring that all leaves comply with established procedures to avoid possible claims of discriminatory practices. When workers' compensation and FMLA leaves occur simultaneously, make sure to advise the employee that the leaves run concurrently.

Foreign Corrupt Practices Act of 1977

The Foreign Corrupt Practices Act (FCPA) of 1977 made it unlawful for certain classes of people and entities to make payments to foreign government officials to assist in obtaining or retaining business. Made up of antibribery provisions, the FCPA prohibits people and entities from making any offer, payment, promise to pay, or authorization of the payment of money or anything of value to any person, while knowing that all or a portion of such money or thing of value will be offered, given or promised, directly or indirectly, to a foreign official to influence the foreign official in their official capacity, induce the foreign official to do or omit to do an act in violation of their lawful duty, or to secure any improper advantage in order to assist in obtaining or retaining business for or with, or directing business to, any person.

In 1988, amendments applied the antibribery provisions to foreign persons, prohibiting them from engaging in any of these activities within the United States.

The FCPA requires companies whose securities are listed in the United States to keep accurate records and maintain accounting controls to ensure that the records accurately and fairly represent corporate financial transactions.

Genetic Information Nondiscrimination Act of 2008 (GINA)

When research into the use of human genomic information made it possible to identify genetic predisposition to particular diseases, many people became uncomfortable with the idea of information so personal being made available to insurance companies or employers that could use it for discriminatory purposes. For more than 10 years, Congress worked on legislation that would prevent that from happening. President George W. Bush signed the resulting legislation, the Genetic Information Nondiscrimination Act (GINA), into law in May 2008.

GINA prohibits employers from unlawfully discriminating against employees or their family members in any of the terms or conditions of employment included in Title VII. The Act defines genetic information as the results of genetic tests for employees and their family members or as information about genetic diseases or disorders revealed through genetic testing.

The act makes it unlawful for employers to request, require, or purchase genetic information but does not penalize them for inadvertently obtaining the information. GINA allows employers to obtain the information for wellness or health programs they offer when the employee authorizes access to the information in writing. In those cases, the information obtained through genetic testing may be provided only to healthcare professionals or board-certified genetic counselors providing services to employees. This information may be provided to employers only in aggregate form that does not identify specific employees.

Employers may request the information as required by the Family and Medical Leave Act (FMLA) or similar state laws but may use it only as required by those laws. Employers can also use genetic information if federal or state laws require genetic monitoring of biological effects from toxic substances in the workplace, but only if the employee receives written notice and provides informed, written consent to the monitoring and the monitoring complies with federal and state laws. Any test results may be provided to employers only in aggregate form without identifying individual information.

The DOL issued a request for comments on the implementation of GINA prior to beginning the rule-making process. The submission period ended in December 2008, and the DOL began evaluating regulatory needs with the Department of Health and Human Services and the Treasury Department since aspects of the law impact agencies in those departments as well.

Glass Ceiling Act of 1991

In 1991, Senator Robert Dole introduced legislation known as the Glass Ceiling Act, which was eventually signed into law as an amendment to Title II of the Civil Rights Act of 1991.

An article in the *Wall Street Journal* in 1986 had coined the term *glass ceiling* to describe the limitations faced by women and minorities when it came to advancing into the senior ranks of corporate management. The act established a commission whose purpose was to determine whether a glass ceiling existed and, if it did, to identify the barriers to placing more women and minorities in senior management positions. The commission found that although CEOs understood the need to include women and minorities in the ranks of senior management, this belief was not shared at all levels in the organization. The study went on to identify three barriers that prevented women and minorities from advancing to senior levels:

Societal Barriers Societal barriers result from limited access to educational opportunities and biases related to gender, race, and ethnicity.

Internal Structural Barriers Internal structural barriers encompass a wide range of corporate practices and shortcomings over which management has some control, including outreach and recruiting programs that do not try to find qualified women and minorities, as well as organizational cultures that exclude women and minorities from participation in activities that will lead to advancement, such as mentoring, management training, or career development assignments.

Governmental Barriers Governmental barriers are related to inconsistent enforcement of equal opportunity legislation and poor collection and dissemination of statistics that illustrate the problem.

The commission also studied organizations that have successfully integrated glass ceiling initiatives into their operations and found some common traits that can be adopted by other organizations. Successful initiatives begin with full support of the CEO, who ensures that the initiative becomes part of strategic planning in the organization and holds management accountable for achieving goals by tracking and reporting on progress. These comprehensive programs do not exclude white men but do include a diverse workforce population. Organizations implementing programs to increase diversity benefit from improved productivity and bottom-line results for shareholders.

As a result of the study, the EEOC conducts glass ceiling audits to monitor the progress that organizations make toward including women and minorities at all levels.

Illegal Immigration Reform and Immigrant Responsibility Act of 1996 (IIRIRA)

The Illegal Immigration Reform and Immigrant Responsibility Act of 1996 reduced the number and types of documents allowable to prove identity, employment eligibility, or both in the hiring process and established pilot programs for verification of employment eligibility. It also allowed for sanctions against employers who failed to comply with the hiring requirements.

Immigration Reform and Control Act of 1986 (IRCA)

The Immigration Reform and Control Act (IRCA) was enacted in 1986 to address illegal immigration into the United States. The law applied to businesses with four or more employees and made it illegal to knowingly hire or continue to employ individuals who were not legally authorized to work in the United States. Unfair immigration-related employment practices were defined as discrimination on the basis of national origin or citizenship status.

Employers were required to complete Form I-9 for all new hires within the first three days of employment. Employers were also required to review documents provided by the employee that establish identity, employment authorization, or both from lists of acceptable documents on the Form I-9. IRCA requires employers to maintain I-9 files for three years from the date of hire or one year after the date of termination, whichever is later, and allows, but does not require, employers to copy documents presented for employment eligibility for purposes of complying with these requirements. The act also provides that employers complying in good faith with these requirements have an affirmative defense to inadvertently hiring an unauthorized alien. Substantial fines for violations of both the hiring and recordkeeping requirements were provided in the law.

In addition to fines, employers that knowingly hire unauthorized workers are subject to both civil and criminal penalties for the following violations:

- Civil Violations
  - Knowingly hired, or to have knowingly recruited or referred for a fee, an unauthorized noncitizen for employment in the United States or to have knowingly continued to employ an unauthorized noncitizen in the United States
  - Failing to comply with Form I-9 employment verification requirements
  - Committing or participating in document fraud for satisfying a requirement or benefit of the employment verification process or the INA
  - Committing document abuse
  - Unlawful discrimination against an employment-authorized individual in hiring, firing, or recruitment or referral for a fee
  - Failing to notify DHS of a Final Nonconfirmation (FNC) of an employee's employment eligibility
  - Requiring an individual to post a bond or security or to pay an amount or otherwise to provide financial guarantee or indemnity against any potential liability arising under the employment verification requirements
- Criminal Violations
  - Engaging in a pattern or practice of hiring, recruiting or referring for a fee unauthorized noncitizens

According to the USCIS, employers "may retain Form I-9 using either a paper or electronic system, or a combination of both . . ." Any electronic system you use to generate Form I-9 or retain completed Forms I-9 must include:

- Reasonable controls to ensure the system's integrity, accuracy, and reliability
- Reasonable controls designed to prevent and detect the unauthorized or accidental creation of, addition to, alteration of, deletion of, or deterioration of an electronically completed or stored Form I-9, including the electronic signature, if used
- An inspection and quality assurance program that regularly evaluates the system and includes periodic checks of electronically stored Form I-9, including the electronic signature, if used
- An indexing system that allows users to identify and retrieve records maintained in the system
- The ability to reproduce legible and readable paper copies

Form I-9 are periodically updated, and employers are responsible for using the most current version. Stay up-to-date by visiting www.uscis.gov/i-9.

E-Verify

E-Verify is a free service offered through the USCIS. It is a tool that helps employers comply with IRCA's requirement that employers must verify the identity and employment eligibility of new employees. Accessed through the Internet, the employer inputs basic information gleaned from the Form I-9 and receives a nearly instant "employment authorized" or "tentative nonconfirmation" (TNC) reply from the website. The employer then prints the results. A TNC result will give the employee more information about the mismatch and a statement of their rights and responsibilities under the law. It is important to note that an employer may not terminate an employee for the initial TNC; it is only when a final nonconfirmation is received that an employer may terminate under E-Verify.

To get started in the program, an employer must first enroll the company, distribute a memorandum of understanding (MOU), and commit to using E-Verify for every new employee at the affected hiring site. Under federal law, the use of E-Verify may be designated to certain locations, although this may be restricted under some state laws.

Amendment to IRCA: Immigration Act of 1990

The Immigration Act of 1990 made several changes to IRCA, including adding the requirement that a prevailing wage be paid to H-1B immigrants to ensure that U.S. citizens did not lose jobs to lower-paid immigrant workers. The act also restricted to 65,000 annually the number of immigrants (with an additional 20,000 for applicants with an advanced degree) allowed under the H-1B category and created additional categories for employment visas, as shown in Table C.5.

TABLE C.5 Employment visas

Visa	Classification
	Visas for temporary workers
H-1B	Specialty occupations, DOD workers, fashion models
H-1C	Nurses going to work for up to three years in health professional shortage areas
H-2A	Temporary agricultural workers
H-2B	Temporary workers: skilled and unskilled, nonagricultural
H-3	Trainees
J-1	Visas for exchange visitors
	Visas for intracompany transfers
L-1A	Executive, managerial
L-1B	Specialized knowledge
L-2	Spouse or child of L-1
	Visas for workers with extraordinary abilities
O-1	Extraordinary ability in sciences, arts, education, business, or athletics
	Visas for athletes and entertainers
P-1	Individual or team athletes
P-1	Entertainment groups
P-2	Artists and entertainers in reciprocal exchange programs
P-3	Artists and entertainers in culturally unique programs
	Visas for religious workers
R-1	Religious workers
	Visas for NAFTA workers
TN	Trade visas for Canadians and Mexicans

In 2023, the United States increased the number of available H-2B visas in part to address the shortage of seasonal workers in industries such as hospitality and tourism.

For more information, visit the "Working in the US page" found at `www.uscis.gov/working-united-states/working-us`.

International Labour Organization (ILO)

The *International Labour Organization (ILO)* was established in 1919 by the Treaty of Versailles to address working conditions and living standards in all countries. It has a tripartite structure consisting of member states' government, employers, and workers. The ILO currently has 185 member countries that agree to the labor standard development outcomes of *ILO conventions* and recommendations. Conventions are legally binding directives, whereas recommendations are nonbinding guidelines.

In 2000, the ILO adopted the Declaration of Fundamental Principles and Rights at Work, which includes the commitment by businesses to support, respect, and protect international human rights; the recognition of worker rights to organize and collectively bargain; to abolish child labor; and to eliminate unlawful discrimination.

International Trade Organizations

For many reasons, some countries have found it to be mutually beneficial to enter into trade agreements. These agreements clarify expectations and establish rules that impact tariffs, employment visas, and employee rights between blocs of trading countries. Though not without controversy, the most prominent of these agreements are reviewed next.

European Union (EU)

The European Union is the world's largest international trading bloc, formed of a common market around which tariffs are reduced and free trade is established. It is designed to clarify the rules of trade, people movement (immigration), and social rights between member countries. Examples include standardized taxes and the rights of most service providers to practice in all member countries. Nineteen of the member countries use the euro as their form of currency.

The EU has both social and political influence over HR practices. The Social Charter of the EU was first adopted in 1989, establishing the 12 fundamental rights of workers. Since their passage, the EU has been working to translate the rights into specific directives to be observed by member countries. Various treaties have been adopted to reinforce the fundamental rights, including employee rights to data protection, the rights of asylum, equality under the law, nondiscriminatory treatment, protection against unfair dismissal, and access to social security. These directives in some form or another apply to all organizations, both local and foreign owned.

The EU currently has 27 member states: Austria, Belgium, Bulgaria, Croatia, Cyprus, Czech Republic, Denmark, Estonia, Finland, France, Germany, Greece, Hungary, Ireland, Italy, Latvia, Lithuania, Luxembourg, Malta, Netherlands, Poland, Portugal, Romania, Slovakia, Slovenia, Spain, and Sweden.

The Schengen area is the geographic locations where legal residents may move freely between member countries without special visas. Ireland and the United Kingdom have declined to participate.

Mercosur

Mercosur is a Southern trading bloc made up of five countries: Argentina, Brazil, Paraguay, Uruguay, and Bolivia. Venezuela was suspended in 2016 for failing to incorporate trade and human rights elements into its laws; also in 2016, Bolivia was in the final stages of becoming a member. Chile, Colombia, Ecuador, Guyana, Peru, and Suriname are considered associate members. Founded in 1991, Mercosur aims to form a common market, allowing for a common external tariff and free movement of goods, services, and people across member nations. A Common Market Council makes decisions, and a Trade Commission deals with tariffs and foreign affairs. The Economic and Social Consultative Forum was established in 1994 to serve in an advisory role to the Trade Commission about labor and social issues. One major goal of Mercosur is to establish a trade agreement with the European Union.

Mine Safety and Health Act of 1977 (MSHA)

The Mine Safety and Health Act of 1977 established the Mine Safety and Health Administration (MSHA) to ensure the safety of workers in coal and other mines. The act establishes mandatory safety and health standards for mine operators and monitors operations throughout the United States. MSHA has developed a comprehensive website (www.msha.gov) that is a resource for miners and mine operators, providing access to information on prevention of accidents, information on year-to-date fatalities, and guidance on specific mine hazards. The site also contains a link to the complete text of the act.

Occupational Safety and Health Act of 1970 (OSHA)

For more than 100 years beginning in 1867, sporadic legislation was enacted by different states and the federal government to address specific safety concerns, usually in regard to mine safety or factory conditions, but there was no comprehensive legislation requiring employers to protect workers from injury or illness. That changed with the Occupational Safety and Health Act of 1970 (the OSH Act), a comprehensive piece of federal legislation that continues to have an impact on employers in virtually every company in America.

Although normally this law is referred to as OSHA, this appendix talks at length about both the act and the agency that is known by the same initials. For the sake of clarity, the law is referred to as the OSH Act throughout the discussion.

In the years prior to passage of the OSH Act, there was a growing recognition that employers were largely unwilling to take preventive steps to reduce the occurrence of injuries, illnesses, and fatalities in the workplace. On December 6, 1907, a total of 362 miners died in an explosion at the Monongah coal mine in West Virginia—the worst mining disaster in American history. In that year alone, a total of 3,242 coal miners lost their lives. As a result, in 1910 Congress established the Bureau of Mines to investigate mining accidents.

There was a long period of time in the United States when it was cheaper for employers to fight lawsuits filed on behalf of workers killed or injured on the job than it was to implement safety programs. Because the courts rarely held employers accountable for worker injuries, many chose this approach. Employer attitudes in this regard didn't change until the shortage of skilled workers during World War II gave employees plentiful options for places to work—and they opted to work for employers that provided safe environments over those that didn't.

The tragic nature of large accidents in the railroad and mining industries captured public attention and created pressure on the federal government to take action. This led Congress to enact legislation requiring safety improvements in the coal mining and railroad industries, but these measures were specifically targeted to those industries. Little attention was paid to equally dangerous workplace safety and illness issues that didn't produce the spectacular accidents prevalent in mines or on railroads. In the late 1960s, some 14,000 American workers lost their lives each year due to injuries or illnesses suffered while on the job. The federal government had been working on solutions but was mired in bureaucratic turf battles over which agency should have control of the process. The Department of Health, Education, and Welfare wanted legislation that applied only to federal contractors, and the DOL, spurred by Secretary W. Willard Wirtz's personal interest in the subject, wanted to protect *all* American workers. After several years of this infighting, the proposal by the DOL was sent to the Congress and enacted as the Occupational Safety and Health Act of 1970. A key component of this legislation was the creation of the Occupational Safety and Health Administration (OSHA), which now sets safety standards for all industries. OSHA enforces those standards with the use of fines and, in the case of criminal actions, can call on the Department of Justice to file charges against offenders.

The intent of Congress, as stated in the preamble to the OSH Act, is to ensure safe and healthful working conditions for American workers. To accomplish this purpose, the act establishes three simple duties:

- Employers must provide every employee with a place to work that is "free from recognized hazards that are causing or are likely to cause death or serious physical harm."
- Employers must comply with all safety and health standards disseminated in accordance with the OSH Act.
- Employees are required to comply with occupational safety and health standards, rules, and regulations that have an impact on their individual actions and behavior.

As mentioned previously, the OSH Act created OSHA and gave it the authority to develop and enforce mandatory standards applicable to all businesses engaged in interstate commerce. The definition of interstate commerce is sufficiently broad to cover most businesses, except only those sole proprietors without employees, family farms employing only family members, and mining operations, which are covered by the Mine Safety and Health Act (discussed earlier in this appendix). The act encouraged OSHA to work with industry associations and safety committees to build upon standards already developed by specific industries, and it authorized enforcement action to ensure that employers comply with the standards. OSHA was charged with developing reporting procedures to track trends in workplace safety and health so that the development of preventive measures would be an ongoing process that changed with the development of new processes and technologies.

The OSH Act also created the National Institute of Occupational Safety and Health (NIOSH) as part of the Department of Health and Human Services. NIOSH is charged with researching and evaluating workplace hazards and recommending ways to reduce the effect of those hazards on workers. NIOSH also supports education and training in the field of occupational safety and health by developing and providing educational materials and training aids and sponsoring conferences on workplace safety and health issues.

In 2011, OSHA celebrated 40 years in the business of protecting American workers. Its focus in the coming years includes increasing enforcement of the standards through additional hiring, and making sure vulnerable workers, such as those who speak English as a second language, are heard. How this translates into the workforce remains to be seen, but we can infer from the statements several key points, discussed next.

More Inspections

With OSHA pushing for an increased budget, it stands to reason that the hiring of additional enforcement officers means more inspections and fines.

Emphasis on Safety Communication

The 2010 National Action Summit for Latino Worker Health and Safety helped to launch OSHA's Diverse Workforce Limited Proficiency Outreach program, designed to "enhance (vulnerable) workers' knowledge of their workplace rights and improve their ability to exercise those rights." Conducting training and providing material in a language all workers can understand is a logical outcome from this focus.

Reporting of Injuries

In 2016, OSHA issued a new rule prohibiting employers from discouraging workers from reporting an injury or illness, including through safety-incentive programs rewarding employees for no injuries being reported. This rule requires employers to inform employees of their right to report work-related injuries and illnesses free from retaliation, which can be satisfied by posting the already required OSHA workplace poster. The rule also clarifies the existing implicit requirement that an employer's procedure for reporting work-related injuries and illnesses must be reasonable and not deter or discourage employees from reporting, and it incorporates the existing statutory prohibition on retaliating against employees for reporting work-related injuries or illnesses. These provisions became effective.

Finally, the OSH Act encourages the states to take the lead in developing and enforcing safety and health programs for businesses within their jurisdictions by providing grants to help states identify specific issues and develop programs for enforcement and prevention.

Employer Responsibilities

The OSH Act has three requirements, two of which pertain to employers. Not only must employers provide a workplace that is safe and healthful for employees, but they must also comply with established standards. OSHA has established other requirements for employers as required by the law:

- Employers are expected to take steps to minimize or reduce hazards, and ensure that employees have and use safe tools, equipment, and personal protective equipment (PPE) that are properly maintained.
- Employers are responsible for informing all employees about OSHA, posting the OSHA poster in a prominent location, and making employees aware of the standards that apply in the worksite. If employees request a copy of a standard, the employer must provide it to them.
- Appropriate warning signs that conform to the OSHA standards for color coding, posting, or labels must be posted where needed to make employees aware of potential hazards.
- Compliance with OSHA standards also means employers must educate employees about safe operating procedures and train them to follow the procedures.
- Businesses with 11 or more employees must maintain records of all workplace injuries and illnesses and post them on Form 300A from February 1 through April 30 each year.
- Within eight hours of a fatal accident or one resulting in hospitalization for three or more employees, a report must be filed with the nearest OSHA office.
- An accident report log must be made available to employees, former employees, or employee representatives when reasonably requested.
- When employees report unsafe conditions to OSHA, the employer may not retaliate or discriminate against them.

Under an OSHA rule effective January 1, 2017, certain employers must electronically submit injury and illness data that they are already required to record on their on-site OSHA Injury and Illness forms. Analysis of this data will be a factor used by OSHA to determine how to allocate its enforcement and compliance resources. Some of the data will also be posted to the OSHA website.

The reporting requirements were phased in over two years:

- Establishments with 250 or more employees in industries covered by the recordkeeping regulation had to submit information from their 2016 Form 300A by July 1, 2017. These same employers were required to submit information from all 2017 forms (300, 300A, and 301) by July 1, 2018. Beginning in 2019 and every year thereafter, the information must be submitted by March 2. These employers are required to submit OSHA Form 301, where prior to this new rule, they could submit either an OSHA Form 301 or other equivalent documentation such as workers' compensation records.
- Establishments with 20 to 249 employees in certain high-risk industries had to submit information from their 2016 Form 300A by July 1, 2017 and their 2017 Form 300A by July 1, 2018. Beginning in 2019 and every year thereafter, the information must be submitted by March 2. A list of industries covered by this provision can be found at www.osha.gov/recordkeeping/NAICScodesforelectronicsubmission.html.

OSHA State Plan states must adopt requirements that are substantially identical to the requirements in this final rule within six months after publication of this final rule.

Employer Rights

Employers have some rights as well, including the right to seek advice and consultation from OSHA and to be active in industry activities involved in health and safety issues. Employers may also participate in the OSHA Standard Advisory Committee process in writing or by giving testimony at hearings. Finally, employers may contact NIOSH for information about substances used in work processes to determine whether they are toxic.

At times, employers may be unable to comply with OSHA standards because of the nature of specific operations. When this happens, they may apply to OSHA for temporary or permanent waivers to the standards along with proof that the protections developed by the organization meet or exceed those of the OSHA standards.

Employee Rights and Responsibilities

When the OSH Act was passed in 1970, employees were granted the basic right to a workplace with safe and healthful working conditions. The act intended to encourage employers and employees to collaborate in reducing workplace hazards. Employees have the responsibility to comply with all OSHA standards and with the safety and health procedures implemented by their employers. The act gave employees the specific rights to do the following:

- Seek safety and health on the job without fear of punishment.
- Know what hazards exist on the job by reviewing the OSHA standards, rules, and regulations that the employer has available at the workplace.
- Be provided with the hazard-communication plan containing information about hazards in the workplace and preventive measures employees should take to avoid illness or injury, and to be trained in those measures.
- Access the exposure and medical records employers are required to keep relative to safety and health issues.
- Request an OSHA inspection, speak privately with the inspector, accompany the inspector during the inspection, and respond to the inspector's questions during the inspection.
- Observe steps taken by the employer to monitor and measure hazardous materials in the workplace, and access records resulting from those steps.
- Request information from NIOSH regarding the potential toxic effects of substances used in the workplace.
- File a complaint about workplace safety or health hazards with OSHA and remain anonymous to the employer.

OSHA Enforcement

OSHA's success is the result of strong enforcement of the standards it has developed. As demonstrated in the 19th and 20th centuries, without the threat of financial penalty, some business owners would choose to ignore injury- and illness-prevention requirements.

Construction and general industry continue to be the sources of the most frequently cited OSHA standards' violations through 2018. That being the case, OSHA established fines and penalties that can be assessed against businesses when violations occur. Table C.6 describes the violation levels and associated penalties for noncompliance that are in effect as of January 2024. Students should note that OSHA plans to update these penalties every January to adjust for inflation.

TABLE C.6 Categories of penalties for OSHA violations

Violation	Description	Fine
Willful or repeated	Evidence exists of an intentional violation of the OSH Act or "plain indifference" to its requirements; OSHA previously issued citations for substantially similar conditions.	Up to $161,323 per violation
Serious	Hazards with substantial probability of death or serious physical harm exist.	Up to $16,131 per violation
Other than serious and posting requirements	An existing hazard could have a direct and immediate effect on the safety and health of employees.	Up to $16,131 per violation
Failure to abate	The employer failed to abate a prior violation.	Up to $16,131 per day beyond the abatement date

Source: Adapted from https://www.osha.gov/penalties

OSHA Recordkeeping Requirements

OSHA requires employers to record health and safety incidents that occur each year and to document steps they take to comply with regulations. Records of specific injuries and illnesses are compiled, allowing OSHA and NIOSH to identify emerging hazards for research and, if warranted, create new standards designed to reduce the possibility of similar injury or illness in the future. These records include up-to-date files for exposures to hazardous substances and related medical records, records of safety training meetings, and OSHA logs that record work-related injuries and illnesses.

As of January 1, 2002, OSHA revised the requirements for maintaining records of workplace injuries and illnesses in order to collect better information for use in prevention activities, simplify the information collection process, and make use of advances in technology. Three new forms were developed:

- OSHA Form 300, Log of Work-Related Injuries and Illnesses
- OSHA Form 300A, Summary of Work-Related Injuries and Illnesses
- OSHA Form 301, Injury and Illness Incident Report

Completion of the forms doesn't constitute proof of fault on the part of either the employer or the employee and doesn't indicate that any OSHA violations have occurred. Recording an injury or illness on the OSHA forms also doesn't mean that an employee is eligible for workers' compensation benefits.

The following paragraphs cover the basic requirements for OSHA recordkeeping, including who should file OSHA reports, which employers are exempt from filing, and what injuries are considered work-related.

Who Must Complete and File OSHA Forms?

All employers with 11 or more employees are required to complete and file the OSHA forms just discussed.

Are There Any Exemptions?

Employers with 10 or fewer employees aren't required to file the forms. In addition, OSHA has identified industries with low injury and illness rates and exempted them from filing reports. These include the retail, service, finance, insurance, and real estate industries. Unless OSHA has notified a business in writing that reports must be filed, the business is exempt from the requirement.

What Must Be Recorded?

OSHA regulations specify which employees are covered for reporting purposes. Injury or illness to any employee on the employer's payroll must be recorded, regardless of how the employee is classified: full-time or part-time, regular or temporary, hourly or salary, seasonal, and so on. Injuries to employees of temp agencies, if under the employer's direct supervision on a daily basis, must also be recorded. The owners and partners in sole proprietorships and partnerships aren't considered employees for OSHA reporting purposes.

Privacy concern cases are new protections developed by OSHA to protect employee privacy by substituting a case number for the employee name on the OSHA Form 300 log. Cases where this is appropriate include injury or illness that involved an intimate body part or resulted from a sexual assault; HIV infection, hepatitis, or tuberculosis; needle-stick injuries involving contaminated needles; and other illnesses when employees request that their names not be included on the log.

An injury or illness is generally considered to be work-related if it occurred in the workplace or while performing work-related duties off-site. The basic OSHA requirement records any work-related injury or illness that causes death, days away from work, restricted or limited duty, medical treatment beyond first aid, or loss of consciousness. Diagnosis of an injury or illness by a physician or other healthcare professional, even if it doesn't result in one of the circumstances listed, must also be reported.

Once the employer has determined that the injury or illness is work-related, the employer must determine whether this is a new case or a continuation of a previously recorded case. To a certain extent, this decision is left to the employer's common sense and best judgment. OSHA considers a new case to have occurred when an employee hasn't had a previous injury or illness that is the same as the current occurrence or when the employee has recovered completely from a previous injury or illness of the same type.

Annual Summary

At the end of each year, employers must review the OSHA Form 300 log and summarize the entries on Form 300A, which must then be certified by a company executive as correct and complete and posted, as previously mentioned, in February of the following year.

Retention

The OSHA Form 300 log and annual summary, privacy case list, and Form 301 Incident Report forms must be retained for five years following the end of the calendar year they cover.

Employee Involvement

Employers are required to provide employees and employee representatives, former employees, or a personal representative of an employee with information on how to properly report an injury or illness, and they're also required to allow employees or their representatives limited access to the records of injury and illness.

The OSHA Form 300 log must be provided to these requestors by the end of the following business day.

The OSHA Form 301 Incident Report must be provided by the end of the next business day when the employee who is the subject of the report requests a copy. When an employee representative requests copies, they must be provided within seven calendar days, and all information except that contained in the "Tell Us About the Case" section must be removed.

OSHA Assistance

OSHA provides many sources for employers and employees to obtain information about workplace health and safety issues. Chief among these is an extensive website (`www.osha.gov`) that provides access to the laws, regulations, and standards enforced by OSHA as well as general information on prevention. In addition to the website, OSHA publishes a number of pamphlets, brochures, and training materials that are available to employers. While OSHA exists to protect workers' safety rights, there are services such as consultation and voluntary participation programs that exist specifically to aid employers in complying with the standards.

OSHA Consultants

Educating employers and employees about workplace health and safety issues is key to preventing injuries and illnesses in the workplace. OSHA provides training programs for consultants who work with business owners in establishing effective health and safety programs. These free consultation services give employers an opportunity to learn which of the standards apply in their worksite, involve employees in the safety process, and correct possible violations without a citation and penalty. Once the consultant becomes involved, the employer must abate any violations, or the consultant will refer the violation to an OSHA inspector.

The *Safety and Health Achievement Recognition Program* (*SHARP*) recognizes small, high-hazard employers that have requested a comprehensive OSHA consultation, corrected any violations, and developed an ongoing safety management program. To participate in the program, the business must agree to ask for additional consultations if work processes change.

Partnerships and Voluntary Programs

The *Strategic Partnership Program* is a means for businesses and employees to participate in solving health and safety problems with OSHA. Partnerships currently exist in 15 industries, including construction, food processing, logging, and healthcare, to develop solutions specific to their businesses.

The *OSHA Alliance Program* provides a vehicle for collaboration with employer organizations interested in promoting workplace health and safety issues. The program is open to trade and professional organizations, businesses, labor organizations, educational institutions, and government agencies, among others.

The *Voluntary Protection Program (VPP)* is open to employers with tough, well-established safety programs. VPP participants must meet OSHA criteria for the program and, having done so, are removed from routine scheduled inspection lists. The program serves to motivate employees to work more safely, reducing workers' compensation costs, and to encourage employers to make further improvements to safety programs. Acceptance into the VPP is an official recognition of exemplary occupational safety and health practices.

Health and Safety Inspections

The OSH Act authorizes both OSHA and NIOSH to investigate health or safety hazards in the workplace. The majority of OSHA inspections are focused on industries with higher hazard risks based on injury and illness rates. Some inspections occur at the request of an employer or employee in a specific organization. Less than 1 percent of OSHA inspections occur as part of the agency's Enhanced Enforcement Program that monitors employers with a history of repeat or willful violations.

NIOSH inspections, known as *health hazard evaluations*, always occur in response to the request of an employer, an employee, or a government agency.

No matter which agency conducts an investigation, employees who request or participate in them are protected by the OSH Act from retaliation or adverse employment actions.

OSHA Inspections

Most OSHA inspections are conducted without notice by a compliance safety and health officer (CSHO) who has been trained on OSHA standards and how to recognize safety and health hazards in the workplace. OSHA has established a hierarchy of situations to give priority to inspection of the most dangerous workplace environments.

During an inspection, OSHA follows a distinct procedure. In advance of the inspection, the CSHO prepares by reviewing records related to any previous incidents, inspections, or employee complaints. The inspector also determines what, if any, special testing equipment will be necessary for the inspection. Upon the inspector's arrival at the worksite, the inspection commences with an opening conference, proceeds to a workplace tour, and ends with a closing conference:

1. The CSHO arrives at the worksite and presents credentials. If the credentials aren't presented, the employer should insist on seeing them before the inspection begins. It's critical that any employee who may be the first person approached at the worksite be instructed as to who should be contacted when a CSHO arrives. Employers have the right to require the inspector to have a security clearance before entering secure areas. Any observation of trade secrets during the inspection remains confidential; CSHOs who breach this confidentiality are subject to fines and imprisonment.
2. The CSHO holds an *opening conference* during which the inspector explains why the site was selected, the purpose of the visit, and the scope of the inspection, and discusses the standards that apply to the worksite. The CSHO requests an employee representative to accompany the CSHO on the inspection along with the management representative. If no employee accompanies the inspector on the tour, the CSHO will talk to as many employees as necessary to understand the safety and health issues in the workplace.
3. The next step is a tour of the facilities. During the tour, the inspector determines what route to take, where to look, and which employees to talk to. During this part of the inspection, the CSHO may talk privately to employees, taking care to minimize disruptions to work processes. Activities that can occur during an inspection include the following:
   - Reviewing the safety and health program
   - Examining records, including OSHA logs, records of employee exposure to toxic substances, and medical records
   - Ensuring that the OSHA workplace poster is prominently displayed
   - Evaluating compliance with OSHA standards specific to the worksite
   - Pointing out unsafe working conditions to the employer and suggesting possible remedial actions
4. The inspector holds a *closing conference* where the inspector, the employer, and, if requested, the employee representative discuss the observations made and corrective actions that must be taken. At this time the employer may produce records to assist in resolving any corrective actions to be taken. The CSHO discusses any possible citations or penalties that may be issued, and the OSHA area director makes the final determination based on the inspector's report.

Should the OSHA area director determine that citations are necessary to ensure employer compliance with OSHA, the director will issue the citations and determine the penalties to be assessed according to established guidelines that consider various factors, including the size of the company. The OSHA area director also determines the seriousness of the danger(s), how many employees would be impacted, and good-faith efforts on the part of the employer to comply with the standards, among others.

During the course of an OSHA inspection, an employer may raise an affirmative defense to any violations observed by the inspector. Possible affirmative defenses include the following:

- It is an isolated case caused by unpreventable employee misconduct. This defense may apply when the employer has established, communicated, and enforced adequate work rules that were ignored by the employee.
- Compliance is impossible based on the nature of the employer's work, and there are no viable alternative means of protection.
- Compliance with the standard would cause a greater hazard to employees, and there are no alternative means of protection.

The employer has the burden to prove that an affirmative defense exists. If it is successfully proven, the OSHA area director may decide that a citation and penalty aren't warranted.

Employers have specific responsibilities and rights during and after the inspection:

- Employers are required to cooperate with the CSHO by providing records and documents requested during the inspection and by allowing employees or their representatives to accompany the inspector on the worksite tour.
- Should a citation be issued during the inspection, the employer must post it at or near the worksite involved, where it must remain for three working days or until the violation has been abated, whichever is longer. It goes without saying, of course, that the employer is required to abate the violation within the time frame indicated by the citation.
- Employers may file a *Notice of Contest* within 15 days of a citation and proposed penalty. If there will be an unavoidable delay in abating a violation because the materials, equipment, or personnel won't be available, the employer may request a temporary variance until the violation can be corrected.

Within 15 days of receipt of a citation by an employer, employees have the right to object in writing to the abatement period set by OSHA for correcting violations. Employees who have requested an inspection also have the right to be advised by OSHA of the results of the inspection.

NIOSH Evaluations

The NIOSH mandate contained in the OSH Act is to identify and evaluate potential workplace hazards and recommend actions to reduce or eliminate the effects of chemicals, biological agents, work stress, excessive noise, radiation, poor ergonomics, and other risks found in the workplace. NIOSH established the *Health Hazard Evaluation (HHE)* program to respond to concerns about these and other risks expressed by employers, employees, unions, and government agencies.

In response to a request, NIOSH will provide a written acknowledgement within a few weeks. They then review the request and, depending on the nature and severity of the hazard being described, responds in one of three ways:

- NIOSH may have written materials that address the concern or may refer the request to another government agency better equipped to respond. If written materials aren't available, a project officer is assigned to assess the need for further assistance.
- The project officer telephones the requestor to discuss the request. In some cases, the request is resolved during the call.
- The project office may determine that the appropriate response is a site visit.

If a site visit is required, NIOSH will conduct an investigation, gathering information by touring the site, meeting with management and employees, and reviewing relevant records maintained by the employer. The project office may also use other investigative procedures such as sampling devices or medical tests to gather information. During a site visit, employees, employee representatives, and NIOSH project officers have seven legal rights considered nonnegotiable by NIOSH:

- NIOSH has the right to enter the workplace to conduct an HHE.
- NIOSH has the right to access relevant information and records maintained by the employer.
- NIOSH has the right to meet privately with management and employees for confidential interviews.
- An employee requestor or other employee representative has the right to accompany NIOSH during the evaluation inspection. NIOSH may also request participation from other employees if necessary to complete the evaluation.
- Employee representatives have the right to attend opening and closing conferences.
- Employees and managers have the right to participate in the investigation by wearing sampling devices and to take part in medical tests or in the use of sampling devices.
- The interim and final HHE reports must be made available to employees; the employer must either post the final report in the workplace for 30 days or provide NIOSH with employee names and addresses so that the report can be mailed to them.

Once the information-gathering phase is complete, NIOSH analyzes the data collected during the HHE and compiles a written report that is provided to the employer, employee, and union representatives.

Many activities that occur during either an OSHA consultation or NIOSH HHE seem similar and may cause confusion about which type of assistance is appropriate for any given situation. Table C.7 provides guidelines for determining which agency should be involved.

TABLE C.7 OSHA consultation versus NIOSH HHE

OSHA consultation	NIOSH HHE
Identify workplace hazards.	Identify the cause of employee illness.
Suggest ways to correct hazards.	Evaluate the potential for hazard from exposure to unregulated chemicals or working conditions.
Assist in creating an effective safety and health program.	Investigate adverse health effects from permissible exposures to regulated chemicals or working conditions.
Assist in reducing workers' compensation costs.	Conduct medical or epidemiologic hazard investigations.
Assist in improving employee morale.	Investigate higher-than-expected occurrences of injury or illness.
	Evaluate newly identified hazards.
	Investigate the possible hazard of exposure to a combination of agents.
	Evaluate the potential for hazard from exposure to unregulated chemicals or working conditions.

Organisation for Economic Co-operation and Development (OECD): Guidelines for Multinational Enterprises (MNEs)

The mission of the Organisation for Economic Co-operation and Development (OECD) is to promote policies that will improve the economic and social well-being of people around the world. This group works with government agencies and makes recommendations to address social, economic, and corruption/fairness issues in business dealings across boundaries (geographic, social, and political), all with a focus on the well-being of global citizens. The Guidelines for Multinational Enterprises lists responsible business conduct. They provide voluntary principles and standards in the areas of employment and industrial relations, human rights, environment, information disclosure, combating bribery, consumer interests, science and technology, competition, and taxation.

The OECD recently updated its guidelines in 2023, marking the first revision since 2011. These updates address the social, environmental, and technological issues that have emerged over the past decade. Key changes include strengthened recommendations for risk-based due diligence, especially regarding human rights and environmental impacts, and enhanced expectations for transparency in business practices, including lobbying activities. The updated guidelines also emphasize the importance of aligning business operations with international climate goals and biodiversity protection.

The governments committed to adhering to the principles are responsible for establishing a National Contact Point (NCP). The NCPs establish relationships with other participants, the business community, labor unions, and any other group needing implementation support of the Guidelines. Governments must commit to the following through their NCP: visibility, accessibility, transparency, and accountability. The NCPs facilitate grievances, called "specific instances," although they are not judicial bodies. The NCPs facilitate problem-solving through methods of conciliation and mediation.

Additionally, OECD Watch supports nongovernmental organizations (NGOs), helping them identify and hold businesses accountable for sustainable development and the eradication of poverty through policy development, education, and interactions with businesses and unions.

Patient Protection and Affordable Care Act of 2010 (PPACA, ACA, Obamacare)

On March 23, 2010, President Barack Obama signed into law a healthcare reform bill that had several employer implications. It established criteria to ensure that Americans had access to affordable healthcare.

It is important to note that the PPACA does not require that employers provide healthcare insurance. It does, however, impose penalties on large employers who fail to provide access to affordable "minimal essential coverage." A large employer is defined as those who employed an average of at least 50 full-time equivalent employees during the preceding calendar year, with an employee working 30 hours a week counted as one full-time worker, and the others prorated.

The PPACA has been significantly modified since its inception, often tied to American elections. As of this publication, here are the key provisions affecting employers:

- **Reporting Requirements:** Applicable large employers (ALEs) must file annual information returns with the IRS and provide statements to employees about the health insurance coverage offered. Forms 1094-C and 1095-C are used to report this information.
- **Preventive Services:** Employer-sponsored health plans must cover a set of preventive services without charging employees co-payments, co-insurance, or deductibles. This includes services such as vaccinations, screenings, and contraceptive methods.
- **Nondiscrimination Rules:** The ACA prohibits employer health plans from discriminating in favor of highly compensated individuals regarding eligibility and benefits. This means benefits and contributions must be fairly distributed among all employees.
- **Coverage for Adult Children:** Employers must extend coverage to employees' adult children up to age 26, regardless of whether the child is a dependent for tax purposes.

- **Essential Health Benefits:** Employer-sponsored plans, particularly those offered through the small group market, must cover essential health benefits such as emergency services, maternity care, mental health services, and prescription drugs.
- **Waiting Period Limitations:** Employers cannot impose waiting periods longer than 90 days before new employees are eligible for health coverage.
- **Summary of Benefits and Coverage (SBC):** Employers must provide a standardized Summary of Benefits and Coverage document to employees, detailing the health plan's coverage and costs. This requirement is designed to help employees understand and compare different health plans.
- **W-2 Reporting:** Employers are required to report the total cost of employer-sponsored health coverage on employees' W-2 forms. This is for informational purposes and does not affect the employees' taxable income.

Pension Protection Act of 2006 (PPA)

The main focus of the Pension Protection Act of 2006 was to require employers to fully fund their pension plans to avoid future cash shortfalls in the plans as employees retire. Beginning in 2008, companies had seven years to bring their plans into compliance; for those that didn't comply, the act provided a penalty in the form of a 10 percent excise tax. The act also specified funding notices that must be provided by defined benefit plans.

One of the biggest changes to pension rules made by the PPA was to allow employers to automatically enroll employees in 401(k) plans. Employees who do not want to participate must now opt out of the plan. Another change was that plan advisers may now provide investment advice to plan participants and their beneficiaries under certain conditions.

Largely as a result of the Enron scandal, the PPA included a requirement for defined contribution plans that include employer stock to provide at least three alternative investment options and allow employees to divest themselves of the employer's stock.

When the Economic Growth and Tax Relief Reconciliation Act of 2001 (EGTRRA) was enacted, Congress increased contribution limits for 401(k) plans and individual retirement accounts (IRAs) and allowed catch-up contributions for taxpayers older than 50 years of age. These changes were set to expire in 2010, but the PPA made them permanent. Employees older than age 50 will be able to make 401(k) catch-up contributions to retirement funds. For 2009, the maximum contribution is $5,500; this amount may be adjusted for inflation in multiples of $500 each year.

Privacy Act of 1974

The Privacy Act of 1974 was an attempt by Congress to regulate the amount and type of information collected by federal agencies and the methods by which it was stored in an effort to protect the personal privacy of individuals about whom the information had been collected. The act requires written authorization from an individual prior to releasing information to another person. The act does not currently apply to private employers.

First, the act provides individuals with the right to know what kind of information is being collected about them, how it is used and maintained, and whether it is disseminated. The act prevents this information from being used for purposes other than that for which it was collected, and it allows individuals to obtain copies of the information, review it, and request amendments to inaccurate information. The act requires the government to ensure that information collected is not misused. Except under specific circumstances covered by the Privacy Act, such as law enforcement or national security needs, the information collected by one agency must not be shared with another. Damages for violation of these requirements may be sought in federal district court and, if found by the judge to be warranted, are subject to reimbursement of attorney's fees and litigation costs, as well as a fine for actual damages incurred by the individual of up to $1,000 paid by the federal government.

Rehabilitation Act of 1973, Sections 501, 503, and 505

The Rehabilitation Act of 1973 was enacted to expand the opportunities available for persons with physical or mental disabilities. The act prohibits discrimination in hiring, promotion, training, compensation, benefits and other employment actions. The employment clauses of the act apply to agencies of the federal government and federal contractors with contracts of $10,000 or more during a 12-month period. Section 501 addresses employment discrimination, while Section 505 details the remedies available for those who have been subjected to unlawful employment practices. The EEOC has enforcement responsibility for Section 501. Under Section 503, individuals with disabilities who think a federal contractor has violated the requirements of the Rehabilitation Act may also file complaints with the Department of Labor through the Office of Federal Contract Compliance Programs (OFCCP).

Sarbanes–Oxley Act of 2002 (SOX)

Although the main focus of *Sarbanes–Oxley Act (SOX)* compliance is the reporting of financial transactions and activities, HR professionals may be called on to participate in SOX reporting requirements. SOX requires information that materially affects an organization's financial status to be reported to the Securities and Exchange Commission (SEC), in some cases immediately, when the organization becomes aware of the information. Some instances where this would apply to HR management are the following:

- Ensuring that material liabilities from pending lawsuits or settlements of employment practices' claims are reported in the financial statements.
- Participating in the review and testing of internal controls for hiring, compensation, and termination practices.
- Reporting immediately any material changes to the organization's financial condition. Although in most cases this wouldn't be an HR responsibility, the settlement of a large class action lawsuit could potentially reach the threshold of a material change.

Failure to provide this information within the time frames required by SOX can result in criminal penalties, including incarceration, for employees who obstruct legal investigations into financial reporting issues. SOX also prohibits employers from retaliating against whistleblowers who report financial conduct that they reasonably believe violates federal laws designed to protect shareholders from fraudulent activity.

Service Contract Act of 1965 (SCA)

The McNamara–O'Hara Service Contract Act of 1965 requires any federal service contractor with a contract exceeding $2,500 to pay its employees the prevailing wage and fringe benefits for the geographic area in which it operates, provide safe and sanitary working conditions, and notify employees of the minimum allowable wage for each job classification, as well as the equivalent federal employee classification and wage rate for similar jobs.

The SCA expands the requirements of the Davis–Bacon and Walsh–Healey Acts to contractors providing services to the federal government, such as garbage removal, custodial services, food and lodging, and the maintenance and operation of electronic equipment. Federal contractors already subject to the requirements of Davis–Bacon, Walsh–Healey, or laws covering other federal contracts, such as public utility services or transportation of people or freight, are exempt from the SCA.

Uniformed Services Employment and Reemployment Rights Act of 1994 (USERRA)

Congress enacted the Uniformed Services Employment and Reemployment Rights Act (USERRA) in 1994 to protect the rights of reservists called to active duty in the armed forces. The act provides reemployment and benefits rights and is administered through the Veterans Employment and Training Service (VETS) of the Department of Labor. USERRA applies to all public and private employers in the United States, including the federal government. The DOL issued revised rules for employers that became effective on January 18, 2006. These revisions clarified some of the requirements previously issued. Its stipulations include the following:

Coverage

- All employers, regardless of size, are required to comply with USERRA regulations.
- Members of all uniformed services are protected by USERRA.
- USERRA prohibits discrimination due to past, current, or future military obligations.
- In addition to service during times of war or national emergency, USERRA protects any voluntary or involuntary service such as active duty, training, boot camp, reserve weekend duty, National Guard mobilizations, and absence due to required fitness for duty examinations.

Notice Requirements

- In most circumstances, employees must give verbal or written notice to the employer that they have been called to active service. If an employee is unable to give notice, a military representative may provide the notice.
- If military necessity prevents advance notice, or if giving notice is impossible or unreasonable, employees are still protected by USERRA.
- To be eligible for reemployment rights, service members must report back to work within time frames that vary according to the length of service. Table C.8 shows the reporting time requirements established by USERRA for returning to work based on varying lengths of service.

TABLE C.8 USERRA reemployment reporting times

Length of service	Reporting time
1 to 30 days *or* absence for "fitness for service" exam	The first regularly scheduled full workday that begins eight hours after the end of the service completion.
31 to 180 days	Submit application for reemployment no later than 14 days after the end of service or on the next business day after that.
181 or more days	Submit application for reemployment no later than 90 days after the end of service or on the next business day after that.
Disability incurred or aggravated	Reporting or application deadline is extended for up to two years.

Duration

- The employer must grant a leave of absence for up to five years, although there are several exceptions that extend coverage beyond five years.

  Types of leave protected without limits include the following:
  - Boot camp
  - Initial service period
  - Waiting for orders
  - Annual two-week mandatory training
- Employees are permitted to moonlight during off-duty hours without losing reinstatement rights.

- Employees do not lose reinstatement rights if they leave their jobs to prepare for mobilization, but the mobilization is canceled.

Compensation

- USERRA does not require employers to pay employees during military absences, unless the employer has an established policy of doing so.
- Employers may not require employees to apply accrued vacation pay to their military leaves, but employees may choose to do so.

Benefit Protection

- Employees on military leave are entitled to the same benefits employers provide for others on a leave of absence.
- Employees continue to accrue seniority and other benefits as though they were continuously employed.
- For leave greater than 30 days but less than 240 days in duration, the employer must offer COBRA-like health coverage upon request of the employee; for service less than 31 days, and at the employee's request, the employer must continue health coverage at the regular employee cost.
- Returning service members are entitled to participate in any rights and benefits provided to employees returning from nonmilitary leaves of absence.

Pension Protection

- Employee pension rights are protected by USERRA.
- Vesting and accrual for returning service members are treated as though there was no break in employment.
- Employer pension contributions must be the same as though the military leave did not occur.
- For defined contribution plans, service members must be given three times the period of the military leave absence (not to exceed five years) to make up contributions that were missed during the leave. Plans with an employer matching component are required to match the makeup funds.

Reinstatement

- The employer must "promptly" reinstate regular employees to positions that the employees would have earned had they remained on the job, referred to as an *escalator position.* The act does not specify a definition of "promptly," since the timing will depend on the length of the leave. For example, an employee on leave for annual two-week training would be expected to be reemployed on the first workday following the end of leave. On the other hand, someone who has been serving on active duty for five years may be promptly reemployed after notice to vacate the position is given to the incumbent.
- Temporary employees do not have reinstatement rights.
- Seasonal or fixed-term contract employees are not entitled to reinstatement.

- Reemployment rights are forfeited if the employee has been discharged dishonorably or other than honorably from the service, has been expelled as a result of a court martial, or has been absent without leave (AWOL) for 90 days.

Continued Employment

- Employees returning to work from leaves of more than 30 but less than 181 days may not be discharged without cause for six months after the date of reemployment.
- Employees returning to work from leaves of 181 days or more may not be discharged without cause for one year from the date of reemployment.

Disabled Veterans

The employer must make reasonable accommodation to provide training or retraining to reemploy a returning service member disabled as a result of service; if reasonable accommodation creates an undue hardship, reemployment can be made to a position "nearest approximate" in terms of status and pay and with full seniority to which the person is entitled.

United States–Mexico–Canada Agreement (USMCA)

The United States–Mexico–Canada Agreement (USMCA) is a comprehensive trade agreement that replaced the North American Free Trade Agreement (NAFTA). Negotiated between the United States, Mexico, and Canada, the USMCA came into effect on July 1, 2020.

The USMCA affects employers through stricter rules of origin, particularly in automotive manufacturing. It imposes higher North American content requirements for tariff-free trade, influencing supply chains and sourcing decisions. Labor and environmental standards are bolstered, necessitating compliance with laws on working conditions, minimum wages, and environmental regulations. Intellectual property protections are strengthened, impacting industries reliant on intellectual property like technology and pharmaceuticals. Digital trade provisions eliminate customs duties on electronic transmissions and protect cross-border data flows, benefiting e-commerce and digital service sectors. Dispute resolution mechanisms are established to address trade disputes between member countries. Overall, employers must adapt to the USMCA's provisions by ensuring compliance with labor, environmental, intellectual property, and digital trade standards, potentially requiring adjustments to business practices, supply chains, and legal strategies.

The agreement aims to modernize and rebalance North American trade, addressing concerns such as labor rights and environmental protections, while also aiming to encourage more domestic manufacturing and job creation.

United States Patent Act of 1790

A *patent* allows inventors exclusive rights to the benefits of an invention for a defined period of time. Generally, the term of a new patent is 20 years from the date on which the application for the patent was filed in the United States or, in special cases, from the date an earlier related application was filed, subject to the payment of maintenance fees. U.S. patent grants are effective only within the United States, U.S. territories, and U.S. possessions. Patents protect an inventor's "right to exclude others from making, using, offering for sale, or selling" the invention in the United States or "importing" the invention into the United States. Patent laws in the United States define three types of patents:

- *Design patents* protect new, original, and ornamental designs of manufactured items. Design patents are limited to 14 years.
- *Utility patents* protect the invention of new and useful processes, machines, manufacture or composition of matter, and new and useful improvements to the same. Utility patents are limited to 20 years.
- *Plant patents* protect the invention or discovery of asexually reproduced varieties of plants for 20 years.

Wage Garnishment Law, Federal

The Federal Wage Garnishment Law is found in Title III of the Consumer Credit Protection Act (CCPA) of 1968 and applies to all employers and employees. Employers are required to withhold funds from an employee's paycheck and send the money to an entity designated in the court order or levy document.

Title III of the CCPA protects employees in three ways:

- Prohibits employers from terminating employees whose wages are garnished for any one debt, even if the employer receives multiple garnishment orders for the same debt.
- Sets limits on the amount that can be garnished in any single week. Currently, the weekly amount may not exceed the lesser of two figures: 25 percent of the employee's disposable earnings, or the amount by which an employee's disposable earnings are greater than 30 times the federal minimum wage (currently $7.25 an hour).
- Defines how disposable earnings are to be calculated for garnishment withholdings.

Earnings that may be garnished include wages, salaries, bonuses, and commissions. Other income from pension plans or employer-paid disability may be subject to garnishment as well. The law does not protect employees from termination if the employer receives garnishments for more than one debt.

Walsh–Healey Public Contracts Act of 1936

The Walsh–Healey Public Contracts Act requires government contractors with contracts exceeding $10,000 (for other than construction work) to pay their employees the prevailing wage for their local area as established by the Secretary of Labor.

Worker Adjustment Retraining and Notification Act of 1988 (WARN)

The WARN Act was passed by Congress in 1988 to provide some protection for workers in the event of mass layoffs or plant closings. The Act requires that 60 days' advance notice be given to either the individual workers or their union representatives. The intent of Congress was to provide time for workers to obtain new employment or training before the loss of their jobs occurred. The WARN Act is administered by the Department of Labor and enforced through the federal courts.

Employers with 100 or more full-time employees or those with 100 or more full- and part-time employees who work in the aggregate 4,000 hours or more per week are subject to the provisions of the WARN Act. The employee count includes those who are on temporary leave or layoff with a reasonable expectation of recall.

The WARN Act established that a mass layoff occurs when either 500 employees are laid off or at least 50 employees making up 33 percent of the workforce and are laid off. A plant closing occurs when 50 or more full-time employees lose their jobs because a single facility shuts down, either permanently or temporarily. In cases where the employer staggers the workforce reduction over a period of time, care must be taken that appropriate notice is given if the total reductions within a 90-day period trigger the notice requirement.

The WARN Act also established rules on notice. For instance, notice is required to be given to all affected employees or their representatives, the chief elected official of the local government, and the state dislocated worker unit. Notice requirements vary according to which group the notices are being sent to, but they must contain specific information about the reasons for the closure, whether the action is permanent or temporary, the address of the affected business unit, the name of a company official to contact for further information, the expected date of closure or layoff, and whether bumping rights exist.

The WARN Act provides for three situations in which the 60-day notice is not required, but the burden is on the employer to show that the reasons are legitimate and not an attempt to thwart the intent of the act:

- The faltering company exception applies only to plant closures in situations where the company is actively seeking additional funding and has a reasonable expectation that it will be forthcoming in an amount sufficient to preclude the layoff or closure and that giving the notice would negatively affect the ability of the company to obtain the funding.
- The unforeseeable business circumstance exception applies to plant closings and mass layoffs and occurs when circumstances take a sudden and unexpected negative turn that could not have reasonably been predicted, such as the cancellation of a major contract without previous warning.
- The natural disaster exception applies to both plant closings and mass layoffs occurring as the result of a natural disaster, such as a flood, an earthquake, or a fire.

Workers' Compensation

Workers' compensation laws require employers to assume responsibility for all employee injuries, illnesses, and deaths related to employment. These laws are enacted and enforced by the individual states. The laws provide benefits for employees that cover medical and rehabilitation expenses, provide income replacement during periods of disability when employees are unable to work, and pay benefits to their survivors in the event of an employee's death.

The amount of compensation paid is based on actuarial tables that take into account the seriousness of the injury, whether the disability is permanent or temporary, whether it is a full or partial disability (such as the loss of an eye or hand), and the amount of income lost because of the injury. In most cases, employers fund workers' compensation obligations by purchasing coverage through private insurance companies or state-sponsored insurance funds. The premiums for workers' compensation coverage are based on a percentage of the employer's payroll in various job categories. The percentages are different and depend on previous claim activity in each category. The rate charged for a roofer, for example, is much higher than that for an office worker because of the inherent danger of the job and the number and severity of claims that result.

In some states, companies may self-fund workers' compensation programs, meaning that they pay the total costs of any injuries or illnesses when they occur instead of paying insurance premiums. These are known as *nonsubscriber plans* and are rare; generally, self-funded insurance plans make economic sense only for very large organizations with the financial base to support the payment of large claims when they occur.

Although increased emphasis on safety programs and training has led to a reduction in the number of nationwide workers' compensation claims filed each year, the insurance rates are increasing largely because of increased medical costs. This is most evident in California, where employers saw costs double between 2000 and 2003, but it has also led to state reform of workers' compensation programs in Florida, West Virginia, Washington, and Texas.

Implementing programs aimed at reducing the cost of workers' compensation coverage for their organizations is one way HR professionals can show a positive impact on the bottom line. Implementing safety training and injury prevention programs is one way to reduce job-related injury and illness and to prevent claims. The costs of individual claims can be reduced by ensuring the availability of jobs that meet "light-duty" medical requirements so that employees are able to return to work earlier, shortening the length of their leave.

Quick Reference Guide: Agencies, Court Cases, Terms, and Laws; General Recordkeeping Guidelines

Table C.9 presents information on agencies, court cases, terms, and laws, and Table C.10 provides general recordkeeping guidelines.

TABLE C.9 Agencies, court cases, terms, and laws

Name	Description
Adverse impact	According to the Uniform Guidelines on Employee Selection Procedures, adverse impact is a substantially different rate of selection in hiring, promotion, or other employment decision, which works to the disadvantage of members of a race, sex, or ethnic group. Occurs when the selection rate (hiring, training, promotion, etc.) for protected class groups is less than four-fifths, or 80 percent, of the selection rate for the group with the highest selection rate.

Name	Description
Albemarle Paper v. Moody	Required that employment tests be validated; subjective supervisor rankings aren't sufficient validation; criteria must be tied to job requirements.
Automobile Workers v. Johnson Controls, Inc.	In response to a sex-based discrimination suit filed by women "capable of bearing children," the U.S. Supreme Court found that "decisions about the welfare of the next generation must be left to the parents who conceive, bear, support and raise them, rather than to the employers who hire those parents."
Bates v. United Parcel	Established that when employers apply an unlawful standard that bars employees protected by the ADA from an application process, the employees don't need to prove they were otherwise qualified to perform essential job functions. The employer must prove the standard is necessary to business operations.
Black Lung Benefits Act (BLBA)	Provided benefits for coal miners suffering from pneumoconiosis due to mine work.
Bureau of Labor Statistics (BLS)	An agency within the DOL that was established to study and publish statistical economic and industrial accidents' data.
Burlington Northern Santa Fe Railway Co. v. White	Established that all retaliation against employees who file discrimination claims is unlawful under Title VII, even if no economic damage results.
Circuit City Stores v. Adams	Arbitration clauses in employment agreements are enforceable for employers engaged in interstate commerce except for transportation workers.
Citizen and Immigration Services, United States (USCIS)	A component of the Department of Homeland Security charged with overseeing lawful immigration to the United States. Individuals wishing to live or work in the United States must submit applications through the USCIS; employers must comply with Form I-9 and/or E-Verify for new hires.
Civil law	Regulations set by countries or legislative groups about the rights of people (different from common laws, which are set by judges).
Clause	A part of a document, agreement, proposal, or contract that gives more detail.

TABLE C.9 Agencies, court cases, terms, and laws *(continued)*

Name	Description
Clayton Act	Limited the use of injunctions to break strikes; exempted unions from the Sherman Antitrust Act.
Commercial diplomacy	The effort by multinational corporations to influence foreign government policy on issues such as tariffs, banking, and other financial regulations; antitrust/competition laws; workplace standards such as safety; data privacy; and corporate conduct in areas such as corruption, governance, and social responsibility.
Congressional Accountability Act (CAA)	Required all federal employment legislation passed by Congress to apply to congressional employees.
Consolidated Omnibus Budget Reconciliation Act (COBRA)	Allows employees and their families to temporarily continue their health insurance coverage after experiencing a qualifying event, such as job loss or reduction in work hours, that would otherwise result in the loss of benefits. COBRA applies to employers with 20 or more employees and requires that coverage be offered at group rates, though beneficiaries must pay the full premium plus an administrative fee.
Davis v. O'Melveny & Myers	Established that arbitration clauses in employment agreements won't be enforced if they're significantly favorable to the employer and the employee doesn't have a meaningful opportunity to reject the agreement.
Department of Labor (DOL)	Charged with the administration and enforcement of U.S. labor laws.
Disability	A physical or mental condition that limits, but does not prevent, the performance of certain tasks.
Disparate impact	Occurs when protected class groups are treated differently than other groups in employment-related decisions; includes practices that are neutral on the surface but have a negative effect on protected groups (such as requiring a high school diploma in areas where minority groups have a lower graduation rate than nonminority groups).
Due process	The way a government enforces laws; in the United States, the way a government enforces its laws to protect its citizens (e.g., guaranteeing a person a fair trial).

Name	Description
Energy Employees Occupational Illness Compensation Program Act (EEOICPA)	Provided compensation for employees and contractors subjected to excessive radiation during production and testing of nuclear weapons.
Energy Policy Act of 1992	Allowed employers to provide a nontaxable fringe benefit to employees engaged in qualified commuter activities such as bicycling and mass transit.
Epilepsy Foundation of Northeast Ohio v. NLRB	Extended *Weingarten* rights to nonunion employees by allowing employees to request a coworker be present during an investigatory interview that could result in disciplinary action.
Equal employment opportunity (EEO)	U.S. laws that guarantee equal treatment and respect for all employees.
Equal Employment Opportunity Act (EEOA)	Established that complainants have the burden of proof for disparate impact; provided litigation authority for the EEOC; extended the time to file complaints.
Equal Employment Opportunity Commission (EEOC)	U.S. agency charged with investigating complaints of job discrimination based on race, color, religion, sex (including pregnancy, gender identity, and sexual orientation), national origin, disability, age (40 or older), or genetic information, and with taking action to stop the discriminatory behavior when found.
Extraterritorial laws	Laws from a multinational enterprise's home country that have application in other countries. U.S. laws with extraterritorial application include Sarbanes–Oxley, Foreign Corrupt Practices Act, Americans with Disabilities Act, Age Discrimination in Employment Act, and Title VII of the Civil Rights Act of 1964. These laws give American workers the right to sue in the United States for unlawful acts that occurred outside of the country.
Federal Employees Compensation Act (FECA)	Provided benefits similar to workers' compensation for federal employees injured on the job.
Federal Insurance Contributions Act (FICA)/Social Security Act	Required employers and employees to pay Social Security taxes.
Federal regulations	In the United States, laws that apply in every state (as opposed to laws unique to every state).
Federal Unemployment Tax Act (FUTA)	Required employers to contribute a percentage of payroll to an unemployment insurance fund.

TABLE C.9 Agencies, court cases, terms, and laws *(continued)*

Name	Description
Forum shopping	Looking for a legal venue most likely to result in a favorable outcome; the practice of trying to get a trial held in a location that is most likely to produce a favorable result.
Griggs v. Duke Power	Required employers to show that job requirements are related to the job; established that lack of intention to discriminate isn't a defense against claims of discrimination.
Immigration and Nationality Act (INA)	Eliminated national origin, race, and ancestry as bars to immigration; set immigration goals for reunifying families and preference for specialized skills.
Intellectual property	Creations or inventions protected by law; an original invention or something created by the mind, which is usually protected by patents, trademarks, or copyrights.
Internal Revenue Service (IRS)	The U.S. government agency responsible for collecting taxes and enforcing tax laws.
Jespersen v. Harrah's Operating Co.	Established that a dress code requiring women to wear makeup doesn't constitute unlawful sex discrimination underTitle VII.
Jurisdiction	The right and power to interpret and apply the law, often within a certain geographical region.
Labor-Management Relations Act (LMRA; Taft–Hartley)	Prohibited closed shops; restricted union shops; allowed states to pass "right to work" laws; prohibited jurisdictional strikes and secondary boycotts; allowed employers to permanently replace economic strikers; established the Federal Mediation and Conciliation Service; allowed an 80-day cooling-off period for national emergency strikes.
Labor-Management Reporting and Disclosure Act (LMRDA; Landrum–Griffin)	Controlled internal union operations; provided a bill of rights for union members; required a majority vote of members to increase dues; allowed members to sue the union; set term limits for union leaders.
Licensing	Giving permission to use, produce, or sell; a written contract in which the owner of a trademark or intellectual property gives rights to a licensee to use, produce, or sell a product or service.

Name	Description
Lobbying	The act of monitoring and seeking to influence new labor laws and regulations by contacting local, state, and national representatives of the U.S. government.
Longshore and Harbor Workers' Compensation Act	Provided workers' compensation benefits for maritime workers injured on navigable waters of the United States or on piers, docks, and terminals.
Mental Health Parity Act (MHPA)	Required insurers to provide the same limits for mental health benefits that are provided for other types of health benefits.
National Labor Relations Act (NLRA; Wagner Act)	Protected the right of workers to organize and bargain collectively; identified unfair labor practices; established the National Labor Relations Board (NLRB).
Needlestick Safety and Prevention Act	Mandated recordkeeping for all needle-stick and sharps injuries; required employee involvement in developing safer devices.
NLRB: *IBM Corp.*	NLRB reversed its 2000 decision in *Epilepsy*, withdrawing *Weingarten* rights from nonunion employees.
NLRB: *M. B. Sturgis, Inc.*	Established that temporary employees may be included in the client company's bargaining unit and that consent of the employer and temp agency aren't required to bargain jointly.
NLRB v. J. Weingarten, Inc.	U.S. Supreme Court: Established that union employees have the right to request union representation during any investigatory interview that could result in disciplinary action.
Norris–La Guardia Act	Protected the right to organize; outlawed yellow-dog contracts.
Payne v. The Western & Atlantic Railroad Company	Defined employment at will.
Personal Responsibility and Work Opportunity Reconciliation Act	Required employers to provide information about all new or rehired employees to state agencies to enforce child support orders.
Pharakhone v. Nissan North America, Inc.	Established that employees who violate company rules while on FMLA leave may be terminated.

TABLE C.9 Agencies, court cases, terms, and laws *(continued)*

Name	Description
Phason v. Meridian Rail Corp.	Established that when an employer is close to closing a deal to sell a company, WARN Act notice requirements are triggered by the number of employees actually employed and the number laid off on the date of the layoff, even if the purchasing company hires some of the employees shortly after the layoff.
Proprietary	Relating to an owner or ownership; rights of property ownership relating to key information, materials, or methods developed by an organization.
Public Contracts Act (PCA; Walsh–Healey Act)	Required contractors to pay prevailing wage rates.
Railway Labor Act	Protected unionization rights; allowed for a 90-day cooling-off period to prevent strikes in national emergencies. Covers railroads and unions.
Repa v. Roadway Express, Inc.	Established that when an employee on FMLA leave is receiving employer-provided disability payments, the employee may not be required to use accrued sick or vacation leave during the FMLA absence.
Retirement Equity Act	Lowered the age limits on participation and vesting in pension benefits; required written spousal consent to not provide survivor benefits; restricted conditions placed on survivor benefits.
Rule of law	A political system in which the law is supreme; all citizens are subject to the laws of their country, no individual is above the law, and everyone must obey it.
Service Contract Act	Required government contractors to pay prevailing wages and benefits.
Sherman Antitrust Act	Controlled business monopolies; allowed court injunctions to prevent restraint of trade. Used to restrict unionization efforts.
Sista v. CDC Ixis North America, Inc.	Established that employees on FMLA may be legally terminated for legitimate, nondiscriminatory reasons, including violations of company policy if the reason is unrelated to the exercise of FMLA rights.

Name	Description
Small Business Job Protection Act	Redefined highly compensated individuals; detailed minimum participation requirements; simplified 401(k) tests; corrected qualified plan and disclosure requirements.
Small Business Regulatory Enforcement Fairness Act (SBREFA)	Provided that a Small Business Administration (SBA) ombudsman act as an advocate for small business owners in the regulatory process.
Smith v. City of Jackson, Mississippi	Established that ADEA permits disparate impact claims for age discrimination comparable to those permitted for discrimination based on sex and race.
Supra-national laws	Agreements, standards, and laws that transcend national boundaries or governments. Examples include directives and regulations from the EU to its member countries.
Taxman v. Board of Education of Piscataway	Found that in the absence of past discrimination or underrepresentation of protected classes, preference may not be given to protected classes in making layoff decisions.
Taylor v. Progress Energy, Inc.	Established that the waiver of FMLA rights in a severance agreement is invalid. FMLA clearly states that "employees cannot waive, nor may employers induce employees to waive, any rights under the FMLA."
Uniform Guidelines on Employee Selection Procedures (UGESP)	Established guidelines to ensure that selection procedures are both job-related and valid predictors of job success.
Velazquez-Garcia v. Horizon Lines of Puerto Rico, Inc.	Established that the burden of proof that a termination wasn't related to military service is on an employer when an employee protected by USERRA is laid off.
Visas and work permits	Documents used by various countries to control immigration and job placement of foreign workers. Most countries require a work permit whenever a foreign individual is transferred or takes a job in the country for a period of six months or more.
Washington v. Davis	Established that employment selection tools that adversely impact protected classes are lawful if they have been validated to show future success on the job.

TABLE C.9 Agencies, court cases, terms, and laws *(continued)*

Name	Description
WorldTrade Organization (WTO)	An international body in which members negotiate tariffs and trade barriers, and trade disputes are reviewed and adjudicated.
Works council	Groups that represent employees; organizations that function like trade unions and represent the rights of workers. Work councils are most common in Europe and the United Kingdom.

TABLE C.10 General recordkeeping guidelines

Record type	Length of retention	Requirements
Affirmative action plan/data	Two years	Applications and other personnel records that support employment decisions (e.g., hires, promotions, terminations) are considered "support data" and must be maintained for the present AAP and the prior AAP. Records required by 41CFR60-300.44(f)(4), 60-300.44(k), and 60-300.45(c) must be kept for a period of three years from the date of making the record. This also applies to records required by 41CFR60-741.44(f)(4) and (k).
Applications for employment	One year from making the record or making the hiring decision, whichever is later; two years if a federal contractor or subcontractor has 150 or more employees and a government contract of at least $150,000	If a charge or lawsuit is filed, the records must be kept until the charge is disposed.

Record type	Length of retention	Requirements
Drug test records	One year for non-DOT employers	Department of Transportation records for commercial drivers: 1 year: Negative drug test results. Alcohol test results less than 0.02. 2 years: Records related to the alcohol and drug collection process. 3 years: Previous employer records. 5 years: Annual MIS reports. Employee evaluation and referrals to SAPs. Follow-up tests and follow-up schedules. Refusals to test. Alcohol test results 0.02 or greater. Verified positive drug test results. EBT calibration documentation.
EEO-1	Annually, unless a federal contractor or subcontractor	The current EEO-1 report must be kept on file. Federal contractors and subcontractors must produce three years' worth of EEO-1 reports, if audited by the OFCCP.
Employment benefits	Until no longer relevant to determine benefits due to employees	Except for specific exemptions, ERISA's reporting and disclosure requirements apply to all pension and welfare plans, including summary plan descriptions, annual reports, and plan termination. Pension and insurance plans for the full period the plan is in place.
Family Medical Leave records	Three years	Basic employee data, including name, address, occupation, rate of pay, terms of compensation, daily and weekly hours worked per pay period, additions to/deductions from wages, and total compensation. Dates of leave taken by eligible employees. Leave must be designated as the FMLA leave. For intermittent leave taken, the hours of leave. Copies of employee notices and documents describing employee benefits or policies and practices regarding paid and unpaid leave. Records of premium payments of employee benefits. Records of any dispute regarding the designation of leave.
Form I-9	Three years after date of hire or one year after date of termination, whichever is later	For example, if an employee works for a company for two years, the employer must retain the I-9 for one more year after the employment ends (three years from the hire date). If an employee works for five years, the employer must keep the form for one year after their employment ends.

TABLE C.10 General recordkeeping guidelines *(continued)*

Record type	Length of retention	Requirements
Merit and seniority pay systems	Two years	Includes wage rates, job evaluations, seniority and merit systems, and collective bargaining agreements or any other document that explains the basis for paying different wages to employees of opposite sexes in the same establishment.
Payroll records, etc.	Three years (EEOC, FLSA, ADEA): Payroll records, collective bargaining agreements, sales and purchase records. Two years: Timecards and piecework tickets, wage rate tables, work and time schedules, and records of additions to or deductions from wages	If a charge is filed, all related records must be kept until the charge is settled. Basic payroll records that must be kept according to the FLSA are: ▪ Employee's full name and Social Security number ▪ Address, including zip code ▪ Birth date, if younger than 19 ▪ Sex and occupation ▪ Time and day of week when employee's workweek begins ▪ Hours worked each day ▪ Total hours worked each workweek ▪ Basis on which employee's wages are paid (e.g., "$9 per hour," "$440 a week," "piecework") ▪ Regular hourly pay rate ▪ Total daily or weekly straight-time earnings ▪ Total overtime earnings for the workweek ▪ All additions to or deductions from the employee's wages ▪ Total wages paid each pay period ▪ Date of payment and the pay period covered by the payment

Record type	Length of retention	Requirements
Personnel records	One year from making the record or taking the action, whichever is greater (EEOC). Three years if applicable under the Davis–Bacon Act. Two years if a federal contractor or subcontractor with 150 or more employees, or government contract of $150,000 or more	Records related to promotions, demotions, transfers, performance appraisals, terminations, requests for reasonable accommodations.
Polygraph test records	Three years	Polygraph test result(s) and the reason for administering.
Selection and hiring records	One year after creation of the document or the action is taken, whichever is later. Two years if a federal contractor or subcontractor with 150 or more employees, or government contract of $150,000 or more	Job ads, assessment tools, credit reports, interview records, and other documents related to hiring decisions.
Tax records	Four years from date tax is due or paid	Amounts of wages subject to withholding. Agreements with employee to withhold additional tax. Actual taxes withheld and dates withheld. Reason for any difference between total tax payments and actual tax payments. Withholding forms.
Work permits	No retention requirements	Employers must keep current work permits for minors.

Appendix D

Resources

Thousands of references are available for every aspect of human resources, so it's just not possible to include every great resource here. The resources included in this appendix are those that add dimension or different perspectives to the information presented in this book. Although the best preparation for the PHR/i and SPHR/i exams is diverse experience, these resources will provide a more in-depth refresher than is possible in this book. Note that you may be able to earn recertification credits by joining eligible associations and reading certain books, so taking the time to build your network and library can provide benefits beyond exam preparation.

Before we begin, here are some tips:

Information About the Test For information about eligibility requirements and test dates, the best source is the Human Resource Certification Institute (HRCI). There are two sources for information from HRCI. The first is the *Certification Policies and Procedures Handbook* (described in the introduction of this book), which is free of charge and published annually). The handbook provides all the information necessary to apply for the exams and includes pricing, deadlines, and general information. The second source is the HRCI website (`www.hrci.org`). The website contains a great deal of information about the exams and also allows you to view the handbook online, download a copy, or request that a hard copy be mailed to you. Another helpful information source is HRCI's *A Guide to the Human Resource Body of Knowledge* (*HRBoK*™). This guide serves as a general resource for all HR professionals and can be purchased from several national online booksellers.

Professional Associations Professional associations are often a great source of information about current trends in a particular practice area. Some of them are member-only sites, but even those often have useful information available to nonmembers.

As mentioned earlier, many sources of HR information are available. The inclusion of these resources is not an endorsement of the information contained in them. They are provided only as suggestions for further reading should you feel the need for more detail in one of these areas. For ease of use, the list is combined and organized according to functional area.

Business Management, Leadership, and Strategy

Resources included with business management, leadership, and strategy cover general human resource books and resources for other business disciplines with which HR professionals interact on a daily basis.

Books

Beugre, Constant. (2018). *The Neuroscience of Organizational Behavior*. Edward Elgar Publishing Ltd.

Crainer, Stuart. (2002). *The Ultimate Business Library: The Greatest Books That Made Management*. Capstone.

Dunn, Kris. (2023). *Best Boss Ever: An Insider's Guide to Modern People Management*. SHRM.

Gardenschwartz, Lee, and Rowe, Anita. (2010). *Managing Diversity: A Complete Desk Reference & Planning Guide, 3rd ed.* SHRM.

Haski-Leventhal, Debbie. (2021). *Strategic Corporate Social Responsibility: A Holistic Approach to Responsible and Sustainable Business, 2nd ed.* Sage Publications.

Lencioini, Patrick. (2015). *The Advantage: Why Organizational Health Trumps Everything Else in Business*. Jossey-Bass.

Mathis, Robert L., Jackson, John H., Valentine, Sean R., and Meglich, Patricia. (2016). *Human Resource Management, 15th ed.* Cengage Learning.

Northhouse, Peter G. (2021). *Leadership: Theory and Practice, 9th ed.* Sage Publications.

Professional Associations

American Management Association, `www.amanet.org`.

Balanced Scorecard Institute, `www.balancedscorecard.org`.

National Human Resources Association, `www.humanresources.org`.

ROI Institute, `www.roiinstitute.net`.

Society for Human Resource Management, `www.shrm.org`.

Workforce Planning and Talent Acquisition

These resources are some of the many related to workforce planning and talent management.

Books

Davila, Norma, and Pina-Ramirez, Wanda. (2018). *Effective Onboarding (What Works in Talent Development)*. Association for Talent Development.

Herring, Cole, and Sadler, Brandon. (2023). *Leading in a Multi-Generational Workforce*. Independently published.

Lauby, Sharlyn. (2022). *The SHRM Essential Guide to Talent Management: A Handbook for HR Professionals, Managers, Businesses, and Organizations*. SHRM.

Miller-Merrell, Jessica. (2023). *Digitizing Talent: Creative Strategies for the Digital Recruiting Age*. SHRM.

Phillips, Jean M. (2023). *Strategic Staffing, 4th ed.* Sage Publications.

Professional Associations

American Staffing Association, `www.staffingtoday.net`.

Association for Talent Acquisition Professionals, `https://atapglobal.org`.

Public Sector HR Association, `www.pshra.org`.

National Association of Personnel Services, `www.naps360.org`.

Learning and Development

These resources provide additional information about developing talent within organizations.

Books

Cook, Aubrey. (2023). *The eLearning & Instructional Design Roadmap: An Un-boring Guide for Newbies, Career-Changers, and Anyone Who Wants to Build Better eLearning*. Oddly Sharp, LLC.

Kirkpatrick, James D., and Kirkpatrick, Wendy Kayser. (2016). *Kirkpatrick's Four Levels of Training Evaluation*. Association for Talent Development.

Knowles, Malcolm S., Holton, Elwood F., Swanson, Richard A., and Robinson, Petra A. (2020). *The Adult Learner, 9th ed.* Routledge.

Weise, Michelle R. (2020). *Long Life Learning: Preparing for Jobs That Don't Even Exist Yet.* Wiley.

Professional Associations

Association for Educational Communications & Technology, www.aect.org.

Association for Talent Development, www.td.org.

The Learning Guild, www.learningguild.com.

Total Rewards

Additional information about compensation and benefit issues and processes is available in the following resources.

Books

Martocchio, Joseph J. (2022). *Employee Benefits, 7th ed.* McGraw-Hill.

WorldatWork. (2021). *The WorldatWork Handbook of Total Rewards: A Comprehensive Guide to Compensation, Benefits, HR & Employee Engagement, 2nd ed.* Wiley.

Professional Associations

American Payroll Association, www.americanpayroll.org.

Employee Benefit Research Institute, www.ebri.org.

International Foundation of Employee Benefit Plans, www.ifebp.org.

International Society of Certified Employee Benefit Specialists, www.iscebs.org.

WorldatWork (formerly American Compensation Association), www.worldatwork.org.

Employee Engagement

These resources provide additional information on the important topic of employee engagement.

Books

Byrne, Zinta S. (2022). *Understanding Employee Engagement: Theory, Research, and Practice (Applied Psychology Series), 2nd ed.* Routledge.

Mashek, D. (2023). *Collabor(h)ate: How to Build Incredible Collaborative Relationships at Work (Even If You'd Rather Work Alone).* Practical Inspiration Publishing.

Scandura, Terri A. (2021). *Essentials of Organizational Behavior, 3rd edition.* Sage Publications.

Professional Associations

Chartered Institute for Personnel and Development, www.cipd.org.

Society for Industrial and Organizational Psychology (SIOP), www.siop.org.

Employee and Labor Relations

These resources provide additional information on employee and labor relations.

Books

Daniels, Aubrey C. (2021). *Bringing Out the Best in People: How to Apply the Astonishing Power of Positive Reinforcement, 3rd ed.* McGraw-Hill Ascent Audio.

Fleischer, Charles H. (2022). *The SHRM Essential Guide to Employment Law: A Handbook for HR Professionals, Managers, Businesses, and Organizations, 2nd ed.* SHRM.

Harvard Law School. (2021). *Make the Most of Online Negotiations.* Harvard Publishing. www.pon.harvard.edu/freemium/make-the-most-of-online-negotiations.

Levy, Paul E. (2019). *Industrial Organizational Psychology, 6th ed.* Worth Publishers.

MacMillan, Charlene. (2021). *Labor-Management Relations: A Handbook for Labor Relations Professionals.* PublishDrive.

Professional Associations

National Diversity Council, www.nationaldiversitycouncil.org.

National Public Employer Labor Relations Association, www.npelra.org.

Global Human Resource Management

These resources are some of the many related to the practice of international human resource management.

Books

Hofstede, Geert. (2010). *Cultures and Organizations: Software of the Mind, 3rd ed.* McGraw Hill.

Hunt, Steven T. (2022). *Talent Tectonics: Navigating Global Workforce Shifts, Building Resilient Organizations and Reimagining the Employee Experience.* Ascent Audio.

Tarique, Ibraiz, Briscoe, Dennis R., and Schuler, Randall S. (2022). *International Human Resource Management: Policies and Practices for Multinational Enterprises (Global HRM), 6th ed.* Routledge.

Professional Associations

International Association for Human Resource Information Management (IHRIM), www.ihrim.org.

International Labour Organization, www.ilo.org.

Worldwide ERC, www.worldwideerc.org.

HR Information Management, Safety and Security

These resources provide additional information on the new functional area of the exams, HR Information Management and HR Information Management, Safety, and Security.

Books

Calder, Alan, and Watkins, Steve. (2019). *IT Governance: An International Guide to Data Security and ISO 27001/ISO27002, 7th ed.* Kogan Page.

Eubanks, Ben. (2022). *Artificial Intelligence for HR: Use AI to Support and Develop a Successful Workforce, 2nd ed.* Kogan Page.

Grubb, Sam. (2021). *How Cybersecurity Really Works: A Hands-On Guide for Total Beginners.* No Starch Press.

Harris, Stacy. (2021). *Introduction to HR Technologies: Understand How to Use Technology to Improve Performance and Processes.* Kogan Page.

Julian, Michael. (2021). *10 Minutes to Live: Surviving An Active Shooter Using A.L.I.V.E.® 2nd ed.* BCG Publishing.

Various Authors. (n.d.). OSHA Publications, www.osha.gov/publications.

Walsh, Michael J. (2021). *HR Analytics Essentials You Always Wanted To Know (Self-Learning Management Series).* Vibrant Publishers.

Professional Associations

American Society of Safety Professionals, www.asse.org.

International Organization for Standardization (ISO), www.iso.org/sectors/management-services/hr.

National Association of Safety Professionals, www.naspweb.com.

National Safety Council, www.nsc.org.

Appendix E

Summarizing the Summaries: What Meta-Analyses Tell Us About Work Engagement

Dr.Erin M. Richard Ph.D.

Assistant Professor of Leadership and Human Resource Development, Louisiana State University

Work engagement (also referred to as employee engagement) is somewhat of a buzzword in organizations today, but many organizational scientists remain skeptical about the construct and its overlap with other job attitudes. It's common for management fads to gain popularity so quickly that the practices or interventions associated with the topic start to outrun the science. For some time, engagement was in danger of becoming one of those fads, but fortunately, the science has begun to catch up with the practice. In fact, work engagement is now one of the most researched topics in organizational science (Carasco-Saul et al., 2015). Because it can be difficult to digest the results of such a large number of studies, some researchers have attempted to statistically summarize this research using meta-analyses. In a meta-analysis, the results of multiple studies are combined in order to obtain the best possible estimate of the true relationship between variables. In this appendix, I summarize three meta-analyses on work engagement that I believe offer some key take-home messages on the topic.

Christian, Garza, and Slaughter, 2011

Is work engagement really just "old wine in a new barrel"? A key criticism of engagement is that we've simply taken older constructs such as job satisfaction and involvement and repackaged them as something new. Christian et al. (2011) addressed this criticism in their meta-analysis published in *Personnel Psychology*.

One of the most common definitions of engagement is *a psychological state consisting of vigor, dedication, and absorption* (Schaufeli et al., 2002). However, engagement has been defined in many different ways, and the lack of consensus on a definition has been one of the criticisms of the construct. Christian and colleagues reviewed the research on work engagement in order to come up with an agreed-upon definition that (a) summarized the key components of most definitions, and (b) distinguished it from other concepts. The result was the following definition of work engagement:

> A relatively enduring state of mind referring to the simultaneous investment of personal energies in the experience or performance of work. (Christian et al., 2011, p. 95)

Christian and colleagues emphasized two key components of this definition, which can be traced back to work by Kahn (1990):

- Work engagement refers to a psychological connection with the performance of *work tasks* (rather than an attitude toward the organization or job situation).

- Work engagement involves the investment of *multiple* resources (i.e., physical, emotional, and cognitive energy) into one's work.

These components of the definition help distinguish engagement from other job attitudes. First, the target of engagement is the work itself; it refers to how one feels when performing work tasks. This focus distinguishes it from job satisfaction, which is an evaluation of the overall job situation, and it distinguishes it from job involvement, which refers to psychological identification with the overall job situation. When we consider that the focus of engagement is on work tasks themselves, it also helps distinguish engagement from organizational commitment, which is an attachment to the organization (or members of an organization). Second, because engagement refers to the simultaneous investment of multiple resources (e.g., physical, emotional, and mental energies) into one's work, Christian and colleagues argue that attitudes like job involvement, which is mainly cognitive, or affective commitment, which is mainly emotional, may be better represented as components of engagement rather than equivalent to engagement.

Christian and colleagues' meta-analysis statistically combined the results of 91 different studies that had examined potential causes and consequences of engagement. They found that engagement was related to job performance across studies, and more importantly, it predicted variation in job performance above and beyond the other three job attitudes. Christian and colleagues' work also offers clues as to how we might increase employees' work engagement. Predictors of engagement included task variety (getting to do many different things at work) and task significance (perceived importance of those tasks). Employees who were more conscientious and higher in trait positive mood also showed higher levels of engagement.

The implications of these findings are that having engaged employees gives companies a competitive advantage and that engagement might be increased through employee selection and job redesign. However, the way in which companies measure engagement varies greatly. To ensure that an organization is measuring something distinct that will be uniquely linked to performance, Christian and colleagues suggest using measures that conceptualize engagement in line with their definition.

Depending on how it's defined and measured, employee engagement can represent a construct that is distinct from other job attitudes and that represents an important predictor of productivity. Work engagement is higher in employees who perceive variety and significance in their tasks and in employees who are high on trait conscientiousness and positive mood.

Maricutoiu, Sulea, and Iancu, 2017

One common but somewhat controversial view of engagement is that it is the opposite of burnout (e.g., Maslach & Leiter, 1997). *Burnout* refers to a psychological state characterized by three dimensions: exhaustion (a feeling of being emotionally and physically drained), depersonalization (cynicism or a detached attitude), and inefficacy (a reduced sense of personal accomplishment). Although there is evidence to suggest that engagement and burnout are different things (e.g., Langelaan et al., 2006; Schaufeli et al., 2008; Schaufeli &

Salanova, 2014), the fact remains that the two are highly correlated, and most researchers believe that one likely influences the other. The question is: *Which comes first? Low work engagement or burnout?*

To answer this question, Maricutoiu and colleagues (2017) meta-analyzed 25 studies that measured engagement and burnout at two different time periods. They found evidence for reciprocal causation (i.e., the two variables likely influence each other). However, the negative effect of burnout (particularly exhaustion) on engagement appears to be stronger than the effect of engagement on burnout. The effects also might take some time to show up. They found that significant relationships only appeared when the lag between measurements was 12 months.

There is evidence that burnout may reduce work engagement over time, and vice versa: Low levels of work engagement may lead to higher burnout. However, detecting these effects seems to require at least a year between measurement occasions, suggesting that the effects might take some time to develop.

Knight, Patterson, and Dawson, 2017

According to a meta-analysis by Knight et al. (2017), four different types of organizational interventions are targeted at increasing work engagement:

- **Personal resource building interventions:** Focuses on increasing employees' optimism, resilience, or positive views of themselves (e.g., self-efficacy)
- **Job resource building interventions:** Focuses on increasing work resources, such as autonomy, social support, or feedback
- **Leadership training interventions:** Attempts to build job resources and motivate employees indirectly by increasing the knowledge and skill of their leaders
- **Health-promoting interventions:** Attempts to increase engagement by promoting healthier lifestyles aimed at building and sustaining personal resources

The purpose of Knight and colleagues' meta-analysis was to estimate the average effectiveness of these interventions and determine which kinds of interventions are most effective. Unfortunately, they found only 20 studies that used controlled designs to examine intervention effectiveness. This limited their statistical ability to detect differences in effectiveness between different types of engagement interventions. However, they were able to draw a few preliminary conclusions.

First, they found that engagement interventions have a small but reliable positive effect. Specifically, work engagement for employees receiving an intervention was an average of 0.29 standard deviations higher than the engagement of the control groups. Second, interventions seem to have stronger effects on the individual dimensions of engagement (i.e., vigor, dedication, and absorption) compared to overall engagement. On average, the intervention groups scored 0.95 standard deviations higher on vigor, 0.75 standard deviations higher on dedication, and 0.78 standard deviations higher on absorption compared to the control groups. Third, there was a great deal of variability in the effectiveness of engagement interventions across studies, and Knight and colleagues (2017) point out that more research is needed to determine what makes some interventions more effective than others. For example, the four types of interventions identified here did not differ significantly in their effectiveness; however, there was some preliminary evidence that group-based interventions (which had medium to large effects on engagement) may be more effective than individual-based interventions.

More research needs to be conducted on the effectiveness of organizational interventions for increasing work engagement. However, the preliminary evidence suggests that such interventions are indeed effective, particularly those that are group-based.

References

Carasco-Saul, M., Kim, W., & Kim, T. 2015. Leadership and Employee Engagement: Proposing Research Agendas through a Review of Literature. *Human Resource Development Review*, *14*: 38–63.

Christian, M., Garza, A., & Slaughter, J. 2011. Work Engagement: A Quantitative Review and Test of Its Relations with Task and Contextual Performance. *Personnel Psychology 64*: 89–136.

Kahn, W. A. 1990. Psychological Conditions of Personal Engagement and Disengagement at Work. *The Academy of Management Journal 33*(4), 692–724.

Knight, C., Patterson, M., & Dawson, J. 2017. Building Work Engagement: A Systematic Review and Meta-Analysis Investigating the Effectiveness of Work Engagement Interventions. *Journal of Organizational Behavior 38*, 798–812.

Langelaan, S., Bakker, A. B., Van Doornnen, L. J., & Schaufeli, W. B. 2006. Burnout and Work Engagement: Do Individual Differences Make a Difference? *Personality and Individual Differences 40*, 521–532.

Maricutoiu, L., Sulea, C., & Iancu, A. 2017. Work Engagement or Burnout: Which Comes First? A Meta-Analysis of Longitudinal Evidence. *Burnout Research 5*, 35–43.

Maslach, C., & Leiter, M. 1997. *The Truth About Burnout*. Jossey-Bass.

Schaufeli, W. B., & Salanova, M. 2014. Burnout, Boredom and Engagement in the Workplace. In M. C. Peeters, J. de Jonge, & T. W. Taris (Eds.), *An Introduction to Contemporary Work Psychology* (pp. 293–320). Wiley Blackwell.

Schaufeli, W. B., Salanova, M., Gonzalez-Roma, V., & Baker, A. B. 2002. The Measurement of Engagement and Burnout: A Two Sample Confirmatory Factor Analytic Approach. *Journal of Happiness Studies 3*, 71–92.

Schaufeli, W. B., Taris, T. W., & van Rhenen, W. 2008. Workaholism, Burnout and Engagement: Three of a Kind or Three Different Kinds of Employee Well-Being? *Applied Psychology: An International Review 57*, 173–203.

Appendix F

Neuroscience Principles and Applications for HR Leaders

Reut Schwartz-Hebron

Founder of the Key Change Institute

Introduction

The design of human resources (HR) and organizational development (OD) systems involves access to a diverse knowledge base in which HR competencies may develop and thrive. In fact, successfully facilitating coaching, developing leaders, building teams, and providing training all rely on studies from numerous fields, particularly those that seek to understand effective change management. One of the more recent contributions to these processes comes from studying neuroscience.

Unlike other cells in the body, brain cells, or neurons, have the ability to directly communicate with each other. Understanding how behaviors, responses, preferences, and choices are represented in neural pathways in the brain has immediate and highly practical applications to change facilitation at every level.

Neuroscience findings clarify why it is difficult for some employees to change or let go of previous ways of doing things. They explain why some change processes can get difficult, complicated, confusing, or frustrating and how to get past change obstacles. The research provides us with specific principles so that we can guide and support the rewiring of new responses and behaviors at the individual level.

The result of combining neuroscience with transformation-related methodologies are true "inside-out" science-based models. For the first time, we have access to models that tie adoption of new ways of doing things on an individual level with leadership development, training in general, and wide-scope organizational change. We can bring the missing link of change acquisition to the organizations, teams, and individuals we support. Neuroscience principles shed light on questions like how to gain buy-in when people don't see the need for change, how to bridge the knowing–doing gap to get from awareness to adoption, and how to correctly identify and effectively overcome different types of resistance.

These and many others are questions that neuroscience can now answer, and they are particularly relevant for HR leaders. Mastering how to apply key neuroscience principles allows HR leaders to provide unique value by enhancing organizational well-being and retention, diminishing undesired behaviors, establishing acquisition and usage of new processes and systems, ensuring skill acquisition and improved performance, and increasing overall growth. Learning to apply neuroscience principles has been redefining the role of HR leaders as internal change guides and partners who provide direction, focus, and clear steps for their clients to achieve desired outcomes. Out of the emerging studies related to neuroscience research and change management, the following three principles are perhaps the most important.

The Principles

Of the different neuroscience principles that apply to change facilitation, perhaps the most critical ones to be aware of are:

1. Understanding the unlearning-relearning process and how to successfully manage it
2. Redefining resistance, how to identify its different types, and how to effectively overcome it
3. Engaging the right system in the brain to facilitate change acquisition and behavioral change

Principle 1: The Unlearning-Relearning Process

Up until about 15 years ago it was not uncommon to find research indicating that our development and ability to change is dramatically reduced after the age of five. Although we do learn and develop most dramatically early in life, new science and, particularly the study of "plasticity," countered the belief that our abilities to learn new skills or change is halted in later years. Both the science and application of how adults unlearn and then relearn is covered next.

The Science

According to neuroscience, concepts, beliefs, thoughts, and, as a result behaviors, responses and habits are represented in "neural pathways." Although the formation of new neurons is limited late in life, new pathways can be formed by making new connections between existing neurons. The neural pathway—the sequence of communication between neurons that represents a specific response—can form and be adjusted at *any time*, no matter how old we are. The main difference is that later in life, new neural pathways and hence new responses, habits, and behaviors typically don't simply form; they need to re-form or change. When you were little and someone yelled at you, a neural pathway was created in your brain to represent your response. If you withdrew, one pathway was formed. If you got defensive, a different pathway formed. If you got angry and responded aggressively, yet a different pathway formed. Furthermore, if you continued to withdraw every time someone yelled at you as the years went by, this initial pathway was reinforced much like a riverbed gets deeper and wider as more water flows through it. The difference between the early formation of neural pathways, and hence responses and behaviors early in life and adopting new skills, responses, and thinking patterns later in life, is that as an adult you need to simultaneously form new neural pathways while letting go of previously reinforced relevant neural pathways. Early enough in life you only need to learn, but later in life you often need to unlearn and relearn.

Although most of us are somewhat fluent when it comes to learning, we recognize that unlearning is more difficult, and we typically try to navigate it with awareness and motivation. Unfortunately, understanding unlearning is one of those aspects of change that can sometimes catch us off guard. Most of us weren't taught to effectively manage our unlearning processes, so we developed commonsense solutions like trying to will ourselves to achieve desired outcomes, which unfortunately does not align with scientific findings as being effective.

Neuroscience teaches us that *unlearning is a specific process*. It has steps and obstacles between steps. Using the science allows us to navigate change successfully and guide others to adopt new skills, behaviors, and responses that allow for unlearning more quickly and seamlessly than we were able to do before.

Application

To more intuitively understand the difference between learning and the unlearning-relearning process, try to think of a time you needed to learn something brand-new such as adopting effective time management skills. Take a moment and try to identify the steps you took in order to initially learn how to effectively manage your workload. Perhaps you studied time management techniques online. You may have broken the new learning down into smaller, more manageable chunks, and used trial and error to learn through practice. Whatever approach you took, since there is currently a lot of emphasis on active learning as we grow up, most people know how to learn and are proficient at taking those steps. Now, however, take a moment and think of a time you needed to *unlearn* something. Continuing with our effective time management example to simplify things, imagine someone else didn't have the foresight of learning the topic early on. Instead, this individual developed less-than-ideal habits, behaviors, and thinking patterns around time management. Maybe this individual agrees to take on more than capacity permits and then procrastinates. In this second example, unlearning is required to successfully adopt new effective time management skills; this individual will need to go through the steps of letting go of previous ways of doing things.

Understanding how to facilitate transformation and change when people need to let go of previous ways of doing things is of great importance in numerous avenues of organizational growth. Two particularly interesting such applications are leadership development and organizationwide cultural change.

Traditionally, leadership development uses a variety of models and methodologies to manage the acquisition of effective leadership practices. Prior to learning about the need to facilitate the unlearning-relearning process, leadership development focused almost solely on teaching effective leadership skills. Although learning from what highly effective leaders do and trying to adopt new, more desirable ways of behaving, thinking, and responding is valuable and important, neuroscience findings indicate we also need to manage the process of letting go of previous practices. If a leader is overly controlling and micromanages her team, it is important to provide her with highly effective team management skills. However, without guiding her to successfully complete the unlearning-relearning process, whatever new behaviors this manager can sustain through awareness and motivation will most often be shortly lost. We now know that the habits and patterns associated with previous patterns such as being controlling and micromanaging don't get "unwired" or "overwritten" when we focus on acquiring new skills. If we are highly motivated, we can typically sustain the new desired state for a few weeks, but soon enough the presence of previous response patterns will make it very difficult to sustain this success. If a leader doesn't listen to his team's opinions and perspectives and is defensive whenever anyone asks to provide him with feedback, it is important to provide him with effective listening skills. However, it is not unusual for leaders in this position to have strong, preexisting, less-than-ideal response patterns. If those are sufficiently reinforced as previous neural pathways, they will most likely be stronger than any new skills. Without guiding this leader to let go of these previous responses, it is highly unlikely he will adopt new needed behaviors in a lasting way.

Cultural change is another great example for the importance of managing the unlearning-relearning process. Traditionally, the main focus for adopting new desired culture is to define and clarify the new cultural environment. Workshops and training will then be conducted to facilitate understanding, engagement, and practice of specific behaviors, processes, structures, and other aspects that are aligned with the new culture. Although these are important, neuroscience helps us recognize that cultural change is often preceded by an existing culture. Omitting the focus on facilitating unlearning will leave the effort more vulnerable to failure. An organization hoping to adopt a new culture of diversity and inclusion may focus on new behaviors and responses such as collaboration, open debate, honest communication, effective accountability, personal integrity, empowering independent thinking, innovation, and shared decision making. Every organization is different, but if, for example, the culture prior to this initiative is of the thinking that there is always only one "right" answer, overly critical negative thinking, focusing on what isn't working, and argumentativeness, some response patterns will need to be unlearned before the desired culture could be acquired in a lasting way. Furthermore, though the scope of cultural change initiatives is typically organizationwide, neuroscience principles can be designed to reach transformation on the individual level.

The benefit of having access to these scientific findings means understanding why there is a need to manage unlearning and how to guide people through it. It's easy to see why, without adding this new knowledge, obstacles of some change efforts may be unnoticed or unclear. Understanding unlearning is one of the great examples of how neuroscience findings demystify change challenges, contributing to long-term acquisition and making change facilitation more predictable and successful.

Principle 2: Redefining Resistance

Successfully managing resistance to change is an extremely vital (but, the most misunderstood) aspect of change facilitation. Understanding resistance in the context of neuroscience research sheds new light on the very definition of resistance and how to effectively overcome it.

The Science

Resistance to change is defined as a phenomenon that delays or slows change adoption or implementation. It is often described as a set of behaviors such as denial, inaction, avoidance, cynicism, and refusal to cooperate. Prior to recent developments in neuroscience, the causes for resistance focused on perceived threats such as disagreement, sense of losing control, loss of influence or perceived value, and insufficient understanding of why the change is needed. As a result of how resistance was defined in the past, change models were designed to resolve or prevent these aspects of it.

Neuroscience provides us with a new way of looking at resistance to change. We now know that whenever we need to unlearn something, we will experience a natural degree of discomfort as part of the process of forming new neural pathways. This discomfort is inherent, and most will respond to it in one of two ways: Avoid it or work through it. If avoided, new pathways will not form. However, it is important to recognize that working through and fully experiencing the discomfort will actually help re-form new neural pathways and work to reinforce the change. This new finding diverts us from the assumption that we need to avoid or prevent resistance. It also directs senior HR professionals to build change systems that help employees recognize this resistance and accept that it is part of the process of forming new behaviors.

Most traditional references to resistance define it as a reaction to an external perceived threat. Although it is important to maintain an effective *external* environment for change, neuroscience directs us to look at the way people respond to that *internal* resistance, regardless of environmental conditions.

Unfortunately, unlike external resistance, which is observable, internal resistance is invisible and people are often unaware of it. Those who successfully overcome their internal resistance adopt new ways of doing things by continuously experiencing the "pull" to do things the old way but continue to move in the new direction despite that pull. For example, if they want to adopt better presentation skills and are uncomfortable speaking in public, they embrace the discomfort and practice the very thing they are uncomfortable with. If someone is uncomfortable with conflict and wants to adopt a more assertive communication style when needed, their internal resistance and the discomfort associated with it show up as they are trying to adopt new responses, but they practice new responses despite it.

Whereas external resistance is a hindrance to change facilitation, internal resistance from a neuroscience perspective is not a blocking element. In fact, internal resistance provides us with an important, deep transformative opportunity. The experience of the discomfort combined with the choice to move forward despite the discomfort is an extremely powerful rewiring mechanism. Internal resistance is not a phenomenon that should be prevented. Instead, it is a powerful change mechanism at the heart of accelerated transformation efforts that form lasting change.

Application

Just like unlearning, understanding how to effectively overcome internal and external resistance is of great importance in most if not all behavioral OD intervention strategies. Two good examples of such interventions are coaching and team building.

Traditionally, coaching models focus on building understanding, acceptance, and motivation as a foundation for achieving a successful transformation process. If the individual is highly motivated and positive toward the need for change, we may assume he is not resisting change. However, with the new knowledge we draw from neuroscience, this conclusion needs to be somewhat revisited. A highly motivated individual will still experience internal resistance. He may be very clear about the importance of the change and may very much want to adopt the new way of doing things, yet due to the experience of the internal resistance, still fail to acquire desired behaviors, thinking habits, or responses. Think about people who truly want to adopt a healthier diet but despite their motivation and acceptance of the need for change struggle to adopt new habits in a lasting way. The same struggle applies when we want to adopt more effective communication strategies, think more strategically, give and accept feedback more effectively, and acquire a wide range of other highly effective skills. Motivation to improve is important, but if it comes as an initial drive and grows thinner with time, it is often not enough to overcome the long haul of day-to-day, continuous effort to re-form neural pathways. New science-based models recognize the presence of internal resistance even if people are highly motivated, providing individuals with effective accountability structures to support transformation as needed. This is why mentoring can be such a powerful tool to support change.

Similarly, if the individual is frustrated, avoidant, stubborn, angry, or passive, we often assume she is resisting in response to less-than-ideal external factors. As a result, we attempt to minimize the resistance to change by building trust, explaining how the change will affect the individual, engaging individuals in the change process, and focusing on benefits the change will have. However, though all these practices are valuable and important, because we may not take external resistance into account, we may not manage the response patterns individuals bring to the party. Knowing that people often respond ineffectively to their internal discomfort allows us to incorporate more evolved skills into coaching practices. Thanks to neuroscience, new coaching models combine creating the right environment and providing people with "change-readiness skills." By getting people to adopt effective ways to respond to their internal discomfort, we allow even particularly resistant-seeming individuals to become highly cooperative with the coaching process.

Team building is another great example of how a new understanding of resistance to change can be extremely valuable. Although this can apply to a wide variety of scenarios, imagine two small teams from two different cultures being merged into one team. Team 1 comes from a centralized culture. They bring clear structures, are able to follow directives, and have the ability to quickly align with new procedures. Team 2 comes from a decentralized culture. They enjoy the freedom of making independent, flexible decisions on a case-by-case basis and the ability to quickly offer creative solutions. Bringing these diverse teams together creates friction as the team is required to redefine the way it operates. Traditional team development models would rightfully focus on clarifying what the new way of operating will be and how it will affect different team members, including and engaging team members in the process, and focus on building transparency and trust. However, with all of this important work, individuals on the team may still not respond in the desired way. Team members may understand the need for change but be so accustomed to the nuances of the old way of doing things that they will fail to make the transition. Others may try to continue doing things the way they've always done, just now under the radar. Some may become argumentative. Subgroups may form, leading to a variety of secondary team dynamics issues. Despite the best effort to minimize the external factors that could lead to resistance, resistance is often very much brewing under the surface. When accompanied by neuroscience-based knowledge, managing team building is designed to support overcoming internal resistance. Doing so by providing effective accountability structures supports the individuals who are positively struggling to adopt all the nuances of the transition. It is also designed to preemptively or continuously provide team members with skills to respond effectively to their internal resistance to minimize ineffective external resistance responses.

This new understanding of resistance to change means we can answer questions around why some change efforts fail despite the fact we do everything "by the book." It enables us to accelerate change efforts at every level and guide people through change in a way that will make early motivation turn into lasting results. It means we can effectively support the transformation of difficult individuals and effectively resolve the challenges that are at the very heart of a variety of difficult change efforts.

Principle 3: Engaging Behavioral Change

When it comes to change acquisition, perhaps the most wonderful benefit of recent neuroscience developments is the removal of what once were invisible obstacles. This third principle removes much of the mystery when, for some unseen reason, people who are part of a change process just seem to go back to their desk and adopt old routines as if nothing much changed. It clarifies why individuals and teams who accept the need for change and are supported through it still don't adopt the new culture or don't follow new processes.

The Science

This third principle has to do with two different systems in the brain: the *explicit* system, which is linked to awareness, and the *implicit* system, which is linked to experience. Simply put, if we engage both systems, people will adopt new habits. Engaging only the explicit system is not enough. People will leave with new understanding, knowledge, and even acceptance but will, for the most part, not put the new behaviors into practice. A good analogy to make intuitive sense of the difference between the two systems is to think about learning how to swim. Imagine you are standing by a pool and given verbal instructions on how to float, move your limbs, and breathe. If you are focused, you will probably be able to repeat the instructions, indicating that you acquired the information and know-how to swim. However, if you were asked to jump and swim right away, you would most likely find it difficult. This is because when you were taught to swim outside the pool, only your explicit system was engaged. To move from awareness to application, the implicit system needs to be engaged as well. The same thing happens when we try to teach new managers how to effectively lead their teams.

To adopt a new skill in a way that will translate into applying it, you'll need to engage your brain through *both* knowledge and experience. The pitfall is that experience in neuroscience terms has very specific requirements and is somewhat different than the everyday definition of the word. Experience in neuroscience terms is a specific event, framed in a specific time and location, initiated by the acquiring individual, and with some sense of emotional importance. Also, unlike the everyday use of the term, because of the way the implicit system operates, it doesn't have to be something the acquiring individual has done, and it doesn't have to be taking place in the present. If you watch someone else being treated with disrespect, it can be just as much your experience as it is theirs, as long as you had an emotional response to the situation. Furthermore, recalling or remembering an event in which you or someone else was treated unfairly is just as much an experience for the implicit system as being treated unfairly in the here and now—that is, as long as you initiated the memory rather than responded to encouragement from someone else to retrieve that particular event. This means that as long as we follow the brain's rules, recalling examples and remembering case studies is the equivalent of going through experiences in "real life."

Furthermore, to establish behavioral change, relevant experiences need to be tied to new interpretations or conclusions. For example, if you want to adopt more assertive behaviors but at some point in your life linked being dismissed or ignored with the conclusion that you are less valuable, having new experiences won't be enough. You'll need to change the interpretation you assign to experiences of being dismissed in order to adopt more assertive behaviors in the future. Unfortunately, these conclusions or interpretations are often hidden and invisible, but they don't have to be. Changing the meaning people assign to experience can be facilitated and can be as easy as asking for it. You just need to know that it is something you need to focus on for behavioral change to occur.

Engaging the implicit system through examples that follow neuroscience requirements and linking those experiences to new, more effective interpretations is a powerful behavioral change combination. We may be accustomed to navigating change through logical discussion, which ignores the implicit system. We may be used to facilitating change by trying to motivate and support others and, by so doing, eliminate the need for much initiative on their part. We've simply never had access to the specific do's and don'ts of how to engage behavioral change before and so may not realize how big those small missteps are in terms of blocking change acquisition. However, when done right, engaging the implicit system means bypassing the "awareness trap," shortening long change processes, and being in awe of how versatile we can be if we match the models we use with what our brain needs in order to change.

Application

Although behavioral change requires engaging both the explicit and the implicit systems, organizations tend to be very good at using the first and insufficiently applying the other. Knowing how to effectively engage both systems at every level of learning, transformation, and change in organizations leads to accelerated transfer of new knowledge into practice in a lasting way. Examples for the importance of this third principle are numerous; training is a particularly important example and is worth a deeper dive.

Traditionally, training models focus on providing participants with new knowledge, processing that knowledge, and practice. In that context, if we were to train customer care representatives how to better respond to complaints, we would typically tell them what the right approach is, illustrate it by showing them examples of effective and ineffective responses, practice, and then discuss and review the specific practiced examples.

It is easy to see that traditional models engage the explicit system. They do so first by providing knowledge and illustrating best practices. Interestingly, although it may seem like getting participants to practice is equivalent to engaging the implicit system and discussion is equivalent to creating the important link between experience and interpretation, the small nuances in design prevent the engagement of the implicit system. For example, it is not uncommon for the practice to be using examples provided by the facilitator. While using examples of specific events that are properly framed in the context of time and location, this practice removes the need for the experience to be initiated by participants and usually is not associated with any emotional importance for participants. By so doing, these minor aspects make the practice under traditional training models highly valuable for understanding but not an experience that can form new behaviors.

Furthermore, though not in all cases, it is not unusual for traditional training models to provide the desired conclusions for an experience without asking participants for their interpretation. Going back to our customer care training example, imagine that some of the participants link the distress and anger in the customer's voice to being threatened. This subconscious interpretation may lead some of them to respond unpleasantly. To replace this link with a new interpretation, it is not enough to explain to these participants logically that the client isn't attacking them and that the right approach is to combine empathy with healthy boundaries and practical guidance to resolve the issue. These participants need to sufficiently practice linking new examples in which the same client behavior is actively linked to a new interpretation.

Conclusion

We can think of the most impactful neuroscience contributions to change facilitation in recent years as forming a triangle. Understanding the unlearning-relearning process is one strategy, redefining resistance is another, and understanding how to engage the right system in the brain to achieve behavioral change completes the trio. There are, of course, many other valuable findings and principles, but even just this taste, combining these three principles, makes a powerful recipe for increasing change acquisition success rates.

Suggested Reading

Begley S. 2007. *Train Your Mind Change Your Brain: How a New Science Reveals Our Extraordinary Potential to Transform Ourselves*. Ballantine Books.

Bi, G., & Poo, M. 1998. Synaptic Modification in Cultured Hippocampal Neurons: Dependence on Spike Timing, Synaptic Strength, and Postsynaptic Cell Type. *Journal of Neuroscience, 18* (24).

Blakeslee, S. 2000. A Decade of Discovery Yields a Shock About the Brain. *New York Times*, Jan. 4.

Bloom, F. E., & Larsen, A. 1985. *Brain, Mind, and Behavior*. Freeman.

Boyke, J., Driemeyer, J., Gaser, C., Buchel, C., & May, A. 2008. Training-Induced Brain Structure Changes in the Elderly. *Journal of Neuroscience*, *28* (28).

Bruer, J. 1999. *The Myth of the First Three Years: A New Understanding of Early Brain Development and Lifelong Learning*. Free Press.

Buonomano, D., & Merzenich, M. M. 1998. Cortical Plasticity: From Synapses to Maps. *Annual Review of Neuroscience*, *21* (1).

DiSalvo, D. 2011. *What Makes Your Brain Happy and Why Should You Do the Opposite*. Prometheus Books.

Hebb, D. O. 1949. *The Organization of Behavior*. John Wiley & Sons.

Jacobs, C. S. 2010. *Management Rewired: Why Feedback Doesn't Work and Other Surprising Lessons from the Latest Brain Science*. Portfolio.

LeDoux, J. 2002. *Synaptic Self: How Our Brains Become Who We Are*. Penguin.

Medina, J. 2008. *Brain Rules: 12 Principles for Surviving and Thriving at Work, Home, and School*. Pear Press.

Schacter, D. 1996. *Searching for Memory: The Brain, the Mind, and the Past*. Basic Books.

Schwartz, J. M., & Begley, S. 2002. *The Mind and the Brain: Neuroplasticity and the Power of Mental Force*. HarperCollins.

Seung, S. 2012. *Connectome: How the Brain's Wiring Makes Us Who We Are*. Houghton Mifflin Harcourt.

Siegel, D. J., & Hartzell, M. 2004. *Parenting from the Inside Out: How Deeper Self-Understanding Can Help Raise Children Who Thrive*. Penguin.

Siegel, D. J. 2010. *Mindsight: The New Science of Personal Transformation*. Bantam.

Index

A

B

C

D

E

F

G

H

I

J

K

L

M

N

P

Q

R

S

T

U

V

W

Y

Z

Online Test Bank

To help you study for your PHR, PHRi, SPHR, and SPHRi certification exams, register to gain one year of FREE access after activation to the online interactive test bank—included with your purchase of this book!

To access our learning environment, simply visit www.wiley.com/go/sybextestprep, follow the instructions to register your book, and instantly gain one year of FREE access after activation to:

- Hundreds of practice test questions, so you can practice in a timed and graded setting.
- Flashcards
- A searchable glossary

SYBEX
A Wiley Brand